Organizational Control

Organization scholars have long acknowledged that control processes are integral to the way in which organizations function. While control theory research spans many decades and draws on several rich traditions, theoretical limitations have kept it from generating consistent and interpretable empirical findings and from reaching consensus concerning the nature of key relationships. This book reveals how we can overcome such problems by synthesizing diverse, yet complementary, streams of control research into a theoretical framework and empirical tests that more fully describe how types of control mechanisms (e.g. the use of rules, norms, direct supervision, or monitoring) aimed at particular control targets (e.g. input, behavior, output) are applied within particular types of control systems (i.e., market, clan, bureaucracy, integrative). Written by a team of distinguished scholars, this book not only sheds light on the long-neglected phenomenon of organizational control, it also provides important directions for future research.

SIM B SITKIN is Professor of Management and Faculty Director of the Fuqua/Coach K Center on Leadership and Ethics at the Fuqua School of Business, Duke University.

LAURA B. CARDINAL is Professor of Strategic Management at the C. T. Bauer College of Business, University of Houston.

KATINKA M. BIJLSMA-FRANKEMA is Associate Professor of Organization Theory at VU University in Amsterdam and Professor of Organization Sciences at the European Institute for Advanced Studies in Management (EIASM) in Brussels.

Organizational Control

Edited by

SIM B SITKIN,
LAURA B. CARDINAL AND
KATINKA M. BIJLSMA-FRANKEMA

CAMBRIDGE
UNIVERSITY PRESS

Shaftesbury Road, Cambridge CB2 8EA, United Kingdom

One Liberty Plaza, 20th Floor, New York, NY 10006, USA

477 Williamstown Road, Port Melbourne, VIC 3207, Australia

314–321, 3rd Floor, Plot 3, Splendor Forum, Jasola District Centre, New Delhi – 110025, India

103 Penang Road, #05–06/07, Visioncrest Commercial, Singapore 238467

Cambridge University Press is part of Cambridge University Press & Assessment, a department of the University of Cambridge.

We share the University's mission to contribute to society through the pursuit of education, learning and research at the highest international levels of excellence.

www.cambridge.org
Information on this title: www.cambridge.org/9780521731973

First published 2010

A catalogue record for this publication is available from the British Library

Library of Congress Cataloging-in-Publication data
Organizational control / edited by Sim B Sitkin, Laura B. Cardinal, Katinka M. Bijlsma-Frankema.
    p. cm. – (Cambridge companions to management)
  Includes bibliographical references and index.
  ISBN 978-0-521-51744-7 (Hardback) – ISBN 978-0-521-73197-3 (Pbk.)
  1. Organization. 2. Management. I. Sitkin, Sim B II. Cardinal, Laura B.
III. Bijlsma-Frankema, Katinka, 1946– IV. Title. V. Series.
  HD31.O728 2010
  302.3′5–dc22

                                                                    2010016809

ISBN   978-0-521-51744-7   Hardback
ISBN   978-0-521-73197-3   Paperback

Contents

Figures

Tables

Contributors

KATINKA M. BIJLSMA-FRANKEMA is Associate Professor of Organization Theory at VU University, Amsterdam and Professor of Organization Sciences at the European Institute for Advanced Studies in Management (EIASM) in Brussels. She received her M.A. in sociology from the University of Groningen and her Ph.D. in organization sciences from the University of Amsterdam. Current research interests include trust, control, and performance of teams and organizations; learning processes within and between teams; organizational cultures; and managerial cognitions. She has recently edited *Trust under pressure* (2005) and special issues on control in *The Journal of Managerial Psychology* (2004), on trust in *Personnel Review* (2003), and on trust and control in *International Sociology* (2005) and *Group and Organization Management* (2007).

JOHN SEELY BROWN is a visiting scholar and advisor to the Provost at the University of Southern California (USC) and Independent Co-Chairman, Deloitte Center for The Edge. Prior to that he was Chief Scientist of Xerox Corporation and Director of its Palo Alto Research Center (PARC) – a position he held for nearly two decades. He is a member of the National Academy of Education, a fellow of the American Association for Artificial Intelligence and of the American Association for the Advancement of Science (AAAS), and a trustee of the MacArthur Foundation. He serves on numerous public boards (Amazon, Corning, and Varian Medical Systems) and private boards of directors. He has published over 100 papers in scientific journals, and two books (with Paul Duguid *The social life of information* [2000 and 2002], and with John Hagel *The only sustainable edge* [2005]). He received a B.A. from Brown University in 1962 in mathematics and physics and a Ph.D. from the University of Michigan in 1970 in computer and communication sciences. In May 2000 Brown University awarded him an honorary Doctor of Science Degree, which was followed by an honorary Doctor of Science in Economics conferred by the London Business School in July 2001, an honorary Doctor of Humane Letters from Claremont Graduate School in May 2004, and an honorary doctorate from the University of Michigan in 2005. He is an avid reader, traveler and motorcyclist. Part scientist, part artist, and part strategist, his views are unique, distinguished by a broad view of the human contexts in which technologies operate and a healthy skepticism about whether or not change always represents genuine progress.

LAURA B. CARDINAL is Professor of Strategic Management at the C.T. Bauer College of Business, University of Houston. She earned her Ph.D. from the University of Texas at Austin. Her areas of expertise include managing innovation and research and development capabilities, diversification and performance, and understanding the evolution and adaptation of control systems. She serves on the editorial boards of *Strategic Management Journal* and *Organization Science*. Previously, she served as the interest group chair for the Competitive Strategy Interest Group of the Strategic Management Society and as the program and division chair of the Technology and Innovation Management Division of the Academy of Management. She is a National Science Foundation grant recipient and has published in journals such as *Strategic Management Journal, Organization Science, Academy of Management Journal,* and *Journal of Accounting and Economics.*

VIVEK CHOUDHURY is Associate Professor and Head of the Information Systems Department at the College of Business at the University of Cincinnati (UC). He is also currently an SAP fellow at the College. Prior to joining UC in 2000, he taught at the College of Business at Florida State University and, before that, at the University of Pittsburgh. He earned his doctorate in information systems from the University of California, Los Angeles (UCLA). His research interests include: management of offshored/outsourced information technology (IT) projects, trust in electronic commerce, and knowledge management. His publications have appeared in such outlets as *Information Systems Research, MIS Quarterly, Journal of Strategic Information Systems, Journal of Small Business Research, Electronic Markets, E-Service Journal, and Competitive Intelligence Review.* He serves, or has served, on the editorial boards of *MIS Quarterly, Information Systems Research*, and *IEEE Transactions on Engineering Management.*

ANA CRISTINA COSTA is a senior lecturer at Brunel Business School, Brunel University, London. She holds a Ph.D. in trust in organizations from Tilburg University in the Netherlands. Prior to joining Brunel University she was an assistant professor at the Delft University of Technology in the Netherlands. Her research primarily focuses on the development of trust in organizations and how it affects performance. More specifically she is interested in the role played by trust in contexts of cooperation and collaboration within and between organizations where concepts such as social capital, knowledge, and innovation are central. Her work has been published in journals such as *Group and Organization Management, European Journal of Work and Organizational Psychology, International Sociology,* and *Personnel Review.*

RICK DELBRIDGE is Associate Dean (Research) and Professor of Organizational Analysis at Cardiff Business School, a senior fellow of the Economic and Social Research Council (ESRC)/Engineering and Physical Sciences Research Council (EPSRC) Advanced Institute of Management Research, and a fellow of the Sunningdale Institute. His research interests include the management of innovation and critical perspectives on work and organization. His work has appeared in a wide variety of leading journals including *Academy of Management Review, California Management Review, Human Relations, Industrial Relations, Journal of Management Studies,* and *Organization Studies and Sociology.* His books include *Life on the line in contemporary manufacturing* (2000) and *The exceptional manager* (2007). He is Associate Editor of *Organization* and an editorial board member of several other leading international journals.

ROGER L. M. DUNBAR is Professor of Management at the Stern School of Business, New York University. He is interested in sensemaking processes as they relate to organizational design and control, and how language use frames understandings and determines meaning. With Bill Starbuck, he edited a special issue of *Organization Science* (March–April 2006) that focused on organization design. He is a senior editor at *Organization Studies.* He was born in Dunedin,

New Zealand, and studied at the University of Otago. He received his doctorate from Cornell University and his first academic appointment was at Southern Methodist University. He spent five years at the International Institute of Management, part of the Science Center of Berlin, Germany, before moving to New York University. He has held visiting appointments at the Free University in Berlin, the University of Auckland and the Victoria University of Wellington in New Zealand, and the University of Wollongong in Australia.

ELIZABETH GEORGE is an associate professor of management at the School of Business and Management, Hong Kong University of Science and Technology. She earned her Ph.D. from the University of Texas at Austin. Her research interests include identity of individuals in organizations, nonstandard work and workers, and institutionalization processes. Her work can be found in journals such as *Academy of Management Review, Administrative Science Quarterly,* and *Organization Science.*

JOHN HAGEL III, Director of Deloitte Consulting LLP, has nearly thirty years' experience as a management consultant, author, speaker, and entrepreneur. He has helped companies improve their performance by effectively applying information technology to reshape business strategies. He is Co-Chairman of the Silicon Valley-based Deloitte Center for The Edge, which conducts original research and develops substantive points of view for new corporate growth. Before joining Deloitte Consulting, he was an independent consultant and writer, and he held significant positions at leading consulting firms and companies. From 1984 to 2000 he was a principal at McKinsey and Co., where he was a leader of the strategy practice. He is the author of a series of bestselling business books, beginning with *Net gain* and including *Net worth, Out of the box,* and *The only sustainable edge.* He has won two awards from the *Harvard Business Review* for best articles in that publication and has been recognized as an industry thought leader by a variety of publications and professional service firms.

MARIANN JELINEK is the Richard C. Kraemer Professor of Strategy at the Mason School of Business, College of William and Mary in Williamsburg, VA, and Visiting International Professor of Strategy and Entrepreneurship at the Technical University of Eindhoven in the Netherlands. She received her Ph.D. from the University of California at Berkeley (1973), and her D.B.A. from the Graduate School of Business at Harvard (1977). Her research interests have centered on innovation, strategic change and technology, in *The innovation marathon* (1990; 1993) with C. B. Schoonhoven and *Institutionalizing innovation* (1979). She has published six books and more than fifty articles in journals such as *Organization Science, IEEE Transactions in Engineering Management, Academy of Management Review,* and *Harvard Business Review,* and has served on various editorial boards for more than twenty years. She was director of the Innovation and Organization Change program at the National Science Foundation from 1999 to 2001, and has been an academic fellow of the Center for Innovation Management Studies since 2002. Recent work includes studies funded by the National Science Foundation on industry–university relationships around innovation, and on the R&D "lab" of the future in an age of global economic links and computer technology.

SOPHIA SOYOUNG JEONG is a doctoral student in management at the Moore School of Business at the University of South Carolina. Her current research interests include ethical judgment and decision-making, prosocial behavior, trust, and cross-cultural organizational behavior.

LAURIE J. KIRSCH Professor of Business Administration and Senior Associate Dean, joined the Joseph M. Katz Graduate School of Business at the University of Pittsburgh after completing her Ph.D. at the University of Minnesota. Her research explores the exercise of control, governance, and knowledge transfer in the information systems context. She has published in leading scholarly journals such as *MIS Quarterly, Management Science, Organization Science, Information Systems Research,* and *Accounting, Management and Information Technologies.* Her research has been funded by the National Science Foundation and the Advanced Practices Council of the Society for Information Management International. She is very active in the International Conference on Information Systems (ICIS) and the Academy of Management. She serves, or has served, on the editorial boards of *MIS Quarterly, Management Science, Information Systems Research,*

Information and Organization, Decision Sciences, MISQ Executive,
and *The Journal of Strategic Information Systems.*

M. AUDREY KORSGAARD is Professor of Organizational Behavior and
Management at the Moore School of Business of the University of
South Carolina. She received a Ph.D. in psychology from New York
University. Her research addresses the topics of trust and prosocial
behavior and their relationship to interpersonal and intragroup
cooperation and conflict. She has studied these issues in a variety of
work settings, including virtual teams, investor–entrepreneur relations, and joint ventures. She currently serves on the board of the
Journal of Management and previously served as Associate Editor of
the *Journal of Management* and served on the boards of *Entrepreneurship Theory and Practice* and *Journal of Organizational Behavior.*

MARKUS KREUTZER is a senior lecturer of strategic management at the
University of St. Gallen (Switzerland). He recently completed his Ph.D.
at this university and wrote his thesis on *Controlling strategic initiatives:
a contribution to corporate entrepreneurship.* His current research
interests are in the areas of strategy processes, strategic initiatives,
and organizational control. His research was published in *Harvard
Business Manager, IO New Management, Organisationsentwicklung,*
and *Zeitschrift für Unternehmensberatung.*

CHRISTOPH LECHNER holds the EMBA Chair of Strategic Management
at the University of St. Gallen (Switzerland). He is Director of its Institute
of Management and Academic Director of its Ph.D. program in strategy
and management. His present research interests are in the areas of
strategy processes, alliance and network strategy, and corporate competi-
tiveness. He has written five books as well as numerous articles in outlets
such as *Academy of Management Journal, Journal of Management,
Journal of Business Research, Journal of Management Studies, Long
Range Planning, Sloan Management Review,* and *Wall Street Journal.*
He is a member of the editorial boards of *Strategic Management Journal,
Long Range Planning,* and *Journal of Strategy and Management.*

CHRIS P. LONG is an assistant professor of management at the
McDonough School of Business, Georgetown University. He earned
his Ph.D. from Duke University. His research examines how leaders

create contexts within which individuals can achieve high levels of performance (e.g., innovation, efficiency), satisfaction, and commitment. Much of his current work focuses on how leaders integrate their efforts to promote control, trust, and fairness in both traditional organizations and new organizational forms in order to accomplish organizational performance objectives within complex and dynamic business environments.

MISTY L. LOUGHRY is an associate professor of management at Georgia Southern University. She earned her Ph.D. from the University of Florida. Her research examines peer control, control of teamwork, and peer evaluations of teamwork. She is a co-principal investigator on two National Science Foundation grants aimed at improving teamwork in college classrooms. Her research has been published in journals including *Organization Science, Small Group Research,* and *Educational and Psychological Measurement.*

BRUCE M. MEGLINO is Business Partnership Foundation Professor at the Moore School of Business of the University of South Carolina. He received a Ph.D. in business administration from the University of Massachusetts. He conducts research on work values, helping behavior, and rationality. He has been elected a fellow of the American Psychological Association, the Society for Industrial and Organizational Psychology, and the American Psychological Society. He serves on the boards of the *Journal of Applied Psychology* and *Journal of Management.*

WILLIAM OCASIO is the John L. and Helen Kellogg Distinguished Professor of Management of Organization at the Graduate School of Management, Northwestern University. His research focuses on understanding how attention in organizations is shaped by three sets of factors: (1) organizational structures and processes; (2) political capital and dynamics; and (3) culture, language, and institutional logic. He is currently the Division Chair of the Organization and Management Division of the Academy of Management, and Senior Editor at *Organization Science.* He holds an M.B.A. from Harvard University and a Ph.D. in organizational behavior from Stanford.

CUILI QIAN is currently a Ph.D. student of strategy in the Management of Organization Department at Hong Kong University of Science and

Technology. Her current research focuses on corporate governance and corporate social responsibility in emerging economies, and multi-national corporations' staffing and control of subsidiaries.

SIM B. SITKIN is Professor of Management and Faculty Director of the Fuqua/Coach K Center on Leadership and Ethics at Duke University's Fuqua School of Business. His current research focuses on leadership and control systems and their influence on how organizations and their members become more or less capable of change and innovation. He is widely known for his research on the effect of formal and informal organizational control systems and leadership on risk taking, accountability, trust, learning, change, and innovation, including a book, *The legalistic organization*, numerous articles in journals and edited books, and teaching cases. He has served as Senior Editor of *Organization Science*, Associate Editor of the *Journal of Organizational Behavior*, as a member of the Board of Governors of the Academy of Management, and has also worked as a consultant and executive educator with many large and small corporations, non-profit and government organizations worldwide.

MATT STATLER is Associate Director, International Center for Enterprise Preparedness (InterCEP), New York University. He conducts research and coordinates special projects focused on how businesses can become more strategically prepared for disasters and other crises. Before joining InterCEP, he served as Director of Research at the Imagination Lab, a non-profit Swiss foundation. In that role, he designed and facilitated strategy processes for major corporate, non-governmental, and educational organizations, while guiding a multi-disciplinary research team that produced dozens of academic publications. Previously he had worked in A.T. Kearney's Nonprofit Practice, and as Managing Director at Weberize, an internet consulting firm. His educational background includes a B.A. in both philosophy and Spanish literature from the University of Missouri, Columbia. He spent one year at the University of Heidelberg as a Fulbright Scholar, and then obtained a Ph.D. in philosophy from Vanderbilt University. Written with the support of the Mellon Foundation, his dissertation examined the role of repetition in education and focused specifically on the philosopher's allegorical return to the cave. His organizational research has appeared in a number of academic journals and edited volumes, including the *Oxford handbook of organizational decision making* (2008), and, his most recent, *Everyday strategic preparedness: the role of practical wisdom in organizations* (2007).

JOHN VAN MAANEN is the Erwin Schell Professor of Organization Studies in the Sloan School of Management at MIT. He has been a visiting professor at Yale University, the University of Surrey in the UK, and Insead in France. He has published a number of books and articles in the general area of occupational and organizational sociology, including *Tales of the field* (1988) and *Organizational transformations and information technology* (with JoAnne Yates, 2001).

ANTOINETTE WEIBEL is a professor at the University of Liechtenstein and a research fellow of the Center for Research in Economics, Management and the Arts (CREMA). She is vice-president of the First International Network of Trust Researchers (FINT) and an active member of the Academy of Management as well as of the European Group of Organization Studies. Her research interests are intrinsic motivation trust, control and reward systems, and virtuous behavior.

FRANZ WOHLGEZOGEN is a doctoral candidate at the Department of Management and Organization, Kellogg Graduate School of Management, Northwestern University. His research focuses on the cognitive underpinnings of strategy formation and implementation, and the challenges of strategizing interorganizational relationships. He has conducted research examining the impact of stakeholder feedback to publicized strategy on firms' commitment to these strategies, and he is currently examining the effect of firms' diversity of alliance partners on their subsequent alliance portfolio strategies. He holds an M.A. in strategy and international management from the University of St. Gallen, Switzerland, and was a management consultant and educator in Europe and Asia prior to joining the Ph.D. program.

Foreword

We are please to introduce *Organizational Control* by Sim Sitkin, Laura Cardinal, and Katinka Bijlsma-Frankema, the newest volume in our Cambridge Companions to Management series. The series is intended to advance knowledge in the fields of management by presenting the latest scholarship and research on topics of increasing intellectual importance. The volumes offer in-depth treatment of management topics that explore and extend our current knowledge and identify future opportunities for research. Each book in the series is one with a sufficient body of research, and holds significant future promise to inform debates, reviews, and empirical research.

Because management scholarship is increasingly international, scholars can no longer limit their reading to scholarship from their own countries, or restrict their conversations to their neighbors. Innovative intellectual work in management is now conducted throughout the world. Each of the volumes in this series is led by prominent scholars who bring together researchers from several countries in order to reflect multi-national perspectives and foster cross-national debate on the topic.

We appreciate the opportunity to work with Cambridge University Press to bring this series to you. Their rigorous independent scholarly reviews of proposals and manuscripts, and approvals via a board of renowned scholars helps ensure that only the highest-quality scholarship is published. We are confident scholars will find the books in this series stimulating and useful to their own programs of research and to the education of their graduate students.

This volume on control is an exemplar of the series. Organizational control is central to organizing, and this is reflected in the prominent place of theorizing about control in the field several decades ago. Despite the fundamental nature of the phenomenon, this area of study has been and remains seriously neglected. This volume seeks to spur theory and empirical research on control by taking on the serious conceptualization issues in control directly. It is based on the proposition that organizational control, as a fundamental and consequential feature of organizations, merits a revitalization of attention to both theory and empirical research. The foundations of control theorizing are reviewed and separated from much of the mischaracterization that helped undermine cumulative knowledge development. This forms the basis for the several new scholarly efforts gathered here to provide a foundation for renewed attention. This volume brings together new approaches to organizational control theory and research by a diverse group of scholars with different scholarly viewpoints to show the vibrancy and future potential of the domain for generative scholarship. The editors are to be congratulated for this ambitious treatment of an issue that is fundamental to management and organization. We are proud to have assisted in bringing what we believe to be a new foundational text in the field to you.

Cary Cooper, Lancaster University Management School
Jone L. Pearce, University of California, Irvine
Series editors

PART I

Introduction and history

1 | *Control is fundamental*

SIM B SITKIN
Duke University

LAURA B. CARDINAL
University of Houston

KATINKA M. BIJLSMA-FRANKEMA
VU University, Amsterdam

Organizational control is a fundamental aspect of organizing that has been largely neglected by organizational scholars for several decades. This volume brings together new approaches to organizational control theory and research by a diverse group of scholars with different scholarly viewpoints to show the vibrancy and future potential of the domain for generative scholarship. The purpose is to provide a springboard and touchstone for a renewal of work in this area.

Priming a renaissance in control research

Control systems have long been recognized as a fundamental aspect of all organizations (Scott, 1992) through which managers seek to align employee capabilities, activities, and performance with organizational goals and aspirations (Cyert and March, 1963; Merchant, 1985). Despite the fundamental nature of the phenomenon, its recognized importance, and some significant foundational work on organizational control, this area of study has been and remains seriously neglected. Specifically, organizational control is today underconceptualized in terms of its key constructs and its determinants and effects. As a result, organizational control has been subjected to only minimal theoretical and cumulative empirical study in recent years.

The atrophy of control research in the domain of organization and management presents a striking contrast with a rise in recent attention to control in the managerial accounting literature, where it has achieved some prominence (Birnberg and Snodgrass, 1988; Davila, 2005; Davila and Foster, 2007; Henri, 2006; Hopwood, 2005; Merchant and Simons, 1986; Simons, 1991, 1994, 1995; Whitley, 1999). Although the growth of attention to control in accounting research is indeed encouraging and useful, our enthusiasm is tempered by the recognition that this research in accounting represents a specialized view of organizational control. Further, when compared to the phenomenon itself – which is so fundamental to a broad array of organizational practices – the relevant organizational theories are rarely drawn upon in the broader accounting control literature.[1]

This volume is based on the proposition that organizational control, as a fundamental and consequential feature of organizations, merits a revitalization of attention to both theory and empirical research. There are well-established (if largely forgotten or misunderstood) foundations for such work (e.g., Anthony, 1952; Blau and Scott, 1962; Etzioni, 1961, 1964, 1965; Fayol, 1949; Gouldner, 1954; Meyer and Rowan, 1977; Ouchi, 1977, 1978, 1979, 1980; Ouchi and Price, 1978; Perrow, 1970, 1972; Tannenbaum, 1968) as well as new scholarly efforts that could provide a promising springboard for renewed attention.

Conceptualizing organizational control: the intended contributions of the volume

This book aims to *advance the study of organizational control as a fundamental phenomenon, its key characteristics, relevant determinants, and effects.* The perspective chosen to pursue this quest can be distinguished from other approaches in three ways.

First, theoretically, we distinguish control as a coercive efficiency-enhancing tool from control as a source of sensemaking and identity formation. Thus, by acknowledging that control is a consequence and a source of human sensemaking and meaning giving, a wider-than-typical range of possible relevant factors related to control determinants and effects become worth studying.

Second, our perspective favors *configurational* approaches over single control elements studied in isolation, because the latter approach is seen as artificial in the light of sensemaking as a phenomenon. The book seeks to present theoretical explication of why multiple controls are used in particular combinations in certain contexts and the implication of how controls are balanced, adapted to circumstances, and evolve over time. In line with this preference, a promising direction for future research is studying configurations of control and other factors that promote commitment to organizational goals and effort directed at these goals, for instance, trust- or collaboration-promoting activities. Studying such configurations will promote awareness of organizational paradoxes and dilemmas flowing from simultaneous needs for control, which is expected to deepen our understanding of control in future research.

Third, the approach chosen implies a certain awareness of the *developmental nature* of organizational phenomena, such as control. By opening the book with a section in which the study of control is put in a *historical perspective*, the idea that present conceptualizations of control can be understood as part of a *process with a past and a future* is made salient. Dynamic theoretical and empirical research on how controls first come into use and how their use changes over time may add more to our understanding of control than cross-sectional studies.

By collecting the most generative of new scholarly approaches in one volume, this book was created to make control salient again to organizational researchers. By exploring a range of promising conceptualizations, developed in the past and in present scholarly work, the contours of a viable agenda for future research can be sketched. In particular, we hope to provide the theoretical and empirical foundations for priming a resurgence of cumulative work on this important topic.

Conceptualizing organizational control

The purpose of this volume is to provide a generative basis and stimulus for future work on control in organizations. Thus, the book is organized into four parts that reflect the types of stimuli we hope to offer.

Part I, **Introduction and History**, offers a context for exploring new conceptualizations and studies of organizational control. To open the volume, **Roger Dunbar** and **Matt Statler** provide a perspective on the history of organizational control research in **"A historical perspective on organizational control."** They begin by assessing how ancient Chinese, eighteenth-century Europeans, and, more recently, Americans used alternative conceptualizations of agency to formulate different types and patterns of organizational control. They articulate the underlying assumptions that have shaped how control has been developed, conceptualized, and written about. They propose a new narrative perspective on control that not only draws upon traditional approaches to control, but also is well-suited to the new complex and distributed forms that are emerging in contemporary organizations and can help guide future research on control.

Part II focuses on **Conceptions of organizational control,** leveraging and extending promising recent work on the conceptualization of control. Traditional approaches to control are extended to include more integrative, multi-faceted, and dynamic conceptions through the use of a configurational approach. In addition, two challenges to traditional approaches are offered, based on critical theory and the emergence of new organizational forms rarely taken into account in traditional organizational control theory. Thus, this section both extends and sharpens existing control theory and also examines the concept of control from fresh angles.

"A configurational theory of control," by **Laura Cardinal, Sim Sitkin,** and **Chris Long,** examines the fundamental building blocks of organizational control and develops a synthesis of complementary, yet traditional, views of control. The authors contend that research on organizational control has been stifled by a highly fragmented literature and static theoretical frameworks and has not progressed substantially since Ouchi's (1977, 1978, 1979, 1980) work in the 1970s and 1980s, with the possible exception of the work of critical theorists (e.g., Adler, 2007; Adler *et al.*, 2007; Barker, 1993; Jermier, 1998). In this chapter, Cardinal, Sitkin, and Long build on prior control research, but also extend it. They outline four problems in the control literature that have stymied the development of an empirical stream of research: lack of conceptual consensus, fragmentation, singularity, and lack of attention to control development. These authors develop a framework that integrates prior theories that have addressed control systems, control mechanisms, and control targets. Their framework permits us to explain the adoption and adaptation of individual organizational control mechanisms, as well as the overall evolution of organizational control systems over time.

Rick Delbridge contrasts critical perspectives with "mainstream" views of organizational control in his chapter, **"Critical perspectives on organizational control: reflections and prospects."** He begins by suggesting that management and employees are agents with divergent interests that at best temporarily overlap. Delbridge looks at the historical development of critical management studies (CMS) and states that CMS seeks to understand the effects of control on those at work, given the shortcomings of management practices and structures. He suggests that CMS questions the overly narrow views of performance in economic terms that concern "mainstream" management research. The author delineates four power-and-knowledge themes that provide challenges for "mainstream" control researchers: questioning the taken-for-granted, beyond efficiency and profit maximization, ontology and epistemology, and challenging structures of domination. He further suggests that control researchers sidestep the issue of whether managers rationally choose forms of control because we are uncomfortable with power and ethical implications of managerial control. Delbridge contributes to our understanding of organizational control by incorporating the concept of identity in our theories of organizational control and helps us comprehend a more nuanced and complex appreciation of agency within social structures.

The chapters in Part III, **Identity, attention, and motivation in organizational control**, develop an array of issues, honing in on specific types of control, contexts in which control issues arise, and especially interesting or important determinants and effects of organizational control.

John Van Maanen's "Identity work and control in occupational communities" taps the case of urban police officers to explore how control in occupational communities fundamentally depends on individual and collective identity work in order to affect organizational member behavior. By reflecting the limits of managerial authority and influence, the chapter highlights the limits of formal and hierarchical control when compared with the relative power of peer and informal control over police behavior. When control works, Van Maanen suggests, it must do so through its influence on the ongoing efforts of organizational members to build and sustain their sense of self-identity and identity with their co-workers. This chapter provides a springboard for future work that links nuanced in-depth studies of control in individual organizations or professions and experimental studies of how identity-based influence in organizations works and is guided by control systems, leaders, and peers.

"Organizational identity and control: can the two go together?" by **Elizabeth George** and **Cuili Qian**, explores the previously underattended idea that organizational control can have a positive effect on employee motivation through promoting employee adoption of an organizational identity. They criticize the general assumption underlying most conceptualizations of control: that there is a divergence of interest between the organization and the individual, such that individuals are likely to take care of their own interests ahead of those of the organization. The authors argue that this need not be the case and that control theory could benefit from taking individual motivation into account. They propose that identity is a strong motivator of behavior and that by understanding how identity shapes behavior, some of the insights about identity could be integrated into conceptualizations of control. George and Qian discuss four ways in which identity can be incorporated into managerial control: membership-based control, prototype-based control, identity salience-based control, and identity coherence-based control. These types are distinguished regarding their effect on two functions of identity (e.g., uncertainty reduction and self-esteem enhancement), and the managerial tasks involved.

William Ocasio and **Franz Wohlgezogen's** "Attention and control" examines how five types of control affect attention in organizations and, through their effect on attention, influence decisions and actions with respect to organizational goals. Specifically, they differentiate hierarchical, outcome, behavioral, cultural, and channel controls. These authors explore how each type of control affects attention and what the drawbacks of each form of control are for attention. By drawing upon insights concerning both regulative and normative controls, and structural and situation-specific controls, and how each one influences attention in direct and indirect ways, their work opens valuable avenues for future research by linking these two literatures.

In "**The role of motivational orientations in formal and informal control,**" **Audrey Korsgaard, Bruce Meglino,** and **Sophia Jeong** outline a framework that takes into account motives and mode of reasoning to understand the effectiveness of organizational control. Traditional research has historically focused on whether goals and means are understood and transparent in comprehending control use (Ouchi, 1979; Thompson, 1967). Korsgaard *et al.* expand that view by incorporating the two constructs (motivational bases and judgment processes) in order to understand employee responses to formal and informal control. Motivational mechanisms can be shaped by self-interest (i.e., personal) or other interest (i.e., the good of the organization). Judgment processes involve either heuristic reasoning that is effortless and automatic (i.e., based on values or norms) or rational deliberation (i.e., based on consequences). Organizational control mediated by behavior–consequence contingencies is expected to be more effective when an employee has a rational self-interest orientation. Conversely, organizational control mediated by social influences is expected to be more effective when the employee has adopted another orientation. Their perspective offers a framework for managers to adapt their operating practices using contextually tailored modes of control and presents a theoretical perspective for future research that moves beyond examining only goals and means as the primary lens to understanding organizational control and effectiveness.

The authors in Part IV, **Relational control**, challenge existing perspectives on organizational control that exclusively consider inside the organization as the focal unit of control, the centrality of controlees in understanding the appropriate mode of control, and managers as the sole source of control. By broadening the theoretical boundaries of organizational control theory these authors not only challenge conventional wisdom, but offer new avenues not previously explored in organizational control research.

In **"Relational networks, strategic advantage: new challenges for collaborative control," John Hagel, John Seely Brown,** and **Mariann Jelinek** address the rising phenomenon of control in networks of organizations. They note that nearly all writing about organizational control has focused on control within organizations, with the exception of work on how formal joint ventures are managed. In contrast, they stress that there is much to learn from how informal (but powerful) networks of organizations have emerged and become quite successful in part because of how they manage control under such complex, adaptive, and emergent circumstances. The core control in these new forms can best be characterized, according to Hagel, Brown, and Jelinek, as relational rather than transactional. The functioning of these "relational networks" is lubricated by trust, which guides their selection of partners, connections among practices, and development of learning opportunities. The shift from analyzing control at the firm level to analyzing control at the network level presents both a significant new thrust in control research and also offers the opportunity for new insights from a new, rapidly emerging form of organizing.

"Toward a theory of relational control: how relationship structure influences the choice of control," by **Laurie Kirsch** and **Vivek Choudhury**, argues that the traditional Ouchi-based (1977, 1978) view of control is incomplete because it examines the feasibility of control mode from only the controller's perspective. They suggest that as work has become more team oriented, peer based, virtual, and distributed, the nature of the relationship between both controller and controllee needs to be considered. The authors develop a typology of relationships that examines the degree and type of risks and delineates the mode of control that builds trust within each type of relationship. Kirsch and Choudhury examine the differences in relationships by taking into account both the form (interdependence) and the depth (degree of importance and contact) of the relationship. Their integrated model incorporates the feasibility and need for control for both controller and controllee in control theories reflecting the complexity of modern-day organizations.

Misty Loughry, in **"Peer control in organizations,"** argues that although peer control is widespread in organizations, it is not well understood. She consequently aims to systematize our current understanding of peer control. Her perspective on peer control questions the assumption that managers exclusively exercise control. In the first part of the chapter, she discusses the scope of the peer control concept, starting from a broad description: "Peer control occurs when workers who are at the same organizational level or in the same field exert lateral control over their peers." In the second part, she distinguishes four types of peer control, following from two dimensions (e.g., formal versus informal, and management designed versus worker designed). Several examples of each type are presented. In the third part of the chapter, she discusses the potential benefits and drawbacks of peer control, drawing upon five theoretical perspectives that can be used to examine informal peer control. The chapter concludes with suggestions for areas meriting greater attention in future research on peer control: levels of analysis, characteristics of workers, characteristics of the organizational context, the broader control system, and supervisor effects.

In Part V, **Managerial and strategic control**, the following chapters examine new theories and empirical opportunities for enhancing our understanding of how organizational control mechanisms and systems are adopted, function in organizations, and can influence the "levers of control" (Simons, 1995) that are utilized.

In **"Control to cooperation: examining the role of managerial authority in portfolios of managerial actions,"** Chris Long presents a new theoretical direction for control research by refining and complementing the work of control theorists who focus primarily on how managers use power and control to influence the interests and actions of their employees. Long questions two underlying assumptions of these control theorists: first, that superior–subordinate goal conflict is omnipresent within organizations; and second, that managers possess a quantity and quality of resources necessary to effectively implement whatever controls they seek to apply. He proposes that a systematic consideration of issues related to managerial authority may help scholars to formulate more comprehensive and realistic pictures of managerial attention and action. He specifically argues that a manager's interest in preserving, protecting, and promoting his or her managerial legitimacy and authority forms a primary motivation for managerial action. The interests that managers have in developing or maintaining that authority by taking legitimate actions lead managers to balance their efforts to implement controls with the efforts they make to promote trust and fairness. These efforts are discussed in terms of managerial actions which lead to the separate aims, along with possible tensions between the aims and how a balance can be struck between them.

"**Consequences and antecedents of managerial and employee legitimacy interpretations of control: a natural open system approach,**" by **Katinka Bijlsma-Frankema** and **Ana Cristina Costa**, explores a natural and open system approach (Scott, 1992) to control, by combining institutional theory and organizational culture theory to challenge and complement traditional approaches to control. The authors challenge two dominant ideas from these approaches: first, that managers rationally choose control forms, and second, that control is interpreted negatively by employees. Building on institutional theory, their proposition is that key to the valence of interpretations and behavioral consequences of control is whether, given the explicit or implicit legitimization of a control mode by management, it is legitimate in the eyes of those controlled. If a control mode is deemed appropriate by organizational members, they will accept it, voluntarily comply, and positive consequences for the organization can be expected in the form of in-role and extra-role behaviors. Based on a historic analysis of management models, they distinguish four sources of legitimacy, on which managers and employees can draw to form their interpretations of the legitimacy of a control mode. Tensions among the four sources may demand juggling different interpretations. The authors develop a theoretical framework for research on organizational control to understand why control is found appropriate in some situations, and hence accepted, but not in other situations. The framework focuses on the relation between managerial and employee legitimacy interpretations of the control modes in an organization, how both groups draw on the four sources distinguished, and how these interpretations were developed in the past.

In "**Managerial objectives of formal control: high motivation control mechanisms,**" Antoinette Weibel addresses a key challenge faced by managers as they try to implement formal control – the need to anticipate and address the unintended consequences of formal control. In the literature, this relationship has been mostly portrayed as negative: formal control is thought to signal distrust and employees are proposed to react to this distrust signal by reducing their intrinsic motivation and their voluntary engagement. Weibel argues that formal control, if "properly" enacted and combined in a complementary way, can boost rather than harm intrinsic motivation. She draws on self-determination theory to propose an integrative alternative in which formal control can positively influence three drivers of intrinsic motivation (autonomy, competence, and relatedness support). Thus, Weibel lays the basis for future work on the positive effects of formal control by outlining how formal controls can address both extrinsic and intrinsic motivation to the extent they attend to the three key drivers resulting in "high motivation control."

In "**Control configurations and strategic initiatives,**" Markus Kreutzer and **Christoph Lechner** seek to understand strategic initiatives through the lens of organizational control. By bringing organizational context into the realm of organizational transformation they develop a typology of strategic initiatives that enhances both theory and practice by linking the internal organization with external market developments. Six types of strategic initiatives are derived from the core components of return on invested capital (ROIC). The authors take a configurational approach to control to explore how strategic initiatives are guided, monitored, and controlled, thus capturing the complexities faced by pursuing different business objectives. Kreutzer and Lechner's rich, descriptive framework offers a platform for future research examining the intervening behaviors required by the initiatives and encouraged by the control configuration. Further, their framework helps us understand the difficulty firms face in achieving optimal fit between strategic initiatives and organizational control.

Advancing the study of organizational control

The control studies in this book not only shed a different light on the phenomenon of control, they also imply directions for future research. Three core recommendations come to the fore in the ideas presented: (1) the need to develop dynamic theoretical models of organizational control to be tested on longitudinal data; (2) the need for more research on how control functions at different levels of analysis and how its determinants and effects cross levels using combinations of qualitative and quantitative data; and (3) the need for traditional control theory to be significantly – even radically – rethought to account for new organizational forms, nonhierarchical sources of control; and the use of more multifaceted control choices by managers, peers, and others in and between organizations.

It is an exciting time to examine the issues surrounding control in organizations. With new forms of organization emerging, with a more diverse workforce, and during a period of ever-faster change, the need for scholars to increase their understanding of organizational control could not be more strongly felt, both in the academic world and in the world of practicing managers. This volume is intended to provide just such a springboard for a resurgence of interest and future work on the topic of control in organizations.

Note

1 Exceptions include research by Kenneth Merchant and Robert Simons.

References

Adler, P. 2007. The future of critical management studies: a paleo-Marxist critique of labour process theory. *Organization Studies*, 28: 1313–1345.

Adler, P., Forbes, L., and Willmott, H. 2007. Critical management studies: premises, practices, problems, and prospects. *Annals of the Academy of Management*, 1: 119–180.

Anthony, R. N. 1952. *Management controls in industrial research organizations*. Cambridge, MA: Harvard University Press.

Barker, J. 1993. Tightening the iron cage: concertive control in self-managing teams. *Administrative Science Quarterly*, 38: 408–437.

Blau, P. and Scott, W. R. 1962. *Formal organizations: a comparative approach.* San Francisco: Chandler Publishing Company.

Birnberg, J. G. and Snodgrass, C. 1988. Culture and control: a field study. *Accounting, Organizations and Society,* 13: 447–464.

Cyert, R. M. and March, J. G. 1963. *A behavioral theory of the firm.* Englewood Cliffs, NJ: Prentice-Hall.

Davila, T. 2005. The promise of management control systems for innovation and strategic change. In C. S. Chapman (ed.), *Controlling strategy. Management, accounting, and performance measurement:* 37–61. Oxford University Press.

Davila, A. and Foster, G. 2007. Management control systems in early-state startup companies. *The Accounting Review,* 82: 907–937.

Etzioni, A. 1961. *A comparative analysis of complex organizations: on power, involvement, and their correlates.* New York, NY: Free Press.

1964. *Modern organizations.* Englewood Cliffs, NJ: Prentice-Hall.

1965. Organizational control structure. In J. G. March (ed.), *Handbook of organizations:* 650–677. Chicago: Rand McNally.

Fayol, H. 1949. *General and industrial management.* C. Storrs (trans.). London: Pitman.

Gouldner, A. 1954. *Patterns of industrial bureaucracy.* New York, NY: Free Press.

Henri, J. F. 2006. Management control systems and strategy: a resource-based perspective. *Accounting, Organizations and Society,* 31: 529–558.

Hopwood, A. G. 2005. After 30 years (Editorial). *Accounting, Organizations and Society,* 30: 585–586.

Jermier, J. 1998. Introduction: critical perspectives on organizational control. *Administrative Science Quarterly,* 43: 235–256.

Merchant, K. A. 1985. *Control in business organizations.* Marshfield, MA: Pitman.

Merchant, K. A. and Simons, R. 1986. Research and control in complex organizations: an overview. *Journal of Accounting Literature,* 5: 183–203.

Meyer, J. W. and Rowan, B. 1977. Institutionalized organizations: formal structure as myth and ceremony. *American Journal of Sociology,* 83: 340–360.

Ouchi, W. G. 1977. The relationship between organizational structure and organizational control. *Administrative Science Quarterly,* 22: 95–113.

1978. The transmission of control through organizational hierarchy. *Academy of Management Journal,* 21: 173–192.

1979. A conceptual framework for the design of organizational control mechanisms. *Management Science,* 25: 833–848.

1980. Markets, bureaucracies, and clans. *Administrative Science Quarterly,* 25: 129–141.

Ouchi, W. G. and Price, R. L. 1978. Hierarchies, clans, and Theory Z: a new perspective on organization development. *Organizational Dynamics*, 7: 62–70.

Perrow, C. 1970. *Organizational analysis: a sociological view.* Belmont, CA: Wadsworth.

1972. *Complex organizations: a critical essay.* Glenview, IL: Scott, Foresman.

Scott, R. W. 1992. *Organizations: rational, natural, and open systems.* Englewood Cliffs, NJ: Prentice-Hall.

Simons, R. 1991. Strategic orientation and top management attention to control systems. *Strategic Management Journal*, 12: 49–62.

1994. How new top managers use control systems as levers of strategic renewal. *Strategic Management Journal*, 15: 169–189.

1995. *Levers of control: how managers use innovative control systems to drive strategic renewal.* Boston, MA: Harvard Business School Press.

Tannenbaum, A. S. 1968. *Control in organizations.* New York: McGraw-Hill.

Thompson, J. D. 1967. *Organizations in action.* New York: McGraw-Hill.

Whitley, R. 1999. Firms, institutions and management control: the comparative analysis of coordination and control systems. *Accounting, Organizations and Society*, 24: 507–524.

2 | A historical perspective on organizational control

ROGER L. M. DUNBAR
New York University

MATT STATLER
New York University

Organizational control: an old, familiar story

Repeatedly through the ages, people have come together to talk and learn about ways of exercising organizational control. From such interactions norms have emerged about effective behavior patterns, and some of these norms have been rendered explicit in codes, principles, laws, adages, edicts, and maxims, that is, in the discursive artifacts that people use to exercise political power and claim moral authority. As people have wanted to explain how an organization has exercised control at a particular time and place, they have constructed stories relating the situational facts to behavioral norms and institutional conditions. Over time, the assumptions that people have made about organizational control have changed too, and these assumptions have influenced the stories they have told. This chapter traces how organizational control has historically been understood.

We begin with one of the very few instances where contemporary organizational scholars have directly addressed the content of this deep human heritage. Specifically, Rindova and Starbuck (1997) describe how the ancient Chinese saw organizations and used conceptualizations of agency relationships to construct alternative ways to exercise organizational control. Next, we move to eighteenth-century Europe and then America and consider how the exercise of organizational control unfolded over time in the West. In particular, we describe how industrial bureaucracies developed and how people would often resist the associated organizational constraints. We consider how this resistance spawned efforts, in turn, to make organizational control more sensitive to human needs and more democratic. We identify the ontological, epistemological, and ethical assumptions that seem to have shaped organizational control research over the years and we suggest that a new set of assumptions is needed in order to accommodate a "narrative perspective" on organizational control. The benefit of a narrative perspective is that it can incorporate age-old organizational control ideas, while explaining how control occurs in contemporary organizations.

Agency relationships: an ancient control pattern

Rindova and Starbuck (1997: 146) discuss an ancient text, "The Officials of Chou," which described organizing processes in China around 1100 BC. The text advised leaders to organize by using rules to define departments, allocate responsibilities, specify coordination practices, define operating procedures and exceptions, and to carry out performance audits. This ancient proposal seems to advocate an approach to control very similar to what, today, we would describe as a modern bureaucracy (Weber, 1978).

The text suggests that control within organizations depends on hierarchical agency relationships linking superiors and subordinates. Ideally, these relations are harmonious, and superiors and subordinates show respect for one another in terms of etiquette, social rank, and the performance of duties. Such respect establishes a context of social order wherein organizations can function. Centuries later, Confucius warned superiors that they should always show consideration to subordinates, for, if they did not, they might find that organizing rules would not work. It seems the ancient Chinese recognized not only that rules were the basis of organization, but that if organizations were to be effective, those with power must also show respect for the social context constructed by the rules.

China was embroiled in wars from around the middle of the fourth century BC and over the next 200 years, a single, centralized state gradually emerged. The new Chinese rulers also relied on laws to organize but in contrast to the views of Confucius they did not see consideration as an important aspect of superior–subordinate relationships. Instead, texts advocated the control of superior–subordinate relations by the use of incentives, suggesting, for example, that superiors could use income, rank or position to reward those who did as they directed. Texts noted, however, that if leaders offer incentives, subordinates try to obtain them and in doing so, they can become manipulative and cannot be trusted. Texts advised superiors to anticipate such situations by distrusting subordinates, withholding power from them, concealing thoughts from them, and inspiring fear in them. They justified the approach by noting that though people can be energetic, intelligent, and capable, people who are offered incentives can become independent, self-interested, and deceitful. At the time, control and power were perceived to be closely intertwined, and so approaches to control were expected not only to motivate subordinates but also to guard against any attempt by them to take over superior's power.

These ideas – using rules to structurally organize, and alternative types of agency relationships to implement organizational control – remain familiar today. That is, texts still suggest that one should use rules to constitute stable organizational platforms from which to exercise control (Weber, 1978). They also suggest that the use of additional rules and procedures can facilitate the assignment of resources, the allocation of tasks, the coordination of action, and the assessment of performance (Arrow, 1974). Hierarchical relationships still divide organizations into members at upper levels with power and status who direct and reward, and members at lower levels who do tasks and are subject to upper level direction (Fayol, 1949). In implementing control, one current approach emphasizes superior and subordinate cooperation and mutual respect, while the other advocates the use of rewards and punishments to motivate subordinates to adhere to rules and perform at high levels (McGregor, 1960).

It would require a small army of historians, political scientists, and philosophers to explain how ancient Chinese governance traditions influenced the subsequent evolution of organizational practice in China or elsewhere. Yet the two alternative beliefs about the appropriate construction of human agency relationships are familiar enough. They seem to constitute a pair of basic patterns that continue to clarify alternative ways organizational control can be conceptualized, implemented in practice, and experienced by organizational actors (cf. Adler, 1999; Bijlsma-Frankema and Costa, Chapter 13).

A genealogy of organizational control: tracing contemporary lines of evolution

Just as the Chinese constructed rule-based organizational platforms from which to undertake organizational control efforts, later Europeans also used similar constructions. Yet as reliance on hierarchical agency relationships increased in Europe and later in the United States, the number of recorded incidents where people resisted rather than accepted control structures also seems to have grown, creating a continuing issue for organizational control implementation. We select representative studies to explain how prescriptions for achieving organizational control were developed and implemented. We then selectively review studies that explain why people resisted organizational control and other studies that have sought ways to overcome this resistance (for review, see Mumby, 2005).

Bureaucracy: the rule platform underlying organizational control

Over time, organizations develop the technologies and skills that are necessary to do particular tasks. As they do tasks better, they tend to grow and, historically, in the process, they have usually also become more hierarchical and more bureaucratic so that organizational control becomes an increasingly important issue. Interests then often emerge that are linked not just to ownership but also to different aspects of the growing organization (Weber, 1978). Over time and based on calculation and rationalization, organization owners and managers identify rules to standardize how tasks are done usually with the aim of having them done more efficiently. Also, rewards and other sanctions are often introduced to encourage employees to adhere to organization standards.

In recent European and American history, the evolution of bureaucratization and organizational control seem to be closely linked. Langton (1984), for example, described how Josiah Wedgwood built his pottery factory over the second half of the eighteenth century and how he developed procedures to run it. Pottery was manufactured in small workshops at the start of the eighteenth century. As tea and coffee drinking increased in Britain and living standards also improved, however, the demand for better and cheaper pottery grew. After much experimentation, Wedgwood perfected what he called Queen's Ware pottery – attractive earthenware that he could make cheaply and quickly. Before he could mass-produce, however, he needed infrastructure – roads and canals – to transport his pottery (without breakage) to markets. With others, he petitioned parliament to build roads and canals in Staffordshire. As the roads and the canals were built, so Wedgwood also built his factory. Langton (1984) describes how over three decades, Wedgwood discovered and then imposed bureaucratic factory rules and behaviors, the aim being to control and improve factory efficiency. As Wedgwood put it, his intent was "to make ARTISTS ... of mere men ... and make such machines of the men as cannot err," (McKendrick, 1961: 34, as cited in Langton, 1984: 333).

The pottery industry was traditionally organized around master–worker relations and relied on superior–subordinate respect rather than rewards for adherence to standard rules. In fact, employee discipline in the industry was not strong. In contrast to this lack of discipline characteristic of employee relations in small potteries, Wedgwood and other large firms sought to achieve tight employee discipline by rewarding strict adherence to factory rules. Eventually, the products made in traditional pottery workshops could not compete with the cheaper and better products made by the larger firms and so gradually, the small firms disappeared. As larger firms flourished, the work done within them was increasingly standardized and worker activities were constrained because Wedgwood was convinced that factory task performance required rules and rule enforcement. In fact, his rules supported not only task performance but also factory administration. For example, he had rules for worker attendance and punctuality, other rules to prevent waste, and so on. Indeed, he "published an incredibly detailed set of rules governing both production and conduct" (Langton, 1984: 344) and based on his rules, he fined or dismissed violators. Other rules identifying positions in the factory defined a career ladder that enabled him to reward those who respected the rules with higher salaries and higher status. Throughout his life, Wedgwood continually added to and adjusted his factory rules (Langton, 1984).

As fortune would have it, John Wesley, the founder of Methodism, began preaching in Staffordshire. Wesley and Wedgwood were soon close friends and mutual supporters. Wesley preached that to be saved, people had to lead more sober and respectable lives, a position that was nicely consistent with Wedgwood's desire for rule-based discipline based on factory rules. Influenced by his friend's theological framework, Wedgwood saw his organization control process as one of all-round positive moral change that converted "traditional potters into rational, industrial functionaries" (Langton,

1984: 342–344) who then generated better and improved product quality, huge production volumes, high wages for workers, and a huge fortune for Wedgwood (Kanigel, 1997).

Implementing industrial controls

Despite the many benefits generated by his factory, Wedgwood also encountered employees who refused to adhere to his organizational control rules. As he believed that organizational control depended on adherence to organizational rules, it was important for Wedgwood and also firm owners like him to understand this resistance. To uncover some of the issues involved, we consider the contributions of Frederick Taylor, another highly influential figure in the development of organizational control ideas.

Taylor grew up in Philadelphia and from an early age, he was fascinated with all things scientific, technical, and measurable. During the three years that he spent in Europe, he learned French and German after which he attended Exeter Academy before returning to Philadelphia. Despite his privileged upbringing and his interests in the scientific and the abstract, Taylor became an apprentice patternmaker in a metal foundry. Foundry work was dangerous, equipment breakdowns were common, and often, workers faced injury. They had to learn what to do and how to survive by working with and copying the more experienced foundry workers. Remarkably, Taylor concluded that this type of on-the-job training was, on balance, a good experience. His reasoning was that if a bit of brutality knocked ambitious spirits back and convinced people to do what they were told, to fit in, and to serve, then it was justified. He claimed later that as he had been a worker, he had learned and understood what work contexts were like and also how workers thought. He believed these understandings gave credibility to his ideas about organizational control.

Taylor finished his apprenticeship in 1878 and obtained a management position at Midvale Steel. There, workers were paid piece rates and if they earned too much, bosses cut their piece rate. If workers found ways to do things faster, their earnings increased and then, again, their piece rate would be cut. To avoid provoking management to cut piece rates in this way, workers learned to hold back production so that everyone worked at the same pace and earned the same wage. As an apprentice, Taylor had participated in such output restriction efforts and so he knew how workmen could control output levels. As a manager, however, he intended to break these output controls.

To do so, he took men aside and showed them how to work faster. If they did not then work faster, he fired them. Next, he would hire and train new people and, if they did no better, he fired them too. Workers described Taylor as a brutal liar with no idea what he was doing. They said the reason their machines broke down was because they did as he told them. Taylor responded that if a machine broke down, the worker using it would pay for its repair. Taylor warned management that his methods would meet with worker resistance and they had agreed to back him. His battle to control Midvale's production levels lasted two years. Reflecting on the experience, Taylor said that he did not want initiative from the men – he just wanted them to obey his orders.

Taylor believed that organization control could be achieved based on knowledge, but he also thought he did not have enough knowledge to exercise the degree of control that he wanted. For example, the workmen at Midvale knew how to go slow even as they could convince management they were working as hard as they could. Taylor could see through most of this but he was not sure that if the men actually did as he said, they would achieve the results he hoped for. He took comfort, however, from the fact that the men did not know what results to expect either, for their knowledge was based simply on shop lore, guesswork, and rules-of-thumb (i.e., situated knowledge that was also often subject to work restriction norms). Taylor was confident that the knowledge he generated using careful measuring methods divorced of work restriction norms determined what could be done in a "more scientific" way and so was superior to any knowledge the workers might possess. He also felt that his superior knowledge was justification enough for the way in which he would dismiss worker complaints and protests.

Taylor generated work knowledge by systematically breaking work cycles down into minute pieces and using experimentation, time-and-motion studies, and data records to find out just how fast different machine tools could go. He chose simple work cycles and most often, his control goal was high production speed. To develop control methods to achieve the highest speeds, he believed everything needed to be tracked, recorded, and standardized. He also believed that all factories would eventually develop and implement this type of knowledge. Taylor divided factory personnel into managers who knew about how machinery worked and how it could be made to work, in contrast to workers who he did not expect to think about how machinery could work at all. Instead, the role of the worker in Taylor's mind was to do as directed and be motivated to do it faster by a piece-rate incentive schedule that was designed by Taylor. Hierarchical role distinctions pervaded Taylor's approach.

In the 1890s, Taylor became a consultant and started presenting papers. His claim was that the way he used piece rates aligned worker and management interests. In order to establish alignment, however, it was necessary for management to study and analyze each job and determine the best way for the work to be done. Based on this knowledge, management could then set output levels that defined a production floor (i.e., workers had to achieve the floor before they would be entitled to additional rewards based on the piece-rate system). Once a production floor and a piece rate were set, Taylor was adamant that organizations could not change them. He reasoned that only if workers believed that they could depend on an unchanging reward structure, would they work to achieve high production levels.

For everyone, then, the process for setting the level of the production floor and the piece-rate schedule was crucial. While determining the appropriate levels for piece rates, Taylor was secretive and slow as he knew his judgments would ultimately be critical for all concerned. Once he understood the work and had set a production floor and a piece rate, however, he sought to share his knowledge with the workers and show them how to achieve high production levels. His aim was high production rates for firms and high rewards for workers – this was the interest alignment he had in mind that he also believed would ultimately ensure the acceptance of his approach. He did not consider how his organizational perspective pervasively emphasizing hierarchical role differences could also have implications for organizational control effectiveness.

Taylor never implemented his organizational control approach on any scale. At Bethlehem Steel, for example, he was hired as a consultant to reduce plant costs. He saw how some people had a greater aptitude for particular types of work than others and so he studied the abilities needed for particular jobs and selectively hired people who had these abilities. One of his selective hires was "Schmidt," a man with exceptional strength and an ability to load pig iron. Taylor studied and trained Schmidt so that eventually, he may have loaded pig iron at rates never seen before or since. Taylor thought of Schmidt as a great success because he did what Taylor told him (i.e., he loaded large quantities of pig iron to the benefit of Bethlehem Steel) and, due to the piece rate set by Taylor, he was also very well paid. Schmidt's co-workers, however, hated him and continually harassed him. Taylor's approach was also impractical because of the time it took to work out an appropriate level for a production floor and the piece-rate incentive. Even if these levels were determined appropriately, management would most likely again confront new rounds of worker resistance and scorn.

The human relations paradigm

Taylor called his approach, "scientific management." While his approach had its adherents, it also ushered in a backdrop of debate about whether the "hard" science approach advocated by Taylor was actually appropriate for studying and controlling humans. Some (e.g., Trist and Murray, 1990) rejected the approach outright, claiming it was dehumanizing on ethical and epistemological grounds. Others (e.g., Likert, 1961a) rejected it on pragmatic grounds, for it had become clear that Taylor's methods generated extensive labor resistance and many disputes, and these costs and delays ultimately destroyed the economic value that might have been associated with his approach.

It was striking that Taylor's methods showed neither interest nor respect for any role that the people actually doing the controlled tasks might play in the control process. Shifting from an exclusive focus on task design mechanics and reachable output levels, therefore, scholars refocused attention on just how the organizational control efforts were implemented and how this process might psychologically influence how people reacted. This led to a series of field studies in different locations that examined a wide range of managerial initiatives and considered how people attributed meaning to them.

In the famous Hawthorne studies, Elton Mayo tried to hedge against the socialism and syndicalism growing during the late 1920s by looking for factors that actually motivated workers (Mayo, 1933). His psychological methods inquired whether the causes of conflict between management and labor could be identified and, if so, if they could be rationally controlled. The studies involved factory workers making telephone equipment in Cicero, Illinois. The study aim was to track the performance consequences of a large number of interventions such as turning the lights up or down to make rooms brighter or darker, authorizing or canceling coffee breaks, and so on. A "problem" arose as it was realized that most interventions and almost any sort of change all seemed to increase production. The authors attributed output increases not just to the conditions that their intervention changed, but also to the changed attitudes and social relations that the experiments brought about at the Cicero work site. In particular, the researchers noted how as people were happily working as a team and had no sense of coercion, feelings of autonomy seemed to emerge and people would simply do things to help themselves and their organization. An implication for organizational control was that leaders needed social skills that could foster teamwork. A leader's superior social skills seemed to act as if they were a continuing throughput control, enabling ongoing cooperation in on-the-job situations while simultaneously also disarming worker alienation.

In the mid-1940s, MIT's Research Center for Group Dynamics included Kurt Lewin, Ronald Lippitt, Leland Bradford, and Kenneth Benne and they shared concerns about the role of hierarchy and the future of participatory democracy in organizations. Lewin's field theory (Lewin, 1943) framed "group dynamics" in terms of how personal, situational, and contextual forces affected group behaviors. Granting the unavoidable and shaping influence of contextual factors, the group rejected both behaviorist and experimental methods and, instead, adopted a participatory, action research approach to the development of situated knowledge about organizations (Bradford *et al.*, 1964; Lewin, 1946).

As an explicitly humanist project that focused on the emotional and psychological outcomes of small groups these efforts, intended to involve organizational members in an understanding of their own group dynamics, were a clear alternative to the authoritarian ideology that in the name of industrial management consistently imposed rule adherence on work situations. These experiments, in contrast, suggested that democratic structures enabling participatory dialogue and representation could successfully resolve disputes and achieve performance objectives without trampling on workers (Bradford *et al.*, 1964). Like Mayo (1933), the MIT researchers also concluded that democratic processes could probably serve as important throughput controls, helping maintain employee satisfaction and production levels over time.

In the United Kingdom, the origins of the Tavistock Institute were in the Directorate of Army Psychiatry, where empirical research focused originally on soldiers was motivated by a frenzied attempt to build a land army quickly during the second world war. A Rockefeller Foundation grant in 1946 enabled this research team to continue and found the Tavistock Institute. The group was guided initially by dynamic personality theories (e.g., Freud, Jung, Adler), with Tommy Wilson and then Eric Trist as the first directors. Moving beyond Freudian psychological drive theories, Tavistock researchers adopted object relations theories and focused attention on how relationships between and among people evolved (Trist and Murray, 1990).

The Institute carried out three significant organizational control research projects. One of them, looking at management–worker relations, took place at the Glacier Metal Company and identified process consulting as a method for alleviating and controlling conflict (Jaques, 1951). Another focused on an emergent method of coal mining in which members of self-regulating work groups rotated through different tasks and thereby gained a greater understanding of each other's responsibilities, reducing the potential for anger to develop towards team members (Trist and Bamforth, 1951). A third project focused on the education of medical professionals, training them in techniques to avoid the counter-transference issues that arose when the professionals projected their own problems on to their patients (Menzies, 1970). Working with action-oriented research methods, the Tavistock staff developed consultancy practices to foster organizational awareness and process-oriented controls. Inasmuch as Tavistock research had initially used scarce resources to address large-scale military control problems, the later studies demonstrated how human-oriented process control techniques had value and significance for civilian organizations.

At Ohio State University in the post-second world war period, Ralph Stogdill got military personnel, manufacturing industry employees, university administrators, students, and others to fill out questionnaires (Stogdill, 1948) and then used statistical factor analysis to identify patterns that might be associated with effective leader behavior. His analyses suggested that leaders who were perceived to demonstrate "consideration" and "initiating structure" achieved higher performance and greater employee satisfaction. Leader consideration meant that organization members perceived a leader to be concerned about the welfare of a group. Considerate managers were perceived to be friendly and approachable, to treat associates as equals, and to be available for discussion and consultation. The behaviors associated with initiating structure, in contrast, included the extent to which a leader defined roles, initiated and organized activities, and articulated goals. Given particular tasks, structure-initiating managers would define performance standards and organize ways to assess progress.

Like Stogdill, Rensis Likert at the University of Michigan used questionnaires and statistical analyses to identify the keys to worker satisfaction and productivity. Likert (1961b) identified three leader behaviors he called task-oriented, relationship-oriented, and participative behaviors, which he found were associated with better task performance and higher employee satisfaction. Task-oriented behaviors occurred as employees determined how tasks were to be done while their managers adopted a facilitative role, attending to goal-setting, planning, coordination, and securing resources. Relationship-oriented behaviors occurred as managers ensured workers had intrinsic and extrinsic rewards. Participative behaviors occurred as employees had a voice in managerial decision-making processes. In this light, the combination of work-facilitating behavior by managers and a degree of ongoing employee decision-making appeared to complement one another and to function again as informal throughput control devices, lessening resistance to direction while continually reinforcing individual motivation.

All of these studies suggest that in order to achieve organizational control, it may not always be necessary to monitor workers closely (e.g., checking on exactly how many shovel-loads Schmidt took to fill the hopper with pig iron and paying him for everything he did). The general insight instead was that managers could allow employees a degree of autonomy in determining goals and how best to achieve them. Participative management ultimately has managers standing shoulder to shoulder with workers, modeling desirable behavior and helping to resolve differences. As managers also behave less formally, they are more able to consistently facilitate these throughput controls. Leaders support rather than command as they seek out and respond to team issues and suggest ways forward.

The Michigan studies also concluded that as groups perceive themselves as teams (i.e., not simply as sets of unrelated individuals), they
work better together. Likert (1961a, 1967) identified four possibilities
for organizational control systems and he named them exploitive
authoritative, benevolent authoritative, consultative, and participative. He endorsed the participative control system as being the most
effective. Based on this conceptualization of a participative control
system, Blake and Mouton (1964) developed a training program – the
"managerial grid" – to help organizations implement participative
organizational control systems. This program with its emphasis on
"team management" became widely popular in the 1970s. Essentially,
the message was that by balancing concerns for production and
people, management achieved more effective organizational control.

The Carnegie school

March and Simon (1958) depicted organizations as information processing or calculating machines dedicated primarily to a search for
efficiency. Using theory and empirical evidence, they presented a series
of propositions summarizing organizational knowledge as it stood in
the 1950s. In their book's second edition, however, they moved some
distance away from this mechanical metaphor and depicted organizations as being "systems of coordinated action among individuals
and groups whose preferences, information, interests, or knowledge
differ" (March and Simon, 1993: 2). They argued that coordinated
action enables organizations to survive as organizations have "control
over information, identities, stories and incentives." They also
warned, "Effective control ... is limited, however, by the uncertainties
and ambiguities of life, by the limited cognitive and affective capabilities of human actors, by the complexities of balancing trade-offs
across time and space, and by threats of competition" (March and
Simon, 1993: 2).

In reassessing their earlier work, March and Simon (1993) suggest
that alternative logics guide attention at different organizational
levels, and so are likely to influence the control processes implemented
at these different levels. At middle and lower levels, for example,
control efforts are usually guided by a logic of consequences (i.e.,
control initiatives are supposed to influence task-related efficiency
and effectiveness). Tasks like inventory optimization or production

maximization often require extensive amounts of data processing and so today, instead of having people do these tasks, organizations program computers that then monitor ongoing situations, apply particular routines, and initiate responses exercising control in a way that is directed towards promoting efficiency and effectiveness. Unlike people, computers are not subject to bounded rationality constraints or limited calculating abilities (March and Simon, 1993: 10), the substitution of computers as control agents has often enabled control improvements at middle and lower organizational levels.

To the extent that an organization relies on different knowledge bases that are located in different organizational units, people must exercise control at higher organizational levels (Ocasio, 1997). In particular, as each organizational unit has different priorities, there is potential for conflict and organization members to have to identify and apply a logic of appropriateness to resolve this conflict. For example, a system of rules may determine what is organizationally appropriate. For example at the North American Space Agency (NASA), the ideal rule might be that safety concerns should always have priority over scheduling concerns (Dunbar and Garud, 2009). Over time and as environments and organizational interests change, those at the highest levels adjust and adapt the priorities that determine what is organizationally appropriate.

By using a logic of consequences and a logic of appropriateness in their control processes, organizations emphasize stable task performance at middle and lower levels, and change in the form of evolving appropriateness criteria at upper levels. As control rules at lower levels repeatedly promote efficiency and effectiveness, this consistency may in itself change what people at upper levels consider to be appropriate. Over time and as appropriateness criteria change, organizations adjust what and how they do things (March and Simon, 1993: 15).

The process paradigm

Researchers have considered how a logic of consequences and a logic of appropriateness may function together to guide attention in exercising organizational control (Ocasio and Wohlgezogen, Chapter 7; Tsoukas, 1996). How organizations pay attention to events depends, on the one hand, on the stable rules and task units that constitute the platform enabling an organization to do things at middle and lower levels and, on the other hand, on how an organization is set up at the highest levels to assess appropriateness and so deal with change that emerges over time. In this way, different logics are guiding complementary organizational control processes at different levels. At one level, attention is focused on achieving efficient task performance. At another level, attention focuses on applying appropriateness criteria to make adjustments triggered by changes due to interactions with surrounding units or to unfolding reality (e.g., Garud and Rappa, 1994).

As an illustration, Sitkin *et al.* (1994) examined the control processes associated with the total quality management (TQM) movement. Propagated in the 1980s as a set of basic principles – "doing things right the first time, striving for continuous improvement, and fulfilling customer needs" (Snell and Dean, 1992: 470; as quoted in Sitkin *et al.*, 1994: 538) – TQM spread rapidly because it promised in part a means of handling the uncertainty and complexity of dynamic business environments. Sitkin *et al.* point out, however, that TQM proponents do not adequately conceptualize how contingencies endemic to a firm's particular situation may influence its control efforts and, for this reason, TQM control systems can become insufficiently attuned to organizational environments.

In order to prescribe what a TQM-based control system should do, Sitkin *et al.* argue for a conceptualization that acknowledges and differentiates the consequences of well-understood and poorly understood conditions. If situations are well understood, control can rely on monitoring and standardized procedures to achieve desired outcomes. If situations are not well understood, because they are changing, novel, or unfamiliar, control depends on monitoring what is occurring and determining what are appropriate responses. They suggest that organizational effectiveness reflects the balance of attention allocated to (a) achieving particular, well-established goals; and (b) learning about unfolding events and determining priorities based on appropriateness criteria. Sitkin *et al.* write that "managers can gain competitive advantage from this apparent paradox if they are able to recognize that the everyday situations they confront almost inevitably involve both the exercise of control and the capacity to learn" (1994: 540–541).

The significance for organizational control of Sitkin *et al.*'s theoretical contribution is that they portray control, risk, uncertainty, and change as being irreducibly intrinsic to the organizational environment. Levels of uncertainty may be higher or lower but even if they are low, uncertainty cannot be fully overcome through the predictions of scientific inquiry. In this sense, the goal of organizational control studies cannot be to empirically demonstrate universal control principles appropriate to all situations. Instead, organizational control studies seek to demonstrate how means for control are appropriate in some circumstances but not in others (Kirsch and Choudhury, Chapter 10; Kreutzer and Lechner, Chapter 15; Long, Chapter 12). This pragmatic view opens the door for control studies to "examine the degree to which ... effectiveness-enhancing activity patterns (e.g., rapid recognition of contextual change, speedy decisions, and learning over time) become synonymous with practices that facilitate learning-oriented quality in organizations" (Sitkin *et al.*, 1994: 558).

Exploring change processes and organizational control, Cardinal *et al.* (2004: 411) build on Cyert and March's (1963) position defining control as an alignment of capabilities, activities, and performance with organizational goals and aspirations. Their aim is to theorize about what drives change in organizational control systems, and their specific focus is on the balance between formal and informal controls as this evolves over time. Presupposing a dynamic ontology in which change occurs inside and outside the organization, they look at input, behavioral, and output control mechanisms. Their data draws on a ten-year case study of the Blue Whale Moving Company, a small logistics firm operating in a mid-sized metropolitan area. They utilize grounded theory, reporting on their data and the consequent emergent theoretical constructs (Glaser and Strauss, 1967).

The study presents an in-depth story of an entrepreneur, "Miller," a likable chap who, together with a partner, "Armstrong," thought that Blue Whale could edge out a good margin on the existing moving business by focusing on internal employee relationships and external relationships with clients and customers. They paid employees a decent wage and implemented informal employee controls that focused on "hygiene, attire, attitude and strength" (Cardinal *et al.*, 2004: 415), and balanced this with a monitoring of traditional firm performance measures.

By focusing on informal and formal control processes over a ten-year period, the study identifies key events that affected the constitution of the evolving balance in this organization's control system. Cardinal *et al.* point out that when firms emphasize formal control mechanisms then – depending on other contextual factors – this emphasis can have a blowback effect that can create new imbalances. Furthermore, they theorize that organizational control systems can be latent rather than explicit, and that even when a balance shifts, traces of earlier formal and informal controls still remain. In this light, the focus of control research shifts away from the explicit impacts of laws, regulations, cultures, and formal or informal mechanisms of whatever sort and moves, instead, toward the tacit assumptions that shape those same artifacts and practices. These tacit assumptions shape strategic decision-making at a rhetorical as well as at a performative level, in a particular manner of speaking or as a mode of activity. To wit: after Blue Whale surfaced from a period of acrimonious legalism, a pair of professional managers reinstated a balance of formal and informal controls, including everything from punitive fines for tardy task completion to "celebratory beer parties" (Cardinal *et al.*, 2004: 424).

The process view of organizational control recalls the basic patterns identified in ancient China. However, rather than forcing a stark either/or choice between one or other conceptualization of an agency relationship, it shows how hierarchically instituted and enforced incentives and sanctions are able to be blended and balanced over time, and how cooperation and mutual respect among superiors and subordinates can change and then be reestablished. Qualitative, longitudinal research methods can help explain how balance in a control system can be lost and then also how it can reemerge.

Reflecting on the trajectory: tracing out basic assumptions

The genealogy that has been presented allows us to look back across the history of organizational control and consider the different ontological, epistemological, and ethical assumptions different studies have made. By identifying these assumptions we may raise more questions than we answer – indeed, we realize future research will be able to apply these basic philosophical categories with greater rigor and in greater depth. Our purpose here is to trace out how historically different assumptions underlie organizational control studies and how they also shape the contemporary state of the field. Indeed, we suggest that historical assumptions remain present in contemporary theories and practices even as studies of organizational control evolve in new directions. In view of the scholarship in this volume, then, the implications beg for further consideration.

The history of organizational control studies is shaped by ontological assumptions made about what control is, along with the nature of its temporal status and its causality. Traditional organizational control research seems to frame the essence of control in terms of formal, logical principles defining unchanging agency relationships that continuously allow the exercise of control in a machine-like, instrumental manner (e.g., Taylor, 2003). In contrast, human relations researchers seem to assume that the essence of organizational control is tied to affective rather than logical phenomena, to human motivation and emotions rather than to rationality (e.g., Trist and Murray, 1990). However, in this literature, human motivation is also viewed as static, taking effect in different contexts in consistent and necessary ways over time. The more recent process paradigm perspective frames the essence of organizational control in terms of situation-specific appropriateness (e.g., March and Simon, 1993). This implies that the essence of organizational control differs across cases, and the elements of organizational control also change over time depending on researchers' assumptions and contingent on the events that unfold in a particular context, as well as the appropriateness criteria that an organization is emphasizing (Cardinal *et al.*, Chapter 3).

These ontological assumptions are interwoven with epistemological assumptions about how organizational control processes can be known. Scholars working in the traditional paradigm see control primarily through a lens that is shaped by engineering knowledge and applied physical science knowledge. Scholars working in the human relations paradigm see control using humanist concepts drawn from psychology and other social science fields. Finally, while process-oriented scholars acknowledge both of these knowledge sources, in addition, they draw in systems theory knowledge and network concepts to further broaden the way they understand organizational control processes (Beer, 1975).

Consistent with their ontological and epistemological assumptions, scholars make different assumptions concerning the research methods most appropriate for the study of organizational control. Some researchers have favored empirical testing and quantitative analytic methods drawn from the physical sciences, others have focused on empirical observation and the monitoring of human reactions *in situ*,

while others have engaged in participant observation, employing
qualitative analysis methods to generate case study descriptions of
what occurs in control situations. Researchers also differ in their
assumptions about what the primary unit of analysis should be. The
traditional paradigm focuses primarily on control outputs, for
example, did production rise or not? The human relations paradigm
focuses on a range of inputs, throughputs, and outputs, for example,
how do employees feel as they arrive at the workplace? How does
the manager behave? How was news of the production increase
presented? The process paradigm addresses all of these variables
related to the situational context and adds the views that organizational actors have concerning what is appropriate. For example,
what is the nature of the cultural context in which the organization
operates and what priorities does this imply? How is it considered
appropriate for employees to interact with one another and with the
organization's management and technologies during the production
increase period?

These epistemological assumptions are still further interwoven with
ethical assumptions about the value that organizational control should
serve, the character of human agency or intentionality, and the consequences that follow when control systems are implemented and take
effect. Ethical theorists differ about whether the value of human
action should be ascribed to intentions or to consequences (cf. Derry
and Green, 1989), but both options can be considered to be "ultimate
ends." In this sense, traditional studies most often assume that the
ultimate end of organizational control is increased output and so
the relative value of a method relates to the degree to which it generates "more" output than other methods. Those working in the human
relations paradigm accept that "more" can have value, but they frame
ultimate ends in terms of workplace humanization. Given two equally
productive control systems, they can be distinguished based on the
extent to which they enhance employee well-being and quality of life.
Process scholars also do not dispute the value of either more output or
enhanced human well-being, but they frame the ultimate end of
organization control in terms of increased participation in workplace
decision processes. Hence, the value of organizational control can be
further differentiated based on the extent to which it allows stakeholders to engage in and contribute to the processes an organization
uses to adjust to changing circumstances (Loughry, Chapter 11).

As we saw following the basic pattern established in ancient China, assumptions about human agency or intentionality shape organizational control research. Traditional control research frames the individual as a rational actor who seeks to maximize pleasure and minimize pain as the extrinsic outcomes of work activity. From this perspective, the worker is amenable to control to the extent that extrinsic incentives are sufficient. While human relations researchers accept rationality in human actors, they recognize that both intrinsic and extrinsic rewards are important. From this perspective, the incentives that make actors accept controls include not just financial incentives but also non-economic rewards such as recognition and fulfillment. For process researchers, the focus is on the bounded character of human rationality, informational incompleteness, and on the ambiguous nature of the causal factors that bear upon people as they make decisions about acting in organizational contexts. From this perspective, the incentives and disincentives at any decision point are contingent and situation-specific, and cannot be generalized to other actors even if they are in similar situations.

Based on their ontological, epistemological, and ethical assumptions, researchers have different beliefs concerning what organizational control systems should achieve if they are properly implemented. For those working in the traditional paradigm, the desired, proximate consequence of organizational control is purely formal – whatever the context and the means, the ultimate end is "more," whatever this may mean in a particular context. In contrast, organizational control that is based on human relations assumptions should enhance and certainly not detract from the quality of organizational life. Similarly, the consequences of a process-based control system will include many adjustments and changes reflecting the views of wider participation as may be brought about by stakeholder forums, process consulting practices, and other methods that draw more diverse contributions to the organizational control process that reflect a variety of interests and identities.

These assumptions allow us to trace with greater precision how the basic pattern that Rindova and Starbuck (1997) identified with respect to ancient Chinese governance has then unfolded in contemporary European and American organizational control research. Table 2.1 presents a summary account of these assumptions.

Table 2.1 A genealogy of organizational control

Assumptions	Traditional	Human relations	Process
Ontological			
What is the substance of control?	Logical principles of form	Human motivation	Situational appropriateness
What is the temporal status of control?	Static	Static	Dynamic
What is the nature of control's causality?	Machine-like instrumentality	Machine-like, but including emotions	Ongoing change and adjustment processes
Epistemological			
Through what knowledge lens is control understood?	Engineering	Psychology and other human and social sciences	Social and human sciences, systems and network analysis
By what methods can control be known?	Quantitative methods, empirical testing	Quantitative methods, empirical testing, and monitoring	Qualitative and quantitative methods and case studies
What is the primary unit of analysis for control studies?	Output variables	Input, throughput, and output variables	Contextual conditions, input, throughput, and output variables
Ethical			
What value does control ultimately serve?	Increased productivity	Humanization of the workplace	Democratization of the workplace
What is the nature of human intentionality?	Rational, seeking extrinsic rewards	Rational, seeking extrinsic and intrinsic rewards	Boundedly rational, constantly adjusting based on situational appropriateness
What consequences should control have when implemented in organizations?	Gains in production	Enhanced attention to human resource departments, personal and organizational development	More stakeholder forums, process consulting

Discussion: making sense of organizational control or turning it into a black box

Despite the changes in assumptions underlying organizational control studies over the years, organizational control as actually practiced seems to reflect a mixture of all of the assumptions – the traditional, human relations, and process perspectives. This mixture of assumptions may reflect the fact that control assessment itself is often done by people with high positions in organizational hierarchies who often adopt a traditional perspective and simply consider whether the outcomes they intended to control have in fact been achieved. As outcomes match their expectations, they consider the organization to be in control. As outcomes do not match their expectations, they want to know what has not worked and needs to be changed. Their attention focuses on rules for channeling resources, behavior, and information flows to and from environments and between organizational units. Their continuing question is whether the organizational rules and routines they have developed are consistently and logically directed toward achieving the output goals they desire. They obtain an answer as they make top-down sense of the situation using narrative frameworks that reflect their understanding of the overall purpose, meaning, and direction of the firm and the issues it is dealing with. Narrative frameworks, by providing answers to basic questions about the identity and trajectory of the firm, provide an overall perspective that shapes the development and implementation of more detailed control mechanisms (Pajunen, 2008).

As well as dealing with top-down controls directed toward organizational output goals, managers who work supervised organizational units must also deal with real-world forces that directly affect what their unit must do in order to achieve desired results. In a production unit, for example, there may be issues surrounding the quality of the materials worked on and available labor skills. At this level, the manager's control assumptions are likely to relate to either the human relations or process perspective. Although local units may require procedures to deal with ongoing issues, these practices may only indirectly relate to the criteria being used by positions high in a hierarchy to guide and assess performance (e.g., the hierarchy may want to tell a story about record-breaking organizational growth and profits, rather than a story about how local units deal with continuing input crises). At different organizational levels, organization members may be using different control frames (Chreim, 2006).

To manage the real-world forces affecting unit performance, managers identify and discuss the associated issues with members of their organizational unit. Exchanges then generate ideas about factors influencing these forces, how they affect performance, and how they may be dealt with. Over time, understandings emerge that unit members summarize and share in stories identifying the issues likely to arise, the signals that have to be monitored, and the actions that must be taken. They also usually include illustrative examples of how issues have arisen and been dealt with in the past. Hence, the narratives summarize a unit's task knowledge and experience and identify ways in which units can mold and change ways of doing things so as to deal with real-world issues even as they also meet hierarchically imposed control criteria.

Organizational control is influenced by the direction provided by hierarchically imposed overall goals that are in turn shaped by the particular set of narrative frameworks developed by those holding hierarchical positions. Organizational control also reflects understandings that develop within local units through the narratives that emerge and explain how to manage the real-world forces affecting performance. At all levels, stories are dynamic, unfolding and changing as they are developed and shared through continuing interactions between organization members (Gephart, 1978).

As organizations get larger, the hierarchy grows so that there are more people at higher levels. This leads to nested sets of agency relationships (i.e., at each hierarchical level, there are agency relationships between each position and the quasi-independently functioning units directly below). People in hierarchies know about the output measures they impose on the units below. To emphasize the importance of these outputs, people in hierarchies often make subordinates' rewards contingent on performance measures that they define as important. Often, however, people in hierarchies do not appreciate the real-world forces that organizational units below are controlling. Instead, their focus is on the output measures that are important to them and they see within unit controls that are dealing with local real-world forces as simply "black boxes" beyond their concern.

As unit outcomes are inconsistent with expectations, people in hierarchies have to assess what went wrong in what they see as a "black box." They often assume that the directives and criteria they impose are the most important if not the only control structures managers under them are dealing with. In fact, they most often do not know the forces that local units are dealing with or how they are being managed, and so they focus attention not on any control processes that may be in place but, instead, on the individuals with hierarchical responsibility for managing the units that have not achieved expected outputs. Not knowing how these individuals exercise control within their units, those in the hierarchy most often choose to focus on the reward and punishment levers they can impose on the units with the intent of "motivating" managers to achieve results that those in the hierarchy desire.

In fact, as people in hierarchies reward people below based on performance relative to metrics imposed from above (e.g., meet a budget, fulfill a quota), those in the supervised units become increasingly sensitive to imposed metrics. Attention narrows and becomes more aggressively focused upon achieving outputs desired by the hierarchy. Depending on results achieved relative to hierarchical expectations, praise or blame is heaped on unit managers. Unlike people in the hierarchy, however, people at lower supervised levels must continue to manage the real-world forces their unit faces. As the rewards and punishments grow, however, the temptation also grows to find ways to simply ignore real-world forces (e.g., relax checking procedures or safety checks) in order to score higher on approved metrics.

People narrow their attention to metrics reflective of what the hierarchy measures and monitors to gain the rewards superiors offer. In doing so, they also often become skeptical of hierarchically directed processes. Reality as perceived by the hierarchy consists of desired results that are linked to rewards and punishments while many other things also impacting reality may be simply ignored. As a result, people tell stories about how rewards and punishments lead to unfairness and control failures. Such a process can break an organization into divided camps as some people feel angry and alienated, their efforts unappreciated and unrecognized, even as others reap rich rewards because their performance looks like what management expects. People in hierarchies doling out rewards based on the output measures they have imposed may, in contrast, be increasingly confident that it is they who are exercising control and they may also believe they are flushing out the irresponsible and incompetent.

From an organizational control standpoint, hierarchically imposed output control goals supported by rewards and punishments refocus attention away from the way that supervised units manage real-world forces. Yet there will be no sense of alarm in the hierarchy as the reward and punishment system draws attention away from local control efforts because this is exactly as the controls are designed to function. The result is an unrecognized organizational control illusion for people in hierarchical positions as their reward and punishment process encourages managers to abandon attention to narratives directing how to manage real-world forces at supervised unit levels (Dunbar, 1981: 106; Langer, 1975).

This illusion is exacerbated by the impact that computer technologies have had on the implementation of organizational control processes. With their ability to generate and store unlimited amounts of data, computers make it possible to monitor and store detailed information describing how events to be controlled unfold over time. Modern communication technologies then make access to this data widely available. Further, computers can be programmed not only to generate and accumulate data on controlled events but also to actually implement controls taking a wide range of organizational interests and relationships into account. A consequence is that rather than being dependent on hierarchical agency relationships as historically was the case, modern organizations are much more dependent on computers and their preprogrammed agency systems. While in the past, people directly determined how agency-based control was implemented, today people who design and program computers indirectly but effectively determine how organizational control implemented by computers either works or fails. Those responsible for design of the control system simply assume that the computer is "going to work" as it should (Vaast and Levina, 2006).

In this regard, Cavetti et al. (2007) suggest that the meaning of agency in control contexts has changed and needs to be reformulated. Computers in organizations are agency systems with tremendous calculative and data-processing power along with a wide range of monitoring and updating abilities. They can be programmed to link data on unfolding events to a range of response options that can reflect stakeholder interests and control goals. Computers must be preprogrammed to unleash this power, however, and to implement organizational control automatically. This means that there is a continual need for situational understanding both in the design of organizational control systems that are computer-based, and also afterward when the system should continually adjust to changing circumstances. Organizations develop situational understanding based on the records that document the reasons for the design of the control system, and in the stories that record the issues that have arisen and continue to arise in implementing the control process. Performance records combined with stories constitute the knowledge organizations rely upon as they explain and implement control in a computer-dominated world.

Toward a narrative perspective on organizational control

We have traced out how illusions of control emerge when high-level people lose their sensitivity to how people in lower organizational units are exercising control, or as computer technologies suppress sensemaking process details at all organization levels. To deal with such developments, one needs a method that is able to register details of the control process and the multitude of things that can go wrong in the process of exercising control in modern organizations. We believe a "narrative perspective" is such a method. We characterize a narrative perspective on organizational control in terms of the ontological, epistemological, and ethical assumptions that it makes.

At an ontological level, this perspective frames the essence of control substance as a multiplicity of narratives. These narratives may cohere with each other or they may be contradictory, but they emerge at different organizational levels and serve different functions at different times. Their temporal status is dynamic rather than static; they can but need not change at every story retelling and as sensemaking events unfold. The nature of their causality can be characterized both in constructivist terms as being the creation of meaning, and more precisely in terms of sensemaking, whereby every time actors recount a narrative they are also attempting to enact organizational control on themselves and on those who hear them (Weick, 1995).

At an epistemological level, a narrative perspective requires scholars to use a lens shaped by narrative studies, including the humanities and the humanist social sciences, to understand organizational control. The methods of analysis appropriate to the narrative object of study include philosophically informed literary criticism and rhetorical analysis as well as the interpretative, hermeneutic traditions of discourse analysis (Polkinghorne, 1987). By looking through this lens and using these methods, control scholars can focus on the historically and contextually specific meaning narratives have for organizational actors (George and Qian, Chapter 6; Pentland, 1999; Van Maanen, Chapter 5). Narrative control scholars may also examine specific symbols or artifacts to analyze how an organization's identity is constituted, inasmuch as that identity is comprised of multiple narratives and provides actors with an answer to the strategic question, "who are we?" (cf. Gioia *et al.*, 2000).

At an ethical level, the narrative perspective frames have coherent meaning as the "ultimate end" of organizational control. Even though the multiplicity of narratives can never be boiled down to a single story – indeed by definition, such a fantasy may be fascist – if an organization is to function effectively, the black box situation described above must somehow be addressed. In such situations, the competing or contradictory narratives need to reconcile in a way that is coherent with the overall identity of the organization as well as with the changing circumstances dealt with by organizational units. This reconciliation requires a new integrative story, and so the intentionality of the individual actors seeking such a narrative is framed and developed not only by boundedly rational, adjusted expectations that are geared to intrinsic and extrinsic rewards, but also by active imaginations that *creatively* give experience new meaning and enact a shared vision of organizational control (cf. Garud and Karnoe, 2001).

Based on these ontological, epistemological, and ethical assumptions, we can reframe the consequences of narrative perspective for organizational control, and identify alternative ways of addressing the challenges presented by black box situations. Broadly speaking, organizations have to engage in storytelling practices. Ideally, these practices unfold at all levels, acknowledging and integrating different actors and organizational circumstances. Top-down, formal organizational control may be exercised, for example, through storytelling practices involving internal and external branding (e.g., Denning, 2006). Bottom-up, informal control may be exercised through storytelling practices that involve spontaneous discussions around a water cooler (e.g., Gabriel, 2000). These practices may be identified, designed, and implemented explicitly, or they may propagate themselves implicitly through behavioral cues or subtle shifts in the physical work environment. But whatever specific shape the

Table 2.2 *A narrative perspective on organizational control*

Ontological assumptions	
What is the substance of control?	Multiple narratives
What is the temporal status of control?	Dynamic
What is the nature of control's causality?	Make experience meaningful: sensemaking
Epistemological assumptions	
Through what lens is control understood?	Narrative studies, as presented in the humanities and the social sciences
By what methods can control be known?	Literary criticism, rhetorical analysis, hermeneutic discourse analysis
What is the primary unit of analysis for control studies?	Stories, narratives, organizational identity artifacts and descriptions, symbols
Ethical assumptions	
What value does control ultimately serve?	Coherence of multiple narratives
What is the nature of human intentionality?	Creative, enacted meaning
What consequences should control have when implemented in organizations?	Encourage storytelling practices

storytelling practices take, their significance for organizational control can only be fully appreciated from the standpoint of the integrated view that a narrative perspective ultimately incorporates. Table 2.2 summarizes the assumptions underlying a narrative perspective on organizational control.

Conclusion

This story began in the distant past, with the founding of ancient organizations, with the beginning of politics, economics, and enterprise intended to pool risk, along with the collective joining of forces to take actions promising beneficial returns. As collective efforts take place, patterns of interactions emerge between and among individuals and groups, as well as agency relationships between people, groups, organizations, and technologies. Provisionally, people begin to estimate a specific set of actions and their relative value for themselves and agency relationships. As the value associated with particular actions is discussed among those concerned, sensemaking processes gradually constitute emergent control mechanisms. As the value of particular actions is imposed on to a group rather than discussed, rules act as constraints, and actions can be differentiated in terms of the extent to which they conform with expectations or not. In such situations, conflict often emerges, and sooner or later the organization risks spiraling out of control.

Whatever the specific control mechanisms might be (i.e., formal or informal, or based on market, hierarchy, or clan, etc.), their significance is communicated and explained to others through narratives that also acknowledge agency relationships. For this reason, we suggest the narrative is more than a means of advancing informal control mechanisms. Specifically, narratives provide the medium through which organizational control is performatively enacted, implemented, and transformed through practice. Although recent organizational control studies have begun to address this phenomenon, we suggest that future researchers must reflect upon the ontological, epistemological, and ethical assumptions that they make. By reflecting critically on what control is, how it can be known, and why it is pursued, scholars can more precisely appreciate how and why distinctions are drawn between formal and informal, tacit and explicit, and emergent and designed organizational control. In turn, managers can develop and implement control systems by telling stories that are coherent across hierarchical levels and appropriate in environments that are increasingly characterized by uncertainty and dynamic change.

References

Adler, P. S. 1999. Building better bureaucracies. *Academy of Management Executive*, 13 (4): 36–47.

Arrow, K. J. 1974. *The limits of organization*. New York, NY: Norton.

Beer, S. 1975. *Platform for change*. New York: Wiley.

Blake, R. R. and Mouton, J. S. 1964. *The managerial grid*. Houston, TX: Gulf.

Bradford, L. P., Gibb, J. R., and Benne, K. D. (eds.). 1964. *T-group theory and laboratory method: innovation in re-education*. New York, NY: Wiley.

Cardinal, L. B., Sitkin, S. B., and Long, C. P. 2004. Balancing and rebalancing in the creation and evolution of organizational control. *Organization Science*, 15 (4): 411–431.

Cavetti, G., Levinthal, D., and Ocasio, W. 2007. Neo-Carnegie: the Carnegie school's past, present, and reconstructing the future. *Organization Science*, 18: 523–536.

Chreim, S. 2006. Managerial frames and institutional discourse of change: employee appropriation and resistance. *Organization Studies*, 27 (9): 1261–1287.

Cyert, R. M., and March, J. G. 1963. *A behavioral theory of the firm.* Englewood Cliffs, NJ: Prentice-Hall.

Denning, S. 2006. Effective storytelling: strategic business narrative techniques. *Strategy and Leadership*, 34 (1): 42–48.

Derry, R. and Green, R. 1989. Ethical theory in business ethics: a critical assessment. *Journal of Business Ethics*, 8: 521–533.

Dunbar, R. L. M. 1981. Designs for organizational control. In P. C. Nystrom and W. H. Starbuck (eds.), *Handbook of organizational design*, vol. II: 85–115. New York, NY: Oxford.

Dunbar, R. L. M. and Garud, R. 2009. Distributed knowledge processes and indeterminate meaning: the case of the Columbia shuttle flight. *Organization Studies*, 30 (4): 397–421.

Fayol, H. 1949. *General and industrial management.* London: Pitman and Sons.

Gabriel, Y. 2000. *Storytelling in organizations, facts, fictions and fantasies.* Oxford University Press.

Garud, R. and Karnoe, P. (eds.). 2001. *Path dependence and creation.* Mahwah, NJ: Erlbaum.

Garud, R. and Rappa, M. 1994. A socio-cognitive model of technology evolution. *Organization Science*, 5 (3): 344–362.

Gephart, R. P., Jr. 1978. Status degradation and organizational succession: an ethnomethodological approach. *Administrative Science Quarterly*, 23: 553–581.

Gioia, D., Schultz, M., and Corley, K. 2000. Organizational identity, image and adaptive instability. *Academy of Management Review*, 25 (1): 63–81.

Glaser, B. G. and Strauss, A. L. 1967. *The discovery of grounded theory: strategies for qualitative research.* Chicago, IL: Aldine.

Gordon, R. and Howell, J. 1959. *Higher education for business.* New York, NY: Columbia University Press.

Jaques, E. 1951. *The changing culture of a factory.* London: Tavistock.

Kanigel, R. 1997. *The one best way: Frederick Winslow Taylor and the enigma of efficiency.* New York, NY: Viking.

Langer, E. J. 1975. The illusion of control. *Journal of Personality and Social Psychology*, 32 (2): 311–328.

Langton, J. 1984. The ecological theory of bureaucracy: the case of Josiah Wedgwood and the British pottery industry. *Administrative Science Quarterly*, 29: 330–354.

Lewin, K. 1943. Defining the "field at a given time." *Psychological Review*, 50: 292–310.

1946. Action research and minority problems. *Journal of Social Issues*, 2 (4): 34–46.

Likert, R. 1961a. *New patterns of management*. New York, NY: McGraw-Hill.

1961b. An emerging theory of organizations, leadership and management, in L. Petrullo and B. M. Bass (eds.), *Leadership and interpersonal behavior*. New York, NY: Holt, Reinhart and Winston.

1967. *The human organization*. New York, NY: McGraw-Hill.

McGregor, D. 1960. *The human side of enterprise*. New York, NY: McGraw-Hill.

McKendrick, N. 1961. Josiah Wedgwood and factory discipline. *The Historical Journal*, 4: 30–55.

March, J. G. and Simon, H. A. 1958. *Organizations*. New York, NY: Wiley.

1993. *Organizations* (2nd edn.). Oxford, England: Blackwell.

Mayo, G. E. 1933. *Human problems of an industrial civilization*. New York, NY: Macmillan.

Menzies, I. E. P. 1970. *The functioning of social systems as a defence against anxiety: a report on a study of the nursing service of a general hospital*. London, England: Tavistock.

Mumby, D. 2005. Theorizing resistance in organizational control: a dialectical approach. *Management Communication Quarterly*, 19 (1): 19–44.

Ocasio, W. 1997. Towards an attention-based view of the firm. *Strategic Management Journal* (Summer Special Issue), 18: 187–206.

Pajunen, K. 2008. The nature of organizational mechanisms. *Organization Studies*, 29 (11): 1449–1468.

Pentland, B. T. 1999. Building process theory with narrative: from description to explanation. *Academy of Management Review*, 24: 711–724.

Polkinghorne, D. E. 1987. *Narrative knowing and the human sciences*. Albany, NY: State University of New York Press.

Rindova, V. P. and Starbuck, W. H. 1997. Ancient Chinese theories of control. *Journal of Management Inquiry*, 6: 144–159.

Sitkin, S. B., Sutcliffe, K. M., and Schroeder, R. G. 1994. Distinguishing control from learning in total quality management: a contingency approach. *Academy of Management Review*, 119 (3): 537–563.

Stogdill, R. M. 1948. Personal factors associated with leadership. A survey of the literature. *Journal of Psychology*, 25: 35–71.

Taylor, F. W. 2003. *Scientific management*. London, England: Routledge.

Trist, E. and Bamforth, K. 1951. Some social and psychological consequences of the Longwall method of coal getting. *Human Relations*, 4: 3–38.

Trist, E. and Murray, H. 1990. *The social engagement of social science: a Tavistock anthology. Volume I: The socio-psychological perspective.* Philadelphia, PA: University of Pennsylvania Press.

Tsoukas, H. 1996. The firm as a distributed knowledge system: a constructionist approach. *Strategic Management Journal*, 17 (Winter): 11–25.

Vaast, E. and Levina, N. 2006. Multiple faces of codification: organizational redesign in an IT organization. *Organization Science*, 17 (2): 190–201.

Weber, M. 1978. *Economy and society.* Berkeley, CA: University of California Press.

Weick, K. E. 1995. *Sensemaking in organizations.* San Francisco, CA: Sage.

PART II

Conceptions of organizational control

3 | A configurational theory of control

LAURA B. CARDINAL
University of Houston

SIM B SITKIN
Duke University

CHRIS P. LONG
Georgetown University

Organization theory scholars have long acknowledged that control processes are integral to the way in which organizations function (Blau and Scott, 1962; Etzioni, 1965; Tannenbaum, 1962). While control theory research spans many decades and draws on several rich traditions (Dunbar and Statler, Chapter 2), several theoretical problems have kept it from generating reasonably consistent and interpretable empirical findings and from reaching consensus concerning the nature of key relationships.

As new forms of organizational relations (networks, alliances, mass customization, supply chains, consortia, contract employees, telecommuting, virtual teams, etc.) emerged in the late twentieth century, traditional organizational control theories were viewed as less and less relevant by organizational scholars. As a result, attention to organizational control research waned, with the exception of critical theorists (e.g., Adler, 2007; Tsoukas, 2007) and accounting researchers (e.g., Davilia and Foster, 2007; Whitley, 1999). For example, despite the importance of the topic and the pervasiveness of the control phenomenon in organizations, organizational control research has not been sufficiently cumulative. The control literature is rich, but deceptive.

Although most organizational scholars might be shocked by our assertion, we observe that there is very little *empirical* work on control in the organizational literature relative to other classic and fundamental organizational phenomena (e.g., design–effectiveness, planning–performance, diversification–performance relationships). From a distance, it may appear as though there is a great deal of empirical work and that there is broad support for the few dominant control theories (e.g., Merchant, 1985; Ouchi 1977, 1979). However, the empirical work within the managerial control tradition has, with few exceptions, only considered a few elements of control at a time. A closer examination makes clear that constructs often have not been tested empirically and, when they have been studied, they have not been operationalized in ways that build a cumulative base of knowledge. It is telling that it would be impossible to conduct a meta-analysis on control research, in striking contrast with other organizational areas of study with similarly rich traditions. As we sought to understand the origins, attributes, and evolution of control we came to more fully appreciate Oliver's observation that "The study of organizational control has a long history in administrative science and yet the need to examine the processes and implications of this phenomenon has never been greater" (Oliver, 1998: letter from the editor).

Although there has been a very recent resurgence of interest in control theory (Cardinal *et al.*, 2004; Chen *et al.*, 2009; Kirsch *et al.*, 2010), before we can begin to understand the role that control serves in nascent organizations or complex economic and social organizational relations, a more consistent and robust theory of control is called for that builds on but fundamentally alters some key precepts from more traditional control research. We came to this deeper appreciation of where control theorists have been and where they need to go because we were unable to apply existing control theories regarding the use of both singular and multiple controls (e.g., Ouchi, 1977, 1979; Long *et al.*, 2002; Simons, 1995) to theorize about the full array of controls. In response, we offer a synthesis of diverse, yet complementary, streams of traditional control research into a theoretical framework that describes how types of *control mechanisms* (e.g., the use of rules, norms, direct supervision or monitoring) aimed at particular *control targets* (e.g., input, behavior, output) are applied within particular types of *control systems* (e.g., market, clan, bureaucracy) over time.

We identify four problems (lack of conceptual consensus, fragmentation, singularity, and lack of attention to control development) that have made it difficult to consistently and precisely operationalize control and to build a cumulative stream of research. In the next sections, we address each of the four problems. We address the problem of lack of conceptual consensus by precisely defining key concepts and terms used throughout the literature. We also systematically apply these concepts throughout our analysis, thus demonstrating that the concepts *can* be consistently applied and that they are theoretically distinguishable. By clarifying the core control terms and introducing precision to the operationalization of control-related constructs, we are able to demonstrate that the fragmentation of the literature is artificial and that key control constructs can be synthesized. Further, we are able to reflect the complexity of the control phenomenon and also show how this complexity can be systematically incorporated into our theoretical and empirical research in ways that alter our conclusions. Finally, we are able to illustrate the value of understanding control from a developmental viewpoint. This not only provides another lens to understand the complexity of control, but it also can help us to begin to comprehend how organizational control legacies might be created over time and across different development sequences (Cardinal *et al.*, 2004). It is our hope that the frameworks we provide in this chapter will be helpful for clarifying and explaining the composition of control in organizations in ways that will prove useful in the further development of research on this topic.

Control theory

Many definitions and constructs and theoretical approaches have been used to describe organizational control. Traditional research describes "control" as one of the four primary functions of management (the others are organizing, planning, and coordinating) (Fayol, 1949). Historically, definitions have focused on the manager as the primary developer and implementer of organizational controls. Theories have posited various ways by which organizational control might be achieved, including: leadership and the development of formal policies (Barnard, 1938; Selznick, 1957), the application of rational-legal authority and rules (Weber, 1946), activation of cultural norms and rituals (Trice and Beyer, 1984, 1993), adherence to incentive systems (Dale, 1958; Whyte, 1955), reliance on direct supervision (Mintzberg, 1979), or through the design of work environments such as assembly lines (Richardson and Walker, 1948; Taylor, 1911).

Problems with control research in the management science tradition

The control literature suffers from four problems which have contributed to the decline in attention to control theory: lack of conceptual consensus, fragmentation, singularity, and lack of attention to control development. We contend that the four problems we identify next have made it difficult to conduct empirical work on organizational control in a cumulative manner.

Lack of conceptual consensus. In spite of its long history and strong traditions, control research has been plagued by a lack of conceptual consensus. The most glaring example of this is that work on organizational control suffers from a dual problem in the use of terms and concepts. Specifically, we uncovered two consistent problems: (1) *false differentiation* – the use of *different terms* to refer to *identical concepts* and (2) *false consensus* – the use of *identical terms* to refer to *different concepts*. One critical effect of these inconsistencies has been that, previously, control researchers have not offered a coherent and cumulative body of work.

To illustrate how this problem manifests itself in the control literature, we describe one instance, using the concept of the "clan" (Ouchi, 1979, 1980, 1981). Ouchi describes the clan as a system of control mechanisms that rely upon the influence of "a deep level of common agreement between members on what constitutes proper behavior, and it requires a high level of commitment on the part of each individual to those socially prescribed behaviors" (Ouchi, 1979: 838). First, this illustrates the false differentiation problem because theorists have used *different terms* to describe concepts that are similar to the clan. For example, in describing essentially identical concepts, Merchant (1985), Lebas and Weigenstein (1986), and Birnberg and Snodgrass (1988) used the term "cultural control," Dermer (1988) used the term "consensual control," and Makhija and Ganesh (1997) used "rituals, traditions, and ceremonies," and even Ouchi used the terms "ritual control" (Ouchi, 1977) and "clan mechanisms" (Ouchi, 1979). Still others have used the terms "input control" (Snell, 1992), "social control," and "people control" (Eisenhardt, 1985). Second, this illustrates the false consensus problem, in that researchers have used the term "clan control" to describe a variety of control concepts. In some cases it has been described as a specific control mechanisms, e.g., informal control modes (Ouchi,

1979, 1980), in other instances as a configuration of control mechanisms (i.e., organizational control system) (Jaworski *et al.*, 1993; Roth *et al.*, 1994), and in still other writings as a singular control mechanism, e.g., a ritual (Cardinal, 2001; Eisenhardt, 1985; Kirsch, 1996, 1997; Ouchi, 1979). Clan control is also often treated as one anchor on the formality–informality continuum (Makhija and Ganesh, 1997; Martinez and Jarillo, 1989; Ouchi, 1979). Though this problem may appear inconsequential or trivial, researchers cannot move theoretical and empirical research forward without a clear consensus on levels of analysis (Glick, 1985), and we attribute the dearth of empirical work at least in part to control researchers' inability or unwillingness to establish a consensus on how to label and measure key constructs.

Fragmentation. In spite of its long history and strong traditions, the control literature currently consists of a fragmented and largely independent collection of typologies and concepts. As a result, control research has not coalesced around common frameworks that generate cumulative, systematic research on control issues. For example, researchers who study individual control mechanisms typically study only formal control (Cardinal, 2001; Kirsch, 1996; Sitkin, 1995; Snell, 1992), and generally they ignore the overall systems of multiple controls within which those mechanisms are operationalized. In addition, research on organizational control systems work has remained very general, has not examined the specific interrelated components of these systems, and has not moved much beyond Ouchi's (1977, 1979, 1980) original conceptualizations toward empirical examinations of related issues. (Note – exceptions include Cardinal *et al.* [2004], Jaeger and Baliga [1985], Jaworski [1988], Jaworski *et al.* [1993], Long *et al.* [2002], and Sitkin and George [2005]).

Singularity. Because organizations are multi-faceted, control issues are also multi-faceted – but research to date does not reflect this complexity. Individual studies and theories of control also have been too singular in their conceptualizations and empirical focus. Historically, control theory has focused on choosing one type of control over another (e.g., market versus clan or behavior versus output). Part of this problem can be attributed to the prescriptive nature of many existing control theories (Sitkin *et al.*, 1994). The contingent nature of the early control work resulted in control research taking on a prescriptive "either/or" nature rather than a multi-faceted nature. Thus, the critical issues for advancing control theory concern how to balance and integrate the various facets over time rather than focusing on picking one type of control (Cardinal, 2001; Cardinal *et al.*, 2004; Sutcliffe *et al.*, 2000).

Lack of attention to control development. Van de Ven and Poole (1995: 511) point to the value of theories that "provide stronger and broader explanatory power of organizational change and development processes." In contrast to what Van de Ven and Poole advocate, traditional views of control were developed to describe a relatively stable organizational world in which task requirements and organizational boundaries were more clearly defined and economic and social relationships were less dynamic (Whitley, 1999). Yet despite the widespread recognition that organizations have been changing at an increasingly dramatic and unrelenting pace, control researchers have not effectively responded to these developments by incorporating more dynamic approaches. This is unfortunate because, by definition, developmental theories are critical to understanding the emergence, adoption, and adaptation of organizational control in both founding and mature firms (Van de Ven and Huber, 1990; Van de Ven *et al.*, 1984). Thus, it is important for control researchers to generate new insights on how to sequence and balance multiple facets of control and to extend control theory to reflect more fully the emergence and the dynamism of organizations and their control requirements (Cardinal *et al.*, 2004; Long and Sitkin, 2006).

Clarifying control terms and concepts

In an effort to systematically address the current problems with control theory, we begin by describing the control concepts that we will apply to create an integrative, configurational perspective on organizational control. To address the current lack of conceptual consensus in the control literature, we present definitions of key control-related terms and concepts: organizational control, formal and informal control mechanisms, control systems, and control targets. We focus specifically on these concepts because they collectively represent the core elements of traditional control research and comprise the basic building blocks of control theory.

Organizational control. Consistent with the management science tradition, *control* is defined as any process whereby managers direct attention, motivate, and encourage organizational members to act in ways desirable to achieving the organization's objectives (Jaeger and Baliga, 1985; Merchant, 1988; Ouchi, 1977, 1979; Snell, 1992).[1] Theories of organizational control developed within this tradition describe how managers measure and monitor the work of organizational actors by comparing their performance against established standards and providing rewards or sanctions based on these evaluations. Key organizational control concepts utilized within the management science tradition include: control mechanisms, formal and informal controls, control systems, and control targets. Each is discussed next.

Formal and informal control mechanisms. Control mechanisms describe the individual, molecular units of organizational control (e.g., standards, policies, norms) that are applied in control processes. Traditionally, researchers have suggested that control mechanisms are either formal or informal based on their position along a single "formality" continuum (Anthony, 1952; Barnard, 1938; Blau and Scott, 1962; Makhija and Ganesh, 1997; Merchant, 1985). However, control researchers (e.g., Cardinal *et al.*, 2004; Long *et al.*, 2002; Roth *et al.*, 1994; Sitkin and George, 2005) have recently suggested that formal and informal represent distinct dimensions and that individual control mechanisms can exhibit both formal or informal attributes.

Formal control mechanisms include a range of officially sanctioned (and usually codified) institutional mechanisms such as written rules and procedural directives (Sitkin, 1995; Sitkin and Bies, 1994). These could include a union job description or formal job specifications. IBM's famous written formal, organization-wide dress code (e.g., a blue suit and white shirt for men) represented a formal control mechanism.

Informal control mechanisms include values, norms, and beliefs that guide employees' actions and behaviors. For example, software companies with no formal dress code may exhibit norms that strongly discourage employees from wearing shirts and ties and encourage workers to attire themselves in T-shirts and sandals (Kirsch and Choudhury, Chapter 10).

Control systems. Organizational control systems are configurations of multiple formal and informal control mechanisms. They are distinguished primarily by the relative emphasis that managers place on the specific combinations of formal and/or informal control mechanisms of which they are comprised (Jaworski *et al.*, 1993; Roth *et al.*, 1994).

Three types of organizational control systems dominate the literature: market, bureaucratic, and clan (e.g., Ouchi, 1977, 1979; Williamson, 1975). In *market control systems* managers primarily focus on evaluating transaction outcomes (i.e., prices), rather than how well subordinates adhere to organizational rules or norms (Ouchi, 1979; Williamson, 1975). Internal market control systems differ from the pure external market systems that transaction cost economists suggest involve no managers and no monitoring. Instead, in intra-organizational market control systems managers draw upon market-style pricing mechanisms, such as "intra-company transfer prices" (Ouchi and Price, 1978: 63), commission-based incentives, and results-based performance programs to align the motivations and actions of employees with organizational goals. In contrast, *bureaucratic control systems* differ from internal market control systems by emphasizing the specification, monitoring, and enforcement of rules (Ouchi and Price, 1978) and primarily apply formal control mechanisms, such as rules and regulations, specialized jobs, and hierarchies (Lebas and Weigenstein, 1986; Weber, 1946).

Although most organizations exhibit discernable levels of formal control (Roth *et al.*, 1994), managers within *clan control systems* place relatively greater emphasis on informal control mechanisms (Ouchi, 1979). Within these clan control systems, managers use traditions and beliefs to motivate members to align their values with those of the collectives with which they are affiliated (Roth *et al.*, 1994; Sitkin and George, 2005). Finally, building from the increasing recognition of formal and informal as independent control dimensions (Cardinal *et al.*, 2004; Jaworski *et al.*, 1993; Roth *et al.*, 1994; Sitkin and George, 2005), researchers have increasingly investigated *integrative control systems* in which managers apply moderate to high levels of *both* formal and informal control mechanisms (Cardinal *et al.*, 2004; Jaworski *et al.*, 1993; Lebas and Weigenstein, 1986; Roth *et al.*, 1994; Simons, 1995). See Table 3.1 for a comparison of the four control systems.

Control targets. Researchers have conceptualized *control targets* as specific elements of organizational transformation processes (i.e., inputs, behaviors, or outputs) to which control mechanisms are intended to be applied. While some aspects of control mechanisms may be applicable across targets (e.g., whether the control is formal or informal), other aspects of the control mechanisms are specific to a

Table 3.1 *Distinguishing control configurations by reliance on formal and informal controls*

		Reliance on formal controls	
		LOW	HIGH
Reliance on informal controls	HIGH	Clan configuration	Integrative configuration
	LOW	Market configuration	Bureaucratic configuration

type of target (e.g., input controls might be aimed at individual skills or credentials, whereas behavioral controls would focus on specific actions and output controls would focus on a final product). By directing control mechanisms toward these targets, managers attempt to align the goals and risk preferences of their subordinates with those of the organization (Cardinal, 2001; Eisenhardt, 1985; Kirsch, 1996; Merchant, 1985; Snell, 1992). Managers select *input targets* ("input control") to direct how material and human resource elements of their production processes are qualified, chosen, and prepared. For example, organizations manage human inputs through training and socialization to regulate the knowledge, skills, abilities, values, and motives of employees (Arvey, 1979; Van Maanen and Schein, 1979; Wanous, 1980). Similarly, organizations manage material inputs by qualifying vendors, equipment, or raw materials. Managers choose *behavior targets* (referred to as "behavior control" or "process control") – such as process rules and behavioral norms – when they want to ensure that individuals perform actions in a specific manner. Finally, managers employ *output targets* ("output control") – such as profits, customer satisfaction levels, and production volumes and schedules – to align output quantity/quality with specific production standards (Mintzberg, 1979; Ouchi, 1977, 1979).

Developing a configurational approach to organizational control

Having addressed the first of four problems in the control literature by clarifying key terms and concepts, we now move on to address the fragmentation and singularity problems we cited previously by introducing our configurational perspective on organizational control. In developing this perspective, we go beyond past work that has looked only at single targets or mechanisms of control in isolation (Cardinal, 2001; Kirsch, 1996; Snell, 1992) or has operationalized control systems in very general ways (Ouchi, 1979). Our control configurations advance control research by clarifying relationships among control systems, specific control mechanisms, and control targets and then specifying the role that each concept plays within a particular configuration of control elements.

In developing our perspective, we first discuss the advantages and the limitations of typologies and taxonomies in organizational control research. We then describe how our configurational theory of organizational control integrates various elements of control in ways that facilitate more systematic and accurate investigations of control development and implementation. Thereafter, we present four control configurations and discuss relationships between and among their component parts.

Typologies, taxonomies, and configurations

Configurations focus on the systemic nature of phenomena, describing a common alignment of elements within and across a set of overarching dimensions (Galbraith and Kazanjian, 1986; Miller, 1986, 1987). Configurational models can be conceptually driven or empirically driven, such as those presented by Miles and Snow (1978) and Miller and Friesen (1984). While the value of taxonomies relative to typologies is debated, Meyer, Tsui, and Hinings (1993) suggest that both make valuable contributions, and in many ways, they are complementary as they create organizing structures. The benefit of developing configurational models is that they serve as points of integration for established lines of literature by "consolidating past gains" and "synthesizing broad patterns" (Meyer *et al.*, 1993: 1,175) of observations. For example, Miller (1986) developed a configurational model integrating classic research on strategy and structure. The three primary dimensions of his configuration model were strategy, structure, and the environment. Within each primary dimension (e.g., structure), Miller identified relevant subdimensions, such as bureaucratization and centralization of power.

Doty and Glick (1994) also highlight a dual role of configurations in developing theory. Both contributions stem from the perspective of configurations as ideal types. The first contribution is that of midrange theory, or an explanation of the internal consistency within ideal types. This involves developing an understanding of how and why the elements interrelate with one another (Doty and Glick, 1994; Miller, 1986). Second, configuration models typically posit an effect of the fit between ideal types and actual organizations on organizational performance, which Doty and Glick (1994) refer to as "grand theory."

Even though it is generally recognized that organizations do not use controls in isolation, most research has been focused on one or two individual elements of control (e.g., only a few input control mechanisms or only formal control mechanisms). Despite calls for synthesis and testing of control theory ideas, prior work has not made the various linkages that allow for a synthesized view. To begin to address this issue, we advocate that organizational control is best depicted as configurational, a "multidimensional constellation of conceptually distinct characteristics that commonly occur together" (Meyer *et al.*, 1993: 1,175). Although both typologies and taxonomies are considered types of configurations, implied in the conventional wisdom is that a true configurational approach is a synthesis of the best of both. Typologies are considered conceptual frameworks (McKelvey, 1982), but they have often been criticized for not being testable. In contrast, taxonomies are empirically driven, but have been considered atheoretical. In this chapter, we use the terms configuration and typology (we do not refer to taxonomies) in precisely this way; a typology is a conceptual framework that is difficult to test, and a configuration describes a concept that is both theory-driven and empirically testable. Configurational theorists delineate two key principles to classifying configurations – coherence and holism (Meyer *et al.*, 1993; Miller and Friesen, 1984). First, the elements in the configuration must coalesce in understandable ways to create overall coherence. Second, the patterning of the elements (rather than the elements individually) must be understood in terms of a holistic form. We propose that existing control theory offers the basic building blocks to develop a configurational model of control.

Toward a more coherent and comprehensive theory of organizational control

We wish to draw from several, previously independent approaches to studying control to offer a less simplistic, more integrative notion of how control systems are actually configured in practice. Because prior research had not simultaneously examined control mechanisms, systems, and targets, we offer a framework that allows for more complex configurations of the distinct facets of control that could better capture and explain the actual use of controls.[2]

Researchers have long portrayed control systems as one of three primary types of governance systems: market, clan, and bureaucracy (Lebas and Weigenstein, 1986; Ouchi, 1977, 1979). Going beyond this three-type approach, Ouchi (1979, 1980) alludes to the blending of all three control systems into one system, and Anthony (1952: 47) foreshadowed later work on the effectiveness of integrative systems: "Management control is most effective when the formal and informal techniques are skillfully blended." Subsequently, the notion of the integrative control system was further developed (i.e., Lebas and Weigenstein, 1986; Roth *et al.*, 1994; Sitkin and George, 2005).

Our observations regarding formal and informal control mechanisms and control targets suggest that control researchers could fruitfully utilize a broader perspective that moves beyond the singular perspectives of control typical of past work. Several versions of the singularity problem in control research could benefit from such a theoretical and empirical shift. Researchers (e.g., Makhija and Ganesh, 1997; Merchant, 1988) typically treat control as formal *or* informal (i.e., as categorical or as end points along a single continuum), rather than acknowledging and theorizing about both formal and informal controls as co-existing in a delicately balanced and dynamic configuration in organizations (Roth *et al.*, 1994; Sitkin and George, 2005; Sutcliffe *et al.*, 2000). Anthony (1952) highlights the importance of informal control mechanisms and points out that it is easy to overemphasize formal controls. The problem identified by Anthony is illustrated by Jaworski (1988) and Merchant (1988). While Jaworski's (1988) theory suggests that control targets can only be formal, Merchant goes further and questions whether informality should be used as a core theoretical element in our theories and states, "Managers do not design informal systems" (Merchant, 1988: 42).

Table 3.2 *Distinguishing control configurations by additional details*
concerning control mechanisms, control targets, and control systems

		Reliance on formal controls					
		LOW			HIGH		
		Clan system			**Integrative system**		
		Formal	Informal		Formal	Informal
HIGH	Input	Low	High	Input	High	High
	Behavior	Low	High	Behavior	High	High
	Output	Low	High	Output	High	High
		Market system			**Bureaucratic system**		
		Formal	Informal		Formal	Informal
LOW	Input	Low	Low	Input	High	Low
	Behavior	Low	Low	Behavior	High	Low
	Output	High	High	Output	High	Low

(Left axis label: Reliance on informal controls)

However, researchers who have categorically rejected the notion that informal control mechanisms can be explicitly designed (Jaworski, 1988; Merchant, 1988) are challenged by Cardinal *et al.* in a recent study (2004). They found that firm leaders can explicitly design both formal and informal controls and, at least some of the time, these authors found those "designed" controls to be rather effective.

In Table 3.2, we propose a control configuration approach that integrates, refines, and extends previous approaches to organizational control.

The three primary dimensions for our configurational model include control systems, control mechanisms, and control targets. The first dimension in the configuration is derived from Ouchi's typology. However, since his approach is a typology, he does not outline the sub-elements across each type (i.e., market, hierarchy, clan). Instead, the types are treated as mutually exclusive. Researchers who have focused on *control systems* (e.g., Ouchi, 1977, 1979; Roth *et al.*, 1994; Simons, 1995) have not explicitly and systematically linked specific *control mechanisms* and *control targets* into control system conceptualizations and operationalizations.

Table 3.3 describes the elements from existing control research that we integrate to create a more theoretically grounded and empirical

Table 3.3 *Comparing control systems and control targets*

	Control systems	Control targets
Categories	• Market • Bureaucratic • Clan • Integrative	• Input • Behavior • Output
Description	Controls systems are configurations of formal and informal control mechanisms. Control systems are classified according to the predominant control mechanisms used.	Controls mechanisms are classified according to the transformation processes they target.
Underlying theoretical perspective	Agency theory	Organizational theory
Illustrative authors	Jaworski *et al.* (1993) Lebas and Weigenstein (1986) Ouchi (1979, 1980) Roth *et al.* (1994)	Cardinal (2001) Eisenhardt (1985) Kirsch (1996, 1997) Merchant (1985) Ouchi (1977, 1979) Snell (1992)

configurational approach. The second and third dimensions for our configurational model include the formality of the control mechanisms (the relevant subdimensions are formal and informal) and the targets of control (the relevant subdimensions are input, behavior, and output). The most extensive body of empirical work on organizational control has focused only on the application of *formal* input, *formal* behavior, and *formal* output control mechanisms (Cardinal, 2001; Kirsch, 1996; Long *et al.*, 2002; Merchant, 1985; Snell, 1992), while ignoring *informal* control mechanisms and how specific control mechanisms are configured into control systems.

Table 3.2 organizes the four types of control systems with their corresponding configurations of the control mechanisms and targets associated with each system to form a complete configuration. The four types of control configurations are: market, bureaucratic, clan, and integrative. Within each control configuration, control mechanisms were classified according to whether they were formal or informal and whether the control mechanisms were applied to inputs, behaviors, or output targets. The single control mechanisms are represented in our configuration based on the relative emphasis on six control mechanisms: formal input, formal behavior, formal output, informal input, informal behavior, or informal output control.

Market configuration. The "market control system" has been described in the literature as exhibiting low levels of both formal and informal control (e.g., Ouchi, 1979; Wilkins and Ouchi, 1983; Williamson, 1975). We predict in a market configuration that high levels of both formal and informal output control would be exhibited. Free market control mechanisms described by Williamson (1975) and Ouchi (1979) would be expected to take the form of output controls (e.g., 100 percent commission).

A striking and a potentially valuable aspect of our framework is that even though this departure from the literature on market control seemed like a very sensible way to depict a market system, market systems were not typically or explicitly described in the control literature in this way before.

Bureaucratic configuration. Though Ouchi (1980) and Ouchi and Price (1978) describe pure markets as having no rules, rules are the fundamental mechanism for control in a bureaucracy. For bureaucratic control rules exist for employees on how to behave, how and when work will be completed, and what quality and quantity of outputs should be produced. Further, managers monitor activities, outputs, skills, and training standards for employees, which can be related to their retaining their employment. Our conception of the bureaucratic control configuration fits quite neatly with the descriptions of Ouchi (1977, 1979, 1980, 1981) and Roth *et al.* (1994). That is, bureaucratic control is high on all types of formal control and low on all types of informal control.

Clan configuration. Most work on clans (e.g., Jaeger and Baliga, 1985; Ouchi and Price, 1978) depicts clans as near-pure informal control settings. In fact, much of the work on informal, clan-like control has stressed that low levels of formality are an essential feature of the clan configuration (e.g., Jaeger and Baliga, 1985; Makhija and Ganesh, 1997; Ouchi and Price, 1978). However, observations by

Roth *et al.* (1994) and Sitkin and George (2005) that all formal organizations are more formal than has sometimes been recognized, suggest that it is highly unlikely to find a uniformly low level of formal control. Thus, we would expect to see some use of formal control, even in clan configurations.

Integrative configuration. In contrast with the historical treatment of bureaucratic and clan control systems as opposite ends of the formal–informal continuum, researchers have begun to treat formal and informal control as independent constructs (Cardinal *et al.*, 2004; Jaworski *et al.*, 1993; Roth *et al.*, 1994). This simultaneous examination of both formal and informal controls creates a fourth, less well-understood system: the integrative system. *Integrative control systems* utilize high levels of *both* formal and informal control mechanisms (Jaworski, 1988; Jaworski *et al.*, 1993; Lebas and Weigenstein, 1986; Roth *et al.*, 1994).

Driving the configurational approach to a greater level of specificity. Our configurational approach highlights two substantial changes in the way theorists have traditionally viewed control in organizations. First, scholars need to better reflect how managers direct both formal and informal mechanisms at specific control targets. Second, our configurations demonstrate that the control system and control target typologies should not be viewed as mutually exclusive, but as part of a more integrated configurational approach. Third, we have tightened the concepts and definitions used in the control literature so that we could consistently develop our configurational approach, thus helping move the control literature toward conceptual consensus while also facilitating future empirical operationalization of key constructs. Fourth, instead of viewing when and why managers choose to focus on single control targets (i.e., singularity) as the most critical factor in control research (Eisenhardt, 1985; Kirsch, 1996; Ouchi, 1977, 1979) our configurational approach suggests why scholars might benefit from investigating how combinations of control mechanisms affect organizational processes and effectiveness.

It is our hope that this broader configurational approach is more descriptively valid, more inclusive, more useful, and more empirically testable because of its specificity and external validity. Control mechanisms rarely exist in isolation, and considering combinations provides a more realistic picture of how control is applied in organizations.

We show how control mechanisms and control targets are systematically linked to different control systems in a way that is both theoretical and practical – giving managers tools and giving researchers better descriptive and explanatory power. Distinguishing mechanisms of control *through their targets* also gives us the ability to ground our understanding of control systems in specific patterns of control mechanism use and non-use.[3]

Perspectives on the evolution of control systems

One of the benefits of our configurational approach to organizational control is that, by clarifying how the components of control systems interact, we are able more directly to focus attention on issues related to control system development and, thereby, address the fourth problem we identify with the control literature. By highlighting the importance of these issues, we anticipate that control researchers will be encouraged to move past their current emphasis on variance theories in mature firms (Mohr, 1982), to formulate process theories that explain "how things evolve over time and why they evolve this way" (Langley, 1999: 692).

To be clear, we are not saying that there are no process studies in the literature that can be related to the study of control. For example, research on divisional corporate strategy (Hoskisson *et al.*, 1991) or strategy implementation (Govindarajan and Fisher, 1990; Govindarajan and Gupta, 1985) provide very useful insights that speak to the control systems used by organizations. In addition, several entrepreneurship researchers (Covin and Slevin, 1990; Hanks *et al.*, 1993; Kazanjian and Drazin, 1990) have studied selective aspects of control systems longitudinally. However, because most control research has been focused primarily on mature control systems in large corporations and because such process work in strategy has remained entirely untapped by mainstream control research, scholars have not, as yet, generated a sufficient level of knowledge about the formation of control systems or how such developmental processes facilitate adaptations of fledgling new firms (infancy) to become more established firms (adolescence).[4] Our perspective, however, provides a basis for integrating this research with traditional control research to provide a more complete picture of how control systems develop and change over time (Cardinal *et al.*, 2004).

Three models of control evolution

Although this research is very general and has only recently become the subject of more critical evaluations (Cardinal *et al.*, 2004), we have identified three core theories regarding control system development or control adaptation and change that have been proposed in the literature. Figures 3.1a, 3.1b, and 3.1c depict the sequences suggested by each of these theories.

The first model, represented by Ouchi (1979, 1980) and shown in Figure 3.1a, utilizes Williamson's (1975) market failures framework to describe how organizations that initially employ market control systems eventually adopt more formal, bureaucratic control systems in response to rising transaction costs. The theory suggests that bureaucracies then fail when performance evaluation becomes overly ambiguous, thus bringing about the adoption of clan systems. To accommodate the need for ambiguous management, "clans differ fundamentally from bureaucracies in that they do not require explicit auditing and evaluation" (Ouchi, 1980: 137). Although they are better at functioning

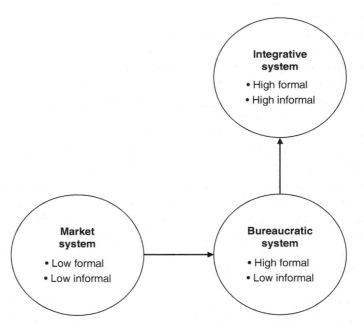

Figure 3.1a Control system sequencing described by control theorists

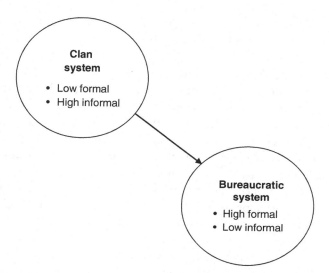

Figure 3.1b Control system sequencing according to Barker (1993)

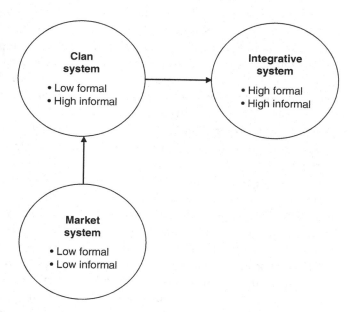

Figure 3.1c Control system sequencing described by life-cycle theorists

under ambiguous conditions, clans lack the explicit price mechanism of the market and the explicit rules of the bureaucracy.[5]

A second approach reflects the current emphasis of critical theorists (e.g., Delbridge, Chapter 4; Jermier, 1998), who note that control mechanisms, which at first appear non-coercive, may, over time, become coercive and more powerful than traditional bureaucratic controls (e.g., Barker, 1993; Jermier, 1998). Barker (1993) presents this perspective in his examination of self-managing teams, which examined the development of several newly formed, self-managing teams in a traditional hierarchical organization. Consistent with the sequence posited by critical theorists, the teams he observed developed through several phases: (a) in phase 1, the teams experience value consensus and formed a clan-like system; (b) in phase 2, the teams began to develop a bureaucratic control system by increasingly codifying each team's values as rules or guidelines to be followed; (c) in phase 3, the rules were stabilized and became even more formal and rationalized. The highly institutionalized control systems Barker observed in phase 3 actually exerted tighter control than the bureaucratic hierarchy that predated the installation of the self-managing teams (Figure 3.1b).

In the third model (Figure 3.1c), life-cycle theorists (e.g., Adizes, 1979, 1989; Greiner, 1972; Kimberly, 1979) and entrepreneurship researchers (Covin and Slevin, 1990; Hanks et al., 1993; Kazanjian and Drazin, 1990) draw upon life-cycle theory to address broader issues of organizational evolution and propose another model that treats control as one of many components in the evolution process. Even though there are many variations of the life-cycle model, existing models suggest that organizations progress through similar stages (Quinn and Cameron, 1983; Van de Ven and Poole, 1995).[6] Life-cycle theorists suggest that organizations first evolve through a creativity or entrepreneurial phase where founders employ market control systems and enact the "control of activities . . . [in response to] immediate marketplace feedback" (Greiner, 1972: 42) in the form of market and customer demands (Adizes, 1979, 1989). As organizations then evolve through a collectivity stage, managers develop a clan control system and direct employees using interpersonal communication and informal control mechanisms. This creates high cohesion and commitment toward the founder and the organization. Eventually, organizations move through a formalization and a control stage. During these stages, managers attempt to create efficiencies and direct employees by codifying some norms as rules using a variety of control mechanisms (Adizes, 1989).

Challenging and synthesizing the three approaches

Though many firms may follow a sequence specified by one of the schools of thought that were described, a more recent study (Cardinal *et al.*, 2004) found that control sequencing in a newly founded firm developed differently than any one of these models alone predicted. In their study, the founding firm exhibited four distinctly different configurations in the use of control mechanisms that closely matched the four control systems (market, clan, bureaucratic, and integrative) discussed in the literature (see Figure 3.2 for the sequencing of control systems).

In its early development, the firm quickly evolved from a market control system (phase 1) into a clan control system (phase 2) that retained some selected market control characteristics. Then, instead of retaining the informal control mechanisms from phase 2, as

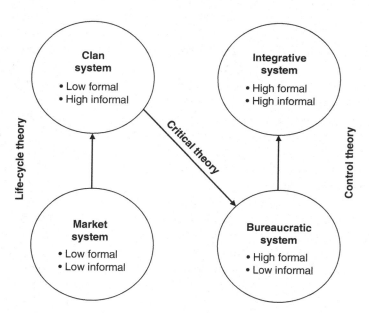

Figure 3.2 The applicability of different theories in explaining the evolution of organizational control

would be predicted by developmental theories, the firm's management completely renounced its use of informal control mechanisms and, in phase 3, adopted a rigid bureaucratic system. This is at variance with developmental theories, which would suggest that informal controls are retained while formal mechanisms are overlaid on them to create an integrative control system. Instead, the firm's development of an integrative control system was to take place only after a period in which the now-latent elements of its clan control system virtually disappeared and its market control system partially disappeared.

Cardinal *et al.* (2004) could only explain what they observed in the founding firm by drawing upon a combination of all three perspectives discussed previously. Specifically, they found that Ouchi's (1979) perspective addressed shifts from one control system to another as each system failed; life-cycle theory accurately predicted the shift from an initial market control system to a clan control system; and Barker's (1993) critical theory study helped to explain the shift from a clan system to a more bureaucratic one and then the shift within a bureaucratic system to a more legalistic bureaucratic system that became punitive. Because the firm they studied followed a path different than that described by control, critical, or life-cycle theorists, their findings highlight some blind spots in the traditional perspectives on control system development. For instance, by suggesting that every organization develops its control system according to a pre-set, defined pattern presents a limited and incomplete view of control system development. In addition, by suggesting that managers merely add new control mechanisms to existing control mechanisms fails to acknowledge that managers often temporarily or permanently set aside some control mechanisms before implementing others in their place.

Our focus on control configurations provides a way of more closely examining the dynamics of control system development over time. Because we disaggregate control systems into their component parts, we are able to examine changes in the emphasis on specific components as well as how critical combinations of changes actually result in substantial shifts in the composition of control systems. As a result, we open up the black box of control system evolution to more clearly discern why different development patterns might exist.

Implications of a dynamic, configurational approach to organizational control

Our configurational approach highlights several suggestions for improving the way theorists have traditionally viewed control in organizations. First, scholars should better reflect how managers use combinations of formal and informal mechanisms and direct them selectively at specific control targets. Second, our configurational approach demonstrates that control system and control target configurations should not be viewed in a mutually exclusive way, but as a more complex, integrated theory of organizational control. Third, we have tightened the concepts and definitions used in the control literature so that we could consistently develop our configurations, thus helping move the control literature toward conceptual consensus while also facilitating the empirical operationalization of key constructs. Fourth, instead of viewing when and why managers choose to focus on single control targets as the most critical factor in control research, our configurational approach suggests that scholars might benefit from investigating how combinations of control mechanisms affect organizational processes and effectiveness cross-sectionally and over time.

Conclusion

Organizational control is in practice a complex and dynamic phenomenon. This chapter has tried to draw on the extensive prior work on control and put it into a broader, more integrative, more specific, and more dynamic configurational framework. If more empirical research is to be done in a cumulative way, it is necessary that researchers' theories of organizational control allow for both the systematic incorporation of specific control mechanisms and targets; they should also recognize that individual pieces of the control puzzle do not operate in isolation. If organizational control research is to be more practically relevant, those conducting it must take account of the complexity and dynamism that organizations and their members actually confront. Finally, unless clearly hypothesized paths of implementation and change are built into organizational control theories, it will be difficult to build a better understanding of how controls emerge, are designed, and fail in organizational settings. Thus, this attempt at building an infrastructure and scaffolding for control theory and empirical research is done in the hope that the structure can rise quickly and cumulatively when it is grounded in a common frame and language.

Notes

1 Our definition reflects the management science tradition and its emphasis on organizational goals and managerial intentionality. Control definitions based on critical theory or developmental approaches to control would not adopt a similar definitional stance.

2 A recent exception includes Cardinal *et al.* (2004).

3 While we do not draw on the concept "mode of control" in this chapter, we differentiate mode of control from control mechanisms, targets, systems, and configurations. Modes of control are roughly equivalent to a row or a column through which control configurations are composed. They are isolated from the whole pattern that comprises a control configuration focusing on either a single row or a single column of control mechanisms. For example, a formal mode would use all formal control mechanisms and a behavior mode would use all behavior control mechanisms. For further information see Kirsch and Choudhury (Chapter 10).

4 Aldrich (1999) describes the stages of nascent entrepreneurship as having three transitions and four periods: adult population (conception), nascent entrepreneur (gestation), fledging new firm (infancy), and established new firm (adolescence).

5 Though Ouchi (1979, 1980) occasionally refers to organizational blending of these control systems, his core argument emphasizes the shedding of one configuration of control attributes as the next type of control system is adapted.

6 Some theories suggest more stages, while others are concerned with the transitions from a single unit firm into a multi-division firm and issues of corporate centralization and decentralization (Quinn and Cameron, 1983). Adizes's (1979) theory on life-cycle is the most complete theory; it is the most fine-grained, and it is the only life-cycle theory that deals with decline and death (Quinn and Cameron, 1983). Because it is more detailed, it also provides better coverage of the early entrepreneurial phases.

References

Adizes, I. 1979. Organizational passages – diagnosing and treating life cycle problems of organizations. *Organizational Dynamics*, 8: 3–25.

1989. *Corporate life cycles.* Edgewood Cliffs, NJ: Prentice Hall.

Adler, P. S. 2007. The future of critical management studies: Paleo-Marxist critique of labour process theory. *Organization Studies*, 28: 1,313–1,345.

Aldrich, H. E. 1999. *Organizations evolving*. Thousand Oaks, CA: Sage Publications.

Anthony, R. N. 1952. *Management controls in industrial research organizations*. Cambridge, MA: Harvard University Press.

Arvey, R. D. 1979. *Fairness in selecting employees*. Reading, MA: Addison-Wesley.

Barker, J. R. 1993. Tightening the iron cage: concertive control in self-managing teams. *Administrative Science Quarterly*, 38: 408–437.

Barnard, C. I. 1938. *The functions of the executive*. Cambridge, MA: Harvard University Press.

Birnberg, J. G. and Snodgrass, C. 1988. Culture and control: a field study. *Accounting, Organizations and Society*, 13: 447–464.

Blau, P. and Scott, W. R. 1962. *Formal organizations: a comparative approach*. San Francisco, CA: Chandler Publishing Company.

Cardinal, L. B. 2001. Technological innovation in the pharmaceutical industry: managing research and development using input, behavior, and output controls. *Organization Science*, 12: 19–36.

Cardinal, L. B., Sitkin, S. B., and Long, C. P. 2004. Balancing and rebalancing in the creation and evolution of organizational control. *Organization Science*, 15: 411–431.

Chen, D., Park, S. H., and Newburry, W. 2009. Parent contribution and organizational control in international joint ventures. *Strategic Management Journal*, 30: 1,133–1,156.

Covin, J. G. and Slevin, D. P. 1990. New venture strategic posture, structure, and performance: an industry life cycle analysis. *Journal of Business Venturing*, 5: 123–135.

Dale, J. D. 1958. *Wage incentives and productivity*. New York, NY: George Elliot.

Davila, A. and Foster, G. 2007. Management control systems in early-state startup companies. *The Accounting Review*, 82: 907–937.

Dermer, J. 1988. Control and organizational order. *Accounting, Organizations and Society*, 13: 25–36.

Doty, D. H. and Glick, W. H. 1994. Typologies as a unique form of theory building: toward improved understanding and modeling. *Academy of Management Review*, 19: 230–251.

Dunbar R. L. M. and Statler, M. 2010. A historical perspective on organizational control research. In S. B. Sitkin, L. B. Cardinal, and K. M. Bijlsma-Frankema (eds.), *Organizational control*. Cambridge University Press.

Eisenhardt, K. M. 1985. Control: organizational and economic approaches. *Management Science*, 31: 134–149.

Etzioni, A. 1965. Organizational control structure, In J. G. March (ed.), *Handbook of organizations*: 650–677. Chicago, IL: Rand McNally.

Fayol, H. 1949. *General and industrial management*. C. Storrs (trans.). London: Pitman.

Galbraith, J. R. and Kazanjian, R. K. 1986. Organizing to implement strategies of diversity and globalization: the role of matrix designs. *Human Resource Management*, 25: 37–54.

Glick, W. H. 1985. Conceptualizing and measuring organizational and psychological climate: pitfalls of multilevel research. *Academy of Management Review*, 10: 601–616.

Govindarajan, V. and Fisher, J. 1990. Strategy, control systems, and resource sharing: effects on business-unit performance. *Academy of Management Journal*, 33: 259–285.

Govindarajan, V. and Gupta, J. 1985. Linking control systems to business unit strategy: impact on performance. *Accounting, Organizations and Society*, 10: 51–56.

Greiner, L. E. 1972. Evolution and revolution as organizations grow. *Harvard Business Review*, 50: 37–46.

Hanks, S. H., Watson, C. J., Jansen, E., and Chandler, G. N. 1993. Tightening the life cycle construct: a taxonomic study of growth stage configurations in high-technology organizations. *Entrepreneurship, Theory, and Practice*, 18: 5–29.

Hoskisson, R. E., Hitt, M. A., and Hill, C. W. L. 1991. Managerial risk taking in diversified firms: an evolutionary perspective. *Organization Science*, 2: 296–317.

Jaeger, A. M. and Baliga, B. R. 1985. Control systems and strategic adaptation: lessons from the Japanese experience. *Strategic Management Journal*, 6: 115–134.

Jaworski, B. J. 1988. Toward a theory of marketing control: environmental context, control types, and consequences. *Journal of Marketing*, 52: 23–39.

Jaworski, B. J., Stathakopoulos, V., and Krishnan, H. S. 1993. Combining combinations in marketing: conceptual and empirical evidence. *Journal of Marketing*, 57: 57–69.

Jermier, J. M. 1998. Introduction: critical theory perspectives on control. *Administrative Science Quarterly*, 43: 235–256.

Kazanjian, R. K. and Drazin, R. 1990. A stage-contingent model of design and growth for technology based new ventures. *Journal of Business Venturing*, 5: 137–150.

Kimberly, J. R. 1979. Issues in the creation of organizations: initiation, innovation, and institutionalization. *Academy of Management Journal*, 22: 437–457.

Kirsch, L. J. 1996. The management of complex tasks in organizations: controlling the systems development process. *Organization Science*, 7: 1–21.

1997. Portfolios of control modes and IS project management. *Information Systems Research*, 8: 215–239.

Kirsch, L. J., Ko, D. G., and Haney, M. H. 2010. Investigating the antecedents of team-based clan control: adding social capital as a predictor. *Organization Science*, 21: 469–489.

Langley, A. 1999. Strategies for theorizing from process data. *Academy of Management Review*, 24: 691–710.

Lebas, M. and Weigenstein, J. 1986. Management control: the roles of rules, markets, and culture. *Journal of Management Studies*, 23: 259–272.

Long, C. P. and Sitkin, S. B. 2006. Trust in the balance: how managers integrate trust-building and task control. In R. Bachmann and A. Zaheer (eds.), *Handbook of trust research*: 87–106. Cheltenham, UK: Edward Elgar.

Long, C. P., Burton, R., and Cardinal, L. B. 2002. Three controls are better than one: a simulation model of complex control systems. *Computational and Mathematical Organization Theory*, 8: 197–220.

Makhija, M. V. and Ganesh, U. 1997. The relationship between control and partner learning – related joint ventures. *Organization Science*, 8: 508–527.

Martinez, J. I. and Jarillo, J. C. 1989. The evolution of research on coordination mechanisms in multinational corporations. *Journal of International Business Studies*, 20: 489–514.

McKelvey, B. 1982. *Organizational systematics: taxonomy, evolution and classification*. Berkeley, CA: University of California Press.

Merchant, K. A. 1985. *Control in business organizations*. Marshfield, MA: Pitman Publishing.

1988. Progressing toward a theory of marketing control: a comment. *Journal of Marketing*, 52: 40–44.

Meyer, A. D., Tsui, A. S., and Hinings, C. R. 1993. Configurational approaches to organizational analysis. *Academy of Management Journal*, 36: 1,175–1,195.

Miles, R. E. and Snow, C. C. 1978. *Organization strategy, structure, and process*. New York, NY: McGraw-Hill.

Miller, D. 1986. Configurations of strategy and structure: towards a synthesis. *Strategic Management Journal*, 7: 233–249.

1987. The genesis of configuration. *Academy of Management Review*, 12: 686–701.

Miller, D. and Friesen, P. 1984. *Organizations: a quantum view.* Englewood Cliffs, NJ: Prentice Hall.

Mintzberg, H. 1979. *The structuring of organizations.* Englewood Cliffs, NJ: Prentice Hall.

Mohr, L. B. 1982. *Explaining organizational behavior.* San Francisco, CA: Jossey-Bass.

Oliver, C. A. 1998. Critical theory perspectives on control. *Administrative Science Quarterly,* 43: letter from the editor.

Ouchi, W. G. 1977. The relationship between organizational structure and organizational control. *Administrative Science Quarterly,* 22: 95–113.

1979. A conceptual framework for the design of organizational control mechanisms. *Management Science,* 25: 833–848.

1980. Markets, bureaucracies, and clans. *Administrative Science Quarterly,* 25: 129–141.

1981. *Theory Z: how American business can meet the Japanese challenge.* Reading, MA: Addison-Wesley.

Ouchi, W. G. and Price, R. L. 1978. Hierarchies, clans, and theory Z: a new perspective on organization development. *Organizational Dynamics,* 7: 62–70.

Quinn, R. E. and Cameron, K. 1983. Organizational life cycles and shifting criteria of effectiveness: some preliminary evidence. *Management Science,* 29: 33–51.

Richardson, F. L. and Walker, C. R. 1948. *Human relations in an expanding company.* New Haven, CT: Labor and Management Center, Yale University.

Roth, N. L., Sitkin, S. B., and House, A. 1994. Stigma as a determinant of legalization. In S. B. Sitkin and R. J. Bies (eds.), *The legalistic organization:* 137–168. Thousand Oaks, CA: Sage Publications.

Selznick, P. 1957. *Leadership in administration.* New York, NY: Harper and Row.

Simons, R. 1995. *Levers of control: how managers use innovative control systems to drive strategic renewal.* Boston, MA: Harvard Business School Press.

Sitkin, S. B. 1995. On the positive effect of legalization on trust. In R. J. Bies, R. J. Lewicki, and B. H. Sheppard (eds.), *Research on negotiations in organizations:* 185–217. Greenwich, CT: JAI Press.

Sitkin, S. B. and Bies, R. J. 1994. The legalization of organizations: a multi-theoretical perspective. In S. B. Sitkin and R. J. Bies (eds.), *The legalistic organization:* 19–49. Thousand Oaks, CA: Sage Publications.

Sitkin, S. B., Sutcliffe, K. M., and Schroder, R. G. 1994. Distinguishing control from learning in total quality management: a contingency perspective. *Academy of Management Review,* 19: 537–546.

Sitkin, S. and George, E. 2005. Managerial trust-building through the use of legitimating formal and informal control mechanisms. *International Sociology,* 20: 307–338.

Snell, S. A. 1992. Control theory in strategic human resource management: the mediating effect of administrative information. *Academy of Management Journal*, 35: 292–327.

Sutcliffe, K. M., Sitkin, S. B., and Browning, L. D. 2000. Tailoring process management to situational requirements: beyond the control and exploration dichotomy. In R. Cole and W. R. Scott (eds.), *The quality movement and organizational theory*: 315–330. Thousand Oaks, CA: Sage Publications.

Tannenbaum, A. S. 1962. Control in organizations. *Administrative Science Quarterly*, 7: 236–257.

Taylor, F. W. 1911. *The principles of scientific management*. New York, NY: Harper.

Trice, H. M. and Beyer, J. M. 1984. Studying organizational cultures through rites and ceremonials. *Academy of Management Review*, 9: 653–669.

　1993. *The cultures of work organizations*. Englewood Cliffs, NJ: Prentice Hall.

Tsoukas, S. 2007. Introduction to the forum on the future of critical management studies: a Paleo-Marxist view. *Organization Studies*, 28: 1,309–1,311.

Van de Ven, A. H. and Huber, G. P. 1990. Longitudinal field research methods for studying processes of organizational change. *Organization Science*, 1: 213–219.

Van de Ven, A. H. and Poole, S. 1995. Explaining development and change in organizations. *Academy of Management Review*, 20: 510–540.

Van de Ven, A. H., Hudson, R., and Schroeder, D. M. 1984. Designing new business start-ups: entrepreneurial, organizational, and ecological considerations. *Journal of Management*, 10: 87–107.

Van Maanen, J. and Schein, E. H. 1979. Toward a theory of organizational socialization. *Research in Organizational Behavior*, 1: 209–264. Greenwich, CT: JAI Press.

Wanous, J. P. 1980. *Organizational entry: recruitment, selection and socialization of newcomers*. Reading, MA: Addison-Wesley.

Weber, M. 1946. *From Max Weber: essays in sociology*. H. H. Gerth and C. W. Mills (eds.), New York, NY: Oxford University Press.

Whitley, R. 1999. Firms, institutions and management control: the comparative analysis of coordination and control systems. *Accounting, Organizations and Society*, 24: 507–524.

Whyte, W. R. 1955. *Money and motivation: an analysis of incentives in industry*. New York, NY: Harper.

Wilkins, A. L. and Ouchi, W. G. 1983. Efficient cultures: exploring the relationship between culture and organizational performance. *Administrative Science Quarterly*, 28: 468–481.

Williamson, O. E. 1975. *Market and hierarchies: analysis and antitrust implications*. New York, NY: Free Press.

4 | Critical perspectives on organizational control: reflections and prospects

RICK DELBRIDGE
Cardiff Business School

Critical perspectives on organizational control begin with the recognition that organization is neither inevitable, nor a given subject only to efficiency requirements. Actors are conceived as knowledgeable agents with potentially divergent motives and interests and organization is seen as socially constructed and political in its nature. Thus in shorthand terms, while wary of simplistic dichotomies, one might position critical approaches in distinction to "mainstream" or functionalist accounts of organization on a number of counts. Radical approaches of various hues emphasize the relationship between the design of work, control, and the nature of economy and society within which organization occurs. Early critique, informed by readings of Marx, challenged conventional assumptions that the design of work and patterns of employment were "created" by the scientific, technological, and organizational advances of the industrial revolution and as such "neutral" or "appropriate" in response to prevailing economic conditions (Fox, 1974; Marglin, 1974). These analyses sought to locate developments within wider patterns of asymmetrical power relations and material outcomes.

Early critical work centered on the labor process, the changing nature of skills, and the degradation of power and social positions of workers (Braverman, 1974). Edwards (1979) argued that to understand the underpinning reasons for workplace hierarchy and the transformation of the labor process during the late nineteenth and early twentieth centuries, scholars needed to focus on the characteristics of the economic system, that is, capitalism. Such theorizing placed an explicit focus on the power relations between the owners and their managers and the employees subject to organizational control (the contest between capital and labor). These approaches benefited from the recognition of the divergent interests of organizational members under capitalism and also placed analysis in the meaningful historical, socio-political and economic contexts of society; society is conceived as the source of values and ideologies that inform organizational members' interests rather than an "environment" held as distinct from organization.[1] However, such "structuralist" arguments were challenged by other critical scholars, often inspired by readings of Foucault, who argued that insufficient attention had been paid to issues of subjectivity, identity, and resistance. Thus concerns with the contests around "technical and material interests" in organization and society have been developed through a growing emphasis on "meaning-making" and the increasingly central examination of how power and domination are socially constructed (see Delbridge and Ezzamel, 2005). Over the past decade various approaches to the critical evaluation of the management and organization of economic activity under contemporary capitalism have emerged and been labeled collectively as "critical management studies" (CMS).

This chapter begins with an outline of the historical development of critical approaches to understanding organization in general and control in particular. In doing so, I provide an overview of the work that has led to the development of CMS. Although it remains a dynamic but heterogeneous community (or communities), it is possible to outline certain central characteristics that inform CMS in terms of both the conduct and objectives of research. These center around the questioning of assumptions, conventions, and the taken-for-granted; moving beyond instrumentalism and concerns only with performance in narrowly defined economic terms; a commitment to reflexivity and making of multiple meanings; and the challenging of dominant groups, discourses, and structures. Each of these characteristics brings issues of power and knowledge to the fore. The chapter proceeds to examine each of these aspects of CMS and the implications for understanding and researching organizational control. It concludes by reflecting upon some key issues that are currently at the forefront of critical perspectives on control and by considering ways in which these might inform future research.

Labor process analysis

Critical scholars have complained that, "The treatment of control in mainstream writing is ambiguous at best, marginal at worst" (Thompson and McHugh, 2002: 101) but Thompson and McHugh go on to add that, "The apparent absence of control from the mainstream is, however, somewhat misleading. The issues are there but they are articulated in different language and concepts." Others have noted similarly that while "control lies at the heart of organization theory . . . explicit discussion and debate of organizational control has become increasingly less common" (Delbridge and Ezzamel, 2005: 603).[2] Control is thus seen as an *implicit* focus of much mainstream organization studies which suffer from attendant weaknesses because of the failure to make these issues explicit and central to analyses.

Critical scholars' concerns with the mainstream treatment of control begin with the use of language and concepts, such as coordination, inputs, outputs, performance standards, feedback loops, and monitoring that appear neutral and hide the outcomes of organizational control. Moreover, the ambivalence of mainstream writers on organization and management to the effects of social controls has, according to Pfeffer (1997), contributed to the emergence of critical perspectives. These critical perspectives span various material, discursive, power–knowledge and domination/emancipation aspects of organization but often start with a concern to analyse control relations.[3] CMS has gained popularity and widened its membership considerably over the past decade but draws upon a substantial history of critical research on organization and work, much of this scholarship concentrates on the labor process in individual workplaces and explores the effects of control on those at work.

Research specifically focused on organizational control under the banner of CMS is most commonly conducted in the form of labor process analysis (LPA).[4] LPA is generally understood to have started with the work of Braverman (1974). His thesis builds from Marx's analysis of the capitalist labor process and argues that there is an inevitable tendency toward the degradation of skill under capitalism as capitalists seek profits in increasingly competitive economic markets. It thus begins with the acknowledgement of the fundamental but unpredictable conflict inherent in capital and labor relationships. This opens up the understanding of managerial control as central but negotiated in capitalist organizations. As Braverman (1974) comments, "what the worker sells, and what the capitalist buys, is not an agreed amount of labor, but the power to labor over an agreed period of time." The owner appropriates "surplus value" from the efforts of employees (i.e., pays people less than the economic value that can be realized from their labor) in order to accrue profits. Under such conceptions of the employment relationship, efficiency, control, and exploitation are inseparable.[5]

This "structured antagonism" (Edwards, 1986) has been the subject of considerable empirical research, most notably through the intensive case studies of "industrial sociologists," such as Gouldner (1954), Lupton (1963), Burawoy (1979), and Cavendish (1982), many of which were conducted before the language and concepts of LPA had been more widely established but which shared certain key concerns for the examination and explanation of workplace patterns of power, control, and resistance. Early LPA work critiqued Braverman (1974) for failing to treat managers and workers as active agents and extended his work to incorporate alternative management strategies. For example, Friedman (1977) stressed that some workers may be better able to resist controls, or managers may see occasions when it is in their interests to allow employees some discretion – resulting in a strategy of "responsible autonomy" rather than the "direct control" – assumed by Braverman (see also Gouldner, 1954, for a discussion of how discretion or "indulgence" is part of workplace relations, and Burawoy, 1979, on the "manufacturing of consent," in which game-playing and rule-breaking on the part of workers contributes to managerial controls).

LPA approaches such as that of Braverman were criticized by other critical scholars for overstating management's objective of controlling labor, that is, treating control as an end in itself rather than the means to achieving profits (Noon and Blyton, 1997), and for focusing too narrowly on the point of production (e.g., Burawoy, 1981). Along with his study of the emergence of multiple management control strategies over the course of capitalist economic development (Edwards, 1979), the work of Edwards and his radical economist colleagues was important in recognizing that employers consciously create segmented labor markets that fragment the working population, particularly along race and gender divisions, and thus weaken their position especially during times of economic crisis (Edwards *et al.*, 1975).

Gordon (1976) extended the conceptualization of these dynamics to argue that any form of economic system, such as capitalism, can continue only if the nature of organization and control is such that it reproduces the social (or "class") relations of that system. He contrasts the concepts of "quantitative efficiency" (the relation-ship between inputs and outputs in production) and "qualitative efficiency" (the reproduction of the class relations of a mode of production). In so doing, Gordon adds an important nuance to the structuralist arguments of Marx and Engels (1848) in the *The communist manifesto* and the LPA researchers that they inspired. Gordon offers a way around debates over whether economic competition *or* class struggle drive capitalism, and he argues for the recognition of the interdependence of these in capitalist development. These arguments have a series of implications for how we might understand the hegemony of capital and its managers (Delbridge, 2007) and also draw our analyses into the wider social and political context of organization and management control.

To address concerns with the narrowness of much early LPA, Burawoy (1983) developed a "politics of production," which provides the conceptual link between the labor process at workplace levels of organization and socio-economic levels of aggregation such as, for example, global politics. This work retained a focus on the organization but builds from this in order to explore the similarities and differences in terms of the institutions of the state in different contexts and the varieties of concepts and approaches that were to be found. Thus attention was directed to the cultural and historical contexts that inform organization and control at micro levels of analysis (Elam, 1990). Concerns to explore social processes such as control at various levels of organization – from "micro" through to "macro" – have remained central in much of the work of critical scholars.

Having traced its emergence to Marxist-inspired accounts and explanations of material and social aspects of work, it is important to recognize the wide range of theories and approaches that now constitute LPA. In particular, a post-structuralist turn, inspired by readings of Foucault, has prompted considerable attention to issues relating to the constitutive role of language/discourse, power, identity, and resistance. Under such approaches, there is a critical appreciation of the power of language in constituting the world. Post-structuralists join with other LPA scholars in recognizing the significance of context (or "situatedness") and the importance of mechanisms of control, but differ in the ontological status that they ascribe to certain aspects of such social processes and in their epistemology. For example, while post-structuralism does not deny the existence of a material world, it stresses that subjects can identify and articulate this material world only through their ability to engage with it discursively, "Control mechanisms and their consequences are experienced by subjects in the form of discursive practices as they engage in networks of power relations" (Delbridge and Ezzamel, 2005: 608).

The post-structuralist turn has also prompted reevaluations of the conception of power. Drawing on Foucault, power is seen as relational – and both disciplining and enabling – rather than as the property of sovereign authority to be wielded over the oppressed. In studying power, the post-structuralist approach conceives all organizational actors as embedded in power/knowledge networks which enable and discipline through discursive practices in mutable ways over time. Some post-structuralists have thus conceived individuals as subjects engaged in ongoing identity projects, engaging in resistance as a means through which they establish or reaffirm their identities (Ezzamel and Willmott, 1998). This adds considerable nuance to any simplistic assumptions about the homogeneous nature and interests of "workers" or "managers," thus emphasizing the contingency and diversity of individuals. Issues of identity have emerged as a significant research subject for critical scholars across the ontological spectrum. Thus concerns around "technical or material interest" in organization that marked early LPA have been joined by an increasing emphasis on "meaning-making" in organization theory with critical interpretive scholars examining how power and domination are socially constructed (Delbridge and Ezzamel, 2005).

During the last decade, there has been a significant broadening of the theoretical resources and approaches that one may consider to represent forms of LPA (O'Doherty and Willmott, 2001). LPA places great significance on what people do and the contexts in which they act, emphasizing control and the indeterminacy of workplace relations and engaging with political economy and class relations. Thus, LPA contributes to an overtly political research agenda that engages with, among other things, skills, autonomy, and organizational systems; individual and organizational identities; managerial strategies of control and workplace relations; contest, power relations, and discursive strategies of legitimation; the organizational and workplace effects of product and labor markets; and the influence of historical, socio-cultural, and politico-economic contexts more widely.

The theories, approaches, and agenda remain broader still for critical management studies. As Jermier (1998) notes, critical theorists have turned their attention to numerous social processes – patriarchy and the mistreatment of women, racism and its effects on minorities, post-colonialism and its legacy of subjugation, environmentalism and capitalism's effects on the planet – and drawn yet more widely on theories to advance our understanding of these. In the following section I outline the substance of CMS before turning to some key issues in relation to organizational control.

Critical management studies

CMS is a catch-all term for a heterogeneous group of researchers and body of work that displays neither internal consistency nor clear differentiation from more mainstream analysis (Adler *et al.*, 2007). The burgeoning interest in CMS that has emerged in the last ten years has contributed to this breadth and consequent lack of coherence but the defining of "critical" has been a constant issue for reflection and debate. A decade ago, Jermier commented in his introduction to the *Administrative Science Quarterly* special issue on "Critical perspectives on organizational control," "As with many concepts that have long academic careers, taking a critical perspective has become a catch-phrase and something of a cliché. Most academics think their work is critical because the topics they study are important and because they criticize other research." However, he then proceeds to draw attention to the distinctive approaches of critical perspectives in analyzing social relations, specifically the "thoughtful examination of the structures of control in society and of the political implications of academic work" (Jermier, 1998: 236).

The defining feature of CMS is a question that has also been addressed by Fournier and Grey (2000). They too recognize that just "being critical" is not sufficient, "Much of the recent managerialist literature is extremely 'critical' of management ... [but] it remains that simply offering a critique of management does not in itself earn one a place in the CMS 'camp'" (Fournier and Grey, 2000: 28, note 4).[6] They also note the theoretical pluralism of CMS – citing neo-Marxism, post-structuralism, deconstructionism, and feminism, among others – and the absence of any single demarcation between critical and non-critical. Nonetheless, they conclude that boundaries are drawn and recognized around key issues, in particular, the questioning of assumptions and the taken-for-granted (denaturalization), moving beyond concerns only with performance in narrowly defined economic terms (performativity), a commitment to understanding of multiple meanings (reflexivity), and the challenging of dominant groups, discourses, and structures (change).

CMS, most particularly in the work of post-structuralist researchers, has drawn attention to the power and influence of discourses that construct and sustain "techniques of control" (Hasselbladh and Kallinikos, 2000). Such accounts recognize that the argument that "there is no alternative" (TINA), that is, the apparent self-evidence of a specific, orthodox way of representing the world (e.g., organizations have structures and goals), works as a powerful influence in favor of the *status quo* (see Adler *et al.*, 2007). Hence the concerns noted earlier about the *apparently* neutral language of both mainstream organization theory and management practice. A central objective of CMS is to challenge these institutionalized forms of understanding and hold these to *radical critique*. "Radical" here refers to concerns to attend to socially divisive and environmentally destructive discourses and/or structures, such as capitalism, patriarchy, and neo-imperialism, that condition local action and conventional wisdom in organizations and wider society. "Critique" involves challenging these patterns in the belief that these are contingent and mutable, that is, that they require reproduction and are thus neither necessary nor unavoidable (Adler *et al.*, 2007). For critical scholars it is not just language that cannot be neutral; they also ask searching questions of the nature of knowledge and the place of science and scientists. Jermier (1998: 237–238) notes, "Critical theorists hold that no knowledge is neutral. Even science is an integral part of society and cannot be insulated from broader struggles for control … Critical theorists maintain that social scientists (in particular) serve interests and take sides on important issues, even when they strive for impartiality and aspire to serve the public interest." This stance goes to the heart of the distinction between all forms of traditional and critical social theory: the former assist (often unwittingly) in the process of social reproduction, while the latter consciously aspire to subvert it. Since scholars cannot rid their theories of and empirical inquiries of normative content and partisan consequences, critical theorists maintain that it is best to acknowledge one's partiality openly. Thus the inescapable question for a critical theorist is, "Whose side are you on?"[7] This normative content, for CMS researchers, emphasizes not just how the world is but how it could be. A characteristic of CMS is thus that it has a project for change, though there is no consensus on what nor how. In principle, therefore, CMS research challenges the norms and conventions of society and the economy (i.e., it stands up to TINA) and puts forward alternatives.[8]

Themes in CMS and their implications for researching control

Though CMS is a broad, and broadening, church, it is thus possible to identify some common themes and underlying concerns across the range of research and theorizing that may be labeled "critical" in approach. In a recent summary statement on the field, leading CMS scholars Paul Adler, Linda Forbes, and Hugh Willmott (2007) have indicated that the CMS community is collectively motivated, to varying degrees and with various intentions, by concerns with the social inequalities and environmental destructions of the broader social and economic systems in which individual managers and firms are operating and which their actions serve and reproduce. They confirm the view that CMS has an agenda for change; research is conducted with a view to radically transforming management practices and organizational systems. The shortcomings of management practices and organizational structures are analyzed and critiqued on the basis of their embeddedness in wider historical contexts and broader patterns of relations of domination. These are the focus for research and critique for it is understood that they can never become "total" or irresistible since by their very existence they provoke the means of their resistance. Thus, what might be considered by dominant parts of society as "deviant behavior" is in fact a *consequence*, not simply a condition, of control (Adler *et al.*, 2007); that is, deviance and resistance are produced through the processes of controlling. In other words, critical organization theorists place control explicitly at the heart of their analyses.

Drawing on the work of Jermier, Fournier, and Grey, and Adler and colleagues, I can therefore identify a number of key themes that are common to work in the broad school of CMS. The themes are: the questioning of the taken-for-granted; moving beyond instrumentalism and assumptions of performativity; the concern for reflexivity and meanings in research; and the challenging of structures of domination. These four themes coalesce around an underlying set of issues of "power-and-knowledge." Each of these has particular relevance for aspects of researching organizational control, and they are outlined in the following sections.

Questioning the taken-for-granted

CMS advocates the challenging of "natural" orders and conventions, for example in questioning the need and purpose of control and in problematizing assumptions of managers as experts holding legitimate positions of authority. This approach highlights the social construction and institutionalization of these conventions in order to hold these up to critique. For example, in contrast with mainstream and functionalist concerns with efficiency, the critical management theorist focuses on the inherent power relations of positioned practices and roles, making transparent the inequalities of such roles and positions, and questioning the rationales and consequences of capitalist conventions. A classic early example is the work of Marglin (1974), who challenged assumptions about the rationality and technical efficiency of the development of the organization of production following the industrial revolution. He explains the emergence of hierarchy and bureaucracy in production (i.e., the division of labor in the putting out system and centralized organization of factories) through the desire for increased control on the part of capital and its management agents rather than technical rationalization. More broadly, much early critical work critiqued the profound differences of discretion, opportunity, and material rewards that resulted from the increasing industrialization of economies. In particular, critical scholars such as Fox (1974) rejected conventional views that technologies and organization develop in ways that are necessary or appropriate to the demands of the "neutral" economic conditions of the time.

Fournier and Grey (2000: 18) describe this as the "denaturalization" project of CMS, "If we conceive of twentieth-century management theory as being involved in a double movement of constructing organizational reality and rationality while effacing the process of construction behind a mask of science and 'naturalness,' we can see CMS as being engaged in a project of undoing this work, of deconstructing the 'reality' of organizational life or 'truthfulness' of organizational knowledge by exposing its 'un-naturalness' or irrationality." Critical researchers are thus highly skeptical of mainstream management arguments, which invoke notions of "imperative" in response to developments such as globalization or conceptions of the capitalist market like competition. This refocuses questions of control around power, knowledge, and legitimacy and contributes to the CMS agenda for change – in regard to material conditions, power asymmetries, environmental impacts, and so on – by throwing the negotiated orders and structured antagonisms of capitalism into sharp relief. Such ambitions mean that CMS is home to a dynamic and ever-changing set of concerns as it targets developments in the economy and society.[9]

Beyond instrumentalism and performative intent

While challenging the discourses of efficiency and profit maximization that are central to capitalism, CMS also addresses the implications of these assumptions and strategies directly. This is captured in what Fournier and Grey (2000: 17) describe as the non-performative intent of CMS which they counterpose with the performative intent of mainstream management theory, "A performative intent ... means the intent to develop and celebrate knowledge which contributes to the production of maximum output for minimum input; it involves inscribing knowledge within means–ends calculation. Non-critical management study is governed by the principle of performativity which serves to subordinate knowledge and truth to the production of efficiency. In non-critical management study, performativity is taken as an imperative towards which all knowledge and practice must be geared." In rejecting the instrumental means–ends rationality of profit maximization and performance targets, CMS seeks to move beyond such "performativity" and asks what control is for and how it can be evaluated.[10]

CMS thus requires analysis of organizational control to be about far more than material or financial measurements of inputs and outputs, and about a wider range of issues than profitability or other performance variables. That is not to say that critical researchers ignore the significance of performance measurement, budgeting arrangements and so on, but rather to acknowledge that they center their attention on the social processes and consequences of these. This has proven particularly relevant in examinations of the crises that unfettered capitalist corporations have wrought with regard to financial markets, employees, communities, and the environment. Thus, CMS brings ethical and political questions to the fore and requires a broader-based assessment of the purposes and outcomes of processes of control.

These first two themes involve critical reflection on who or what controls whom, why control is exercised, and with what wider implications and outcomes. Such reflection on the nature of organizational control is mirrored in CMS concerns with the meanings, purpose, and practicalities of research itself.

Reflexivity and meaning

A central and growing concern in CMS involves the recognition of how the research of researchers is influenced by their social positions and personal histories and how their accounts, and the readings of these, are conditioned by the use of language in constituting and conveying the objects and subjects of research. There has been considerable methodological and philosophical reflexivity on the part of critical researchers (Fournier and Grey, 2000). This means that both researchers' philosophical assumptions about the nature of the social world they are researching (ontology) and how knowledge of that world may be acquired (epistemology) are considerations given significant attention. As has been discussed, such concerns have not resulted in homogeneity in research approach, ontological assumptions, epistemologies, or methods across the CMS community, far from it. But they do require a sensitivity to, and reflexivity around, their implications. For example, in considering conceptions and theories of organizational control, there is a need to consider how research contributes to, rather than challenges, the hegemony of dominant mainstream and conventional managerialist discourses. Too much of mainstream organization theory assumes that a "scientific" and positivist approach is normal, natural, and appropriate without explicit reflection on the implications and limitations of such. CMS researchers have drawn on a wide range of methods but generally place significant value on getting close to the subjects of their research. As Jermier observes, "Most critical theorists employ methods that allow them to ground their research in the accounts of individuals and groups whose perspectives are ordinarily devalued or neglected." He goes on to recognize, however, that "critical theorists also aim to reveal socioeconomic conditions that produce and reinforce asymmetrical structures of control . . . the critical theorists' most controversial task is to go beyond informants' reports to articulate the socioeconomic context that envelops their informants' worlds without relying exclusively on either pre-existing theory or mere speculation" (Jermier, 1998: 240). Thus critical researchers are familiar with the challenges of interpreting micro-level observational data in their wider contexts and in seeking to explain more macro-levels of activity on the basis of the analysis of micro-data. I discuss below two approaches within CMS (analytical concepts of identities and critical realist conceptions of agency and social structures, respectively) that have developed partially at least in response to these challenges.

Debates around ontological assumptions, the ontological status of key concepts, and epistemological concerns are central features of CMS. Indeed, such issues have been central to much debate within the CMS community, particularly between neo-Marxist and post-structuralist LPA researchers, for quite some time. Increasingly, these debates have moved beyond polar positioning to find some common ground for mutual engagement. Fournier and Grey (2000: 26) suggest that these contests have promoted a greater reflexivity on the part of CMS and helped its dynamism and vitality, "We do not see these divisions as demarcating clear 'camps' or fixed positions within CMS, but rather as defining lines of movement, arguments, and shifting alliances that constitute the very criticality of CMS, for it is these polemics that allow for the doubt, questioning, and reflexivity that feed and sustain critique." Indeed, recent dialogues between different ontological positions *within* CMS (e.g., Delbridge and Ezzamel, 2005; and Reed, 2005, versus Contu and Willmott, 2005) have helped to highlight the central importance of taking ontology seriously in social science research and to both more clearly articulate the meaningful differences, convergences, and potentials of these different approaches.[11]

Challenging structures of domination

CMS seeks to place the understanding of organizational control within its meaningful historical backdrop and the politico-economic context of capitalism. There are long-standing traditions of assessment and evaluation of the historical developments of management control in capitalist economies (e.g., Edwards, 1979; Marglin, 1974) and critique of the dehumanized, depersonalized, and alienating nature of work in contemporary organizations. At these broad levels of analysis and debate, Jermier (1998) proceeds to argue that two key themes in critical theory are the misuse of power in society, resulting in the mistreatment of some individuals and groups, and the justification for aligning science with the interests of the mistreated. CMS researchers have taken various views and approaches in seeking to address these. At one end of the spectrum, there lies a radical and even revolutionary commitment to change which is expressly "anti-management," eschewing dialogue with managers while seeking to undermine management through critique. Under such conceptions, notions of "better management" are rejected, "The argument is that management is irredeemably corrupt since its activity is inscribed within performative principles which CMS seeks to challenge" (Fournier and Grey, 2000: 24).

At the other end of the CMS spectrum there are more contingent and localized levels of engagement. Here CMS is held to contribute to the promotion of "better" management, varyingly defined as "more humane," "less oppressive," or "less socially divisive," with the intention of lessening the distortion of the asymmetrical power relations of capitalist organization (e.g., Alvesson and Willmott, 1996; Fournier and Grey, 2000; Watson, 1994). In this approach, there are various views on how "transformation" might or should be achieved but there is a consistent commitment to engagement *with* management practitioners in order to seek change. There is also recognition of the heterogeneity of "management" and that managers are themselves managed and thus subject to control and potential exploitation. Contemporary critical accounts of organizational control in, for example, post-bureaucratic and knowledge-intensive organizations seek to lay bare the underlying power relations of organization, explore and critique the apparently neutral *language* of knowledge creation, management expertise, and participation, and examine the material effects of changing social relations in the workplace and their wider societal interrelationships.

Although much early LPA concentrated on the situation of "workers," particularly in industrial settings, over the past decade or so CMS researchers have increasingly engaged with and explored the experiences of managers and professional employees in processes of domination. For example, Perlow's (1998) study of professionals in a knowledge-intensive setting explored the fragile "boundaries" between the product development engineers' work and home lives. She identified the combination of coercive and subtle normative controls that resulted in the engineers working long hours to the detriment of their "nonwork lives" and also highlighted professional employees' active participation in their subjugation through their senses of identity, ethics, and commitment. Additionally, the author showed how wider social relations inform an individual employee's sense of obligation. This is just one example of the burgeoning critical literature that has reflected on various issues of control and their impact on managers and professionals as subjects of such processes rather than agents. Much recent work under the CMS banner has thus sought to evaluate managers' experiences, particularly with regard to various economic and social changes and organizational developments, including the rise of information and communication technologies, the advent of "post-industrial" network organization, and the proliferation of forms of insecure employment and the demise of careers.

This work has reflected shifts in the nature of the economy and employment patterns, with studies of work in service sector contexts and of "experts" working in knowledge-intensive organizations, highlighting departures from the conventional understandings of management control that derive from industrial settings. These economic and organizational developments have exacerbated the negotiated, ambiguous, and fragile nature of the structured antagonism of workplace relations and complicated the nature of these relationships by introducing imprecise or ambiguous concepts such as "knowledge creation" and "customer service quality" that can be drawn upon in the negotiation of organizational control. Even though critical research tends to emphasize the difficulties such developments present for employees, some work has also drawn attention to the opportunities that such complexity and ambiguity present. For example, Rosenthal (2004) draws attention to the possibilities of control as "worker resource" in front-line customer service settings. In such circumstances, employees may subvert or resist management control through their interactions with, and influencing of, customers. This of course raises new problems for supervisors and managers. The presence of another set of active agents in the processes that surround organizational control (i.e., customers) makes such relations even less predictable and emphasizes the importance of assessing rather than assuming the outcomes of these processes.

Of course, analysis of the interrelationships of employees is of potential interest to all organization control researchers but this goes further in CMS. The challenge to the structures of domination is emblematic of CMS concerns with locating the analysis and explanation of local social relations in deeper social and historical contexts. Recent work that has revisited the prospects for building contemporary analyses from the early theory of Marx by Paul Adler exemplifies this approach. A central argument of Adler (2007) is that recent LPA has not paid sufficient attention to the structural foundations and contradictions of capitalism. Specifically, Adler draws attention to the progressive "socialization" of the labor process, which results in the increasing interdependence of both the structure of industry and of subjective self-identities, and capitalist valorization processes, which describe the profit imperative and the processes through which profits are accrued, at least in part through the extraction of surplus value from workers' efforts. His "paleo-Marxist" view thus sees the basic contradiction at the heart of capitalism as existing at a deeper layer of causality than that of class struggle; it exists in the relation between the forces of production and the relations of production. These forces of production are constituted by technology, materials, and workers' productive faculties and the relations of production are the relations of ownership and control over these productive forces. Adler argues that analyses of workplace relations should incorporate a stronger interpretation of the conditioning impact of the structural forces of capitalism. He goes so far as to suggest that workplace relations are "largely pre-ordained" by capitalism's macrostructure with the actions of owners, managers, and workers of secondary importance. As reflected in the earlier discussion on the ontological variation within CMS, not all critical researchers share Adler's views and his emphasis on deep structures.[12]

In a broadly sympathetic reading of Adler's position, Delbridge (2007) develops a research framework that not only draws from but also extends his arguments through combining insights from the concept of hegemony most commonly associated with Gramsci and the ontological conceptions of critical realism. Incorporating critical realism emphasizes the central significance of agency theory in the reproduction/transformation of social structures involving conscious action and unintentional reproductive/transformative consequences (Hay, 1994). It also recognizes the historicity, that is, the preceding structural contexts and mechanisms or social structural forces that impact upon action but reject notions of structural determinism. Adler's article brings together organizational research with "individual," "technical," and "social" aspects of work and organization. But his discussions of management and organizational developments such as Taylorism and lean production and their impact upon, *inter alia*, skills and the micro-social relations of production, can (and should) be located in their wider historical, political, and economic contexts. A critical realist theory of hegemony provides the analytical concepts and a framework through which this can be achieved. Through this approach the study of organizational control is reengaged with its historical, economic, and institutional contexts while retaining the significance of the agency of actors in specific local circumstances in interpreting the empirical outcomes at any given moment.

Power–knowledge

The four themes reviewed thus far are closely related and not discrete in nature. A central feature of each of these themes is power and its relationships to knowledge and action. CMS strongly promotes the view that the apparent neutrality of knowledge works to obscure processes of enduring domination and power asymmetries. For many decades the contested and negotiated aspects of organizational control have been central to the research of those seeking to advocate change within, or beyond, capitalism. Conceptions of *power-and-knowledge* recognize the intimate relationship between the two and work to ensure that existing "realities" and social and economic relations are not accepted as necessary or immutable.

A clear articulation of this can be found in a paper by Hasselbladh and Kallinikos (2000), which examines the processes and patterns of rationalization and institutionalization of formal organizing. They draw attention to the significance of writing and formal codification in promoting and objectifying rationalized patterns. They further evaluate how different forms of objectification make discourses and techniques of control possible, and demonstrate how these themselves become institutions. They thus show how the processes and operations that constitute the "knowledge regimes" of society make actors, patterns of action, and formal organizing possible. In Foucauldian terms, they provide an evaluation of how the construction of objects and subjects, classification, causal reasoning, truth, and positions of authority are discourses and techniques of control that belong to no one but that act to define and bring to material effect the ideals and rationalized patterns of organization and society.

The "hidden" aspects of power have been central concerns in CMS. One major area where CMS has contributed has been in examining the nature of normative or cultural control where employees "internalize the rules and will continue to follow rules and orders even when the organization's overt power is weakened or even absent" (Etzioni, 1964: 51). The interplay of "value-based management" and bureaucratic structures and the ways they are experienced by workers has been the subject of considerable empirical research (e.g., Kunda, 1992). Such ideas have been at the heart of a number of prominent managerial initiatives, most notably the "strong organizational culture" arguments of Peters and Waterman (1982; see also Deal and Kennedy, 1982) and the enduring influence of "soft human resource management" as the source of employee commitment and, through this, organizational control. Critical scholars have explored the evidence of normative controls in practice. Some (e.g., Barker, 1993; Sewell, 1998) have been pessimistic of the prospects for employees to escape the powerful influence of "concertive" or "chimerical" controls underpinned by peer pressures to conform to managerial objectives and the panoptic surveillance heralded by increasingly sophisticated information technology and performance measurement. Others (e.g., Delbridge, 1998) have acknowledged the increasingly challenging context for employees that exists in high-surveillance and low-trust workplaces but have found evidence of knowledgeable workers exercising personal agency and of enduring individual and collective resistance.

In addressing such aspects of organizational control as power, knowledge, and knowledgeability, CMS thus builds upon, but goes beyond, what Greenwood and Hinings (2002: 411) identified as the distinction of a sociological approach to organization theory in its concern with "who controls and the consequences of that control." This they contrasted with "management theory" with its concern with efficiency and "how to understand and thus design efficient and effective organizations." However, rather than juxtaposing power and efficiency, CMS researchers see these as inextricably linked as aspects of capitalism (Clegg *et al.*, 2006). Approaches to power differ across the spectrum of research under the CMS label but resonate to varying degrees with the work of Marx (particularly the early work that inspired Gramsci's development of the concept of hegemony) and Foucault. Foucault problematized the assumptions of "bad" power by recognizing the mundane and dispersed nature of power, which is conceived and experienced through "everyday ways of sense making that are more or less institutionalized in disciplinary knowledge" (Clegg *et al.*, 2006: 9). Power is therefore not a "thing" or a property of people but a relation between things and people. From this position, critical management theorists have sought to challenge taken-for-granted assumptions about the nature of corporations, management, and knowledge about these.

In a recent extension of the work of Marx and other conventional LPA on labor value, Sewell (2005) has discussed the "indeterminacy of knowledge." His intention is to both inject greater dynamism into what he sees as unnecessarily static and overly deterministic LPA accounts and to draw attention to the increasing significance of discourses of "knowledge" in contemporary organization. Sewell identifies the role of managers in linking abstract and tacit knowledge with practical organizational knowing (where knowledge informs action). This is a process that entails objectifying or codifying organizational knowledge and then the setting of targets on the basis of the leading performers whose know-how becomes shared knowledge through processes of codification and communication. Sewell's appeal is therefore for an engagement with the array of power relations relating to the elicitation and representation of knowledge. His article encourages us to appreciate the subtle disciplinary mechanisms at work that seek to perpetuate management control within a context of indeterminacy of knowledge. Again, issues of knowledge creation, knowledge workers, and knowledge management are concerns for mainstream organization theorists but there is distinctiveness in the assumptions, conceptualizations, and objectives of how these are addressed in CMS. Given these overlapping concerns but divergent approaches, in what ways might a critical research agenda on organizational control be relevant to mainstream researchers?

A contemporary critical research agenda

Critical research on control places emphasis on the importance of language and meanings, examines the interrelational (dualisms or dualities) of structures and actions, and locates analyses in the historical, institutional, politico-economic, and socio-cultural contexts that constrain and enable action. This involves a number of analytical challenges that might be shared with mainstream researchers, perhaps most significant among these are the situating of organizational action and the making of conceptual and empirical linkages across levels of analysis. Let me conclude by outlining two approaches to these issues that stem from different ontological standpoints within the CMS community but which have enlivened critical thinking from across the spectrum and may provoke further theoretical reflection. The first approach addresses the ways in which the concept of identity, primarily stemming from post-structuralist perspectives in critical theory, have been developed to make sense of the complex and dynamic relationships among self, work, and organization (for an overview see Alvesson *et al.*, 2008). The second is the critical realist informed attempt to develop a more sophisticated understanding of agency within enduring social structural contexts (for an overview see Mutch *et al.*, 2006). Each of these is potentially influential within a CMS research agenda but may have value, and implications, for mainstream organization control researchers.

Much recent CMS research has highlighted the importance of employee identities, both their sense of self and the socially constructed identities that are developed collectively, in understanding people's experiences of organization.[13] This has offered new insights into various aspects of normative controls while also locating these in their meaningful economic, discursive and/or material societal contexts. For instance, recent reviews of the empirical evidence have highlighted the "conflicted collaboration" that appears to characterize contemporary industrial workplaces, i.e., workers experience simultaneously both interdependence and disconnection (Delbridge, 2007). For example, the evidence on the experience of teamworking under lean manufacturing regimes is best described as *both* coercive and collaborative; workers are subject to fragmentary stresses and tensions while at the same time they are more tightly coupled interdependently within teams. This is contributed to, and further compounds, a fracturing of identities (Jenkins and Delbridge, 2007) where employees' senses of self, personal value, and satisfaction are drawn from an increasing spectrum of sources and interactions beyond the workplace. Thus individuals' views on their value and their sense of self at work are informed by various stimuli outside the organization and which exercise potential influence over extended periods of time. Van Maanen (Chapter 5) similarly notes the multiplicity of identifying references that are available to, or confront, individuals. Though I share his skepticism to the extent to which each of these possibilities might be equally likely (and would also question how fleetingly, situationally determined they are), the potential for (self-) subordination that these open up is apparent.

In recent work in professional and knowledge economy workplaces, critical scholars have identified the emergence of managerial controls exercised through individuality and exhortations to "be yourself." Recent theorizing by Fleming and Sturdy (2009) has suggested that there is an emerging new form of managerial control, which they label "neo-normative," which is derived from the individualizing discourse of market rationalism (individual employees are seen as self-interested and atomistic) and encouraged to be "authentic," as diverse and creative individuals. Among other things, this acts to blur the symbolic distinctions between "home" and workplace. It also acts to apparently "remove" the need and expectation of corporate forms of control; control is self-disciplinary in nature. Such developments focus attention on the management of identities as a central feature of contemporary organizational control. Alvesson *et al.* (2008) recognize the increasing managerial interest in controlling employees through appeals to their feelings, values, self-image, and identifications (Willmott, 1993). They argue that managers are themselves increasingly concerned with how organizational control is accomplished "through the self-positioning of employees within managerially inspired discourses . . . [resulting in] the employee as a managed identity worker who is enjoined to incorporate the new managerial discourses into narratives of self-identity" (Alvesson *et al.*, 2008: 16). Thus *identity control* is increasingly recognized by critical researchers as a space and focus of contest. For post-structuralist researchers, including those at the forefront of work exploring identity and organization, the situatedness of control is important and from their ontological position context is understood as discursively constituted.

They thus speak of "a" context rather than "the" context and emphasize the potential for different actors to construct contexts through discourse. The concepts of identity and discourse provide the means for connecting individuals, organization, and action in understanding control and its effects. These interconnections are important aspects of interpreting and analyzing organizational control for both critical and mainstream researchers. In particular, this work helps sensitize mainstream researchers to the importance of language and to ensure that organization is understood to be socially constructed and involve knowledgeable actors with potentially divergent interests.

An alternative to the discursive conception of context is derived from critical realism. Critical realism is founded upon an "objectivist social ontology in that it focuses on social reality as consisting of objectified social structures that exist independently of the various ways in which they can be discursively constructed and interpreted by social scientists and other social actors" (Reed, 2001: 214). Drawing on Emirbayer (1997), Mutch *et al.* (2006) make clear that this is not to suggest structural determinism, but it does place emphasis on contextuality, process, causal explanation, and a stratified ontology or levels of reality. At the surface level of the empirical (the focus for mainstream positivist research) are events that are understood through the senses of individuals. Events are generated by underlying and intransitive structures which cannot be directly observed but can be known by their contingent effects. These are what Layder (1997: 20) has termed the "collective properties of social life that historically emerge to form objective features that provide the wider background context and the immediate settings of activities." When considering organizational control, these may be understood to be the discourses, institutions, traditions, and patterns of social relationships that constitute capitalism. Critical realists conceive these structures as generative mechanisms that give rise to empirical tendencies (e.g., the structured antagonism of capitalist employment relations) but do not determine the outcomes of action. Mutch *et al.* (2006) show that it is an understanding of the ways that actors connect with their contexts that allows an assessment of stability and change in processes of organization, including control. Thus the outcomes of processes of controlling (even, for example, the experiences of working under Fordist management practices in a car factory) cannot be assumed but must be researched, evaluated, and the specific empirical evidence then explained in the light of both local contingent factors and wider social and historical forces.

Critical realism has recently begun to influence aspects of mainstream organization theory, in particular institutional theory (see Palmer *et al.*, 2008; Thornton and Ocasio, 2008). For example, Leca and Naccache (2006) have used critical realist concepts to distinguish between institutional logics that act as generative mechanisms and have the potential to exert influence through institutions, which inform but do not determine action. Such a framing may be of use to mainstream researchers seeking to determine interlinkages between levels of analysis and across periods of time when explaining aspects of the processes and outcomes of organizational control. Critical realist concepts provide ways of both (a) evaluating patterns of organization over time, and (b) understanding these at local, micro levels as observable empirical outcomes. Thus, post-structuralist approaches to understanding identity and critical realist conceptions of agency/structure both share concerns with locating knowledgeable actors in meaningful contexts in ways that situate analyses of organizational control. They both challenge mainstream researchers to make control an explicit focus for research and to incorporate approaches that reflect upon taken-for-granted conventions and avoid purely performative assumptions of the purposes and consequences of organizational control.

CMS is a dynamic and vibrant community of researchers but it is certainly not coherent or uniform in outlook, ontology, or objectives. Though it does come together in challenging the assumptions, realities, and results of capitalism, in some ways it is easier to say what CMS is not. And what it stands in distinction to, in antagonism with, is the orthodoxy of much organization theory (what a leading critical theorist, Gibson Burrell, described as North Atlantic theories of organization, or NATO!). Nonetheless, it may be that mainstream researchers will find some benefit through greater understanding and engagement across ontological and political divides within organization theory. For critical management scholars, the future research agenda remains varied and emergent, but it is to be hoped that it retains Horkheimer's (1972: 213) emphasis on describing and criticizing exploitation, oppression, and social injustice, his recognition of the impossibility of disinterested or "objective" social science, and meets his objectives to unite theory with struggles for social change (see Jermier, 1998: 238–239).

Notes

1 Of course, as the chapter by George and Qian in this volume discusses, it is entirely possible for employees and managers to share interests. Critical scholars have recognized this in cases where, for example, a workplace is under pressure to improve performance or close (Cressey and MacInnes, 1980). As I will explain in this chapter, however, for critical researchers the fundamental nature of capitalist economy and society results in mistreatment and processes of domination that make any convergence of interests partial and temporary.

2 Concerns with the treatment of control have also been voiced from within the mainstream organization research community, see Cardinal *et al.* (Chapter 3) in this volume, and also Cardinal *et al.* (2004), who found that current control research was insufficient to make sense of their ten-year longitudinal study of a founding organization.

3 For example, one of the first major radical contributions to organization theory proposes the "concept of organization as control of the labour process" (Clegg and Dunkerley, 1980: 1).

4 I use the term "labor process analysis" as a catch-all term for various approaches to labor process theory (see O'Doherty and Willmott, 2001).

5 As Jermier (1998) notes, Marxist notions of economic exploitation through the capitalist labor process have been developed under a wider rubric of "mistreatment" in critical management studies to include oppression, social injustice, and also environmental concerns.

6 Fournier and Grey (2000: 9) cite the critique of management offered by Adam Smith to show that criticizing managers does not in itself constitute CMS.

7 In covering a wide range of work in such a short space, I am forced to generalize. It is certainly not the case that all those working under the CMS banner would have the same answer to this question; one would hope though that it is a question that they all recognize.

8 It should be noted that the *practical* impact, or lack of it, is one major issue of concern for commentators on CMS (see Fournier and Grey, 2000).

9 Given the fundamental critique of capitalism at the heart of critical theory, critical scholars were not surprised by the global financial crisis in the second half of 2008 and were quick to establish websites such as http://sites.google.com/site/radicalperspectivesonthecrisis/finance-crisis to provide forums for commentaries.

10 Bijlsma-Frankema and Costa (Chapter 13) provide a natural and open systems approach to control, which also moves beyond rational and closed conceptualizations.

11 The contributions of both critical structuralist and post-structuralist theorization of organizational control are briefly outlined in Delbridge and Ezzamel (2005).
12 The paper was debated in a special section of *Organization Studies* (Volume 28, Number 9, 2007).
13 More recently mainstream control researchers have also begun to examine the role of identity, see for example George and Qian (Chapter 6) and Van Maanen (Chapter 5) in this volume.

References

Adler, P. 2007. The future of critical management studies: a paleo-Marxist critique of labour process theory. *Organization Studies*, 28 (9): 1,313–1,345.
Adler, P., Forbes, L., and Willmott, H. 2007. Critical management studies: premises, practices, problems, and prospects. *Annals of the Academy of Management*, 1: 119–180.
Alvesson, M. and Willmott, H. 1996. *Making sense of management: a critical introduction*. London: Sage.
Alvesson, M., Ashcraft, K., and Thomas, R. 2008. Identity matters: reflections on the construction of identity scholarship in organization studies. *Organization*, 15: 5–28.
Barker, J. 1993. Tightening the iron cage: concertive control in self-managing teams. *Administrative Science Quarterly*, 38 (3): 408–437.
Braverman, H. 1974. *Labor and monopoly capital*. New York, NY: Monthly Review Books.
Burawoy, M. 1979. *Manufacturing consent*. Chicago, IL: University of Chicago Press.
    1981. Terrains of contest: factory and state under capitalism and socialism. *Socialist Review*, 58: 83–124.
    1983. Between the labor process and the state: the changing face of factory regimes under advanced capitalism. *American Sociological Review*, 48: 587–605.
Cardinal, L. B., Sitkin, S. B., and Long, C. P. 2004. Balancing and rebalancing in the creation and evolution of organizational control. *Organization Science*, 15: 411–431.
Cavendish, R. 1982. *Women on the line*. London: Routledge and Kegan Paul.
Clegg, S. and Dunkerley, D. 1980. *Organization, class and control*. London: Routledge and Kegan Paul.
Clegg, S., Courpasson, D., and Phillips, N. 2006. *Power and organizations*. London: Sage.

Contu, A. and Willmott, H. 2005. You spin me round: the realist turn in organization and management studies. *Journal of Management Studies*, 42 (8): 1,645–1,662.

Cressey, P. and MacInnes, J. 1980. Voting for Ford: industrial democracy and the control of labour. *Capital and Class*, 11: 5–37.

Deal, T. and Kennedy, A. 1982. *Corporate cultures*. Reading, MA: Addison-Wesley.

Delbridge, R. 1998. *Life on the line in contemporary manufacturing*. Oxford University Press.

2007. Explaining conflicted collaboration: a critical realist approach to hegemony. *Organization Studies*, 28 (9): 1,347–1,357.

Delbridge, R. and Ezzamel, M. 2005. The strength of difference: contemporary conceptions of control. *Organization*, 12(5): 603–618.

Edwards, P. K. 1986. *Conflict at work*. Oxford, UK: Blackwell Publishing.

Edwards, R. 1979. *Contested terrain: the transformation of the workplace in the twentieth century*. London: Heinemann.

Edwards, R., Reich, M., and Gordon, D. 1975. *Labor market segmentation*. Lexington, MA: D. C. Heath.

Elam, M. 1990. Puzzling out the post-Fordist debate: technology, markets and institutions. *Economic and Industrial Democracy*, 11 (1): 9–37.

Emirbayer, M. 1997. Manifesto for a relational sociology. *American Journal of Sociology*, 103 (2): 281–317.

Etzioni, A. 1964. *Modern organizations*. Englewood Cliffs, NJ: Prentice-Hall.

Ezzamel, M. and Willmott, H. 1998. Accounting for teamwork: a critical study of group-based systems of organizational control. *Administrative Science Quarterly*, 43: 358–396.

Fleming, P. and Sturdy, A. J. 2009. "Just be yourself!" Towards neo-normative control in organizations? *Employee Relations*, 31: 569–583.

Fournier, V. and Grey, C. 2000. At the critical moment: conditions and prospects for critical management studies. *Human Relations*, 53 (1): 7–32.

Fox, A. 1974. *Beyond contract*. London: Faber and Faber.

Friedman, A. 1977. *Industry and labour: class struggle at work and monopoly capitalism*. London: Macmillan.

Gordon, D. 1976. Capitalist efficiency and socialist efficiency. *Monthly Review*, 24: 19–39.

Gouldner, A. 1954. *Patterns of industrial bureaucracy*. New York, NY: Free Press.

Greenwood, R. and Hinings, C. R. 2002. Disconnects and consequences in organization theory? *Administrative Science Quarterly*, 47: 411–421.

Hasselbladh, H. and Kallinikos, J. 2000. The project of rationalization: a critique and reappraisal of neo-institutionalism in organization studies. *Organization Studies*, 21 (4): 697–720.

Hay, S. 1994. Structure and agency and the sticky problem of culture. *Sociological Theory*, 12 (1): 57–70.

Horkheimer, A. 1972. Traditional and critical theory. *Critical theory: selected essays*: 188–243. New York, NY: Seabury Press.

Jenkins, S. and Delbridge, R. 2007. Disconnected workplaces: interests and identities in the "high performance" factory. In S. Bolton and M. Houlihan (eds.), *Searching for the human in human resource management*: 195–218, Basingstoke: Palgrave.

Jermier, J. 1998. Introduction: critical perspectives on organizational control. *Administrative Science Quarterly*, 43: 235–256.

Kunda, G. 1992. *Engineering culture: control and commitment in a high-tech corporation*. Philadelphia, PA: Temple University Press.

Layder, D. 1997. *Modern social theory*. London: University College London Press.

Leca, B. and Naccache, P. 2006. A critical realist approach to institutional entrepreneurship. *Organization*, 13 (5): 627–651.

Lupton, T. 1963. *On the shop floor: two studies of workshop organization and output*. Oxford, UK: Pergamon.

Marglin, S. 1974. What do bosses do? The origins and functions of hierarchy in capitalist production. *Review of Radical Political Economics*, 6 (2): 60–112.

Marx, K. and Engels, F. 1848/1998. *The communist manifesto*. New York, NY: Penguin.

Mutch, A., Delbridge, R., and Ventresca, M. 2006. Situating organizational action: the relational sociology of organizations. *Organization*, 13 (5): 607–626.

Noon, M. and Blyton, P. 1997. *The realities of work*. Basingstoke: Macmillan.

O'Doherty, D. and Willmott, H. 2001. Debating labour process theory: the issue of subjectivity and the relevance of poststructuralism. *Sociology*, 35: 457–476.

Palmer, D., Biggart, N., and Dick, B. 2008. Is the new institutionalism a theory? In R. Greenwood, C. Oliver, K. Sahlin, and R. Suddaby (eds.), *The Sage handbook of organizational institutionalism*: 739–768. Thousand Oaks, CA: Sage.

Perlow, L. 1998. Boundary control: the social ordering of work and family in a high-tech corporation. *Administrative Science Quarterly*, 43 (2): 328–357.

Peters, T. J. and Waterman, R. H. 1982. *In search of excellence*. New York, NY: Harper and Row.

Pfeffer, J. 1997. *New directions for organizational theory: problems and practices.* Oxford University Press.

Reed, M. 2001. Organization, trust and control: a realist analysis. *Organization Studies*, 22: 201–228.

2005. Reflections on the realist turn in organization and management studies. *Journal of Management Studies*, 42 (8): 1,621–1,644.

Rosenthal, P. 2004. Management control as an employee resource: the case of front-line service workers. *Journal of Management Studies*, 41 (4): 601–622.

Sewell, G. 1998. The discipline of teams: the control of team-based industrial work through electronic and peer surveillance. *Administrative Science Quarterly*, 43: 397–427.

2005. Nice work? Rethinking managerial control in an era of knowledge work. *Organization*, 12 (5): 685–704.

Thompson, P. and McHugh, D. 2002. *Work organizations: a critical introduction.* Basingstoke: Palgrave.

Thornton, P. and Ocasio, W. 2008. Institutional logics. In R. Greenwood, C. Oliver, K. Sahlin, and R. Suddaby (eds.), *The Sage handbook of organizational institutionalism:* 99–129. Thousand Oaks, CA: Sage.

Watson, T. 1994. *In search of management.* London: Routledge.

Willmott, H. 1993. Strength is ignorance; slavery is freedom: managing culture in modern organizations. *Journal of Management Studies*, 30 (4): 515–552.

PART III

Identity, attention, and motivation in organizational control

5 Identity work and control in occupational communities

JOHN VAN MAANEN
Sloan School of Management, MIT

This chapter is about identity construction and display in the workplace.[1] It is concerned directly with a few of the many ways work selves and work lives are animated and made meaningful and what this might mean to managers in organizations where strong, valued, collective work identities are at play. I take as axiomatic that work is a natural locale for the study of identity since we spend so much of our adult life at it. But the significance of work is by no means only quantitative. As Hughes (1951) noted long ago, our work is as good a clue as any to our sense of self, our course of being, our way of life. "What do you do for a living?" is an all too familiar probe to which we must have a ready answer or risk censor.

There are a number of ways work can bestow meaning on the self. Some are set by historical and institutional processes that are rather distant and removed from specific individuals going about their trade. Others emerge from the kinds of things people do in the ordinary context of going about their work. The former draws on a relatively stable, categorical ordering of occupational status and provides something of a shell or vessel within which people labor (Hauser and Warren, 1997). Such processes govern the prestige of a given occupation in a socially recognized universe of occupations (e.g., being a police officer rather than a postal worker) or the prestige of the specific social context in which the occupation is taken up, especially the type and status of the organization or organizational segment in which the work is pursued (e.g., the Los Angeles Police Department rather than the Azusa Police Department, or as a member of the SWAT team in the Patrol Division rather than as a member of the Officer Friendly squad in the Community Relations Division). Work also provides meaning by its contrast to other human activities relative to some worldview, religion, or ideology (e.g., work rather than play, leisure, contemplation, or self-development). Matters such as these reflect the status ordering of occupations, the place of work within broad social contexts and suggest – at least to outsiders – the physical, social, and moral nature of a given line of work versus others. Societal notions of "dirty work" develop in this context and are somewhat above and beyond the control of individual role occupants to alter.[2] Awareness of the prestige of an occupation (or lack thereof) is however another matter entirely and may well effect the ease or difficulty individuals have identifying themselves with their work.

Work also bestows meaning on individuals through their daily activities – the bundle of tasks that comprise the occupation. The intricacies and skills involved in the work process itself is one example (e.g., the thrill of an expertly handled car chase, the pride that comes from a superbly orchestrated drug bust). The results of the work are another – both the products (e.g., a captured villain, a child rescued from danger) and the by-products (e.g., a raise, a reprimand, a promotion). By and large, the meaning of work in these more or less internal domains relies on cultural conventions or codes specific to the occupation and arise (and change) in the day-to-day conduct of the trade. Outsiders rarely have much appreciation for the insider's perspective on the occupation's processes or products and therefore are in no position to judge individual performance with the same appetite, knowledge, evaluative criteria, and consequence that practitioners bring to the task.

Of central interest to me in this article are the ways individuals define, sharpen, and solidify their work identities in organizational settings. These matters concern the performance or playing out of an occupational role in an always-specific temporal, spatial, and interactional context. In particular, I want to sketch out how the words and deeds of police officers in large urban departments allow them to affirm and sustain a particular and valued work identity. Work identity rests of course on both an immediate situated identity and a broader social identity.[3] I treat the work identity more or less enacted and performed by individuals as akin to claims of personal character in an organization and use it, as do subordinates, peers, and superiors who read and honor such identity claims, to stand for a postulated "real person" who transcends situation and role. In broad strokes, it reflects a person's sense of distinctiveness, agency, dignity, special skills, ethics, and morality (or lack thereof). At work, it emerges within a context of occupationally similar colleagues who share (roughly at least) the same occupational role.

This exercise is an initial try at linking something of a theory of work identity to matters concerning organizational control by using the everyday world of police officers as a heuristic (and altogether opportunistic) grounding device. My writing of this world is fashioned more as an analytic ethnography than a substantive one because I am more interested in putting forth and illustrating a few concepts than representing a way of life (although the two are not unrelated).[4]

The theory sketched out here stands as a complement rather than a corrective to a good deal of previous work on occupational culture and control.[5] This earlier work emphasizes the shaping of social identity through the processes by which individuals learn their trade, come to value it, and thus become members of specific work organizations and/or occupational communities. Social identity concerns the self-consciousness that comes from membership in an occupational category and, when fully elaborated, provides members with a more or less shared sense of the collective culture – its mandate, license, heroes, history, legacy, special ethos, rules of thumb, unique problems, in-groups and out-groups, and so forth. While much empirical work has been focused on work identity generally, this work is often not always grounded in specific organizational settings where particular work identities are displayed and played out.[6] What I argue here is that occupational or work identities have considerable organizational relevance. When work identities are highly valued, strong, salient, and held in common by numerous colleagues in close proximity, management control becomes in varying ways problematic.

Resistance is of course one response of members of an occupational community to managerial efforts to direct their work, but it is not the only response and may well be the exception rather than the rule. Indeed, I will argue that control of members in at least one occupational community – police officers in big-city departments – depends largely on the degree to which managers intentionally or unintentionally respect and reinforce everyday identity claims made by members of the occupational community who fall under their area of responsibility. Identity in this context works to limit formal and hierarchical control by underpinning various forms of informal and peer control. That this occurs rather matter-of-factly, routinely, and continually is a point that should not be missed. Nor is it missed in other settings where it often seems the organization is itself designed to support, encourage, sustain, and perhaps even magnify the importance of valued occupational identities (to the self as well as others) – doctors in most hospitals (e.g., Friedson, 1963; Millman, 1977); engineers in some high-tech companies (e.g., Kunda, 1992); and professors in many research universities (e.g., Boyer, 1987).

Control is treated in organization studies in a number of ways. Some analysts rely on taxonomies emphasizing coercive, instrumental, and normative tactics (Etzioni, 1965; Scott, 1998); others look to input, throughput and output controls (Cardinal, 2001); still others look to more subtle, less direct control strategies, such as concertive controls exercised by work colleagues (Barker, 1999) or control through "leniency arrangements" or "indulgency patterns" (Gouldner, 1954) or control by self-regulation, professional oversight and/or peer pressures (Friedson, 1975). My treatment here leans toward the latter, more subtle control processes but points also to the widely acknowledged view that control is multi-faceted, not singular, and dynamic in the sense that control strategies come and go, varying over time in their effectiveness (or lack thereof).[7] Ultimately, however, control processes derive whatever power they may have at a given time from the eager or reluctant consent of those who are said to be controlled.[8] When it comes to those who harbor highly valued work identities, matters of managerial control become complicated and complicit in ways that link both the would-be controllers and controlled in identity games that carry more or less identifiable rules of play.

What some of these rules are and how they operate on the ground in the day-to-day work life of urban police officers are put forward in this chapter. The police are a peculiar occupational group because the nature of their work makes a large degree of self-control unavoidable. Yet the occupation lacks the institutional status and social prestige that leads managers (and outsiders) in other organizations to trust institutionally legitimated professionals to control themselves (Banton, 1964; Black, 1980; Manning, 1977, 2003; Rubenstein, 1973). Critically, the police are so widely dispersed (particularly in the heart of the organization, the patrol division) that their work cannot be observed. Much of what the police do and are supposed to do occurs outside the managerial gaze. The result is then a façade of organizational control (pseudo-control) that measures things that can be measured and ignores things that cannot. To wit, the police have parking ticket quotas and arrest statistics but make no attempt to count how many crimes have been prevented. The question raised here is what directs police action given that they operate within what most organizational theorists, following Gouldner (1954), would call a mock bureaucracy, wherein both the managers and the managed commonly overlook official rules and procedures? My answer rests on the work identities shaped and adopted by street-savvy officers. Control in police organizations is thus primarily an occupational matter that is used, counted on, and largely taken-for-granted by managers. But before diving empirically into the police world, a quick review of what we know of occupational communities is provided.

Occupational communities

One of the more persistent themes in sociology generally has been the presumed dichotomy between communal or collegial and rational or administrative forms of work organization. Although theories of organizations typically adopt the latter perspective, a conception of work organized in terms of occupational communities approximates the former. Broadly, an occupational community can be seen as a group of people who consider themselves to be engaged in the same sort of work; whose social and personal identity is drawn from such work; and who, to varying degrees, recognize and share with one another job specific (but, to varying degrees, contentious) values, norms, and perspectives that apply to but extend beyond work-related matters (Van Maanen and Barley, 1984, 1985).

Occupational communities build and sustain relatively unique work cultures consisting of, among other things, task rituals, standards for proper and improper behavior, work codes surrounding relatively routine practices and, for the members at least, compelling accounts attesting to the logic and value of their rituals, practices, standards, and codes. Moreover, a continuing – and problematic – quest for occupational self-control that allows work identities to emerge from displays (and claims) of personal agency serves as something of a special motive for most members of any given occupational community.[9]

In many ways, the notion of an occupational community stands as an alternative to an organizational frame of reference for understanding why people behave as they do in the workplace. Yet it is a perspective of considerable worth when seeking to explain or, more prosaically, figure out why seemingly well developed rational principles of organizational design including authority relationships, incentive systems, assigned decision rights, performance assessments, and so forth, work so poorly in certain settings. Several analytic aims are served by this approach.

First, a focus on occupations preserves some of the existential, everyday reality of the first-hand experiences of people at work. Social worlds coalesce around the objects produced, the services rendered, the interactions that occur in the workplace (and elsewhere), and the identities sought and assumed, honored, and dishonored by those within the community. To focus on occupation as the semantic tag that ties together the bundle of tasks that constitute a given line of work brings such social worlds and their many meanings to light.

Second, by examining these social worlds, we broaden our understanding of social control in organizations. It is self-evident that a fundamental problem of organization – or, more properly, the management of organizations – is the control of the labor process. Occupational matters are undeniably central to this problem since all positions have histories marking their rise (and fall) in terms of the amount of self-control occupational members have over their labors. The ongoing struggle of stable and shifting, formal and informal, large and small groups to develop and occupy some niche in the occupational structure of society is played out every day in organizations where administrative principles of control (i.e., codification, measurement, standardization, discipline, etc.) compete with traditional or communal principles of control (e.g., peer pressures, work symbols and ideologies, interaction rituals, valued practices).

Third, a focus on work and occupation casts a slightly different light on problems of diversity and conflict in the workplace than that cast by organizational theories. From an administrative standpoint, "deviance" among organizational members is defined in terms of exceptions to managerial wishes and expectations. The sources of such deviance are often ignored or muted since administrative solutions are sought in terms of correcting the "system" so that expectations can be met. That deviance is willful is a point often made in organizational studies but seldom elaborated on beyond bland references to the ubiquitous "informal" groups contained within an organization. Even when deviance is treated seriously and in some depth by organizational theorists concerned with the individual and group orientations of organizational members, it is often treated as merely the result of non-work factors such as subcultural norms imported into the workplace from outside (Katz, 1965); too rigorous, tight, punitive, or otherwise unenlightened management practices (Pfeffer, 1998); narrow, standardized, efficiency-focused technologies (Blauner, 1964; Thomas, 1994); one-shot, special favors granted by bosses to favored employees (e.g., Rousseau, 2004); situational opportunities seized on by employees to improve earnings, advance careers, or reduce risk (Dalton, 1959; Mars, 1982); and so on. Even though these sources of informal adjustments or member deviance are no doubt present in all organizations, willful violation of managerial dictates may also correspond to a pervasive logic embedded within the historically developed practices of occupational members doing what they feel they must. What is deviant organizationally may be occupationally correct (and vice versa).[10]

Finally, a focus on common tasks, peer relations, shared symbols or any and all of the elements that comprise an occupation brings forth a concern for how a given line of work can be said to influence a person's social conduct and identity in the workplace. Goffman (1961: 87–88) makes this point nicely when he suggests: "A self (then) virtually awaits the individual entering a position; he needs only to conform to the pressures on him and he will find a 'me' ready-made for him ..." Although a position is organizationally created and sanctioned, the work that comprises such a position often has a history and a set of everyday contingencies of its own. Even rigidly defined and monitored positions are almost always more than most organization designers, authorities, and, alas, researchers make them out to be (e.g., Roy, 1960). Some of these positions may offer an occupant far more than a job. Indeed, some may offer a rewarding and valued "me." The identity bestowing or limiting characteristics of positions are, in short, frequently matters that are job specific and worked out and honored or dishonored by colleagues within a given (and bounded) occupational community. Such communities could involve high-status executives (Morrill, 1996), West Point cadets (Lipsky, 2003), or drug-dealing gang members (Venkatesh, 2008). Here I look at the police.

Identity work

There is I think a general neglect within social science to examine the ways human beings develop and sustain a sense of uniqueness from one another as a social phenomenon. The term "identity" is used in a bewildering variety of ways and has, of late, become something of a cultural cliché. The scholarly literature spans sociology, economics, psychology, anthropology, philosophy, linguistics, literary theory, and cultural studies. Within this burgeoning literature are many theories of identity but it is nonetheless abundantly clear that human beings conceive of themselves in a vast number of ways and that these conceptions are all shaped by the specific cultural context in which they emerge.

Given this as a starting point, a good deal of the discourse on identity is built on broad ideas about the kind of social relations and institutional forms that surround us. Theories of modernity, for instance, take as a given the progressive prying loose or disembodying of persons from the traditional ties of place, tribe, clan, and family. Modern society is highly rationalized and operates largely through the production (and reproduction) of individuals who can easily be slotted into what seems to be an ever-increasing set of categories such as nation, race, ethnicity, region, sex, religion, class, interest group, lifestyle, occupation, job, generation, voting block, and so on (and on). Identity is thus tied to assumed group membership and people become aware of themselves mostly as members of a particular category or mix of categories. Within a category, individuals are subject to similar socialization processes such that personal differences are often considered maladaptive (at best) or deviant (at worst).[11]

Identity in current social theory rests largely on the social context within which people operate. Goffman (1959) suggests that individuals have as many selves as there are social contexts within which these selves are lodged. And these situated selves may or may not congeal. Post-modern theorists push the multiplicity and segmentation of individuals – as initiated by modernity – to the limit by denying any cohesion of the self from one social context to the next. A situated identity is all that is possible. Any transcendent identity – existing across social time and space – is illusory for, in Gergen's (1991) view, the self is so fully saturated in fragmented, fleeting, inconsistent, disconnected social relations that whatever identity the person holds at the moment is depthless and flat. Nothing is left of an individual's sense of the self except an incessant play of images without continuity or consistency.

Or is it? We might best think of the saturated and shifting (or perhaps shiftless) self as a hypothesis and then ask whether or not people try to identify themselves and others in a reasonably coherent fashion across social situations and times. Do they, for example, make connections between their past and present? Do they succeed? Are they concerned with continuity? Are people worried that an identification made of them (or by them) in one social context may not carry over into another? Are identity claims respected and accepted or disputed and denied by others? Are these questions even answerable in any persuasive way? I think they are but, before considering them concretely in the police world, an analytic framework must first be sketched out.

Acts of identity

The key idea underpinning my approach to the formulation of identity in the modern (or post-modern) world is that people are constantly interpreting themselves and others and that the very act of interpretation is synonymous with meaning making.[12] Personal identity is thus the meaning of the self to the self or to others. Such meaning rests of course on the responses of others such that a personal identity not reflected back more or less favorably on the part of significant others is unlikely to be held with much confidence (or for very long). As Goffman (1959) ironically notes and documents, our identity may well be our most personal and prized possession but it is on loan to us from others.

Meaning is of course also a contextual matter and so therefore is identity. Selves are contextualized when connected to other persons, to beliefs, to ideas, to situations, to feelings, to objects in the world, to particular times, to specific places, and so forth. Any connection – attributed, claimed, denied, or ignored – is an act of identification and is a building block of identity formulation. If these acts are repeated time after time and are sustained by others, bits and pieces of personal identity are formed and perhaps stabilized. In this fashion, identity results.

Making a connection is a rhetorical activity – an attempt to persuade, a claim, an attribution. It can occur in many ways. For example, a patrol officer who identifies himself as an "honest cop" invokes a connection between himself and a desirable ethical value. Such a claim may or may not be honored by others (or even the self) but it is nonetheless a part of any identity formation process. Countless claims (and counterclaims) are no doubt made in the course of a

workday, a week, a year, or a career. Some stick, some do not. Some
are deeply held and felt, some are not. Identity formation is thus
mostly a rhetorical process of deploying identifications by acts that
connect the self to the world.

Connections are of many types but two stand out as generic forms –
synchronic and diachronic. Synchronic connections are those that
identify the self with a condition, a state, a value, a person, a place,
a feeling, and so on. They are atemporal and rest on specific tropes –
metaphors, synecdoches, metonymies – that link the self to
something else. Diachronic connections link the self across time and
take narrative or storied form. Selves in a story become characters
with a past, a present, and, presumably, a future. Narratives are
obvious (and formidable) instruments of identity and the police make
much use of them. Stories are often the only entertainment available in
patrol cars, they are the essence of long and late nightshifts spent
waiting for something to happen (Van Maanen, 1974; Manning,
1977, 1989; Young, 1991).

Identifications emerge not only through talk but also through performance. As folklore suggests, actions often speak louder than words.
An officer who walks into the squad room before roll call and stands
chatting away with one group of officers rather than with another
group makes an identifying statement. The way an officer issues a
traffic citation or interviews a crime victim identifies as well by the
indifference, enthusiasm, or sympathy shown (and presumably felt).
A high-five slap of hands, a fist-bump with a colleague, or a sound pat
on the back may make a more powerful statement than simply the
verbal comment "good work." Identification through performance
works not only by the message conveyed but also by the manner of
its execution. But, as communication, identification of both the verbal
and non-verbal sort must rely on established cultural codes or else they
would be unintelligible. Some of these are broad, drawn from meanings that float in the society at large, some are narrow, drawn from
meanings that are tied to a given occupational community.

What I am sketching out is a rhetorical, semiotic, and communication framework for the study of identity. I assume that identity is
always up for grabs and it is not a matter that can be settled once and
for all. This does not mean that I think we are in some sort of
perennial identity crisis or suffer from a kind of existential dread that
comes from not knowing who we are. On these matters I follow both

Schutz (1964) and Berger and Luckman (1966) who argue that our social worlds are already deeply suffused with assumptions about identity, about self, about others and that those with whom we regularly interact share these background understandings such that identity is an explicit concern only in certain times and places.[13] Most interpretation is implicit and only becomes explicit as an active, conscious matter when people are encountered who are not yet known, when novel situations are experienced, or when our assumptions about identity (our own as well as others) are, for whatever reason, challenged. A patrol officer who thinks of herself as a model of professional conduct may think again after receiving a sudden and public dressing-down from a respected (by her) fellow officer who identifies her as "negligent, weak, flighty, and carrying a bad attitude problem."

Active interpretation of the self and others is a common phenomenon only when persons are showered with unexpected, sometimes traumatic, experiences that violate their sense of routine, normality, or propriety. This is of course why transition points are so important to the establishment of identity and why socialization theories stress the novel, the irregular, or the unexpected, since such situations place new claims on the self. Yet socialization theories are typically concerned with what agents do to the subjects of socialization. The self that emerges most clearly from socialization studies in the workplace is one that is deemed occupationally or organizationally relevant and proper. This is the work identity that must be more or less taken up and accepted by recruits if they are to be regarded by colleagues as members in good standing within the trade. Students of socialization as an organizational form of control look to acts of identification aimed toward others that are intended to produce a group of like-minded persons. Students of identity as a form of self-control must look to acts of identification coming from both the self and others (toward both the self and others) that are intended to document one's standing as a distinctive member within a group.

Of importance to any concern for identity is of course the strength of an act of identification. The remarks "I work for the police department" and "I am a cop" are both identifications. But, each remark can be heard and held as quite different in quality and intensity. Addressing the strength and importance of a given identification can be handled in many ways. Some, for example, are theory driven as when an analyst of a Freudian bent privileges certain phases in life, certain key relationships and certain interactional patterns as the keys to identity.[14] But actors on stage in the everyday world make identity judgments too and seem quite able to do so without recourse to psychoanalytic thought or any other analytic aid beyond those provided by the communities in which they live. Participants in ordinary conversation generally have a good sense of those self and other identifications that are strong and weak, those that are important or not. Insults, jokes, irony, compliments, persuasion, and satire would be impossible without such abilities. At issue here is word choice, topical choice, gesture, timing, awareness of audience, style, figures and modes of speech, posture, invocations of context, a twinkle of the eye, or a tongue put firmly in cheek. Through such means identifications are seen, spoken, heard, felt, written, and read as to their salience to the self and to others.

In everyday life therefore identities are continually being communicated both explicitly and implicitly by actions (and inactions) as well as by verbal exchanges of all sorts – from brief interjections to much longer conversations and narratives. But how do a vast number of identifications add up to something like a personal identity? Here I follow both the ethnomethodological and symbolic interactionist principles in which the conventionality and stability of interpretation are constituted through asserting and documenting agreement in a given human community. Identity is thus dependent on the work that takes place in a particular interpretive community (Fish, 1980). It is grounded by sustained forms of social interaction and stabilized in collaboration with others who can initiate and respond, confirm and disconfirm acts of identification.

Identity formation is a give-and-take process occurring between the self and others. If, for example, Officer Smith gets identified by one of his mates in the patrol division as a "real battler, a rough and ready guy, always willing to mix it up" and Officer Smith finds this identification attractive or flattering, he may use it in his narratives with patrol buddies who more or less support the identification by repeating it to others and back to Officer Smith. At some point later he may be confronted on the street by an "asshole" (to use the technical term favored by the police) who takes a swing at him. If he answers by punching out and flattening his adversary, he identifies himself again as a battler. As the incident is talked about among members of his squad, Officer Smith once again hears the identification of himself as a rough-and-ready guy and finds himself reconfirmed. Later he might be encouraged by others to volunteer for tasks that require toughness and provide him with more chances to prove his nature and get reconfirmed by both himself and others. Here such opportunities serve as identity enhancers and thus direct and influence action. If he hasn't heard the identification in a while, he may have to seek out certain situations to discover whether or not he is still the sturdy battler.

In such a fashion, identities are built (and dismantled). They are personal but thoroughly social and provisional in origin as well as maintenance. Strictly speaking, personal identity refers to those understandings of the self (by the self) that are internal but stable, transcending time and place. Yet they must rest on situated identities that are public, socially enacted, negotiated and momentary, bounded by space, time, and circumstance. Officer Smith's talk and action occur within defined situations and his responses to those situations are read by others in shared ways. Situated and personal identities are related in the sense that we presumably wish to enter and exit situations with our personal identity intact. Much of the time, if we are fortunate, this is not a problem but inevitably tensions between situated and personal identities arise. The challenge on such occasions for the individual is to not only bring forth on a given occasion a convincing self (a situated identity) but also to believe in that self (a personal identity) as well.

Identity work, as laid out here, deals with the interplay of social, personal, and situational identities. From the interplay comes the differentiation of individuals within a particular occupational community. How police officers – in particular, patrol officers – distinguish themselves one from the other and how such identity work promotes a certain order or control regime within the organization is the question I want now to explore. I look in three domains for answers to the question. These domains are hardly exhaustive of the uncountable spaces, times, performances, tropes, and narratives by which identities are established but the three areas are – as I will argue – of considerable importance and concern to the police. The first concerns what is done and concentrates on the work ethics of police officers dealing with the focus, intensity, and interest of their work. The second takes up the way or how the police handle their work activities and looks at the social poetics of police work captured through the skill, style, and face displayed by officers at work. The third domain is a most critical one for the police and considers how officers judge the trustworthiness of their colleagues (and, by implication, themselves as well). There is of course much overlap among the three. All have moral implications and where officers stand in one domain may well suggest where they stand in the others.[15]

Work ethics of the police

Patrol work is a social and spatial activity. Officers are assigned to precincts, work units, and given territorial responsibility. There are good beats and bad, similar colleagues and not so similar, comfortable places to be and uncomfortable places, safe zones and unsafe zones. Officers, by reading and occupying space, place themselves and others. Those who seek out active assignments over quiet ones or prefer night shifts to days identify themselves. Those who work solo or in tight, long-lasting partnerships or as members of certain cohesive squads in the department are identified – and identify themselves – by the company they keep. Precinct preferences identify as well.

Overriding a good deal of these social and spatial particulars is the metaphoric use of a station house (inside)/street (outside) distinction made by the police (Glaeser, 2000; Manning, 1977; Moscos, 2008; Young, 1991). This is a distinction that gives rise to identifications across hierarchies, across functions, and across officers. A patrol car team, for example, when leaving the station, radios a message to a police dispatcher saying that they are heading out, hitting the bricks, going to the street. Outside is where action can be found, the place where self-respecting police officers are supposed to be and where officers can exert agency and prove themselves. Inside, by contrast, is the place of boring paperwork, the place of supervision, restraint, and lack of agency. Outside is a place of relative freedom and autonomy. Inside is the place where those who do not know what is happening outside are located, a place of theory rather than practice, a place where "brown-nosers" hang out.

Such a distinction is not entirely unambiguous, however, for inside the station is also where coffee, company, and comfort can be found, a place for relaxation and a place where there is occasionally no work to do – certainly, for many, no "real work" to do.[16] Sometimes it can be a place where identifying acts of resistance can be set as is, for instance, the case when patrol officers stay in when their sergeant wants them out attending to police tasks on the streets. While advancing in age and hierarchy or shifting from patrol to certain other police functions typically means spending more time inside than out, all officers develop reputations early in their careers for their interest in and worth as street cops.

This interest and worth is not taken lightly for it is regarded in many ways as a measure of the officer's personal commitment to police work. Every level of the police hierarchy uses some version of the inside versus outside dichotomy when comparing themselves to the next higher level. Sergeants spend more time out than lieutenants who spend more time out than captains and so on up to the Assistant Chiefs and Chief of Police who spend more time out than the civic leaders to whom they must answer. Or so each claims.

For many if not most officers, personal character inevitably forms more on the outside where discretion and personal choice reside than on the inside where routines and rituals mark the working day. "Real police work" is done on the outside. Paperwork, meetings, training sessions, strategic planning sessions, administrative work, record keeping, lock-up work (all regarded by some – especially young, lower level officers – as "shit work") are done on the inside; thus, the more time one spends (or has spent) outside, on the proverbial street, the more one can credibly claim to be a real police officer. What it is one does outside is of course a critical matter and with such considerations the ethics of police work emerge more sharply and contentiously. Contested identities emerge from almost any discussion of work ethics in American police agencies. At issue is the proper attitude toward the work and the attitude displayed, inferred, claimed, or implied by an officer is thought to reveal the person, not the uniform. Here is where control and identity intersect.

Sergeants and other supervising personnel in police agencies know all this of course although the further they are from the street, the less they will know of the characters they seek to influence. A part of such knowledge resides with their own experience for all American police officers begin their careers with a lengthy stint in the patrol division. But, closer to the ground, where everyday assignments are parceled out and duties allocated, considerable knowledge of those over whom one has formal authority is present. If not, troubles are sure to arise. Yet, generally, sergeants know well who likes to work with whom, who prefers district A to district B, who enjoys the late turn rather than the early one, who will walk a beat without complaining and who will not, and so on (and on). By trying to match up such identity preferences, sharp supervisors can exercise considerable control over what gets done under their respective watches.

What occurs is, in effect, the sorting out and distribution of identity rewards: Officer Brown is charged with an identity-sustaining (or enhancing) task by Sergeant Jones who in so doing is reasonably confident that such a task will be handled well. Identity rewards – what Anteby (2008) calls "identity incentives" – are thus a potential and potent form of managerial control.[17] However, as a tool of the supervisor's trade, they must be handed out sparely, selectively, and judiciously if they are to retain their power. Moreover, since there are different work identities at play in the police world, allowing and encouraging the expression of certain desired identities (and not others) is often a tricky matter.

Some officers, for example, believe others are lazy, inert, without initiative. What they find wanting in their counterparts is a commitment to their work as police officers. Younger patrolmen, in particular, say they are surprised at what they call the "job mentality" of some of their colleagues – notably the older ones – who they say lack an independent spirit and take little interest in performing their duties in an aggressive, timely, and professional fashion. Police administrators often invoke this line when they identify "uniform carriers" who cannot be counted on to do much more than they are explicitly told (if that). They are annoyed by the way they approach police tasks. In the words of a police sergeant: "Being a cop is not harmless. A good street cop has to have drive and be willing to go out of their way to get some work done. If you see some kid blow a red light or smoking a joint you've got to go after him, chase him down. Or if someone pisses you off a couple of times, you gotta get 'em. Make it personal and try to achieve something. If you're taking a burglary report, go around the neighborhood and talk to people and find out if they saw or heard anything funny. It's really a matter of taking pride in the job and getting results" (Van Maanen, 1981: 227).

This is a work ethic that stresses a goal and task orientation. A good officer from this perspective is marked by a drive to maintain order, catch crooks, act autonomously, and go beyond commands, mere punctuality, or official job description. Initiative and success are linked and results come to those officers who seek them out. They know, as Manning (1974) notes, enforcing the law sometimes means breaking it. Real police officers do not simply "snuggle down in a warm and cozy patrol car, enjoy the scenery and go only where dispatch tells them to go." Those who identify others as uniform carriers or simple-minded order followers do not necessarily blame them for their lack of initiative. Often they regard them as products of an older, out-of-date, militaristic organization (and historical period) that emphasized (inappropriately) strict notions of command, control, and obedience. But they do see the work ethics of this earlier period as flawed and those that are seen to hold on to them identify themselves quite clearly as certain kinds of people.[18]

Other officers – notably older ones – have a rather different spin on work ethics. Rather than celebrating narratives that suggest organizational change, they bemoan them and worry about the efficiency-minded efforts of their superiors and the softening or weakening of the right kind of attitude and self-control displayed by their younger patrol colleagues. They are often convinced that the spirit and pride of being a police officer has taken a fall and many officers now lack the discipline it takes to be a police officer.[19] Good officers don't go off looking for something wild and crazy to do or worry about exceeding a quota while on patrol but go by the book and attend to their assigned and traditional duties – maintaining law and order on their patch. Efficiency and effectiveness of the police is contrasted to notions of readiness, duty, and staying out of trouble, and is a critical matter in this regard and must be displayed. Discipline can be inferred by the way the hair is cut, a uniform is worn, a gun holstered, a tie knotted, an order executed. Where there is respect for higher ranking officers (a somewhat rare commodity) it comes from the greater knowledge of police action and action plans these superiors are thought to possess – a matter often determined by the amount of time these superiors spend or have spent on the street and the reputations they have gained as a result.

Many police practices serve as reminders to patrol officers of the need for discipline. Shotguns are checked in and out, locked in position in the squad car. Reports must be properly filled out and filed. Radio communications are continually monitored and messages sent and received in special code. Patrol cars must be equipped and positioned in certain ways. Security and safety are not only precautionary police concerns but they are the products of police action. Secrecy is necessary since the enemies of the police – and there are many – wish to know what the police are up to, and secrecy is best maintained through order, a strict division of labor, and hierarchy. Discipline means sacrifice of course and its basis lies in the vow, the oath of office all officers are sworn to uphold. This sets the police off from other, less noble, pursuits and gives their work a special luster, value, and importance. Those who stress discipline, sacrifice, and living up to an oath are also those officers most likely to find colleagues in their midst who lack the true "police spirit," who are regarded as inauthentic sorts, unworthy of the uniform, who only play at being a police officer and treat their work as if it were a mere job rather than a calling.

Acts of identification that signal such a stance are many. A seeming obsession for making rank might be one, the drawing of strict lines of separation between work and leisure another. Still another might come from showing less than a keen interest in the street tales of veteran officers, who, in turn, read such indifference as a lack of respect for the uniform. Some duty-conscious officers complain that too many of their cohorts back off from their police responsibilities and point to the fact that many officers ride to and from work in plain clothes, have no sense of obligation to intervene in police-relevant situations they witness off-duty and talk about their occupation as if they simply fell into it accidentally. Some complain that others are so dependent on technology that they no longer know any "real" police skills (Meehan, 2000). Occasionally they mention those officers who they think are ashamed of what they do and thus when they are at work they are "faking it," merely playing a role rather than being a police officer. For some officers, policing is a twenty-four-hour-a-day matter, a seven-day-a-week responsibility, a way of being – in uniform or out. It is not a job but a way of life, a way of being premised on considerable sacrifice. A quite strong sense of self and feeling of importance results.

From such concerns come self and other distinctions of just who embraces and just who distances themselves from the police role and what that role rightly means – the uniformed role in particular. Senior officers in many departments have a choice of wearing a uniform at work and those that choose to do so or not are thought to reveal their identities in telling ways. Within any rank, some officers seem to work only to not work, taking as much time off from the job as they can by coming to work late and leaving early, running personal errands on the job, not monitoring the ongoing work on a shift, not helping others out, taking frequent sick leaves, and never putting in an extra day (or hour) unless coerced to do so by superior officers, or "milking" their calls and staying "out of service" for long chunks of time while on duty. They are viewed as slackers whose work ethics are out of line with what the trade requires. An officer who challenges such practices may well win the respect of others and then can ask more of his colleagues who identify more closely with the "real cop" role.

The issue here is not to analyze whether these claims and derogations are justified or not. What matters is that the police identify one another and themselves as committed to the work in a particular fashion and the attitude they assume is closely monitored and felt. The highest praise an officer can give another is that he or she is just like me and approaches the job from the right frame of mind – whether that job is treated as a career, a calling, an opportunity, a burden, a job, a dead end, a duty, or an imposition. How officers carry out and talk about their work establishes their work ethics, and these are seen as identity markers with action and control consequences as to who will do what and how well they will do it.

Another example concerns those officers who display an intense interest in their pay and work to maximize the amount of overtime they earn through court appearances, extra duty, or second jobs. They talk about providing for their families or having a taste for the finer things in life or even their aim of putting away as many bad guys as possible through the making of numerous arrests. All police officers regard money as important of course but some – regardless of the vocabulary of motives they put forth to explain it – are seen to go beyond the pale, whose work ethics are shaped (or stripped) by squeezing out as much money from the job as possible and being certain that every minute of work time is properly remunerated. Those who criticize their colleagues for their crass materialism are, of course, positioning themselves as righteous, dedicated sorts driven only by the internal benefits of the work and the larger goals they serve (goals only partly and imperfectly met by putting in hours or making arrests).

Much of this identity work is conditional on the opportunities that flow from work itself, opportunities that are of course controlled by others in the agency. To wit, an officer assigned to a drug enforcement unit or a gang squad is far more likely to make abundant arrests than an officer assigned routine patrol duties. Within patrol, some officers enjoy writing tickets (well beyond whatever quota might be imposed on them by the department or their sergeant) or making numerous vehicle checks, stops, and searches as ways of seeking "hits" (stolen cars, outstanding warrants, "on view" liquor or drug violations, etc.). Although there is of course variation attributable to mood, weather, health, time, and the like, most officers display work interests that they can defend – and that others learn to more or less count on whether they appreciate those interests or not.

The main – and official – function of patrol consists of answering dispatched calls, backing up other officers on their calls, and clearing up the paper that results from assigned calls. Such calls may entail helping clear the scene of a traffic accident, dealing with a helpless person who needs assistance ("helpless" often being little more than the official tag for a drunken or drugged person), sorting out a family squabble, taking a report from someone whose car has been stolen, responding to a suicide threat, and so on. Much of the time between calls for many patrol units is spent driving around going to and from places that have impinged themselves on officers in some way as trouble spots – places where real police action might be found. The nature of these trouble spots points to the kinds of police work given officers find attractive and, as such, identify.

Patrolling also involves its share of arbitrary activities – especially when boredom looms large and the usual trouble spots are unyielding. If the day – more commonly the night – is passing without much to do, patrolling may well be about what cops call "fucking off" as a way to reduce or avoid boredom and the lethargy it fosters rather than to find work. It concerns doing something unrelated to police work when there is nothing else to do. Fucking off may be about getting away from the squad sergeant with whom an officer lives in conflict. It may be about taking a lengthy time out in a local coffee stop or enjoying a city view far from a busy highway. Fucking off is then a way of asserting individual agency and hence identity and all officers develop characteristic ways of doing so in the face of tedium and organizational controls they regard as largely irrelevant to the job. How officers choose to duck some of their duties – when, where, how, how long, why, and so forth – sheds light on their work ethics and is of more than a little concern to others in the department.

It is important to also note that certain tasks and assignments in the patrol division deprive officers of agency. Without agency, identity suffers and it should be no surprise that fucking off in such situations makes escaping work an identity marker of some interest. When there is little or no police work to be done beyond, say, routine patrol, outwitting one's sergeant, playing practical jokes, securing some alcohol, taking a snooze are understandable responses, although not all will be equally amused or impressed when hearing of or witnessing such acts and thus display their own identity by taking offense. As a general rule, the less agency allowed on a particular police assignment, the less potential there is to make a difference in the performance of the task through a display of personally valued skills. In such cases it is more likely that officers will reassert their agency in non-work-related activities and thus take control and introduce some unauthorized diversions into their everyday routines.

Escapades and legendary tales emerge in this domain, suggesting a rather unbreakable link between identity and agency as well as the salience and importance of personal identity to officers caught up in such situations.[20] Sergeants and other higher-ups in the department are usually well aware that fucking off is an act of identity (although they would surely not use the phrase "an act of identity"). Overlooking such practices is common but, again, as with proactive identity rewards, selective. Overlooking certain officially taboo practices carries value and can sometimes be exchanged for hard work on other matters that might otherwise be resented and resisted by particular officers. "You owe me one" is an expression heard frequently in police agencies and is itself a control device that grows directly out of the identity work of the police among the police.

In sum, work ethics are very much an issue for police officers. All officers it seems can be located as to their commitment to the police role and, while considerable variation is to be found in the way commitment is read, measured, and assessed, there are clear and forceful views of what it means to be properly in the police role. Generational differences are apparent as are differences among ranks and differences by assignments, but all would agree that work ethics are attached to the person and a good deal of variety exists across officers. But it is this variety that often allows astute superior officers to get their bidding done through the selective identity games they play such as allowing certain quotas to be ignored by some officers but not others, by trading patrol assignments for shift changes, by overlooking unauthorized "time outs" at work for extra efforts on traffic duties, and so on (and on).[21]

Work ethics, however, have more to do with one's choice, focus, and intensity of work involvement(s) than the quality of such work (or escapade). Police officers are also concerned with the face, skill, and style displayed by themselves and others at work. The chief way performance is made visible to the police is through stories – narration and renarration of work sequences to colleagues and superiors. From such stories come what I describe next as the social poetics of police work, which, like the work ethics claimed, attributed, displayed, and judged by police officers, provide another domain in which personal identity is fashioned.

The social poetics of patrol

Poetics in literature concerns the ways writers as narrators achieve particular effects in their texts and on their readers. It emphasizes the close examination of the making of texts by looking at how specific authors blend invention and convention, innovation and tradition in their work. Like in fashion, social poetics deals with the processes of creativity in the social world and thus displays a keen interest in how individuals appropriate certain cultural forms (established ways of saying or doing things) for use in specific and ever changing social situations.[22] A social poetics analyzes how performances – as production and communication – take shape such that they are read (by the self and others) as creative, typically individual, adaptations or solutions to both the novel (exceptional) and common (familiar) problems faced by members of some specified community. Agency is at the center of social poetics and it is found in those differences in doing things that make a difference. Officers who perform a police action in a particular way identify themselves by the choices they make, by their artful (or artless) style of execution and by the greater or lesser degrees of mastery conveyed to knowledgeable others by their actions. Competence is at issue and, to the police, wide discrepancies exist.

That work is often understood by the police as a performance of a certain sort is clear when stories of the work are told. "Let me tell you about last Friday night ..." leads into a story or series of stories about episodes and characters, about duties performed and avoided, about what happened to whom, where, when, and why. The primary audience for these tales is other police officers. In fact, the chief way work performances of patrol officers are made visible to others is through the telling and retelling of work experiences – both informally (mostly word of mouth) and formally (mostly in writing). The police on the ground usually work alone or in pairs and most of their colleagues and especially their superiors do not often see what they do. But a good deal of police work does get narrated and attended to in various ways.[23] In important ways, the tales that are told within the agency serve to shape and direct the actions of the members.

Stories of patrol work consist mainly of relatively closed action sequences in which troubles arise (beginnings), actions are taken (middles), and outcomes achieved or thwarted (endings). The plot is standard, one of crisis, intervention, and result (Manning, 1982). Some action sequences are of course preferred to others, notably those taking place on the outside and involving real police work. Instances in which the police are unsure of what to do or are unable to do anything at all muddy if not destroy the middle and end of the standard tale and hence are less likely to be told because they are not seen as "real work." Calls to attend to disputes among neighbors (rarely requiring any action to be taken) or to investigate burglar alarms (overwhelmingly false) are examples in this regard. Such tasks are handled with dispatch and relative disinterest for they do not lead to good stories.

A reportable and identifying story must be "police relevant" in that there is some form of danger posed to people or public safety of the sort that the police could remove or eliminate through their actions (Bitner, 1970, 1990). Situations that do not promise some possibility for police action (and thus narratability) are not sought out or liked. Incidents most worthy of creating a story are those that provide a challenge to a police officer's abilities and might involve a sequence of events that lead to a particularly sought after ending, such as the rare capture of a red-handed thief. The best stories are those that portray officers exercising their imagination, their special skills and abilities in response to an opportunity sought or good fortune seized.

The social poetics of patrol work inevitably involve the police notion of commonsense – a kind of presence of mind that leads an officer to a shrewd analysis of a problematic situation and can be acted on in certain ways to achieve or at least try to achieve a desirable goal. The choice of what to do in a given situation reflects the amount of commonsense possessed by an officer. The best stories elaborate complexity and provide multiple-choice opportunities. All officers seek to display their commonsense and, based on the feedback and confirmation they receive from others, come to understand and (usually) sustain a positive sense of self.

Commonsense is not thought to be evenly distributed across officers or always realized by an officer at the time (although there is usually plenty of it on hand after an incident has, in police parlance, "gone down"). At the center of police tales and poetics are choices about what to do in a vexing situation, about what measures to take given always particular if not peculiar circumstances. This is one reason why police procedurals are disregarded and why the thick rulebooks they are issued remain in the trunks of their prowl cars. An officer's reaction to a car identified as stolen depends for example not on some standard operating procedure but on a variety of contextual matters such as where it is at the time it is spotted, whether it is in motion or stopped, whether it appears abandoned or in use, whether the engine is still warm, whether the thieves could still be about, and so on. Each of these contextual features opens up different lines of possible action that call for police judgment and action.

Commonsense as displayed in the stories officers tell and are told about them is then built up over time and becomes associated with the identity of a particular officer. Those officers with lots of commonsense have therefore lots of memorable and creditable stories circulating in the agency about their exemplary use of it. There is of course a structure to commonsense based partly on just where officers are assigned and the opportunities they have to take part in events that can demonstrate their commonsense (or lack thereof). Since commonsense assumes agency or choice, it is most readily displayed outside on the street rather than inside in the station. Patrol officers can build identity then by telling stories about their own work while administrators can build identity only by telling stories about the work of others or by placing themselves in the past. Since identity must be continually attended to, administrators are at some disadvantage when it comes to displaying commonsense – beyond what is revealed by their choice of the stories of others to tell – because they no longer have a continuous flow of outside experiences to draw on for use in their narratives.

. The poetics of various patrol activities allow individual officers to develop something of their own characteristic style of work that reflects not only their work ethics but the quality of their work as well. Performance identifies the performer and through such a linkage a piece of work is signed. As stories are told, officers develop their own signatures. How they issue moving vehicle violations, deal with the public in a crowd control situation, intervene in street corner quarrels, or interrogate criminal suspects are identifying acts. In a family dispute, an officer can take, for example, the jovial "let me be your buddy" approach of a friendly helper, or assume the worldly "you can tell me anything, it won't shock me" posture of a nonchalant professional. They may favor impersonality and cutting things short by adopting a "don't tell me too much 'cause I'm not your friend" line or take a technical turn by pushing those they deal with to tell them "what's the problem around here, anything for us?" Some may be slightly embarrassed by the whole matter and simply rush to finish the job and get back to their patrol cars. Depending on whom they are talking to and what effects they are trying to achieve, officers place themselves in a particular position, select a tone, display or conceal implements of their trade, assume a bodily pose, choose a vocabulary, and so forth. Taken as a whole, these performances are recognized as involving particular skills. They are not the kind of skills assessed by annual performance reviews, but they are the skills that count to valued colleagues and are talked about and judged by others in the department. Reputations as being good or bad on the family beef call emerge and Officer Baker, for example, becomes known to his colleagues (and himself as well) as someone who is "affable and calms people down" or "short-tempered and irritates everyone" or "tough and easily takes control."

Known skills such as an ability to talk to people, write crisp and well-formulated reports, locate trouble of a certain kind, or handle the wheel expertly and coolly in a high speed chase are some of the ways police identify one another and themselves through the poetics of their work. Certain skills often become the basis for the control of work through its distribution as when a patrol sergeant or dispatcher gives a certain call to Peter and not Paul. Signatures are often reinforced indirectly as is the case when officers note that they had taken a call the day before yesterday that Mary would have loved or that their work would have been much easier if only Joe had been along. In principle, there are as many different poetics in police work as there are culturally recognized skills. And these skills are much discussed such that good and bad performers (and performances) become known. Storytelling itself is a performance whose identifying poetics include topic and word choice, wit, elliptic or hyperbolic style, displayed emotion, and means of convincing emplotment (e.g., tragedy, satire, irony, romance, comedy).

It is important to point out that for the police the doing of the work is often more the source of identity than is the result of the work. This performance or process orientation for the police is perhaps more pronounced than in other lines of work since police work – in particular, patrol work – rarely has a product to serve as an object of pride. Much police work is undertaken to restore order and achieve something akin to an imperceptible state of calm or peace (clearing an accident, quieting a neighborhood). Some patrol officers claim that their job is simply "to keep the assholes from taking over the city" (Van Maanen, 1978). Even when arrests are made in criminal cases, the arresting officers, if they are from the patrol or uniformed division, see little of the final product and rarely learn if their reports and activities are helpful in making or breaking the case. They are left with a sequence of action and only a tentative or provisional end imposed by the division of labor and the administrative logic that attends to their work.

Yet, the sequence of action (including purposeful inaction) it seems is more than enough to allow a rich poetics of patrol work to develop. The police have no doubt that their work allows for many different kinds of mastery and each kind has its own poetics that can be achieved, recognized and, critically, talked about as such. Mastery of performance in police circles is acquired, as all would attest, only through many years of experience and practice. Stories multiply, converge, thicken, spread, such that some officers are able, within the genre of work to which their mastery applies, build what Bourdieu (1986) calls "cultural capital." Identity adheres in and across these work genres since what a person does well is considered a good measure of just who they are under the skin.

Trust among the police

Identity is fundamentally a dynamic matter. It is not achieved once and for all but is always provisional and therefore represents, as suggested before, something of a quest – a quest for personal dignity, for recognition, for grace, for the respect of others (conditional, of course, on the display of respect), for a sense of place and stability. Effective supervisors recognize this of course and, to their credit, grant honor and respect to those whose actions correspond to their own ideas of what skillful police work entails. Respect and honor signal confirmation of identity. This is of course something of a subtle, modest gift yet one the giver may well expect – vaguely – to be paid back in some fashion in the future (e.g., the willingness to help out on a distasteful task, the foregoing of a lunch break when a squad is shorthanded, the taking on of extra paperwork, working a shift with a hapless rookie, etc.).

Personal identity is what we think of as the deep, unshakable, authentic, honest, sincere "true self," the inner essence of, so to speak, our being and representing our moral worth among others. Among the police, the most discussed and worrisome moral value is trustworthiness. This concern goes beyond admired or disdained work ethics or social poetics displayed by colleagues and cuts to the core of character judgments. All police officers point out just how important it is "to be able to rely on one another," "to count on your backups," "to trust your partner blindly." One of the striking features of trust to the police is the heavy negative moral weight put on the behavior of co-workers taken to be inauthentic, phony, deceitful, fake, false, insincere, and thus dishonest. The performed or presented self should line up with the true self – the situated with the real. From this perspective, the most damaging lies are those that directly involve the self (Manning, 1974). The officer who says he cares deeply for his patrol colleagues yet is rarely seen to glide by and offer aid on those potentially troublesome calls his colleagues handle will have his trustworthiness questioned. This is dirty work at the individual level.

Performances, tropes, and narratives provide the materials that allow police officers to assess the trustworthy character of themselves and their colleagues. To have an identity is to be a "real person" and that means putting a "true self" out for inspection. The true self must be both claimed and displayed, it must not be hidden or withheld among colleagues. To be trustworthy is therefore to be known by others (and presumably one's self) as a readable, straightforward, candid (in the right situations, for the right reasons), and predictable sort of person. Trustworthy officers "show themselves," "speak their mind," and "can be counted on." They are "open and honest," "reliable," "straight shooters," "know what they are doing," and "say what they think not what you want to hear." To be trustworthy is to have a "true self" that is known. Identity is premised on such reasoning because a person without an easily identifiable and relatively stable identity has nothing solid – no character or principles – to be true or false to beyond the consistency of their inconsistency.

The patrolman who claims, "I have my values, my hard stops, and everybody around here knows what they are and where I stand" is saying he is trustworthy. He is assuring himself and others that he can be counted on as to what he will and will not do. It may well be that because the police are so preoccupied with criminals who achieve their goals through misrepresentation, guile, and cunning, they perhaps value trustworthiness more so than other occupational groups. Violations of trust are, after all, precisely the kinds of behavior they are paid to prevent. What repeated violations of trust reveal is a lack of personal identity without which there can be no promises met, no reliability or predictability, no person behind the mask.

Distrust between police officers frequently results, as they point out, from not knowing one another's stories – their narratives and performances. Common is the expression of shock or disgust with the behavior of a fellow officer through the use of the pointedly tart question, "What's his story?" It may be simply this colleague has yet to amass any stories or that the puzzled officer has not yet heard them. Whatever the source, however, not knowing one another's stories means they can not know the other's identity and thus can hardly gauge the other's trustworthiness. Over time, by telling and showing one another more and more bits and pieces of their work lives, their family lives, their likes and dislikes, their pasts and presents, their skills and lack of skills, their aims and frustrations, officers begin to identify one another and judge one another's trustworthiness. Those who are not out and about on the street, are not seen in the station house, are not apparent at squad parties or local gathering spots are not trusted. Supervisors are obviously disadvantaged in this regard.

Two general matters are of most interest in these sorts of identity games. First, since trustworthiness is taken to be a mark of one's character, it should be relatively constant across social situations. Second, it should be relatively consistent across time. This is one reason why officers like to get to know their colleagues in a variety of situations and times – inside the station and out, in different action settings, with partners and peers, with ranking officers, with various publics, at home and at social occasions, at play and at work, drunk and sober, in tense situations and relaxed ones, at different points in their careers and in different work roles. The "true self" is thought to reveal itself by a certain consistency of behavior across all these settings and times.

This is not to say that the police expect each other to behave in exactly the same way across time and space. It is not precise in any arithmetic way with one side of an equation expected to equal the other side. But it is to say that the police regard as untrustworthy those who, for example, give widely discrepant accounts of events in different social situations or those who appear obsequious and ingratiating with some officers and unbending and aloof with others. The aggressive, street savvy patrol officer who, when promoted to sergeant, turns suddenly into a rule-minded zealot obsessed with procedural regularities will be shunned by stupefied former colleagues as an unpredictable sort devoid of character.[24] The valued sameness in different places and times is then a matter of degree. Few patrol officers expect their workmates to speak to a drunk citizen or a district court judge in the same way they speak to friends, or to behave the same way at home as they do at work, or to show the same enthusiasm for the job as a twenty-year veteran as they did as a rookie. Too close a match between situations and times would reflect a sort of unaccountable stiffness or rigidity and be regarded as potentially false as social chameleons whose colors always match their surroundings and thus have no true color at all. A person who has a pat line for all situations or seems to be constantly selling themselves as a good and honorable sort may well be taken by others as "stiff," "hiding something," "unable to act spontaneously," or being "too slick" and will be seen therefore as untrustworthy, unable to be candid. Those who say yes (or no) to everything, who never show resistance (or vice versa) are seen to lack personal interest and pride in what they do. Those who are seemingly always upbeat and cheerful, never bitchy or morose (or vice versa) wherever they happen to be are thought to be depthless sorts of people who have no opinion of their own, no soul to reveal, no character or, if they do have character, they are, for some reason, most unwilling to expose it.

At the heart of the matter is a deep concern over the potential betrayal of and disloyalty to one's colleagues. Those who show sudden shifts of allegiance, do not reciprocate for favors bestowed on them by others, or appear virtually inflexible, create suspicion as to whether they even have the capacity to act in a trustworthy fashion. Without such a capacity, trust is impossible. As a moral value, trust implies a predictable and more or less unflinching commitment to opinions, ethics, ideas, persons, places, and so on. It also implies that the trusted officer within the "blue brotherhood" makes good on promises extended to others, provides aid to others when (appropriately) asked, and pays others back for their gifts of help, assistance, and occasional forbearance. These are matters that cannot be made or altered over-night and a certain stability is expected. If changes or breaches occur, they must be carefully accounted for and orchestrated over time and typically be only of a modest sort. Those who are seen to give up their principles (or, worse, their colleagues) too quickly, too easily, or too abruptly are regarded as morally bankrupt, empty of character, unworthy of respect, and beyond trust.

Within the moral discourse surrounding trust exists a shadowy character in the police world, the despised, untrustworthy officer who is a traitor to one's own kind: a dissembler, a dirtbag, a rat, a depraved and dangerous anti-hero of the occupation. The despised have, however, a peek-a-boo, now-you-see-them-now-you-don't pres-ence. Everyone seems to know of untrustworthy colleagues but few get identified as such – at least completely so. They are apparently everywhere and nowhere at once and are perhaps best thought of as allegorical members of the trade. Their function it seems is to mark the moral boundaries of the police world across which members must not pass. Yet, despite the difficulties the police face when pointing to specific untrustworthy colleagues, their interest in establishing and maintaining their own credentials and those of others as trustworthy remains lively.

As I have mentioned, coming to know others depends in large measure on learning their stories. There must then be places and times where these stories can be exchanged so that officers who do not often work together can get to know one another as human beings rather than simply as members of the same organization. Such socializing is often sponsored directly by the organization and serves in part as a control tactic because it is assumed that if colleagues have a more intimate knowledge of one another, their relationships and work performance will improve. Some of my previous work has taken up this theme for the police do think of social events, of squad parties, of pub crawls, of holiday feasts, of departmental picnics, of promotion celebrations, of retirement fetes, of breakfast gatherings, of wakes and funerals, of reunions and get togethers of all sorts, planned and spontaneous, as oracles of identity – occasions that are believed to reveal "true selves" (Van Maanen, 1986, 1992). On these occasions, participants can "let their hair down," "say what's really on their mind," "toss convention to the wind," or, most generally, "be themselves."

What happens of course is usually less than what is hoped for. The veterans with long service in the department who, for example, find their younger efficiency-minded or technology-obsessed colleagues mystifying will learn few of their stories because the identity they display in the stories they tell will be promptly challenged or attacked by the veterans as inappropriate to the police role (and the reverse). The dance of intimacy, as Goffman (1959) tells us, depends on the exchange and honoring of revelation by counter-revelation. When narratives are challenged, identity is on trial and a defense usually mounted. Exchange is blocked. If there is a lack of respect for the mind that is spoken, the atmosphere clouds and often all that can be uncovered is a dislike among officers.

While it is true that one can trust other officers without liking them, both judgments rest on a good deal more than an occasional social gathering. Parties may help for they sometimes mix up ordinary social relations and provide another time and place in which the stability of character can be displayed and tested. Yet, more often than not, like-minded officers seek one another out at parties and small clusters form. Most partygoers know that to speak one's mind across clusters, to be open and honest with less familiar colleagues is to risk misunderstanding. Recognizing this, officers across organizational segments such as the patrol and detective divisions or across hierarchical ranks must identify each other without much direct input from one another and feel sure that even if they were to talk, their counterparts would not open up or tell them the truth. Thus telling one's own stories as well as learning the stories of others is not a smooth, casual, or easy-to-orchestrate matter.

Patterns of trust in police agencies are therefore rather restrictive and premised usually on a long interactional history. They extend often to only those officers who are linked by early partnership, long-term squad membership or divisional posting, shared police academy experiences, close and extended residential proximity, and so on. Because trustworthiness is tied directly to personal identity, an assessment of continuity and consistency is crucial to the matter and such assessment takes time, usually a long time.

Social poetics and work ethics play a role here too for those who are seen to emphasize the wrong kinds of interests and skills or hold on to the wrong kind of work values and interests can not be trusted by those who possess the right ones. This is of course a matter of perspective. For example, those officers who some feel compromise their work obligations by not backing-up fellow officers or by avoiding certain kinds of calls are "faking" their identity as responsible and hard-working police officers and cannot be trusted, just as those who by taking advantage of their disability insurance or the sick leave policy in the department for monetary gain are seen by many to display a most inappropriate commitment to the police mission and are not "real cops" despite the claims they make. The officer who is the master of escapade cannot suddenly turn into a pillar of workaday respectability without losing the trust of those who knew him earlier. To lose the trust of one's colleagues (of fail to gain it in the first place) is to leave one excluded from the informal ties, reciprocal exchanges, and small workaday rewards and self-validating pleasure offered by the job. At stake is one's identity and it is always on the line.

Some concluding remarks

Students of work life have repeatedly suggested that those drawn to worthy occupations that have long histories are expected to acquire a strong sense of belonging to a traditional establishment that sets them off from others (Abbott, 1995; Barley and Kunda, 2006; Hughes, 1958). Police work is certainly no exception to this rule and those engaged in the police life do form an occupational community that emphasizes loyalty to colleagues, independence of thought and action, strong work identities, and emotional distance from high ranking members of their trade, ordinary citizens and, of course, most villains. Police culture forms at the bottom of the organization where most of the members labor and thus valorizes working the street while mocking police management and command.[25] Police work as patrol is responding to calls, looking for action (or distraction), and producing quick, decisive, and altogether pragmatic solutions for the messy problems that are met in the street in such a way that those solutions stick and do not come back to haunt an officer or the department. Paperwork is a necessary evil, despised but handled with the understanding that a mistake – even a trivial one – could be costly.

At an organizational level of analysis, it is hardly surprising that police organizations are marked by a good deal of self and occupational control. To take the patrol function specifically: coordination demands across and even within units are slight to modest; the relationship between ends (keeping the peace) and means (patrol activities) are not well understood despite at least a half-century of seriously trying; the problems of order faced on the street remain rather unpredictable both spatially and temporally; much of the work is carried out unobserved by others in the agency and even less so by the public at large; and the environment or field in which the police operate is highly politicized and volatile. High status professionals carve out considerable autonomy in such domains and so do relatively low-status police officers. Cops may not control significant organizational resources beyond their craft-like knowledge of the job and of their territories and clientele but they nonetheless operate for the most part on their own with considerable discretion as to what they will do. This is more or less consistent with what theorists of a contingency, resource dependency, neo-institutional, and even a population ecology bent might say.[26] But, critically, what it is people do with their autonomy at work is not well developed in the organizational literatures. In the foregoing analytic and ethnographic notes, I have tried to open up the organizational control discourse to some of the day-to-day control tactics and stratagems that operate largely on a cultural plane but seem so common and deeply embedded within some organizations that they are almost taken-for-granted and hence rather invisible.

Again at the organizational level, this taken-for-granted character of using identity as a control mechanism is not a particularly astonishing matter. It has been picked up of late by a number of organizational scholars (e.g., Ibarra, 2003; Kogut and Zander, 1996; White, 1992; Wrzesniewski and Dutton, 2001). Organizational economists Akerlof and Kranton (2005: 11) say, for example, "the ability of organizations to place workers into jobs with which they identify and the creation of those identities are central to what makes organizations work."

I agree. But few researchers – including Akerlof and Kranton beyond their engaging review of several classic work ethnographies – have spelled out in any detail what those identities might be specifically or how particular actions might follow from such identities.

Bringing the notions of occupational communities, cultures, and identities into the scholarly discourse surrounding organizational control allows for a greater understanding of how self-control operates. I have argued here that such an understanding turns on a nuanced awareness of the always variegated work identities present in an organization. When such identities are valued and desired by both managers and the managed, individual acts of identity follow that may well be consistent with organizational aims and managerial preferences. Control is virtually automatic. Rarely, however, are such perfect matches to be found since jobs and roles in organizations consist of multiple tasks, some of which are identity-sustaining (even enhancing) and some of which are not. Control then rests on the tricky ways these bundles of work are lumped and split into tasks that are affirming or disconfirming of identity and then allocated selectively across those who make up a given work group.

Control is always a mix-and-match matter. Direct face-to-face orders come along with the use of particular constraining technologies that are held in high or low regard and are backed up by official rules and procedures that have more or less authoritative status. Pay policies, production quotas, bonuses, promotional opportunities, disciplinary measures, supervisory oversight and monitoring and highly rationalized appeals to meet or exceed targets are found in all organizations. In police organizations, the influence of all of these approaches – save perhaps appeals "to serve and protect" – are rather minimal. Pay bands are narrow, negotiated, and set beyond the workplace, no bonuses or special rewards are delivered beyond symbolic ones, promotions are few and far between with only one in ten or so patrol officers expected to make it to the sergeant's rank before retiring, disciplinary measures are used quite sparingly and take considerable time to unfold. What are left are peer pressures and self-control. Official rewards of course combine with the unofficial, but, as I have argued here, police organizations by maintaining and often embracing the self-image of its workforce builds managerial control by engaging officers in a tacit agreement: identity engaging and sustaining work for the meeting of managerial goals.

Identity pursuits on the part of most patrol officers by and large meet management's desire for compliance. Sergeants can usually and routinely rely on the arousal of positive identity feelings to induce appropriate action and effort on the part of their charges. Allowing officers to "do what I want to do and express who I am" keeps the organization afloat and, by and large, allows it to meet its rather loosely and internally defined public service goals. Outsiders may not see the police doing much but, rest assured, the police would not agree.

This suggests that perhaps too much classic organization control research is focused on constraint and the power to impose restrictions. This approach assumes that an organizational member's aspirations for autonomy, freedom, dignity, and respect compete with the achievement of organizational goals. Yet a member's voluntary engagement in particular activities can be achieved in many ways. And the way managers and supervisors create opportunities for the support and enactment of valued identities is one of those ways. We know organizations help shape these identities but the fact that they also become highly desirable with action consequences that follow such desirability has not been closely examined. Here I have suggested that police organizations help shape the identity of police officers, allow opportunities for its expression, routinely but selectively grant indulgences to identity-sustaining actions that fall beyond official lines of approval, and count on those who come to the organization to deeply engage with the police identity.

The broad culture is learned rather swiftly at the outset of an officer's career and serves to help neutralize the noticeable taint or stigma associated with doing the so-called dirty work of a society, work that appears no one else wants to do (Bitner, 1970; Moscos, 2008; Van Maanen, 1974). The stigma is, in part, institutional, reflecting the working class character of the police organizations and, in part, social, reflecting the degraded status possessed by most of the "clients" of regular police attention and action. The trade also carries a physical stain because of violence and proximity to violence sometimes involved in the work as well as a moral stain because of the corrupt, criminal, or scandalous revelations that surface from time to time in numerous police agencies.

There is of course nothing like a shared stigma to draw people together and many have remarked on the tight, cohesive culture of solidarity that mark police agencies (Black, 1980; O'Neil *et al.*, 2007; Skolnick, 1966). Socialization into such a culture provides recruits with a self-consciousness of the collective as defined by members rather than the society. Ennobling aspects of the work are prominently drawn on by agents of socialization as a way of helping recruits cope with whatever stigma – however slight – they might feel. Recruits learn of the sacred public trust they are given and the importance of the police role to society. They hear of police heroism in the face of danger. Potential stigma is thus actively managed.

By and large, American police departments seem to be reasonably successful in this regard – particularly the large, urban ones. Turnover within the occupation is low, a long line of aspirants to the trade forms whenever departmental openings are offered, and a self-image of "helping people" is almost universally quoted by the police as a motive for joining and staying with the force (Greene and Mastrofski, 1988; Langworthy *et al.*, 1995; Reis, 1971). Those for whom a stigma looms large, who, for example, regard the police as despicable henchmen for the ruling class or brutal enforcers of the status quo or deceitful con artists out to line their own pockets at the expense of the local citizenry or lowly, unskilled, useless civil servants forced to interact with the scum of the earth would no doubt never join the police or leave after joining if such feelings persist or emerge. If they did not, the tension between their personal, situational, and social identities would be extreme for their "true selves," if revealed by word or deed to colleagues, would then be a source of considerable discomfort and pain as a target for the degradation of others.

Socialization as a control device helps to bring social, situational, and personal identities in line and by so doing helps create an occupational community of notable strength. Occupational members – as set off from the rest of society – are given means by which they can satisfactorily present and manage their roles in society. The organization is of course critical in this regard. The police have resources, powerful supporters in high places, an oath of office and other public-spirited vows, honorable goals, past and present heroes, evocative insignias, legal protections, sophisticated technologies, codes of conduct, mission statements, and mottoes (e.g., "Making Detroit Safer," "New York's Finest") as sources of collective pride. Yet police recruits also learn swiftly that those who do not wear the badge and with whom they must interact often treat them as rather faceless, anonymous, street-level bureaucrats (Lipsky, 1980). All officers soon recognize that as representatives of the state *par excellence*, their presence is not always welcome. Even if a good citizen's heart is pure and conscience clean, a police car parked in front of one's house is not a benevolent sign in this society (nor is it likely to be overlooked by the neighbors). The police know this and talk a good deal about their ability to "secure the peace" by merely showing up. They know that a seemingly idle patrol car or officer is still doing something – communicating a social identity – through mere presence. As they learn their work, they come to appreciate and talk about the symbolic character of the police role and their own shared position in the scheme of things.

Yet the police also know that such matters say little about them as individuals *qua* individuals – as unique persons with special interests, skills, values, and character. The categorical police role is then something of screen behind which a good deal of individual variation is concealed. Outsiders rarely sense such variation beyond the socially marked distinctions of rank, age, gender, ethnicity, function, and so on. What I have somewhat breathlessly argued in this chapter is that while the police agree that work ethics, poetics, and trust are central matters, of concern to all occupational members, these are also precisely the matters officers use to distinguish themselves from one another and thus become individuals within the workplace. Those officers who, for example, seek court time and seemingly relish making heaps of arrests are seen by others (and themselves) as quite different than those who do not seek such work. Those who blissfully pass on work to others, or finesse it, or avoid it altogether put their work ethics on display. All is complicated of course by the multidimensional aspects of the work. The station house sergeant who is labeled by patrol officers the "Olympic Torch (who never goes out)" may lose status to some by his inside inclinations but gain some back again by his much appreciated ability to "brighten" the paperwork of subordinates and thus help "cover their asses" by his suggestions of just what to put in and leave out of formal reports (Van Maanen, 1983).

It may well be that the unity or solidarity of the police occupational culture has been much overstated.[27] Police values and attitudes are far from uniform. Some of this is structural. In most good-sized departments, officers can be posted to: the mounted (horse) patrol; the traffic, juvenile, internal investigations, or records division; the bomb, gang, or tactical operations squad; the drug enforcement, crime prevention, or equipment repair unit; the community relations, crime statistics, or police training function; the personnel or police communications department; or the detective bureau with its numerous specialties such as homicide, computer crimes, and bank fraud. Each will have its own poetics and perhaps special measures of trust and ethics on which officers will vary. Each will be seen to some as embracing or eschewing "dirty work" as locally defined. This division of labor is gendered as well with women more frequently assigned to administrative and service units than men (Martin, 1980; Worden, 1993). The patrol division – my interest throughout most of this chapter – is itself quite varied in the kinds of assignments it offers while serving also as the gateway to postings elsewhere in the organization. Officers seen by some of their patrol colleagues as "unwilling to share the load" or "backing away from the action" or perhaps simply as "shy and quiet" will be encouraged by word and deed to move on to a more appropriate posting (or out of the agency altogether) if they cannot find an acceptable niche (both to themselves and to others) within the division. And, again, this is what allows identity controls to be effective in the hands of knowledgeable managers. Were the same identity rewards offered to all or were all identities the same, postings, leniencies, and respectful attitudes would lose the considerable influence they now possess.

Many niches in police agencies exist and officers typically find them or make them. Identity is thus linked to the work and ordinarily – with time, effort, and the confirmation of others – stabilized. What the occupational culture provides are those dimensions on which personal differences matter. Yet, across the board, trust is crucial in the police world and character judgments inevitably turn on this moral matter. Trust will almost certainly not be taken for granted by officers unacquainted with one another or even vouchsafed among all those who are acquainted. The basis of trust is a certain consistency of behavior across time, space, and situation along with the belief that help given will be returned. Only those whose "true self" is shown, known, and tested can be trusted.

On this last point, some readers may find it rather archaic to be reading of a "true self." As I mentioned at the outset, the self, we have been told, is today shattered, fragmented, contradictory, entirely situational (e.g., Jameson, 1991). Post-modern theorists argue that individuals today are completely absorbed or – to use the Adlers' (1991: 219) evocative term – "engulfed" by the social contexts that surround them. Since these contexts are radically different from one another because of the ever-growing and varied roles we are asked to play in everyday life, any authentic sense of self must recede from view as impossible to maintain. To be sustained, a "true self" must be anchored in social relations. But if our social relations are multiple, disconnected, pull us in many directions, invite us to play a number of non-overlapping roles, they become more or less incoherent. Some celebrate such conditions as providing the structural means of freeing the person from the social (Baudrillard, 1995). Others express grave concern as does Giddens (1991) when he suggests that our lives have become ever more unpredictable, ever more disembedded from the familiar and stable, and thus whatever trust we have in our knowledge of the self or others is continually eroding.

While no doubt useful as a warning against both essentialism and the easy presumption of a transcendent human nature, I am, in the end, skeptical of this post-modern portrait of the individual as isolated, situationally conformist, segmented, and altogether fungible. The police view such a person as morally flawed – without enduring character – and who struggles, successfully for the most part, to maintain a sense of themselves and their colleagues as having coherent identities that do not drastically shift over time or across social situations. Contradictions raise questions and officers are held to account for them as best they can. But trust among colleagues would be impossible were not a continuity of identity – a "real self" – assumed. Perhaps, in other lines of work, post-moderns multiply and prosper. Certainly trust is unlikely to have quite the same central value and distinguishing mark of acceptable character in other occupations as it does to the police. But I think it unlikely to be irrelevant to the conduct of any work that takes place in an occupational community so typically marked if not defined by the intense interaction and identity work that goes on among members. Thus, to again invoke the words of Everett Hughes (1971: 149): "If a problem turns up in one occupation it is nearly certain to turn up in others."

Notes

1 A number of friends and colleagues have read and commented on various drafts of this paper. Sim Sitkin, Laura Cardinal, and Katinka Bijlsma-Frankema provided a detailed critique of a late draft, as did Michel Anteby and Heng Xu. Earlier drafts were made more coherent from the help I received from Kate Kellogg, Blake Ashworth, Barry Staw, Ed Schein, and Peter Manning. They were all close readers, generous in their time given and advice offered. I am grateful to them all.

2 By this remark I mean merely that social identity, as attached to the performance of dirty work in society, is modified, if at all, more by collective associations and actions than by individual acts of interpretation and negotiation. Professionalization is one such collective process by which members of a given line of work attempt to increase their status, respect, and rewards within a society and unload unwanted tasks – dirty work – to other occupational groups (Abbott, 1981; Sarfatti-Larson, 1977; Van Maanan and Barley, 1985). But dirty work designations run deep, pertain to the moral status of certain kinds of work, and are not likely to disappear entirely even if the respectability of those who perform it is uplifted (Ashforth and Kreiner, 1999; Hughes, 1971; Emerson and Pollner, 1976). That people carve out meaning and dignity while attending to low status work or in socially distasteful occupations is not at issue. They do. But efforts to bootstrap the collective endeavor to higher realms of social standing and reward typically fall flat. See, for example, the ethnographic work on sewer men (Reid, 1993), doormen (Bearman, 2005), crack dealers (Bourgeois, 2003), and temp workers as "warm bodies" (Barley and Kunda, 2006). Even the homeless carve out a degree of meaning and dignity to their work of getting through the day (and night) despite their socially disdained position (Snow and Anderson, 1993).

3 The notion of a situated identity emerges most cogently from Goffman's (1959, 1961, 1967) analysis of the interaction order. It refers to that aspect of identity that is public, socially enacted and more or less momentary since it is bounded strictly in space and time. It is negotiable only within a defined situation that regulates the actions and responses of both the self and others. Social identity refers to the self-consciousness that results from membership in a particular social category such as an occupation or role and is further discussed a bit later in this paper. For considerably more elaborate treatments of situated and social identity, see, Turner (1968), Alexander and Lauderdale (1977), Stryker and Burke (2000), and especially Holland *et al.* (2001).

4 The ethnographic materials dealing with the police, unless otherwise noted, come from my own studies of police organizations – focused particularly on patrol divisions. A good deal about the settings and methods followed in these studies has been published and I will not repeat these accounts here other than to say that they rest on fifteen months of participant-observation in a large, urban, American police agency (in the early 1970s), nine months of fieldwork in the Metropolitan Police Department in London during the academic year 1985–6, and a number of additional forays – for the most part, "flying visits" – in other big city departments in the United States. On these methods, see Van Maanen, 1978, 1981, 1988.

5 Such work is considerable and, in sociology, dates back to both Durkheim (1997/1883) and Weber's (1946) interests in the role of work in society. The idea of occupational community is hardly new. Gertzl (1961: 38), for example, used the phrase to reflect the "pervasiveness of occupational identification and the convergence of the informal friendship patterns and colleague relationships." Salaman (1974) elaborated on the same themes when characterizing the work worlds of architects and railroaders. More recent synthetic treatments are found in Hodson and Sullivan (2001) and Barley and Kunda (2006).

6 There are of course notable exceptions. Consider, for example, Pratt (2000), Kunda (1992), Fine (1996), Covaleski *et al.* (1998), and Creed *et al.* (2002). These are studies grounded in particular work worlds in which observed talk and action is linked to particular not general work identities and a reader comes away with a sense of the specificity of a given work world.

7 See, for example, the useful and, because of its longitudinal character, unusual study by Cardinal *et al.* (2004) that looks at specific managerial control practices put into place during the first ten years in the organizational life of a southwestern moving company. They show that control practices are many, sometimes complementary, sometimes contradictory but, in different periods, clustering around formal and informal forms of control. Of special note, there seems to be no strict path dependence from, say, the informal to formal but rather a waxing and waning of each cluster thus suggesting that an extended reliance on one form of control foreshadows the rise of the other. "Balance" is, they argue, the key to managerial control yet, as they show, it is elusive and difficult if not impossible to codify and maintain. On the nature of informal and peer control in organizations, see Loughry (Chapter 11 in this volume).

8 The notion of "consent" is a contentious one in organizational and occupational studies. Neo-Marxist scholars raise the possibility of "false consciousness" whenever consent is flagged as legitimating a given control regime in capitalistic contexts (e.g., Burawoy, 1979; Jermier, 1998; Willis, 1977). They have their points to make and, by and large, they are thoughtful and worthy ones. My view on these matters is agnostic and pragmatic because sorting out what is "false" and what is "real" depends a good deal on one's epistemological stance and the too easy displacement of lived experience for theory. I have no doubt that consent is in many places and many times manufactured and manipulated by those whose persuasive resources are munificent and powerful but I know too that there are always weapons of the weak that must not be underestimated. When put into play, false consciousness often dissolves. There are thus many ways to read consent.

9 Several good reviews (and examples) of the "quest for self-control" are found in Fantasia (1988), Hodson (2001), and Simpson (1985). A few useful empirical studies of late include Pratt *et al.* (2006), Alvesson and Willmont (2002), and Bearman (2005). The "quest for dignity" is a somewhat broader matter but it too is developing a solid research literature. See, for example, Roscigno and Hodson (2004) and Sennett (2007). This latter quest – and its many failures – has of course been at the core of virtually all of Erving Goffman's writings but made particularly poignant in *Stigma: notes on the management of spoiled identity* (1963).

10 It is worth noting too that our identity claims – who we are – can also take the form of just who we are not. In the police world, for example, the street cop is determinedly not a management cop (Ianni, 1982). And "not being a management cop" may allow for a sharper street cop identity to emerge since the latter always stands in contrast to something else. Hence the possibility arises that at times the appearance rather than the reality of opposition is what is at stake when making identity claims. I am grateful to Sim Sitkin for pointing this out.

11 This is of course a gross simplification of some quite subtle and serious social study. Theories of modernity track back to Durkheim, Marx, and Weber and there are important differences among them that are ignored here. All emphasize, however, the progressive loosening of social bonds among people as nationalization, industrialization, urbanization, mechanization, professionalization, and so forth take hold. As modernity advances, work becomes fragmented, rationalized, separated from the home, the family, the neighborhood. Social roles narrow and multiply, conformity within roles is demanded but it is conformity within increasingly delimited spheres. The literature here is massive. Giddens (1991) provides an elegant sociological treatment of both modernity and postmodernity and their respective discontents.

12 I am hardly staking out any new ground in this section and have written on these matters before (see, in particular, Van Maanen, 1978, 1979, 1988). I should note however that when it comes to the study of identity I rely heavily on Cooley, 1922/1902; Mead, 1934; and Goffman, 1959; as well as a long line of symbolic interactionist writers of whom I am the most fond of Rock, 1979; Lyman and Scott, 1970; Hewitt, 1979, 1989; and, especially, Manning, 1989. Good collections of work in this tradition include McCall and Simmons (1978) and Kortarba and Fontana (1984). Of most use to me in this article is, however, a remarkable study of the merging of the East and West Berlin police agencies occurring after the fall of the wall by Glaeser (2000). Much of my thinking about the personal identity of American police officers as set forth here is influenced by this work.

13 Scholarly treatments on the consciousness of the self includes Strauss (1959), Geckas (1991), Hewitt (1979, 1989), Tajfel (1982), Tajfel and Turner (1986), and Giddens (1991). What often brings the self to the surface is, in Zussman's (1996) phrase, "autobiographical occasions." These are encounters and episodes in which we are under some pressure to produce a story of our life such as a job interview, an anniversary, a homecoming, a professional convention, a first date, a retirement banquet, or a therapy session. On these occasions, we are ordinarily required to reflect on our lives and provide a satisfactory account for them (to both the self and others). Vinitzky-Seroussi (1998) provides a marvelous treatment of high school reunions as powerful autobiographic occasions wherein the past is usually (but not always) reconstructed to fit the present. As suggested in this work, one reason we talk so much about the past (and memory) is that there is so little of it left. Ibarra (2003) is also quite good on the self-consciousness that obtains when career transitions are undertaken by those of high status (MBA graduates of the Harvard Business School who were ten to fifteen years into their respective high flying careers when they decided to undertake dramatic career shifts).

14 Lest the good work produced by psychologists and social psychologists on identity and its consequences go unrecognized in this chapter, the thoughtful and comprehensive review by Swann *et al.* (2009) must be mentioned. Personal identity it seems is now competing with traditional renderings of personality (and its Big Five mystical nature-and-nurture trait factors) as the master marker of the individual. The brick-by-brick, experimental approach of those psychologists and social psychologists who study identity – a subtle form of ethnography, if unrecognized as such – highlights negotiated interactions, self-validation, and self-consistency as general yet critical features of identity formation and maintenance and thus echoes many of the points made in this chapter as applied to a specific occupational community. See, for example, Swann (1999) and McAdams (1996). On matters of control and identity, Sitkin and Sutcliffe (1991) have a field study on pharmacists who must routinely negotiate their identities – occupational/professional and organizational – in light of legal problems that may arise when suspicious prescriptions (and customers) appear. Here the pharmacists say that their occupational/professional identity overcomes the organizational one. This work is a superb example of the everyday relevance of identity work (and the need to study it more closely).

15 By pointing to "moral implications," I mean to convey that identity – to the self and to others – is not neutral. Moral is used here in the Durkheimian sense to refer not to some universal standard but to what a

given group defines as good. Judgments of the self and others as good or bad are involved and, while they are culturally shaped, they are most assuredly not relative (nor necessarily generous).

16 As used by the police, "real work" is most often taken to mean their law enforcement duties more so than their peace keeping ones (although officers do not always agree on what precisely these duties mean and just how they are to be separated in practice). To be sure, crook catching is always "real work" while tasks undertaken inside the station house rarely qualify as real work to patrol officers. But, beyond this point, work ethics are involved. To some officers, real work means attending to "reportable" business of almost any type (but not the reporting process itself which is mere "paperwork"); to others, only certain kinds of reportable business qualifies as real work. All officers use the phrase, however, as a gloss for those tasks they find most fulfilling as police work and therefore most closely connected to their social identity as police officers. For more on the notion of "real work" to the police, see Van Maanen (1974), Manning (1977), Bitner (1967), Brown (1988), Young (1991), and, most recently, Moscos (2008).

17 I must note that I am much taken with Michel Anteby's superb and recently published *Moral gray zones* (2008). This ethnographically informed monograph provides a close look at a dying occupational community formed among craftsmen working for a French manufacturing firm in the aeronautics industry. In marvelous detail, Anteby shows how these craftsmen approached their work and managed to carve out a good deal of autonomy (and dignity) within the organization. "Identity incentives" refer specifically to the willingness – indeed sometimes eagerness – of managers to allow for the making of "homers" (finely crafted artifacts of a highly symbolic sort having nothing whatsoever to do with the assigned work of the craftsmen). These artifacts are crafted with company materials and often on company time. What is shown clearly is the power of such practices and just how they served to not only regulate the interaction order in the plant among craftsmen and managers but to insure that official work was itself carried out well. One would have to return to Gouldner's (1954) wonderful study of the indulgency patterns he discovered in the Gypsum plants he roamed in the 1950s to find as detailed and nuanced a treatment of the various kinds of leniency practices that are no doubt found in all organizations, then and now.

18 Fabien (1983) develops the useful idea of "allochronism" to refer to a strategy people sometimes use to discount and override the experiences of others. He uses it to suggest how ethnographers treat informants (and their cultures) in their texts and on the ground. Glaeser (2000) borrows

it to show how West Berlin police treated the stories told by the East Berlin police when the two organizations were brought together in the early 1990s. It is the labeling of others as backward, as displaced in time ("where their clocks tick differently") that places them in a position where they are disallowed as unable to fully take part in the present. Younger police officers of my acquaintance who often type their older colleagues as "hopelessly out of it," as "living in a different time," or as "unable to get with it," are using the same discounting – if not dehumanizing – strategy. The response of those so labeled is inevitably one of anger, defensiveness, and often sadness. Dialogue is thus foreclosed by allochronism.

19 Discipline follows organizational contours as well as personal ones. Some departments stress honor, sacrifice, or discipline through, for example, the giving of medals, boot camp-like training, decorative or dress regalia, the use of considerable ceremonial protocol, and strict codes of conduct governing relations between the ranks. All police organizations display quasi-military characteristics but some more so than others (e.g., Jermier and Berkes, 1979; Manning 1996; Skolnick and Bayley, 1986; Wilson, 1968). Within most police agencies, however, the ties that bind officers to their work are perhaps becoming more contractual and instrumental rather than normative and expressive. To some, the ceremonially minimalist organizational form of the so-called "professionalized" police department is a sad commentary on the occupation (see Young, 1991).

20 My favorite escapade story is one Manning (2001) tells of the Alamo Run, a police caper made possible by the use of personal cellular phones in squad cars. The story tells of how patrol officers in Dallas challenged one another at work to drive to San Antonio, snap a Polaroid photograph of themselves and their patrol car in front of the Alamo National Monument and return to Dallas before their shift was finished. Until the escapade was discovered and stopped by departmental officials, calls that were assigned to the unit speeding to and from San Antonio were taken by other units in the patrol squad who kept in touch with their gleeful, on-the-road compatriots by phone.

21 This variation infrequently makes it into published reports on the police life. On this matter I too must cop a plea for I am guilty of underplaying the variety of work ethics among the police in favor of a rather general one I once tagged the "lay low and keep out of trouble" ethic (Van Maanen, 1973, 1974). I cannot claim ignorance either since I was quite aware at the time of a few officers who regarded the "lay low" ethic a faulty and demoralizing one. Indeed, they were the very ones that made the rule apparent for me. Moreover, in the late-1970s, I counted over fifty different official assignments available to officers of the lower ranks

in the agency I studied and knew quite well that there were personal differences and varying work styles across the officers who filled these slots (Van Maanen, 1983). This article is something of a corrective in this regard. Manning (2005) has good things to say about the many flaws associated with research on police agencies and a number of equally good things to say about what to do to fix them.

22 Social poetics is a relatively new topic within the social sciences. It has been developed most notably by Herzfeld (1985, 1997) in anthropology, Brown (1987, 1989, 1992) in sociology, and Gergen and Gergen (1988) in social psychology. In many ways, it gives constructivism added vigor by directing attention to creativity and innovation. Analytically, it is not too far away from the practice theory of Bourdieu (1992) and Lave (1993). Both approaches assume agency and push for finding the sources of originality and mastery in the informing traditions, inter-action patterns, implicit knowledge, social relations, and transmitted wisdom represented in any "community of practice."

23 A good deal of police work – particularly "real work" – is narrativized in written reports and read and signed off by ranking officers. Peers also read these reports as well if they are particularly interested in the story. All can retell the narratives appearing in reports, filling in the missing details and restoring the sequence of events as necessary, by drawing on a rich store of background knowledge – both general to the trade and perhaps specific to the story. Some of the stories – verbal and written – become classic tales of the field and spread throughout the department (and sometimes beyond as the Alamo Run tale recounted in note 20 illus-trates). On the characteristics of those stories that travel well in police organizations, see Muir (1979), Manning (2003), and Young (1991).

24 I am not suggesting that personal change is entirely unacceptable but such change must be accounted for carefully, in culturally accepted ways. On the nature of acceptable (and unacceptable) accounts in general, see Scott and Lyman (1968). Change can be disclaimed as well (Hewitt and Stokes, 1975). How personal change is shaped by narrative is a topic on which much ink is being used these days. See, for example, Fine (1996), Vinitzky-Seroussi (1998), Cole (1996), Bruner (1990), Schudson (1989), and Sarbin (1986). On studying narratives, see Reissman (1993) and Czarniawska (1997).

25 There is, as Manning (1977) points out, some irony in adopting the perspective of patrol officers as the defining ethos of the occupational culture for this perspective also keeps the lower order participants in their place at the bottom of the organization. The police culture celebrates patrol work and thus resources and personnel are directed into a line of work with a limited career structure and a most traditional – some might

say conservative if not reactionary – outlook toward the work. Some 60–70 percent of sworn officers serve in the patrol divisions of most American police agencies with perhaps 15–20 percent in middle management positions and 1–5 percent in the top command posts. This distribution has been rather steady over the years. Except for the Chief of Police (for whom an outside search might be organized), police careers are flat, local, internal, and tightly constrained.

26 Such consistency rests on the overdetermined character of police autonomy as well as the relatively general levels of analysis put into play by those in the various theory groups mentioned in the text. Thus, in passing (and in part), contingency theorists could treat the independence of street cops as the inevitable result of the uncertainty and unpredictability surrounding their work; resource dependancy theorists could treat autonomy as a result of the structural inability of supervisors to monitor their charges; neo-institutionalists could see police autonomy as result of ingrained images of the police role long established as canonical in Anglo-American societies; and population ecologists could view police officer independence as an appropriate "fit" with the environment given the spatial character and diversity of the work and the difficulty, if not impossibility, of measuring the "public good" the police are said to produce. That there is no silver bullet here is my point. All are relevant if incomplete (and to this list I add another in this paper).

27 Three reasons can be put forward for this state of the art. First, a good deal of current research on police work adopts rather uncritically the classic fieldwork studies of twenty to twenty-five or more years ago that focused primarily on white, urban, male patrol officers (e.g., Muir, 1979; Reiss, 1971; Rubenstein, 1973; Skolnick, 1966). Second, structural changes in police organizations are often passed over and thus tensions arising from the introduction of new technologies, increased recruitment of women and minorities, and the penetration of other occupational groups into police worlds (notably lawyers, computer technicians, social researchers, organizational consultants, and "civilian" record clerks, communication operators and social service workers) are underplayed. Third, the external environment within which the police operate has historically been understudied (with, of course, exceptions such as Bayley, 1976; Reiner, 2001; Wilson, 1968). Union politics, city elections and governance, budgetary practices, local economic ups and downs all influence the police in various ways and thus unsettle the occupational culture. On these matters (and more), see Greene and Mastrofski (1988), Scheingold (1992) and, as mentioned in a previous footnote, Manning (2005) from whom this list of research woes is lifted.

References

Abbott, A. 1981. Status and status strain in the professions. *American Journal of Sociology*, 86: 819–835.

1995. *The system of professions*. Chicago, IL: University of Chicago Press.

Adler, P. A. and Adler, P. 1991. *Backboards and blackboards*. New York, NY: Columbia University Press.

Akerlof, G. E. and Kranton, R. E. 2005. Identity and the economics of organizations. *Journal of Economic Perspectives*, 19: 9–32.

Alexander, C. N. and Lauderdale, P. 1977. Situated identities and social influence. *Sociometry*, 40: 223–233.

Alvesson, M. and Willmont, H. 2002. Identity regulation as organizational control: producing the appropriate individual. *Journal of Management Studies*, 39: 619–644.

Anteby, M. 2008. *Moral gray zones*. Princeton, NJ: Princeton University Press.

Ashforth, B. E. and Kreiner, G. E. 1999. How can you do it? Dirty work and the challenge of constructing a positive identity. *Academy of Management Review*, 24: 413–434.

Banton, M. 1964. *The policeman in the community*. New York, NY: Basic Books.

Barker, J. R. 1999. *The discipline of team work*. London: Sage Publications.

Barley, S. R. and Kunda, G. 2006. *Gurus, hired guns, and warm bodies: itinerant experts in a knowledge economy*. Princeton, NJ: Princeton University Press.

Baudrillard, J. 1995. *Simulacra and simulation* (Sheila Faria Glaser, trans.). Ann Arbor: University of Michigan Press.

Bayley, D. 1976. *Forces of order: police behavior in Japan and the United States*. Berkeley, CA: University of California Press.

Bearman, P. S. 2005. *Doormen*. Chicago, IL: University of Chicago Press.

Berger, P. L. and Luckmann T. 1966. *The social construction of reality*. Garden City, New York: Anchor Books.

Bitner, E. 1967. The police on skid row: a study of peace keeping. *American Sociological Review*, 32: 699–715.

1970. *The functions of the police in modern society*. National Institute of Mental Health, Crime and Delinquency Issues Series. Rockville, MD: Center for Studies of Crime and Delinquency.

1990. *Aspects of police work*. Boston, MA: Northeastern University Press.

Black, D. 1980. *Manners and customs of the police*. New York, NY: Academic Press.

Blauner, R. 1964. *Alienation and freedom: the factory worker and his industry*. Chicago, IL: University of Chicago Press.

Bourdieu, P. 1986. The forms of capital. In J. G. Richardson (ed.), *Handbook for theory and research for the sociology of education*: 241–258. Westport, CT: Greenwood Press.

1992. *The logic of practice* (Richard Nice, trans.). Stanford: Stanford University Press.

Bourgeois, P. 2003. *In search of respect: selling crack in El Barrio*. New York, NY: Cambridge University Press.

Boyer, E. I. 1987. *College: the undergraduate experience in America*. New York, NY: Harper and Row.

Brown, M. K. 1988. *Working the street: police discretion and the dilemmas of reform*. New York, NY: Russell Sage Foundation.

Brown, R. H. 1987. *Society as text*. Chicago, IL: University of Chicago Press.

1989. *A poetic for sociology*. Chicago, IL: University of Chicago Press.

1992. *Writing the social text: poetics and politics in social science discourse*. Chicago, IL: Aldine.

Bruner, J. 1990. *Acts of meaning*. Cambridge, MA: Harvard University Press.

Burawoy, M. 1979. *Manufacturing consent*. Chicago, IL: University of Chicago Press.

Cardinal, L. B. 2001. Technological innovation in the pharmaceutical industry: managing research and development using input, behavior and output controls. *Organizational Science*, 12: 19–36.

Cardinal, L. B., Sitkin, S. B., and Long, C. P. 2004. Balancing and rebalancing in the creation and evolution of organizational control. *Organizational Science*, 15: 411–431.

Cole, M. 1996. *Cultural psychology: a once and future discipline*. Cambridge, MA: Harvard University Press.

Cooley, C. H. 1922/(1902). *Human nature and the social order*. New York, NY: Charles Scribbner and Sons.

Covaleski, M. A., Dirsmith, M. W., Heian, J. B., and Samuel, S. 1998. The calculated and the avowed: techniques of discipline and struggles over identity in big six public accounting firms. *Administrative Science Quarterly*, 43: 293–327.

Creed, W. E. D., Scully, M. A., and Austin, J. R. 2002. Clothes make the person? The tailoring of legitimating account and the social construction of identity. *Organizational Science*, 13: 475–496.

Czarniawska, B. 1997. *Narrating the organization: dramas of institutional identity*. Chicago, IL: University of Chicago Press.

Dalton, M. 1959. *Men who manage*. New York, NY: Wiley.

Durkheim, E. 1997(1883). *The division of labor in society*. New York, NY: Free Press.

Emerson, R. and Pollner, M. 1976. Dirty work designations: their features and consequences in a psychiatric setting. *Social Problems*, 23: 243–254.

Etzioni, A. 1965. Organizational control structure. In J. G. March (ed.), *Handbook of organizations*: 650–677. Chicago, IL: Rand McNally.

Fabien, J. 1983. *Time and the other: how anthropology makes its object.* New York, NY: Columbia University Press.

Fantasia, R. 1988. *Cultures of solidarity.* Berkeley, CA: University of California Press.

Friedson, E. 1963. *The hospital in modern society.* New York, NY: Free Press.
    1975. *Doctoring together: a study of professional social control.* Chicago, IL: University of Chicago Press.

Fine, G. A. 1996. *Kitchens: the culture of restaurant work.* Berkeley, CA: University of California Press.

Fish, S. 1980. *Is there a text in this class? The authority of interpretive communities.* Cambridge, MA: Harvard University Press.

Geckas, V. 1991. Self-concept as a basis for a theory of motivation. In J. A. Howard and P. L. Callero (eds.), *The self-society dynamic: cognition, emotion, and action:* 321–337. Cambridge University Press.

Gergen, K. 1991. *The saturated self: dilemmas of identity in contemporary life.* New York, NY: Basic Books.

Gergen K. and Gergen, M. 1988. Narrative and the self as relationship. In L. Berkowitz (ed.), *Advances in experimental social psychology:* 17–56. New York, NY: Academic Press.

Gertzl, B. G. 1961. Determinants of occupational community in high status occupations. *Sociological Quarterly*, 2: 37–40.

Giddens, A. 1991. *Modernity and self-identity: self and society in the late modern age.* Stanford: Stanford University Press.

Glaeser, A. 2000. *Divided in unity: identity, Germany and the Berlin police.* Chicago, IL: University of Chicago Press.

Goffman, E. 1959. *The presentation of self in everyday life.* Garden City, New York: Anchor.
    1961. *Encounters.* Indianapolis: Bobbs-Merrill.
    1963. *Stigma: notes on the management of spoiled identity.* Englewood Cliffs, NJ: Prentice-Hall.
    1967. *Interaction ritual.* Chicago, IL: Aldine.

Gouldner, A. 1954. *Patterns of industrial bureaucracy.* New York, NY: Free Press.

Greene, J. R. and Mastrofski, S. D. (eds.). 1988. *Community policing: rhetoric or reality?* New York, NY: Praeger.

Hauser, R. M. and Warren, J. R. 1997. Socioeconomic indexes for occupations: a review, update, and critique. *Sociological Methodology*, 27: 177–298.

Herzfeld, M. 1985. *The poetics of manhood: contest and identity in a Cretan mountain village*. Princeton: Princeton University Press.

1997. *Cultural intimacy: social poetics in the nation-state*. New York, NY: Routledge.

Hewitt, J. P. 1979. *Self and society: a symbolic interactionist social psychology*. Boston, MA: Allyn and Bacon.

1989. *Dilemmas of the American self*. Philadelphia, PA: Temple University Press.

Hewitt, J. P. and Stokes, R. 1975. Disclaimers. *American Sociological Review*, 40: 1–11.

Hodson, R. 2001. *Dignity at work*. New York, NY: Cambridge University Press.

Hodson, R. and Sullivan, T. 2001. *The social organization of work*. Belmont, CA: Wadsworth.

Holland, D., Lachicotte, W., Skinner, D., and Cain, C. 2001. *Identity and agency in cultural worlds*. Cambridge, MA: Harvard University Press.

Hughes, E. C. 1951. Work and self. In J. Rohrer and M. Sherif (eds.), *Social psychology at the crossroads*: 215–243. Chicago, IL: Aldine

1958. *Men and their work*. Glencoe, IL: Free Press.

1971. *The sociological eye*. Philadelphia, PA: Transaction Books.

Ianni, E. 1982. *Two cultures of policing: street cops and management cops*. Philadelphia, PA: Transaction Books.

Ibarra, H. 2003. *Working identity: unconventional strategies for reinventing your career*. Boston, MA: Harvard Business School Press.

Jameson, F. 1991. *Postmodernism, or, the cultural logic of late capitalism*. Durham, NC: Duke University Press.

Jermier, J. M. 1998. Introduction: critical perspectives on organization control. *Administrative Science Quarterly*, 43: 235–256.

Jermier, J. M. and Berkes, L. 1979. Leader behavior in a police command bureaucracy: a closer look at the quasi-military model. *Administrative Science Quarterly*, 24: 1–23.

Katz, F. 1965. Explaining autonomy in formal work groups in complex organizations. *Administrative Science Quarterly*, 10: 204–223.

Kogut, B. and Zander, U. 1996. What firms do? Coordination, identity and learning. *Organization Science*, 7: 502–518.

Kortarba, J. A. and Fontana, A. (eds.). 1984. *Self in society*. Chicago, IL: University of Chicago Press.

Kunda, G. 1992. *Engineering culture*. Philadelphia, PA: Temple University Press.

Langworthy, R., Hughes, T., and Sanders, B. 1995. *Law enforcement recruitment, selection, and training: a survey of major police departments in the US*. Washington, DC: Academy of Criminal Justice Sciences, Police Section.

Lave, J. 1993. The practice of learning. In S. Chaiklin and J. Lave (eds.), *Understanding practice*: 3–32. Cambridge University Press.

Lipsky, M. 1980. *Street-level bureaucracy: the dilemmas of the individual in public services*. New York, NY: Russell Sage Foundation.

Lipsky, D. 2003. *Absolutely American: four years at West Point*. Boston, MA: Houghton Mifflin.

Lyman, S. M. and Scott, M. B. 1970. *A sociology of the absurd*. New York, NY: Meredith.

Manning, P. K. 1974. Police lying. *Journal of Contemporary Ethnography*, 3: 283–306.

1977. *Police work: the social organization of policing*. Cambridge, MA: MIT Press.

1982. Producing drama: symbolic communication and the police. *Symbolic Interactionism*, 5: 223–242.

1989. *Symbolic communication: signifying calls and the police response*. Cambridge, MA: MIT Press.

1996. United States of America. In T. Jones and T. Newburn (eds.), *Plural policing*: 34–54. London: Routledge.

2001. Information technology in the police context: the "sailor" phone. In J. Yates and J. Van Maanen (eds.), *Information technology and organizational transformation: history, rhetoric, and practice*: 205–222. Newbury Park, CA: Sage.

2003. *Policing contingencies*. Chicago, IL: University of Chicago Press.

2005. The study of policing. *Police Quarterly*, 8: 23–43.

Mars, G. 1982. *Cheats at work: an anthropology of the workplace*. London: Unwin.

Martin, S. E. 1980. *Breaking and entering: policewomen on patrol*. Berkeley, CA: University of California Press.

McAdams, D. P. 1996. Personality, modernity, and the storied self: a contemporary framework for studying persons. *Psychology Inquiry*, 7: 295–321.

McCall, G. J. and Simmons, J. L. (eds.). 1978. *Identities and interactions: an examination of human associations in everyday life*. New York, NY: Free Press.

Mead, G. H. 1934. *Mind, self, and society* (C. W. Morris, ed.). University of Chicago Press.

Meehan, A. J. 2000. The transformation of the oral tradition of the police through the introduction of information technology. *Sociology of Crime, Law and Deviance*, 2: 107–132.

Millman, M. 1977. *The unkindest cut: life in the backrooms of medicine*. New York, NY: Morrow.

Morrill, C. 1996. *The executive way*. University of Chicago Press.

Moscos, P. 2008. *Cop in the hood.* Princeton: Princeton University Press.

Muir, W. K. 1979. *Police: streetcorner politicians.* University of Chicago Press.

O'Neil, M., Marks, M., and Singh, A. (eds.). 2007. *Police occupational culture: new debates and directions,* Vol. VIII (Sociology of crime, law and evidence). Greenwich, CT: JAI Press.

Pfeffer, J. 1998. *The human equation: building profits by putting people first.* Boston, MA: Harvard Business School Press.

Pratt, M. G. 2000. The good, the bad, and the ambivalent: managing identification among Amway distributors. *Administrative Science Quarterly,* 45: 456–493.

Pratt, M. G., Rockmann, K., and Kaufmann, J. 2006. Constructing professional identity: the role of work and identity learning cycles in the customization of identity among medical residents. *Academy of Management Journal,* 49: 235–262.

Reid, D. 1993. *Paris sewers and sewermen: realities and representations.* Cambridge, MA: Harvard University Press.

Reiner, R. 2001. *The politics of the police.* New York, NY: Oxford University Press.

Reis, A. J. 1971. *The police and the public.* New Haven, CT: Yale University Press.

Reissman, C. 1993. *Narrative analysis.* Newbury Park, CA: Sage.

Rock, P. E. 1979. *The making of symbolic interactionism.* London, UK: Macmillan.

Roscigno, V. J. and Hodson, R. 2004. The organizational and social foundations of worker resistance. *American Sociological Review,* 69: 14–39.

Rousseau, D. M. 2004. Under the table deals: idiosyncratic, preferential or unauthorized? In R. Griffin and A. O'Leary-Kelly (eds.), *Dark side of organizational behavior:* 262–290. San Francisco, CA: Jossey-Bass.

Roy, D. 1960. Banana time: job satisfaction and informal interaction. *Human Organization,* 18: 158–168.

Rubenstein, J. 1973. *City police.* New York, NY: Farrar, Straus, and Geroux.

Salaman, G. 1974. *Community and occupation.* Cambridge University Press.

Sarbin, T. (ed.). 1986. *Narrative psychology.* New York, NY: Praeger.

Sarfatti-Larson, M. 1977. *The rise of professionalism: a sociological analysis.* Berkeley, CA: University of California Press.

Scheingold, S. A. 1992. *The politics of street crime: criminal process and cultural obsession.* Philadelphia, PA: Temple University Press.

Schudson, M. 1989. The present in the past versus the past in the present. *Communication,* 11: 105–113.

Schutz, A. 1964. *Collected papers II: studies in social theory*. The Hague: Martinus Nijhoff.

Scott, W. R. 1998. *Organizations: rational, natural and open systems*. Upper Saddle River, NJ: Prentice Hall.

Scott, M. B. and Lyman, S. M. 1968. Accounts. *American Sociological Review*, 33: 46–62.

Sennett, R. 2007. *The craftsman*. New Haven, CT: Yale University Press.

Simpson, R. L. 1985. Social control of occupations and work. *Annual review of sociology*, 11: 415–436.

Sitkin, S. B. and Sutcliffe, K. M. 1991. Dispensing legitimacy: the influence of professional, organizational, and legal controls on pharmacist behavior. *Research in the sociology of organizations*, 8: 269–295.

Skolnick, J. H. 1966. *Justice without trial: law enforcement in democratic society*. New York, NY: Wiley.

Skolnick, J. H. and Bayley, D. H. 1986. *The new blue line: police innovation in six American cities*. New York, NY: Free Press.

Snow, David A. and Anderson, L. 1993. *Down on their luck: a study of homeless street people*. Berkeley, CA: University of California Press.

Strauss, A. 1959. *Mirrors and masks: the search for identity*. San Francisco, CA: Sociology Press.

Stryker, S. and Burke, P. J. 2000. The past, present, and future of an identity theory. *Social Psychology Quarterly*, 63: 284–297.

Swann, W. B. 1999. *Resilient identities: self, relationships, and the construction of social reality*. New York, NY: Basic Books.

Swann, W. B., Johnson, R. E., and Bosson, J. K. 2009. Identity negotiation at work. In B. Staw and A. Brief (eds.), *Research in organizational behavior: 29*. Amsterdam: Elsevier.

Tajfel, H. 1982. *Social identity and intergroup relations*. Cambridge University Press.

Tajfel, H. and Turner, J. C. 1986. The social identity theory of intergroup behavior. In S. Worchel and W. G. Austin (eds.), *Psychology of intergroup relations: 7–24*. Chicago, IL: Nelson-Hall.

Thomas, R. 1994. *What machines can't do: politics and technology in the industrial enterprise*. Berkeley, CA: University of California Press.

Turner, R. 1968. The self concept in social interaction. In C. Gordon and K. Gergen (eds.), *The self in social interaction: 132–145*. New York, NY: Wiley.

Van Maanen, J. 1973. Observations on the making of policemen. *Human Organization*, 32: 407–418.

    1974. Working the street: a developmental view of police behavior. In H. Jacob (ed.), *The potential for reform of criminal justice*

(Sage criminal justice system annual review), III: 83–130. Beverly Hills, CA: Sage.

1978. On watching the watchers. In P. K. Manning and J. Van Maanen (eds.), *Policing: a view from the streets*: 309–350. New York, NY: Random House.

1979. The self, the situation, and the rules of interpersonal relations. In W. Bennis, E. H. Schein, F. Steele, and J. Van Maanen (eds.), *Essays in interpersonal dynamics*: 43–101. Homewood, IL: Dorsey Press.

1981. Notes on the production of ethnographic data in an American police agency. In R. Luckham (ed.), *Law and social enquiry*: 189–230. New York, NY: International Center for Law in Development.

1983. The boss: the American police sergeant. In M. Punch (ed.), *Control in the police organization*: 275–317. Cambridge, MA: MIT Press.

1986. Power in the bottle: drinking patterns and social relations in a British police agency. In S. Srivasta (ed.), *Executive power*: 204–239. San Francisco, CA: Jossey-Bass.

1988. *Tales of the field.* University of Chicago Press.

1992. Drinking our troubles away: managing conflict in a British police agency. In D. Kolb and J. M. Bartunek (eds.), *Hidden conflict in organizations*: 78–99. Newbury Park, CA: Sage.

Van Maanen, J. and Barley, S. R. 1984. Occupational communities: culture and control in work organizations. In B. Staw and L. L. Cummings (eds.), *Research in organizational behavior*, VI: 287–365. Greenwich, CT: JAI Press.

1985. Cultural organization: fragments of a theory. In P. Frost, M. Louis, and L. Moore (eds.), *Organization culture*: 31–53. Newbury Park, CA: Sage.

Venkatesh, S. 2008. *Gang leader for a day: a rogue sociologist takes to the streets.* New York, NY: Penguin.

Vinitzky-Seroussi, V. 1998. *After pomp and circumstance: high school reunion as an autobiographical occasion.* University of Chicago Press.

White, H. C. 1992. *Identity and control: a structural theory of social action.* Princeton: Princeton University Press.

Weber, M. 1946. *From Max Weber: essays in sociology* (H. H. Gerth and C. W. Mills, ed. and trans.). New York, NY: Oxford University Press.

Willis, P. 1977. *Learning to labor.* New York, NY: Columbia University Press.

Wilson, J. Q. 1968. *Varieties of police behavior.* Cambridge, MA: Harvard University Press.

Worden, A. 1993. The attitudes of women and men in policing: testing conventional and contemporary wisdom, *Criminology*, 31, 203–237.

Wrzesniewski, A. and Dutton, J.E. 2001. Crafting a job: revisioning employees as active crafters of their work. *Academy of Management Review*, 26: 179–201.

Young, M. 1991. *An inside job: policing and police culture in Britain.* Oxford, UK: Clarendon Press.

Zussman, R. 1996. Autobiographical occasions. *Contemporary Sociology*, 25: 143–148.

6 Organizational identity and control: can the two go together?

ELIZABETH GEORGE AND CUILI QIAN
Hong Kong University of Science and Technology

Organizational control theorists traditionally have conceptualized control as any process by which organizations or their representatives channel individuals' and groups' efforts toward the attainment of organizationally desired objectives (Eisenhardt, 1985; Flamholtz et al., 1985; Jaworski, 1988; Ouchi, 1977, 1979). The underlying assumption in this conceptualization of control is the divergence of interests between the organization and the individual such that individuals are likely to take care of their own interests ahead of those of the organization. These theorists argue that organizations need to control individuals through either formal mechanisms (Blau and Scott, 1962) or by co-opting them into either the culture or values of the organization (Ouchi, 1979). We argue that this conceptualization of control takes into account only a part of the relationship between individuals and organizations, and it offers a limited view on human motivation. Indeed individuals and organizations might not have divergent interests, and organizational members need not forego their own interests in favor of those of the organization in order to retain their membership in these organizations. In fact, the research on organizational identification suggests that individuals can benefit in many ways from their organizational membership (Dutton et al., 1994; Pratt, 1998), and that organizations play a major role in shaping how individuals define themselves (George and Chattopadhyay, 2005). Furthermore, individuals like Cervantes's Don Quixote might be driven by a strong belief in who they are, and their actions might be shaped by their commitment to this identity rather than external rewards or punishments (March and Weil, 2005). We explore this idea and we argue that identity is a driver of behavior; consequently, it is a basis of control. In this context, the focus of control, and therefore of the managerial tasks related to control, might change from the traditional ways of controlling employees' behaviors or outcomes to identity-based control.

We propose that a more complete conceptualization of control should take into account all manner of relationships between individuals and organizations. Although traditionally control has been used to constrain individual action and direct it toward the organization's goals, an expanded view of control can focus on its motivational or enabling aspects, which can benefit both individuals and organizations. Specifically, we propose that control is the process whereby managers align the interests of both organizations and their members, such that employees' actions, both in terms of direction and intensity, are beneficial to the organization. We build our view of this aspect of control on social identity theory (Tajfel and Turner, 1986) and self-categorization theory (Turner, 1987), and we argue that understanding the basic identity-related relationship of individuals with organizations will help us understand how individual behavior is shaped in organizations. (See Weibel, Chapter 14, for an alternate, yet complementary, view of the motivational consequences of control practices.) In this conceptualization of control we do not begin with the will of the organization, but rather we are open to the possibility that the shaping of the interests (of both employees and the organization) is a mutually negotiated process.

We propose that within this alternate view of the individuals' relationship with organizations, the key role of management – with regard to control – changes from imposing the organization's will on employees to facilitating social identity completeness or coherence for individuals. Once employees realize the shared interests between themselves and the organization, they are motivated to engage in behaviors that are mutually beneficial. This fulfills the purpose of organizational control. We explore and expand on these ideas. We first very briefly review the literature on organizational control to see what role individual motivation can have in our understanding of control. We then discuss identity as a fundamental motivator of human behavior, with a focus on the two drivers of identification: uncertainty reduction and self-esteem enhancement. Finally, we explore different ways in which identity plays a role in shaping or controlling individual behavior.

Traditional approaches to control

Theorists have offered multiple taxonomies and typologies of control, ranging from Etzioni's (1961) three principles of coercion, material rewards, and normative control to Ouchi's (1980) control by markets, bureaucracies, or clans. Scholars have identified several forms of control that have been discussed in the literature, such as input control, behavior control, market control, cultural control, and output control (Cardinal, 2001; Cardinal *et al.*, 2004; Jaworski, 1988; Kirsch, 1996; Ouchi, 1979). Each form of control has been associated theoretically with a set of antecedent conditions. Among these conditions are (a) the extent to which it is feasible to measure the performance that is desired (Ouchi, 1977); (b) the extent to which the task is programmable (Eisenhardt, 1985); or that one knows the process through which inputs are transformed to outputs (Ouchi, 1977); (c) the extent to which it is feasible to observe the behaviors involved in the completion of the task (Govindarajan and Fisher, 1990); and (d) the extent to which the organization has knowledge about the task in evaluating and rewarding the behaviors that are observed (Kirsch, 1996).

Empirical studies have focused on identifying and revising the antecedent conditions of organizational control mechanisms and their subsequent consequences on individuals, business units, and organizations (Cardinal, 2001; Eisenhardt, 1985; Govindarajan and Fisher, 1990; Kirsch, 1996; Snell, 1992). For example, Eisenhardt (1985) examined compensation practices for retail salespersons in fifty-four stores and found that task programmability is strongly related to the choice of compensation package. The cost of measuring outcomes and business uncertainty was also found to affect compensation. In a study of thirty-two information systems, Kirsch (1996) found that the antecedents of different forms of control varied. For instance, the extent to which behavioral control was used was determined by the interaction between observed behavior and the project sponsor's level of systems development knowledge, while the extent of use of outcome control was a function of observed behavior and measurable outcomes.

It is interesting to note that these studies typically do not consider the motivation of those who are to be controlled as an antecedent of the appropriate form of control to be used. Even though some studies have taken into account differences between individuals – such as different levels of human capital (Eisenhardt, 1985) or knowledge (Kirsch, 1996) – none of the studies we reviewed considered the possibility that individuals might have different relationships with the organization, which would be amenable to different forms of control. Ouchi and Johnson's (1978) study of the relationship between types of organizational control and employees' emotional well-being in two American organizations suggests that the type of controls used affects the relationship between individuals and organizations, and this relationship would then in turn affect the type of controls that would be appropriate. Their empirical test, however, only considered the first half of this argument – that is, the relationship between the type of control and three individual-level outcomes: emotional well-being, affiliative behavior, and attachment to the company. Further, the explanatory power of these studies is modest at best (adjusted R2 ranging from .02 to .25), suggesting that there is room for improving our understanding of control in organizations. In this chapter, we argue that individual motivation might be an important consideration in the form and effectiveness of control in organizations. Though the preference of individual employees implicitly has been assumed to be one of resistance to control, and this might indeed represent the preferences of a significant proportion of those involved in organizations, we suggest that there is an alternative. Drawing on the sizable literature on organization identity, which suggests that individuals derive positive meaning and self-identity from their association with organizations (cf. Ashforth and Mael, 1989; Dutton *et al.*, 1994), we try to expand the control literature by presenting an alternative that considers a new source of control – identity. Identity-based control not only takes the employees' motivation into account and aligns the interests of employees and those of organizations, but also it has distinct implications for the roles of managers in the control process.

Identity as a motivator

We propose four different ways in which identity can be incorporated into managerial control. Before we elaborate on each we briefly review the manner in which individual identities shape behaviors. Identity is a strong motivator of behavior since individuals are strongly driven to have a coherent and consistent identity and then to maintain it (Dutton *et al.*, 1994). Although individuals have personal and social identities, we focus only on the latter, because it has been more closely associated with organizational membership (Ashforth and Mael, 1989). A person's *social identity* consists of "those aspects of an individual's self-image that derive from the social categories to which he perceives himself as belonging" (Tajfel and Turner, 1986: 16). An individual's self-image includes many social identities that correspond to the various roles played by the individual, such as employee, family member, and citizen.[1] The degree to which an individual identifies with a particular social category, such as the organization, the family, or the nation, is a psychological construct that reflects the degree of similarity between the qualities attributed by individuals to that particular category (or its typical representative), whether good or bad, and the qualities that the individual currently incorporates in his or her self-image (Doise, 1988; Dutton *et al.*, 1994; Weinreich, 1986). Individuals who identify with a category demonstrate emotional involvement with and commitment to this category (Ellemers *et al.*, 1999; Tajfel and Turner, 1986), and perceive that they share a common fate with other category members (Ashforth and Mael, 1989).

Social identities serve two purposes: they help individuals reduce uncertainty about appropriate forms of behavior in a context, and these identities help them retain a positive sense of themselves (Tajfel and Turner, 1986; Turner, 1987). Membership in an organization, for instance, gives employees guidance on the perceptions, attitudes, and behaviors that are appropriately demonstrated by prototypical members of that organization and thus helps reduce any uncertainty the individual might otherwise have experienced (Mael and Ashforth, 1992). Newcomer socialization helps new employees learn about a variety of things about the organization from the tangible, like organizational benefits, to the intangible, such as the core values of members of the organization. This information can be drawn on later by individuals to guide them on what they can expect from the organization and its members as well as what are appropriate behaviors for members of that organization (see Ashford and Black, 1996). Therefore, organizational membership provides some degree of certainty or predictability of what could otherwise be seen as a series of relatively uncertain social interactions.

Categorizing oneself as part of the collective also helps the individual to experience positive self-esteem. This can occur in several ways: when an individual acts based on social identity, and other members of the group respond to the individual as if he or she were a valued member of the group, this interaction can help the individual experience positive self-esteem. Being viewed by other members of a group as a valued colleague can help individuals feel positive about themselves. Categorization as a group member has also been associated with in-group favoritism and a sense that the group has valued attributes (Tajfel and Turner, 1986). These valued attributes are then associated with each member of the group, resulting in individuals experiencing positive self-esteem from membership in that group. A well-defined social identity has the potential to reduce social uncertainty as well as enhance positive self-esteem; it thus can facilitate the well-being of the individual.

There is a significant body of literature suggesting that organizations are an important source of an individual's social identity (Ashforth and Mael, 1989; Dutton *et al.*, 1994). Identification with organizations can meet a number of the employees' needs, such as self-esteem enhancement (Erez and Earley, 1993), uncertainty reduction (Hogg and Terry, 2000), self-verification (Polzer *et al.*, 2002), and affiliation (Bartel and Dutton, 2001). Since we spend a great part of our adult lives in and around organizations, we tend to define ourselves in part in terms of our membership in these organizations. Thus, organizational membership is key to both reducing uncertainty in our social world, as well as potentially helping us to maintain positive self-esteem. In the following section we use these two functions of identity, uncertainty reduction, and self-esteem enhancement, to explain how identity plays an important part in controlling individuals' behaviors in organizations. We describe four bases of control, membership-based control, prototype-based control, identity salience-based control, and identity coherence-based control.[2] A summary of our key points can be found in Table 6.1.

Identity-based control

Membership-based control

Individuals derive positive self-esteem when they work in organizations that are regarded as prestigious. Dutton *et al.* (1994) argued that people are likely to identify more with organizations that they believe have positive external images relative to other organizations because association with such positively viewed organizations could bring the employees some form of "reflected glory" and consequently boost their self-esteem. Membership in prestigious organizations implies

Table 6.1 *The types and managerial implications of identity-based control*

Types of identity-based control	Functions of identity			Managerial task
	Uncertainty reduction	Positive self-esteem enhancement		
Membership-based control	☑ Employees are motivated to work in an organization that is distinct from others since it provides them clarity on how they should behave and how they are different from others.	☑ Employees are motivated to maintain organizational prestige and distinctiveness since membership in this prestigious organization enhances their own self-esteem.		Clarify which behaviors or actions contribute to the prestige and distinctiveness of the organization.
Prototype-based control	☑ Employees are motivated to act consistently with the group prototype.	☑ Employees who are prototypical are treated as valued members by others in the organization.		Help clarify the essence or prototype of the group, and the extent to which employees share these characteristics.
Control based on managing multiple identities				
Identity salience-based control	☑ Employees act on the basis of an identity that is distinctive, comprehensive, and easily accessible.	☒		Clarify the organizational prototype, exploring how comprehensive this prototype is, and how often and easily it is invoked in the work context.
Identity coherence-based control	☑ Employees are motivated to maintain coherent identities.	☑ Coherence in identities across situations helps individuals retain positive self-esteem across contexts.		Make sure that the identities are not in conflict. Remove structural blocks that make conflicting demands on employees' identities.

that the individual might have the same valued attributes as those of the organization. Numerous studies have supported this argument and have found that the prestige of the organization is significantly and positively associated with individuals' identification with the organization (e.g., Iyer *et al.*, 1997; Kreiner and Ashforth, 2004; Reade, 2001).

Organizations that are perceived to have distinct practices and values relative to comparable firms provide employees with a clear referent for the purposes of identification (Ashforth and Saks, 1996). Dutton *et al.* (1994) argued that people will identify with organizations that are distinctive relative to other organizations because incorporation of an organization's distinctive features into the employees' social identity satisfies the need to accentuate their own distinctiveness in comparison with members of other organizations. Mael and Ashforth's (1992) study of alumni's identification with a university examined and found support for the idea that distinctiveness is a predictor of organizational identification.

While Hogg and Terry (2000) suggested that individuals attend separately to their uncertainty reduction and self-enhancement needs, others like Long and Spears (1997) have argued that individuals simultaneously attend to these two needs by identifying with groups that are both better and distinct from other groups. George and Chattopadhyay (2005) found support for the latter argument in their study where organizational prestige and distinctiveness formed a single factor that predicted an individual's identification with the organization.

Since individuals derive positive identity from being associated with organizations that are prestigious and/or distinctive, and if they are aware of this, it is likely that those individuals would be motivated to act in ways that would preserve the prestige and distinctiveness of the organization and their membership in that organization. In other words, these organizational characteristics of prestige and distinctiveness both define the organization and its members and are created by the organization and its members. The behaviors in which the individual would engage would further the interests of the organization, because these interests also coincide with those of the individual. Thus, managers may not need to control employees by monitoring their behaviors or evaluating their outputs. Rather, the individuals are internally driven to engage in behaviors that maintain or enhance the prestige and distinctiveness of the organization, that is, those that help them retain their organizational membership, enhance their self-esteem, and reduce their uncertainty.

These arguments make the assumption that individual employees are aware of how their actions contribute to the organization's prestige and distinctiveness. In instances where this assumption holds, it is likely that employees would engage in actions that would benefit the organization, and indirectly, themselves. However, when the causal link between employee actions, organizational prestige, and distinctiveness is not clear, then the managers must clarify for the individual which behaviors or actions contribute to these attributes of the organization. For instance, managers first could help employees understand the sources of an organization's financial success and next explain the role that the individual plays in creating that success. This understanding could help individuals in the daily enactment of their jobs, such that they know what to do in order to help their organization, and themselves, succeed. Thus, the drive for self-esteem enhancement, identified by social identity theorists (Tajfel and Turner, 1986), could act as the motivator for individual employee actions that would benefit both the individual and the organizations. This is consistent with the argument of Van Knippenberg and colleagues that leader behaviors could affect followers' or employees' identification with the collective, and that this effect on identification may in turn affect followers' attitudes and behaviors (Van Knippenberg *et al.*, 2004). In our conceptualization of control, the manager's task shifts from one of constraining employees, or indeed providing incentives to shape their behavior, to providing information that helps employees retain a positive sense of self.

Prototype-based control

Social identity theory (Tajfel and Turner, 1986) and, more particularly, self-categorization theory (Turner, 1987) have suggested that people incorporate characteristics of the groups to which they belong into their social identity; thus they see themselves as interchangeable with other members of their group or category. Brewer and Gardner (1996) suggested that attributes of the group, such as commonly held values, are represented in the form of a group prototype, which is internalized to construct this social identity. Though members of the category might vary on their level of "prototypicality," all of them would have some of the characteristics that define the category in order for them to be considered (by themselves and others) as members of that group or category. For example, categories such as "Tory," "Democrat," or "Green" would evoke prototypes of individuals who might be members of various political parties. Although individuals can vary the degree to which they match the prototype, they would have some common attributes that would identify them (to themselves and others) as members of those categories. Such a prototype helps guide the individual in determining the behaviors, attitudes, or values that ought to be shown by members, and thus it plays a role in reducing the social uncertainty that the individual might feel. Further, prototypical members of the group are treated as valuable by others in the group, thus causing the individual to have enhanced self-esteem. If the prototype is positive, the more prototypical those individuals regard themselves to be and the more positive their self-esteem is likely to be.

The group or category prototype has at least two important implications for organizational control. First, the prototype, rather than organizational rules and strictures, would control individual behavior. Since individuals have internalized these prototypes, their behavior would be guided by the prototype. Building on Ocasio and Wohlgezogen's (Chapter 7) arguments, we suggest that prototypes might guide behavior by channeling individuals' attention toward information that is consistent with the prototype. Second, as in the case of organizational attributes such as prestige and distinctiveness, it is in the individual's psychological interest to have a clear prototype of a group, as well as to engage in behaviors that will sustain or perpetuate that prototype. This sets up a strong internal drive to engage in behaviors that are prototypical. Acting consistently with the prototype would also be in the individual's interest because it would reduce the cognitive energy needed to decipher appropriate behaviors, values, and attitudes in the organizational context.

Again, we assume that the group prototype is clear to individuals. In the case that it is clear, members would be able to shape their behaviors to match the prototype. However, some researchers suggest that groups that are heterogeneous in terms of characteristics such as gender or nationality (where these characteristics are particularly meaningful in that context) are less likely to have a clear prototype than are more homogenous groups (Chattopadhyay *et al.*, 2004). If the prototype is not clear, then the managerial task would be both to help individuals determine the essence or prototype of the group and to understand the extent to which they share these characteristics. Once that has been accomplished, according to self-categorization theory (Turner, 1987), group members would be more likely to engage in behaviors that are consistent with the prototype. Van Maanen (Chapter 5) notes that members of the police force spend a great deal of time clarifying and elaborating on what constitutes police work; thus these actions then shape their own behaviors as well as their judgments of others. Organizational socialization activities help to clarify organizational prototypes and behaviors associated with these prototypes. Similarly, group leaders can play a role in shaping the group prototype. (See Haslam, 2001 for a review of leadership from the perspective of self-categorization theory.) A critical component in the power of this prototype is the extent to which members find it representative of their group. In either case, whether the prototype is generated by the organization, the group, or the leader, the power of the prototype in motivating behavior is a function of the extent to which individual members of the group believe that they are prototypical.

Control based on managing multiple identities

Our discussion of the relationship between control and identity has so far assumed that individuals have one major social identity, the one that is related to their organizational membership. However, we know that organizations are only one of the many social categories to which individuals belong. Any employee also belongs to a gender group, an occupation, a familial group, an ethnic group, a nation, and so on. Each of these categories could be incorporated into the individual's social identity, such that the individual then potentially can act based on any one or more of those identities. This can be problematic if some of the social identities that define an individual are at odds with his or her identity as an organizational member. In other words, if our multiple identities are not simultaneously salient in any given situation, then we can partition the identities such that the same individual is both a loving parent and also a tough boss. However, if both the parent and the work identities are invoked in the same situation, and the demands that they make on the individual are at odds, then the management of these multiple identities becomes a problem. Turner's (1987) principle of functional antagonism suggests that stronger identification with one social category reduces identification with other social categories. Identification implies accentuation of intra-category similarities and inter-category differences, thus making simultaneous multiple identifications unwieldy. In the organizational domain, Chatman *et al.* (1998) used Turner's argument to explain a modest negative correlation between the salience of identities based on demographic characteristics and identities based on organizational membership. Ashforth and Mael (1989) similarly theorized that individuals do not integrate multiple identities because this integration might be cognitively taxing and might compromise the usefulness of each identity. These arguments and the idea of a salience hierarchy in identity theory "imply that social identities are discrete psychological phenomena such that as one identity becomes salient, others necessarily become less so" (Ashforth and Johnson, 2001: 46).

There are at least two ways in which managing multiple identities can be related to the controls used in organizations. First, the choice of which one of the identities is acted on is a function of the salience of that identity. If organizational identity is the most salient, then the individual will act as a member of the organization, and presumably will work to maintain the organization's interests. In order to motivate the individual to act in the organization's interests, the manager must make organizational identity relatively more salient than other identities, particularly in instances where there might be conflict between identities, for example, between organizational identity and team identity.

A second way in which the management of multiple identities and control are related is based on Steele's (1988) thesis that individuals seek to maintain a sense of continuity in their identity across time and situations. It is psychologically taxing for individuals to have multiple discordant identities. This is especially the case if more than one identity can apply to a situation. In this situation the managerial task of motivating behaviors involves making sure that the organizational identity of an individual is not inconsistent with other central social identities held by that individual. We elaborate on the management of salience and of harmonious social identities and their relationship with control next.

Identity salience-based control

Self-categorization theorists have argued that the key to understanding social identity salience is to understand what attributes of a situation will activate a particular social identity rather than an alternate identity (Haslam, 2001). Hogg and Terry (2000) argued that identity salience depends partially on the extent to which an identity accounts for context-specific behaviors and/or situationally relevant similarities and differences among people. Identity salience and identity coherence differ in that salience relates to the extent that any one identity is regarded as relevant in a particular situation, whereas identity coherence deals with the extent to which multiple identities are consistent with each other. We use an example of surgical teams to explore the idea of identity salience. If a surgical team consists of male and female surgeons, anesthesiologists, and nurses, would individuals act based on gender, based on occupation, or based on identity? The answer to that question is found among the conditions under which an identity is salient.

First, a salient identity is one that is distinctive and is constructed such that intergroup differences are greater than intragroup differences (see Haslam, 2001 for a review). Thus, if a female surgeon believes she has more in common with a group of surgeons than a group of women, then her occupational identity would be more salient to her than her gender-based identity. In contrast, if all of the nurses are female, and there are a few female surgeons and anesthesiologists, then a female nurse is likely to find her gender identity to be as salient as her occupational identity since gender and occupation maximally differentiate between the three groups.

Second, a salient identity is one that provides a more comprehensive account for the individual in the context rather than other identities (Haslam, 2001). Previously we noted that self-categorization theorists have argued that a key function of social identities is to reduce uncertainty in social interactions. If organizational membership provides a comprehensive guideline for navigating the social context in which the individual operates, then organizational identity is salient. However, if the individual finds that organizational membership does not help predict or respond to events at work, and that other identities have to be invoked to deal with those situations, the organizational identity will not be salient. Referring to the surgical team again, an occupational identity is likely to be more salient than a gender-based identity in the performance of a surgical procedure because the occupational identity would most likely provide guidance on the appropriate actions in that context, than would the gender-based identity. In contrast, a gender-based identity might be more salient in the discussion of policies related to working hours or shifts, since these are more likely to be gender-related, rather than occupation-related, issues on work–family balance.

Finally, in order for an identity to be salient it must be easily accessible (Haslam, 2001). This accessibility is a function of the history of the individual. When we identify with a group, then we are more likely to invoke the identity that stems from that group membership when we encounter a new situation. When an identity is often in use, that identity is most easily recalled, and is most likely to be the one that the individual refers to for guidance on how to process information and respond to the environment. The accessibility of the identity also stems from how others in the situation deal with the individuals. For instance, a gender-based identity is relatively easily accessible if others in the situation act as if they regard the individual as representative of his or her gender group.

Putting these three factors together we argue that identity plays a role shaping behavior when that identity is distinctive, comprehensive, and easily accessible. This is particularly important when the organization is only one of several sources of social identity for the individual, and managers would like the organizational identity to motivate behavior. Whether employees will work toward collective interests as well as their own self-interests depends on the extent to which employees identify with the group, and group identity is salient (Van Knippenberg *et al.*, 2004). The manager's task then involves helping to make the organizational identity the most salient to the individual employee, so that the employee's behavior is guided by that organizational identity. This could entail clarifying the organizational prototype, exploring how comprehensive this prototype is, and understanding how often and easily it is invoked in the work context. This is a managerial task that has remained relevant over the years from the times of the East India Company, which dealt with British employees who went "native" in the colonies (Dalrymple, 2002), to more modern managers who tried to help expatriate employees overcome their ethnocentric biases in international assignments (Osland, 1995). In both these instances reminders of organizational membership, through practices, rituals, or symbols, help keep organizational identity salient and increase the odds that individuals' behaviors will reflect organizational interests rather than the interests of other identities individuals might hold.

Identity coherence-based control

The management of multiple social identities involves not simply cycling through the identities as each identity assumes or wanes in its salience. Researchers have argued and demonstrated that simultaneous identification with multiple potential targets can occur. Barker and Tomkins (1994), Scott (1997), and Van Knippenberg and Van Schie (2000) examined multiple identifications among traditional employees and found that employees can identify simultaneously with the organization and its subunits or the organization and their work group. George and Chattopadhyay (2005) found that contract workers could identify simultaneously with client and employer. Ashforth and Johnson (2001) speculated that multiple identities can be simultaneously salient when there is an overlap between the identities; thus cuing one identity would make the other identity more cognitively accessible. Similarly, Hornsey and Hogg (2000) argued that identities can coexist if their central and defining values are compatible rather than dissonant. Scott *et al.* (1998) suggested that when individuals' multiple identities are tightly aligned with one another, the pressure stemming from competing demands from these multiple identities can be mitigated. Consistent with these arguments, Mlicki and Ellemers (1996) and Wenzel (2000) demonstrated that individuals could identify simultaneously with both their nation (Poland and Germany, respectively) and with Europe because the defining characteristics of the two identities were compatible. Cinnirella (1997) found similar results with Italian respondents but the opposite with British respondents. He speculated that this could be a result of the pro- and anti-Europe discourses in the respective countries that rendered the Italian and European identities compatible but made the British and European identities incompatible. In the organizational domain, Chattopadhyay *et al.* (2004) argued that individuals can simultaneously identify with their gender or race and with their work group when the two identities are compatible. These arguments and empirical findings suggest a more complex phenomenon than that suggested by Turner's (1987) principle of functional

antagonism. Individuals are likely to simultaneously attend to multiple identities to the extent that those social identities are compatible
with each other, and acting based on one identity will not result in
actions that are inconsistent with another identity.

Since all employees are likely to have multiple social identities, the
key to managing them is trying to make sure that the identities are not
in conflict. In other words, when an individual is a member of more
than one category at the same time, without the two identities making
competing or conflicting demands on that person, then it is possible to
act consistently with both category memberships at the same time.
This is true both for instances where the identities are nested within
each other (such as being a member of a work team and a member
of an organization), and in instances where the identities need not
overlap completely (such as being a woman and an organizational
member). Google and other organizations that have been nominated
as exemplary employers recognize this fact by providing services such
as onsite dry cleaning, car maintenance, or childcare, which take care
of employees' non-work identity-related responsibilities and thus help
employees to focus their attention on work (Avant, 2007). Managers
in these companies understand that if organizational membership
requires that individuals have to act in ways that are inconsistent with
their gender or family role identities, then individual behavior might
not necessarily favor the interests of the organization. In a different
context, Sitkin and Sutcliffe (1991) found that pharmacists chose to
follow professional norms when they were faced with conflicting
controls imposed on them by their organization and their profession.
The benefit of having coherent identities is that it enables the individual to retain positive self-esteem across contexts, as well as helping the
individual minimize the effort needed to manage differing identity-
based demands made on the individual across contexts. Consequently,
the challenge for managers is to assist individuals in holding on to key
social identities, as well as an organizational identity, at the same time.

Alternately, a way of thinking of this managerial task is of removing
organizational blocks that prevent individuals from maintaining a
coherent set of social identities. Though not conceptualized as such,
Anteby's (2008) argument that managers selectively are lenient in the
application of sanctions against workers who violate workplace rules
in order to enact occupational identity is an example of removing
blocks that prevent the formation of a coherent identity, which

includes organizational as well as occupational membership. In his study, managers recognized the importance of craftsmanship to some categories of workers, and they used this knowledge to get workers to do what they (the managers) wanted in exchange for allowing the workers to practice their craft. In Anteby's (2008) study, the interests of the managers and workers were not aligned, and in being lenient managers had to compromise a part of their interests in order to gain a larger good. However, we make the argument that it is not necessary for either organizations or individual employees to lose when employees act on their multiple identities. This is consistent with the point made by authors who argue for the benefits of a diverse workforce, suggesting that positive skills and values related to other identities, such as gender, might be useful in the organizational context (see Williams and O'Reilly, 1998 for a review). Therefore, we suggest that organizational design could be aligned with employees' identities so as to capitalize on employee differences, without putting undue pressure on employees to choose between different identities. Managers could seek out and eliminate organizational structures that make conflicting demands on employees' identities. Going a step further, Sitkin and Lind (2006) argue that leadership involves not only creating or altering organizational structures but also explaining these structures in order to help individuals interpret them correctly. Regarding the arguments presented in this paper, we would say that the actions of their leaders could help individuals align their many social identities with their organizational membership-based identity.

Some ideas for future research

In this paper, we propose that organizational control theorists should take into account individual/organizational relationships that are based on the interests of both parties coinciding with each other, rather than being divergent. Building on this possible relationship we propose four types of identity-based control that could result in the same behavioral outcomes as those achieved by traditional organizational controls. We suggest that using an alternative perspective to examine organizational control may enrich the control literature. There are several avenues for future research that flow from our arguments. First, it would be fruitful to examine empirically if the drivers of behavior that we propose in this model account for additional variance in employee behaviors over that accounted for by more traditional conceptualizations of control. For example, we could examine if the extent to which individuals identify with organizations explains more of the variance in individual behaviors than that explained by more traditional mechanisms of behavioral control. Future researchers also could explicitly test how managers use identity-based control to achieve organizational goals. Qualitative studies could be undertaken to gain a situated understanding of how managers make organizational identity salient, clarify prototypes, facilitate identity coherence, or help individuals to understand the link between their actions and organizational prestige and distinctiveness. Further, the interactive effects of traditional control mechanisms with identity-based control on employee behaviors might add to our understanding of the effectiveness of organizational control.

Third, in the future, researchers could consider the differences in use of identity-based control across cultures. As Brewer and Chen (2007) highlighted, cross-cultural differences might be involved when invoking the self that is defined in terms of roles and relationships with significant others (relational self) versus the self construal that is based on being a prototypical group member (the collective self). It would be interesting to explore the extent to which identity-based control is more or less relevant to one rather than another of these social self construals. Sampling managerial control based on different nationalities also may provide us with a broader range of differences in practices of control.

Finally, future researchers could consider the limits to our arguments. We based our theorizing about control on the assumption that individual and organizational interests coincide. This assumption has been supported in many studies on organizational identification (cf. Ashforth and Mael, 1989; Dutton et al., 1994). However, it is very likely that there are certain domains in which this assumption will not hold. For example, individuals who work under exploitative conditions are not likely to respond to managerial attempts to make their organizational identity salient. Under those conditions, identity-based control would not be relevant, because the organizational identity that is invoked is not appealing to the individual employee. In addition, it would be useful to look at instances where multiple identities within the organizational domain (such as team membership-based identity and organizational membership-based identity) are in conflict. What would be the result of managerial attempts to make organizational membership-based identity salient when identity as a team member is strong and the team's interests apparently do not coincide with those of the organization?

Conclusion

We began this paper by arguing that traditional ways of thinking about control have assumed that the interests of organizations and workers are inherently in opposition. We then pointed out that this need not be the case, and that control theorists could benefit from considering the individual motivation of employees. We then proposed that identity is a strong motivator of behavior and by understanding how identity shapes behavior, we might be able to integrate some of the insights about identity into our conceptualization of control. The role of identity in control is not completely new. Alvesson and Willmott (2002) made the argument that identity can take the form of a yoke that ties individuals to organizations in ways that are beneficial to the organization (and presumably of little or no benefit to the individual). Thus, though they did consider identity as a shaper or controller of behavior, their assumption of the relationship between individuals and organizations was no different from that held by previous control theorists. Anteby (2008), in contrast, suggested that the organization can be a location for identity enactment by the individual and that in the absence of the organization and its actions, the individual employee's professional identity would not be fully developed. Our thinking on the relationship between identity and control lies in between these two sets of arguments. We agree that identity can be constraining when it is imposed by others. Ouchi's (1979) conceptualization of clan control as a form of alignment of individual and organizational goals used the organization as the starting point, and suggested that socialization processes bring the individual in line with the organization. Even this view of control that takes individuals into account places the individual's goals and interests in a subordinate position to those of the organization. As a result, individuals need socialization in order to be convinced of the benefits of organizational membership. We argue, in contrast, that the goals and interests of the organization might be the same as that of the individual. Put simply, individuals need membership in social entities in order to negotiate their way in a social world. As suggested by social identity and self-categorization theories, this group membership helps to reduce the uncertainty that the individual might feel, and it also helps the individual maintain a positive sense of self. Managers could view their task as one of helping individuals realize the benefits of goal congruence between the individual and the organization, generating commitment toward the organization. Therefore, working in the organization does not necessarily require subjugation of oneself and one's interests, but rather working in the organization makes the individual's identity more coherent and sustainable. We believe that control theorists can benefit from this understanding of the relationship between individuals and organizations.

Notes

1 In our arguments here we do not distinguish between the relational social self and the collective social self (Brewer and Gardner, 1996). We believe that social identity control is likely to be similar irrespective of whether the social identity is derived from an individual's relationships with significant others in the organization or from a more abstract notion of membership in the organization.

2 These four have been derived from the work in social identity theory and self-categorization theory but do not represent an exhaustive list of possible ways in which identity and control are related. Rather, they should be viewed as a starting point in incorporating ideas from identity theories into the organizational control literature.

References

Alvesson, M. and Willmott, H. 2002. Identity regulation as organizational control: producing the appropriate individual. *Journal of Management Studies*, 39: 619–644.

Anteby, M. 2008. Identity incentives as an engaging form of control: revisiting leniencies in an aeronautic plant. *Organization Science*, 19: 202–220.

Ashford, S. and Black, S. 1996. Proactivity during organizational entry: the role of desire for control. *Journal of Applied Psychology*, 81: 191–214.

Ashforth, B. E. and Johnson, S. A. 2001. What hat to wear? The relative salience of multiple identities in organizational contexts. In M. A. Hogg and D. J. Terry (eds.), *Social identity processes in organizational contexts*: 31–48. Philadelphia, PA: Psychology Press.

Ashforth, B. E. and Mael, F. 1989. Social identity theory and the organization. *Academy of Management Review*, 14: 20–39.

Ashforth, B. E. and Saks, A. 1996. Socialization tactics: longitudinal effects on newcomer adjustment. *Academy of Management Journal,* 39: 149–178.

Avant, J. 2007. *Fortune magazine names parent-friendly Google as best employer.* See www.babble.com/CS/blogs/strollerderby/archive/2007/01/13.

Barker, J. R. and Tomkins, P. K. 1994. Identification in the self-managing organization: characteristics of target and tenure. *Human Communication Research,* 21: 223–240.

Bartel, C. and Dutton, J. 2001. Ambiguous organizational memberships: constructing organizational identities in interactions with others. In M. A. Hogg and D. J. Terry (eds.), *Social identity processes in organizational contexts:* 115–130. Philadelphia, PA: Psychology Press.

Blau, P. R. and Scott, R. 1962. *Formal organizations: a comparative approach.* San Francisco, CA: Chandler Publishing Company.

Brewer, M. B. and Chen, Y. 2007. Where (who) are collectives in collectivism? Toward conceptual clarification of individualism and collectivism. *Psychological Review,* 114: 133–151.

Brewer, M. B. and Gardner, W. 1996. Who is this "we"? Levels of collective identity and self-representations. *Journal of Personality and Social Psychology,* 71: 83–93.

Cardinal, L. B. 2001. Technological innovation in the pharmaceutical industry: the use of organizational control in managing research and development. *Organization Science,* 12: 19–36.

Cardinal, L. B., Sitkin, S. B., and Long, C. P. 2004. Balancing and rebalancing in the creation and evolution of organizational control. *Organization Science,* 15: 411–431.

Chatman, J. A., Polzer, J. T., Barsade, S. G., and Neale, M. A. 1998. Being different yet feeling similar: the influence of demographic composition and organizational culture on work processes and outcomes. *Administrative Science Quarterly,* 43: 749–780.

Chattopadhyay, P., George, E., and Lawrence, S. 2004. Why does dissimilarity matter? Exploring self-categorization, self-enhancement and uncertainty reduction. *Journal of Applied Psychology,* 89: 892–900.

Chattopadhyay, P., Tluchowska, M., and George, E. 2004. Identifying the in-group: a closer look at the influence of demographic dissimilarity on employee social identity. *Academy of Management Review,* 29: 180–202.

Cinnirella, M. 1997. Towards a European identity? Interactions between the national and European social identities manifested by university students in Britain and Italy. *British Journal of Social Psychology,* 36: 19–31.

Dalrymple, W. 2002. *White Mughals*. New Delhi, India: Penguin Books.

Doise, W. 1988. Individual and social identities in intergroup relations. *European Journal of Social Psychology*, 18: 99–111.

Dutton, J. E., Dukerich, J. M., and Harquail, C. V. 1994. Organizational images and member identification. *Administrative Science Quarterly*, 39: 239–263.

Eisenhardt, K. M. 1985. Control: organizational and economic approaches. *Management Science*, 31: 134–149.

Ellemers, N., Kortekaas, P., and Ouwerkerk, J. W. 1999. Self-categorization, commitment to the group and group self-esteem as related but distinct aspects of social identity. *European Journal of Social Psychology*, 29: 371–389.

Erez, M. and Earley, P. C. 1993. *Culture, self-identity and work*. Oxford, UK: Oxford University Press.

Etzioni, A. 1961. *A comparative analysis of complex organizations: on power, involvement, and their correlates*. New York, NY: Free Press.

Flamholtz, E. G., Das, T. K., and Tsui, A. S. 1985. Toward an integrative framework of organizational control. *Accounting, Organizations and Society*, 10: 35–50.

George, E. and Chattopadhyay, P. 2005. One foot in each camp: the dual identification of contract workers. *Administrative Science Quarterly*, 50: 68–99.

Govindarajan, V. and Fisher, J. 1990. Strategy, control systems, and resource sharing: effects on business-unit performance. *Academy of Management Journal*, 33: 259–285.

Haslam, S. A. 2001. *Psychology in organizations: the social identity approach*. Thousand Oaks, CA: Sage.

Hogg, M. A. and Terry, D. J. 2000. Social identity and self-categorization processes in organizational contexts. *Academy of Management Review*, 25: 121–140.

Hornsey, M. J. and Hogg, M. A. 2000. Assimilation and diversity: an integrative model of subgroup relations. *Personality and Social Psychology Review*, 4: 143–156.

Iyer, V., Bamber, E., and Barefield, R. 1997. Identification of accounting firm alumni with their former firms: antecedents and outcomes. *Accounting, Organizations and Society*, 22: 315–336.

Jaworski, B. J. 1988. Toward a theory of marketing control: environmental context, control types, and consequences. *Journal of Marketing*, 52: 23–39.

Kirsch, L. J. 1996. The management of complex tasks in organizations: controlling the systems development process. *Organization Science*, 7: 1–21.

Kreiner, G. and Ashforth, B. E. 2004. Evidence toward an expanded model of organizational identification. *Journal of Organizational Behavior,* 25: 1–27.

Long, K. and Spears, R. 1997. The self-esteem hypothesis revisited: differentiation and the disaffected. In R. Spears, P. J. Oakes, N. Ellemers, and S. A. Haslam (eds.), *The social psychology of stereotyping and group life:* 296–317. Oxford, UK: Blackwell.

Mael, F. and Ashforth, B. E. 1992. Alumni and their alma mater: a partial test of the reformulated model of organizational identification. *Journal of Organizational Behavior,* 13: 103–123.

March, J. and Weil, T. 2005. *On leadership.* Oxford, UK: Blackwell.

Mlicki, P. and Ellemers, N. 1996. Being different or being better? National stereotypes and identifications of Polish and Dutch students. *European Journal of Social Psychology,* 26: 97–114.

Osland, J. S. 1995. Working abroad: a hero's adventure. *Training and Development,* 49: 47–51.

Ouchi, W. G. 1977. The relationship between organizational structure and organizational control. *Administrative Science Quarterly,* 22: 95–113.

1979. A conceptual framework for the design of organizational control mechanisms. *Management Science,* 25: 833–848.

1980. Markets, bureaucracies, and clans. *Administrative Science Quarterly,* 25: 129–141.

Ouchi, W. G. and Johnson, J. B. 1978. Types of organizational control and their relationship to emotional well being. *Administrative Science Quarterly,* 23: 293–317.

Polzer, J. T., Milton, L. P., and Swann, W. B. Jr. 2002. Capitalizing on diversity: interpersonal congruence in small work groups. *Administrative Science Quarterly,* 47: 296–324.

Pratt, M. G. 1998. To be or not to be: central questions in organizational identification. In D. Whetten and P. Godfrey (eds.), *Identity in organizations: building theory through conversations:* 171–207. Thousand Oaks, CA: Sage.

Reade, C. 2001. Antecedents of organizational identification in multinational corporations: fostering psychological attachment to the local subsidiary and the global organization. *International Journal of Human Resource Management,* 12: 1,269–1,291.

Scott, C. R. 1997. Identification with multiple targets in a geographically dispersed organization. *Management Communication Quarterly,* 10: 491–522.

Scott, C. R., Corman, S. R., and Cheney, G. 1998. Development of a structurational model of identification in the organization. *Communication Theory,* 8: 298–336.

Sitkin, S. B. and Lind, E. A. 2006. *The six domains of leadership: a new model for developing and assessing leadership qualities.* Carrboro, NC: Delta Leadership Inc.

Sitkin, S. B. and Sutcliffe, K. M. 1991. Dispensing legitimacy: the influence of professional, organizational, and legal controls on pharmacists' behavior. *Research in Sociology of Organizations,* 8: 269–295.

Snell, S. A. 1992. Control theory in strategic human resource management: the mediating effect of administrative information. *Academy of Management Journal,* 35: 292–327.

Steele, C. 1988. The psychology of self-affirmation: sustaining the integrity of the self. In L. Berkowitz (ed.), *Advances in experimental social psychology,* 21: 261–302. New York, NY: Academic Press.

Tajfel, H. and Turner, J. C. 1986. The social identity theory of intergroup behavior. In S. Worchel and W. G. Austin (eds.), *Psychology of intergroup relations* (2nd edn.): 7–24. Chicago, IL: Nelson-Hall.

Turner, J. C. 1987. *Rediscovering the social group: a self-categorisation theory.* Oxford, UK: Blackwell.

Van Knippenberg, D. and Van Schie, E. C. M. 2000. Foci and correlates of organizational identification. *Journal of Occupational and Organizational Psychology,* 73: 137–147.

Van Knippenberg, D., Van Knippenberg, B., Cremer, D. D., and Hogg, M. A. 2004. Leadership, self, and identity: a review and research agenda. *The Leadership Quarterly,* 15: 825–856.

Weinreich, P. 1986. The operationalism of identity theory in racial and ethnic relations. In J. Rex (ed.), *Theories of race and ethnic relations:* 299–320. Cambridge, UK: Cambridge University Press.

Wenzel, M. 2000. Justice and identity: the significance of inclusion for perceptions of entitlement and the justice motive. *Personality and Social Psychology Bulletin,* 26: 157–176.

Williams, K. Y. and O'Reilly, III. C. A. 1998. Demography and diversity in organizations: a review of 40 years of research. In B. M. Staw and L. L. Cummings (eds.), *Research in organizational behavior,* 20: 77–140. Greenwich, CT: JAI Press.

7 | Attention and control

WILLIAM OCASIO AND
FRANZ WOHLGEZOGEN
Northwestern University

Many an exasperated parent, trying to get a fidgety child to listen and follow instructions, has utilized the phrase "pay attention" with a big exclamation mark at the end. Coaches, teachers, and mentors, willing their hopefuls to realize their full potential and to forsake distractions and temptations (and to make their guardians proud), implore them to "focus, focus, focus ..." Attempts to influence and control others' behavior work through attention. If individuals' attention is not directed at what needs to be done, chances are very low that it will ever get done.

What is true for the interpersonal context holds true for the organizational context: the structuring and management of attention is central to control processes in organizations. An organization must succeed at directing members' minds or it never will manage to direct their actions. Many definitions of organizational control implicitly or explicitly stress the role of cognitive processes and especially attention.

For example, control has been characterized as "measurement and control systems [which] focus attention and cause persons in the organization to orient their efforts to succeeding on the measured dimension" (Pfeffer, 1982: 131); and have more recently been defined as "any mechanism that managers use to direct attention, motivate, and energize organizational members to act in desired ways to meet an organization's objectives" (Long et al., 2003).

Although it appears that it is true by definition that controls affect attention, it is important to examine in detail *how* different types of control affect attention in different ways. Despite their overlapping focus, theories of attention and theories of control have been developed separately. In this chapter we strive toward and argue for a stronger connection between the two literatures. We suggest that bringing together attention and control allows us to explicate some fundamental cognitive effects and deficiencies of different types of controls, and this also provides us with a valuable theoretical lens that can be used to enrich empirical designs.

In this chapter we briefly review the organizational literature on attention and differentiate five control mechanisms in organizations that influence attention: *hierarchal controls, outcome controls, behavioral controls, cultural controls,* and *channels.* For each of the five control types, we explicate the attentional mechanisms, and the effects and drawbacks. We conclude with an evaluation of the attention-based view of organizational control and some suggestions for further research.

Attention basics

What is attention?

Attention is one of the most fundamental tasks of the brain, one that is crucial for the performance of other cognitive tasks. Although the term seems self-explanatory, over the years psychologists have proposed various conceptualizations of attention (Moray, 1967; Posner and Rothbart, 2007; Swets and Kristofferson, 1970), submerging numerous mental processes under the term. Three processes appear most consistently in the literature: selection, vigilance, and regulation – the what, how, and when of attention. Selective attention, the process that has received most research, describes choosing to notice a particular external stimulus; due to its computational limitations, the human brain cannot process all external stimuli simultaneously and thus has to choose which external stimuli to attend to and which to screen out. The selection mechanism is important so that a person can act coherently when faced with competing and distracting sources of stimuli. The selective nature of attention necessitates a trade-off regarding the allocation of attention (Kinchla, 1992), resulting in better processing of one stimulus and worse processing of others. In short, selective attention determines *what* is being attended to: a high degree of selectivity narrows the range of issues that could be attended to, a low degree of selectivity makes a broader range of issues available to be focused upon. Attentional vigilance describes the capacity of an individual to sustain concentration on a particular stimulus (e.g., waiting for a particular signal to occur or change). Empirical evidence suggests that with "attentionally" taxing tasks, sustained attention is limited in duration and an individual's probability to detect the stimuli decreases over time (Swets and

Kristofferson, 1970). We can see this as a matter of degree, of *how* attentive an actor is toward a stimulus: during periods of sustained attention, attention toward a stimulus is high, when sustained attention can no longer be maintained, attention is low.

Current neuroscience adds a third – and so far least well understood – attentional process: the ability to deal with interruptions (Parasurman, 1998). This function relates to memory and planning components of the mind, which are essential for the development of skill and maintenance of efficient task performance. This third process enables us to process multiple targets quasi-simultaneously, by switching back and forth between different stimuli. We call this process attentional regulation.[1] Vigilance and regulation can be seen as supplementary forces: the former allows individuals to attach their attention firmly and without interruption to a particular stimulus (for a limited period of time), the latter allows individuals to detach their attention from that stimulus, reallocate it to a different stimulus, and then come back to the first. Effective decision-making in organizations would be impossible if one or the other of these two forces were missing. Attentional regulation is essentially about timing and sequencing, about when a stimulus is attended to: high regulation allows actors to freely attach, detach, and reattach attention to a stimulus, low regulation means less freedom to detach and reattach. We see a natural trade-off between vigilance and regulation: an actor cannot sustain attention firmly on a stimulus and at the same time flexibly switch back and forth between stimuli.

Attention-based theories in organizational theory

Carnegie school scholars Simon, Cyert, and March were the first organizational theorists to recognize and theoretically explore the importance of attention in organizations. Simon's now widely cited and employed model of bounded rationality follows from the attentional limitations of the human brain, the necessity to be selective in the allocation of attention (1957). Given this limitation, Simon sees one of the primary functions of organizations in influencing individual decision processes by allocating and distributing the stimuli that shape actors' attention. In short, Simon saw the organizational structure to influence decision-making by shaping actors' attention.

Subsequent research in the Carnegie school tradition highlighted the impact of routines on attention (March and Simon, 1958); how the process of sequential rather than simultaneous attention can help resolve conflict; how organizational learning can lead to a revision of attention rules (Cyert and March, 1963); and that the allocation of attention is a rational act (March and Olsen, 1976). Further, the "garbage can" decision process points to the possibility that attention can not only be directed by tightly coupled organizational structures, but also by the loose coupling of decision-makers, issues, pre-existing answers, and decision-making opportunities (Cohen *et al.*, 1972; March and Olsen, 1976).

Ocasio's attention-based view of the firm (Ocasio, 1997) builds on the Carnegie school's research and combines it with insights from social psychological research about attentional processes to build a comprehensive model of organizational decision-making that builds on three inter-related premises: (a) actors' decision-making depends on which issues and answers they focus their attention on; (b) what they focus their attention on depends on the situational influences they are subjected to; and (c) the situational influences they are subjected to depend on how the organization's resources, rules, and relationships are coming together to shape specific communication and decision-making channels.

In subsequent research, Ocasio and Joseph (2006) have gone beyond the influence of the individual communication or decision-making channel, and have instead elaborated on the impact of networks of coupled channels, different network structures, and different degrees of coupling between channels. They show that a tight coupling of specialized cross-level channels enables the development of corporate capabilities.

Many recent publications have invoked attention-based explanations for a wide range of issues, such as performance effects of particular strategies (Chakrabarti *et al.*, 2007), strategic choice (Hung, 2005), strategic change (Cho and Hambrick, 2006), firm innovativeness (Yadav *et al.*, 2007), challenges in post-merger integration processes (Yu *et al.*, 2005), and firms' differential forecasting abilities (Durand, 2003), to name but a few. However, despite this wide application of the perspective, only little theoretical progress has been made to *deepen* our understanding of organizational attention and its consequences. One of the few notable exceptions to the rule is the research by Barnett on real options in strategic management (2003; 2005). Reminding us of the actors' attentional limitations, he successfully shows how the use of real options can affect actors' commitment, effectiveness of coordination, and external legitimacy of the organization.

Given the natural affinity between the control literature and the attention-based view of the firm, we are optimistic that a closer examination of the attentional effects of different controls and control configurations will advance our understanding of organizational control and organizational attention.

Five ways to control attention

There are many ways in which control can be conceptualized and differentiated (Cardinal *et al.*, 2004; Ouchi, 1979; Pfeffer, 1998; Schreyogg and Steinmann, 1987). Our purpose in this chapter is to point out how different types of control affect attention processes in different ways, and how this, in turn, directs actors' decision-making and behavior toward the organization's goals. In line with our goal of stimulating the control literature to consider and incorporate an attention-based view, we opt for breadth rather than depth, to reveal how a wide and diverse range of control types influence attention. Thus, we discuss both regulative controls – the explicit and enforced rules, systems, and directives, directly conceived for and aimed at particular control objectives – and normative/cognitive controls – the social and cultural arrangements that legitimate and make salient particular values, beliefs, and practices to a social group and thus influence decisions and behavior indirectly.

In addition we differentiate structural and situational controls. We see structural controls as overarching and pervasive systems, those that are not explicitly limited to particular issues or contexts. Such controls are global, in the sense that they may influence all decision-making opportunities, even those that are additionally guided by more concrete and situational controls. Their influence, though, is through relatively abstract and general constraints, which leave the actor a significant amount of agency in figuring out how to translate these high-level guidelines into actionable rules for a concrete situation. As situational controls we understand those controls that are explicitly tied to a particular decision-making opportunity. They are invoked as a result of a particular event, and provide more detailed directions for decision-making and behavior for a particular situation, leaving less agency and room for interpretation to the actor.

Given these two dimensions, we differentiate five categories of control mechanisms for this chapter: *hierarchical controls, outcome controls, cultural controls, behavioral controls*, and *channels*. Though the first four control mechanisms are commonly studied in the control literature, channels have received less attention. We define *channels* here as anticipated formal opportunities for communication. They shape individuals' cognition and behavior by establishing a momentary temporal and spatial context in which communication takes place, and determine participants and resources for interaction. Channels make particular stimuli and decision-making patterns salient without prescribing them explicitly.

We use each of the five categories to discuss distinct types of influence on the attention of those actors who are being controlled. Hierarchical, outcome, and channel controls primarily have an impact on attentional regulation. They serve as intermittent reminders, directing and redirecting distracted actors' attention back toward organizational goals. Behavioral and cultural controls affect actors' selective attention: they influence which stimuli an actor is more likely to attend to. These "selection rules" tend to be more pervasive and restrictive than the attention regulation patterns influenced by hierarchical and channel controls, which allow a degree of flexibility. Outcome controls can affect both attentional selection and regulation. Behavioral and channel controls primarily have an impact on actors' attentional vigilance. These control mechanisms determine actors' allocation of attentional resources for a limited period, but ensure that attention is sustained during that period. Actors' attention will be more strongly shaped than with structural, global controls. We will show that behavioral and channel controls thus can structure and automate attentional processes and – in the case of channel controls – allow for directed yet relatively unstructured communication and interaction and the emergence of issues and answers in the organization.

We do not see the five categories of control mechanisms as mutually exclusive. In fact, we expect that a combination of all five is at work in most if not all organizations, though with different relative elaboration and weight of each category. In this chapter we remain largely agnostic to the questions of whether these mechanisms are purposely and deliberately designed and combined by organizational members (Cardinal *et al.*, 2004); to which degree these choices are influenced by the wider social context and by an organization's history; or whether

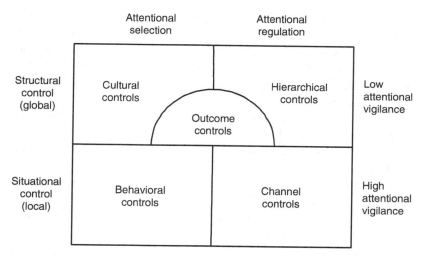

Figure 7.1 Framework for control categories and attention processes

the mechanisms and their combination emerge over time, without a "grand design" or a "chief architect" ensuring consistency or compatibility. We also attempt to refrain from taking either a too instrumentalist or too critical perspective on control and attention. Instead we try to present a balanced account that provides food for thought and points of departure for both camps.

Control types and attention processes

Hierarchical controls: attentional regulation

Some of the earliest work on organization theory relates to the use of organizational structures – the network of member roles and relationships, and rules and procedures – to realize organizational control. Weber's (1978 [1928]) conceptualization of bureaucracy details how a fixed structure of clearly specified roles or offices, connected through official, explicit rules, creates an organizational hierarchy of formal, rational-legal authority. The role definitions and rules create fixed divisions of labor, clear reporting and supervisory relationships between offices, and clear performance criteria. Bound by official rules, individual actors are assigned particular responsibilities and decision-making rights. Within the established boundaries of their authority they can exercise discretion in order to reach their performance goals. In this early formulation of hierarchies we find all the elements that are relevant for a structural control of attention: (a) roles, with their specific decision-making rights and responsibilities or goals; (b) the relations between roles; and (c) rules and procedures that guide actors' behavior and decision-making.

The differentiation of roles and their rights and responsibilities is a prerequisite step to achieve and coordinate the division of labor in organizations. But the definition of roles does not only distribute tasks to allow actors to focus their efforts and specialize, it also distributes and focuses attention to accommodate actors' attentional limitations (Ocasio, 1997; Simon, 1957). These limitations constrain the range of external stimuli actors can process, the range of decision alternatives they can conceive of, and the range of consequences of their actions they can foresee.

Roles address these limitations by scoping out responsibilities and by specifying decision-making rights. Responsibilities and decision-making rights limit issues, responses, and consequences an actor has to attend to: an actor will screen out those stimuli which are outside of his responsibilities; he will generally ignore those responses he cannot implement or trigger given his decision-making rights, which are not considered conducive to fulfill his immediate responsibilities; and he will consider only the consequences of actions or inactions that affect his realm of responsibility. Responsibilities are often made explicit and concrete by specifying particular outcomes an actor has to ascertain as we will discuss in the next section. But, in addition to assigning sets of issues and responses to particular actors, responsibilities also structure the relations between actors.

Effectively, role-specific responsibilities take the total of all issues deemed relevant and critical to the achievement of the organization's objectives, cluster them into manageable sets, and distribute them among organizational members. The clustering could follow a functional, a geographic, a product-related, or a customer-related logic. By specifying priorities, responsibilities also communicate which issues an actor can legitimately ignore and refuse responsibility for, thus freeing up attentional resources (for a more detailed discussion of the role of "plausible deniability" see Browning and Folger, 1994). Although this is a necessary flip side to selective focus, it is a root cause for interrole and interunit coordination difficulties and silo thinking. Some have pointed out that the strict adherence to prescribed attentional blinkers can give rise to significant organizational pathologies, that is, immoral or unethical behavior (Bakan, 2004). Extreme consequences are suggested by Arendt's account of the "banality of evil" (1965), exemplified by Nazi administrator Adolph Eichmann's court testimony that he bore no responsibility and was simply "doing his job."

Specific role prescriptions notwithstanding, hierarchies also impact actors' attention by stratification (i.e., by demarcating peers, superiors, and subordinates). Peers and superiors exert subtle and not-so-subtle pressures for conformity and may sanction non-conforming behavior – essentially normative effects (see Loughry (Chapter 11) for a thorough review of direct and indirect control exerted by peers and superiors). But cognitively they provide domains which are attended with priority. An actor will be more attentive to his peers', immediate superiors', and subordinates' activities, utterances, and attitudes than to other actors because they are both more available and more directly consequential to the actor. These stimuli from an actor's domain are unlikely to captivate his attention for sustained stretches of time (only pathological employees will fix their attention on a colleague or a superior and wait for an extended period for some kind of signal and do nothing else in the meantime). Instead, stimuli are most often attended to in a flexible, cursory fashion, with actors jumping from stimulus to stimulus: listening to a co-worker spreading rumors, watching the boss from the corner of one's eye, quickly breathing down the neck of a subordinate, and then focusing back on the task at hand. This interrole influence produces a degree of intragroup stability, consistency of behavior, and coordination, but it can also lead to tensions, communication lags, and coordination problems between units and between levels in the hierarchy.

In order to address coordination challenges many organizations utilize multiple, crisscrossing structures (e.g., line and staff reporting relations, project teams, communities, committees, etc.). Such multi-layered structures can cure some attention-related control problems, such as myopic attentional focus, silo thinking, and control loss through layers of hierarchy (Williamson, 1970). Since multi-layered structures place multiple requirements on actors embedded in them, they offer the opportunity for greater control from different directions and multiple pathways (Evans, 1975), but they also harbor the potential for conflict by asking actors to attend to multiple sets of issues more or less simultaneously and may thus overstretch actors' attentional capabilities and compromise their ability to sustain attention on any one issue properly.

Outcome controls: attentional regulation and selection

As discussed above, responsibilities constitute a limited set of issues an actor has to attend to with priority. In that sense, responsibilities can be viewed as codified role expectations, set to compel an actor to ensure attainment of a particular outcome (e.g., a customer relations role's responsibility to ensure customer satisfaction) or the prevention of one (e.g., a legal council's responsibility to steer the company clear of litigation and prevent legal liabilities). A special case of *explicit and codified* role expectations that has received significant scholarly attention is the case of outcome controls, such as goals, objectives, budgets, or deliverables for employees' work (Cardinal, 2001; Eisenhardt, 1985; Thompson, 1967). Outcome controls translate responsibilities into a more concrete and traceable form. They work as a yardstick to judge progress or success and as a reminder to redirect attention after distraction and interruptions. To be effective, outcome controls usually rely on the use of incentives or sanctions that are clearly aligned with a desired outcome or level of effort.

Most important, outcome controls do not specify the processes or behavior to achieve the desired outcomes. Thus, outcome controls allow actors to choose a course of action toward a set goal that best leverages their individual knowledge and skills. However, this can also lead to dysfunctional behavior and "strategic inattention," which can put an organization's survival in jeopardy and – in some cases – its directors in jail. For example, research suggests that goals direct attention toward issues and answers that lead to immediate payoffs, at the (in many cases foreseeable) expense of long-term results (John and Weitz, 1989; Smyth, 1968). Ridgeway (1956) noted early that it is highly consequential how goals are formulated: if the number of shoes are set as the only production goal in a factory, only small shoes will get produced; if the production goal of screws is formulated in terms of tons, only large, heavy screws will be produced. In extreme cases, the relentless pursuit of a goal can lead to the disregard of ethical and legal standards – Enron's and WorldCom's shareholder "value creation" by all legal and illegal means come to mind as vivid examples.

From an attention perspective, outcome controls have an intriguing double effect. On the one hand, their explicit specification of expectations can have a powerful, regulative effect for behavior and decision-making, bringing attention back to focus on the goal or objective *on occasion*. A particular goal or objective may not be ever-present to an individual, and may not pervasively and consistently influence all behavior and decisions. But it will serve as a reminder and as a compass to guide future decisions and action. It will prompt an individual to review past decisions and judge whether they have contributed toward reaching the goal, and allow a realignment of strategies for future decisions. This routine of "review and realignment" may occur periodically, either externally prompted (e.g., by a status update request) or internally motivated (prudent or anxious introspection before an external review). When this routine fails to occur periodically, the outcome control ceases to be effective.

On the other hand, outcome controls have a normative effect because expressed goals often contain an evaluative dimension. Goals are usually set not just because they are expedient, but because they are important to the organization. As such, goals and objectives may express, and allow the monitoring of compliance with, values and ideals that are relevant beyond the specific control target for which they are set. They become intertwined with the larger culture of the organization – not just in the sense of becoming infused with values (over time), but also in the sense of enforcing and codifying culture. The attentional effect is very different from the regulative dimension: goals do not function as a compass instrument that is occasionally consulted, but as a moral compass that operates constantly. When the normative effect is strong, goals can have a pervasive, even subconscious effect on behavior and decision-making by shaping attentional selection (i.e., what issues are attended to with priority and which are considered secondary and expendable). Companies like Wal-Mart and Dell, for example, have successfully implanted the goal of lowering cost in their employees' minds so that cost reductions have become not merely an issue that is attended to during special meetings or designated initiatives, but *the standard* against which (almost) all activities and decisions are judged. As a result of this selective attention, other considerations, for example, issues of product and service quality, or the organizations' and brands' image, have not been attended to sufficiently.

Attentionally, output controls are especially important for larger, differentiated organizations because they provide easily interpretable signals to the entire organization and thus can potentially impact the attention of the entire organization. Standardized, widely shared outcomes allow even those not directly involved in or close to the decision-making processes to interpret specific events, make comparisons across time and units, and generally take a quick reading on the status of the organizations. These signals allow for coordination across units (Gittel, 2000; Ouchi, 1978) and adjustment of attentional priorities (Cyert and March, 1963).

Cultural controls: attentional selectivity

As a counterpoint to rational, technological, and structural–functionalist perspectives on organizations, a broad literature evolved that emphasizes the symbolic aspects of organizations and management, and the role of value and belief systems in shaping action and decision-making in organizations (Smircich, 1983).[2] However, the concrete mechanisms by which culture influences individual actors' behavior are disputed by sociologists and cultural theorists. A major division in the debate concerns the question of whether culture provides individuals with a unified and unifying set of values and ultimate ends to guide behavior, or whether it provides the tools and means as fuel for behavior (Swidler, 1986). We remain impartial to this debate and merely wish to point out the different attentional effects of both mechanisms.

The *values view* of culture is prominently represented by Weber's conceptualization of historically constructed ideas (Weber, 1948 [1916]) and Parsons' (1937) abstract and general values that are immanent in social systems. Both see culture providing the end(s) toward which we strive; thus culture shapes action by defining what people want. According to Parsons, culture serves as a standard for selecting among open alternatives in a given situation (Parsons and Shils, 1951). Closely tied to this view of culture is the idea that culture is diffused within a group by socialization processes (Pfeffer, 1998; Van Maanen, 1975). Actors absorb values and criteria for legitimate behavior by observation and imitation, or by instruction through "orientation trainings," folklore, and so forth (Kreps, 1986). The culturally assimilated then share a common identity given their shared values, and a commitment to something larger than themselves (Gioia and Chittipeddi, 1991; Peters and Waterman, 1984; Siehl and Martin, 1981).

Taking the view of culture as supplying or supporting the ends not the means, we can see culture as the "normative glue" (Smircich, 1983) that holds an organization together by providing values, ideals, and beliefs that members share (Louis, 1983; Schein, 1983; Van Maanen, 1991). Manifested in mission or vision statements, stories, and language, these values, ideals and beliefs can become points of identification (Deal and Kennedy, 1982; Peters and Waterman, 1984) and orientation. Actors who identify with the organization's overall culture thus find a common ground and a basis for communication and decision-making because they share some unquestioned and often unquestionable assumptions about the purpose and priorities of the organization.

This can work as a perceptual filter: actors who assimilated the organizational culture (subconsciously) translate the values and ideals into rules on how to allocate their attention. However, the translation from values and ideals into attention rules is hardly precise, and depends to a large degree on the actor's interpretation of the cultural elements. Even if actors converge in their interpretation, due to thorough socialization or detailed codification of cultural elements in the organization, culture is best thought of as providing a somewhat fuzzy boundary between relevant and irrelevant issues, and legitimate and illegitimate solutions. While culture does narrow the scope of actors' attention, it mostly does not predictably pinpoint particular issues or solutions as goals or processes would.

Even though the pervasive but fuzzy impact of culture on attention can be seen as a weakness of cultural controls, since it might fail to *unambiguously* direct actors' attention toward the fulfillment of organizational goals, it is also a strength. Because values, ideals, and beliefs provide rather general and broad directions, they become essential in situations where more precise forms of control provide conflicting and contradictory cues. Cultural controls may help by providing overarching priorities and principles by which more particular conflicts can be resolved. Thus values, ideals, and beliefs help actors to disentangle themselves from the thorny problems of the particular and refocus their attention on the "real" or "ultimate" ends to find a way toward a solution that not only resolves the immediate conflict but also ensures consistency across decision-making situations and congruence with the organization's cultural priorities.

So far we have focused on culture's impact on an actor's own internal attention processes. But in strong cultures, the impact of values, ideals, and beliefs goes beyond filtering and directing actors' cognition and behavior: it can compel actors to actively direct and police other actors' behavior to ensure cultural conformity. Thus, culture increases actors' attentional alertness to cultural deviation and motivates sanctioning of deviant behavior. This links to Ouchi's concept of clan control (1979): to achieve goal congruence organizational members are not only inspired to be loyal to the clan but also to actively monitor each other's loyalty. However, overzealous cultural enforcement can have negative consequences: it can lead to rigidity and cultural stagnation and to fear of engaging in and "using" the culture in novel ways for fear of being considered deviant and being policed. Such a "political correctness paranoia" wastes attentional resources and narrows perception unnecessarily.

One drawback of the values perspective on culture, as Swidler (1986) argues, is its overemphasis on the unit act, its assumption that values dictate the ends and organizational actors calculate piece by piece which means will be conducive to reaching these ends. This would require rational means/ends calculations for every action, which is unrealistically taxing on actors. Instead, actions may be integrated into "larger assemblages," so-called "strategies of action" (Swidler, 1986: 276), or logics (Fligstein, 1990; Thornton and Ocasio, 1999). Cultural artifacts, such as habits, sensibilities, and worldviews, become the raw material with which such strategies of action are constructed.

From a *logics view* of culture, cultural artifacts are appropriated and strategically employed within the constraints of the overall cultural logic rather than sacred fixtures that are obediently followed. The emphasis here is less on cultural ideas (values, ideals, and beliefs) and more on cultural practices: language, gossip, stories and myths, and rituals and worldviews. Through these practices actors share modes of behavior and outlook (Hannerz, 1969), rather than goals and values. Identity – from this perspective – is based on "what we do" and "how we do things around here" rather than the "beliefs we hold" (see also George and Qian [Chapter 6] for a discussion on the motivating and controlling effects of such activity-based identity conceptions).

Cognitively, logics provide schemata and categories that function as perceptual templates by providing "default assumptions about [objects'] characteristics, relationships, and entailments under conditions of incomplete information" (DiMaggio, 1997: 269). Logics help to simplify cognition and behavior; they allow actors to take cognitive shortcuts to increase cognitive efficiency at the expense of accuracy. In the extreme case they allow automatic attentional processing. The disadvantage of logics (or schemata, categories) is that they can become a "hammer looking for nails," that is, they can lead to misclassification of events, inappropriate responses, or inaccurate recall, if information or a stimulus is perceived as schema consistent and thus processed without much scrutiny (Fiske and Linville, 1980).

The attentional effect is that issues or solutions that do not fit a particular schema may be either ignored or misclassified, and are thus effectively unavailable for decision-making. Unexpected and novel external stimuli may go unnoticed or may be misinterpreted and misfiled into existing categories. Novel solutions may remain inconceivable or may be conceived as illegitimate if they require elements or tools that the organizational culture does not supply or condone. In that sense, logics work as a cognitive filter: for a given decision they remind the actor what issues or solutions the organizational culture deems relevant and legitimate. We see the effect of this evaluation as equivalent to that of outcome controls: they, too, provide a yardstick for evaluating choices. In the case of cultural controls this yardstick is implicit and normative, in the case of outcome controls it is explicit and regulative.

Despite the many possible pathways of influence culture may have on actors' attentional processes, we must be cautious not to overstate how strong this influence is and how pervasively it affects all organizational members – especially in large, differentiated, decentralized organizations. Long ago, sociologists suggested that in more populous and heterogeneous groups, culture's effectiveness of compelling group members to honor group norms and sanction norm breaking may decrease (Wirth, 1940). Thus, we have to expect that overarching organizational cultures may fail to sufficiently direct the attention of actors in large differentiated organizations. The lack of effectiveness of an overarching organizational culture does not mean that there is a cultural vacuum. On the contrary, most organizations are host to many different sub- and counter-cultures with varying degrees of overlap (Hatch, 1997). These sub- and counter-cultures still have the described cognitive effects – they define local standards of appropriateness, relevance, rationality, etc. Such plurality can cumulatively reduce perceptual blind spots, but it also diminishes the unifying and attention-orientating effect of shared culture.

Behavioral controls: attentional selectivity and vigilance

One way to ensure that organizational actors pursue organizational goals, is to give them instruction on what to do to get there rather than trying to explain the overall goal of the journey (Cardinal, 2001; Ouchi, 1977). Instead of giving actors a map with marked points of departure and destination and letting them figure out how to get from A to B, it provides step-by-step or *ad hoc* driving directions: which highway signs to look for and when to take a left or a right. This can be achieved by (a) programming particular behavior through rules and procedures, and monitoring actors' adherence to these programs, or by (b) intervening and (re)directing actors' efforts in an *ad hoc* fashion. Both rely on systematic and close surveillance of actors' behavior. Both are inherently situational: (pre-)programmed behavior is prescribed for particular circumstances, and *ad hoc* interventions are triggered by a particular event. This also means that the behavioral rules have little to no direct influence on the actors outside of the specific situation for which they are intended.[3] This differentiates behavioral controls from hierarchical controls, outcome controls, and cultural controls, which we described as more "universally relevant" and shaping cognition, yet not continuously cognitively available. Behavioral controls are the reverse: they are only relevant for particular situations, yet when they are activated they produce sustained attention on specific issues and solutions and can push aside more global behavior prescriptions. This dominance of (even small) situational cues over general behavioral tendencies (in short, the power of the situation) has been the cornerstone of much experimental research in social psychology in the last decades (Lewin, 1951; Ross and Nisbett, 1994).

From the controlled actor's perspective, the impact of behavioral control on attention seems trivial. While rules and procedures can vary in detail – leaving different degrees of agency to the actor, but always less than hierarchical or output controls alone would – the impact on attention is the same regardless: they point out some or all issues to attend to, contingencies to watch out for, solutions to consider, and decision criteria to apply for choosing among these alternative solutions.

This takes the decision of how to allocate attentional resources partially or completely out of the actors' hands. Less or no deliberation on behalf of the actor is necessary to decide which external stimuli to process, or how to respond to them. A good example of highly detailed programming is food preparation in most restaurants: both the McDonald's employee stacking a Big Mac, and the cook at French Laundry preparing "Oysters and Pearls" do not ponder how to process and compose the ingredients, they follow the recipe as accurately as possible. The key here is that both processes, that is, preparing the burger and the fancy appetizer, require very different levels of manual skill, and even different levels of vigilance, but the allocation of the attentional resources is not flexibly controlled by the actor – as it would be if we merely defined a responsibility for burgers or fancy appetizers. With behavioral controls, the attentional processing is automatic: the actor knows exactly what signals to watch out for and how to respond to them, but he has to be vigilant for the duration of the process.

Standardized procedures, routines, and criteria – be they for physical activities or for decision-making (Sutcliffe and McNamara, 2001) – save attentional resources with regard to coordinating the interdependent activities. By limiting and making predictable each actors' performance outcomes (Cyert and March, 1963), standardized procedures enable actors to more easily coordinate behavior with others and thus ensure a consistent response. Additionally, the supervisor's task of monitoring and policing deviations from the program is also facilitated, given the template of expected behavior against which actual behavior can be compared.

Ad hoc interventions in actors' behavior, without prior programming, may also have an attention-economizing effect on the controlled actor. Imagine an actor working under supervision with the prospect of *ad hoc* intervention, faced with a complex task that involves an unmanageable number of or unknown contingencies, without a prescribed process or detailed objectives. The actor will attend and react to readily available external stimuli as he sees fit, but given the absence of actionable goals or behavioral prescriptions, and the presence of the supervisor, he may limit his search of important issues or optimal responses, because he may expect the supervisor to provide feedback and guidance. Stage actors improvising and looking for the director's or audience's response to their performance, or a masseuse reacting to a client's verbalizations of pain and pleasure, are examples of this control approach. The availability of feedback and guidance limits an actor's anxiety to miss important signals and his concerns about choosing the best possible response, since he will count on the supervisor to bring important missed signals to his attention and to prevent inappropriate action from being taken. For the supervisor, this approach can be attentionally taxing, since actors' behavior is basically unpredictable and there is not a clear standard against which it can be compared.

However, few organizational processes fall into either of these two extremes, complete programming and monitoring, or exclusively *ad hoc* intervention. Complete programming is often unattainable because not all contingencies that might occur and derail a standardized procedure can be predicted and tackled with a preconceived response (see, for example, the total quality controls processes in Sitkin *et al.*, 1994). Also, procedures accommodating too many contingencies can become too complex for actors to follow accurately and thus produce more errors and problems than they prevent. Exclusive reliance on *ad hoc* intervention is often unfeasible due to supervisors' limited attentional resources. If they are the *only* source for guidance, they have to attend all aspects of an actor's behavior in order to identify the need for intervention to bring the actor back on track toward the organization's goals. This is not feasible if supervisors have a wide span of control or complex processes to monitor.

Given these issues, most processes will involve some guidance through procedural constraints coupled with the possibility of *ad hoc* review, intervention, and deliberation at critical decision points. This strikes an attentional balance: it pre-structures processes as much as possible by defining decision points, response alternatives, and decision criteria where feasible, thus allowing automatic attentional processing and facilitated monitoring, and it still leaves room for intervention and deviation from the defined procedure, which requires controlled attentional processing. It also balances the attentional workload between the actor and the supervisor.

Compared to outcome control and hierarchical controls, behavioral controls allow a more responsive and intensive form of control. Unlike outcome controls, which need to ensure compatibility, behavior controls address local particularistic conditions (Ouchi, 1978) and thus avoid the ambiguity that universal output controls can create. Since supervisors can assess and react to actors' behavior continuously rather than having to wait for an outcome to make an assessment and formulate a response, deviation from organizational goals can be detected earlier, and can be remedied more quickly. However, there are two disadvantages. One is the potential subjectivity of supervisors' evaluations of actors' behaviors (and thus subjective interventions may or may not help to steer actors behavior toward organizational goals). The second drawback is the aforementioned significant amount of supervisors' attention (especially for complex behavior-based systems) that is being consumed.

Channel controls: attentional regulation and vigilance

Channels are defined above as anticipated formal opportunities for communication; they rely on similar normative and cognitive mechanisms as does culture, but more directly address and shape the situational circumstances to influence actors' attention processes. The cultural view of organizational control usually assumes that the influence of culture (or of a subculture) is consistent across situations and contexts. In other words: an actor's cultural imprint is assumed to always be with him and thus the same set of values or practices are assumed to bear on his choices and actions in different situations. However, half a century of social psychological research contradicts this view (Lewin, 1951; Ocasio, 1997; Ross and Nisbett, 1994).

If we leave the view of culture as a monolithic block behind and instead take the view of culture as fragmented and the actor as standing at the intersection of many different cultures (departmental, professional, national, company, industry, etc.) then we must assume that depending on the specific situation very different normative elements will become activated (DiMaggio, 1997). In other words: the actor's decision about which logics to follow and which schema and scripts to apply will be strongly influenced by the circumstances of a particular situation. This significantly loosens the perceptually constraining effect of "one strong culture."

Researchers increasingly recognize that actors' decision-making may not be most effectively influenced by directly prescribing decision-making rules (see, e.g., Sutcliffe and McNamara, 2001), or by relying on the (waning) power of overarching cultural norms, but instead by shaping the decision-making *situation* itself. Underlying this emphasis is the realization that actors' attention is guided by the momentary, and *local* pressures of the situation – resulting from the particular, temporal, and spatial circumstances (Ocasio, 1997) – rather than by universal, abstract, high-level, regulative or normative rules or resources. Or as Manning (1977) suggested, it is the *immediate context* of rules, not the rules themselves, or the rules about the rules, that are consequential for social behavior.

The control mechanism of choice to influence the situation is the communication and decision-making channel. Though the concept of channel plays an important role in early administrative theory (Allison, 1969; March and Simon, 1958; Simon, 1957; Thompson, 1967), it has not received much attention in contemporary research. Simon (1957: 103) recognizes the role of "channels of communication ... through which information for decision making flows" and sees them as "partly based on, and partly separate from, the lines of formal authority."

Similarly, March and Simon (1958: 188) point to the importance of channels for decision-making when stating that "communication traverses definite channels, either by formal plan or by the gradual development of informal programs." Allison (1969) points more explicitly to the effects such channels have on decision-making when he describes channels as:

regularized ways of producing action concerning types of issues, [which] structure the game by pre-selecting the major players, determining their points of entrance into the game and distributing particular advantages and disadvantages for each game. Most critically, channels determine "who's got the action" ... (Allison, 1969: 710)

Notice that channels "regularize" decision-making by determining the set up of the "game," rather than by directly prescribing the rules of the game. A similar idea underlies March and Olsen's "garbage can" model of decision-making (Cohen *et al.*, 1972; March and Olsen, 1976): participants, problems of concern to participants, and pre-existing solutions are dumped into a garbage can, and the interaction of all three lead to a decision through a process of organized chaos.

From the above, we can conclude that channels are an important mechanism of control that influences actors' attention by shaping the situation. Specifically, they determine:

(a) the spatial and temporal context, and thus determine the amount of interruptions and disturbances, the actors' perceived environmental pressures, and the transparency of the process to observers, etc.;

(b) the participants, and thus the diversity of information and perspectives, the degree of shared understanding of rules, issues, and solutions, and the balance of power in the decision-making situation; and participant roles and relationships for the specific channel;

(c) the resources available, i.e., the information and communication infrastructure that can be used to enable and guide communication and decision-making.

However, no situated interaction exists just "in the moment." Instead, it is nested in and linked to its cultural environment and the behavioral regulations, structural arrangements, and relation between actors that exist in the organization independent of the specific situation. The relationship between the situation and the environment are non-trivial, however. Even though the situated interaction is influenced by the pre-existing behavioral rules, cultural norms, and roles and relationship, the specific stimuli present in the channel can overturn or suppress these inputs. This is well established in experimental social psychological research: participants in a study enter the lab each with their own cultural "baggage," and yet are affected by the situational interventions and manipulations of the experimenter. Similarly, well-managed strategy retreats, brainstorming sessions, or outdoor team-building workshops can elicit very different behavior than everyday interactions in the office would – and they should, otherwise they would be pointless and frivolously expensive exercises. Conversely, attentional processes or behaviors that emerge and potentially are repeated in channels may become habitual and may be applied in situations outside the channel. Thus cultural artifacts, like schemata or stories, behavioral routines, and newly established relationships can spread beyond the channel and become fixtures in the organizations' non-situational control system.

We deliberately define channels as *anticipated, formal* opportunities for communications. This excludes spontaneous, informal interactions, which are elusive to purposive control, and in which non-situational factors such as actors' hierarchical positions and their respective right and responsibilities, or general cultural prescriptions, may guide behavior. However, if the interaction is anticipated, due to previous occurrences, or from an announcement of the planned interaction, actors develop preconceptions with regard to the participants, rules, and resources involved in the interaction. This gives the channel a degree of permanence and concrete existence, and fuels its institutional power, the basis for its normative (activating internalized rules) and cognitive influence (making salient particular taken-for-granted categories, schemas, and scripts on actors' attention). Also, since we are interested in channels as devices for organizational control, we focus on formal, that is to say officially legitimated, forums of interaction.

Though the channel is an intensive, local control mechanism, it would be a mistake to see it as predetermining the outcome of the communication that is taking place. In fact, the single most interesting aspect about channel controls is how they *allow issues and solutions to emerge* that were not planned and could not have been drawn up before the channel interaction.[4] Channels are not devices that enable actors to broaden their horizon and increase the quantity of issues they can attend. Instead, they facilitate intensive *and* generative decision processes. Channel interaction involves a degree of vigilance – a sustained attention to what is going on in the channel – and heedfulness (Weick and Roberts, 1993) – an acute awareness of and adjustment to other players in the channel, but it does not prescribe a procedure and thus does not take the concrete pattern of what is attended, or how, out of the participating actors' hands. In this regard channels are fundamentally different from controls that *restrict* actors' attention, because channels can effectively *stimulate* actors' attention to focus on issues and answers they would not have considered otherwise, while still giving it some broad direction. This stimulation of attention can occur as a result of the relatively free interaction among actors in the channels and their attempts to reconcile their divergent views and to deal with ambiguity and goal conflict in a particular situation (Cyert and March, 1963; March and Olsen, 1976). This form of interaction allows actors' private knowledge and specific capabilities to enter into the communication and decision-making processes.

The emergence of otherwise inconceivable issues and answers can be an important contribution toward the achievement of organizational goals. As we have pointed out in previous sections, many control mechanisms produce significant blind spots that are a necessary, but potentially dysfunctional, side effect of influencing actors' attention. Schreyogg and Steinmann (1987) suggest that such blind spots, particularly regarding the validity of premises for decisions and strategies, are a fundamental and insurmountable flaw of all "focused" controls, and therefore highlight the importance of unfocused controls. We see channels as such an unfocused control because they allow actors to bring issues to the table that are not planned for or directly stimulated, yet still allow for a higher degree of control over actors' attentional processes (e.g., more vigilance) than global cultural norms would. It can be argued that not all channels stimulate an active questioning of premises and strategies that leads to an expansion of actors' attention. Depending on how channels situate a decision and who they allow to participate, rules and scripts that become salient to participants can be more or less restrictive. Thus, we can say that channels can be more or less distinctively or consequentially structured.[5] But at the extreme low and high points the concept of situated interaction becomes trivial.

If a channel provides a very distinctive structure to the interaction, and thus allows little deviation from the particular situational norms they make salient, it really resembles a behavioral control that virtually prescribes a particular procedure for interaction. In this case it is really the salient behavioral rules that are doing the "control work," not the situation in itself.

Organizations do not rely on channel controls in isolation, but combine them with some form of high-level behavior control (e.g., a standard procedure for a six-sigma team, or some basic rules for a brain-storming session). Still, there can be a distinctive impact of the setting, the spatial and temporal circumstances on the interaction that is distinctive from the procedure's impact on the interaction, which subtly shift the relations between actors, actors' perceptual filters, and their interpretative schema. This makes channels an important control mechanism to consider.

The fact that channels allow for agency and for emergent processes is simultaneously their most important strength and their biggest weakness. By establishing a venue for relatively open and "loose" interaction, agency problems and dysfunction political behavior can arise. Most of us have had first-hand experience with and rolled our eyes at individuals "hijacking" or "derailing" a meeting by pitching issues that are of greatest personal relevance to them but nobody else. This is but one instance of problems and tensions that can occur in channels. However, the obscure agenda pushed with annoying persistence by an outsider in a meeting could turn out to be the one crucial piece of the puzzle that no one else has paid attention to. Or it could be a completely irrelevant distraction.

What we can conclude from the above discussion is that channel controls become more important for large differentiated organizations, in which knowledge is decentralized. In those – more and more commonplace – types of organizations overarching cultural controls may be less effective and too unspecific to direct actors' attention, outcomes may be hard to measure, and behavior may be difficult to program or supervise. In short: knowledge-intensive organizations may find that channel controls are, if not the dominant, the most crucial controls to affect actors attentional processes in order to align their behavior with organizational goals.

Value of attention-based view for future research

What do we gain from paying more attention to attentional processes? It allows us to both gain a deeper understanding of how organizational controls work, and recognize a wider set of issues – such as situational factors, actors' interactions, and so on – that come to bear on how effectively controls direct actors toward organizational goals. The attention-based view of organizational control helps to explicate the link between structural and cultural interventions, individual cognition, and behavior. They allow us to evaluate different types and different configurations of control based on the effectiveness of their impact on attentional processes. The identification of attention as a crucial mediator between organizational controls and actors' behavior leads us to a better understanding of the cognitive underpinnings of different control mechanisms. Throughout this chapter, we have used the attention perspective to identify advantages and disadvantages of the five types of organizational controls we describe. Thus, the attentional perspective allows scholars to theorize and empirically test *in more detail* the cognitive mechanisms at play in different control configurations.

Further, we have shown that actors' attention can be influenced through many different pathways. We stated at the beginning of the chapter that we believe that all five of the control types we describe are active in most organizations, and they may not all provide consistent impulses to actors. Such inconsistencies arising from conflicting organizational controls can lead to confusion of actors, and diffuse rather than focus of their attention. Unpredictable and inconsistent decision-making that fails to contribute to the attainment of organizational goals can be a result. It is important to recognize that under such conditions suboptimal behavior is not simply a result of willfully deviant behavior and conflicts of interests, but deficient allocation of attention. We believe that more research should be directed at how actors and organizations deal with inconsistent and conflicting control mechanisms.

We have also provided a more differentiated view of attention processes by not reducing organizational attention merely to a matter of focus or selective attention. Instead we have shown three different attentional processes – selection, regulation, and vigilance – and have suggested how they are affected by the five control categories.

The most valuable insight of the attention-based view is the "situatedness" of attention, and the importance of situational factors for the effectiveness of organizational controls. Thus, the attention perspective urges scholars to consider controls not as universal structural or cultural mechanisms but instead as situationally contingent and embedded mechanisms. Thus, we hope that the attention-based view stimulates researchers to look more closely at situational factors and their impact on actors' cognition and behavior, and to look more closely at channel controls. The situational perspective on organizational control helps us understand that in complex organizations many different forms of control co-exist, but not all affect the behavior of an actor simultaneously all the time. Instead, particular sets of controls become prevalent at different times, depending on the situational characteristics or the channel.

One aspect that we have alluded to in the text but that requires further research is the relative power of global structural or cultural versus situational factors in predicting behavior in different control configurations. To better understand the impact of different types of control on behavior we have to gain a better understanding of which types of situational factors eclipse global structural or cultural factors, and which global structural or cultural factors, in turn, drown out situational stimuli. In other words: which types of channels insulate actors strongly from their larger environment and let them focus more narrowly on immediate situational aspects, and which encourage a more comprehensive perception that leads actors to look beyond immediate factors?

Finally, our discussion of channel controls has emphasized the often-neglected interactions between actors as a potential factor for the effectiveness of particular controls. The emphasis on actors' interactions frees us from a passive, submissive view of organizational actors, and instead allows us to explore issues of misunderstandings, conflict, and political struggle and strife within the control system. Pushing the emphasis on interactions further conceptually leads us to see channels not only as devices for exercising control but also as arenas for struggle over control or platforms giving control to particular actors. This would give rise to a concept of emergent control, where control systems trigger and to some degree shape political processes in the organization, and where powerful actors strategically use attention structures to expand their status and influence in the organization.

Conclusion

In this chapter we have reaffirmed that attention is central to conceptions of organizational control. We have argued that all systems of control involve attention, and that attentional processes mediate between controls and actors' behavior. To explore in detail how controls impact attention, we have delineated the different effects of five types of control – hierarchical, output, behavioral, cultural, and channel controls – and the three interrelated attention processes of selection, regulation, and vigilance. We have asserted the importance of situational factors and thus the need for scholars to rediscover the underused concept of channels and channel controls. We finished with some observations regarding the benefits of an attention-based view for research on organizational control and pointed out a number of potential issues for future research, suggesting more scholarly attention toward situational factors and emergent processes of control resulting from actors' interaction in channels as particularly promising.

Notes

1 In the literature on attention (e.g., Parasurman, 1998; Posner and Rothbart, 2007) the terms "executive control" or "executive attention" are used instead of "attention regulation." We use the term "regulation" instead of "control" so as not to confuse it with the discussion of organizational control.

2 Though culture is a pervasive phenomenon and organizations are embedded in and are influenced by their cultural context (Smircich, 1983), we focus here on culture *within* the organization and its impact on organizational members' cognitive processes.

3 However, repeated identical *ad hoc* interventions and repeatedly following the same procedures can lead to routinized behavior. When actors begin to expect a particular intervention in a particular situation, or follow a particular procedure following a triggering event without deliberate choice, behavioral controls may cease to have a regulative effect but instead become normative.

4 This crucial difference of channels relative to other forms of control is similar to Sitkin, Sutcliffe, and colleagues' (Sitkin *et al.*, 1994; Sutcliffe *et al.*, 1999) conceptual distinction between control processes, which aim at increasing the reliability and predictability of organizational action and exploration processes, which contribute to improving the resilience and learning of the organization. The concept of channels, however, emphasizes (a) that such explorative processes are firmly situated in the immediate temporal and spatial context in which they occur, and (b) that these contextual factors can be influenced to guide the interaction in the channel, and thus constitute a form of organizational control.

5 Social psychologists make a similar distinction between strong and weak situations (Mischel, 1977). Strong situations have a more determinist effect on individual behavior and make only a limited number of behavioral patterns acceptable. Because of their pronounced influence on behavior, strong situations make factors such as individual predispositions or general cultural norms less consequential – just as distinctive channels eclipse other influences on actors' attention.

References

Allison, G. T. 1969. Conceptual models and the Cuban missile crisis. *The American Political Science Review*, 63 (3): 689–718.

Arendt, H. 1965. *Eichmann in Jerusalem: a report on the banality of evil* (revised edn.). New York, NY: Viking Compass.

Bakan, J. 2004. *The corporation: the pathological pursuit of profit and power*. New York, NY: Free Press.

Barnett, M. L. 2003. Falling off the fence? A realistic appraisal of a real options approach to corporate strategy. *Journal of Management Inquiry*, 12 (2): 185.

2005. Paying attention to real options. *R&D Management*, 35 (1): 61–72.

Browning, L. D. and Folger, R. 1994. Communication under conditions of communication risk: a grounded theory of plausible deniability in the Iran-contra affair. In S. B. Sitkin and R. J. Bies (eds.), *The legalistic organization*: 251–280. Thousand Oaks, CA: Sage.

Cardinal, L. 2001. Technological innovation in the pharmaceutical industry: the use of organizational control in managing research and development. *Organization Science*, 12 (1): 19–36.

Cardinal, L. B., Sitkin, S. B., and Long, C. P. 2004. Balancing and rebalancing in the creation and evolution of organizational control. *Organization Science*, 15 (4): 411–431.

Chakrabarti, A., Singh, K., and Mahmood, I. 2007. Diversification and performance: evidence from East Asian firms. *Strategic Management Journal*, 28 (2): 101–120.

Cho, T. S. and Hambrick, D. C. 2006. Attention as the mediator between top management team characteristics and strategic change: the case of airline deregulation. *Organization Science*, 17 (4): 453–469.

Cohen, M. D., March, J. G., and Olsen, J. P. 1972. A garbage can model of organizational choice. *Administrative Science Quarterly*, 17 (1): 1–25.

Cyert, R. M. and March, J. G. 1963. *A behavioral theory of the firm*. Englewood Cliffs, NJ: Prentice-Hall.

Deal, T. E. and Kennedy, A. A. 1982. *Corporate culture*. Reading, MA: Addison-Wesley.

DiMaggio, P. 1997. Culture and cognition. *Annual Review of Sociology*, 23: 262–287.

Durand, R. 2003. Predicting a firm's forecasting ability: the roles of organizational illusion of control and organizational attention. *Strategic Management Journal*, 24 (9): 821–838.

Eisenhardt, K. M. 1985. Control: organizational and economic approaches. *Management Science*, 31 (2): 134–149.

Evans, P. B. 1975. Multiple hierarchies and organizational control. *Administrative Science Quarterly*, 20 (2): 250–259.

Fiske, S. T. and Linville, P. W. 1980. What does the schema concept buy us? *Personality and Social Psychology Bulletin*, 6 (4): 543–557.

Fligstein, N. 1990. *Transformation of corporate control*. Cambridge, MA: Harvard University Press.

Gioia, D. A. and Chittipeddi, K. 1991. Sensemaking and sensegiving in strategic change initiation. *Strategic Management Journal*, 12 (6): 433–448.

Gittel, J. H. 2000. The paradox of coordination and control. *California Management Review*, 42 (3): 101–117.

Hannerz, U. 1969. *Soulside: inquiries into ghetto culture and community*. New York, NY: Columbia University Press.

Hatch, M. J. 1997. *Organization theory: modern, symbolic, and postmodern perspectives*. New York, NY: Oxford University Press.

Hung, S. C. 2005. The plurality of institutional embeddedness as a source of organizational attention differences. *Journal of Business Research*, 58 (11): 1,543–1,551.

John, G. and Weitz, B. 1989. Salesforce compensation: an empirical investigation of factors related to use of salary versus incentive compensation. *Journal of Marketing Research*, 26 (1): 1–14.

Kinchla, R. A. 1992. Attention. *Annual Review of Psychology*, 43 (1): 711–742.

Kreps, G. L. 1986. *Organizational communication – theory and practice*. New York, NY: Longman.

Lewin, K. 1951. *Field theory in social science*. New York, NY: Harper.

Long, C. P., Burton, R. M., and Cardinal, L. B. 2003. Creating control configurations during organizational foundings. *Academy of Management Best Conference Paper*: 6.

Louis, M. R. 1983. Organizations as culture-bearing milieux. In L. R. Pondy, P. Frost, G. Morgan, and T. Dandridge (eds.), *Organizational symbolism*: 39–54. Greenwich, CT: JAI Press.

Manning, P. K. 1977. *Police work: the social organization of policing*. Cambridge, MA: MIT Press.

March, J. G. and Olsen, J. P. 1976. *Ambiguity and choice in organizations*. Bergen, Norway: Universitetsforlaget.

March, J. G. and Simon, H. A. 1958. *Organizations*. New York, NY: Wiley.

Mischel, W. 1977. The interaction of person and situation. In D. Magnusson and N. S. Endler (eds.), *Personality at the crossroads: current issues in interactional psychology*: 333–352. Hillsdale, NJ: Erlbaum.

Moray, N. 1967. Where is attention limited? A survey and a model. *Acta Psychologica*, 27: 84–92.

Ocasio, W. 1997. Towards an attention-based view of the firm. *Strategic Management Journal*, 18 (Summer Special Issue): 187–206.

Ocasio, W. and Joseph, J. 2006. Governance channels at General Electric: 1950–2001. In R. M. Burton, B. Eriksen, D. D. Haakonsson, and C. C. Snow (eds.), *Organizational design: the dynamics of adaptation and change*. Boston, MA: Springer.

Ouchi, W. G. 1977. The relationship between organizational structure and organizational control. *Administrative Science Quarterly*, 22 (1): 95–113.

1978. The transmission of control through organizational hierarchy. *Academy of Management Journal*, 21 (2): 173–192.

1979. A conceptual framework for the design of organizational control mechanisms. *Management Science*, 25 (9): 833–848.

Parasurman, R. 1998. The attentive brain: issues and prospects. In R. Parasurman (ed.), *The attentive brain*. Cambridge, MA: MIT Press.

Parsons, T. 1937. *The structure of social action*. New York, NY: McGraw-Hill.

Parsons, T. and Shils, E. A. 1951. *Toward a general theory of action-theoretical foundations for the social sciences*. Cambridge, MA: Harvard University Press.

Peters, T. J. and Waterman, R. H. 1984. *In search of excellence*. New York, NY: Warner Books.

Pfeffer, J. 1982. *Organizations and organization theory*. Boston, MA: Pitman.

1998. Understanding organizations: concepts and controversies. In D. Gilbert, S. Fiske, and G. Lindzey (eds.), *Handbook of social psychology* (4th edn.), 2: 733–777. New York, NY: McGraw-Hill.

Posner, M. I. and Rothbart, M. K. 2007. Research on attention networks as a model for the integration of psychological science. *Annual Review of Psychology*, 58: 1–23.

Ridgeway, V. F. 1956. Dysfunctional consequences of performance measurement. *Administrative Science Quarterly*, 1: 240–247.

Ross, L. and Nisbett, R. E. 1994. *The person and the situation: perspectives of social psychology*. New York, NY: McGraw-Hill.

Schein, E. 1983. The role of founder in organizational culture. *Organizational Dynamics*, 12: 5–23.

Schreyogg, G. and Steinmann, H. 1987. Strategic control: a new perspective. *Academy of Management Review*, 12 (1): 91–103.

Siehl, C. and Martin, J. 1981. *Learning organizational culture*. Graduate School of Business, Stanford University.

Simon, H. A. 1957. *Administrative behavior*. New York, NY: Macmillan.

Sitkin, S. B., Sutcliffe, K. M., and Barrios-Choplin, J. R. 1992. A dual-capacity model of communication media choice in organizations. *Human Communication Research*, 18: 563–598.

Sitkin, S. B., Sutcliffe, K. M., and Schroeder, R. G. 1994. Distinguishing control room learning in total quality management: a contingency perspective. *Academy of Management Review*, 19: 537–564.

Smircich, L. 1983. Concepts of culture and organizational analysis. *Administrative Science Quarterly*, 28: 339–358.

Smyth, R. C. 1968. Financial incentives for salesmen. *Harvard Business Review*, 46 (January/February): 109–117.

Sutcliffe, K. M. and McNamara, G. 2001. Controlling decision-making practice in organizations. *Organization Science*, 12 (4): 484–501.

Sutcliffe, K. M., Sitkin, S., and Browning, L. 1999. Tailoring process management to situational requirements. In R. Cole and W. Scott (eds.), *The quality movement and organization theory*: 315–330. Thousand Oaks, CA: Sage.

Swets, J. A. and Kristofferson, A. B. 1970. Attention. *Annual Review of Psychology*, 21 (1): 339–366.

Swidler, A. 1986. Culture in action: symbols and strategies. *American Sociological Review*, 51: 273–286.

Thompson, J. D. 1967. *Organizations in action–social science bases of administrative theory*. New York, NY: McGraw-Hill.

Thornton, P. H. and Ocasio, W. 1999. Institutional logics and the historical contingency of power in organizations: executive succession in the higher education publishing industry, 1958–1990. *American Journal of Sociology*, 105 (3): 801–843.

Van Maanen, J. 1975. Police socialization: a longitudinal examination of job attitudes in an urban police department. *Administrative Science Quarterly*, 20 (2): 207–228.

1991. The smile factory: work at Disneyland. In P. Frost, L. Moore, M. R. Louis, C. Lundberg, and J. Martin (eds.), *Reframing organizational culture*: 58–76. Newbury Park, CA: Sage.

Weber, M. 1948 [1916]. The social psychology of world religions. In H. H. Gerth and C. W. Mills (eds.), *From Max Weber*: 267–301. London, UK: Routledge.

1978 [1928]. Bureaucracy. In R. Roth and C. Wittich (eds.), *Economy and society*: 956–980. Berkeley, CA: University of California Press.

Weick, K. E. and Roberts, K. H. 1993. Collective mind in organizations: heedful interrelating on flight decks. *Administrative Science Quarterly*, 38: 357–381.

Williamson, O. E. 1970. *Corporate control and business behavior*. Englewood Cliffs, NJ: Prentice-Hall.

Wirth, L. 1940. The urban society and civilization. *American Journal of Sociology*, 45 (5): 743.

Yadav, M. S., Prabhu, J. C., and Chandy, R. K. 2007. Managing the future: CEO attention and innovation outcomes. *Journal of Marketing*, 71 (4): 84–101.

Yu, J., Engleman, R. M., and Van de Ven, A. H. 2005. The integration journey: an attention-based view of the merger and acquisition integration process. *Organization Studies*, 26 (10): 1,501.

8 The role of motivational orientations in formal and informal control

M. AUDREY KORSGAARD,
BRUCE M. MEGLINO,
AND SOPHIA SOYOUNG JEONG
University of South Carolina

A fundamental challenge to organizations is ensuring that members act to achieve organizational objectives. This challenge arises from the inevitable circumstance wherein an individual's self-interests are not consonant with the goals and objectives of the organization. Broadly speaking, organizations address this challenge through organizational control, which is defined as a process that directs, motivates, and encourages employee behaviors that are congruent with organizational objectives (Ouchi, 1977, 1979; Snell, 1992). Organizational controls vary along numerous dimensions, such as formality, target, and scope (Cardinal, Sitkin, and Long, Chapter 3). In this chapter, we focus on one distinction among control practices, the motivational mechanisms that underlie the operation of controls. Often, organizational control takes the form of mechanisms or systems that appeal to an individual's self-interests. These mechanisms involve linking incentives or other personal consequences to actions that further the organization's objectives. Alternatively, organizations may seek to guide employee behavior through indirect social influence processes. Such mechanisms affect behavior via social structures and processes such as organizational culture, normative influence, and identification. Control exercised through indirect social influence directs members' attention toward the cooperative accomplishment of organizational goals. In short, organizations exert control through two distinctly different motivational mechanisms; that is, by appealing to employees' rational self-interest or through indirect social influence processes that de-emphasize the self.

Understanding the distinction in these motivational mechanisms is important, for research and theory suggest that there is substantial variation in the degree to which individuals are motivated by self-interest and are disposed to engage in rational reasoning (Cropanzano et al., 2005; Ferraro et al., 2005). Recent theory and research on cooperative and moral behavior suggests that this variation is attributable to differences in two factors: (a) the *motive*, that is, the degree to which an individual's behavior is motivated by self-interest versus other interest; and (b) the *mode of reasoning*, that is, the degree to which the individual's underlying judgment process is rationally versus heuristically driven (Loewenstein and Small, 2007; Meglino and Korsgaard, 2006; Tenbrunsel *et al.*, in press). By simultaneously considering variations in motives and judgment processes, this research provides important insights into the motivational mechanisms underlying organizational controls and the actions organizations can take to increase the effectiveness of these controls.

This chapter proceeds as follows. First, we briefly discuss the differences between formal and informal controls and the motivational mechanisms underlying their effects. We next introduce a typology of individual orientations based on underlying motives and modes of reasoning. We then integrate these orientations with formal and informal controls to examine implications of various control practices and approaches.

Organizational control

Typologies of organizational control

One of the major distinctions in organizational controls is the degree to which they are formal or informal. Formal control mechanisms refer to explicit and codified arrangements that specify, track, and/or reinforce desired inputs, behaviors, or outcomes. Informal controls refer to social structures and processes, such as norms, culture, and values to direct and guide employee behaviors (Cardinal *et al.*, 2004; Cardinal *et al.*, Chapter 3). Formal and informal organizational control can vary in terms of whether the target is input, behavior (process), or output. Input control refers to control over the resources and requirements for goal achievement, and it includes formal controls such as selection and training as well as informal controls such as socialization (Snell, 1992). Behavioral or process controls address the activities and strategies that lead to goal achievement. Job design and standardization of policies are examples of formal practices; group norms are an example of informal practices. Output controls such as outcome-based pay address the consequences of performance.

Formal and informal control may refer to specific mechanisms or practices, or to a cluster of practices organized into a coherent, systemic configuration. While some scholars suggest such configurations are consistently formal or informal (e.g., the market versus clan system, Ouchi, 1977, 1979), contemporary research suggests that formal and informal controls may coexist within a given configuration (Cardinal *et al.*, 2004, Chapter 3).

Although all of these various practices and configurations are designed to foster the achievement of organizational goals, they operate on the behavior of individuals in fundamentally different ways. In some cases, controls constrain variation in capability and behavior. For example, formal input controls that specify the selection of well-qualified employees constrain variation in performance by ensuring a uniformly high degree of capability. Another example is a job design (Taylor, 1911) that imposes strict and precise rules and procedures constraining and minimizing variation in employee behavior, thereby achieving efficiency. Alternatively, organizational controls may operate on employees' volitional control by inducing employees to act in accordance with organizational objectives. As noted above, such inducements may emphasize the personal consequences of adhering to organizational objectives or they may operate through indirect social influence processes that do not require conscious attention to self-interests. We focus specifically on controls that operate through these motivational mechanisms.

Organizational control and contingent consequences

A critical feature of organizational control is the degree to which (and how) volitional employee behavior is tied to expected consequences. These consequences, which can include a pay increase/decrease, a promotion/demotion, continued employment, discipline, etc., are extrinsic and instrumental. Moreover, though the linkage between the behavior and the consequence may not be completely and accurately specified in all cases, the existence of a contingency is almost universally known in advance.

In some cases, such as in performance management systems or pay-for-performance plans, the contingency is specified within the control mechanism itself. This is also the case for formal disciplinary procedures. In these cases, there is an explicit, codified relationship between the behavior and the consequences. Note that the contingency may specify a behavior (e.g., discipline systems for violation of safety behavior) or an outcome (e.g., incentives for reduced frequency of customer complaints). For other control mechanisms, the contingency is implied. For example, procedures, policies, and standards often specify the required input, behavior, or output, but the consequences of violating the standard are not made explicit. However, the overarching principle of violation of employee policy holds. For example, job applicants may be told that they should accurately report their prior work history. Even though the consequences of lying may not be indicated on the application form, individuals implicitly understand that they are likely to be dismissed if they are found to have misrepresented themselves. Similarly, while formal documentation may only specify an employee's job duties, employees implicitly recognize that failure to carry out these duties can lead to discipline or dismissal. In other cases, the contingency may be either explicit or implicit depending on the situation. For supervisory directions, for example, the consequences of compliance or non-compliance may be explicit in that the supervisor may promise rewards or sanctions. Alternatively, the consequences may be implied by virtue of the difference in power between the supervisor and the employee. Similarly, monitoring may be explicitly linked to rewards (e.g., performance management systems) or it may be implicitly linked to negative consequences in that employees understand that some type of violation or substandard performance, if detected, will lead to corrective action.

Even though the aforementioned contingencies are all formal control practices, informal control may also regulate behavior through contingencies. For example, social exchanges, which form the basis of various social processes such as psychological contracts (Schalk and Rousseau, 2002), perceived organizational support (Rhoades and Eisenberger, 2002), and leader–member exchange (Schriesheim *et al.*, 1999) can be understood as a mode of informal control that relies on inducing desired behavior through anticipated consequences. Such relationships constitute a loose and voluntary exchange of benefits; thus, this type of control involves an implicit understanding that consequences are linked to the performance of certain behaviors. Thus, the myriad social exchange relationships that develop within an organization may, under certain circumstances, affect behavior through the imposition of positive or negative consequences. Indeed, social exchange theory suggests that employees who are beneficiaries of favorable exchange relationships with members of the organization will be motivated to act in ways that benefit the organization in anticipation of receiving benefits in the future (Blau, 1964).

The motivational impact of behavior–consequence contingencies suggests that an employee's choices and actions are mediated by a consideration of anticipated personal consequences. This process presumes that individuals are motivated by self-interest and are mindful of personally relevant consequences. In other words, organizational controls involving behavior–consequence contingencies require that individuals be sufficiently self-interested and rational when considering their choice to comply. If employees do not focus on, and rationally evaluate, the possible consequences of their action, the control practice cannot be expected to shape employee behaviors. In short, the success of certain organizational controls is heavily dependent on employees being motivated by self-interest and engaged in a rational, deliberative choice process. On the other hand, certain forms of organizational control do not require rational deliberations by the employee. We discuss these in the following section.

Organizational control and indirect social influence

For some organizational controls, the employee is aware of the expected behavior but the choice to comply with the behavior is not predicated on the personal consequences of doing so. Thus, even though explicit or implied contingencies may be present in the situation, these contingencies are not the primary drivers of the employee's behavior. Instead, employees' responses are motivated through a process of indirect social influence. Indirect social influence is a heuristic-based process wherein individuals comply or conform to requests and expectations with little conscious consideration (Cialdini and Goldstein, 2004). This mode of influence involves the activation of cognitive structures such as goals, norms, and values that guide behavior outside the individual's conscious awareness. An example of indirect social influence is when an employee complies with a supervisor's request without actively considering the personal consequences of doing so.

Although behavior can be motivated by contingent consequences or indirect social influence, these motivational processes can change over time. That is, behavior that is initially motivated by contingent consequences can evolve to a point where it is ultimately motivated by indirect social influence. This is perhaps most evident in the case of normative influence. That is, individuals may initially comply with a group or an organizational norm as a means of attaining social or material gain and avoiding sanctions (Kelman, 2006). Such overt influence may involve monitoring behavior or administering consequences contingent upon compliance. As such, its effectiveness is dependent upon the individual engaging in some degree of rational, self-interested reasoning. However, if individuals eventually come to identify with the group or organization and internalize its values, they could more reflexively respond to norms or expectations without consideration of the consequences of (non-)compliance.

When individuals identify with the group, they are apt to accept social influence out of a general principle that group members should conform to the norms and expectations of the group (Kelman, 2006). That is, individuals may adhere to controls because they desire to conform to the group and not because they consider the consequences of complying with a specific request (George and Qian, Chapter 6). In such cases, the salience of the individual's group identity and the presence of social cues or expectations are sufficient to induce conformity. Similarly, when individuals have internalized group or societal norms, social influence does not require rational deliberation. Adherence to such norms is based on a more reflexive assessment of what is "right" and "correct" in a given social structure.

Early in an individual's membership in a group or organization, formal and informal controls are likely to affect behavior through expected consequences. This implied behavior–consequence contingency serves to focus the attention of new members because the contingency specifies the behaviors that are valued by the group or organization. Over time, as individuals become socialized into the group or organization, informal control may operate through identification and internalization. One sees this in some forms of socialization, particularly in the armed services. Military recruits initially follow rules and obey orders to avoid being disciplined or rejected. Ultimately, they adhere to controls because they are committed to following the standards of the organization (identification) and/or believe doing so is fundamentally right (i.e., internalization). This dynamic transition from consequence-based compliance to relatively mindless compliance implies that indirect social influence can underlie both informal controls such as group norms and formal controls such as organizational policies and procedures. Moreover, indirect social influence can mediate formal or informal controls that evoke internalized societal norms, such as obedience to authority or reciprocity. For example, because it evokes legitimate authority and the norm of obedience to authority, direct supervision may affect employee behavior through indirect social influence.

The preceding distinction between controls based on a behavior–consequence contingency or on indirect social influence underscores the importance of matching the type of control with the corresponding motivational mechanism. That is, the presence of different motivational bases suggests that the success of different forms of organizational control will depend on an employee's level of self-interest. However, an equally important contingency is an employee's judgment process; specifically, the extent that informal and formal control are based on rational versus heuristic reasoning. Thus, a full discussion of the mechanisms underlying control must involve a consideration of how individuals process information as well as the extent to which they act in their own self-interest. In the following section, we discuss how the theory of other orientation offers a useful framework for understanding how and why self-interest and rationality vary.

The theory of other orientation: a framework of motives and judgments

As noted in our introduction, the mechanisms underlying various types of controls mirror those that underlie helping and cooperative behaviors in organizations. Research suggests that, to understand these forms of behavior, one must examine both the motive and judgment processes underlying an individual's actions. Below, we present one such framework, the theory of other orientation (Meglino and Korsgaard, 2004), which integrates motives and reasoning processes to produce four basic orientations. Differentiating between these orientations provides insight into when individuals are susceptible to indirect social influence and when individual behavior is guided by rational self-interest.

Self- and other interest

The first dimension of the framework illustrated in Figure 8.1 is the distinction between *self-interest* and *other interest* as motives. Self-interest is defined as intentions or behaviors wherein the ultimate goal

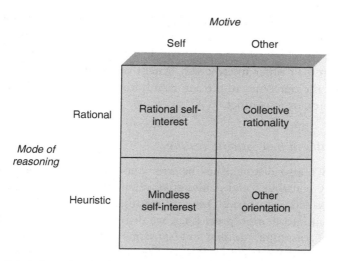

Figure 8.1 A framework of motives and modes of processing

is to benefit the self (Cropanzano *et al.*, 2007). In contrast, other interest refers to intentions or behaviors that are directed at the goal of benefiting others. Self- and other interest are thought to reflect distinct motivational systems (Brewer, 2004). The relative strength of self- and other interest is likely to vary as a function of distinct individual differences, such as values (Korsgaard *et al.*, 1997) as well as contextual factors (Vohs *et al.*, 2006).

Although self-interest and other interest are distinct motives, some researchers (De Dreu *et al.*, 2006) maintain that individuals can simultaneously pursue both self- and other interests under some circumstances. However, other scholars (e.g., Brewer, 2004) consider these motivations as competing with each other. In many circumstances, the conflict between self- and other interest is such that the pursuit of one is achieved at the expense of the other (De Dreu and Nauta, 2007). Moreover, in an effort to reduce complexity and uncertainty (Simon, 1990), individuals may adopt a goal that emphasizes one interest domain, leading them to focus their attention on acts or outcomes relevant to that domain to the exclusion of the other.

It is important to note that self-interest and other interest describe an individual's motive, but not necessarily the resulting acts. Therefore, behavior that benefits others may be motivated solely by a concern for others, by a desire to advance one's own interests, or in service of joint concerns. Conversely, the same motives can be responsible for behaviors that ultimately benefit the self (e.g., recognition for helpful acts). Thus, the extent to which actions that are motivated by self-interest or other interest will benefit others depends, in part, on whether the outcomes to the actor and others are independent, complementary, or in conflict.

Rational and heuristic reasoning

Figure 8.1 also distinguishes between modes of reasoning that are relatively controlled and deliberative versus those that are relatively effortless and automatic. Drawing on research on decision-making and social information processing, we distinguish between two main modes of reasoning, *rational* and *heuristic* (Chaiken and Trope, 1999; Stanovich and West, 2002). Rational reasoning is defined as thinking and acting in a manner that is expected to lead to an optimal or maximum result for a person based on a consideration of the person's values and risk preferences (Bazerman, 1993). As noted above, this is a deliberative process that considers the consequences of one's actions.

Heuristic reasoning involves the application of existing knowledge structures (i.e., rules, norms, scripts) as a means of determining choices and behavior (Stanovich and West, 2002). This process is rapid, relatively effortless and largely outside of the actor's conscious control (De Neys, 2006). It is characteristic of moral intuition (Haidt, 2001), automaticity (Bargh and Chartrand, 1999; Langer, 1989), and social influence (Cialdini and Goldstein, 2004; Malhotra and Bazerman, 2008). This mode of reasoning is distinctive in that it does not require the systematic evaluation of anticipated consequences. However, heuristic reasoning is not necessarily inferior to rational reasoning in achieving desired ends (be those self- or other interested objectives). If the heuristic is valid or relevant to the structure of the situation (i.e., is *ecologically rational*), it is likely to result in high-quality decisions (Snook *et al.*, 2004).

Rational and heuristic reasoning are considered distinct modes of processing. Dual-process models generally assume that unconscious processing is a default mode of information processing and reasoning because it requires less mental effort. Thus, when individuals lack motivation or are inhibited from engaging in rational reasoning, they are apt to rely on heuristic reasoning. For example, research shows that when individuals are highly motivated (e.g., when pursuing specific goals or when they are held accountable) and have high ability (e.g., when they are trained and when they experience lower cognitive load) they are more likely to rely on rational reasoning (see, e.g., Eagly and Chaiken, 1993; McAllister *et al.*, 1979).

Four orientations

The simultaneous consideration of self-interest versus other interested motives and rational versus heuristic modes of reasoning yields four different orientations, which we describe next.

Rational self-interest orientation. The rational self-interest orientation reflects the type of reasoning that underlies classical economics and value-expectancy models of attitudes and motivation (e.g., Ajzen, 2001; Ferraro *et al.*, 2005). Individuals who are represented in this quadrant focus on personal gain and pursue self-serving goals in a manner that maximizes expected personal outcomes.

Mindless self-interest orientation. In some cases, individuals pursue self-interests without engaging rational reasoning. This orientation describes individuals' pursuit of self-serving goals without careful consideration of personal consequences and without seeking to maximize their outcomes. This category includes spontaneous and impulsive behavior (Dawes, 1988). For example, Bazerman *et al.* (1998) distinguish between two components of the self that often come in conflict. The *want* self is concerned with short-term, pragmatic interests, whereas the *should* self is concerned with long-term idealistic and identity-based interests. These selves are associated not only with preferences, but with different judgment processes as well. The *want* self describes choices that are visceral, emotional, and impulsive, whereas the *should* self describes choices that are rational and thoughtful. Short-term pragmatic outcomes dominate the *want* self, whereas long-term idealistic and identity-based outcomes dominate the *should* self. Thus, when short-term interests dominate, an individual may engage in a less deliberative and rational process, resulting in choices and actions that subvert the concerns of others as well as the individual's own long-term self-interests (Wade-Benzoni, 2002).

Collective rational orientation. This orientation occurs when individuals are other-interested but engage in relatively rational reasoning. We describe this orientation as "collective" because it involves weighing outcomes for both the self and others. That is, individuals are motivated to serve their own interests as well as the interests of others and formulate intentions in a rational manner. This may be manifested in situations where individuals are members of a group and their focus shifts to the outcome for the group as a whole. Being members of this group, the individual will benefit from choices and actions that benefit the group as a whole. As well, collective rational orientation can help individuals who are engaged in a conflict of interest with others. An example of collective rationality is how individuals negotiate integrative solutions to conflicts of interest (De Dreu *et al.*, 2006).

Other orientation. This orientation exists when individuals are high in other interest and rely on heuristic reasoning to pursue those interests. Like collective rationality, other orientation may operate when the "other" involves an entity (dyad or group) within which the self is subsumed. However, this orientation is distinguished from collective rationality in that it does not involve the explicit consideration of anticipated consequences. That is, individuals rely more on heuristic reasoning and less on rational reasoning. Specifically, individuals in this mode apply principles or norms of behavior, which obviates the need to consider personal consequences.

The dominance of rational self-interest and other orientation

Research suggests that self-interest and rational reasoning mutually influence one another. Self-interest can stimulate rational judgment such that when personal stakes are high, individuals tend to apply more effort and rigor to their decisions (McAllister *et al.*, 1979). As well, repeated exposure to rational principles can lead individuals to act in a self-interested way (Sonenshein, 2007). Additionally, contextual cues can stimulate rational reasoning, leading to self-interested choices. For example, Irwin and Baron (2001) conducted a series of experiments demonstrating that participants' choices were more strongly influenced by their moral values (e.g., preserving the environment, abortion) when they were asked to make decisions about their willingness to purchase or change items based on moral issues. In contrast, when asked to determine the price for various products and services (presumably a more calculating and rational process), participants' moral values had a weaker effect. Similarly, Tenbrunsel and

Messick (1999) found that the moral aspects of a situation (i.e., the outcomes for others) became less salient and compelling once a decision had been framed in terms of costs and benefits. Specifically, they found that highlighting the costs of socially undesirable behavior actually increased unethical or uncooperative behavior.

In a similar manner, other interest has been shown to prompt heuristic reasoning. Other interest involves a greater sensitivity to the concerns and needs of others. As a result, other interest is likely to lead individuals to be more attentive and susceptible to social cues and expectations. When such cues are consistent with other interest, individuals high in other interest are likely to conform to the norm without regard to anticipated consequences. This relationship is illustrated in a study that examined the impact of other interest and the norm of reciprocity on helping behavior (Korsgaard *et al.*, 2008). In this study, reciprocal helping was significantly greater among individuals who were primed on other interest as opposed to those primed on self-interest. Further, Ybarra and Trafimow (1998) found that public health norms had a stronger impact on the healthy intentions of participants primed with a collective self-concept versus those primed with an individual self-concept. Similarly, recycling norms predicted intentions only for individuals who were highly identified with the group (Terry *et al.*, 1999).

In short, research suggests that motive and mode of reasoning tend to co-vary such that self-interest is related to rational reasoning and other interest is associated with heuristic reasoning. These patterns of co-variance suggest that two orientations, rational self-interest and other orientation (both represented along the main diagonal of Figure 8.1), may be especially common in occurrence. Moreover, we expect that collective rationality, which represents a compromise between other orientation and rational self-interest, is likely to be a less stable or sustainable orientation, further contributing to the dominance of rational self-interest and other orientation. Research suggests that when interests conflict, collective rationality is a difficult state to sustain (De Dreu, 2006; Tenbrunsel *et al.*, in press). Such judgments require the consideration of more numerous outcomes (i.e., self and other) across a broader span of time (Tenbrunsel *et al.*, in press), which can tax the limits of bounded rationality. Further, the presence of rational reasoning is likely to make self-interests salient. Thus individuals who employ a rational model in pursuit of others' interests are likely to develop a heightened awareness of potential tradeoffs between their personal concerns and those of others. In short, we expect rational self-interest and other orientation to be especially important and particularly common motivational states in organizations.

An integration of control systems and orientations

Figure 8.2 depicts the integration of regulating mechanisms underlying formal and informal organizational control with the cognitive and motivational processes underlying the two motivational orientations. Specifically, the model shows how rational self-interest and other orientation shape employees' responses to organizational control.

As indicated previously, each of the two general categories of organizational control shown in Figure 8.2 is associated with two distinct regulatory mechanisms. When the regulating mechanism involves behavior–consequence contingencies, the effectiveness of the control practice necessitates that employees be aware of and consider the potential consequences of complying with the organization's

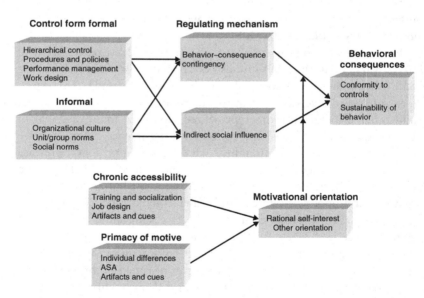

Figure 8.2 The role of motivational orientation in response to informal and formal control

specifications. In contrast, when the regulating mechanism involves indirect social influence, successful control only requires the salience of a specific cue (norm, social information, symbols, etc.) to guide behavior. Here, the employee accepts or adheres to the cued behavior without reflecting on the consequences of the specific action.

Because many forms of formal control involve specification of behavior and links to consequences, formal controls often operate through behavior–consequence contingencies. Additionally, because informal controls are exercised through social influence processes and structures, indirect social influence mechanisms are likely to underlie this mechanism. However, crossover effects can occur between the methods of formal versus informal control and the regulatory mechanism. That is, under certain circumstances, formal controls may operate through indirect social influence and informal controls may operate through behavior–consequence contingencies. Specifically, behaviors may start out being controlled by one process but migrate to the other. There are two forms of such migration. Behavior can initially be controlled by behavior–consequence contingencies but eventually come to be controlled by indirect social influence. As discussed above, early in an employment relationship, informal control is likely to be mediated through compliance, which involves behavior–consequence contingencies. Over time, however, members who successfully adapt and become integrated into the organization often respond to informal controls through the indirect social influence. Behavior can also be mediated by indirect social influence but migrate to being controlled by behavior–consequence contingences. The phenomenon of burnout is illustrative of this transformation. An idealistic individual may act in accordance with values shared with the organization, but as a result of stress, disillusionment, or other forms of disassociation, lose touch with those values and become more focused on the costs and benefits of job performance.

The same process can occur for formal controls. That is, persons may come to identify and internalize formal company goals and principles that were initially controlled using a behavior–consequence contingency. Such would be the case when employees have a sufficiently long tenure in the organization and social processes (e.g., leadership, group processes) support identification and internalization. In such a case, employees' experience with formal controls would come to convey significance that is beyond the behavior–consequence contingency; that is, the formal controls would reinforce the employee's identity and/or core values. Bijlsma-Frankema and Costa (Chapter 13) provide a case for such a transformation wherein the extent to which members of an organization accept control measures depends on whether the practice is fair, reinforces group identity, allows for autonomy, and encourages the development of competency.

It is also possible that a given control technique will influence behavior through both processes at the same time. For example, hierarchical control can certainly be mediated through its ties to consequences in that an employee may be mindful of the rewards and sanctions for complying with a supervisor's directions. Additionally, the employee may also follow the supervisor's direction by virtue of the internalized norm of legitimate authority (i.e., employees reflexively respond to supervisors' requests). The extent to which the influence of this control practice is mediated by one regulatory mechanism or the other may be shaped by whether the broader organizational context promotes rational or heuristic information processing. Cardinal *et al.* (Chapter 3) suggest this sort of process when formal and informal controls co-occur.

The effect of these regulating mechanisms on employee behavior is contingent on the motivational orientation that the employee has adopted. Organizational control mediated by behavior–consequence contingencies is more likely to yield compliance when an employee has adopted a rational self-interested orientation. Alternatively, organizational control that is mediated by indirect social influence is likely to be more effective when an employee has adopted an other orientation. Stated another way, employees who are rationally self-interested should be relatively more sensitive to control via anticipated consequences, and, employees who are other oriented should be relatively more sensitive to control via indirect social influence.

Organizational influences on mode of processing

As shown in Figure 8.2, various dispositional and contextual factors contribute to an individual's motivational orientation. These are broadly grouped into two categories: factors that encourage the primacy of self- versus other interest, and factors that lead to the chronic accessibility of one mode of reasoning over the other. We discuss each of these next.

Primacy of self- versus other interest. The first category encompasses factors that encourage the primacy of self-interest or other interest. Factors that make self-interest salient are expected to lead to greater reliance on rational reasoning. Conversely, factors that make the concerns of others (or the collective) salient are expected to produce a greater reliance on heuristic reasoning. These factors lead to the relative strength of one motivational orientation.

As noted previously, concerns for the self versus others can be seen in certain individual differences. Empirical investigations of individual differences indicate the existence of a broad-based culture comprising prosocial characteristics including empathy, social responsibility, and prosocial values (Schroeder *et al.*, 1995). Similarly, the cultural values of collectivism and interdependent self-construal tend to be associated with concern for others (Triandis, 1995). Given the interplay between other interest and heuristic reasoning, individuals possessing these traits should be more responsive to indirect social control. For example, Ybarra and Trafimow (1998) found that persons with an interdependent self-construal were more subject to normative influences than were persons with an independent self-construal. Thus, individuals who possess other oriented attributes should be more responsive to informal controls than are individuals who lack these attributes.

A similar process can operate at the job level. That is, the characteristics of the job itself can attract individuals with certain values, such as other interest. For example, Holland's (1985) theory of vocational personalities identifies "social" types of individuals who prefer teaching, training, and developmental professions and who also exhibit high levels of other oriented values.

Individual differences are apt to have a role at the collective level as well. Schneider's attraction–selection–attrition (ASA) cycle (Schneider, 1987) describes how persons with similar values can come to dominate a particular organization. This cycle can therefore result in organizations that contain substantial numbers of individuals who are highly self-interested or other interested. Indeed, research by Crandall and Harris (1976) shows that members of volunteer organizations exhibit higher levels of other orientation. In such cases, one would expect employees to adopt a mode of processing that is consistent with their values (i.e., rational in the case of persons who are low in other orientation; heuristic in the case of persons who are high in other orientation). In essence, then, the ASA cycle can influence the relative effectiveness of informal controls at the organizational level.

Note that the direct effect of values that ASA encourages differs from the effect of shared values, which scholars have suggested will enable informal controls to work more effectively (e.g., Ouchi, 1977, 1979). The proposed role of shared values appears to have a basis in what Schein (2004: 111) describes as "internal integration," that is, the tendency for persons with similar values to more easily "establish a system of communication and a language that permits interpretation of what is going on." We propose a mechanism that is different from internal integration. We maintain that shared values will have a different effect on control processes depending upon their impact on the motivational orientation that employees adopt. Specifically, organizational controls mediated by indirect social influence are likely to be more effective if the ASA cycle leads to individuals high in other orientation. However, if the ASA cycle results in a workforce of individuals with a strong rational self-interest orientation, informal controls are likely to be far less effective. The reason for this difference is not based on the "sharedness" of the values but on the effect that values have on how individuals interpret organizational controls. That is, because individuals who are high in other orientation are more sensitive to social influence, the more the organization is staffed with individuals who are high on other-oriented values, the more effective controls based on indirect social influence will be in regulating employee behavior. In contrast, individuals who are rationally self-interested are less likely to comply with social cues for which there is no clear personal benefit.

Research also suggests that other interest can be readily activated in individuals through motive-consistent cues. For example, priming techniques, which involve exposing participants to words that have prosocial meaning, can have a significant impact on other interest and prosocial behavior. Similarly, making salient the concerns of others (as opposed to the benefits to the self) can stimulate prosocial orientation and behavior (Batson, 1990; Grant, 2008). Moreover, other interest can be stimulated by the salience of group identity. Research shows that even a minimal identification with a group can increase cooperation toward other members. Thus, to the extent that artifacts and cues in an organization highlight other interest, employees may possess a high level of other-oriented motivation, which in turn may encourage greater responsiveness to social influence and informal controls. These artifacts and cues can include factors such as the use of language, physical arrangements of groups, and the relative emphasis placed on prosocial activities within and outside the organization. For example, research suggests that a focus or emphasis on external corporate social responsibility (e.g., caring for the environment) leads to greater goodwill among employees' attitudes toward the firm and its members, leading to greater cooperation within the organization (Branco and Rodrigues, 2006).

Chronic accessibility of mode of reasoning. Individuals may persist in a mode of processing because they have previously relied on this process for other activities (Chen *et al.*, 1996). When individuals are repeatedly and consistently prompted to rely on heuristic or rational processing, this process is likely to be chronic or readily accessible for future judgments. Thus, factors that lead to chronic accessibility of rational reasoning should lead individuals to be more responsive to formal controls whereas those leading to chronic accessibility of heuristic reasoning should lead individuals to be more sensitive to informal controls.

Consistent with this view, one can argue that socialization processes within an organization can lead to the dominance of a given mode of reasoning. This is evident from research comparing the problem-solving approaches of individuals trained in economics, who tend to be relatively more effective in applying principles of rational decision-making, with those who were not (Ferraro *et al.*, 2005). Similarly, industries, organizations, and occupations that emphasize risk management can promote a rational, cost-benefit mindset among their employees. This mode may carry over to tasks and problems that do not lend themselves to rational reasoning (Gioia, 1992). Moreover, artifacts and cues may bolster the accessibility to rational reasoning. This tendency was eloquently illustrated in a series of studies demonstrating the impact of relatively subtle visual cues such as images of money on individual judgment and on behavior (Vohs *et al.*, 2006).

When rational reasoning is chronically accessible, employees are apt to respond well to formal controls. Indeed, such controls may actually be more necessary: research suggests that individuals who are trained in economics are not only more adept at rational calculations, but they also are more self-interested and less cooperative. For example, such individuals are less likely to choose ethical or prosocial options when faced with conflicts of interest (Tenbrunsel *et al.*, in press). Thus, in the absence of accountability or other behavior–consequence contingencies, individuals socialized to be rational and self-interested may act with guile and not in the best interest of the organization.

Implications for understanding and leveraging organizational control

The model we have proposed identifies regulating mechanisms that underpin the operation of different forms of organizational control. That is, controls that rely on behavior–consequence contingency, and controls that function through indirect social influence. The model also indicates that each regulating mechanism is consistent with a specific motivational orientation. That is, individuals with a rational self-interested orientation are more responsive to controls involving behavior–consequence contingencies, whereas individuals with an other orientation are more responsive to controls involving indirect social control. Finally, the model specifies ways in which organizations can stimulate different motivational orientation among employees.

The practical benefit of the proposed model lies in its ability to describe how organizations can align their operating practices with the methods they employ to control employee behavior. This form of alignment has implications that are both reactive and proactive. In a reactive sense, the model specifies how an organization can tailor its operating practices to match its dominant form of control. Thus, if an organization is more dependent upon formal controls to assure that employees act to support the organization's objectives, the model specifies techniques that can stimulate the rational processing that enables such controls to be most effective. Thus, in the case of formal controls that rely on behavior–consequence contingencies, the model suggests attracting and retaining employees who are lower in other-oriented values. It also proposes that this type of orientation should pervade other organizational practices such as socialization, training, the design of jobs, and the type of artifacts and cues in the environment. If, on the other hand, the organization places relatively greater emphasis on informal controls, which rely on indirect social influence as the dominant regulating mechanism, the model suggests retention and other practices that favor enhancing other orientation.

One can also view the model as being proactive in that, in addition to addressing the alignment of organizational practices, it specifies regulating mechanisms that support different types of control. This can prompt an organization to focus on the behavior it wishes to control before it decides on the mechanisms it will use to regulate the behavior. If, for example, the behavior in question is very specific, visible, and easily measured (e.g., sales, number of items produced), the organization may wish to employ straightforward behavior–consequence contingencies and structure its supporting practices around rational self-interest.

On the other hand, intense interdependence among employees is a major advantage that organizations enjoy over a reliance on the separate market transactions that characterize techniques such as outsourcing (Simon, 1991). This interdependence makes it extremely difficult to extract the incremental contributions of individual employees. Even though some attempts to accomplish this (referred to as "criterion development") have been successful (Komaki, 1998), such techniques are extremely problematic for all but relatively rudimentary jobs. For such behaviors, the model would propose that organizations rely on indirect social influence and adopt operating practices that support other orientation.

In such cases where desirable behavior is difficult to quantify, informal control systems will be more effective in affecting employee behavior when individuals are other oriented. If individual employees engage in rational cost–benefit calculations as opposed to focusing on the inherently intrinsic and symbolic consequences of informal control mechanisms, an organization cannot be assured that informal control systems will be successful. This is because every agent will have different criteria for weighing the cost and benefits of informal interactions. Such specification is beyond an organization's control, resulting in a wide range of behaviors that diverge from those that are desirable. For example, some people may perceive employee rejection as a significant cost, while others might regard it a negligible by-product. In contrast, if the other oriented employees react heuristically to shared norms, informal control mechanisms will be more effective in producing universal and lasting desirable behavioral outcomes.

Future research

The framework we have proposed prompts a number of issues that are worthy of future research. For example, we focus on the role of orientation on employee reactions to control measures; however, motivational orientation is also likely to affect the choices managers make in employing one form of control versus another. These choices are likely to be shaped by the managers' emphasis on building trust and establishing legitimacy of authority (Long, Chapter 12). As well, the structure of relationships will likely inform managers' choices to employ more or less formal controls and to rely more or less on the group as a conduit for control. Specifically Kirsch and Choudhury (Chapter 10) argue that the depth of interdependence leads to different sorts of risks and thus requires a combination of formal and informal controls that utilize more or less rational mechanisms (e.g., deterrence versus internalization).

The role of time in the processes outlined in the previous framework is another issue worthy of consideration. As discussed previously, the regulating mechanism underlying formal and informal controls may shift over time as employees' relationships to the organization and key members evolve. Moreover, some of these relationships are likely to be recursive. Most notable, experience with a control system is likely to reinforce or undermine certain motivational orientations. For example, the behavior–consequence contingency is learned through experience as well as through organizational cues. Thus, as employees are exposed to formal controls and their enactment, these contingencies are likely to be reinforced and made more salient. This salience, in turn, should prompt greater rational self-interest.

Our proposed model also raises concerns and thus suggests potential research issues involving multinational corporations. Specifically, Eastern cultures encourage greater interpersonal harmony, interdependence, and group cohesion (Hofstede, 1984). In such other oriented cultures, gaining a sense of belonging is more important than in Western cultures, which are more individualistically oriented (Heine *et al.*, 1999; Triandis, 1995). These differences suggest that informal controls may be more effective in Eastern cultures whereas formal controls may be more effective in Western cultures. Although this may present a challenge for the consistent implementation of controls within multinational organizations, it also suggests a fruitful area for future research.

The model that we have proposed in this chapter is an outgrowth of our work, and the work of others, on the psychological processes underlying individual behavior. Traditional models of behavior assume that individuals engage in rational processing and act according to their self-interests. There are, however, myriad examples of situations where these principles do not adequately explain how individuals behave. We believe that expanding the assumptions underlying behavior to include other orientation provides coherent explanations that resolve prior inconsistencies and inadequacies in our understanding of behavior. In the model of control presented here, we have attempted to extend our viewpoint to a domain that has typically not been the purview of organizational behavior. We hope that this framework will provide a novel approach to future research on the functioning of control processes in organizations.

References

Ajzen, I. 2001. Nature and operation of attitudes. *Annual Review of Psychology*, 52: 27–58.

Bargh, J. A. and Chartrand, T. L. 1999. The unbearable automaticity of being. *American Psychologist*, 54: 462–479.

Batson, C. D. 1990. How social an animal? The human capacity for caring. *American Psychologist*, 45: 336–346.

Bazerman, M. H. 1993. Fairness, social comparison and irrationality. In J. K. Murnighan (ed.), *Social psychology in organizations*: 184–203. Englewood Cliffs, NJ: Prentice Hall.

Bazerman, M. H., Tenbrunsel, A. E., and Wade-Benzoni, K. 1998. Negotiating with yourself and losing: making decisions with competing internal preferences. *Academy of Management Review*, 23 (2): 225–241.

Blau, P. M. 1964. *Exchange and power in social life.* New York, NY: John Wiley and Sons.

Branco, M. and Rodrigues, L. C. 2006. Corporate social responsibility and resource-based perspectives. *Journal of Business Ethics*, 69 (2): 111–132.

Brewer, M. B. 2004. Taking the social origins of human nature seriously: toward a more imperialist social psychology. *Personality and Social Psychology Review*, 8 (2): 107–113.

Cardinal, L. B., Sitkin, S. B., and Long, C. P. 2004. Balancing and rebalancing in the creation and evolution of organizational control. *Organization Science*, 15 (4): 411–431.

Chaiken, S. and Trope, Y. 1999. *Dual-process theories in social psychology.* New York, NY: Guilford Press.

Chen, S., Shechter, D., and Chaiken, S. 1996. Getting at the truth or getting along: accuracy- versus impression-motivated heuristic and systematic processing. *Journal of Personality and Social Psychology*, 71: 262–275.

Cialdini, R. B. and Goldstein, N. J. 2004. Social influence: compliance and conformity. *Annual Review of Psychology*, 55 (1): 591–621.

Crandall, J. E. and Harris, M. D. 1976. Social interest, cooperation, and altruism. *Journal of Individual Psychology*, 32: 50–54.

Cropanzano, R., Goldman, B., and Folger, R. 2005. Self-interest: defining and understanding a human motive. *Journal of Organizational Behavior*, 26 (8): 985–991.

Cropanzano, R., Stein, J., and Goldman, B. M. 2007. Self-interest. In E. H. Kessler and J. R. Bailey (eds.), *Handbook of organizational and managerial wisdom*: 181–221. Los Angeles, CA: Sage.

Dawes, R. M. 1988. *Rational choice in an uncertain world*. San Diego, CA: Harcourt, Brace, Jovanovich.

De Dreu, C. K. W. 2006. Rational self-interest and other orientation in organizational behavior: a critical appraisal and extension of Meglino and Korsgaard (2004). *Journal of Applied Psychology*, 91 (6): 1,245–1,252.

De Dreu, C. K. W. and Nauta, A. 2007. The distinct roles of self-interest and other-orientation in organizational behavior: implications for work performance and pro-social behavior. Paper presented at the Society for Industrial Organizational Psychology, New York, NY.

De Dreu, C. K. W., Beersma, B., Stroebe, K., and Euwema, M. C. 2006. Motivated information processing, strategic choice, and the quality of negotiated agreement. *Journal of Personality and Social Psychology*, 90 (6): 927–943.

De Neys, W. 2006. Automatic-heuristic and executive-analytic processing during reasoning: chronometric and dual-task considerations. *Quarterly Journal of Experimental Psychology*, 59: 1,070–1,100.

Eagly, A. H. and Chaiken, S. 1993. *The psychology of attitudes*. Fort Worth, TX: Harcourt, Brace, Jovanovich.

Ferraro, F., Pfeffer, J., and Sutton, R. I. 2005. Economics language and assumptions: how theories can become self-fulfilling. *Academy of Management Review*, 30 (1): 8–24.

Gioia, D. A. 1992. Pinto fires and personal ethics: a script analysis of missed opportunities. *Journal of Business Ethics*, 11 (5/6): 379–389.

Grant, A. M. 2008. The significance of task significance: job performance effects, relational mechanisms, and boundary conditions. *Journal of Applied Psychology*, 93 (1): 108–124.

Haidt, J. 2001. The emotional dog and its rational tail: a social intuitionist approach to moral judgment. *Psychological Review*, 1,089: 814–834.

Heine, S. J., Lehman, D. R., Markus, H. R., and Kitayama, S. 1999. Is there a universal need for positive self-regard? *Psychological Review*, 106: 766–794.

Hofstede, G. 1984. *Culture's consequences: international differences in work-related values*. Beverly Hills, CA: Sage.

Holland, J. L. 1985. *Making vocational choices: a theory of vocational personalities and work environments* (2nd edn.). Englewood Cliffs, NJ: Prentice-Hall.

Irwin, J. R. and Baron, J. 2001. Response mode effects and moral values. *Organizational Behavior and Human Decision Processes*, 84 (2): 177–197.

Kelman, H. C. 2006. Interests, relationships, identities: three central issues for individuals and groups in negotiating their social environment. In S. T. Fiske, A. E. Kazdin, D. L. Schacter, S. T. Fiske, A. E. Kazdin, and D. L. Schacter (eds.), *Annual Review of Psychology*, 57: 1–26. Palo Alto, CA: Annual Reviews.

Komaki, J. L. 1998. When performance improvement is the goal: a new set of criteria for criteria. *Journal of Applied Behavior Analysis*, 31 (2): 263–280.

Korsgaard, M. A., Meglino, B. M., and Lester, S. W. 1997. Beyond helping: do other-oriented values have broader implications in organizations? *Journal of Applied Psychology*, 82: 160–177.

Korsgaard, M. A., Meglino, B. M., Lester, S. W., and Jeong, S. S. 2008. Multiple motives for organizational citizenship behavior. Paper presented at the Society for Industrial and Organizational Psychology, San Francisco, CA.

Langer, E. J. 1989. *Mindfulness*. Reading, MA: Addison-Wesley.

Loewenstein, G. and Small, D. A. 2007. The Scarecrow and the Tin Man: the vicissitudes of human sympathy and caring. *Review of General Psychology*, 11 (2): 112–126.

Malhotra, D. and Bazerman, M. H. 2008. Psychological influence in negotiation: an introduction long overdue. *Journal of Management*, 34 (3): 509–531.

McAllister, D. W., Mitchell, T. R., and Beach, L. R. 1979. The contingency model for the selection of decision strategies: an empirical test of the effects of significance, accountability, and reversibility. *Organizational Behavior and Human Decision Processes*, 24: 228–244.

Meglino, B. M. and Korsgaard, M. A. 2004. Considering rational self-interest as a disposition: organizational implications of other orientation. *Journal of Applied Psychology*, 89: 946–959.

2006. Considering situational and dispositional approaches to rational self-interest: an extension and response to De Dreu (2006). *Journal of Applied Psychology*, 91 (6): 1,253–1,259.

Ouchi, W. G. 1977. The relationship between organizational structure and organizational control. *Administrative Science Quarterly*, 22 (1): 95–113.

1979. A conceptual framework for the design of organizational control mechanisms. *Management Science*, 25 (9): 833–848.

Rhoades, L. and Eisenberger, R. 2002. Perceived organizational support: a review of the literature. *Journal of Applied Psychology*, 87 (4): 698–714.

Schalk, R. and Rousseau, D. M. 2002. Psychological contracts in employment. In N. Anderson, D. S. Ones, H. K. Sinangil, C. Viswesvaran (eds.), *Handbook of industrial, work and organizational psychology, Volume 2: organizational psychology*: 133–142. Thousand Oaks, CA: Sage.

Schein, E. H. 2004. *Organizational culture and leadership* (3rd edn.). San Francisco, CA: Jossey-Bass.

Schneider, B. 1987. The people make the place. *Personnel Psychology*, 40: 437–453.

Schriesheim, C. A., Castro, S. L., and Cogliser, C. C. 1999. Leader-member exchange (LMX) research: a comprehensive review of theory, measurement, and data-analytic practices. *Leadership Quarterly*, 10 (1): 63–113.

Schroeder, D. A., Penner, L. A., Dovidio, J. F., and Piliavin, J. A. 1995. *The psychology of helping and altruism: problems and puzzles*. New York, NY: McGraw-Hill.

Simon, H. A. 1990. A mechanism for social selection and successful altruism. *Science*, 250: 1,665–1,668.

1991. Organizations and markets. *Journal of Economic Perspectives*, 5 (2): 25–44.

Snell, S. A. 1992. Control theory in strategic human resource management: the mediating effect of administrative information. *Academy of Management Journal*, 35 (2): 292–327.

Snook, B., Taylor, P. J., and Bennell, C. 2004. Geographic profiling: the fast, frugal, and accurate way. *Applied Cognitive Psychology*, 18 (1): 105–121.

Sonenshein, S. 2007. The role of construction, intuition, and justification in responding to ethical issues at work: the sense making-intuition model. *Academy of Management Review*, 32: 1,022–1,040.

Stanovich, K. E. and West, R. F. 2002. Individual differences in reasoning: implications for the rationality debate? In T. Gilovich, D. Griffin, and D. Kahneman (eds.), *Heuristics and biases: the psychology of intuitive judgment*: 421–440: Cambridge University Press.

Taylor, F. W. 1911. *The principles of scientific management*. New York, NY: W. W. Norton and Company, Inc.

Tenbrunsel, A. E., Diekmann, K. A., Wade-Benzoni, K. A., and Bazerman, M. H. In press. Why we aren't as ethical as we think we are: a temporal explanation. In A. Brief and B. M. Staw (eds.), *Research in organizational behavior*. Amsterdam: Elsevier.

Tenbrunsel, A. E. and Messick, D. M. 1999. Sanctioning systems, decision frames, and cooperation. *Administrative Science Quarterly*, 44: 684–707.

Terry, D. J., Hogg, M. A., and White, K. M. 1999. The theory of planned behaviour: self-identity, social identity and group norms. *British Journal of Social Psychology*, 38: 225–244.

Triandis, H. C. 1995. *Individualism and collectivism*. Boulder, CO: Westview Press.

Vohs, K. D., Mead, N. L., and Goode, M. 2006. The psychological consequences of money. *Science*, 314: 1,154–1,156.

Wade-Benzoni, K. A. 2002. A golden rule over time: reciprocity in intergenerational allocation decisions. *Academy of Management Journal*, 45 (5): 1,011–1,028.

Ybarra, O. and Trafimow, D. 1998. How priming the private self or collective self affects the relative weights of attitudes and subjective norms. *Personality and Social Psychology Bulletin*, 24: 362–370.

PART IV

Relational control

9 Relational networks, strategic advantage: collaborative control is fundamental

JOHN HAGEL III
Deloitte Center for The Edge

JOHN SEELY BROWN
University of Southern California and Deloitte Center
for The Edge

MARIANN JELINEK
College of William and Mary

A brief glance at the evolution of strategic focus reveals dramatic shifts in relevant context with potent implications for organization and control, rooted in the reversal of a century-old "long wave" centered on internalizing various economic activities to control them, that gave rise to the integrated firm, the corporation, and the conglomerate (Chandler, 1977; Chandler and Salsbury, 1974). Where companies from the mid-1860s to roughly the 1980s created strategic advantage by internalizing activities for greater stability, efficiency, and control, increasingly since then advantage has centered more on faster learning and innovation (IBM_Global_Services, 2006; Prahalad and Krishnan, 2008; Schramm, 2006). But no company can control all the resources needed for innovation (Prahalad and Krishnan, 2008), so creating strategic advantage has increasingly required collaborative, outsourced, strategic alliances (Culpan, 2002; Doz et al., 2001; Doz and Hamel, 1998) and "open innovation" (Chesbrough et al., 2006; Chesbrough, 2003). Moreover, such innovation embraces new business and service models, not just new products: thus new models of business are emerging, centering on networked interactions (Chesbrough, 2006; Sirkin et al., 2008; Tuomi, 2002).

These developments pose critical theoretical and practical challenges for traditional conceptualizations of organizational control. First, most organizational theory of control has fixated on employees of "the firm," yet contemporary relational networks explicitly transcend firm boundaries, to tap into expanded expertise. Much prior discussion addresses control in terms of hierarchical models, economic rationality, and managers' ability to enforce compliance (Bijlsma-Frankema and Costa, Chapter 13), but these are not really options among firms in voluntary association. The evolution of control theory has embraced three central facets, control of *inputs, behavior,* and *outputs* to induce desired results. More recently theorists have moved toward dynamic control theory within the firm over time (Cardinal *et al.*, 2004). Yet the challenge today surpasses organizational boundaries – or rather, *firm* boundaries, for networked activities themselves are quite elegantly organized – a matter to which we shall return. In addition, the contemporary rapid-paced world of constant learning and innovation across firms requires frequent network reconfiguration – building new relationships, adding partners, and creating *ad hoc* assemblages of willing, capable, collaborating partners for changing goals.

A reconsideration of control theory in light of these facts directs our attention to reframing the fundamental meaning of "control"; expanding the system within which control takes place to transcend boundaries of the firm; and extending our understanding of the control transaction to embrace mutual social control; iterative, and possibly intermittent engagements among partners; and changing networks that nevertheless must be coordinated to assure results. Relational networks that seek to build long-term, trust-based relationships across participants to foster innovation constitute an especially challenging case that will be our main focus, but not our only concern (Hagel and Brown, 2008a). Because the precise outcomes cannot be specified in advance, the partners in such networks are profoundly dependent upon one another – more so because each holds expertise or knowledge unknown to the others, yet crucial to shared goals. The organizers in such networks of creation cannot compel compliance, because their partners are not their employees and do have alternative options. Nevertheless, neither the organizers nor their partners are passive objects of others' unilateral power. Instead, members in such innovation networks are usefully construed to be co-controlling their interactions. Just how this might occur is our topic.

This chapter will begin by contrasting the "long wave" of internalized activities and the controls to which they gave rise with the contemporary shift toward collaborative processes, increasingly embracing external partners. Specific examples of networks for innovative product and service design, and, by extension, new collaborative business models will provide our illustrations, underlining the increasing importance of a global perspective on resources and potential alliance for network partners. We next turn in sequence to three levels of managerial practice within such relational networks: identifying and engaging relevant partners; connecting across capabilities, products, and sites; and amplifying opportunities for innovation and learning that are a major reason for networks in the first place. We then take up the broader implications of network control, closing with consideration of the consequences of our perspective for companies and managers, for policy-makers, and for researchers.

From company capabilities to network dynamics

Beyond the market: externalizing collaborative co-creation

If the central fact of business organization for much of the twentieth century was "integration" – internalizing activities in order to control them – a very different trend has characterized business organization since perhaps 1980. First visible in the United States in the reengineering and outsourcing movements, and driven by financial pressures to lower costs and enhance return on assets, firms simply stopped performing activities others could do better, and often cheaper (Hammer and Champy, 1993). Activities that did not directly add value were outsourced or eliminated while refocusing attention on what a given firm did best enabled superior performance (Quinn, 1992). Specialist firms abounded, ready to take on contract manufacturing, software development, industrial design – an endless array of activities formerly the responsibility of an integrated firm precisely because they were often unavailable outside in earlier times – reflecting the growing elaboration of the world economy. In such conditions, old assumptions about what must be internalized come up for reconsideration, as does the very definition of "what business we are in" (Hagel and Singer, 1999). Yet the issues of coordination, quality assurance, and control that drove early firms to internalize these activities did not disappear: indeed, they become still more challenging when geographical, cultural, and institutional distance intervene. As this is being written, melamine contamination of dairy products, candies, chocolates, and infant formula from China are in the news. Not long ago, so were children's toys with lead paint, counterfeit drugs and airplane parts, and "grey market" products (substandard rejected by

Western companies, or "excess" production flowing through
unauthorized channels), as well as cars identical to those produced
for General Motors (GM) that were "rebadged" with the name of the
Chinese maker. Of course, China is by no means the only locus for
such disputes; recent news found similar issues in the United States
(McWilliams, 2008), underlining melamine contamination as a control issue, not a "China" issue. Moreover, such opportunistic behavior
is by no means the only difficulty in collaborative action.

Particularly where partners seek to create something new, to
develop cutting-edge technologies, manufacturing processes or services, or even new business models where "the answer" cannot be
specified in advance, much more is at risk – and it is much more
difficult to ascertain whether a partner is performing in good faith.
Once business moves from predominantly "inside the firm" to predominantly "with the network," a whole new set of control issues
arises. Before we turn to control issues, however, some clarification of
network terminology is required. Networks differ, and within different networks, different issues of relationship, risk, and control arise.

A taxonomy of networks

"Networks" have become increasingly important, both in business
and non-business sectors, as means of collaboration to achieve complex goals. Analysis of relationships, communications flows, and
influence as instances of social capital (e.g., Burt, 1992) has drawn
much attention, but consistent terminology is needed to clarify among
and between different types of networks, such as innovation networks,
relational networks, creation networks, process networks, and relational process networks, among others. Although humans have always
collaborated, much organization theory has preferred to focus on
matters internal to the firm, with relatively less focus on the very
interfirm or interorganizational links that have become so important.

To highlight the dimensions of difference, we point to the character
of the interaction involved. On one extreme, two or more partners
may engage in a one-off exchange, with no expectation of further
interactions: this is a transactional relationship, at arm's length and
emphasizing the transaction. The parties have no obligation to one
another past the transaction; this is the focus of much single-round,
zero-sum game theory analysis. On another extreme, multiple

partners may engage in an ongoing series of interactions: this is a relational exchange, engaging and requiring trust, and focused on continuing interaction. Further still, beyond simple transactions, partners may cooperate with one another to share business processes in their ongoing relationship.

We will use the following explicit taxonomy throughout the paper, starting with the broadest and moving to subcategories of relationships:

- *Innovation networks* – any broad-based mobilization of resources across firm boundaries to deliver new value to the marketplace, including both transactional and relational networks.
- *Transactional networks* – networks that access resources across firm boundaries largely through short-term transactions. There is no necessary expectation of a relationship beyond the immediate transaction, although parties may transact with one another repeatedly.
- *Relational networks* – networks that both rely on and build long-term, trust-based relationships to deliver new value to the marketplace, including both tightly coupled networks like the Toyota supplier network and loosely coupled networks like Li & Fung.
- *Relational process networks* – networks that not only rely on long-term, trust-based relationships but also organize extended business processes into loosely coupled modules of activity that enhance scalability, diversity, and flexibility.

Using this taxonomy, the four examples we highlight in this chapter would break out as follows, distinguished by the nature of their interactions, the duration of continued exchange, and the degree of entrainment among shared business processes (see Table 9.1). These processes in turn create distinct requirements for trust, distinctively different potentials for control, and concomitant potentials for achieving sustained innovation, accelerated learning, and richer opportunities through sharing of tacit knowledge in particular. In these kinds of networks trust is a critical underpinning for open information exchange and learning.

- Dell – Dell operates a relational network of suppliers like Toyota's system, but it relies on original design manufacturers (ODMs) from Taiwan who operate relational process networks to support the design of new computers. From its corporate clients' perspective, Dell's "virtual IT department" services constitute a relational network, linked to software and component suppliers.

Table 9.1 *Innovation networks: any broad-based resource mobilization across boundaries*

Network types:	Transactional networks	Relational networks	Relational process networks
	Often market-mediated, partners access resources through short-term exchanges or transactions.	Ongoing or repeated exchanges, predicated on trust, where partners depend on one another to create and deliver new value. May be loosely or tightly linked.	Ongoing, trust-based relationships where partners devolve essential business processes to one another, collaborating to achieve a conjoint business model.
Examples:	InnoCentive	**Tightly linked:** Toyota's supply chain. Dell's suppliers. For its corporate clients, Dell operates as a "virtual IT department."	Taiwanese original design manufacturers (ODMs)
		Loosely linked: Partners orchestrated by Li & Fung.	VISA's shared process network. Flat panel display development.

- Apple's iPod – Apple's network depended on a key participant in its early iPod efforts, PortalPlayer, which in turn operated a relational process network that underpinned much of Apple's early success in the commercialization of the iPod.
- VISA – VISA operates a relational process network, although it is somewhat of a special case because at least in its early decades its participants all had an ownership stake in VISA.
- Flat panel displays – participants came together in a relational process network.

Innovation networks more broadly have been discussed by Chesbrough (e.g., Chesbrough, 2006; Chesbrough *et al.*, 2006; Chesbrough, 2003) but we focus here on the opportunities and requirements of relational networks, and even more specifically, relational process networks that provide much richer opportunities for sustained and scalable innovation because of their ability to access and develop tacit knowledge among the participants.

From input, output, and behavior control to trust-based relations

Since organizations – and most especially, firms – are intended to achieve particular objectives, some means of assuring achievement of those ends is needed (Tannenbaum, 1968). Control systems have been described in three different targets – control of inputs, outputs, or behaviors (Cardinal, Sitkin, and Long, Chapter 3) – each entailing various tradeoffs (Jensen and Meckling, 1976; Ouchi and McGuire, 1975; Williamson, 1981). Most firms deploy elements of all three systems, although often favoring one or another (Jaeger and Baliga, 1985; Oliver and Anderson, 1995; Ouchi and McGuire, 1975; Snell, 1992). *Behavioral controls* specify the procedures to be followed, and rely on close monitoring and supervision, along with behaviorally based performance assessment (Cheng and McKinley, 1983). *Output controls* monitor results, rather than behavior, and rely on clear standards (Thompson, 1967), as well as outcomes that can be observed and measured (Eisenhardt, 1985; Ouchi, 1979). *Input controls* are suggested for situations where output cannot be easily measured, nor behavior closely monitored; these include "clan" approaches that emphasize social suasion and group social pressure (Ouchi, 1979), resource sharing and socialization (Govindarajan and Fisher, 1990) as well as hiring, training, and selection (Snell, 1992).

These research findings are uniformly rooted in firm-based control situations, although peer pressure and informal socialization are also widely documented in social groups ranging from families to peer groups (Asch, 1958) to societies (Kuran, 1997). Yet their applicability to networks as voluntary associations – where individual survival is not at issue, as in families; where firms have alternative opportunities; or where the enormous social pressure of a repressive society (Kuran, 1997) is not at work – remains an open question. Even if the underlying theory seems apropos, what kinds of control might be suitable in such voluntary business associations? A simplistic answer is that participants join in the first place, cooperate in the second, and continue in the third because they perceive benefits to doing so outweigh the costs (Barnard, 1956). But what benefits, particularly when – for example, because a product is new and innovative – market outcomes may reside in a distant and uncertain future? And, beyond withdrawal of those uncertain future benefits, what controls make sense?

Control under such circumstances poses new challenges, and the mechanisms available to resolving the challenge are our focus: it is not clear that the traditional notions of behavior, input, and output as typically construed are applicable here. Why not? First, because the traditional mechanisms of control presume a hierarchical relationship not present in networks. Network members, after all, are not "employees," and they typically have alternative opportunities for business, while the focal firm seeking their collaboration may have few options. Shifting strategy focus from inside a single firm (with a single, hierarchical order, legitimate authority, and at least a nominally common strategy) to a network is one problem: how shall non-employee participants be enticed to cooperate at all, or to shift to a new strategy, or to share critical insights?

Transactions, and indeed transactional networks, rest on the assumption that price in a marketplace subsumes the essential information needed. By contrast, relational networks undertake much less certain interactions, where value is "to be determined" in the future; where behaviors cannot easily or usefully be specified, because learning is a desired result; and where ongoing relationships, trust, and shared insight are central.

Shifting from static to dynamic capabilities poses another challenge, for we focus particularly on networks aiming to learn and innovate, seeking to create new knowledge by their interactions, rather than simply enacting a prior recipe. Strategy theory on dynamic capabilities opened an important door in providing theoretical grounding for changing configurations of capabilities. Recent work on supply chain innovation, involving other firms beyond the focal organization, also provides insight.

But this creates a dilemma: most work on organizational control focuses precisely on *organizational* control – control of employee actors to ensure coincidence of their acts with the firm's strategic intent, for example, although more sophisticated observers also note that agile response to changing circumstances may sometimes be preferable to reproducing an abstract intent: see Moncreiff (1999). Once we step into networks of collaborating, but independent partners, hierarchical models of control don't work – partners are not employees. Moreover, particularly for innovation networks, outcomes cannot be precisely specified in advance if the collaboration is to benefit from partners' creative capabilities. Thus outcomes must be emergent – and cannot be tightly predetermined contractually. Learning, the most critical desired outcome, is unpredictable in detail.

How, then, to exercise control? Older methods – bringing activities "inside" the organization's boundaries to own them; exercising hierarchical control; depending on clan-like identity – are no longer feasible for external collaboration with equals who are often distant in geography, culture, and expertise. Another critical limitation: because outcomes are emergent and breakthroughs are sought, results have a futurity and an uncertainty that disables transactional remuneration. Transactions require a here-and-now certainty about the exchange of value in the transaction; learning and innovation, by contrast, are rooted in ongoing interchange. This limitation is further exacerbated because all parties in relational networks focused on innovation have a critical need for trust-based interactions – to address uncertainties, emergent outcomes, and sought-for home runs – that only enduring relationships can achieve.

We turn now to brief descriptions of four contemporary networks to illustrate the nature of emerging control practice. As our taxonomy indicated, networks differ along dimensions of duration of relationship, degree of engagement, and trust. Dell Computer's interlocked business network uses virtual networking to drive innovation. Dell's supplier network relies on enduring relationships with suppliers, but of a fairly conventional nature: Intel supplies chips, and Dell and Intel exchange information on customer demands and technical capabilities. Similarly, Apple Computer's iPod and iPhone networks highlight both agility and multiple usages of capabilities that an enduring network can provide. But beneath Apple's successful relational network is the much more process-entrained network of Portal-Player: this network has devolved key development, design, and manufacturing processes to network partners. Though these particular networks center on so-called "high tech" firms, and technology-based products, they are by no means the sole practitioners of these new managerial arts: the birth of the VISA network exemplifies a similar network collaborating to create a new business model, a means of serving customers that was not only new to the world, but quite contrary to then-existing industry practice (Hock, 2005). Finally, we'll look at the international consortium of companies that developed flat panel displays: a central element in contemporary computers, especially laptops – but also in cell phones, video cameras, and more. The project was so challenging that no company, and indeed no *country*, possessed the technical, scientific, manufacturing, and financial resources to achieve it alone (Murtha *et al.*, 2001).

Dell Computer's virtual networking. Dell Computer is widely recognized for its made-to-order business model through which consumers can order a custom-built computer online or by telephone. Dell's customer service representatives are trained to query the customer, ascertain needs, and advise customers to ensure the best choice. Less well known by many is Dell's much larger corporate business: Dell is essentially the IT service function for many firms, maintaining a website with pre-specified choices for hardware and software as negotiated by the corporate customer. The employee chooses from the available online options, seeing what appears to be an internal corporate webpage. Dell manufactures the computer and loads it with the firm's choice of software, then arranges for delivery of the fully loaded equipment to the employee's desk: true "plug-and-play," with no requirement for lengthy set-up processes (Magretta, 1998). Dell operates "as if" it were the corporate IT support department: from the client firm's perspective, an important activity is devolved to Dell, as a relational network partner, intertwined seamlessly with its clients. For firms with hundreds or thousands of desktops to maintain, the advantages are enormous.

Dell's own supply network is far more discrete. For Dell's supply network, the confluence of constant input from consumers, high-demand gamers, and corporate customers translates to valuable information about changing computation requirements. Dell's high volume usage of key components makes the firm a highly desirable customer, with whom chip makers like Intel interact in early design stages: Dell's up-to-the-minute customer knowledge helps to ensure that new chips meet real customer needs. Because it holds mere hours (or less) of inventory, Dell quickly shifts to versions of top chips, Intel gets immediate feedback, and both consumer and corporate clients get effective, low-cost systems. Even though there is substantial trust in the Intel–Dell relationship, the partners' business processes remain discrete.

Dell's initial network pioneered in the design of a "pull" manufacturing system that tied customer requirements for highly customized configurations of a computer to on-demand manufacturing for delivery within days. Its innovative direct selling channels, combined with a lean manufacturing approach, provided sustainable competitive advantage that other computer companies struggled to replicate. More recently, however, reports suggest that Dell is looking for a buyer for its factories – moving further, if it does sell them, into networked partnerships as a fundamental business model; for additional discussion of Dell's approach, see Hagel (2008).

What would be different about such outsourced manufacturing? Among other things, it would be predicated on having a core business process performed by others, requiring a different kind of loosely coupled network arrangement (to which we shall return) to achieve the rapid innovation, agile response to changing customer needs, and high-quality Dell needs. For laptop computers, Dell – like most other laptop makers – relies on ODMs based primarily in Taiwan. ODMs now perform design as well as manufacturing functions for major computer original equipment manufacturers (OEMs) – activities that were formerly considered core proprietary activities. The Taiwanese ODMs have gained market share by offering compelling value – bringing together higher value-added activities as well as offshore manufacturing assembly, leveraging not only lower labor cost but also bringing their customers compressed design cycle times, component cost savings, tighter inventory management, and more adaptive (often local) supply chains.

Apple's iPod network. Apple's iPod is in many regards the story of PortalPlayer, a firm that played a central role in the commercialization of the iPod. The real relational network in this story was Portal-Player's, not Apple's, although it was essential to iPod's success, and thus to Apple's. If Dell's network reflects incremental advances in components, Apple's iPod displays a much more aggressively innovative new product development activity arising directly out of the network. The iPod was not the first portable music player to the market, but its form factor – the geometry of its design, which affects ease of use, style and component integration – all yielded performance quality that swept to market dominance rapidly. In 2008, Apple's market share was over 70 percent of all MP3 players, and 84 percent of all player sales (Elmer-DeWitt, 2008), while iTunes was the largest seller of music in any format in the United States.

Apple's success hinged on advanced performance capabilities: a minute disk drive, rapid development (nine months from concept to product!), and effective collaboration in an open business model with a range of partners. One of the key participants in Apple's network was PortalPlayer, which provided the basic platform for MP3 files, produced the reference design in collaboration with Apple, and orchestrated technical design input for the iPod through its own global network.

Once the iPod was up and out, subsequent development of the iPhone engaged many of the same partners, used similar software and the iTunes website user interface for device setup and updates. iPhone launched Apple into the cell phone business, with a runaway bestseller. But its significance is not launching "a single" new business; the development process multiplexed new features, redefined device categories, and blurred distinctions among product lines – and relied upon a network of capable partners. Apple has persistently utilized its networks' technical developments, features, and user interface enhancements across its products. Thus the 2008 iPod Nano and iPod Touch have features initially developed for iPhone, like Album View, accelerometers to shift between landscape and portrait layout, touch screens, and the common iTune interface, including the App Store (for Applications, small computer programs to download onto iPods and iPhones). The result is a cluster of businesses, leveraging capabilities that sprang from earlier accomplishments of the PortalPlayer relational process network and other network participants. For network partners, these continued developments extend the benefits of participation, making continued participation highly attractive.

The marketplace results suggest the impact and strategic advantage of such collaborative innovation. As of September 2008, some 65 million users had downloaded over 100 million applications – in the first sixty days of the App Store's existence. As of September 2008, 90 percent of all US cars offer iPod integration. iPod Touch and iPhone blend the product categories of MP3 player, game platform, video and TV viewer, among others. With the help of its collaborating partners – game developers, music providers, and software developers as well as the collaborating hardware and components providers – Apple has moved well beyond its initial positioning as "a computer company," shifting customers' expectations along the way, to become . . . what? A portable musical device company? A cell phone company? An experience company? But Apple still makes computers, and indeed has seen its market share rise, along with its profits, in all its product lines; its network partners continue to benefit from these successes. For instance, in October 2008, Apple's 3G iPhone was second only to Motorola's RAZR, which sold for as little as 25 percent of the lowest iPhone price. Moreover, through its iTunes website, Apple was also the number one music distributor in any format in the United States, exceeding Walmart, Best Buy, and Amazon. Tapping into relational networks has enabled Apple to enter and prosper in areas where it had not been previously active, and to do so very rapidly, thereby maximizing the benefits of its collaborative innovation activities, precisely because the company can draw upon the deep expertise of its partners. Apple itself need not recreate the relational network PortalPlayer has already set up and which it manages effectively.

In short, Apple's network of alliances and collaborating partners has supported creation of dramatically new ways of being in consumer electronics, and entertainment, and software, and electronic devices, among other businesses. Apple's relational network and its dynamic processes accelerate capabilities development for all the partners, including Apple, and also speeding the pace of coherent strategic change.

VISA, a global collaborative finance network. VISA's early development rested on an extraordinary relational process network that allowed VISA to focus on building and innovating around a shared processing platform, while the banks in turn could focus on innovating in terms of product design and marketing initiatives to accelerate adoption of this innovative financial service product (Hock, 2005). Although it is hard to remember that when VISA was formed the credit card was still a relatively new innovation, and a troubled one at that, VISA's vision of a global network was a frame-breaking innovation. Moreover, without the common relational process network to solve major problems of transaction exchange and widespread card acceptance across individual banks' customer and retailer networks, credit cards could not have produced either widespread credit transactions or profitability to issuing banks. Having solved the problem in the United States, similar issues reemerged when the credit card network moved across international boundaries, and new agreements and standards had to be negotiated.

The worldwide VISA network evolved as a collaborative participation of some 22,000 owner-member banks that simultaneously competed with one another for customers, and cooperated in honoring one another's charges – to the tune of more than $1.25 trillion annually, across borders and currencies. Dee Hock, the founder and CEO Emeritus of VISA, calls VISA's early organization "chaordic," by which he means it exhibits a self-governing blend of both order and chaos, achieving "enough" harmony to operate, but enough chaos to constantly generate new, emergent capabilities (Hock, 2005).

As with the flat panel displays (see below) or iPod networks, VISA too is more than the sum of its parts – and more than it may be at any instant: there is always more potential because human actions are not deterministic. As problems, threats, or opportunities arise (the need to expand the network abroad, for example, dealing with currency exchange and expanded security), the partners can come together to generate new responses, share best practices, and commission experiments. Yet such networks as these do not arise within any of the standard frameworks we typically think of, as neither ownership rights nor short-term financial gains and incentives are sufficient to foster them. To succeed, banks had to agree to standards for exchange, honoring other banks' credit cards, and respecting cardholders' credit. No individual partner has incentive to start a network according to traditional conceptualizations, because no partner owns it or has a primary claim on its benefits. Instead, the network must be created in order to enable the benefits enhancing each participant's credit card.

Indeed, the conflict between network needs and traditional ownership and financial gain ideas very nearly sank the network from the outset: Bank of America (BofA), the originator of the networked credit card idea, first wanted total control and rule-making authority, while the many smaller banks were enormously wary of being controlled, disadvantaged, or even taken over by BofA or by one of the other large bank partners. Moreover, in the United States, the network even required a Justice Department letter assuring that no antitrust action would be taken so long as anticompetitive effects were not observed, since the services and products of VISA could only be provided by means of joint action (Hock, 2005: 162).

In the VISA network, information – defined as "a difference that makes a difference" – served as a "boundary acid" to dissolve old boundaries and create new patterns of information sharing and cooperation: networked credit card interactions served as the boundary object (Star and Griesemer, 1989). Eventually, the US network was expanded to incorporate global partners – entailing massive additional amounts of information, raising additional issues of security, and adding standards for exchange, equitable rules, and more. What had driven its success was profoundly simple:

At critical moments, all participants had felt compelled to succeed. And at those same moments, all had been willing to compromise. They had not thought of winning or losing but of a larger sense of purpose and concept of community that could transcend and enfold them all (Hock, 2005: 245).

Dee Hock's network control approaches diverge dramatically from the ownership-based, centralized, command-and-control notions of organization embedded in most corporations and in most intercorporate interactions. The network was the point: without the participation of many independent banks around the United States (and later, the world), the VISA card would be of limited value; local credit cards had not been especially successful. Yet without the trust, collaboration, and information sharing of Dee Hock's organizing process, the smaller banks would not have joined to be subservient to BofA. While this seems evident in retrospect, initially BofA envisioned a traditional approach of centralized control, rules, and regulations handed down from the dominant firm. By contrast, Hock's approach relied on engaging the ideas of the participants as equals, open communication and discussion of problems, peer pressure, shared visions, and trust in an ongoing relationship.

Participants "felt compelled to succeed" because they began to perceive the benefits of networked collaboration, open information sharing, and trust that had characterized the organizing process Hock led. "The will to succeed, the grace to compromise," equitable treatment, open sharing of information, trust and open solicitation of opinions and ideas from collaborators were central to Hock's "chaordic" organizing ideas, even if they are far less characteristic of VISA's contemporary and more traditional form.

Flat panel displays. Flat panel displays (FPDs) were the holy grail of the information age: the dream was of giant, wall-hanging flat televisions, available and affordable for any household – but also critical to on-board auto navigation screens, hand-held devices and medical instruments, and many other displays. FPD was a new kind of industry, driven by knowledge that was distributed around the globe that had to be recombined, shared, redeveloped, and redeployed. An international community of players, leveraging unique national capabilities, was critical to creating the new global industry, because no company and no country had all the necessary resources. Immense financial investments were required, but these did not initially make sense until a host of technical problems were addressed, and these could be solved only in collaborative interaction.

Companies "needed to participate in the rapid pace of knowledge accumulation and change in FPD itself," because so much depended on tacit knowledge and experience (Murtha *et al.*, 2001: 4). Moreover, the need for speed – "an awesome fact" here, as in many technology industries (Jelinek and Schoonhoven, 1994) – put a premium on partners' proximity, continuity, and learning. Yet the critical expertise was scattered among American, Japanese, and other firms that needed to "learn to know what they did not know" (Murtha *et al.*, 2001: 170). Only by relying heavily on alliances, decentralized authority, and accountability to and for operations outside their own home countries – and their firms – could these problems be solved.

For example, as Murtha *et al.* (2001: 193) reports, Corning's Display Technologies "coordinates among substrate R&D and production sites in the US, Japan, and Korea, as well between the division and Corning's core R&D organization in the US. Affiliates retain a high degree of autonomy." Joint ventures and collaborative production continue, sharing authority and responsibility across countries and companies to this day.

What is interesting here is that at the outset, though the parties could agree on an end target, it was so far from the capabilities of any company, or any single national cluster of companies, that intermediate steps could not be specified, nor could effective contracts be written. Significant amounts of trust and openness were essential to move forward, as the participants were neither employees nor contractually obligated, nor could their knowledge be owned by any central company. Much of their joint achievement turned on tacit knowledge, developed in collaboration, as they shared insights and experiences, problems and solutions, ideas and even production protocols across firm boundaries. Partial successes – small FPDs – were successfully incorporated into cameras, cell phones, and the like (where the participants competed). These paved the way for still more development and expansion into other products, all the while aiming toward the large FPD computer display screens and wall televisions of today.

Early successes were leveraged into succeeding efforts as network participants shared their insights. Contributing those insights was central to continued participation – and continued network membership was essential to remaining part of the discovery process through which participation in the next round of product, and access to the next round of learning, were assured. At each step, potentially proprietary information was shared with network partners. Participants were constrained to operate on trust because traditional hierarchical controls were not suitable; behavior could not be specified; and multiple cultures were involved, so cultural controls as typically understood would not do. Moreover, speed was of the essence.

Even though ideas at any step along the way had potentially great proprietary value, their value in an ongoing stream of evolution was even more valuable. What did work for control was the incentive of continued participation, earned by collaborative behavior; and the evident advantage of being part of the leading edge of development, well beyond what any single entity could fathom: continued membership meant continued, accelerated learning vastly beyond what non-participants could manage. Clearly, new means of control and new thinking about it are needed to address these needs. We term such learning-oriented, long-term associations relational process networks because they share responsibility for core business processes with trusted partners, with and from whom each member learns, accelerating their own capabilities and those of the network. Central to such networks is that they both rely upon and build trust-based relationships over time.

Global high-tech regions as resource and challenge

FPD offers a good bridge into understanding network evolution, because FPD exemplifies an industry in which distinct, observable clusters of related technical expertise have arisen, evolved, and shifted locales. When the FPD effort began, integrated circuit and microcomputer design was led by US firms, while the older technology of memory chips was dominated by Japanese firms (which also led in some consumer electronics). As the FPD effort proceeded, much manufacturing development at first took place in Japan, to take advantage of a cluster of specialist expertise in precise, miniaturized manufacturing: the geographic proximity of advanced manufacturing facilitated network information sharing across firms.

Eventually, however, Taiwan became a center for flat panel display manufacture, as pioneering Japanese manufacturers licensed their technology to Taiwanese firms, thereby extending the revenue production of the (older) generation manufacturing processes as well as extending the network of participants. Further, by expanding production across the industry, component costs were further reduced, expanding the potential applications for earlier-generation (smaller-sized) displays, even as the advanced manufacturers moved on to the next, larger generation (discussed at length in Murtha *et al.*, 2001). This expansion is an example of network evolution, showing how network benefits are extended as additional partners apply learning developed in an initial collaboration.

Global clusters of creative action – "spikes" – offer both a locus and an exemplar for outlining the challenges of control in collaborative innovation networks, a special case with implications. Such clusters are mutually reinforcing sites of exponential development: near neighbors in the same industry attract others to serve them and their needs; industry incumbents exchange ideas (and, often, personnel as well) (Kenny, 2000). Such clusters of specialist expertise leap ahead of existing mainstream practice, because talent gathers in highly specialized local business ecosystems around the world. As such, spikes have always been a key engine of economic growth as talent seeks to come together in specific locations in quest of richer opportunities to collaborate and rapidly improve performance. As an example, spikes spread westward in the United States – from the textile mills of Lowell, Massachusetts, to the steel mills of Pittsburgh to the automobile assembly plants in Detroit and finally the high-tech companies of Silicon Valley – marking various stages of economic growth.

While Silicon Valley is the contemporary archetype, numerous other spikes are beginning to emerge as technical and scientific capability spreads, often assisted by government support (e.g., Chinese requirements for joint ventures and in-country research as the price of entry to China). Indian education has facilitated software training and development, while import and export rules have been adapted to favor software. Bangalore's software development sector is the result.

FPD made use of several global high-tech regions to achieve the requisite research, development, manufacturing, engineering, scale, and ultimately, innovation required. Note that this is true not just for the FPD case, but it's also clearly a key success factor in both the PortalPlayer and Dell ODM examples. The networked nature of FPD's (or PortalPlayer's and Dell's) broadly distributed international effort differs dramatically from another high technology breakthrough, IBM's massive System 360 effort. IBM transformed the global industry by its development of a new, massively scalable architecture, drawing on resources beyond those of any other company in the 1960s (Chandler, 2001). Where IBM's challenges for the 360 were financial, technical, and (internally) managerial, the FPD project was technically, financially, and managerially beyond any company – so it also added the challenges of innovation network control. For instance, where IBM could hold internal "shoot outs" to adjudicate alternatives, FPD participants' multiple solutions and possibilities required empirical resolution. These could be decided only on the factory floor – did they work? The financial hurdles inside IBM pale in comparison to those facing FPD, which could only be resolved in the marketplace as each sequential size improvement (and its associated manufacturing tricks) achieved applications that could be sold to fund further development. The critical value of multiple partners' contributions to the overwhelming complexity of manufacturing process meant that the network could make technical progress by virtue of its ongoing relationships that was simply impossible for non-participants.

Today, more centers of technical excellence in more diverse technologies have emerged, expanding the challenges and opportunities. On the one hand, "all of us are more knowledgeable, innovative, and informed than any of us is." On the other hand, consorting with strangers in cyberspace where traditional input, output, and behavioral controls don't work, and where trust is essential, requires development of new management practices to achieve the functionality of control without power or hierarchy, detailed contractual obligations, or immediate incentives. What would effective network versions of these controls be like? A closer look at the requisite management practices for global networking can suggest insights.

Relational networks as management practice

Three levels of managerial practice can be identified as the minimum essentials for creating networks, with subsequent levels building on earlier ones. Since relational networks aim for enhanced capability, faster learning, and more rapid problem-solving, especially in service of innovation, managerial practice centers on these criteria for action. Moreover, the nature of contemporary alliances – increasingly global, often reflecting the emergence of new spikes of creativity and expertise, and dynamic in their evolution – is in network requirements. Thus partners may not be found in familiar places – or with familiar faces. Multiple partnerships may bridge different locales, depending on what (new) capability is required, or what new possibilities emerge over time. Where relational networks deliver their greatest benefits, however, is in amplifying the participants' capabilities to learn and thus to innovate (in products, in processes, in business models or in all of these). As with FPD and iPod, whole new product categories can arise; as with Li & Fung, whole new approaches to orchestrating business activities can generate new sources of strategic advantage.

First level of management practice: identify and engage relevant partners

Old paradigms of who's the "developed country" source of ideas, and who's the "developing company" recipient of products, advanced technology, and the like are increasingly obsolete (Doz *et al.*, 2001; Doz and Hamel, 1998; Friedman, 2005, 2008). Thus managers seeking to benefit from emerging spikes of creative capability need to recognize where innovation is that might be relevant, so that appropriate partners can be sought. Both the relevant capabilities – and thus pool of partners – as well as the locus of innovation can change, as new centers of creativity, talent, and skills arise in new places.

Partner selection can be construed as a classic instance of input control: identifying the right partners is an essential first step for possible success. However, it is input into a *network*, not into a firm; partners are typically (but not always) themselves firms. Criteria for consideration will surely include relevant expertise, reputation, reliability, and past experience, and ability to learn and share information, among other factors: partner selection addresses hoped-for, long-term relational behaviors, particularly around trust because it is so crucial to information-sharing, problem-solving, and learning. All this suggests that long-term relationships are a plus – so long as they don't become anchors to obsolete practice, too-limited partner sets, and outdated assumptions. The right partners may be new partners, in new places, with new kinds of knowledge; who's "right" for one project may not be for the next (but may still be valuable for other efforts).

Identifying the right partners, then, requires finding both requisite expertise and appropriate collaborators with whom to build a relationship, where "appropriate" has as much to do with relational behavior as nominal expertise. A critical question is whether a potential partner is trustworthy. But fabricating a relational network will also require attracting the partner's long-term interest and building trust in a firm-to-firm relationship, where desirable potential partners may have many alternatives. The new network will then require generating mutually acceptable control mechanisms, as well as creating new ways of learning, sharing benefits, and exchanging both tacit and explicit information: in short, creating the infrastructure of the network's interactions. Potential partner firms' people, their organizational learning capabilities, openness to learning, and technical expertise are all important inputs in the networked world, essential elements in a networked innovation process that is rooted in trust.

Assuming that potential partners have been identified, both selection and mutual socialization are involved, and these are more difficult when the parties interact across organizational and cultural boundaries, rather than simply within them. Dee Hock's (2005) account of mutuality among the VISA partner organizations, and of his savvy efforts to use group suasion to achieve consensus, highlight the potency of shared visions of system-level benefits in trust-building. Formal member ownership and control of the relational network of VISA recognized a reality vastly different from the enterprise-centric views still prevalent in organization theory, strategy, and managerial practice (and characteristic of VISA today, as a more traditional business). In short, collaboration in a trust-based network across firm boundaries relies on controls substantially different from traditional conceptualizations of control within the firm.

Similarly, the details in Murtha *et al.* (2001) of the shifting locus of major development in FPDs underline the importance of trust, first in underlining how networked trust within a spike can generate shared benefits. But they also reveal the dynamic nature of spikes over time: Japan as a focal player in precision manufacture has been displaced by Taiwan and China as knowledge was licensed out and networks expanded. Misconstruing FPD development as some form of "national" competition – as many policy-makers were tempted to do – simply ignores the criticality of trust-based, network-level phenomena.

In the case of FPD, the development process was so very expensive that it was imperative to extract more revenue from the "old" capabilities by licensing them out, and expanding markets for early generation products. This also added applications, as others made use of the smaller FPDs, at the same time it expanded into product types and markets the original players didn't address. Rapid expansion of FPD in multiple markets enhanced the value of the innovators' coming new generation displays, helping make FPD a widely embraced standard. Direct negative consequences would have arisen if the original innovators had stopped pushing; then, they'd have simply licensed others to eventually surpass them. Meanwhile, however, shifting manufacturing to (much) lower cost locations while the innovators developed the technology further, into larger screens, gave them both higher revenues (license revenue plus expanded sales with lower cost products) to further fund the very expensive ongoing development activity.

Original partners had to share proprietary information, trusting partners' reciprocity; the Japanese had to license their manufacturing processes to others, trusting the benefits of ongoing cooperation to fund FPD; FPD partners today continue delegated decision-making, information sharing, and interactions based on trust. Such relational networks transcend countries, even as they transcend individual enterprises – and they are becoming more common.

Today, many leading-edge devices such as Apple's iPhone and iPod are manufactured in China, where the burgeoning technology cluster will undoubtedly produce other such devices. Very likely, the Chinese engineers, scientists, and technologists offer their own ideas, including some for localized application (Lewin and Peeters, 2006), and some may find global applications: Nokia's cell phone with scrolling screen was originally designed for Asian markets to display ideograms, but its use otherwise is widespread today. Partners to Apple's innovation included Philips, IDEO, Connectix, and WebTV in addition to Portal-Player. For these and many other innovation and networked business activities, broad knowledge of who is capable of contributing, and where and how, will be critical: managers need to be on the lookout for resource opportunities.

As a first impression, these networks might seem assembled by a network organizer who serves as gatekeeper, deciding who could participate in the network. In traditional thinking, the network organizer would define fundamental governance processes to coordinate the activities of the network, for example, determining how disputes will be resolved and how performance will be measured. Yet the traditional view is incomplete. Participants in such a network enjoy choice on both sides.

Network orchestrators will be known not only for the ultimate success of their products in the marketplace, but also for the fairness of their dealings with partners, their willingness to share benefits from collaboration – including learning opportunities, accelerated practice improvements, and financial rewards. In short, rather than a simple power position, network organizers will be enacting a persuasion, an articulation, and a demonstration position. Some sharing of control or mutuality seems essential to maintaining the cooperative network, even if the orchestrating firm is *"primus inter pares."* These characteristics relate both to the inapplicability of traditional centralized controls on the one hand, and the mutual dependency of network members – including the organizer – on the other. Since the relationship is central, ongoing interactions, their fairness and continuing benefit to participants are critical to continued willingness to participate (cf. Barnard, 1956).

The greater the stakes and the less calculable the ultimate outcomes, the more important enduring relationships, reputational capital, and trust among the partners will become. Because new capabilities will be needed for new product categories like FPD, with needed breakthroughs unpredictable in advance, the ability to use and reuse network achievements will be essential to providing extended remuneration. For example, as we noted, Apple's iPhone made use of technologies and partners from the earlier iPod project – and the subsequent iPod Touch traded technologies from iPhone. FPD developers at first could produce only tiny screens – but these became useful for cameras and video display.

Such savvy multiple uses of technology solutions create an ongoing stream of revenues and profits for all; support continued development; and if equitably shared to the satisfaction of the partners, offer substantial inducements for continued collaboration, because the real rewards accrue long-term. Such relational process networks enable participants to get better faster by working with others in the networks than they possibly could working on their own (Hagel and Brown, 2005). This motivates participants to do the right thing in the near-term, that is, sharing insights and information, going the extra mile to solve a problem rather than pursuing opportunistic short-term profit maximization at the cost of the process benefits and the long-term rewards. Successful relational process nets aiming for innovation must therefore focus on building long-term relationships among their participants, creating opportunities for repeated interactions that demonstrate the value of cooperation, and leveraged, shared learning.

Critical management practice for relational networks at this level, then, first involves much more systematically scanning for potentially relevant partners, who may very well be global. Because new centers and new technologies are constantly arising, so, too, are new potential partners. Knowing "where to look" – in terms of the desired arenas of technology, functionality, or science, customer need, latent possibilities, adjacent prospects and trust-building potential – becomes a central management practice that positions a firm for expanded opportunity arising from relational process networks.

Second, firms need a more dynamic view, because what was true of an area yesterday may not be true tomorrow: what's needed is focus on trajectories of capability evolution, rather than simply on capabilities at a given point in time. This, too, depends on trust. Such new capabilities and prospective partners constitute competitive opportunities, but also potential competitive threats, if unrecognized. Firms oriented toward relational networks are more likely to be alert to the possibilities.

Third, firms need to take a more active role in shaping promising spikes – catalyzing growth, technical development, and bridging gaps to enable partners' capability trajectories. Building such relationships early, before the capabilities are fully in place and discernible to the outside world, can create the foundations of trust and mutual respect from which creation networks spring. Building relationships early can also offer additional competitive advantage, foreclosing rivals.

Fourth, firms need new control methods suitable to such relationships' nascent capabilities, trust-building across cultures, and developmental perspectives. Western firms' reliance on highly formal, tightly specified, short-term transactions to access capabilities from specialized third parties will not be appropriate. Nor will a hard-nosed, short-term cost-benefit focus work well. Instead, trust and capabilities can be bootstrapped: a laddered series of value exchanges can serve to create a staircase of accelerating trust. Firms can begin with relatively low value collaborations that are not very tightly specified, so that the partners can begin to develop experience working together and explore opportunities to learn from each other. As their experience and confidence in each other grows, they can move to higher value collaborations where more is at stake. Such trust-building is central to relational networks, which create trust as well as depend upon it.

Alternatively, early high value collaborations that are tightly specified can systematically move to lower levels of specification over time, allowing partners more opportunity to improvise and experiment in collaboration. Companies like Li & Fung and Nike are masters at integrating new partners into their relational networks quickly through such trust-building processes. Long-term, trust-based relationships are key to effectively collaborating in dynamic markets, because trust is the key to the tacit knowledge that drives learning and innovation. It is precisely this tacit knowledge that is most valuable, most impossible to specify in advance, and most fundamentally rooted in trust. Where trust flourishes, tacit knowledge can be shared, to enhance learning, problem-solving, and innovation.

Companies that build successful relational networks are also thoughtful about other aspects of building trust, including attending to potential dependencies. Li & Fung's "30–30" rule addresses trust by explicitly considering partner strength. The rule commits Li & Fung to utilizing a minimum of 30 percent of any partner's capacity in a given year, but never more than 70 percent, leaving a minimum of 30 percent of capacity for the partner's other business. This ensures Li & Fung will be viewed as a significant partner who gets priority, but not as a dominator. Because both sides are making a significant commitment of resources, both invest in building trust.

The safety cushion of 30 percent of capacity avoids total dependency, insuring that partners are more self-reliant and thus more independent, while inviting trust. Moreover, because network partners see other businesses' needs and capabilities, Li & Fung's network is not doomed to tunnel vision. The partner's long-term well-being is served, and with it the long-term potential of the relational network. Maintaining a partner's capability for independent action and avoiding dependency builds trust – and thereby facilitates mutual learning, sharing of insights, and continued relational participation.

Second level of management practice: Connecting across capabilities, products, and sites

The deeper partners get into modular, loosely coupled business activities shared with partners, the more scalable, diverse, and flexible their businesses processes become (Hagel and Brown, 2005, 2006, 2008a, 2008b). Where a firm orchestrates core activities with multiple partners, as Li & Fung does, the relational network becomes increasingly a relational process network. As strategic needs change, new capabilities will be needed; new products don't necessarily reiterate the last innovation network state, but may require new partners, or different configurations. This creates reiterated issues of trust and control, as "old" partners need to embrace "new" partners, or be content not to be included in some activities: perceptions of fairness and legitimate participation arise at each iteration. Li & Fung's 30–30 rule acknowledges the partners' long-term well-being, but also contributes to Li & Fung's freedom of action to reconfigure its relational network: no partner is wholly dependent on the others. All the partners can engage with diverse others; they can utilize their enhanced capabilities elsewhere – potentially further enhancing the original network, adding flexibility, and enabling the network to scale-up at need.

Such reconfigurations occur because highly specialized capabilities from any one spike, or cluster of capability, may well have potentials in multiple applications. Capabilities acquire even more value when they are connected effectively with complementary capabilities available in other spikes around the world. Those who can connect, can create new value-generating configurations: the next wave of value creation in the global economy will come from platforms for connecting capabilities across spikes: rather than building self-contained bilateral relationships like traditional outsourcing relationships with individual outsourcing providers, contemporary companies need to begin developing networks of relationships spanning across diverse participants in multiple spikes, adding and reconfiguring as new capabilities and new application possibilities arise, and connecting partners effectively. These practices dramatically enhance flexibility by virtue of the diverse possibilities they access.

PortalPlayer's connection advantages. One of the most interesting network organizers is PortalPlayer, founded in 1999 by a group of former National Semiconductor executives, and a central player in the introduction of Apple's iPod product line, as we mentioned previously (on 5 January 2007, PortalPlayer was acquired by NVIDIA). PortalPlayer's founders recognized commercial opportunity in the emerging MP3 product category. From the outset, the company was organized as a micro-multinational with its own operations based in both San Jose in the US and Hyderabad in India. They focused on the opportunity to design an MP3 decoder and controller chip with rich firmware explicitly constructed to incorporate technology from a broad range of other companies, so PortalPlayer invested significant efforts in building a global network of technology companies with complementary capabilities to support MP3 development.

PortalPlayer's relational network partners included UK technology providers like the microprocessor company ARM and Wolfson Microelectronics, a specialized provider of digital to analog conversion technology. US participants in the PortalPlayer network included Texas Instruments and Linear Technologies, a small company specializing in power management integrated circuits. From Japan, PortalPlayer recruited Sharp to provide flash memory, Sony for battery technology, and Toshiba for hard disk drive technology. In Taiwan, PortalPlayer developed close relationships with both UMC and TSMC to access silicon foundry capabilities.

PortalPlayer's network was assembled to design and produce innovative prototypes of MP3 players that could meet demanding price points and form factors and performance requirements, using PortalPlayer's platform. That is, PortalPlayer created a relational process network to collaborate on core business processes: its business model is deeply rooted in collaborative innovation and development. When Apple approached PortalPlayer with the idea for a new MP3 product line coupled with an online music store, PortalPlayer mobilized its global design network to help Apple enter the market nine months after the initial product and business concept were approved.

In terms of the iPod product itself, Apple focused on the external design and the user interface, leaving the rest of the design to Portal-Player and its network. Leveraging its initial success with the iPod, PortalPlayer generated over $250 million in revenue with only 280 employees on a variety of products in 2007, and enjoyed ongoing revenue contributions for every iPod and iPhone that Apple sold. On the one hand, PortalPlayer enjoyed an ongoing revenue stream tied to Apple's ongoing success; on the other, PortalPlayer's network enabled vastly accelerated development of multiple generations of product. Furthermore, PortalPlayer's own relational network is how the firm did business: it is a "fabless" semiconductor company, relying on network partners for critical manufacturing capabilities and sharing proprietary knowledge in order to innovate rapidly (as did Apple). Speed, mutual learning, and sharing of proprietary information rests essentially on trust, and PortalPlayer's reputation as a trustworthy participant constitutes important reputational capital.

Alternative connection approaches. Both Apple and PortalPlayer are important contributors to a mighty network of innovation that spans multiple technology hot spots. ODMs in Taipei – companies like Lite-On and Compal – have organized their own relational networks of hundreds of business partners. These relational networks link complementary capabilities in geographic spikes across Asia and North America to support the design of new consumer electronic and other high-tech products, with learning opportunities and accelerated technological development. Yet "high technology" is not the only prospect for connecting capabilities across spikes of capability.

Procter and Gamble (P&G) offers a contrasting, transactional innovation network approach, which clarifies just how relational networks differ from transactional networks. P&G now draws half of its new product ideas from outside the company, and the company's collaborating partners are not only the few large, western firms of comparable size to P&G, but smaller players as well. P&G began insourcing innovation ideas because even with global research facilities and the best talent money could buy, "By 2000, it was clear to us that our invent-it-ourselves model was not capable of sustaining high levels of topline growth" (Huston and Sakkab, 2006: 60).

P&G is an example of how global competition drives networked approaches to innovation. In the face of an explosion of new technologies and escalating competition from widely distributed new spikes, along with growing overseas markets, the company needed more new ideas from all quarters, because it can get better new products faster and cheaper by networking: its printed Pringles chips relied on technology sourced from a small Italian bakery (Huston and Sakkab, 2006). P&G's ability to develop methods to tap into such a solution centers on connecting with varied capabilities, wherever they may reside, marshaling them into an effective, usable network.

Yet, unlike Apple and PortalPlayer, the FPD network, or Li & Fung, P&G's is a transaction-based network. P&G buys or licenses inventions and ideas sourced elsewhere, then develops them into innovations inside. Only the initial idea draws on others, although even that limited expansion has substantially enhanced P&G's volume of new product innovations. The rest of the innovation cycle remains limited to P&G's internal capabilities. In contrast to the more loosely coupled, modular capabilities of relational process networks like those of Apple and PortalPlayer, FPD or Li & Fung, P&G's "connect and develop" may still be too slow and too constrained to compete. Relational process networks' enhanced ability to access tacit knowledge – and thus to rapidly learn and innovate – arises precisely from long-term, trust-based relationships not available in P&G's transactional approach.

The role of network orchestrator. These differences come into focus with the definition of the role of network orchestrator: the "first among equals" that identifies potential participants, defines standards and protocols for interaction, specifies the action points where decisions resolving differences must be taken, and facilitates the network culture to enhance participants' learning. As we shall see, the network orchestrator takes primary responsibility for developing the network. P&G undertakes no such activities, instead identifying useful external technologies, purchasing access to them, and then enhancing, scaling up the manufacturing and then distributing them through their own channels. By contrast, Li & Fung or PortalPlayer devote extensive effort to ensuring their networks' ongoing capabilities evolution, enlisting partners' insights, and developing both knowledge and innovation ideas.

Relational networks can make use of loosely coupled, modularized product designs to innovate – specified only as to interface, or performance – or more tightly coupled, stable product and process designs. Even here, relational networks pay dividends, visible in Japanese automakers' superior products and processes, based on long-term engagement with their prime components suppliers' innovating capabilities (Womack *et al.*, 1990). But loose coupling offers the greatest potential, which hinges upon trust: the greater the trust, the greater the scope for partner innovation. Such loosely coupled relationships both build trust and rely upon it, gaining enhanced ability to improvise and experiment within modules of activity relative to more tightly integrated business networks. Modular structure, loose coupling, and free information exchange also makes it easier to mix and match modules in ways that can deliver more customized value in response to evolving needs and opportunities. Finally, loose coupling also facilitates introducing new participants and new capabilities that can help push current participants to get better faster.

Not only products, but also processes can be loosely coupled – including management processes – to accelerate learning across in global process networks. Few people appreciate what a high-tech product the athletic shoe has become, yet for decades it has been manufactured in China and other developing countries. Nike aggressively seeks out new materials and ways to integrate them into its shoes to push the performance envelope for its customers. New materials and processes imply new business partners with promising new capabilities to enhance Nike's shoe design and manufacturing process networks. New partners become part of a sophisticated tutelage system, working with other network partners with complementary capabilities to teach them how to take more advantage of new materials and manufacturing techniques to improve performance. In return, new partners also gain greater insight into the activities of complementary partners and can refine their own materials and practices. Mutual tutelage, information exchange, and peer influence ratchet up capabilities of the network, not just the individual firms: participants gain multiple capabilities and resources.

Third level of management practice: Amplify innovation and learning opportunities

Benefiting from relational networks centers not just on accessing existing capabilities, but on rapidly developing capabilities available only through the network – learning more and faster by learning together, creating a "choice architecture" to reframe attention and control (Thaler and Sunstein, 2008), and gaining from fresh independent inputs from partners. The focal point of "the organization" is no longer "the enterprise"; instead, it is the network, made up of multiple, interdependent, mutually influencing enterprises that also access external experience. The focal point of any given exchange is not "the transaction"; it is its effect on network capabilities. The deepest pools of potential arise when business processes become collaborative. But such network capabilities and advantages do not "just happen"; instead, they are the artifact of explicit management of the network. This third level of management practice centers on enhancing learning opportunities and exploiting the generative potential of loosely coupled processes shared across diverse network partners.

Potential diversity benefits. Folding these ideas into the rich environment for focused learning and innovation found in spikes of coalescing capability raises the ante. While any given global spike offers benefits, connecting capabilities across spikes can actively evolve a robust, reconfigurable platform – a pool of known partners and capabilities – for repeated learning and innovation that draws on multiple spikes' sheer diversity. Spike participants with diverse specializations can learn from each other to deliver more value to the market, enhancing their network by means of the productive friction of their interactions. Yet "productive friction" seems an oxymoron; like other relational network capabilities, it does not "just happen," but must be carefully built, as we shall discuss.

Process networks enable learning and innovation loops that can fold back in on and reinforce the innovation and learning loops already in play within individual spikes – if the network takes advantage of them. The dynamics are fractal – the individual spikes derive network benefits through participants who engage in relations within the "home spike," while further benefits are found in a larger, multi-spike network. As a result, relational networks at both levels are highly dynamic in terms of potential to deliver growing value over time. However, such dynamism depends utterly on trust that enables active disagreement and productive resolution of differences that arise precisely from the participants' different experiences and expertise, as well as the willingness to expand the network to embrace new participants, capabilities, and ideas. Participants must behave in new ways, contrary to immediate short-term transactional self-interest; and relational network orchestrators must encourage such new behaviors.

Bidirectional influence. Network partners can accelerate and facilitate active improvement by learning from each other, sharing information broadly, then rapidly applying and reapplying what is learned both within the network and beyond it. Such learning arises specifically in surfacing and resolving differences of viewpoint and problems of execution, and bringing differences into discussion. Traditional ideas of control – stereotypically thought of in terms of compelling behavior on the part of the controlled – is clearly inadequate for encouraging such outcomes. Instead, the character of the network prescribes the nature of the controls appropriate to the situation, closer to a network of equals in an architecture of interactions designed to foster trust and learning, and iterative reengagement.

Here, control is usefully thought of as bidirectional mutual influence, as already suggested by Li & Fung's 30–30 rule, or PortalPlayer's ongoing participation in both revenues from the initial iPod product design and in subsequent product generations. Because network participants have an ongoing stake in the network, incentives align with network responsibility, rather than immediate transactional advantage. Instead of zero sum, the game is sum enhancing. Partners can trust in one another to enhance tacit knowledge exchange to drive enhanced innovation and learning – because they, themselves, must share their knowledge to legitimize continued participation, from which ongoing benefits flow. Learning opportunities, information exchange, and experience-based trust, along with the other long-term benefits of continued participation, suggest new understandings of control within such relational networks. Learning opportunities for participants amplify network innovation, while shared information serves as a tool for leveraging innovation possibilities. Active learning is valued partner behavior, whereas sharing what is learned builds trust, demonstrates trustworthiness, and creates forward-looking reputational credits for further exchange downstream, along with subsequent benefits.

Misty Loughry's focus on peer control within a firm offers a relevant parallel (Loughry, Chapter 11): we see network partners similarly, as symmetrical participants in a relational network that is a collaborative creation. In relational process networks, however, an orchestrator who is first among equals serves key governance roles, including gatekeeper, defining standards and protocols for interaction, establishing procedures for dispute resolution, defining performance measurements, and allocating resulting rents. It is the orchestrator who organizes activities into loosely coupled modules – designing opportunities for productive friction that lead to innovation, shared learning, enhanced network participant capabilities, and ultimately shared profits. And it is the network orchestrator who initiates the network management practices we have been describing, such as encouraging productive friction and open information sharing, which enable peer influence.

Network partners wishing to enjoy the benefits of enhanced capabilities, superior learning, and better, faster innovation must both "lend to" and "borrow from" one another's tacit understandings to succeed, while also demonstrating their own network-responsible behaviors. Thus trust-based multi-directional peer control, incentivized by learning and capabilities enhancement as well as profits, is the control mode of choice, orchestrated by the lead firm but also affected by participants. This control operates among and between firms, as network participants: the network and behaviors within it form the "organization" within and through which this new sort of control emerges.

Moreover, this kind of "organizational" control aims at maximizing the learning, innovation, and trust of the network as a whole, rather than at traditional near-term, firm-level goals of minimizing costs, maximizing profit, or seizing transactional advantage. Although costs may indeed go down and profits up, and although exchanges are performed, these immediate outcomes are by-products of the relational network, not its primary focus. Rather than transactions (as in the

P&G network), relational process networks (like those of Portal-Player, Li & Fung, and the FPD partners) aim at ongoing relationships that both foster productive friction, learning, and capability building and emphasize mutual influence and peer control, rather than top-down direction.

New network management techniques. Harnessing the potential for accelerated learning and capability building requires new management techniques that shift focus from a single enterprise to the relational network, actively exploiting the diversity inherent in multiple firms, diverse specializations, particular insights, and varied experience. All this generates productive friction in successful networks: friction, as a result of differences; productive friction, because the differences get resolved. As diverse human resources with varied skill sets and backgrounds come together around challenging problems, they bring different viewpoints and potential solutions. Such differences simultaneously contain both potential conflict and the fuel for creative new approaches that push performance boundaries: effective management of the relational net is what generates the benefits.

Our key point is that productive friction does not just "happen" – it needs to be catalyzed by a thoughtful orchestrator who actively manages the creation, evolution, and maintenance of the network and its good operation, engaging participants in the process. Productive friction emerges, nearly always, around concrete/grounded problems and mismatches among adjacent parties in relational process networks. We are not talking about abstract issues here, but very explicit issues, as in "your chip draws too much power at this point," or "the fit of your part here is not perfect."

Yet much trust and mutual respect underpin forthright disagreement and productive friction, which do not arise without them. Trust in this setting translates to genuinely listening to another's perspective and ideas, seeking to incorporate their essence in a shared solution. Past experience at listening and being listened to offers a robust bridge to deeper trust, as do understanding and respect for partners' diverse viewpoints and skills. The relational network's enduring, iterated exchanges build a powerful foundation for further engagement, because partners have learned to value one another's differences.

The ability to foster productive friction can therefore be very powerful in accelerating learning and capability building, which might well be seen as control at a meta level – network control. Network organizers can be very helpful in ensuring that the key ingredients are in place. As we have noted, it is important to identify participants with the appropriate skill sets and backgrounds, to ensure that the elements are available for a solution, and that creative new approaches can be put on the table: this is, as we noted earlier, the network version of input control.

In this context, the loosely coupled process management techniques described previously become very helpful in scaling networks to include a growing number of participants with a rich diversity of skill sets and backgrounds. This is also behavioral or process control, insofar as peer influence, modeling of expected behavior, and socialization of new members helps outline a template for effective behavior that experience validates in superior results. Yet this kind of control is quite different from the behavioral or process focus of most traditional control conceptualizations, which tend to emphasize explicit specification of activities and systematic monitoring of those activities, versus the kind of implicit norms and mutual exchange we are discussing here. Traditional considerations of normative control do include implicit norms and mutual exchanges of tacit knowledge within a single work group and firm, but the network controls discussed here reside between and among network partners, and they extend over multiple projects. Such network controls aim specifically at scaling the network and its capabilities.

Beyond the traditional control approaches, especially in light of the uncertain and distant eventual marketplace results of breakthrough innovations, some other forms of outcome control like those we suggest are essential, highlighting ongoing relational outcomes rather than those of individual transactions. Network orchestrators must focus participants' efforts on explicit and aggressive performance objectives, of subcomponents, for example, while at the same time removing as many constraints as possible on the solution. Yet it makes sense to loosen constraints only where partners merit trust, and ongoing engagement is anticipated: the distinction from transactional networks is where relational networks, and even more so, process networks create their advantages of enhanced learning, superior speed, and rapid innovation.

This focus on objectives and outcomes rather than specifying activities is quite compatible with the design philosophy shaping loosely coupled, modular process networks. Just as traditional firms typically deploy input, output, and behavioral controls, so, too, do networks.

From our perspective, relational process networks move increasingly toward network performance outcomes over time as the primary form of control, with a very different form of network behavior control through informal norms also playing a role in building trust. Still, it's important to note that individual transactions are not the heart of the matter – the relational network is, with concomitant emphasis on trust, learning, and ongoing network capability enhancement, creating the prospect for increasingly shared business processes.

Partner behaviors that can contribute to such enhanced trust and deeper process engagement include reliable delivery on promises (especially timetables), and rapid-fire response to the predictable failures – an ability to shift to "Plan B" (or C or D) at need, and still deliver superior eventual performance. Prototypes operate as boundary objects, enabling participants to develop shared understanding of potential solutions while testing competing options against the relevant performance requirements (which may themselves change, as participants innovate to improve possibilities). Above all, participants need to be provided with clear action points, that is, decision milestones where differences need to be resolved and agreement reached on the best approach to go forward at that moment. Here is another key aspect of the orchestrator's role: bringing the participants to the action point, as a means to build capability, resolve friction productively, and achieve challenging performance outcomes.

The interplay of process controls – interaction around prototypes, generation of alternatives, and the articulation and resolution of differences to arrive at (perhaps changed) consensus goals – together with the discipline of demanding performance goals themselves – is noteworthy here. While it might be tempting to consider this as solely the network orchestrator's responsibility, we see mutuality, peer control, and collaborative behavioral, process, and attitude controls as a more accurate view. Orchestrators like Li & Fung, Apple, PortalPlayer, or Nike surely do have their own routines, processes, and protocols – but they aim at enhanced network capabilities, rather than any individual transaction. Moreover, the orchestrators themselves are also influenced by their partners, learning from them and adapting their own behavior accordingly, always aiming to enhance network capabilities.

Building process network advantages. ODMs in Taiwan use such techniques to orchestrate design activity across many specialized component and subsystem vendors for new consumer electronic products.

Rather than detailed design blueprints to be handed off to manufacturing or component partners, ODMs focus on defining aggressive component performance targets and establishing appropriate action points where participants must come together to mutually resolve any disagreements that may prevent effective integration of the components and subsystems. Network participants interact around electronic design documents and prototypes to systematically explore design options and improve the product together. (This is in sharp contrast to Detroit automakers' historic insistence on fully specified components, with contracts awarded solely on price, and focused solely on the present transaction [Womack *et al.*, 1990].)

Li & Fung's 30–30 rule acquires additional significance in the context of accelerating learning and capability building. By ensuring that partners always have a minimum of 30 percent of their capacity allocated to other customers, as we noted earlier, Li & Fung nudges partners to gain exposure to new practices and techniques outside the network – encouraging them to act in their own best interests through an architecture of choice (Thaler and Sunstein, 2008). Each partner then brings this learning back into the Li & Fung network when they engage around the performance requirements of the next round of specific products: partners' process enhancements benefit the network.

Li & Fung is also using its own investment in service-oriented IT architectures to accelerate learning and capability building by sharing information – in essence, enhancing informational relations within the network. One of the benefits of automating routine coordination activities is systematic capture of performance data from network partners. This performance data can be used to deliver real-time performance benchmarking information to each partner, telling them how they are doing relative to comparable network participants along twelve different dimensions of performance. Similar performance comparisons have been shown to encourage improvement in a medical settings, for example, where hospitals' differential rates of infection or varied surgical outcomes are compared – examples of evidence-based medicine, and consistent with calls for evidence-based management (Rousseau and McCarthy, 2007).

Trust and the expectation of enduring relationships are critical here: thoroughgoing transparency could be used to extract concessions, but greater benefits arise from identifying and addressing key performance gaps, with coaching on how to improve. Li & Fung has shifted its own focus in response to network potentials: its staff formerly responsible for routine coordination activity now concentrate on coaching and bringing network partners together to explore ways to improve capabilities, using evidence from the IT system's tracking. Best practices, explicit experiments, and real-time data serve to enhance network performance.

Information technology can also support accelerated learning and capability building in other ways as well. Interaction tools like mobile phones, instant messaging, intellectual property (IP) based video conferencing, Wikis, and other forms of collaborative workspaces facilitate richer and more frequent collaboration among distributed participants. Rather than simply focusing on automating tasks and eliminating people, this new generation of technology combines high-tech and high-touch to enable collaboration on demand, fostering rapid-pace learning and thus innovation.

Beyond zero sum. Dynamic specialization within networks can also accelerate learning and capability building. We have already mentioned network scalability; it has an important side effect in that it encourages and rewards rapidly evolving specialization. As more and more diverse participants join a network, each can afford to focus more tightly on its own truly distinctive activities and can rely on other network participants to provide complementary capabilities. At the same time, participants have strong incentives to deepen their own specializations more rapidly to exploit the growth opportunities created by expanding networks. By concentrating on further developing areas where they already have great strength, participants have the potential to learn more rapidly in contrast to companies spread across a broader set of activities.

Thus specialist network partners become increasingly distinct from one another, each bringing more distinctive benefits to the network and each increasingly differentiated from others, reducing competition with them – at the same time increasing potential for productive friction. For example, specialized semiconductor fab (fabrication plant) operators in Taiwan anchor the design process networks that enable specialized semiconductor design firms to focus on strengthening their design capabilities, without the distraction, expense, and challenge of building and operating semiconductor fab facilities, which the fab operators own and manage. Fab operators bring a distinctive viewpoint to discussions, which ODMs now rely on for critical insight.

Productive friction and increasing specialization permit network organizers to shift the incentives for participation from near-term cash rewards to the longer-term opportunity to get better faster by working with others. Successful network organizers increasingly focus on the objective of accelerating learning of all participants as they build long-term relationships with business partners. The key test of these relationships becomes "will all parties be better at what they do as a result of having been in a relationship together than they would have been in the absence of a relationship?"

In fact, without this longer-term opportunity to get better faster, building long-term, trust-based relationships becomes more challenging, since participants become vulnerable to all the zero sum behaviors that economists worry about (e.g., holdup, moral hazard, cheating, shirking). When there is a fixed set of resources, one party loses when the other party gains, focusing everyone on short-term efforts to gain more of the finite resources, inevitably eroding trust and fostering adversarial behavior. By contrast, relational networks can focus everyone on the opportunity to expand total available resources through learning and capability building, thus creating more incentives for collaborative behavior. Such a self-reinforcing cycle lends dynamic stability and enduring benefit to the network (Greif, 2006).

This third level of management practices amplifies innovation and learning opportunities, moving progressively toward the networks that we describe as relational process networks. Rather than focusing narrowly on mobilizing existing capabilities, such creation networks seek to deploy the mechanisms required to accelerate capability building over time. This in turn leads to a third, and much more powerful, form of strategic advantage – more rapid innovation and learning – that becomes critical for success in a rapidly changing global business landscape.

Such loosely coupled relational networks can overcome the organizational inertia that often tends to slow innovation initiatives within large companies, while at the same time providing access to a broad scope of diversified resources. Note that while some organizational theorists point to dynamic capability, they address individual enterprises, rather than the network level that is our focus. Relational networks represent a powerful way to transcend the organizational tensions that often result from trying to build ambidexterity within a single enterprise. External scalability endows these loosely coupled networks as powerful catalysts for both systemic innovation (requiring the collaboration of large numbers of complementary resource contributors) and compound incremental innovation (requiring rapid iteration of small improvements in products and processes).

As such, creation networks may come to dominate a growing number of global industries and markets for two reasons. First, they access all three forms of strategic advantage created by each level of management practice discussed above – enhanced access to tacit knowledge, expanded access to diverse specialized participants in capability spikes around the world, and accelerated innovation and learning: thus they get better, faster. Next, these networks also provide a sustainable foundation for the long-term trust and loosely coupled relationships built through the first two levels of management practice, active selection of participants and connecting diverse resources across locales.

Because theirs is not a world of fixed resources, it is easier for them to sustain trust as participants avoid adversarial practices designed to gain privileged access to scarce resources. Because the networks create new resources through innovation and learning, they foster longer-term trust: participants focus on collaboration to expand total resources. In the absence of trust, loosely coupled networks begin to unravel; networks focused solely on mobilizing existing resources, rather than accelerating capability building, are soon consumed in disputes about allocating fixed rewards. By contrast, opportunities to expand total resources through innovation and learning enables creation networks to leverage loose coupling into a key ingredient to support productive friction, rather than succumbing to dysfunctional friction.

Broader implications of network innovation and control

Relational networks challenge theorists and practitioners alike to reconstrue "organizations" to transcend a historic fixation on rigid structure and fixed boundaries of the firm, in favor of expanded networks of activities and relationships. Not just bilateral external partners, but a wide and variable range of others within a knowledge-based, innovation-focused innovation network will benefit. Theory too will gain from a trust- and relationship-oriented concept of organizational "control" that acknowledges mutual obligations and responsibilities among partners across firm boundaries and the network, as the trade-off for access to enhanced learning and innovation opportunities.

While identifying and engaging potential network partners can be seen as input selection, it operates beyond the boundaries traditionally envisioned for organizational control, across and among firms. Moreover, trust is also highly implicated in this form of input control – to a much greater degree than typically acknowledged in the more asymmetric power relationship between individuals and their firm employer: potential partner firms are more autonomous and have genuine alternatives; the more alternatives the more desirable those firms are as potential partners.

The nature of the behavioral controls visible in successful relational networks diverges substantially from behavioral controls within firms. In part because the partners are more equal, in part because the emphasis is on mutuality, and in part because the focus in relational networks shifts toward the expansion of available resources and benefits, peer influence, implicit and normative controls take on greater importance, and become more future-focused. In addition, because network participants are true partners with a claim on longer-term network benefits, they share responsibility for the good order of network operations to a greater degree than employees. Incentives flow from learning, from enhanced capabilities, as well as from downstream profit flows.

Output controls also differ in relational networks: first, on any given project, the outcomes in performance terms are challenging and primary. Where a new product like the iPod is concerned, performance targets good enough to attract market notice are the aim, and pushing the state of the art (rather than satisficing) is the means. Participants challenge themselves because their joint success creates network outputs downstream: not just the results of the present project, but opportunities for learning, subsequent projects, and additional applications of what has been learned to other activities within the network or beyond it. This rich array of outcomes is available to network participants, and dwindles, if participation ceases. The promise of future benefit flows is intimately entwined with relationships in the network, and with possibilities the network avails.

The promises extend beyond any individual network at a given moment: the success of networks that bridge emergent spikes of developing expertise holds promise for developing economies, for policy-makers, for firms seeking to innovate, and for citizens of our "flat, hot, and crowded" world (Friedman, 2008).

Network management practices will strengthen incentives to cata-
lyze formation of new spikes and more rapid growth of existing spikes
(Ernst, 2003). Connective capabilities across the flat world will paradoxically lead to the proliferation and growing prominence of spikes,
and with them more opportunity for developing economies like
China's, for instance (Ernst, 2007a, 2007b, 2008).

A combination of institutional mechanisms, management practices,
and new generations of IT will offer powerful platforms for expanding
the global reach of participants within each spike of capability. For
example, global process networks and new approaches to managing
modular business processes help to connect participants within spikes
with complementary capabilities around the world, and with relevant
customers in global markets. Emerging IT architectures and interaction tools discussed earlier will also help to expand the scope of
collaboration across spikes by making it easier for individuals in a
large number of companies and locations to interact with each other.
All of these elements will make it even more attractive for people and
companies to come together in specialized local business ecosystems,
because their efforts will be amplified on a global scale. As a result,
these elements will become significant catalysts for the proliferation
and growth of spikes.

Spikes offer powerful environments for learning, only partly driven
by specialized educational institutions, and they will become even
more attractive for learning as participants discover their ability to
connect with individuals and institutions in other, equally specialized
spikes around the world. To connect is to access learning possibilities.
Connection will drive enhanced, accelerated learning where partners
share their insights and jointly engage in productive friction to solve
problems. Excellence within spikes and across spikes will help to
breed even higher levels of excellence by virtue of powerful feedback
loops. Networks are both the means to access these capabilities and to
configure and reconfigure them into effective, profitable engines for
learning, growth, and innovation.

The bottom line

So what? The network characteristics we have outlined, and the
resulting possibilities and constraints for control in networks carry
implications for companies, policy-makers, and academic researchers.

Conventional control theory's firm-centric and often transactional approaches ignore potential levers and incentives, while emphasizing modes of control less available, or inapplicable in extra-firm settings. Shifting focus beyond the firm to the network directs our attention to network trust and learning dynamics, encouraging consideration of the very characteristics that distinguish networks from firms.

For companies

The relational process networks we have described are not transactional: instead, their essence evolves in and through extended interchange among network partners who learn from one another, become more distinctive from each other over time, and learn to depend upon one another for specialized expertise to perform core business functions, thereby fueling much more effective new business models. These models emphasize learning, capabilities development, trust, and enduring, if protean, networks of recurrent engagement.

From the mainstream perspective, the immediate challenge of relational networks and networked creation activities is how to balance the desire for proprietary advantage with realities of the open innovation advantage. Recognizing how inadequate prior, internally oriented approaches are is a powerful driver for change, as in the case of P&G. Yet relational process networks go beyond P&G's transactional network: successful networks like those of early VISA, Apple and PortalPlayer, and Li & Fung create dramatic innovation as a result of their external collaborations. Their success exerts still further push: such collaborative innovation is enough – better that networking innovation capabilities become an enduring competitive advantage – and ultimately, as rivals eventually duplicate these skills, a requisite for survival.

As we have described, new management skills are needed: finding partners, creating dynamic networks characterized by enduring trust relations and reconfigurable capabilities, recognizing innovation possibilities beyond the borders of the firm (or its current network, or its current product/process focus), and generating the internal network processes of mutual trust, shared discipline, intensively productive friction, and demanding performance goals. These are very different desiderata from the typical profit maximization, cost minimization, transactional mantras of contemporary business gospel. Relational innovation networks focus on emergent outcomes, which are nevertheless challenging because participants enlist to make them so. The intrinsic rewards of learning, capability development, access to exciting opportunities, challenging projects, and partners who contribute to one another, underpin the extrinsic rewards of ongoing profits, and continued participation, and superior performance.

For public policy-makers

Those concerned with economic development have long sought to facilitate innovation clusters. Whether within a country, a region, or a city, innovation has fostered growth, jobs, and prosperity. For developed economies, outsourcing and offshoring have been seen as dangerous slippage toward economic downturn – yet the networked picture we see instead emphasizes collaborative creation of new products, jobs, and industries, not mere replacement of activities. What can easily be transported offshore is what is already well-characterized, mature, and not especially innovative: in short, yesterday's business. In sharp contrast, relational process networks of creation are much more interesting: they involve managing the absorptive capacity of firms by growing joint network capabilities that transcend any individual firm's abilities, and they often generate whole new industries – flat panel displays, iPods and iPhones, and downloadable digital content provide examples. Moreover, abundant evidence suggests that addressing the challenges of less affluent markets demands and develops precisely the kinds of innovation all firms will need to compete in a "flat" world (Brown and Hagel, 2005; Lewin and Peeters, 2006).

Policy-makers attentive to these benefits will instantly appreciate the need to foster their own spikes while encouraging firms and networks to collaborate across spikes (Ernst, 2007a, 2007b, 2008). Tax and regulatory arrangements should neither impede nor discourage the workings of global innovation networks. New intellectual property regimes will be needed as well, to assist and recognize how innovation is taking place: collaborative innovation is not at all the same as the simple-product, single-inventor model on which much IP thinking is based. The realities of a global economic arena argue powerfully for harmonized IP, tax, and regulatory policies.

Policy-makers also have a role to play in supporting the infrastructures of energy, communication, logistics, and information exchange to underpin networked innovation activities. Developing nations can play only if they can communicate, and for innovation purposes, that is likely to mean high band-width electronic exchange as well as logistics systems for secure transfer of goods. Computers and computer-controlled design and manufacturing systems need reliable, "clean" electricity. Widespread global exchange of goods demands effective quality control on the manufacturing side – and government involvement will also be central for inspection of food products, assurance of safe and reliable standards, and contract enforcement, no less than in such issues as port security and disease prevention.

Finally, policy-makers would do well to reconsider the standard, backward-looking economic data most countries presently collect. Such data do not assist in the discovery of new spikes, the identification of potential partner firms, or the creation of new networks.

For academic researchers

The facts of networked innovation and relational networks demand that we redefine "organization theory" and "strategy" in light of where and how economic activity, and especially innovation, is happening: in dynamic networks. Limiting theories of organization and strategy to "the firm" is no longer a viable approach (as others have noted: see, for example, Czarniawska, 2008; Davis and Marquis, 2005). Research to illuminate new modes of collaboration is, of course, already widespread, yet much organization theory as well as much control theory remains overly fixated "within the boundaries of the firm," despite the increasing fraction of important economic activity taking place beyond and across those boundaries. Construing "organization" beyond "the firm" is an essential first step; considering mutual influence and deliberately orchestrated peer control in place of hierarchical dominance paradigms is a critical second step.

Emerging practices of cooperative networks, network relationships, and information sharing point us to promising redefinitions or reconsiderations of old fundamentals. As we have argued here, short-term, economic rationality assumptions about organizational and interorganizational logics do not serve where uncertainty and futurity reign. Further, even mature industries and well-understood products and processes can and do benefit from more open approaches, as new business models and improved managerial practices emerge. These, too, are appropriate targets for academic research, looking to the incentive effects of conjoint learning, capabilities development, and accelerated innovation, as well as the rationality of non-fixed-pie assumptions.

Academics in North America have been especially adept at generating curricula to reflect new managerial needs, being among the first to design petroleum and aeronautical engineering, computer science, and biotechnology courses, for example (Mowery and Rosenberg, 1998; Rosenberg, 1982; Rosenberg and Nelson, 1994). The challenge for supporting networks of creation is similar: old "truths" about the disciplinary silos of the past must give way to new, cross-disciplinary courses to bring forth new insights. The new management curriculum needs to embrace the realities of global collaborative business, relational networks, and their innovation benefits.

References

Asch, S. 1958. Effects of group pressure on the modification and distortion. In E. E. Maccoby, T. M. Newcomb, and E. L. Hartley (eds.), *Readings in social psychology:* 174–183. New York, NY: Holt, Rinehart and Winston.

Barnard, C. I. 1956. *The functions of the executive.* Cambridge, MA: Harvard University Press. (Original work published in 1938)

Brown, J. S. and Hagel, J. III 2005. Innovation blowback: disruptive management practices from Asia. *McKinsey Quarterly,* 1: 34–45.

Burt, R. S. 1992. *Structural holes: the social structure of competition.* Cambridge, MA: Harvard University Press.

Cardinal, L. B., Sitkin, S. B., and Long, C. P. 2004. Balancing and rebalancing in the creation and evolution of organizational control. *Organization Science,* 15 (4): 411–431.

Chandler, A. D. J. 1977. *The visible hand: the managerial revolution in American business.* Cambridge, MA: Harvard University Press.

2001. *Inventing the electronic century: the epic story of the consumer electronics and computer industries.* New York, NY: Free Press.

Chandler, A. D. J. and Salsbury, S. 1974. *Pierre S. Dupont and the making of the modern corporation.* New York, NY: Harper and Row.

Cheng, J. L. C. and McKinley, W. 1983. Toward an integration of organization research and practice: a contingency study of bureaucratic control and performance in scientific settings. *Administration Science Quarterly,* 28 (1): 85–100.

Chesbrough, H. W. 2003. *Open innovation: the new imperative for creating and profiting from technology.* Boston, MA: Harvard Business School Press.

2006. *Open business models: how to thrive in the new innovation landscape*. Boston, MA: Harvard Business School Press.

Chesbrough, H., Vanhaverbeke, W., and West, J. (eds.). 2006. *Open innovation: researching a new paradigm*. Oxford University Press.

Culpan, R. 2002. *Global business alliances: theory and practice*. Westport, CT: Quorum Books.

Czarniawska, B. 2008. *A theory of organizing*. Cheltenham, UK: Edward Elgar.

Davis, G. F. and Marquis, C. 2005. Prospects for organization theory in the early twenty-first century: institutional fields and mechanisms. *Organization Science*, 16: 332–343.

Doz, Y. L. and Hamel, G. 1998. *The alliance advantage*. Boston, MA: Harvard Business School Press.

Doz, Y. L., Santos, J., and Williamson, P. 2001. *From global to metanational: how companies win in the knowledge economy*. Boston, MA: Harvard Business School Press.

Eisenhardt, K. 1985. Control: organizational and economic approaches. *Management Science*, 31 (2): 134–149.

Elmer-DeWitt, P. 2008. How to grow the iPod as the MP3 player market shrinks. http://apple20.blogs.fortune.cnn.com/2008/01/29/beyond-the-incredible-shrinking-ipod-market/.

Ernst, D. 2003. Pathways to innovation in the global network economy: Asian upgrading strategies in the electronics industry. East-West Center Working Papers: 1–46. Honolulu, HI: East-West Center.

2007a. Innovation offshoring – root causes of Asia's rise and policy implications. East-West Center Working Papers: Economics Series, No. 90. Honolulu, HI: East-West Center.

2007b. Beyond the "global factory" model: innovative capabilities for upgrading China's IT industry. *International Journal of Technology and Globalization*, 3 (4): 437–460.

2008. Can Chinese IT firms develop innovative capabilities within global knowledge networks? In M. G. Hancock, H. S. Rowen, and W. F. Miller (eds.), *China's quest for independent innovation*: 1–26. Washington, DC: Shorenstein Asia Pacific Research Center and Brookings Institution Press.

Friedman, T. L. 2005. *The world is flat: a brief history of the twenty-first century*. New York, NY: Farrar, Straus, and Giroux.

2008. *Hot, flat, and crowded: why we need a green revolution – and how it can renew America*. New York, NY: Farrar, Straus, and Giroux.

Govindarajan, V. and Fisher, J. 1990. Strategy, control systems, and resource sharing: effects on business-unit performance. *Academy of Management Journal*, 33 (2): 259–285.

Greif, A. 2006. *Institutions and the path to the modern economy: lessons from medieval trade.* Cambridge University Press.

Hagel, J. III. 2008. Unbundling Dell's businesses. www.edgeperspectives. typepad.com/edge_perspectives/2008/09/unbundling-dell.html; November 20.

Hagel, J. III and Brown, J. S. 2005. *The only sustainable edge: why business strategy depends on productive friction and dynamic specialization.* Boston, MA: Harvard Business School Press.

  2006. Globalization and innovation: some contrarian perspectives. World Economic Forum Annual Meeting. Davos, Switzerland.

  2008a. Creation networks: harnessing the potential of open innovation. *Journal of Service Science,* 1 (2): 27–40.

  2008b. From push to pull: emerging models for mobilizing resources. *Journal of Service Science,* 1 (1): 93–110.

Hagel, J. III and Singer, M. 1999. Unbundling the corporation. *Harvard Business Review,* 77 (2): 133–141.

Hammer, M. and Champy, J. 1993. *Reengineering the corporation.* New York, NY: Harper Business.

Hock, D. 2005. *One from many: Visa and the rise of chaordic organization.* San Francisco, CA: Berrett-Koehler Publishers.

Huston, L. and Sakkab, N. 2006. Connect and develop: inside Procter and Gamble's new model for innovation. *Harvard Business Review,* 23 (3): 58–66.

IBM_Global_Services. 2006. The global CEO study. *The Global CEO Study,* 64. Somers, NY: IBM.

Jaeger, A. and Baliga, B. R. 1985. Control systems and strategic adaptation: lessons from the Japanese experience. *Strategic Management Journal,* 6 (2): 115–134.

Jelinek, M. and Schoonhoven, C. B. 1994. *The innovation marathon.* San Francisco, CA: Jossey-Bass.

Jensen, M. C. and Meckling, W. H. 1976. A theory of the firm: managerial behavior, agency costs and ownership structure. *Journal of Financial Economics,* 3: 305–360.

Kenny, M. (ed.). 2000. *Understanding Silicon Valley: the anatomy of an entrepreneurial region.* Stanford, CA: Stanford University Press.

Kuran, T. 1997. *Private truths, public lies: the social consequences of preference falsification* (2nd edn.). Cambridge, MA: Harvard University Press.

Lewin, A. Y. and Peeters, C. 2006. The top-line allure of offshoring. *Harvard Business Review,* 84 (3): 22–24.

Magretta, J. 1998. The power of virtual integration: an interview with Michael Dell. *Harvard Business Review,* 76 (2): 73–84.

McWilliams, J. E. 2008. China, America, and melamine (electronic version). *International Herald Tribune: The Global Edition of the New York Times.*

Moncreiff, J. 1999. Is strategy making a difference? *Long Range Planning,* 32 (2): 273–276.

Mowery, D. C. and Rosenberg, N. 1998. *Paths of innovation: technological change in 20th-century America.* Cambridge University Press.

Murtha, T. P., Lenway, S. A., and Hart, J. A. 2001. *Managing new industry creation: global knowledge formation and entrepreneurship in high technology.* Stanford, CA: Stanford University Press.

Oliver, R. and Anderson, R. 1995. An empirical test of the consequences of behavior and outcome-based sales control systems. *Journal of Marketing,* 58 (1): 53–67.

Ouchi, W. G. 1979. A conceptual framework for the design of organizational control mechanisms. *Management Science,* 25 (9): 833–848.

Ouchi, W. G. and McGuire, M. A. 1975. Organizing control: two functions. *Administrative Science Quarterly,* 20 (4): 559–569.

Prahalad, C. K. and Krishnan, M. S. 2008. *The new age of innovation: driving cocreated value through global networks.* New York, NY: McGraw Hill.

Quinn, J. B. 1992. *Intelligent enterprise.* New York, NY: Free Press.

Rosenberg, N. 1982. *Inside the black box: technology and economics.* Cambridge University Press.

Rosenberg, N. and Nelson, R. R. 1994. American universities and technical advance in industry. *Research Policy,* 23: 323–348.

Rousseau, D. M. and McCarthy, S. 2007. Educating managers from an evidence-based perspective. *Academy of Management Learning and Education,* 6 (1): 84–101.

Schramm, C. J. 2006. *The entrepreneurial imperative: how America's economic miracle will reshape the world (and change your life).* New York, NY: HarperCollins.

Sirkin, H. L., Hemerling, J. W., and Bhattacharya, A. K. 2008. *Globality: competing with everyone from everywhere for everything.* New York, NY: Business Plus.

Snell, S. 1992. Control theory in strategic human resource management: the mediating effect of administrative information. *Academy of Management Journal,* 35 (2): 292–327.

Star, S. L. and Griesemer, J. R. 1989. Institutional ecology, "translations" and boundary objects: amateurs and professionals in Berkeley's museum of vertebrate zoology, 1907–39. *Social Studies of Science,* 19: 387–420.

Tannenbaum, A. S. 1968. *Control in organizations.* New York, NY: McGraw-Hill.

Thaler, R. H. and Sunstein, C. R. 2008. *Nudge: improving decisions about health, wealth, and happiness.* New Haven, CT: Yale University Press.

Thompson, J. D. 1967. *Organizations in action.* New York, NY: McGraw-Hill.

Tuomi, I. 2002. *Networks of innovation.* Oxford University Press.

Williamson, O. E. 1981. The economics of organization: the transaction cost approach. *American Journal of Sociology,* 87 (3): 548–577.

Womack, J. P., Jones, D. T., and Roos, D. 1990. *The machine that changed the world.* New York, NY: Rawson Associates.

10 | Toward a theory of relational control: how relationship structure influences the choice of controls

LAURIE J. KIRSCH
University of Pittsburgh

VIVEK CHOUDHURY
University of Cincinnati

Greg Milstead, the operations manager of a four-store John Deere dealership, wants employees at his stores to meet specific sales and marketing targets.[1] Traditionally, he would set monthly targets and assess, at month-end, whether employees met the targets. Employees themselves would have only a general sense during the month of whether they were on track to meet the goals. As a control system, this approach has its limitations as the ability to take corrective action during the month is constrained by the lack of information for the manager and his employees. Recognizing a need for a better control system, Milstead championed the implementation of an information system to provide the employees with real-time information about how well they were progressing toward the monthly goals. The system proved a great success in providing employees precise knowledge of goals and their progress. In addition, it facilitated an unexpected change in the way in which control is enacted. Control no longer rests solely with the manager. Employees have become much more pro-active in determining how to achieve the goals, and in ensuring that the goals are reached. Moreover, given the transparency provided by the information system, employees now can see how their peers in other stores are progressing against the same targets. This visibility has become a mechanism for encouraging desired behavior, as employees who see they lag behind others have become more motivated to determine how to improve their own performance. Thus, employees and manager have become partners in the exercise of control. As Milstead noted:

We set an annual goal for each store's departments, which translates into monthly goals for employees . . . Employees know what is expected, and they respond. We have smart people. They figure out how to accomplish goals in better ways than management could dictate. And from a management standpoint that is very powerful (*The Leader*: 2).

The seminal work on the choice of controls is arguably Ouchi's (1977, 1978, 1979) framework, which identifies three modes of control: behavior, outcome, and clan. At that time, organizations tended to be bureaucratic in structure with clearly delineated boundaries between units and with clearly defined reporting relationships, typically among co-located employees. Much of the work was relatively routine with identifiable and documented goals. However, since the time when Ouchi developed his framework, organizational work has made the transition to more knowledge work with a greater level of uncertainty in process and goals, greater interdependence among individuals, and hence more focus on teamwork. Further, work groups may span departments, units, or even organizations, and are often distributed across the globe (Bigley and Roberts, 2001; Hagel, Brown, and Jelinek, Chapter 9). Organizational relationships now vary greatly in form, from superior–subordinate hierarchies to matrixed relationships, peer-based groups, and virtual teams. As the organizational environment has become more complex and fluid, management processes, including control, may need to change accordingly (Child and McGrath, 2001; Towry, 2003).

The example above illustrates this point. Historically, the manager exercised outcome control by setting goals for his employees and assessing whether they achieved the goals. Employees were unable to assess their own progress very precisely, and they had little insight into their peers' activities and achievements. Implementing an information system provided employees the transparency needed to check their own progress against the goals on a real-time basis and make adjustments as needed. It also gave them transparency into other employees' progress, which motivated them to adjust their own activities and achieve higher performance. Thus, the way in which control was enacted evolved from management-defined, outcome-based control to a set of integrated control activities implemented by managers and employees.

In contemporary organizations, we are likely to see a variety of control strategies in use. Prior research on the choice of controls has often been based on Ouchi's (1977, 1979) framework, and has largely focused on the choice of controls *from a controller's perspective*. Therefore, the control antecedents in these studies reflect *the feasibility of a control mode* given the degree to which the controller understands the process to transform inputs to outputs (knowledge of the transformation process), to observe the actions of the controllee (behavior observability), or to measure the outputs produced by the controllee (outcome measurability) (e.g., Eisenhardt, 1985; Kirsch, 1996; Snell, 1992).

In contrast, few studies have considered the controllee's views and perspectives, or the role that the *controllees* play in enacting control (there are exceptions, e.g., the work on peer monitoring by Loughry and Tosi (2008) and Loughry, Chapter 11). In addition, prior research has not examined factors that influence the *need* for control in a given context. In this chapter, therefore, we propose an integrated model of control – one that simultaneously considers both the *feasibility* and *need* for specific control modes, and incorporates both *controllee-initiated* and *peer-based* controls. We propose that a useful way to understand the need for control choices is to consider the nature of the *relationship* between controller and controllee – specifically, control choices can be understood partly as a response to the *need to mitigate risks* inherent in different types of relationships (Long, Chapter 12). This understanding can supplement models that focus on the feasibility of a control mode, given characteristics of the controller. This allows us to develop an integrated model of control.

This chapter proceeds as follows. In the next section, background literature on organizational control is reviewed, with a focus on the antecedents of control and how the controller–controllee relationship is typically conceptualized in the literature. Next, a typology of relationships is introduced, and four specific types of relationships are described, as are the risks inherent in each type of relationship and the trust mechanisms appropriate for mitigating these risks. In the following section, we develop arguments relating control choices to the different types of relationships and explain our integrated model of control. The final section discusses the implications of our analyses for future research and offers concluding comments.

Background literature

Control is defined here as any attempt taken by one individual to motivate another to behave in a manner consistent with organizational objectives (Cardinal, 2001; Das and Teng, 1998; Jaworski, 1988;

Ouchi, 1979). Our definition of control emphasizes transactions between a "controller" who exercises control and a "controllee" who is the target of control. Researchers have identified different *modes* of control, including behavior, outcome, and clan control modes (Cardinal, Sitkin, and Long, Chapter 3; Ouchi, 1977, 1979; Roth *et al.*, 1994). Behavior and outcome controls are typically viewed as *formal* controls in the sense that expectations are clearly identified and documented.[2] Managers articulate and evaluate behaviors or outcomes and reward or sanction controllees based on their level of adherence to the specified behaviors or attainment of the specified outcomes (Henderson and Lee, 1992; Ouchi, 1979). In contrast, clan control is viewed as an *informal* mode of control since it is harder to specify precise behaviors or outcomes for controllees. Instead, it relies on a common vision, as well as shared norms and values, to motivate behavior that is consistent with organizational objectives (Fortado, 1994; Kirsch *et al.*, 2002). Each of these control modes is exercised via specific *mechanisms* such as financial incentives, rules, and procedures, team-building approaches, and socialization practices (Cardinal, 2001; Cardinal *et al.*, 2004; Turner and Makhija, 2006).[3]

Antecedents of control

Much of the work on the antecedents of control has been heavily influenced by Ouchi's seminal framework (1977, 1979). As depicted in Figure 10.1, Ouchi's framework posits that the choice of behavior, outcome, or clan control is a function of outcome measurability and knowledge of the transformation process. High levels of outcome measurability suggest that outcome controls can be used. If a controller understands the process needed to transform inputs into outputs, he/she can utilize behavior control. When the controller lacks understanding of the transformation process, and is unable to measure outputs, the framework suggests that only clan control is viable. Eisenhardt (1985), drawing from agency theory, argued that if behaviors are observable, a controller can also use behavior control. Behaviors can be observed by direct monitoring, or they can be revealed through information systems such as reports and boards of directors. There is considerable support for these arguments, at least for the choice of behavior or outcome control (Eisenhardt, 1985; Henderson and Lee, 1992; Kirsch, 1996). There is less empirical evidence about the

		Knowledge of the transformation process	
		Perfect	**Imperfect**
Ability to measure outputs	**High**	Behavior control or output control	Output control
	Low	Behavior control	Clan control

Figure 10.1 Antecedents of control (adapted from Ouchi, 1977, 1979)

antecedents of clan control, but some studies offer insight into the use of clan control (e.g., Cardinal, 2001; Cardinal *et al.*, 2004; Fortado, 1994; Kirsch *et al.*, 2002; Roth *et al.*, 1994; Sitkin and George, 2005).

Controller–controllee relationships

Relationships between controller and controllee are central to the exercise of control. A relationship, in the context of formal controls, is often conceptualized in terms of a specific dyad. Quite often, though not always, the individuals have a superior–subordinate relationship, such as salespersons and their managers or project leaders and their managers (e.g., Cardinal, 2001). In the case of informal controls, specific dyadic or hierarchical relationships are typically not identified, but instead are often viewed as groups. The "clan" in clan control, as an example, is a group of individuals who are dependent on one another and who are committed to achieving group goals, such as a team of doctors and nurses working together (Ouchi, 1979). While different conceptualizations place the control episode with some specific individual or group, few studies have actually examined in depth the nature of the relationship between controller and controllee, instead often making assumptions about the structure and form of the relationship.

There are a few exceptions. Recently, process-oriented researchers have generally taken a more in-depth view of control, and have examined how control is exercised by different controllers and how the exercise of control unfolds over time (e.g., Cardinal *et al.*, 2004; Choudhury and Sabherwal, 2003; Mähring, 2002). Some of this work has specifically examined controller–controllee relationships. For example, in a study of four information systems (IS) project teams, Kirsch (2004) focuses on the "elements" of control. Adding "roles and relationships" to the three elements identified previously by Eisenhardt (1985) – measurement, evaluation, and reward – she examined how the various elements of control changed over time, as four novel and complex projects unfolded. With respect to roles and relationships, she found that informal mechanisms were utilized as these projects began when the project stakeholders were facing considerable uncertainty, that formal mechanisms were added as the nature of the task became more routine, and that, in the last phase of the project, a combination of formal and informal roles and relationships was utilized. Other studies have suggested that expectations about roles can also influence control choices (Choudhury and Sabherwal, 2003; Kirsch, 1997). For example, if a manager expects that a subordinate will exercise self-control, then the manager will structure the subordinate's environment so that it is conducive to self-control (Kirsch and Cummings, 1996).

These studies provide some insight into different forms of relationships, and suggest that relationships are important in the exercise of control. The literature also suggests that the nature of the relationship between controller and controllee can influence the choice of control (Long, Chapter 12), and this relationship can change over time. However, "relationship" as a theoretical construct is not typically modeled in any systematic fashion. To address this deficiency in the control literature, we turn to a typology of relationships that we can utilize as a starting point to better understand the influence of the controller–controllee relationship in choosing controls.

A typology of relationships

Building on earlier work by Fiske (1990), Sheppard and Sherman (1998) present a typology of relationships, based on differences in "form" and "depth" of the relationship. Form is viewed as a type of interdependence in which the perspective of the one initiating the relationship is considered ("How much do I depend on another person or unit?"). In their typology, depth is viewed as a "product of the importance, range, and number of points of contact among parties" (Sheppard and Sherman, 1998: 423). Their typology consists of four types of relationships. Next, each type is described and examples are provided.

The *shallow dependence* type of relationship is characterized by a simple dependence, in which one party's desired outcomes are contingent upon the actions of another. From the perspective of the former person or party, there is unidirectional dependency, because this party is dependent on the actions of the latter. Depth is considered "shallow" because there are few points of contact between the parties. This does not describe an ongoing relationship, but rather it is indicative of a one-time transaction between parties with little or no history. In a shallow dependence relationship, one party supplies goods or services in exchange for something, typically compensation (Fiske, 1990). An example of this type of relationship is any simple transaction such as a web purchase, in which a purchaser depends on a vendor to supply a product in exchange for payment.

In a *deep dependence* relationship, the interactions between parties are frequent and important (i.e., "deep"), and there are many points of contact between them. The dependence is again characterized as unidimensional, meaning that one person's desired outcomes are contingent upon the actions of another. An example of this type of relationship is an ongoing manager–employee organizational relationship in which a manager delegates work to his employee. However, unlike a shallow dependence relationship, the manager's behaviors have consequences for their employees, and managers may control the fate of the employees. Moreover, knowledge asymmetry may be found in this type of relationship because the behavior of one party is often outside the other's area of expertise or authority. Another example of a deep dependence relationship might be a marketing manager who is asked to lead a project team's development of an information system. In this case, there is a need for frequent and intense interactions between the marketing manager and the project team, and the marketing manager's desire for a new information system is dependent on the actions of the project team. Further, knowledge asymmetry is likely to exist in that the marketing manager has expertise in a business function (marketing) while the project team has expertise in software, hardware, and networking technologies.

Shallow interdependence relationships are characterized by relatively few points of contact between parties and, generally speaking, less intense interactions between them (i.e., "shallow"). Yet the relationship is interdependent because the parties must coordinate their activities to be successful; they are both dependent on the actions of others to be successful. Client–vendor relationships can be illustrative of this type when the depth of interaction is relatively shallow between the client and the vendor, but interdependent tasks of the two parties demand coordinated activity.

Finally, a relationship characterized as *deep interdependence* consists of parties that are mutually dependent on each other. There is a deep sense of sameness and connection (Fiske, 1990). To coordinate their activities, there are many points of contact between them. Communication is critical, but "the complexity and speed demanded by their deep interdependence may prevent complete or regular communication" (Sheppard and Sherman, 1998: 425). Distributed teams responsible for producing an information system may exhibit deep interdependence. For example, one team may reside in the United States, and one may be in India, but together the two teams are responsible for producing one complete and integrated information system. The relationship is deep in that frequent and intense communication is needed to coordinate their work. The relationship is also interdependent because the parties are dependent on each other to successfully produce one information system.

Relationship types, risks, and trust mechanisms

Sheppard and Sherman (1998) argue that each relationship type involves a specific kind of risk, as shown in Figure 10.2. Risks are conceptualized more broadly than the agency-based notions of risk that control researchers often draw on. Relationships characterized as shallow dependence contain two risks: indiscretion and unreliability. Indiscretion means that sensitive information is shared when it should be kept quiet. Unreliability is the risk that an individual will not act as expected. In addition to these two risks, relationships described as shallow interdependent run the risk of poor coordination, as shown in Figure 10.2, with the result that tasks are not completed effectively and efficiently by all parties.

Risks inherent in deep dependence relationships include cheating, neglect, abuse, and loss of self-esteem. Because these relationships are typically characterized by knowledge asymmetry and ineffective monitoring of behavior, a person engaged in some specific work task may purposely cheat or may simply neglect to fulfill expectations.

Type of relationship	Risks	Mechanism necessary for trust production
Shallow dependence	Indiscretion Unreliability	Deterrence
Deep dependence	Cheating Neglect Abuse Loss of self-esteem	Obligation
Shallow interdependence	Indiscretion Unreliability Poor coordination	Discovery
Deep interdependence	Misanticipation	Internalization

Figure 10.2 Types of relationships, risks, and trust mechanisms (Sheppard and Sherman, 1998)

In some situations, abuse can be another risk when one person may "exact additional costs . . . by using fate control as a lever" (Sheppard and Sherman, 1998: 425). An example of abuse is a manager who threatens that an employee will lose her job unless she works overtime in poor conditions without pay. Finally, risks to self-esteem occur when an individual receives direct feedback, or lack of feedback, that the individual interprets as lack of success or individual failure.

As shown in Figure 10.2, for relationships characterized as deep interdependence, the risk of misanticipation, or the inability to anticipate others' needs, is key. In this type of relationship, the tasks of the different parties are highly interdependent, and speedy communication among parties is essential. However, because precise procedures and instructions may not be formally documented, and because fast communication is crucial to success, parties exhibiting deep interdependence may not understand what information and actions are needed by others to complete their work tasks. Misanticipation can cause incomplete work, as well as the need for significant rework at a later point in time, when it is often quite costly and difficult.

To mitigate the risks between parties, Sheppard and Sherman (1998) identify and discuss specific mechanisms necessary for producing trust in each type of relationship (shown in the third column of Figure 10.2). In a shallow dependence relationship, deterrence-based mechanisms can penalize parties that are acting in an unreliable or indiscrete manner (Ring and Van de Ven, 1994). These mechanisms can include court-imposed sanctions or a poor credit rating. In a deep dependence relationship, as shown in Figure 10.2, a sense of obligation can produce trust. Roles and responsibilities, employer–employee relationships, and procedures and rules mitigate risks by producing an obligation or a promised way of behaving (Rousseau, 1995; Tyler and Lind, 1992). Mitigating risk in shallow interdependence includes the use of mechanisms to discover information needed to coordinate activities. Sheppard and Sherman (1998) argue that this discovery takes place through communication and research, which can be facilitated through collocation and electronic communication and collaboration systems. Deep interdependence requires internalization (see Figure 10.2), or common understanding and world views "in which one adopts another's beliefs because they are congruent and integrated with one's own" (Sheppard and Sherman, 1998: 430).

Since risk implies a lack of information, we believe that control mechanisms, with the information they convey, can also help mitigate potential risky behavior in each type of relationship. Different control strategies convey different types of information (Long, Chapter 12; Makhija and Ganesh, 1997; Sitkin, 1995; Turner and Makhija, 2006) and thus different control strategies will be needed to address different types of risks. Put another way, different control strategies are needed to build the trust production mechanisms necessary to mitigate the risks in each type of relationship, as identified above by Sheppard and Sherman (1998). *Considering the nature of risks between parties supplements the focus from the controller's knowledge and ability to observe behaviors or measure outcomes, when choosing controls, with the need to mitigate risks inherent in different types of relationships.* Thus, we propose that control choices are not just a function of the feasibility of certain forms of control from the controller's perspective, but also of the need to mitigate risks stemming from particular types of relationships. We turn our attention to this idea next.

Relationship type and control choice

As each type of relationship is discussed next, we first consider the three traditional antecedents of control, stemming from Ouchi's work, and their implications for control choices in that type of relationship. We supplement this analysis by considering the risks inherent in each

Relationship type	Knowledge of trans. process	Outcome measurability	Behavior observability	Mechanism necessary for trust production	Appropriate control modes
Shallow dependence	Low to high	High	Low to high	Deterrence	Outcome (controller-initiated)
Deep dependence	Low to high	High	High	Obligation	Behavior and outcome (controller-initiated)
Shallow interdependence	Low for controllers	High for controllers	High for controllers		Behavior and outcome (controller-initiated)
				Discovery (by peers)	Behavior (peer-based)
Deep interdependence	Low for controllers	High for controllers	Low for controllers		Outcome (controller-initiated)
				Internalization (by peers)	Clan (peer-based)

Figure 10.3 An integrated model of control choices

type of relationship, the trust mechanisms needed to mitigate those risks (as previously discussed), and the control choices that we believe are best suited to helping establish these trust production mechanisms.

In Figure 10.3, we capture the essence of our arguments. For each type of relationship, we indicate the likely levels of knowledge of the transformation process, outcome measurability, and behavior observability, the three antecedents that, in the traditional literature, determine the feasibility of control. We also note the mechanism necessary for trust production to mitigate the specific risk inherent in each type of relationship. This, in turn, determines the need for controls – that is, each relationship type should be controlled by mechanisms most likely to mitigate risks by helping to build the specific trust production mechanism needed for that relationship type. The last column in Figure 10.3, therefore, reflects our integrated model of control in which control choices are simultaneously based on both the feasibility and need for specific control modes, and incorporates both manager (controller) initiated and peer (controllee) based controls (Long, Chapter 12; Loughry and Tosi, 2008; Loughry, Chapter 11). We argue that this integrated model aptly reflects the complexity of contemporary organizations and the corresponding need for control choices to address this complexity. In the following sections we develop our arguments for each type of relationship.

Shallow dependence

As noted, a *shallow dependence* relationship is characterized by a simple dependence in which one party's desired outcomes are contingent upon the actions of another. Consider two examples: a customer purchasing a book online at Amazon.com, or buying a cup of coffee at Starbucks. In both cases, the customer's focus is on the outcome of the behavior, rather than the behavior itself. That is, the customer is interested in obtaining the product in good condition at a fair price, but is not particularly interested in the details of how the vendor fulfills the order.

From the perspective of the traditional control literature, the two purchases noted above are different. In the case of the online purchase, it is not feasible for the customer to observe the vendor's order fulfillment and shipment processes, that is, behavior observability is low. In this situation, the customer is also not likely to know about Amazon's internal operations, that is, the controller's (customer's) knowledge of the vendor's transformation process is also low. However, it is easy for the customer to assess whether the book is shipped promptly and arrives in good condition – his ability to measure the outcome of the process (outcome measurability) is high. As a result, the traditional control literature would suggest that outcome controls are most appropriate in this situation.

In the case of the customer buying coffee at Starbucks, however, it is quite possible for a customer, if he so chooses, to observe the coffee-preparation process – behavior observability may, in fact, be high. Similarly, at least some of the customers may be fairly skilled at preparing coffee, that is, their knowledge of the transformation process may be reasonably high. And, of course, the customer can assess how quickly the coffee was ready and how good it tastes, which suggests that outcome measurability is high. In this case, both behavior and outcome controls would be feasible. Though some of the extant literature would suggest using some combination of both, agency theorists would argue that behavior control is appropriate in this situation (e.g., Govindarajan and Fisher, 1990). Agency theory assumes that agents are risk averse. Structuring an outcome-based contract would unnecessarily shift risk to the agent when a behavior-based control could be fashioned.

Thus, the traditional feasibility-driven perspective may offer different recommendations for choice of controls in two situations that are both characterized by shallow dependence. The relationship perspective, on the other hand, is more firmly prescriptive regarding the choice of controls in this context. As argued by Sheppard and Sherman (1998), deterrence is an appropriate mechanism for producing trust across parties in this relationship in order to reduce risks of unreliability and indiscretion. That is, in this case, the *need* is for controls that create deterrence. Since deterrence-based mechanisms (e.g., poor credit rating) are outcomes of specific transactions, they provide a means for one person (e.g., the consumer) to control the actions of another (e.g., the vendor). Lack of payment, or an implied threat of no repeat business by a consumer, are means to ensure the vendor delivers as promised. Therefore, as seen in Figure 10.3, the relationship perspective would suggest outcome-based control will be utilized when parties are engaged in a shallow dependence relationship – and this would be true for both of the examples discussed.

Deep dependence

In cases of deep dependence, the dependence is again characterized as unidimensional but, unlike shallow dependence, the interactions between the parties are frequent and important, with many points of contact between them. An example is employer–employee relationships. In this type of relationship, risks include cheating, neglect, abuse, and loss of self-esteem (see Figure 10.2). Sheppard and Sherman (1998) point to "obligation" as the trust production mechanism that helps to control the risks inherent in deep dependence relationships. However, with respect to the specific ways to create this sense of obligation, Sheppard and Sherman largely defer to the domain of organizational control theorists, including agency theorists. In fact, there is a great deal of consistency between Sheppard and Sherman's observation that "obligation" is a trust production mechanism and the notion of contracts as a control mechanism in the organizational control and agency literatures. Building a sense of obligation between parties can be achieved, in part, with the appropriate structuring of control mechanisms.

A sense of obligation can be developed through either informal or formal controls. Thus, clan controls, almost by definition, entail creating a set of shared beliefs that result in a sense of mutual obligation.

But we expect that in most cases formal controls will be utilized for deep dependence relationships, because the extant control literature suggests that when formal controls are feasible, they are usually preferred. For example, in a qualitative study of IS project teams, Kirsch (1997) found that managers were reluctant to structure a portfolio of controls without a range of formal mechanisms included; these managers were uncomfortable relying solely on informal approaches to control. In subsequent studies, authors have made similar observations (Choudhury and Sabherwal, 2003; Kirsch, 2004).

We expect that outcomes or targets will be defined by a controller in such a way that they will be measurable, thereby enabling the controller to utilize outcome control. Ouchi's model suggests that if the controller's knowledge of the transformation process is perfect, he will be able to use behavior control. Sheppard and Sherman (1998) note, though, that in deep dependence relationships, one often sees knowledge asymmetry where each party has only limited understanding of the other's domain. This makes the use of controller-initiated behavior control more difficult, although not necessarily impossible – Eisenhardt (1985) argued that even without perfect knowledge of the transformation process, a controller can utilize behavior control by investing in information systems and other monitoring devices to reveal the behavior of the employee.

In such a setting, when outcomes are measurable and behaviors can be made observable, a controller is likely to utilize either behavior control or outcome control (or both) to ensure his employee achieves the goals of the organization (Choudhury and Sabherwal, 2003; Kirsch, 1996; Snell, 1992). Thus, fear of cheating or shirking on the part of the controllee can be mitigated by structuring a contract in which the controller observes the controllee's behavior or rewards the controllee for achieving specific targets. Thus, we predict that deep dependence relationships will be controlled via formal controls (behavior and/or outcome), as shown in Figure 10.3.

Shallow interdependence

Relationships characterized as shallow interdependent involve parties who do not have significant points of contact and frequent interactions, but who nevertheless require significant amounts of coordination to successfully execute their work tasks. Consider the case of a firm in which a vice-president has charged the managers of sales and manufacturing, managers who historically had an arms-length relationship, to work collaboratively and cooperatively to build a product that the market demands and the salesforce can sell. In this scenario, the sales and manufacturing managers can be conceived of as peers, with the vice-president in a superior role. A traditional control theory perspective might model this with the vice-president as controller, and the sales and manufacturing managers as controllees. This perspective would then ponder the controller's choice of controls, based largely on the feasibility of various controls, and probably conclude that the vice-president will use a combination of formal controls. Specifically, he has the authority to set specific targets for both the sales and manufacturing managers, and is likely to be able to measure progress against the targets, thereby enabling the use of outcome control. He may also choose to implement behavioral control, if he is in a position to observe the managers' behaviors via reports, meetings, or personal observation, and depending on the asymmetry of knowledge between the controller and controllees.

An integrated view demands a consideration of the *need* for control and encourages us to think more broadly. Sheppard and Sherman's (1998) analysis points to poor coordination as a major risk in shallow interdependent relationships. They argue that discovery – information gathering and exchange – is the mechanism needed to mitigate this risk. The parties need information about job descriptions, operating procedures, work that has been completed, schedules, and so on. Coordinating work activity calls for clear communication of tasks and roles, as well as expected behaviors and accomplishments.

Behavior controls are a means of communicating roles and expectations (Turner and Makhija, 2006). But it is not the coordination between the vice-president and either manager, though, that would be most problematic in this scenario, but rather the coordination between the sales and manufacturing managers as they work through the process of jointly creating a product that can be built and sold. Thus, the relationship perspective tells us that in a shallow interdependent relationship, it is not enough to have behavior control that makes the behaviors of the sales and manufacturing managers (controllees) visible to the vice-president (controller). Instead, what is needed is peer-based behavior control, that is, behavior control that the managers of sales and manufacturing exercise over each other in order to coordinate their activities and make forward progress.[4] Loughry and Tosi (2008) note that "peers often have better information about coworkers than do managers, they can detect behaviors that other forms of monitoring might miss." For example, the behavior of the manager of manufacturing (sales) may become visible to the sales (manufacturing) manager through meetings, reports, and other types of information systems. The transparency of the behavior would then provide the sales (manufacturing) manager an opportunity to influence the behavior of the manager of manufacturing (sales).

In a scenario characterized by shallow interdependence relationships, therefore, we predict that an integrated approach to control will be utilized. As depicted in Figure 10.3, we argue that both controller-initiated and peer-based formal controls will be used. Specifically, we posit that the manager (or the person in the controller role) will utilize formal controls (behavior and/or outcome). The manager's control efforts will be supplemented by actions taken by the controllees to ensure their peers are working as expected. That is, the "controllees," given their need for discovery to coordinate their interdependent tasks and activities, will structure and utilize peer-based behavior control.

Deep interdependence

Similar to shallow interdependence, parties in a deep interdependent relationship are involved in highly interdependent tasks in which frequent communication is critical to coordinating their work. In contrast, though, these parties are "connected" and share world views. One party does not require written and detailed specifications, procedures, and rules for proceeding because they know what needs to be done, given their "sameness" with the others. Consider the case of a collaboration between project teams in the United States and India, charged with developing one information system and overseen by a manager located in the US. This situation might be modeled with the US manager as the controller, and the project team leaders as the controllees. In this case, the traditional view of control would suggest that the US manager is likely to utilize outcome-based control, setting specific targets for the project leaders to achieve.[5]

The relationship perspective would, however, suggest that even if outcome measurability and/or behavior observability are high, formal controller-initiated controls are not likely to be enough. In a deep interdependence relationship, Sheppard and Sherman (1998) argue that risk stems from misanticipation of each other's needs and behaviors. They posit that internalization is the mechanism needed to foster trust, and that the parties involved in this relationship should adopt each other's beliefs in order to be able to foresee each other's needs. This is possible because of their shared worldviews and congruent beliefs. Internalization maps nicely to a strategy of clan control. The exercise of clan control is based on a common vision among parties and shared norms and value systems. Values and norms must be internalized among parties; thus the need for internalization as a way to build trust also calls for the use of clan control. In this scenario, therefore, we posit that members of the US and India project teams will jointly exercise clan control to find "sameness" and "connections," adopting each other's norms and values, and committing to a common project vision, to assure forward progress on the project.

Thus, as with shallow interdependence, we believe that those involved in a deep interdependence relationship will utilize an integrated control strategy. In the case of deep interdependence, we posit that managers will rely on outcome-based control strategies. Supplementing the manager's control strategies, we posit, are "controllees" who utilize clan control since they share worldviews and hold common beliefs, and since they have a pressing need to coordinate their activities on a real-time basis. This argument is reflected in Figure 10.3.

Discussion and conclusion

In this chapter, we have noted that, in much of the extant literature, the choice of control has been based on the feasibility of exercising a certain mode or type of control, from the controller's perspective. In particular, the controller's knowledge of the transformation process, his ability to observe behavior, and his ability to measure outcomes determine whether a controller will utilize outcome, behavior, or clan control (Eisenhardt, 1985; Ouchi, 1977, 1979, 1980). We have argued that this perspective is incomplete in that it does not take into explicit consideration the attitudes and perceptions of the controllee, or the *need* for specific controls in a given context. A focus on just the feasibility of controls means that the traditional control literature may, in some cases, suggest the same set of controls for an individual buying a cup of coffee at Starbucks, as for a manager overseeing the implementation of a global information system. This is clearly not the intent or the goal of the control literature.

As a first step to addressing this limitation, we propose an integrated model in which both the *feasibility* and the *need* for specific controls are considered, as well as both *controller-initiated* and *peer-based* controls. Such an integrated model is likely to be more nuanced and effective in matching controls to the underlying context. We have proposed a focus on the controller–controllee relationship to better understand the need for control in a specific context, and how both the controller and the controllee influence and implement control choices. Prior work of Sheppard and Sherman (1998) provides a typology of relationships, the risks inherent in those relationships, and the mechanisms needed to produce trust to mitigate the risks. We use this framework, and extend it, by considering the controls needed to mitigate the risks inherent in specific relationships. Considering relationships and risks encourages researchers to move beyond the superior–subordinate focus that is often adopted when conducting empirical studies of control. Instead of focusing solely on the feasibility of control from the superior's perspectives, the relationship perspective encourages researchers to also focus on the controls, which may be controller-initiated or peer-based, needed to manage potentially risky behavior.

Based on differences in form and depth of relationship, Sheppard and Sherman (1998) propose four types of dependencies between parties: shallow dependence, deep dependence, shallow interdependence, and deep interdependence. For each type, they identify specific risks and relevant mechanisms needed to produce trust. We extend their ideas by also noting the types of controls that are relevant to mitigate the risks inherent in each type of relationship.

In the case of shallow dependence relationships, the traditional control literature suggests that behavior and outcome controls are feasible in different settings. A relationship perspective, on the other hand, considers the need for control in these relationships and concludes that outcome-based controls are appropriate.

For a deep dependence relationship, the proposed control strategies are largely the same, regardless of whether the analysis is approached from a control theory perspective based on Ouchi's work, or from a relationship perspective based on Sheppard and Sherman's work.

This is partly because Sheppard and Sherman themselves note that the specific mechanisms for creating a sense of obligation, the recommended trust-building mechanism for this kind of relationship, are the purview of control theory.

Both shallow and deep dependence relationships are considered unidimensional in the sense that the principal's desired outcome is dependent on the actions of the agent. The structure of the relationship is clear and typically hierarchical. Thus, a strategy of formal controller-initiated controls is often adequate.

In contrast, when work tasks are highly interdependent, uncertain, and span disciplines, organizational structures and processes become more complex. The remaining two relationships – shallow interdependence and deep interdependence – reflect this more complex work environment, and, consequently, *demand* more complex control strategies (Hagel *et al.*, Chapter 9) to ensure that the risks inherent in these relationships are managed and organizational objectives are met. For both of these types of interdependent relationships, we propose that organizations will utilize a set of integrated controls to reflect the nature of the relationships. In the case of shallow interdependence, we expect to see a combination of formal manager-initiated controls as well as peer-based behavior control to ensure that activities are coordinated across individuals and work groups. In the case of deep interdependence, we expect to see manager-initiated outcome controls supplemented by peer-based clan control that results from internalized and shared belief systems and values.

Considering the nature of relationships as a supplement to traditional antecedents in determining control modes provides a means of understanding how controls are used in combination. Many studies of control have empirically examined the choice of a single control mode, though some studies have examined how portfolios of control are structured (Cardinal *et al.*, 2004; Jaworski *et al.*, 1993; Long, Chapter 12). For example, based on case study results, Kirsch (1997) argued that controllers select pre-existing mechanisms of formal control, designing new mechanisms if necessary, and supplementing the formal mechanisms of control with informal mechanisms. Recently researchers have also examined how portfolios of control choices change over time (Cardinal *et al.*, 2004; Kirsch, 2004; Mähring, 2002). Though these efforts are significant, they have not yet yielded precise insight into how and why portfolios of control are created.

Further, these studies have also typically been focused on the perceptions and actions of the controller, with the controllee playing a relatively minor role in the selection of control combinations. The focus on relationships, as discussed in this chapter, provides a mechanism for broadening our understanding of the choice of control in contemporary organizations.

The integrated control perspective suggests a number of opportunities for future research. An obvious one is, of course, to test whether the proposed control portfolios suggested here for specific relationship types are, in fact, employed in practice. Another potential research issue is to examine the relative salience of the feasibility perspective prevalent in the extant literature and the need-based perspective suggested here, with a focus on controller–controllee relationships. That is, if the two perspectives suggest conflicting control choices, what do controllers choose? Third, much of our analysis above is based on the use of control strategies to create the trust-production mechanisms needed in specific relationships. This raises some intriguing questions about the nature of the relationship between control and trust. For instance, are they complements or substitutes? Does trust mediate the relationship between control portfolios and the effectiveness of controls? Finally, including the relationship perspective also focuses attention on the cost of controls. For instance, in the case of the shallow dependence relationship, as discussed previously, the relationship perspective clarifies that even if behavior control were possible, it would not be used in most instances. An interesting question to ask, therefore, would be: to what extent do controllers consider the costs when deciding on a portfolio of controls?

Traditional control theory, with its focus on a single control mode and the perspective of the controller, may not provide a complete understanding of control in complex, dynamic, and uncertain organizational environments (Hagel *et al.*, Chapter 9; Long, Chapter 12). We argue that considering the types of relationships, and the risks inherent in the different relationships, will provide a way of understanding more complex control choices. Moreover, it shifts the focus from determining control strictly from a feasibility perspective to also considering what behavior needs to be controlled. The integrated model of control choice developed here provides a framework for deepening our understanding of the choice of controls in contemporary organizations.

Notes

1 See "How the EQUIP™ business system changed a dealership's culture" in *The Leader*, July 2008, an internal newsletter published quarterly by John Deere-AMC, publication number DSALEDU0807.

2 Some researchers are beginning to look at these types of controls in their informal form as well (e.g., Cardinal *et al.*, 2004), but in this paper we stay with the traditional view of behavior and output controls as formal.

3 We seek to differentiate mode of control from control mechanism and control systems. Control mode refers to the type of control used, and can involve multiple control mechanisms to exercise behavior, outcome, or clan control modes. Mode of control is also unique from "control systems that are configurations of multiple formal and informal control mechanisms" (Cardinal *et al.*, Chapter 3).

4 Indeed, from a traditional control theory perspective, we note that neither outcome control nor clan control seems feasible in this scenario. Neither sales nor manufacturing would have the authority to define outcome targets for the other unit, suggesting that outcome control is not feasible. The lack of a deep and ongoing relationship between sales and manufacturing suggests that clan control is not feasible.

5 Though it is possible that a controller in a deep interdependent relationship might also structure behavior-based controls, researchers have found that managers in this situation do not always have the requisite knowledge to utilize behavior control, and that it can be quite difficult to observe behaviors of geographically distributed team members (e.g., Choudhury and Sabherwal, 2003; Kirsch, 2004; Rustagi *et al.*, 2008).

References

Bigley, G. A. and Roberts, K. H. 2001. The incident command system: high-reliability organizing for complex and volatile task environments. *Academy of Management Journal*, 44 (6): 1,281–1,299.

Cardinal, L. B. 2001. Technological innovation in the pharmaceutical industry: the use of organizational control in managing research and development. *Organization Science*, 12 (1): 19–36.

Cardinal, L. B., Sitkin, S. B., and Long, C. P. 2004. Balancing and rebalancing in the creation and evolution of organizational control. *Organization Science*, 15 (4): 411–431.

Child, J. and McGrath, R. G. 2001. Organizations unfettered: organizational form in an information-intensive economy. *Academy of Management Journal*, 44 (6): 1,135–1,148.

Choudhury, V. and Sabherwal, R. 2003. Portfolios of control in outsourced software development projects. *Information Systems Research*, 14 (3): 291–314.

Das, T. K. and Teng, B. 1998. Between trust and control: developing confidence in partner cooperation in alliances. *Academy of Management Review*, 23 (3): 491–512.

Eisenhardt, K. M. 1985. Control: organizational and economic approaches. *Management Science*, 31 (2): 134–149.

Fiske, A. P. 1990. Relativity within moose ("mossi") culture: four incommensurable models for social relationships. *Ethos*, 18: 180–204.

Fortado, B. 1994. Informal supervisory social control strategies. *Journal of Management Studies*, 31 (2): 251–274.

Govindarajan, V. and Fisher, J. 1990. Strategy, control systems, and resource sharing: effects on business-unit performance. *Academy of Management Journal*, 33 (2): 259–285.

Henderson, J. C. and Lee, S. 1992. Managing I/S design teams: a control theories perspective. *Management Science*, 38 (6): 757–777.

Jaworski, B. J. 1988. Toward a theory of marketing control: environmental context, control types, and consequences. *Journal of Marketing*, 52: 23–39.

Jaworski, B. J., Stathakopoulos, V., and Krishnan, H. S. 1993. Control combinations in marketing: conceptual framework and empirical evidence. *Journal of Marketing*, 57: 57–69.

Kirsch, L. J. 1996. The management of complex tasks in organizations: controlling the systems development process. *Organization Science*, 7 (1): 1–21.

1997. Portfolios of control modes and IS project management. *Information Systems Research*, 8 (3): 215–239.

2004. Deploying common systems globally: the dynamics of control. *Information Systems Research*, 15 (4): 374–395.

Kirsch, L. J. and Cummings, L. L. 1996. Contextual influences on self-control of IS professionals engaged in systems development. *Accounting, Management and Information Technologies*, 6 (3): 191–219.

Kirsch, L. J., Sambamurthy, V., Ko, D., and Purvis, R. L. 2002. Controlling information systems development projects: the view from the client. *Management Science*, 48 (4): 484–498.

Loughry, M. L. and Tosi, H. L. 2008. Performance implications of peer monitoring. *Organization Science*, 19 (6): 876–890.

Mähring, M. 2002. IT *Project Governance*. Unpublished doctoral dissertation, Stockholm School of Economics.

Makhija, M. V. and Ganesh, U. 1997. The relationship between control and partner learning in learning-related joint ventures. *Organization Science*, 8 (5): 508–527.

Ouchi, W. G. 1977. The relationship between organizational structure and organizational control. *Administrative Science Quarterly*, 22: 95–113.

1978. The transmission of control through organizational hierarchy. *Academy of Management Journal*, 21 (2): 173–192.

1979. A conceptual framework for the design of organizational control mechanisms. *Management Science*, 25 (9): 833–848.

1980. Markets, bureaucracies, and clans. *Administrative Science Quarterly*, 25: 129–141.

Ring, P. S. and Van de Ven, A. H. 1994. Developmental processes of cooperative interorganizational relationships. *Academy of Management Review*, 19: 841–856.

Roth, N. L., Sitkin, S. B., and House, A. 1994. Stigma as a determinant of legalization. In S. B. Sitkin and R. J. Bies (eds.), *The legalistic organization*: 137–168. Thousand Oaks, CA: Sage.

Rousseau, D. 1995. *Psychological contracts in organizations: understanding written and unwritten agreements*. London, UK: Sage Publications.

Rustagi, S., King, W. R., and Kirsch, L. J. 2008. Predictors of formal control: usage in IT outsourcing partnerships. *Information Systems Research*, 19 (2): 126–143.

Sheppard, B. H. and Sherman, D. M. 1998. The grammars of trust: a model and general implications. *Academy of Management Review*, 22 (3): 422–437.

Sitkin, S. B. 1995. On the positive effect of legalization on trust. *Research on Negotiation in Organizations*, 5: 185–217.

Sitkin, S. B. and George, E. 2005. Managerial trust-building through the use of legitimating formal and informal control mechanisms. *International Sociology*, 20 (3): 307–338.

Snell, S. A. 1992. Control theory in strategic human resource management: the mediating effect of administrative information. *Academy of Management Journal*, 35 (2): 292–327.

Towry, K. L. 2003. Control in a teamwork environment – the impact of social ties on the effectiveness of mutual contracts. *The Accounting Review*, 78 (4): 1,069–1,095.

Turner, K. L. and Makhija, M. V. 2006. The role of organizational controls in managing knowledge. *Academy of Management Review*, 31 (1): 197–217.

Tyler, T. and Lind, E. A. 1992. A relational model of authority in groups. In M. L. Zanna (ed.), *Advances in experimental social psychology*: 115–191. San Diego, CA: Academic Press.

11 | *Peer control in organizations*

MISTY L. LOUGHRY
Georgia Southern University

Peer control occurs when workers who are at the same organizational level or in the same field exert lateral control over their peers. Peer control is widespread in organizations, yet is not well understood. This chapter discusses the scope of the peer control concept, including different types of formal and informal peer controls designed by managers and workers. The potential benefits and drawbacks of peer control are also discussed. Five theoretical perspectives that can be used to examine informal peer control are reviewed. The chapter concludes with suggestions for future research on peer control.

Peer control is widespread in organizations and impacts a variety of important individual and organizational outcomes, but relatively little management research examines peer control as compared to other forms of organizational control, such as supervision/leadership and incentive pay. Yet wider spans of control and greater use of teams and self-managed work groups have decreased organizations' use of direct supervision and increased the importance of interpersonal influence and lateral coordination to direct and motivate work in organizations (Ilgen and Pulakos, 1999; Pfeffer, 1997). Furthermore, although competitive and economic conditions often leave little room for organizations to offer enough incentive pay to have a substantial influence on workers, the discretionary rewards and sanctions that coworkers give one another frequently do have very meaningful influences on workers.

The goals of this chapter are to show that peer control is an important, yet insufficiently understood, element of the organizational control system and to stimulate new research on peer control. First, the scope of the peer control concept is outlined, including formal and informal peer control, management-designed and worker-designed peer control, and beneficial and harmful aspects of peer control. Next, five disciplinary perspectives that have discussed peer control are reviewed to show that peer control is a broad concept to which scholars from various disciplines could contribute useful research. The chapter concludes with suggestions for future research.

Scope of the peer control concept

Peer control, also called lateral control, is a type of control that occurs when people who are at the same organizational level or in the same field exert control over their peers. Thus, peer control occurs among people who do not have hierarchical authority over one another.

The broader concept of control has been variously defined and can be considered as attributes of processes, contexts, people, or groups that influence people's behavior (Jaworski, 1988). Some scholars have defined control as an effort to keep organizational members operating in a coordinated way to accomplish organizational objectives (e.g., Arrow, 1964; Kirsch, 2004). For example, Cardinal, Sitkin, and Long (Chapter 3) define control as "any process whereby managers direct attention, motivate, and encourage organizational members to act in ways desirable to achieving the organization's objectives." However, peer control is not always consistent with accomplishing organizational objectives, so peer control that is both for and against organizational objectives would be included in a complete conceptualization of peer control. Therefore, peer control might broadly be considered as a process whereby peers direct attention, motivate, and encourage organizational members to act in ways desirable to achieving the objectives of the people who initiate the control. Agency theory research defines "peer monitoring" consistent with this, as occurring when individuals notice and respond to their peers' behavior or performance results (Loughry and Tosi, 2008) or oversee their peers' behavior and/or work (Welbourne and Ferrante, 2008). Although these and other definitions of control state that the person or group doing the controlling intends to affect the behavior of another person (Tannenbaum, 1968), some forms of peer control may occur when peers affect one another's behavior without intending to do so (Zajonc, 1965). This is important because some organizational controls, such as internal control processes that separate duties like writing checks and balancing the checkbook, may have control effects even though the peers involved in these duties do not intend to control one another. Because peer control is a broad concept, it may be helpful to examine different types of peer control.

Types of peer control

Formal and informal. Organizations typically use a system of controls that includes both formal control mechanisms, which are officially sanctioned, such as written policies, and informal control mechanisms, such as norms and values (Cardinal *et al.*, Chapter 3). Control systems that include a balanced and integrated mix of formal and informal control mechanisms are thought to work better than those that rely too heavily on one or the other (Cardinal *et al.*, 2004). Although formal controls are often necessary, they can create conflict and distrust between the organization and its members and increase the cost of control when used excessively (Sitkin and Bies, 1994). Informal controls do not always contribute to organizational effectiveness (Loughry and Tosi, 2008). However, those that do may enhance organizational members' well-being, trust in management, and perceptions about the legitimacy of management's decisions relative to formal controls (Bijlsma-Frankema and Costa, Chapter 13; Sitkin and George, 2005). Informal controls are also more difficult for competitors to imitate than are formal controls, and therefore can be a source of sustainable competitive advantage (Turner and Makhija, 2006).

Just as the general concept of control includes formal controls and informal controls, peer control can also be conceptualized as including formal peer controls and informal peer controls. Formal peer controls are those that have written or explicit rules of operation. Informal peer control occurs when peers notice or respond to their coworkers' behavior or results in ways that are not explicitly prescribed.

Management-designed versus worker-designed. In addition to formal and informal, another way that peer control can be categorized is into peer-control mechanisms that are management-designed versus worker-designed. Management designs the peer control system when it creates formal peer control mechanisms within the organization's broader control system, and when it manages the work context in an attempt to influence the informal peer control that occurs among workers. Worker-designed peer controls are those that workers choose to use to control their peers. These include formal peer control mechanisms that workers choose in contexts in which the organization explicitly delegates authority to the workers to self-govern, as in self-managed teams. Worker-designed peer controls also include the informal peer controls that emerge voluntarily among peers, such as when one worker points out a problem that the coworker might not have noticed.

By considering two aspects of peer control, whether it is formal or informal and management-designed or worker-designed, peer controls can be classified into four types. These are shown in Table 11.1, along with examples of peer control mechanisms that fall within each of the four types.

Management-designed formal peer controls

To use management-designed formal peer controls, organizations create rules requiring peers to evaluate, observe, or influence one another and thus act as agents of the organization or its management. Although management designs certain peer control mechanisms, for them to function in the way that management intends, the workers who are governed by the system must cooperate in the system and thereby consent to take part in the control of their peers (Sewell, 1998). For example, management can create a reporting hotline, but when workers observe a coworker stealing, they decide whether or not to report it. Thus, the degree to which workers comply with management's intentions is one variable that will affect the outcomes of management-designed peer control systems.

Some examples of management-designed, formal peer control mechanisms include formal peer evaluations, whistle-blowing hotlines, segregation of duties, formal on-the job training and mentoring programs, and delegating authority to self-managing teams. These are discussed next.

Formal peer evaluations. One way that organizations formalize peer control is by using peer evaluations as part of 360-degree feedback systems or multi-source performance appraisals. These systems require peers to evaluate one another using instruments selected by the organization's management. Their purposes are to encourage workers to increase both their task effort and their efforts at maintaining effective interactions with their peers, and to provide developmental feedback to help members improve their performance.

Table 11.1 *Types of peer control mechanisms with examples*

	Management-designed	Worker-designed
Formal peer control	• Formal peer evaluations (such as in 360-degree feedback systems). • Whistle-blowing hotlines. • Segregation of duties. • Management-designed peer on-the-job training or mentoring systems. • Management delegating self-governing authority to workers (self-managing teams and academia).	*This box would be relevant when management delegates explicit self-governing authority to workers, usually in self-managed teams or academia.* • Explicit work rules (and any explicit associated rewards/sanctions) that self-managing teams create for themselves. • Worker-initiated rules for posting/sharing comparative performance data. • Worker-designed peer on-the-job training or mentoring systems. • Faculty-designed rules for tenure and promotion procedures.

Informal peer control	• Management structuring the work and the work context to encourage or facilitate peer control (e.g., task and reward interdependence, open offices).
	• Management-initiated publicly posting/sharing comparative performance data, newsletters that highlight workers' achievements.
	• Management attempts to influence workers' relationships with each other (e.g., sponsoring social events for workers).
	• Management attempts to manage the organization's culture.
	• Training workers in techniques for relating to one another (e.g., conflict management techniques).
		Workers' discretionary (not explicitly required) noticing and responding to peers' behavior or results.
		• Direct informal peer control
		  ○ Observational monitoring/noticing peers' behavior and results.
		  ○ Advisory monitoring – praising, correcting, training, or mentoring peers.
		  ○ Vertical reporting.
		  ○ Discussing/sharing job-related information about coworkers' behavior, results, or other job-related data.
		• Indirect informal peer control
		  ○ Rejecting/avoiding peers.
		  ○ Gossiping about disliked peers.

The effect of peer evaluation systems on performance is not known. The research has primarily assessed workers' satisfaction with peer ratings and ratings' reliability (such as inter-rater agreement and prediction of assessment center performance) rather than how peer evaluations affect individual or collective performance (Beehr *et al.*, 2001; Bono and Colbert, 2005; Fedor *et al.*, 1999). A meta-analysis found a very small positive effect of peer ratings on performance in longitudinal studies (Smither *et al.*, 2005). One study found that formal peer assessments were associated with increased supervisory ratings over time (Bamberger *et al.*, 2005).

There is some concern that informal behavior among participants, such as intentionally distorting peer ratings, can lead to counter-productive work-group dynamics (Bamberger, 2007). In addition, there is some evidence that peer ratings of poor performers can be too lenient (Atkins and Wood, 2002), in which case the peer ratings would not be useful to detect performance problems and provide feedback for improvement.

Given the limited research on peer appraisals, it is not known whether they are a useful part of formal organizational controls to coordinate work, encourage effort, and constrain inappropriate behavior. Future research that examines how formally requiring employees to evaluate peers affects individual and collective performance would be valuable. The small body of existing research in this area has focused on the feedback from the peer ratings as the mediating mechanism between peer ratings and any performance changes (Smither *et al.*, 2005). Future research could also examine how formal peer evaluation systems affect the informal peer control that emerges (throughout the year, not just at performance evaluation time), and whether informal peer control may mediate or moderate the performance effects of the written peer evaluation system. For example, requiring workers to evaluate one another might change the types of information that workers notice about their peers, how they use that information to informally influence their peers, and the degree to which monitored coworkers heed their peers' advice.

Requiring peer reporting. Reporting or whistle-blowing hotlines, honor codes, and ethics programs in which organizations ask their workers to report coworkers' misdeeds are also formal peer control mechanisms created by management (Mesmer-Magnus and Viswesvaran, 2005). These systems aim to make reporting dishonest peers a formal part of workers' role responsibilities. Research suggests that formal peer reporting systems affect workers' attitudes, including reducing negative attitudes toward peer reporting of coworkers' misdeeds and making workers more likely to claim that they would report dishonest coworkers (Trevino and Victor, 1992).

Future control research on peer reporting could include longitudinal studies that examine outcomes such as inventory shrinkage and accidents in order to provide evidence that peer reporting discourages inappropriate employee behavior. This research might also examine the factors that influence how workers use peer reporting systems and how workers' use of the systems interacts with workers' informal peer control. For example, in some contexts there may be strong peer pressure not to use the organization's hotline to report peers. This might be accompanied by informal pressure on peers to stop behaving inappropriately, perhaps including threats to use the system if the peer doesn't stop the inappropriate behavior. In contrast, informal pressures not to use the peer reporting system could be accompanied by workers' tolerance of peers' inappropriate behavior. Therefore, understanding how the informal peer control works with the formal peer reporting system would be necessary in order to understand how peer reporting systems affect the intended outcomes.

Segregation of duties. Publicly traded companies are required by law to establish sound internal control processes to minimize losses from identifiable risks, and sound business practice requires that all organizations do the same (Hopwood *et al.*, 2008). Accountants, therefore, must evaluate "internal controls" as required part of audits. Organizations frequently use control mechanisms that rely on peer control as part of their documented internal control processes to reduce identifiable risks and discourage dishonest behavior (Willis and Lightle, 2000). Among the most important is "segregation of duties," which means that no individual should perform more than one of the following three functions: (1) authorizing transactions; (2) having custody of assets; and (3) recordkeeping (Hopwood *et al.*, 2008). This makes it likely that if one employee is embezzling money or doing something else dishonest, that another employee will detect it. For example, organizations typically assign different employees to authorize payment, write checks, and balance the checkbook. Mandatory vacations and forced job rotation are also used to increase the chances that a coworker would discover any fraudulent behavior (Hopwood *et al.*, 2008). Where there is especially high risk within one function, organizations may require that at least two employees be involved in the same function. For example, banks give one employee a key to the bank vault and another the vault combination so that two employees must be present to open it. This ensures that no one employee could open the vault and steal the money without being immediately detected.

When dangerous work is performed, organizations sometimes use similar segregation of duties to protect the safety of workers or other people, such as mandating that employees not perform a dangerous task without being assisted or observed by another employee. For example, two employees might be required to check the positions of equipment settings before a dangerous operation is performed, or the first employee to enter a bank in the morning might be required to check for robbers and give an "ok" signal before coworkers can enter.

Segregation of duties increases the chances of timely detection if an employee behaves inappropriately, gets into a dangerous position, or sustains an injury. Although well-accepted accounting practices recommend that organizations use internal control systems that rely on peer control, there is little accounting research on peer control (Chen and Sandino, 2007).

On-the-job training, mentoring, and counseling. Although peer control systems can be used with any employees, they might be particularly useful for new employees. Therefore, many organizations assign a peer on-the-job trainer to supervise the new employees for a designated period of time or until the new employee has met certain performance criteria. New employees may also be assigned a peer mentor to help them fit into the organizational culture and get comfortable in their new role.

There is a large body of literature on mentoring (Eby *et al.*, 2008), but it has not yet focused on the value of peer mentoring for organizational control, although one study found that it was a cost-effective way to deter substance abuse in the workplace (Miller *et al.*, 2007). Future research could examine the impact of peer training or mentoring programs on outcomes such as group or member performance, accidents, or errors. It is likely that there could be control effects on both the trainer/mentor as well as the trainee/protégé. Although performing training and mentoring activities can take time away from the mentor's task work, research suggests that it can increase the mentor's learning, skills, and performance because teaching someone else requires increased attention to and understanding of details of the subject being taught (Pullins and Fine, 2002). Mentoring can also be fulfilling and energizing for mentors and increase their satisfaction (Pullins and Fine, 2002).

Delegating authority for self-governance. In some organizations management formally delegates self-governing authority to groups of workers. In these organizations, peer control is a core element of the organization's control system and is relied upon for much of the control that would be performed by supervision in more vertical control systems. One example is self-managed teams, in which the organization delegates authority and control to teams comprised of peers (Van Mierlo *et al.*, 2005). A second example is academia, in which peer groups are largely responsible for hiring, promotion, and tenure decisions (Carmichael, 1988). In addition, boards of directors frequently include inside members of the organization who have formal responsibility to monitor the executives themselves (Fama and Jensen, 1983a). Management's choice to delegate self-governing authority to groups of workers is a form of management-designed formal peer control. When groups of workers receive formal authority for governing themselves, they often create formal rules for how they will exert peer control. This is discussed next.

Worker-designed formal peer controls

When management delegates authority to groups of workers, the workers sometimes create explicit rules for how the peer control will operate. Workers may also develop systems for sharing information about the performance of individuals or the group as a whole, in order to make members feel accountable to the peer group. In some cases, workers may also design systems for training and mentoring new workers. These are worker-designed formal peer controls.

Although control research has traditionally viewed formal controls as being management-initiated (Jaworski, 1988), there are various examples of workers designing explicit rules for peer control. In self-managed teams, workers sometimes develop codified rules about what behaviors are expected and what the consequences will be if those expectations are violated (Barker, 1993). Universities establish faculty committees to provide peer control of faculty through selection, tenure and promotion; ask for outside letters of support from peers in the same discipline; and rely on peer review by colleagues in the discipline when they use journal publications to evaluate the quality of faculty research (Fama and Jensen, 1983a; Ouchi, 1977). In these situations, groups of faculty members usually develop written rules for how the peer control system will operate. Peer review is also an important part of the control systems in professions such as accounting, law, and education. Therefore, worker-designed formal peer control mechanisms could be examined in these settings.

Management-designed informal peer controls

In management-designed informal peer control, management manages the organizational context to indirectly influence workers' choices of informal peer control so that they are more likely to benefit the organization. It is the worker-initiated informal control that then directly influences coworkers.

One way that management influences the peer control context is through the organizational structure. Although structure is itself a formal control mechanism (Jaworski, 1988), it can also affect informal control. The organizational structure assigns roles to workers and establishes relationships between those roles, which affects the amount of attention that workers pay to one another (Ocasio and Wohlgezogen, Chapter 7). Several other ways that managers can influence the informal peer control context are discussed next.

Sharing comparative performance data. Some organizations share individual performance data with peers in order to stimulate social comparison and informal peer control among organizational members. This may increase accountability to peers and reduce social loafing (Hollenbeck *et al.*, 1998).

Modern information systems make it easy to give workers extensive and timely information about their own and peers' performance; this social comparison information can motivate low performers to improve even without any direct influence attempts by peers (Kirsch and Choudhury, Chapter 10). Some control scholars view sharing comparative performance information as a way to integrate the control activities of managers and employees, making them partners in the organization's control system (Kirsch and Choudhury, Chapter 10). However, critical theorists express concern that public posting creates excessive total control (Sewell, 1998; Delbridge, Chapter 4).

Nordstrom, Lorenzi, and Hall (1990) found that public posting of individual-level performance data was positively associated with performance and created more social interaction among peers. However, they also speculated that posting comparative performance information contributes to a more competitive relationship among peers, which could have negative consequences in settings where cooperation among workers is needed to accomplish the work.

Because technology is making it easier for organizations to track and share performance statistics, future research that examines the implications of doing so would be useful. Future research on public posting of comparative performance data could examine worker-initiated informal peer control as a mediating mechanism between posting the data and the resulting effects on individual and collective performance. Studies that examine how workers observe their peers' performance, the information that they notice, and peer influence attempts aimed at both enhancing and reducing coworkers' performance would be beneficial. The impact on workers' stress, turnover, and other outcomes could also be examined. It is likely that moderators, such as the type of worker or the level of organizational commitment may influence these relationships.

Task interdependence. Managing task interdependence is another way that managers can design the organizational context to influence the peer control that emerges among workers. Task interdependence refers to the level of collective action, coordination, and mutual adjustment that is required to perform the task (Thompson, 1967). Past research has found that task interdependence is positively associated with performance (Campion *et al.*, 1996; Wageman and Baker, 1997). One reason could be that task interdependence stimulates informal peer control among workers. Kirsch and Choudhury (Chapter 10) suggest that workers will exercise peer control when they have interdependent work relationships in order to access information and coordinate their work. They argue that when the interdependence is shallow (requiring coordination but infrequent interaction), the peer control will take the form of behavior control that communicates expectations about roles and performance. However, when the interdependence is deep (requiring frequent communication and tight coordination), the peer control will take the form of internalized shared vision, values, and beliefs, because the frequent interaction makes explicit statements about expectations less necessary.

Future research that examines how task interdependence influences the worker-initiated informal peer control that emerges would be useful. Higher levels of task interdependence may increase workers' attempts at peer control in order to reduce workers' vulnerability to peers' behavior or production results. Peer control that aims to improve performance might have stronger effects in interdependent work contexts because it could facilitate efficient mutual adjustment and increase the quality or reliability of coworkers' performance. Peer control that enhances coworkers' performance or reliability would benefit collective performance more in interdependent work groups where the whole group's performance would suffer if any one member did not perform as expected. This relationship was supported in a recent study (Loughry and Tosi, 2008).

Reward interdependence. In addition to task interdependence, managers can design the reward interdependence to influence informal peer control among workers. Reward or outcome interdependence occurs when workers' outcomes depend on their peers' behaviors or results. The nature of the reward interdependence can be cooperative or competitive (Deutsch, 1949). Cooperative reward interdependence is commonly achieved by basing some of workers' pay or other rewards or punishments on collective performance (Welbourne *et al.*, 1995). This gives workers a self-interested reason to exert informal peer control aimed at improving peers' performance. Furthermore, because both peers and supervisors understand that collective rewards make workers' dependent on each others' performance, reward interdependence may legitimize informal peer control and make peers and supervisors more comfortable with it (Welbourne and Ferrante, 2008). In contrast, without reward interdependence, informal peer monitoring might be perceived as violating hierarchical authority relationships or "trying to be the boss."

Competitive reward interdependence results when organizations reward workers based on their relative performance, such as when the top performers get a bonus or award. Although competition among workers can cause everyone to work hard in hopes of achieving a promotion or other competitive prize (Akerlof, 1976), little is known about how these contests affect peer control. It is likely that competitive interdependence creates a strong interest in observing peers. However, it is also likely to deter beneficial forms of peer control that seek to enhance peers' performance or assist poor performers, and cause some instances of informal peer control aimed at reducing peers' performance. There is evidence that even pay based on individual performance (without an explicit competitive component) reduces cooperative behavior among coworkers (Weibel, Chapter 14). Therefore, future research that examines how commonly used competitive rewards affect informal peer control would be worthwhile.

Some research suggests that the levels of task and reward interdependence in a job should be aligned, although some reward interdependence may stimulate informal peer control that positively affects performance even when the task is independent (Wageman and Baker, 1997). Some organizations do use reward interdependence when the task is independent, in order to encourage informal peer control (Townsend, 2007). However, the idea that organizations can create beneficial peer control simply by providing group-based rewards may be overly simplistic, as research finds that moderating variables, such as the perceived justice of the incentive system, intervene (Welbourne *et al.*, 1995). There is also a danger that reward interdependence may cause workers to exert more peer control than is optimal if workers reduce their own task effort to spend time controlling peers or if the peer control causes stress for workers (Baker *et al.*, 1988; Barron and Gjerde, 1997).

Training. Training organizational members on appropriate versus inappropriate ways of influencing peers would be another way that organizations could manage the organizational context to influence peer control among workers (Lavelle *et al.*, 2007). Training could encourage workers to use more direct forms of peer control, such as talking to the peer about their concerns, rather than indirect methods, such as gossiping about or ostracizing peers (Loughry and Tosi, 2008) and aim to create a culture of taking charge to create beneficial changes in the organization (Morrison and Phelps, 1999). Future research could examine how various types of training interventions affect the informal peer control that emerges among workers and how the training affects workers' attitudes, stress, or their behavior in response to peer control attempts by others.

Worker-designed informal peer controls

Worker-designed informal peer controls are important because they are ubiquitous and powerful. In contrast to the other three types of peer controls (management-designed and worker-designed formal peer control mechanisms and management-designed informal peer control mechanisms), which are present in only some organizations, worker-initiated informal peer control is present in virtually every organization. Workers' informal peer control has strong influences in organizations because peers frequently spend a substantial amount of time with one another, which gives them many opportunities to exert informal lateral influence. Often supervisors and subordinates do not spend as much time together, so vertical influence may be more sporadic. Furthermore, the informal nature of lateral relationships is likely to make peers receptive to informal peer influence because people value solidarity and friendships with their peers (Barnard, 1938) and peer relationships strongly influence the quality of life for people in organizations (Roy, 1959).

Workers' informal peer control of work-related behavior can continue beyond the boundaries of the organization because people often socialize with their peers outside of work and have long-term social relationships that continue even when work assignments change. When workers have relationships outside of work, such as living in the same neighborhoods or attending their children's activities, they gain additional opportunities to influence one another. This makes peer relationships very important to people and creates opportunities for peers to apply discretionary rewards and sanctions in contexts outside the organization that can influence peers' work-related behaviors (Westphal and Khanna, 2003).

The reach of worker-designed informal peer control is expanding as electronic forms of communication such as email, blogs, and websites are giving people more opportunities to exert informal peer control and, with minimal time and effort, to influence many peers (Kirsch *et al.*, 2010). For example, many workers can email all of their co-workers with one distribution list.

Finally, worker-designed informal peer control warrants special research attention because, in contrast to formal peer control systems and other organizational controls, which organizations design with the goal of advancing organizational interests, informal peer control can advocate for peers to behave in ways that are consistent with or opposed to the organization's interests (Jaworski, 1988). Thus the direction of informal peer control is one variable that is crucial for understanding its influence in organizations.

Beneficial and harmful aspects of peer control

When considering the broad scope of the peer control concept, in addition to the types of peer controls discussed above, it is important to note that there may be both beneficial and harmful aspects of peer control. Peer control can be harmful or beneficial depending on whose perspective one takes and what outcomes one considers. Parties whose outcomes might be affected by peer control include the organization, the workers who are the targets of the peer control, the peer performing the peer control, and the work group. For each of these, multiple outcome variables could be affected by the peer control.

Benefits. The broader control literature has shown that control systems are necessary for organizations to function and that having an appropriate control structure benefits the organization by improving performance and deterring organizational members from behaving in ways that harm the organization (Cardinal *et al.*, 2004). This literature has demonstrated that some control combinations have positive outcomes for workers in addition to organizations. Demonstrated benefits of specific types of controls include increased innovation among research and development professionals (Cardinal, 2001), reduced burnout and role stress for salespeople (Cravens *et al.*, 2004), and higher job satisfaction, lower role conflict, and less role ambiguity for marketing managers (Jaworski *et al.*, 1993).

Peer control has a number of potential benefits for organizations relative to other types of control. One is that peer control is less costly than supervision, audits, and other forms of control that rely on paid specialists to perform the control function, because workers usually perform peer control while they are also accomplishing their task work (Fama and Jensen, 1983a). Relative to other forms of control, peer control may also leave workers with the feeling that they have more choice or "autonomy" in their work, which is a necessary condition for intrinsic motivation (Weibel, Chapter 14).

Another benefit of peer control is that it may increase the quality and quantity of information that goes into the organization's control system because peers' often understand how well a coworker performs overall, and not just on easily measurable parts of the job (Fama and Jensen, 1983b; Welbourne and Ferrante, 2008). Peers can often monitor a broad range of performance criteria and see information that is difficult for organizations to obtain in other ways (Fischer and

Hughes, 1997). This contrasts with many organizational controls that can only measure certain, sometimes narrow, dimensions of a worker's performance (Jacobides and Croson, 2001). For example, if organizations simply measure the number of tasks completed, some workers might perform just the fast and easy tasks and avoid unpleasant or difficult work, or take short cuts that undermine quality. However, peers can often observe one another working, view their outputs, talk with their customers, and in other ways obtain a richer understanding of an organizational member's work habits than the organization can cost-effectively obtain in other ways. Another way of thinking about this is that peers may be able to accurately assess both task performance and organizational citizenship behaviors (Organ, 1997). Thus, peer control may be able to discourage workers from meeting the measureable goals in the organization's formal control system by using opportunistic methods. Therefore, by including peer control as part of the organization's system of controls, the overall control system might achieve a richer and more accurate picture of each member's contributions, enhancing the legitimacy and justice of the control system (Bijlsma-Frankema and Costa, Chapter 13).

Organizational benefits from informal peer control, such as enhanced coordination of tasks, greater agreement about goals and values, heedful relating, and organizational learning, have been demonstrated in self-managed work teams and high-reliability organizations (Bijlsma-Frankema *et al.*, 2008; Manz and Sims, 1987; Marks and Panzer, 2004; Weick *et al.*, 1999). Information sharing, which frequently occurs as peers monitor one another, has been associated with higher performance in a number of studies (Welbourne and Ferrante, 2008).

In addition to benefitting the organization, some types of informal peer control may benefit the organizational members who are the targets of the peer control. Peer control can provide feedback and clarify roles, and thus could help to reduce ambiguity for workers (Callister *et al.*, 1999). Jaworski *et al.* (1993) found that a form of peer control, which they called "professional control," was negatively associated with role ambiguity. The use of self-managing teams, which rely on peer control, has been associated with higher job satisfaction across multiple studies (Van Mierlo *et al.*, 2005). Peer control may also be able to provide more opportunities for recognition and praise than could cost-effectively be provided by supervisors, award programs, or other aspects of the formal control system. This peer recognition could benefit workers by increasing their feelings of task significance and making them feel appreciated (Hackman and Oldham, 1976). In addition, peer control that helps workers to perform better or to refrain from prohibited behavior could benefit workers by saving them from the unpleasant consequences that the organization's formal control system would provide for poor performance or unacceptable behavior.

Less is known about the potential benefits for individuals who exert peer control, although observing peers has been positively associated with supervisors' evaluations of workers (Welbourne and Ferrante, 2008). Observing peers may lead to learning that enhances a worker's own job performance.

Work groups may benefit from peer control by increasing the reliability of members' performance and facilitating shared understandings among team members. A work-group-level study found that a form of informal peer control was associated with fewer employee behavior problems among front-line workers (Loughry and Tosi, 2008). However, more research is needed to understand the conditions under which peer control benefits work groups.

Risks and drawbacks. Even though control has a number of benefits and is widely accepted as a core management function, control has a negative connotation in the management field (Cardinal, 2001). It is easy to find examples of excessive or unkind control in the popular press, and control systems can become overly legalistic, rigid, and unbalanced, breeding distrust and hostility among workers (Cardinal *et al.*, 2004; Sitkin and Bies, 1994). Some view peer control as particularly dangerous because it could interfere with relationships among coworkers that provide solidarity and support for workers, exacerbate the power imbalance between management and workers, and increase total control to an excessive level (Barker and Cheney, 1994; Delbridge, Chapter 4).

Peer control has a special risk that is not typical of other control systems in that it does not always have the goal of advancing organizational interests (Jaworski, 1988). Although many types of controls can have dysfunctional outcomes because they are poorly designed or fail to function as expected (Kerr, 1975), members at all levels in organizations sometimes purposefully influence peers to work against the organization's interests (Taylor, 1916; Roethlisberger and Dickson, 1939). For example, recent research showed how members of corporate boards of directors use peer control to encourage fellow board members to act against the organization's interests (Westphal and Khanna, 2003).

Another drawback of peer control is that even when peers try to influence one another to act in the organization's interests, they may do so in ways that are actually detrimental to the organization or its members. Peer control could take time away from workers' assigned duties, upset supervisors, who might feel that control is a supervisory role, or contribute to performance problems if the peer performing the control misunderstands what behavior is appropriate (Welbourne and Ferrante, 2008). Peer control can also be done using inappropriate techniques. Informal peer control that uses direct methods, such as noticing what peers do, praising peers for good work, correcting coworkers when they make a mistake, reporting serious misbehaviors such as stealing, discussing how to do the job (Loughry and Tosi, 2008), interacting and providing feedback, and evaluation of work (Jaworski *et al.*, 1993) is more likely to be beneficial. However, workers often choose indirect methods of peer control, such as gossiping about and avoiding poor performers, which have negative outcomes even though the peers exerting the control want their co-workers to perform better (LePine and Van Dyne, 2001; Loughry and Tosi, 2008). An estimated 25–30 percent of US workers report having experienced abusive workplace behavior (bullying), some of it perpetrated by peers who yell, curse at or insult workers, have them perform unappealing tasks, perform under unreasonable deadlines, or exclude, ignore or spread rumors about the victim (Almeida-Bradaschia and Kuwamoto, 2007). High levels of peer pressure and inappropriate forms of peer control could harm individual or collective performance, create an unpleasant work environment, and subject peers to stress (Barron and Gjerde, 1997; Kandel and Lazear, 1992).

Now that the broad scope of peer control has been outlined, it is clear that a variety of research perspectives could contribute to better understanding it. The next section reviews different research traditions that have been written about peer control.

Perspectives on peer control

This section overviews five areas of management research in which the theoretical frameworks include a role for peer control. These are: (1) traditional management research; (2) control research that has sprung from the Ouchi perspective; (3) agency theory; (4) critical perspectives on control; and (5) teamwork research. These five areas are important because, although peer control is not their core topic, they each have a substantial body of research that notes the effects of peer control on outcomes that matter to organizations. However, none of these fields has peer control as a core focus. Therefore, the research that does exist on peer control is scattered, so one purpose of this chapter is to bring together the disparate literature on peer control in order to organize what is known. A second purpose is to show that peer control is an important, yet understudied, variable in these five areas and to encourage scholars in these fields to consider including peer control in their studies.

Peer control issues are relevant in literatures in addition to these five. Peer detection and reporting of employee fraud is one element of internal controls recommended by accounting scholars (Merchant, 1985), but little accounting research examines peer control (Chen and Sandino, 2007; Towry, 2003). Scholars in sociology examine the influence of peers in social systems (Hechter, 1984), but generally do not focus on control systems for work organizations, with the exception of some studies of employee crime (e.g., Hollinger and Clark, 1983). Finally, norms and peer effects are part of the vast literature on organizational culture and climate. Cultural control is discussed elsewhere in this book (Van Maanen, Chapter 5).

Traditional management perspectives

Management scholars have long recognized that members of organizations have important influences on their peers. Taylor (1916) proposed scientific management in part to counter workers' tendencies to influence one another to limit production, which he referred to as "soldiering." Barnard (1938) noted that organizations have informal as well as formal components and that control of individuals must be achieved within the social system. He emphasized the need for workers to feel comfort and solidarity in their peer relationships. The human relations school expanded the study of informal relations among workers, and recognized that the informal influences and loyalties among peers could be even stronger than the organization's formal control systems or workers' rational self-interests (Roethlisberger and Dickson, 1939). Simon (1945) further noted that individuals in peer relationships sometimes submit themselves to peers' authority for reasons such as peers' greater status or knowledge. He explained that the advice, communication, and control that flows informally among peers can be influenced by and have influences on the organization's formal control systems and that these influences can benefit or harm the organization's interests. The social aspects of control and the distribution of control throughout the organization are also mentioned in Tannenbaum's (1968) influential book *Control in organizations*. Dunbar and Statler (Chapter 2) review studies in traditional management dating back to the 1920s and suggest that an implication of the research for organizational control is that it is important for leaders in organizations to have strong social skills in order to foster teamwork and cooperation and reduce alienation among workers.

In spite of occasionally acknowledging that social control matters, traditional management research did not emphasize peer control or how organizational leaders should influence it. Hofstede (1978) complained that the cybernetic models of control that dominated management control research ignored the strong social effects on control. He emphasized that controls within organizations include "many interpersonal processes operating on the same people at the same time" (p. 452) and that factors such as the organization member's status, relationships, and other social factors have strong influences on control that were not being considered in the control literature. Hofstede suggested that a control system is analogous to a living cell that has internal processes to maintain equilibrium in changing environments, and thus includes self-regulating processes in which "control is exercised within the system itself" (p. 455). Some of these concerns began to be addressed with research begun by Ouchi (1977) and more contemporary control researchers who have followed this system perspective (e.g., Cardinal *et al.*, 2004).

Ouchi's contextual framework

Ouchi (1977, 1979) developed a highly influential theoretical framework that suggested that an organization's choice of controls should be driven by the characteristics of the context in which they are being used. He classified organizational control into three categories, which Kirsch (2004) calls "control modes" and Cardinal *et al.* (Chapter 3) call "control targets." *Behavioral controls* specify rules of behavior before the work is performed and then monitor compliance with those rules. *Output controls* measure and reward results without specifying how those results should be achieved. *Clan controls* rely on selecting the right people for the job (ones who have the desired attitudes, values, and commitment, as well as the proper skill set), then using rituals to strengthen the socialization and increase individuals' desire to comply with the shared norms.

Ouchi suggests the use of clan control when neither behavioral nor output controls are feasible because the task is not programmable (rules cannot be established because the relationship between the worker's actions and the result is not known with certainty), and outcomes cannot be accurately measured. Although Ouchi emphasized clan control as a substitute for a more formal evaluation of performance, more recently, scholars have found that clan controls are frequently used to supplement formal controls (Cardinal *et al.*, 2004; Kirsch, 2004; Kirsch *et al.*, 2010). With clan control, strong shared norms and salient rituals help workers to internalize their own control by monitoring and evaluating their own behavior (Peterson, 1984). Clan control, which emphasizes informal and social means of control, is related to peer control, because many instances of these informal controls are initiated by workers (Jaworski, 1988). Jaworski *et al.* (1993) separated clan control into cultural control and professional control, which is a form of peer control that includes cooperation between professionals, familiarity with each other's productivity, job-related discussions among professionals, and the ability to provide accurate appraisals of each other's work.

Many of the important parts of clan control, such as rigorous selection and socialization using rituals and ceremonies, would be under the control of hierarchical management and not peers in most types of organizations (academia would be an exception). However, adherence to group norms and values would be enforced by peer control (Kirsch, 2004). Therefore, understanding peer control is necessary to understand clan control. Work in the Ouchi tradition emphasizes the need for social control and describes when organizations will rely on it most heavily, but it does not emphasize the process or outcomes of peer control specifically. Thus, scholarship in this tradition could both contribute to and benefit from increased research on how and when peer control influences organizational behavior.

Agency theory

Agency theory provides a theoretical framework for examining peer control as a functional aspect of organization control. Agency theory's concept of peer monitoring or mutual monitoring views peer control as a mechanism to align workers' behavior with organizational interests (Fama and Jensen, 1983a, 1983b). Peer monitoring uses information that one agent reports about the others or influences that agents have over each other (Kandel and Lazear, 1992; Towry, 2003). Peer monitoring thus serves a monitoring function by giving organizations better information about workers' behavior and performance results and reducing opportunities for workers to engage in hidden action (Fischer and Hughes, 1997; Holmstrom, 1982). Peer monitoring also serves an incentive function when peers apply rewards and sanctions that influence workers' costs of engaging in various behaviors in order to encourage their peers to comply with their wishes (Barron and Gjerde, 1997; Varian, 1990). Agency theory views peer monitoring as beneficial because it is a low-cost monitoring mechanism, since workers perform the monitoring while accomplishing their work; and because peers often have information about their colleagues that is not available to higher-level agents.

Agency theory views peer monitoring as having a special purpose when it is difficult for organizations to measure individual contributions to collective work (Alchian and Demsetz, 1972). This is both because the peer control is more useful for organizations and because peers may be more willing to exert peer control in settings involving collective efforts and rewards. Agency theory studies have also examined peer monitoring as a mechanism to control default risk in loans to groups of borrowers in developing countries (Islam, 1996; Stiglitz, 1990).

Loughry and Tosi (2008) used an agency theory perspective to study peer monitoring in work groups at a theme park. The study only examined informal peer control in which the direction of the peer influence favored better performance. They found that peer monitoring could be positively or negatively associated with work-group performance, depending on the method of peer control used and characteristics of the context that interacted with the peer monitoring. Performance was measured as the degree to which the work unit was free of employee behavior problems. Direct peer monitoring in which peers noticed their coworkers' behavior or results, praised coworkers, reported dishonest coworkers to management, and discussed how everyone did the job, was associated with better work-unit performance when supervision was low or task interdependence was high. Indirect peer monitoring, when employees gossiped about or avoided poorly performing coworkers, was associated with worse work-unit performance when supervisory monitoring or cohesiveness was high.

Critical control perspectives

Critical theorists have produced some of the most convincing research supporting the assertion that peer control can create strong pressure for workers to increase production. Scholars who take a critical perspective are concerned about the dangers of peer control, which can increase stress on workers and subject them to higher levels of control overall (e.g., Barker and Cheney, 1994; Lazega, 2000). For example, Barker (1993), in an ethnographic study of a manufacturer that converted its work structure to self-managing teams, describes how group members felt more closely monitored by peers in the self-managed teams than they had felt from supervisors under the previous system. Barker reports that workers punished team members who displayed "bad attitudes," made them feel guilty, and pressured them to conform, tolerating less undesirable behavior than the supervisors had formerly allowed. In another study, Ezzamel and Willmott (1998) describe the peer influences in a dress-manufacturing firm that partially replaced hierarchical management with self-managing teams and changed from individual incentives to group incentives. The managers who implemented the system intended to stimulate peer pressure and normative control, and they were successful. Workers felt like all team members were "forced to be the supervisor" (p. 382) in order for the team to earn good bonuses. Pressures for productivity became intense and the firm achieved improvements in work quality and response speed.

The critical perspective describes how peer control can combine with other organizational controls to create a control environment that may impinge on workers' freedom to a higher degree than many would think is appropriate. For example, Covaleski *et al.* (1998) describe peer control among accounting firm partners that dominated the accountants' lives. This peer control was increased by circulating reports that showed partners' performance results compared to peers.

Accountants were required to justify their behavior and results to peers at frequent partner meetings. The peer control also intruded into the accountants' marriages and personal lives, for example, by partners sending performance reports to the partners' spouses with the goal of increasing the pressure to perform well. One partner was criticized for mowing his lawn, which the peer said was not a good use of his time, and for not dressing well while he was mowing, which the peer felt did not present a professional image. Likewise, Sewell (1998) describes how an organization's electronic monitoring combined with teamwork to create a very strong peer control environment and high levels of discipline among workers. Critical theorists also express concern that organizations sometimes assign people to teams primarily to achieve work intensification by increasing peer pressure and internalized pressure to not let the team down, rather than because the task's interdependence makes teamwork necessary (Townsend, 2005).

Teamwork literature

The teamwork literature provides the last perspective on peer control that will be discussed here (LePine *et al.*, 2008). Organizations increasingly use teamwork to perform many types of work because of its established benefits, yet formal individual controls are more difficult to use in team settings because it is hard for organizations to identify individuals' contributions (Kirsch, 2004). Peer control may, therefore, be especially relevant to understanding teamwork, and team settings may be appropriate for research to generate new knowledge about peer control. Because of widespread interest in teamwork in the workplace, researchers are conducting an enormous amount of research on teamwork, so this may be an especially fruitful area for future empirical research to incorporate peer control variables.

Team production methods tend to elicit strong peer control (Barker and Cheney, 1994; Fischer and Hughes, 1997; Sewell, 1998) and there is evidence in the teamwork literature that peer control benefits team production. Group process research has found that team members monitoring their teammates and providing feedback and suggestions are necessary for groups to function well (Hedge *et al.*, 1999). Recent research suggesting that there are five "core components" of teamwork, identified variables that strongly relate to peer control (team leadership, mutual performance monitoring, and backup behavior) as three of the five (Salas *et al.*, 2005). Peer control also reduces free-riding in teamwork settings (Wageman and Baker, 1997). Formal peer evaluations are sometimes used with teamwork to provide further incentives for team members to share workloads in a fair way (Erez *et al.*, 2002). The social interaction in groups, including application of discretionary rewards and sanctions, expressions of approval and disapproval, and influence attempts, are thought to motivate team members to expend effort and to comply with peers' wishes, thereby influencing group performance (Guzzo and Shea, 1992; Hackman, 1992). A recent review of the teamwork literature called for more research to learn about when and how sharing leadership among team members affects team performance (Mathieu *et al.*, 2008).

Areas for future research

This chapter began with a discussion of the scope of the peer control concept, including types of peer controls and potential benefits and drawbacks of peer control. Different theoretical perspectives for understanding peer control were then reviewed. Now, to conclude the chapter, issues for future research will be suggested.

Levels of analyses

Peer control is likely to affect outcomes at the individual, group, and organizational levels. At the individual level, relevant outcomes include job performance, attitudes, and psychological variables such as job satisfaction, satisfaction with coworkers, role conflict, role ambiguity, stress, and subjective well-being (Jaworski *et al.*, 1993; Spreitzer *et al.*, 2005). In turn, these variables might mediate an association between peer control and outcomes such as employee turnover, intentions to quit, or intentions to search for another job. Peer control is likely to influence individuals' performance, in part, by affecting individuals' choices of work processes and which tasks to prioritize as peers push for their preferences (Holmstrom and Milgrom, 1991). Therefore, work processes might be examined as mediating variables.

At the work group and organizational levels, peer control is likely to affect performance (and performance losses, such as employee theft), as well as other variables such as climate, culture, cohesiveness, interpersonal and task conflict, and shared understandings among workers. Peer control might also have legal implications (Sitkin and Sutcliffe, 1991). For example, some forms of peer control might reduce accidents, malpractice, and other behaviors that could create liability for organizations. However, inappropriate forms of peer control might make organizations vulnerable to lawsuits for harassment and violations of employment regulations (Pfeffer, 1994).

Ideally, control research would be able to prescribe when certain controls will be best for specific situations (Merchant, 1988). Because peer control can be helpful or harmful to organizations' interests, peer control research that examines when different types of peer control are likely to be more beneficial or harmful for organizations and their members would be useful. Two areas that may affect both the types of informal peer control that emerge and the outcomes for organizations and their members are personal characteristics of the people in the organization and characteristics of the work context.

Characteristics of workers

The characteristics of workers in the control context are likely to influence the types of peer control that they will exert. For example, extroversion, openness, agreeableness, and conscientiousness have been shown to affect peer responses to low performers (Jackson and LePine, 2003). Research could examine what personality characteristics affect individuals' willingness to engage in different types of peer control, submit to the peer control of others, or work in an environment with strong peer control. This research might look for interactions between the personality characteristics of the controller and the controlee. Because teams research has examined the impact of many personality traits on performance in groups of interdependent peers (Mathieu *et al.*, 2008), researchers could consider whether some of these traits affect how workers exert and respond to peer control.

Even when there is no hierarchical authority among peers, there are often differences in experience, status, and reputation among co-workers. These might influence the types of informal peer control that individuals exert and how they react to peer control by others. For example, workers with less tenure may rely on more experienced peers for advice, feedback, and job-related information (Robinson and Weldon, 1993; Salancik and Pfeffer, 1978). In a study of peer

sanctioning among law firm partners, the partners doing the sanctioning were more likely to be more senior than the person being sanctioned
and to have a relationship in which the person being sanctioned goes to
the sanctioner for advice and sees the sanctioner as a friend (Lazega,
2000). It is possible that peer control by senior people aimed at more
junior people might have different outcomes than the other way
around. There may also be differences in how strong and weak performers engage in and react to peer control and in their implications for
performance and other outcomes. Competent performers would be in a
better position to understand what is required for good performance
and to communicate useful information to peers. Similarly, workers
may feel greater willingness to influence, and greater obligations to
comply with, the wishes of peers with whom they share many similarities such as ethnic, family, or religious ties (Kandel and Lazear, 1992)
and in highly cohesive work groups (Loughry and Tosi, 2008).

A related issue is how peer control differs by the type of work or
workers' level in the organizational hierarchy. For example, peer
control might operate differently among professional and managerial
workers than entry-level workers. Workers who have extensive education and socialization and workers with long apprenticeships are
likely to have substantial job-related knowledge and professional
norms that support certain standards of performance (Ouchi, 1979;
Sitkin and Sutcliffe, 1991). For example, one study found that engineers worked hard to achieve higher status with their peers (Sutton and
Hargadon, 1996), yet for some types of workers higher performance
may not translate into higher status with peers. Workers' organizational commitment is another variable that may be important in peer
control research. Workers with higher levels of organizational commitment may be more willing to engage in and respond positively to
informal peer control aimed at helping the organization.

Characteristics of the organizational context

Elements of the work context also affect peer control. Some of these
were discussed earlier. Workers in organizations and positions with
low turnover might be more likely to see the organization's interests as
aligned with their own, and thus be willing to engage in peer control
that supports better performance (Ouchi, 1979). In addition, workers
in jobs that offer better pay or working conditions than they would be

able to obtain elsewhere might be more willing to engage in peer control that benefits the organization than workers who perceive that it would be easy for them to find alternative equivalent employment.

Another element of the work context that is important in contemporary organizations is the degree to which workers perform their work in the presence of coworkers. The increasingly virtual nature of work is likely to affect peer control, so it will be important for research to examine how peer control functions among workers who are not co-located. Workers who telecommute, travel frequently, or work via computer or telephone with colleagues in different cities or countries may exert and experience peer control in different ways than workers who spend large amounts of time together. Research could take into account the proximity of workers, the degree to which workers can physically observe one another, the amount of time that workers are in the presence of coworkers, and other characteristics of the context that may make peer control different from one organizational setting to another (see Kellogg *et al.*, 2006 for a discussion of how work contexts are changing in modern organizations).

There may also be characteristics of the type of work that are important for understanding peer control. These might include, for example, job characteristics such as task significance and feedback from the job, particularly if that feedback comes from clients or users of the workers' products or services (Hackman and Oldham, 1976). Workers who believe that their work is important and affects others might be more willing to use peer control to enforce high expectations. Therefore, there may be differences in peer control between service organizations and manufacturing environments. Informal controls such as peer control may be especially appropriate for service work because there is more ambiguity about cause–effect relationships and more difficulty in measuring quality than in most manufacturing environments (Jaworski, 1988). Furthermore, workers in service organizations may experience control pressures from clients that could compete with or complement the peer control. Questions about how peer controls operate as part of the organization's control system are considered next.

The broader control system. Because peer control almost always operates as part of a broader control system, it is important for research to study how peer control interacts with and is influenced by other control mechanisms. This leads to questions such as: "When the demands of two controls conflict, which one will prevail?" and

"When does peer control substitute for, complement, or work at odds with another control, or have little effect in the presence of another control?"

Future research could look at other elements of the control system as antecedents that affect the types and amounts of peer control that emerge. Research could address questions such as: when will organizational members exert peer control in ways that support organizational objectives? When are members likely to exert peer control that opposes organizational interests or exert peer control in such a way that it harms the organization? When will organizational members refrain from exerting peer control?

Supervision. Supervision is a mechanism in the control system in nearly all organizations. Supervisors' attitudes are likely to affect the types and amounts of peer control that emerge in work groups (Welbourne and Ferrante, 2008). Supportive management and alignment of interests between management and employees may lead to norms favoring high productivity (Feldman, 1984; Rhodes and Steers, 1981) and thus result in peer control that is more supportive of the organization's goals. In contrast, poor relations between management and workers could lead to peer control that works against the organization's interests. Supervision may also affect the amounts of peer control that emerge among workers by influencing the degree to which employees perceive that the organization's formal control system meets the control needs for the situation. This would be consistent with research that shows that informal peer controls can become latent (inactive) in organizations and reemerge when the rest of the control context changes (Cardinal *et al.*, 2004).

Supervision is also likely to interact with peer control to influence outcome variables such as performance and workers' attitudes. There is some evidence that peer control and supervision can be substitutes (Loughry and Tosi, 2008). Both can limit hidden action, provide information about workers' behavior and results, give guidance to workers, and constrain the range of acceptable performance (Arnott and Stiglitz, 1991; Barron and Gjerde, 1997; Kerr and Jermier, 1978).

In cases in which workers view themselves as having interests that conflict with those of the organization and its managers, the demands of supervisory controls and peer controls may conflict. Research in these environments could examine what factors determine when supervisory versus peer controls have stronger influences. One factor that could be relevant is the degree to which supervisors have control over important rewards and sanctions. The presence of unions might also change the power relationships between supervisors and workers, and thus affect which controls have stronger influences. There may also be different relationships with different outcome variables. For example, in contexts in which supervisors have high power but poor relations with workers, supervision could have stronger effects on measured performance and easily measurable behaviors such as attendance, whereas peer control might have stronger effects on employee attitudes and less measurable aspects of performance that nevertheless might be important for organizations. Van Maanen (Chapter 5) discusses how strong work identities that are shared among peers increase the difficulty of achieving management control.

A recent study of employee drinking points to the complex relationship that is likely between supervision and peer control (Bacharach *et al.*, 2002). The study found that workers' perceptions of permissive drinking norms were the strongest direct predictor of problem drinking among blue-collar workers and these norms both mediated and moderated the effects of other factors in the work context (stress from role conflict, supervisors' policy enforcement, and alienation at work such as powerlessness and lack of autonomy). Supervisors' behavior had an indirect effect mediated through stress and alienation, which had direct effects on both drinking norms and problem drinking behavior. Loughry and Tosi's (2008) theme park study also found a complex relationship between supervision and peer control. Supervisory monitoring and direct peer monitoring were strongly correlated ($r = .52$), yet direct peer monitoring was only positively associated with group performance in work groups with lower levels of supervision.

Challenges in peer control research

Peer control research presents definite challenges. As has been shown, there is not one clear disciplinary perspective from which to draw, yet there is an enormous amount of research that may contain relevant information. Peer control is influenced by ongoing relationships among workers and characteristics of the organizational setting, both of which can change over time (Cardinal *et al.*, 2004). This makes field studies and surveys valuable research techniques, yet gaining access to organizations to gather this type of rich data for research purposes is difficult. Obtaining sufficient sample sizes with matched data from different sources such as workers and their peers and managers, as well as characteristics of the organizational context presents an additional challenge. Then the data may contain rating errors because individuals may have self-interests in providing peer ratings and other responses to researchers' inquiries that that do not reflect their true perceptions (Bamberger *et al.*, 2005). There are also challenges in analyzing peer control data including issues involving levels of analysis and isolating causal relationships (Klein and Kozlowski, 2000; Manski, 1993).

This chapter has reviewed the literature related to peer control. It has shown that peer control is widespread, takes many forms, and has implications for organizations and their members. The suggestions for future research provide a starting point to suggest how scholars from various disciplines might contribute new research to help bring more understanding to this important topic.

References

Akerlof, G. 1976. The economics of caste and of the rat race and other woeful tales. *Quarterly Journal of Economics*, 90: 599–617.

Alchian, A. A. and Demsetz, H. 1972. Production, information costs and economic organization. *American Economic Review*, 62: 777–795.

Almeida-Bradaschia, C. and Kuwamoto, P. E. 2007. Mobbing on the workplace: a worldwide problem. Paper presented at the Annual Meeting of the Academy of Management, Philadelphia, PA.

Arnott, R. and Stiglitz, J. E. 1991. Moral hazard and nonmarket institutions: dysfunctional crowding out or peer monitoring? *American Economic Review*, 81: 179–190.

Arrow, K. 1964. Control in large organizations. *Management Science*, 10: 397–408.

Atkins, P. W. B. and Wood, R. E. 2002. Self versus others' ratings as predictors of assessment center ratings: validation evidence for 360-degree feedback programs. *Personnel Psychology*, 55: 871–904.

Bacharach, S. B., Bamberger, P. A., and Sonnenstuhl, W. J. 2002. Driven to drink: managerial control, work-related risk factors, and employee problem drinking. *Academy of Management Journal*, 45: 637–658.

Baker, G. P., Jensen, M. C., and Murphy, K. J. 1988. Compensation and incentives: practice vs. theory. *Journal of Finance*, 42: 593–616.

Bamberger, P. A. 2007. Competitive appraising: a social dilemma perspective on the conditions in which multi-round peer evaluation may result in counter-productive team dynamics. *Human Resource Management Review*, 17: 1–18.

Bamberger, P. A., Erev, I., Kimmel, M., and Oref-Chen, T. 2005. Peer assessment, individual performance, and contribution to group processes: the impact of rater anonymity. *Group and Organization Management*, 30: 44–377.

Barker, J. R. 1993. Tightening the iron cage: concertive control in self-managing teams. *Administrative Science Quarterly*, 38: 408–437.

Barker, J. R. and Cheney, G. 1994. The concept and the practices of discipline in contemporary organizational life. *Communication Monographs*, 61: 19–43.

Barnard, C. 1938. *Functions of the executive*. Cambridge, MA: Harvard University Press.

Barron, J. M. and Gjerde, K. P. 1997. Peer pressure in an agency relationship. *Journal of Labor Economics*, 15: 234–254.

Beehr, T. A., Ivanitskaya, L., Hansen, C. P., Erofeev, D., and Gudanowski, D. M. 2001. Evaluation of 360 degree feedback ratings: relationships with each other and with performance and selection predictors. *Journal of Organizational Behavior*, 22: 775–788.

Bijlsma-Frankema, K. M., De Jong, B. A., and Van de Bunt, G. G. 2008. Heed, a missing link between trust, monitoring and performance in knowledge intensive teams. *International Journal of Human Resources Management*, 19: 19–34.

Bono, J. E. and Colbert, A. E. 2005. Understanding responses to feedback: the role of core self-evaluations. *Personnel Psychology*, 58: 171–203.

Callister, R. R., Kramer, M. W., and Turban, D. B. 1999. Feedback seeking following career transitions. *Academy of Management Journal*, 42: 428–438.

Campion, M. A., Papper, E. M., and Medsker, G. J. 1996. Relations between work team characteristics and effectiveness: a replication and extension. *Personnel Psychology*, 49: 429–452.

Cardinal, L. B. 2001. Technological innovation in the pharmaceutical industry: the use of organizational control in managing research and development. *Organization Science*, 12: 19–36.

Cardinal, L. B., Sitkin, S. B., and Long, C. P. 2004. Balancing and rebalancing in the creation and evolution of organizational control. *Organization Science*, 15: 411–431.

Carmichael, H. L. 1988. Incentives in academics: why is there tenure? *Journal of Political Economy*, 96: 453–472.

Chen, C. X. and Sandino, T. 2007. Do internal management controls mitigate employee theft in organizations? AAA MAS Meeting Paper, July 30. Downloaded from http://ssrn.com/abstract=1004184.

Covaleski, M. A., Dirsmith, M. W., Heian, J. B., and Samuel, S. 1998. The calculated and the avowed: techniques of discipline and struggles over identity in big six public accounting firms. *Administrative Science Quarterly*, 43: 293–327.

Cravens, D. W., Lassk, F. G., Low, G. S., Marshall, G. W., and Moncrief, W. C. 2004. Formal and informal management control combinations in sales organizations: the impact on salesperson consequences. *Journal of Business Research*, 57: 241–248.

Deutsch, M. 1949. A theory of co-operation and competition. *Human Relations*, 2: 129–152.

Eby, L. T., Allen, T. D., Evans, S. C., Ng, T., and DuBois, D. L. 2008. Does mentoring matter? A multidisciplinary meta-analysis comparing mentored and non-mentored individuals. *Journal of Vocational Behavior*, 72: 254–267.

Erez, A., LePine, J. A., and Elms, H. 2002. Effects of rotated leadership and peer evaluation on the functioning and effectiveness of self-managed teams: a quasi-experiment. *Personnel Psychology*, 55: 929–948.

Ezzamel, M. and Willmott, H. 1998. Accounting for teamwork: a critical study of group-based systems of organizational control. *Administrative Science Quarterly*, 43: 358–396.

Fama, E. F. and Jensen, M. C. 1983a. Separation of ownership and control. *Journal of Law and Economics*, 26: 301–325.

　　1983b. Agency problems and residual claims. *Journal of Law and Economics*, 26: 327–349.

Fedor, D. B., Bettenhausen, K. L., and Davis, W. 1999. Peer reviews: employees' dual roles as raters and recipients. *Group and Organization Management*, 24: 92–120.

Feldman, D. 1984. The development and enforcement of group norms. *Academy of Management Review*, 9: 47–53.

Fischer, P. E. and Hughes, J. S. 1997. Mutual monitoring and best agency contracts. *Journal of Institutional and Theoretical Economics*, 153: 334–355.

Guzzo, R. A. and Shea, G. P. 1992. Group performance and intergroup relations in organizations. In M. D. Dunette and L. M. Hough (eds.), *Handbook of industrial and organizational psychology*, vol. III: 269–313. Palo Alto, CA: Consulting Psychologists Press.

Hackman, J. R. 1992. Group influences on individuals in organizations. In M. A. Dunette and L. M. Hough (eds.), *Handbook of industrial and organizational psychology*, vol. III: 199–267. Palo Alto, CA: Consulting Psychologists Press.

Hackman, J. R. and Oldham, G. R. 1976. Motivation through the design of work: test of a theory. *Organizational Behavior and Human Performance*, 16: 250–279.

Hechter, M. 1984. When actors comply: monitoring costs and the production of social order. *Acta Sociologica*, 3: 161–183.

Hedge, J. W., Bruskiewicz, K. T., Logan, K. K., Hanson, M. A., and Buck, D. 1999. *Crew resource management team and individual job analysis and rating scale development for air force tanker crews* (Technical report no. 336). Minneapolis, MN: Personnel Decisions Research Institutes, Inc.

Hofstede, G. 1978. The poverty of management control philosophy. *Academy of Management Review*, 3: 450–461.

Hollenbeck, J. R., Ilgen, D. R., LePine, J. A., Colquitt, J. A., and Hedlund, J. 1998. Extending the multilevel theory of team decision making: effects of feedback and experience in hierarchical teams. *Academy of Management Journal*, 41: 269–282.

Hollinger, R. C. and Clark, J. P. 1983. Deterrence in the workplace: perceived certainty, perceived severity, and employee theft. *Social Forces*, 62: 398–418.

Holmstrom, B. 1982. Moral hazard in teams. *Bell Journal of Economics*, 13: 324–340.

Holmstrom, B. and Milgrom, P. 1991. Multitask principal-agent analyses: incentive contracts, asset ownership, and job design. *The Journal of Law, Economics, and Organization*, 7: 24–52.

Hopwood, W. S., Leiner, J. J., and Young, G. R. 2008. *Forensic accounting*. Boston, MA: McGraw-Hill Irwin.

Ilgen, D. R. and Pulakos, E. D. (eds.). 1999. *The changing nature of performance: implications for staffing, motivation, and development*. San Francisco, CA: Jossey Bass.

Islam, M. M. 1996. Peer monitoring in the credit market. *Journal of Contemporary Asia*, 26: 452–465.

Jackson, C. L. and LePine, J. A. 2003. Peer responses to a team's weakest link: a test and extension of LePine and Van Dyne's Model. *Journal of Applied Psychology*, 3: 459–475.

Jacobides, M. G. and Croson, D. C. 2001. Information policy: shaping the value of agency relationships. *Academy of Management Review*, 26: 202–223.

Jaworski, B. J. 1988. Toward a theory of marketing control: environmental context, control types, and consequences. *Journal of Marketing*, 52: 3–39.

Jaworski, B. J., Stathakopoulos, V., and Krishnan, H. S. 1993. Control combinations in marketing: conceptual framework and empirical evidence. *Journal of Marketing*, 57: 57–69.

Kandel, E. and Lazear, E. P. 1992. Peer pressure and partnerships. *Journal of Political Economy*, 100: 801–817.

Kellogg, K. C., Orlikowski, W. J., and Yates, J. 2006. Life in the trading zone: structuring coordination across boundaries in postbureaucratic organizations. *Organization Science*, 17: 22–44.

Kerr, S. 1975. On the folly of rewarding A, while hoping for B. *Academy of Management Journal*, 18: 769–783.

Kerr, S. and Jermier, J. M. 1978. Substitutes for leadership: their meaning and measurement. *Organizational Behavior and Human Performance*, 22: 375–403.

Kirsch, L. J. 2004. Deploying common systems globally: the dynamics of control. *Information Systems Research*, 15: 374–395.

Kirsch, L. J., Ko, D., and Haney, M. H. 2010. Investigating the antecedents of team-based clan control: adding social capital as a predictor. *Organizational Science*, 21: 469–489.

Klein, K. J. and Kozlowski, S. W. J. (eds.). 2000. *Multilevel theory, research, and methods in organizations: foundations, extensions, and new directions*. San Francisco, CA: Jossey-Bass.

Lavelle, J. J., Rupp, D. E., and Brockner, J. 2007. Taking a multifoci approach to the study of justice, social exchange, and citizenship behavior: the target similarity model. *Journal of Management*, 33: 841–866.

Lazega, E. 2000. Rule enforcement among peers: a lateral control regime. *Organization Studies*, 21: 193–214.

LePine, J. A. and Van Dyne, L. 2001. Peer responses to low performers: an attributional model of helping in the context of groups. *Academy of Management Review*, 26: 67–84.

LePine, J. A., Piccolo, R. F., Jackson, C. L., Mathieu, J. E., and Saul, J. R. 2008. A meta-analysis of teamwork processes: tests of a multidimensional model and relationships with team effectiveness criteria. *Personnel Psychology*, 61: 273–307.

Loughry, M. L. and Tosi, H. L. 2008. Performance implications of peer monitoring. *Organization Science*, 19: 876–890.

Manski, C. F. 1993. Identification of social effects: the reflection problem. *Review of Economic Studies*, 60: 531–542.

Manz, C. C. and Sims, Jr., H. P. 1987. Leading workers to lead themselves: the external leadership of self-managing work teams. *Administrative Science Quarterly*, 32: 106–128.

Marks, M. A. and Panzer, F. J. 2004. The influence of team monitoring on team processes and performance. *Human Performance*, 17: 25–41.

Mathieu, J., Maynard, M. T., Rapp, T., and Gilson, L. 2008. Team effectiveness 1997–2007: a review of recent advancements and a glimpse into the future. *Journal of Management*, 34: 410–476.

Merchant, K. A. 1985. *Control in business organizations*. Boston, MA: Pitman Publishing.

1988. Progressing toward a theory of marketing control: a comment. *Journal of Marketing*, 52: 40–44.

Mesmer-Magnus, J. R. and Viswesvaran, C. 2005. Whistleblowing in organizations: an examination of correlates of whistleblowing intentions, actions, and retaliation. *Journal of Business Ethics*, 62: 277–297.

Miller, T. R., Zaloshnja, E., and Spicer, R. S. 2007. Effectiveness and benefit-cost of peer-based workplace substance abuse prevention coupled with random testing. *Accident Analysis and Prevention*, 39: 565–573.

Morrison, E. W. and Phelps, C. C. 1999. Taking charge at work: extrarole efforts to initiate workplace change. *Academy of Management Journal*, 42: 403–419.

Nordstrom, R., Lorenzi, P., and Hall, R. V. 1990. A review of public posting of performance feedback in work settings. *Journal of Organizational Behavior Management*, 11: 101–123.

Organ, D. W. 1997. Organizational citizenship behavior: it's construct clean-up time. *Human Performance*, 10: 85–97.

Ouchi, W. G. 1977. The relationship between organizational structure and organizational control. *Administrative Science Quarterly*, 22: 95–113.

1979. A conceptual framework for the design of organizational control mechanisms. *Management Science*, 25: 833–848.

Peterson, K. D. 1984. Mechanisms of administrative control over managers in educational organizations. *Administrative Science Quarterly*, 29: 573–597.

Pfeffer, J. 1994. The costs of legalization: the hidden dangers of increasingly formalized control. In S. B. Sitkin and R. J. Bies (eds.), *The legalistic organization*: 229–346. Thousand Oaks, CA: Sage.

1997. *New directions for organization theory*. New York, NY: Oxford University Press.

Pullins, E. and Fine, L. M. 2002. How the performance of mentoring activities affects the mentor's job outcomes. *Journal of Personal Selling and Sales Management*, 22: 259–271.

Rhodes, S. R. and Steers, R. M. 1981. Conventional vs. worker-owned organizations. *Human Relations*, 34: 1,013–1,035.

Robinson, S. L. and Weldon, E. 1993. Feedback seeking in groups: a theoretical perspective. *British Journal of Social Psychology*, 32: 71–86.

Roethlisberger, F. J. and Dickson, W. J. 1939. *Management and the worker*. Cambridge, MA: Harvard University Press.

Roy, D. F. 1959. Banana time: job satisfaction and informal interaction. *Human Organization*, 18: 158–168.

Salancik, G. R. and Pfeffer, J. 1978. A social information processing approach to job attitudes and task design. *Administrative Science Quarterly*, 23: 224–253.

Salas, E., Sims, D. E., and Burke, C. S. 2005. Is there a "big five" in teamwork? *Small Group Research*, 36: 555–599.

Sewell, G. 1998. The discipline of teams: the control of team-based industrial work through electronic and peer surveillance. *Administrative Science Quarterly*, 43: 397–428.

Simon, H. 1945. *Administrative behavior: a study of decision making processes in administrative organizations.* New York, NY: Macmillan.

Sitkin, S. B. and Bies, R. J. 1994. *The legalistic organization.* Thousand Oaks, CA: Sage.

Sitkin, S. B. and George, E. 2005. Managerial trust-building through the use of legitimating formal and informal control mechanisms. *International Sociology*, 20: 307–338.

Sitkin, S. B. and Sutcliffe, K. M. 1991. Dispensing legitimacy: the influence of professional, organizational, and legal controls on pharmacist behavior. *Research in the Sociology of Organizations*, 8: 269–295.

Smither, J. W., London, M. and Reilly, R. R. 2005. Does performance improve following multisource feedback? A theoretical model, meta-analysis, and review of empirical findings. *Personnel Psychology*, 58: 33–66.

Spreitzer, G., Sutcliffe, K. M., Dutton, J., Sonenshein, S., and Grant, A. 2005. A socially embedded model of thriving at work. *Organization Science*, 16: 537–549.

Stiglitz, J. E. 1990. Peer monitoring and credit markets. *The World Bank Economic Review*, 4: 351–366.

Sutton, R. I. and Hargadon, A. 1996. Brainstorming groups in context: effectiveness in a product design firm. *Administrative Science Quarterly*, 41: 685–718.

Tannenbaum, A. S. 1968. *Control in organizations.* New York, NY: McGraw-Hill.

Taylor, F. W. 1916. The principles of scientific management. In J. M. Shafritz and J. S. Ott (eds.), *Classics of organization theory:* 66–81. Chicago, IL: Dorsey Press.

Thompson, J. D. 1967. *Organizations in action.* New York, NY: McGraw Hill.

Townsend, K. 2005. Electronic surveillance and cohesive teams: room for resistance in an Australian call center? *New Technology, Work, and Employment*, 20: 47–59.

2007. Who has control in teams without teamworking? *Economic and Industrial Democracy*, 28: 622–649.

Towry, K. L. 2003. Control in a teamwork environment – the impact of social ties on the effectiveness of mutual monitoring contracts. *The Accounting Review*, 78: 1,069–1,095.

Trevino, L. K. and Victor, B. 1992. Peer reporting of unethical behavior: a social context perspective. *Academy of Management Journal*, 35: 38–64.

Turner, K. L. and Makhija, M. V. 2006. The role of organizational controls in managing knowledge. *Academy of Management Review*, 31: 197–217.

Van Mierlo, H., Rutte, C. G., Kompler, M. A. J., and Doorewaard, H. A. C. M. 2005. Self-managing teamwork and psychological well-being. *Group and Organization Management*, 30: 211–235.

Varian, H. R. 1990. Monitoring agents with other agents. *Journal of Institutional and Theoretical Economics*, 146: 153–174.

Wageman, R. and Baker, G. 1997. Incentives and cooperation: the joint effects of task and reward interdependence on group performance. *Journal of Organizational Behavior*, 18: 139–158.

Weick, K. E., Sutcliffe, K. M., and Obstfeld, D. 1999. Organizing for high reliability: processes of collective mindfulness. *Research in Organizational Behavior*, 21: 81–123.

Welbourne, T. M. and Ferrante, C. J. 2008. To monitor or not to monitor: a study of individual outcomes from monitoring one's peers under gainsharing and merit pay. *Group and Organization Management*, 33: 130–162.

Welbourne, T. M., Balkin, D. B., and Gomez-Mejia, L. R. 1995. Gainsharing and mutual monitoring: a combined agency-organizational justice interpretation. *Academy of Management Journal*, 38: 881–899.

Westphal, J. D. and Khanna, P. 2003. Keeping directors in line: social distancing as a control mechanism in the corporate elite. *Administrative Science Quarterly*, 48: 361–398.

Willis, D. M. and Lightle, S. S. 2000. Management reports on internal controls. *Journal of Accountancy*, 190: 57–64.

Zajonc, R. B. 1965. Social facilitation. *Science*, 149: 269–274.

PART V

Managerial and strategic control

12 | Control to cooperation: examining the role of managerial authority in portfolios of managerial actions

CHRIS P. LONG
Georgetown University

This chapter presents a new theoretical direction for control research. Managerial controls that comprise the primary focus of this research describe the various initiatives managers undertake to motivate, evaluate, and reward subordinates for performing work in ways consistent with the achievement of an organization's interests, goals, and strategies (Merchant, 1985). From the earliest research on organizations, the act of controlling subordinates has been recognized as one of a manager's primary functions (Blau and Scott, 1962). Since that time, researchers have identified various mechanisms by which managers exercise control in their organizations including the development and implementation of formal policies (Barnard, 1938), rational-legal authority and rules (Weber, 1968[1918]), cultural norms and rituals (Van Maanen and Schein, 1979), or incentive systems, direct supervision, and/or work designs (Mintzberg, 1979).

While traditional control theory focuses primarily on how managers exercise their power through applications of managerial controls, I propose here that a more deliberate consideration of how managers develop and utilize their managerial authority may help scholars formulate more realistic pictures of managerial attention and action (Ocasio, 1997) and better comprehend how managers actually cultivate high levels of superior–subordinate cooperation.

Managerial authority refers to a person's right to exercise power based on the belief that his or her actions are legitimate and in alignment with accepted standards of appropriate conduct. I specifically argue that a manager's interest in preserving, protecting, and promoting his/her managerial authority constitutes a primary motivation for managerial action. I further contend that the desire that managers have in developing or maintaining that authority through actions that will be viewed as legitimate lead them to balance their efforts to implement controls with their efforts to promote trust and fairness. Through their

365

efforts to promote trust, managers attempt to instill their subordinates with positive expectations about the individual treatment they will receive. Through efforts to promote fairness, managers attempt to provide equitable, representative, and civil treatment across the groups of subordinates that they manage.

Although managers may engage in a range of actions to preserve, promote, and protect their authority, I focus here specifically on how managers balance their efforts to promote control, trust, and fairness for two primary reasons. First, because initial research on these relationships suggests that managers who successfully balance levels of control, trust, and fairness can produce important effects on subordinates' perceptions, attitudes, and behaviors. Second, because managers face significant challenges in integrating these activities, it is important to understand how managers effectively reconcile the inherent tensions in their motivations to take these actions and in the organizational and relational effects that the joint development of control, trust, and fairness can produce.

Recent research highlights the importance of these issues by suggesting that managers who effectively integrate their efforts to promote control with their efforts to promote trust and fairness can positively and significantly influence subordinates' attitudes toward superior–subordinate cooperation. For example, Long et al. (2010) observe that subordinates' levels of job satisfaction are increased when managers act fairly and in ways consistent with the controls they apply. In addition, Sengun and Wasti (2007) outline how social controls enhance levels of trust that exchange partners have in each others' abilities and generosity and, as a result, increase the willingness of individuals to engage in risk-taking with those partners.

Though research has shown these issues are important, a review of relevant research reveals that previous scholars have acknowledged, but have not systematically investigated, how trust and fairness concerns influence the design and implementation of managerial control systems (Barnard, 1938; Kim and Mauborgne, 1997). For example, although he does not incorporate these issues into his formal theorizing, Ouchi (1980: 130) does acknowledge the influence of fairness concerns by suggesting that, when implementing organizational controls, managers recognize that "it is this demand for *equity* (i.e., fairness) which brings on transactions costs" and that managers who implement controls are often sensitive to "equity" (i.e., fairness) issues. He also acknowledges the important role that trust plays in these dynamics by stating that managers understand how the transaction costs that motivate control applications "can arise from the underlying nature of the goods or service or from a lack of *trust*" between managers and their subordinates.

I argue that more focused investigations on how managers develop and utilize their authority can significantly increase our understanding of how they integrate and balance their efforts to promote control, trust, and fairness. More importantly, I argue that the perspective on managerial attention and action that I present here may ultimately enable scholars to formulate more accurate and complete conceptualizations of the control systems managers use to "direct attention, motivate, and encourage organizational members to act in desired ways to meet an organization's objectives" (Long *et al.*, 2002: 198).

The ideas I present here provide three key additional and important contributions to organizational research. First, in adopting a more multi-faceted perspective on managerial control activities, this chapter departs from existing research on managerial control systems that focus only on what organizational controls managers apply. By highlighting relationships among control, trust, and fairness, this chapter seeks to focus control research more directly on examining how managers attempt to increase superior–subordinate cooperation by crafting integrative, multi-faceted solutions to critical organizational problems. Second, I introduce and develop the concepts of "trustworthiness-promotion" and "fairness-promotion" through descriptions of various types of relevant activities that managers pursue. Third, by considering how managers integrate and balance these activities with their efforts to promote organizational controls, I synthesize three discrete streams of organizational research to present an agenda for investigating multiple aspects of managerial control systems.

I present my arguments in several sections. I first outline key elements of traditional control theory and describe how these perspectives on control present overly narrow and incomplete views of managerial attention and action. I then describe how a more direct focus on issues related to managerial legitimacy and authority can help scholars develop more comprehensive conceptualizations of managerial control systems. To facilitate this, I introduce the concepts of trustworthiness-promotion and fairness-promotion and describe how this integrative perspective provides a more accurate picture of managerial attention and action than is currently presented within the control literature. I conclude the chapter by outlining some key factors that influence how managers integrate and balance the control, trustworthiness-promotion, and fairness-promotion activities they implement.

Organizational control

The act of applying controls constitutes a fundamental aspect of organizational life. Organizational scholars who maintain a more general perspective often characterize organizational controls broadly as any method that managers use to direct attention and motivate organizational members to act in desired ways (see Barley and Kunda, 1992 for a general review of perspectives). Control theorists, who more directly examine these concerns, provide a more focused lens on control phenomena and classify controls as the specific mechanisms that managers apply to direct individuals' task efforts in ways consistent with the accomplishment of organizational goals (Long et al., 2002).

Control theorists have generally built their theories on the fundamental premise that managers apply organizational controls to address the agency problems that naturally exist in organizations. Agency problems are present when managers must rely on subordinates to perform tasks and, for various reasons, those subordinates may be incapable or unwilling to fully and effectively cooperate with them toward the pursuit of their desired objectives.

To ensure that they are able to efficiently and effectively accomplish their objectives, managers apply a range of *control mechanisms* to their subordinates' work efforts (Barney and Hesterly, 1996). Scholars often distinguish forms of controls by the portion of the production process to which they are targeted (Cardinal, Sitkin, and Long, Chapter 3). Managers generally apply *input controls* before individuals perform tasks using mechanisms to guide the selection and preparation of human and material production resources. For example, managers use training and socialization to regulate employees' skills and abilities or screening methods to obtain a specific quality and quantity of material production inputs. Managers apply *process controls* while employees perform tasks by directing individuals to utilize specific methods of task production. Finally, managers apply *output controls* after individuals complete tasks by measuring the outputs they produce against standards such as desired production quantities or profit levels (Ouchi, 1979).

Much of what constitutes current control theory builds from several key assumptions to identify the conditions under which managers will apply particular forms of control. First, control theorists generally assume that omnipresent superior–subordinate goal conflicts increase the motivations for subordinates to act opportunistically and misrepresent both their abilities (i.e., adverse selection) and work efforts (i.e., moral hazard). While not ubiquitous, these disagreements are assumed to be pervasive enough that managers are advised to be dubious of their subordinates' abilities and intentions. Control theories build from this assumption to suggest that a primary focus of managers' control efforts should be to guard against subordinate incompetence and opportunism (Ouchi, 1980).

Second, control theories generally build on assumptions that managers possess a quantity and quality of resources necessary to effectively implement whatever controls they seek to apply. While time and money are often assumed to be in sufficient supply to implement controls, these theories also assume that power is among the most important resources that managers possess. *Managerial power* is defined as the capacity to assert one's will despite resistance from others (Grimes, 1978; Perrow, 1986). Because control scholars build their theories on the presumption of omnipresent superior–subordinate goal conflict, they tend to emphasize how managers direct their subordinates largely through efforts to exert their managerial power. For example, scholars who build from agency theory principles argue that managers apply controls primarily to mitigate the relational risks that emerge from managerial concerns about subordinate opportunism (Eisenhardt, 1989; Ouchi, 1979; Williamson, 1975). According to this perspective, managers gain their power by acquiring and holding resources that their subordinates desire and then exert their power by dispensing rewards and enacting punishments based solely on their perceived capacity to measure and monitor subordinates' task efforts.

While this view has primarily been developed and presented through theories of formal control (Ghoshal and Moran, 1996; Sitkin and Bies, 1994), I contend that these observations on control research are also relevant to research on informal or social controls, i.e., "values, norms, and beliefs that guide employee actions" (Cardinal *et al.*, 2004: 10). Although control theorists who focus on resolving agency problems have paid less direct attention to informal controls, scholars have utilized a critical theory perspective to conduct more deliberate investigations of informal control development and use. Building from the same basic assumptions outlined previously, these control scholars suggest that a manager's interests in developing and exerting their power both enable and motivate their applications of informal controls (Jermier, 1998). In summarizing this literature, Jermier (1998: 235) concludes that, while managers who apply informal controls do so to "seem more humanistic," their true motivation for applying informal controls "lies in the unstated promise of providing more thorough control for elites" and, thus, in reinforcing their sense of managerial power.

Although the primary ideas that have emerged from existing control theories have garnered substantial empirical support (Eisenhardt, 1989), I contend that these perspectives provide an overly limited view of managerial attention and action. Specifically, I argue that current control theories overemphasize managers' control activities and underemphasize the other, related activities managers take to cultivate important aspects of superior–subordinate relationships. As a result, while control scholars are able to provide important and credible details about *what* forms of control mechanisms managers may initially choose to implement, they have generated significantly less insight into *how* managers apply those controls over periods of time and in ways that actually generate effective levels of subordinate cooperation with their directives (Bijlsma-Frankema and Costa, Chapter 13).

My arguments here are bolstered by research that finds managers who rely primarily on controls to guide their subordinates often compromise the quality of superior–subordinate relations and actually decrease their capacity to secure subordinate cooperation with their directives (Ghoshal and Moran, 1996; Sitkin, 1995). This is because managers who emphasize controls often signal that they trust subordinates less, will actively seek to limit their personal autonomy more and, as a result, stimulate their subordinates to exhibit increasing levels of resistance to their control efforts (Sitkin and Bies, 1994; Sitkin and Stickel, 1996).

An authority-based perspective on managerial action

I believe, however, that our current understanding of how managers achieve superior–subordinate cooperation could be improved if scholars were to shift away from theories that focus primarily on how managers utilize their power to implement organizational controls and toward theories that are used to examine how managers protect and promote their authority through a wider range of managerial actions. I further contend that if this perspective were more fully integrated into our conceptualizations of managerial control systems it would significantly advance our knowledge not only about *what* initial actions managers choose to direct their subordinates but also about *how* managers actually implement those choices over time and in ways that enable them to effectively promote superior–subordinate cooperation.

Key to my position here is the distinction I highlight between the current focus in control research on managerial power and the focus on managerial authority that I advocate. Although closely related, conceptualizations of control that focus on how managers exercise their power emphasize a manager's capacity to force or overtly coerce compliance with their (or their organization's) interests through resistance from subordinates. A perspective that emphasizes managerial authority also focuses on how managers gain and maintain the capacity to efficiently and effectively direct their subordinates, and emphasizes a manager's desire to achieve these ends through the promotion of superior–subordinate cooperation and commitment. An important difference here is that researchers using this perspective would not assume the presence of superior–subordinate conflicts and, in fact, may anticipate that managers may encounter relatively low levels of resistance. This is because the subordinates of managers who possess authority are willing to "suspend judgment in advance of a command or decision" and are, *a priori*, "committed to execute the command before it is issued" (Grimes, 1978: 725). Managers, as a result, are motivated to develop and maintain their authority based on a persistent desire to have subordinates cooperate with their directives and commit to the achievement of the goals they advocate (Dornbusch and Scott, 1975).

To achieve a level of authority where subordinate responses like these are generated, managers must take actions that are viewed as legitimate by those whom they seek to direct (Bijlsma-Frankema and Costa, Chapter 13; Dornbusch and Scott, 1975). In general, perceived legitimacy is dependent on evaluations that one's actions are "desirable, proper, or appropriate within some socially constructed system of norms, values, beliefs, and definitions" (Suchman, 1995: 574). Tyler and Lind (1992: 118) observe that being viewed as legitimate "nearly always facilitates and is often crucial for the effective exercise of authority [. . . and,] once established, functions to enhance acceptance of decisions as long as their authority is viewed as legitimate."

Previous research suggests that managers derive their authority from two, distinct relational sources: authorization and endorsement (Dornbusch and Scott, 1975). From the managerial perspective, a sense of authorization describes a manager's belief that higher governing authorities will support and reinforce his or her decisions and actions. When managers' actions are authorized, their superiors view those actions as legitimate and, as a result, will "back-up" those initiatives if necessary. Endorsement, in contrast, describes the support for their decisions and actions that managers feel from those whom they seek to control. If subordinates view their managers' actions as legitimate, they will judge those actions as worthy of their willing compliance and commitment.

By focusing on the utilization of managerial power, those who advocate current control perspectives generally assume that managers need only rely on authorization to apply the controls they deem appropriate. However, I argue that a more active consideration of issues related to managerial authority dynamics would direct scholars to evaluate how both authorization *and* endorsement influence managerial actions. More specifically, I contend that focused attention on how managers gain endorsement with their directives would enable us to better understand how managers successfully motivate their subordinates to "obey" and, on some level, more willingly accede to their directives. By incorporating issues related to authority, this perspective could lead scholars toward a clearer understanding of how managers elicit high levels of cooperation from those from whom they seek to direct.

The case for multiple managerial actions

The value of this perspective increases with the recognition that, in new organizational forms and modern work environments, managers are, arguably, more keenly aware of issues related to their authority and, specifically, to endorsement. In organizations characterized by flatter organizational hierarchies and decentralized decision-making, it would be difficult for managers to maintain their authority solely through authorization and the support of higher authorities (Lewin *et al.*, 1999). Instead, individual efforts to maintain managerial authority in these environments depends, at least in part, on one's capacity to concurrently gain authorization from their superiors *and* endorsement from their subordinates.

Although managers in these environments still seek authorization and use control mechanisms to direct their subordinates, scholars remain decidedly agnostic about how managers actually concurrently achieve the levels of authorization and endorsement sufficient to achieve high levels of subordinate cooperation. Toward this end, Noorderhaven (1992) outlines a road map that directs scholars to broaden their current focus on managerial action and attempts to motivate a more expansive perspective on control that evaluates how managers promote superior–subordinate cooperation.

The general perspective he advocates is consistent with the substantial interest that trust and fairness concepts have garnered in the organizational literature. In general, these researchers argue that managers often increase levels of superior–subordinate cooperation by promoting positive subordinate perceptions of trust and fairness. Managers who build trust among their subordinates may actually achieve residual efficiencies by reducing agency costs (monitoring costs, bonding costs, search costs, warranty costs) and enabling an organization to gain competitive advantages, solve employee commitment problems, and more closely align subordinates' motivations to organizational requirements (Barney and Hansen, 1994). Similarly, individuals who believe that they are treated fairly are more likely to voluntarily comply with managerial directives, view superiors as legitimate authorities, exhibit extra-role behaviors, and more willingly embrace organizational goals (Tyler and Lind, 1992).

Conceptualizing actions to promote trust and fairness

Even though extensive research has established trust and fairness as a key antecedent of employee cooperation in organizations, researchers have not effectively conceptualized how managers balance their efforts to promote trust and fairness with their efforts to exert organizational controls. One key reason for this is that scholars have yet to fully comprehend how managers actually approach promoting trust and fairness. As a result, our understanding of these managerial actions must currently be gleaned from studies researchers have performed primarily on subordinate reactions to managerial initiatives (few exceptions include: Folger and Skarlicki, 1998 and Whitener *et al.*, 1998). Though these studies provide important insights into the benefits of promoting organizational trust and fairness, they provide a less clear understanding of how managers actually pursue these outcomes.

To fully examine these dynamics, I contend that it is necessary to identify concepts that more directly describe managerial perspectives on these issues. To deepen our discussion on this, in the following sections I introduce and describe the concepts of *trustworthiness-promotion* and *fairness-promotion*. Although related, I argue that these concepts are distinct from one another and from organizational controls both in their primary focus and in the specific outcomes that managers hope to achieve through their implementation.

Trustworthiness-promotion activities. Previous work by Long and Sitkin (2006) describes managers' efforts to promote trust and suggests that the focus of these efforts is to produce (i.e., for subordinates) "a psychological state comprising the intention to accept vulnerability based upon positive expectations of the intentions or behavior of another (i.e., the manager)" (Rousseau *et al.*, 1998: 395). Because trust is largely dependent on an individual's perceived capacity to predict another's positive intentions toward him or her (Mayer *et al.*, 1995), I contend that managers use *trustworthiness-promotion activities* to communicate their underlying motivations in ways that increase the perceived predictability and acceptability of their actions (Rousseau *et al.*, 1998). To do this, managers focus their trustworthiness-promotion activities on providing their subordinates with credible assurances that their individual goals within a particular organizational system will be protected and furthered.

I argue that managers conceptualize their trustworthiness-promotion activities as ways to develop key aspects of the relationships between themselves and the *individual subordinates* under their direction. Because trust is largely dependent on the extent to which an individual feels that her/his personal interests will be protected, managers will enact their trustworthiness-promotion efforts primarily within individual superior–subordinate relationships. Sometimes these efforts will be enacted independently and in isolation, sometimes these efforts will be enacted with multiple subordinates concurrently (e.g., managers leading teams). Regardless of how many individuals managers may engage with at a particular time, I argue that they will focus their trustworthiness-promotion activities on enhancing individual assessments along key dimensions of trustworthiness (Mayer *et al.*, 1995): their task abilities and capacity to help trustors achieve their desired goals (i.e., ability), their willingness in accommodating trustors' individual needs and interests (i.e., benevolence), and their readiness to both support ideals that trustors value and fulfill promises that they make (i.e., integrity and reliability).

Managers may utilize a wide range of formal and informal mechanisms in their trustworthiness-promotion efforts. For example, managers may actively use informal communication channels to demonstrate their concern for subordinates' interests and improve the general quality of their superior–subordinate relationships (Lewicki and Bunker, 1996; Sitkin and Roth, 1993). Under other conditions, managers may redesign formal organizational policies to respond to the specific, trust-based concerns that their employees maintain about organizational procedures (Zucker, 1986).

In addition, I contend that managers will adjust to the situational demands they face by fostering calculative, institutional, or relational trust (Rousseau *et al.*, 1998). For example, managers may build calculative trust with subordinates by promoting positive perceptions of their managerial ability, benevolence, and integrity in ways that display themselves as reliable exchange partners. Managers may build institutional trust (Zucker, 1986) through the careful development of organizational forms (i.e., structures, procedures, processes) that effectively promote their general ability to manage organizational tasks, their concern for employees' needs and interests (i.e., promote benevolence), and their intentions to honor (or at least not violate) employee–management agreements (i.e., promote integrity). In addition, managers may attempt to build relational trust and deepen their relationships with subordinates (Lewicki and Bunker, 1996) by utilizing their ability to identify and forge relational links with subordinates, by benevolently paying attention to subordinates' emotional needs, and by working hard to fulfill promises that they will maintain high-quality interpersonal relationships with subordinates (Sitkin and Roth, 1993).

Fairness-promotion activities. Managers' efforts to promote fairness may take many forms. I argue that, through *distributive fairness promotion*, managers make explicit attempts to equitably distribute rewards and responsibilities (Adams, 1965). Through *procedural fairness-promotion*, managers make attempts to consistently apply rules and procedures and provide employees some control over managerial decisions and decision processes (Tyler and Lind, 1992). Through *interactional fairness-promotion*, managers attempt to treat subordinates in ways that align with the interpersonal treatment that they expect to receive. In promoting interactional fairness, managers exhibit high levels of sensitivity and respect for their employees through their actions and words (Bies and Moag, 1986).

While sharing some similarities with trustworthiness-promotion activities, fairness-promotion activities are distinct in important ways. When managers promote trustworthiness, they attempt to influence subordinates' evaluations about whether their individual, absolute expectations will be realized. In contrast, managers use fairness-promotion activities to positively influence subordinates' expectations that they will be treated well in terms relative to objective standards of fairness or the referents to which they compare themselves. This conceptualization builds from the observations of scholars such as Kim and Mauborgne (1997), who suggest that managers conceptualize promoting fairness primarily as ways that they can positively impact the social comparison processes they assume their subordinates engage.

Although managers attempt to treat groups of multiple individuals "fairly," it is difficult for them to personalize their treatment of individuals and, thus, to promote high levels of trust. I argue that, even though fairness-promotion activities may not be very effective for promoting trust outright, they can be effective for decreasing subordinate distrust in their managers. Sitkin and Roth (1993), who describe dynamics similar to these, would suggest that managers rely on fairness-promotion activities to signal to their subordinates that they are working to protect their general rights and interests. Thus, managers understand that, through their fairness-promotion activities, they may preserve and protect their legitimacy and authority by decreasing the tendency of subordinates to distrust their intentions and behaviors. This, in turn, may decrease the perceived risks inherent in particular exchanges and indirectly promote the development of trust (Dirks and Ferrin, 2002).

Similar to trustworthiness-promotion activities, managers draw upon a wide range of formal and informal mechanisms to build positive perceptions of organizational fairness. For example, in an organization where a "pat on the back" is highly valued, managers attempting to simultaneously promote distributive fairness and interactional fairness may equitably and openly provide subordinates with words of encouragement and appreciation. Under different circumstances, managers hoping to build perceptions that they are procedurally fair may focus on developing formal dispute resolution procedures targeted toward a wide variety of subordinate concerns (Bendersky, 2003).

Multi-faceted systems in managerial control research

To assist in clarifying the differences between the concepts described above, Table 12.1 summarizes the primary components of the three categories of managerial activities that I discuss here.

I contend that the introduction of trustworthiness-promotion and fairness-promotion concepts, together with a conscious consideration of issues related to perceived managerial authority, leads naturally to a reassessment of both the composition of managerial control systems and of how these systems are implemented.

I build from the premise that the overarching goal of a managerial control system is to produce a level of superior–subordinate cooperation sufficient to enable the efficient and effective achievement of organizational goals. Though control mechanisms comprise a crucial but partial factor in the overall control process, discussions of managerial actions that focus only on control mechanisms are insufficient to explain how managers attempt to ensure that subordinate cooperation is secured and organizational objectives are effectively realized. In contrast, I argue that how managers actually gain compliance and commitment to their objectives is a more involved process that engages managers in ongoing efforts to balance their applications of organizational controls with their efforts to promote trustworthiness and fairness.

An important implication of these ideas is that managerial controls are more than merely mechanisms through which managers force,

Table 12.1 *Descriptions of managerial applications of control, trustworthiness-promotion, and fairness-promotion activities*

	Control activities	Trustworthiness-promotion initiatives	Fairness-promotion activities
Primary focus	Manager's efforts to: (1) select (2) train (3) monitor (4) reward subordinates for task completion efforts.	Enhance subordinates' perceptions of a manager's: (1) capabilities (2) interest in accommodating their needs (3) willingness to fulfill promises.	Enhance subordinates' perceptions of: (1) distributive (2) procedural (3) interactional fairness.
Intended outcomes	Align subordinate inputs, behaviors, and outputs with demands of organizational tasks.	Produce calculative, institutional, and/or relational trust in a manager.	Produce employee perceptions that a manager is distributively, procedurally, and/or interactionally fair.
Strengths	Provide managers with the mechanisms to prepare, supervise, and remunerate subordinates for completing task directives.	Provide managers with the mechanisms to address employees' individual concerns.	Provide managers with the mechanisms to address employees' collectively focused concerns (e.g., concerns for equity and consistency).
Weaknesses	(1) May wrest too much control out of employees' hands, signaling to them that their manager cannot be trusted. (2) May lead managers to promote efficiency and effectiveness over fairness.	(1) May lead managers to compromise fairness by focusing too much on the concerns of particular, individual employees. (2) May lead managers to spend too little time directing and controlling the actions of their subordinates.	(1) Can lead managers to compromise employee trust by providing insufficient attention to the particularized concerns of individual employees. (2) May lead managers to spend too little time directing and controlling the actions of their subordinates.

direct, or coerce their subordinates to execute their will. Even though managers may use controls to achieve these means, the end goal of managers' control actions often is to secure subordinate cooperation and commitment with their desired objectives. Because controls alone are insufficient to achieve these ends, scholars could benefit from a greater understanding of the role that controls play within a wider scope of managerial actions. This expanded perspective broadens our views both of the actions managers take as well as their subordinates' evaluations of those actions.

Recent research by Long *et al.* (2010), for example, describes how subordinates' perceptions of the controls they encounter lead them to generate specific expectations about how they should evaluate managers' efforts to promote fairness. In their research, they introduce and develop the concept of *fairness monitoring*, which they describe as a sense-making process that individuals use to determine whether particular, relevant types of fairness are promoted in work contexts. They contend that individuals engage in the forms of fairness monitoring that enable them to most accurately evaluate whether their manager or organization is fair in ways related to the controls they encounter. Consistent with their hypotheses, they observe that individuals who are directed through market controls focus on producing individually based outcomes and tend to primarily monitor whether managers promote distributive fairness; individuals who are directed through bureaucratic controls to focus on executing specific procedures tend to primarily monitor whether managers promote procedural fairness; and individuals who are directed through clan controls to get along and "fit in" with others tend to primarily monitor whether managers promote interpersonal fairness.

Importantly, Long *et al.*'s (2010) work suggests that, in addition to providing subordinates with work directives, the imposition of controls also motivates specific expectations about the treatment those subordinates expect to receive from their managers. Because a manager's level of endorsement and, ultimately, their authority, is based, in part, on whether that manager is able to fulfill subordinates' expectations, this ultimately suggests that scholars may want to broaden their conceptualization of managerial control systems to include specific activities that managers use to fulfill the expectations that subordinates generate from their experiences with particular types of controls. Because many of these expectations relate directly to issues of trust and fairness, this suggests that scholars may want to incorporate an understanding of how managers tend to integrate and balance their control, trustworthiness-promotion, and fairness-promotion efforts into their conceptualizations of managerial control systems.

A focus on complementarities

One potentially useful way of reconceptualizing managerial control systems is to think about how managers establish the complementarities between multiple activities that enable them to enhance superior–subordinate cooperation. Bendersky (2003: 644) defines *complementarities* as "the interplay among the components (i.e., activities), which enables each type of component to influence individuals' attitudes and behaviors more significantly than it could without reinforcement from the others." Though task control, trustworthiness-promotion, and fairness-promotion represent distinct activities, a key part of my argument here is that because they can be jointly applied to address related concerns, managers do not consider or pursue the implementation of these activities in isolation. To the contrary, because the pursuit of multiple activities is often necessary to promote levels of managerial authority sufficient to elicit superior–subordinate cooperation, it would be beneficial for scholars to examine how and why managers integrate and balance their control, trust-promotion, and fairness-promotion efforts to produce complementary effects on subordinates' cooperative attitudes and behaviors.

In some cases, managers will attempt to capitalize on "synergistic complementarities" that exist between activities. For example, when managers implement complementary activities, their synergistic interaction may enhance the effects produced by a complementary activity. Sitkin (1995), for example, outlines three ways that formal controls can increase subordinates' trust by decreasing the perceived risks of complying with managerial directives. First, managers may use opportunities to apply organizational controls to demonstrate their detailed knowledge of organizational operations and elicit a form of *competency-based trust* from their subordinates. Second, they may publicly embrace control mechanisms that constrain their ability to exploit employees, thus decreasing the levels of risk and vulnerability that their subordinates perceive. Third, managers also may take explicit steps to clearly connect employees' compliance with managerial directives to the disbursement of rewards such as salaries, bonuses, and promotions. In doing this, managers provide their employees with confidence that their best chance of achieving personal and professional goals lies with their acceptance of management's explicit instructions (Sitkin, 1995).

The joint influence of complementary activities may also produce positive, interactive effects on related job attitudes and behaviors. For example, Long and colleagues (2010) find that as subordinates' strong managerial control perceptions highlight the importance of particular performance criteria and stimulate subordinates to closely monitor relevant types of fairness information; those subordinates come to view related fairness judgments as especially accurate indicators of their opportunities for organizational success. Thus, when subordinates perceive their supervisor to be fair on the dimension that they monitor, they will exhibit higher levels of job satisfaction because they have confidence that their fairness judgments provide them with clear and unambiguous evidence that their supervisor is providing them with important opportunities to develop and succeed in their work environment.

Even though synergistic complementarities are consistent with more traditional research on this topic, I argue that an additional motivation for managers to integrate their control, trustworthiness-promotion, and fairness-promotion efforts is to compensate for problems that may arise through the application of any one category of activity. This focus stimulates a desire to achieve a different form of complementarity, which I identify as a "compensatory complementarity." When managers attempt to establish compensatory complementarities, they integrate multiple activities in order to decrease or mitigate the negative effects that could be produced if any one type of activity were pursued in isolation. Controls, for example, present managers with efficient ways to communicate and motivate task directives. However, controls that are applied without attention to fairness concerns may stimulate conflicts by compromising subordinates' perceptions that they are equitably rewarded for their efforts (Deutsch, 1982), that they hold sufficient control over organizational decisions and decision processes (Tyler and Lind, 1992), and that they are respected within their organization (Bies and Moag, 1986). In addition, if mishandled, the implementation of controls may be seen as inappropriately wresting control over organizational tasks from subordinates, thereby signaling to those subordinates that their manager may not be concerned with their individual needs and should not be trusted (Ghoshal and Moran, 1996).

Alternatively, trustworthiness-promotion initiatives present managers with effective ways to build and deepen relationships with subordinates by providing managers the means with which they can promote their subordinates' individual interests (Mayer *et al.*, 1995). As described in the leader–member exchange (LMX) research, managers may often tend to develop trusting relationships with only particular subordinates (Scandura *et al.*, 1986; Schriesheim *et al.*, 1998). As a result, trustworthiness-promotion initiatives that are pursued in isolation can compromise subordinate fairness perceptions and stimulate conflicts by leading managers to neglect the respective needs of other subordinates in their "out-group" (Deutsch, 1982). Trustworthiness-promotion initiatives may also increase managers' concerns about efficiency by leading them to question the amount of time they are spending deepening relationships with their subordinates (Spreitzer and Mishra, 1999).

Managers may also utilize fairness-promotion initiatives in an effort to promote a sense among subordinates that everyone in the organization is equitably rewarded, empowered, and respected (Tyler and Lind, 1992). If managers focus only on promoting fairness, they may spend an inordinate amount of time addressing the generalized concerns of multiple subordinates and fail to develop trust because they do not attend to the particular concerns of their individual subordinates. In addition, managers who focus too much on fairness-promotion may begin to feel they are not maintaining efficient, direct control over the organizational task completion efforts. This is because they may perceive that they are devoting too much time attending to their subordinates' desires for equity and respect or have ceded too much decision-making discretion and authority to those subordinates.

Striking a balance between control, trust, and fairness

The few theorists who have examined trust and fairness from a manager's perspective suggest that those who actively initiate programs to build organizational trust and fairness make difficult choices. This is because these programs, at least initially, appear more costly and risky than more traditional mechanisms for managing employees (Wicks *et al.*, 1999). These programs appear more costly because they often require managers to expend time fulfilling obligations to sub-ordinates, ensuring they equitably distribute organizational resources and opportunities, and fully addressing important employee concerns. They appear more risky because they require managers to cede discretion and decision-making authority to lower echelon employees who exhibit different (and often conflicting) interests, needs, and preferences (Spreitzer and Mishra, 1999).

In response to these concerns, I argue that it is important to understand how managers balance the attention they concurrently pay to control, trustworthiness-promotion, and fairness-promotion activities. Drawing from a definition proposed by Cardinal *et al.* (2004: 412–413), balance describes a "harmonious" combination of task control, trust-promotion, and fairness-promotion activities to direct them towards achieving "isomorphism with internal and external requirements and sustaining or smoothly adapting to changes in those requirements."

It is important to note that Cardinal *et al.*'s (2004) definition of balance does not connote an equal distribution of attention or effort to multiple activities (Long and Sitkin, 2006). Instead, these authors suggest that managers attempt to integrate and balance multiple activities in ways appropriate to their interpretations of situational conditions. Applying their ideas to this conceptual effort, I argue that relational, organizational, and individual issues may affect the salience of particular managerial concerns and, as a result, will also affect the emphasis that managers independently and jointly place on building trust, building fairness, and applying controls.

Relational influences on balance

The form and severity of the conflicts that managers experience with their subordinates comprise probably the single most important factor influencing the balance that managers establish between their control, trustworthiness-promotion and fairness-promotion activities (Long and Sitkin, 2006). This is because superior-subordinate conflicts provide managers with information about the level of endorsement they maintain at any given time. If the level of endorsement that managers maintain is not sufficient to accomplish their goals, closely examining the composition of their conflicts can provide them with important information about their subordinates' specific concerns and indirectly suggest potential, remedial options.

In response to these concerns, I argue that managers will often attempt to apply controls and promote both trustworthiness and fairness in ways that limit the potential for superior–subordinate conflicts. This perspective represents an important departure from the general perspective embodied by current control theory that tends to provide a much more limited perspective on relationships between superior–subordinate conflicts and managers' actions. For example, control theorists who focus on issues of power and control merely assume the omnipresence of superior–subordinate goal conflicts. In order to respond to the opportunistic threats that these conflicts represent, control theorists generally suggest that managers should align their organizational control choices with their capacity to measure and monitor their subordinates' task efforts (Ouchi, 1980; Barney and Hansen, 1994).

The perspective on managerial authority that I present, however, motivates the development of a much more detailed perspective on managers' evaluations of superior–subordinate conflicts and of the behavioral responses those evaluations elicit. This line of argument builds from the contention that superior–subordinate conflicts provide managers with information about how and why their subordinates do not wholeheartedly endorse their actions. Thus, managers are motivated to closely examine the conflicts they perceive. In addition, I argue that managers who seek increased levels of endorsement will often act in alignment with the subordinates' preferences these analyses uncover. For example, when faced with conflicts and blatantly distrustful employees, managers may often undertake trustworthiness-promotion initiatives that explicitly assure their subordinates that they possess the ability to manage them, that their interests will be protected, and that they will honor their promises to them (Mayer *et al.*, 1995; Rousseau *et al.*, 1998). The aim for managers who initiate these actions is to give a verifiable "proof source" (Doney *et al.*, 1998) to subordinates and convince them that both conflicts and a distrust of management is damaging to superior–subordinate relations. Following Lewicki and Bunker (1996), managers looking to develop trusting relationships with subordinates would begin by tailoring their trustworthiness-promotion activities by developing calculative trust through repeated superior–subordinate exchanges. Then, as trust deepens, managers would seek to bolster subordinates' "knowledge" that they are trustworthy as they concurrently work toward deepening the sense of common identity with their subordinates. The important point here is that, at each stage, managers would tailor their actions to support the level of trust they were seeking to promote.

Because conflicts often result from the inequities that subordinates perceive, I argue that managers faced with conflicts will often engage in rigorous examinations of their allocation decisions and procedures. Both Leventhal *et al.* (1980) and Lerner (1977) suggest that managers often choose to emphasize both fair allocation mechanisms and equitable reward distributions in order to establish an environment where conflict is kept to a minimum. Although they acknowledge that the specific methods managers employ are determined by situational factors, they outline how (what I would describe as distributive and procedural fairness-promotion) activities provide managers with opportunities to mitigate subordinates' feelings of relative deprivation that can lead to subordinates' resentment of and contempt for authority (Greenberg, 1987).

Even though conflicts may often stimulate managers' efforts to integrate their control, trustworthiness-promotion, and fairness-promotion activities, I acknowledge conditions under which managers may respond to conflicts by focusing primarily on implementing organizational controls. Research on power-use strategies suggests that higher power actors (i.e., superiors) often attempt to resolve conflicts with lower power actors by focusing primarily on trying to control their behaviors. According to this research, higher power actors do not typically initiate conciliatory behaviors (i.e., initiatives to promote trust and fairness) because their relative status stimulates less perspective-taking about the interests of those in lower status positions.

Though managers may often exhibit imbalanced responses to the conflicts they encounter over time, managers who exhibit balanced attention to promoting control, trust, and fairness are more likely to build positive working relationships. When this happens, managers may gain production efficiencies and enable themselves to more easily obtain valuable employee insights that can be incorporated into their future decision-making and planning activities. If managers, however, neglect their subordinates' interests over long periods, their superior–subordinate interactions can develop into "pathological spiraling relationships" where "surveillants come to distrust their targets (i.e., employees), and their targets become unmotivated and untrustworthy" (Enzle and Anderson, 1993: 263).

Organizational influences on balance

The balance that managers strike at any given time not only reflects the emphasis they place on various combinations of activities, it also describes the relative attention that managers pay to issues of endorsement and authorization. In addition to relational factors, factors inherent to managers' relationships with authorizing superiors and institutions may influence the choices they make about the particular control, trustworthiness-promotion, and fairness-promotion activities they implement.

As Whitener et al. (1998) and Meindl (1989) highlight, the structure, policies, and culture in which managers operate significantly affect the decisions they make in promoting trust and fairness. These factors may naturally lead managers to adopt trustworthiness-promotion and fairness-promotion activities that support organizational or institutional norms. For example, managers in highly formal organizational contexts where they perceive high levels of authorization may put most of their effort into developing and implementing elaborate formal controls in order to clarify employment contracts and ensure that organizational decisions are consistently applied. To support these actions, managers may satisfy their organization's legal or institutional obligations by pursuing both calculative and institutional trustworthiness-promotion efforts with their subordinates. This dynamic was described by Sitkin and Roth (1993) and Sitkin and George (2005) who observed that managers faced with problems associated with HIV/AIDS-infected employees responded to institutional-level demands using formal control mechanisms to reduce the scope of risk and uncertainty faced by their employees. These managers also implemented distributive and procedural fairness-promotion mechanisms that allowed them to protect employees' perceived rights to be treated in a fair manner.

In organizations where managers are authorized to develop high-quality interpersonal relationships with their subordinates, they may actively engage in relational trust-promotion activities, interactional fairness-promotion activities, and utilize informal controls. As Wilkins and Ouchi (1983: 475) point out, managers who implement informal control mechanisms attempt to establish "shared frameworks, language and referents," all key elements of relational trust. To successfully develop these common values and frames of reference, managers often may also promote interactional fairness by respectfully, candidly, and truthfully communicating their beliefs to employees (Bies and Moag, 1986).

Individual influences on balance

Because the ultimate responsibility for decisions and actions rests with managers, I contend that several individual-level factors will tend to influence the ways in which managers will integrate their control, trustworthiness-promotion, and fairness-promotion activities. Probably the most prominent of these factors is the individual goals that managers hope to achieve. While control theory already outlines how managers can use control to realize particular goals, how goals simulate the promotion of particular types of trust and fairness is less well understood. However, Shapiro *et al.* (1992: 374) argue that, in initiating actions consistent with the concept of trustworthiness-promotion, managers should "assess the type of relationship you want and the requisite kind of trust necessary to sustain that relationship." This is important because, as Wicks *et al.* (1999: 99) suggest, "trust is good – but a conditional good." In other words, it is possible to both over- and underinvest in trust and neither is desirable "from either a moral or strategic point of view." Managers who overinvest in trust may waste valuable resources creating an overly collegial climate. Managers who underinvest in trust may neglect opportunities to build relationships of a quality they require.

Individual goals may also impact the emphases that managers place on promoting particular types of fairness. For example, Leventhal and colleagues (1980) in their allocator preference theory contend that managers carefully select their allocation procedures based on the goals they hope to attain and the situations in which procedures are developed and applied. According to this theory, when low levels of subordinate endorsement provide managers with clear signals that their capacity to achieve organizational goals may be compromised, managers will be motivated to closely scrutinize their existing procedures and, if necessary, retool those procedures in ways that more effectively facilitate goal accomplishment.

These motivations may lead managers to adjust their efforts to promote distributive fairness principles in order to incite poor performers to increase their task efforts. By tying efforts directly to rewards, managers communicate to employees that there are clear benefits to adhering to the organizational goals they seek to pursue (Lind and Tyler, 1988; Tyler and Lind, 1992; Rousseau et al., 1998). Distributive fairness-promotion initiatives, for example, can readily complement formal controls and calculative trust-promotion initiatives by "strongly reinforce(ing) those individuals whose contributions are most useful and beneficial to the group product, while at the same time deliver(ing) a lower degree of reinforcement to poor performers" (Chen and Church, 1993: 30). Lerner (1977) suggests that these efforts may help managers establish a level of social harmony that makes subordinates more receptive to the idea of cooperating with managers and acceding to their authority (George and Qian, Chapter 6).

A manager's knowledge of transformation processes is a factor familiar to control researchers that may also pose broader implications within an expanded perspective on control. A manager's knowledge of a particular transformation process determines how well he/she understands "the link between the actions subordinates take and the results they achieve" (Snell, 1992: 295). Used extensively in control theory, this measure describes "how well the controller understands the task" (Kirsch, 1996: 4) that his/her subordinates perform (Ouchi, 1979; Eisenhardt, 1989). Managers who possess complete knowledge of transformation processes can specify how subordinates should perform their responsibilities and can develop effective evaluation measures to monitor whether employees have properly carried out instructions (Snell, 1992). Managers who understand the activities to "structure the transformation process of work" (Snell, 1992: 294) can employ this knowledge to select particular types of trustworthiness-promotion and fairness-promotion activities that align with both the tasks they direct and the organizational controls they select. Ultimately, this knowledge of organizational tasks enables managers to review task demands to ensure they are able to efficiently and effectively direct subordinate activities while cultivating cooperative superior–subordinate relationships (Long et al., 2002).

Other individual-level factors may influence managerial decisions and actions as well. For example, managers who are high self-monitors may be particularly sensitive to the level of subordinate endorsement they receive. Thus, when superior–subordinate conflicts arise, those managers may respond quickly by initiating various trustworthiness-promotion and fairness-promotion activities to re-establish themselves in the "good graces" of the populations they seek to affect. In addition, managers who are emotionally intelligent may be particularly sensitive to the legitimacy-based evaluations that their subordinates and superiors make about their work. These individuals may also be more effective at calibrating their activities to the particular interests and concerns of those external audiences.

Discussion and conclusion

This chapter introduces and examines a framework that outlines how managers' interests in preserving, protecting, and promoting their authority lead them to integrate their efforts to apply organizational controls and promote organizational trust and fairness. In this chapter, I describe how this perspective may motivate scholars to integrate previously independent perspectives, broaden theoretical views of managerial attention and action, and, ultimately, generate a more comprehensive and realistic understanding of managers' efforts to direct and control subordinates' work activities.

Even though previous research suggests that issues related to trust and fairness are key considerations in the development and implementation of managerial control systems, this area of study remains underconceptualized. The observations communicated within this chapter help to set the stage for a more systematic treatment of these issues.

I contrast the ideas presented in this chapter with more traditional perspectives on *managerial attention* that have focused primarily on examining how managers leverage their power to exert control over their subordinates' activities (Ocasio, 1997; Ocasio and Wohlgezogen, Chapter 7). By encouraging control scholars to expand their view of managerial attention and focus more on issues related to managerial authority, this chapter places the decisions managers make about directing their employees within a broader social context. Building on this premise, I argue that their ongoing attempts to preserve, protect, and promote their authority lead managers to both evaluate whether their actions are viewed as legitimate and stimulate them to actively cultivate positive social relationships with those whom they manage. I argue that managers use these evaluations to calibrate their actions to not only achieve efficiency and effectiveness gains, but also to develop the high levels of superior–subordinate cooperation that are necessary to achieve key organizational objectives.

This chapter also significantly extends the perspective presented within current control research by outlining an expanded view of *managerial action*. By suggesting that managers integrate the controls they apply with their efforts to promote trust and fairness, I provide support to those who advocate for a broader perspective on organizational control research (Cardinal, 2001; Cardinal *et al.*, 2004). Those who support this position attempt to refine the work of control theorists who suggest that managers rely primarily on formal control mechanisms to align the goals and risk preferences of their employees with their organization (Kirsch, 1996; Merchant, 1985; Ouchi, 1979; Snell, 1992). By extending the work of justice and trust scholars (Greenberg, 1987; Tyler and Lind, 1992) to examine factors that lead managers to promote organizational trust and fairness, this chapter responds to these concerns and previous research that has portrayed trust and fairness initiatives as merely "a class of more general control mechanisms" (Bradach and Eccles, 1989: 104) or as a substitute for control (Das and Teng, 1998). The theoretical distinctions I make among control, trustworthiness-promotion, and fairness-promotion activities helps to increase the conceptual clarity with which these activities are described and places descriptions of various activities in a consistent framework where their attributes and effects can be compared.

I identify trustworthiness-promotion and fairness-promotion activities as distinct but complementary to the controls that managers apply. This chapter creates a basis for increasing our understanding about how managers can achieve specific relational outcomes and how they can integrate multiple activities to enhance their capacity to achieve the more general outcomes of superior–subordinate cooperation and organizational performance. The ideas presented here illuminate potentially important additional relationships not only within but also among organizational control, organizational trust, and organizational fairness.

Through the ideas presented here, I encourage control scholars to broaden their conceptualizations of managerial control systems. I suggest that a view of managerial action that generates a greater understanding of how managers integrate their applications of controls with their efforts to promote trust and fairness provides a more comprehensive and realistic picture of the range of actions that managers actually take. Future knowledge generated using this perspective may assist scholars in understanding how managers enhance their pursuit of organizational objectives by lessening the tensions that may develop between them and their employees while they increase subordinate commitment to organizational goals.

References

Adams, J. S. 1965. Inequity of social exchange. In L. Berkowitz (ed.), *Advances in experimental social psychology*: 279–299. New York, NY: Academic Press.

Barley, S. and Kunda, G. 1992. Design and devotion: surges of rational and normative ideologies of control in managerial discourse. *Administrative Science Quarterly*, 37: 363–399.

Barnard, C. I. 1938. *The functions of the executive*. Cambridge, MA: Harvard University Press.

Barney, J. B. and Hansen, M. 1994. Trustworthiness as a source of competitive advantage. *Strategic Management Journal*, 15: 175–190.

Barney, J. B. and Hesterly, W. 1996. Organizational economics: understanding the relationship between organizations and economic analysis. In S. R. Clegg, C. Hardy, and W. R. Nord (eds.), *Handbook of organization studies*: 115–147. Thousand Oaks, CA: Sage.

Bendersky, C. 2003. Organizational dispute resolution systems: a complementarities perspective. *Academy of Management Journal*, 28: 643–656.

Bies, R. J. and Moag, J. S. 1986. Interactional justice: communication criteria of fairness. In R. J. Lewicki, B. H. Sheppard, and M. H. Bazerman (eds.), *Research in negotiation in organizations*: 43–55. Greenwich, CT: JAI Press.

Blau, P. and Scott, W. R. 1962. *Formal organizations: a comparative approach*. San Francisco, CA: Chandler.

Bradach, J. L. and Eccles, R. G. 1989. Price, authority, and trust: from ideal types to plural forms. *Annual review of sociology*, 15: 97–118.

Cardinal, L. B. 2001. Technological innovation in the pharmaceutical industry: managing research and development using input, behavior, and output controls. *Organization Science*, 12: 19–36.

Cardinal, L. B., Sitkin, S. B., and Long, C. P. 2004. Balancing and rebalancing in the creation and evolution of organizational control. *Organization Science*, 15: 411–431.

Chen, Y.-R. and Church, A. H. 1993. Reward allocation preferences in groups and organizations. *The International Journal of Conflict Management*, 4: 25–59.

Das, T. K. and Teng, B. S. 1998. Between trust and control: developing confidence in partner cooperation in alliances. *Academy of Management Review*, 23: 491–512.

Deutsch, M. 1982. Justice in the "crunch." In M. J. Lerner and S. C. Lerner (eds.), *The justice motive in social behavior*: 343–357. New York, NY: Plenum Press.

Dirks, K. and Ferrin, D. 2002. Trust in leadership: meta-analytic findings and implications for research and practice. *Journal of Applied Psychology*, 87: 611–628.

Doney, P. M., Cannon, J. P., and Mullen, M. R. 1998. Understanding the influence of national culture on the development of trust. *Academy of Management Review*, 23: 601–620.

Dornbusch, S. M. and Scott, W. R. 1975. *Evaluation and the exercise of authority*. San Francisco, CA: Jossey-Bass.

Eisenhardt, K. M. 1989. Agency theory: an assessment and review. *Academy of Management Review*, 31: 57–74.

Enzle, M. E. and Anderson, S. C. 1993. Surveillant intentions and intrinsic motivation. *Journal of Personality and Social Psychology*, 64: 257–266.

Folger, R. and Skarlicki, D. 1998. When tough times make tough bosses: managerial distancing as a function of layoff blame. *Academy of Management Journal*, 42: 100–108.

Ghoshal, S. and Moran, P. 1996. Bad for practice: a critique of the transaction cost theory. *Academy of Management Review*, 1: 13–47.

Greenberg, J. 1987. A taxonomy of organizational justice theories. *Academy of Management Review*, 12: 9–22.

Grimes, A. J. 1978. Authority, power, influence, and social control: a theoretical synthesis. *Academy of Management Review*, 3: 724–725.

Jermier, J. M. 1998. Introduction: critical theory perspectives on control. *Administrative Science Quarterly*, 43: 235–256.

Kim, W. C. and Mauborgne, R. A. 1997. Fair process: managing in the knowledge economy. *Harvard Business Review*, 38: 65–75.

Kirsch, L. J. 1996. The management of complex tasks in organizations: controlling the systems development process. *Organization Science*, 7: 1–21.

Lerner, M. J. 1977. The justice motive: some hypotheses as to its origins and forms. *Journal of Personality*, 45: 1–52.

Leventhal, G. S., Karuza, J., and Fry, W. R. 1980. Beyond fairness: a theory of allocation preferences. In G. Mikula (ed.), *Justice and social interaction*: 167–218. New York, NY: Springer-Verlag.

Lewicki, R. J. and Bunker, B. B. 1996. Developing and maintaining trust in work relationships. In R. M. Kramer and T. R. Tyler (eds.), *Trust in organizations: frontiers of theory and research*: 114–139. Thousand Oaks, CA: Sage.

Lewin, A. Y., Long, C. P., and Carroll, T. N. 1999. The co-evolution of new organizational forms. *Organization Science*, 10: 535–550.

Lind, E. A. and Tyler, T. R. 1988. *The social psychology of procedural justice*. New York, NY: Plenum Press.

Long, C. L., Bendersky, C. B., and Morrill, C. 2010. *Fairness monitoring: contextualizing fairness judgments in organizations.*

Long, C. P. and Sitkin, S. B. 2006. Trust in the balance: how managers integrate trust-building and task control. In R. Bachmann and A. Zaheer (eds.), *Handbook of trust research*. Cheltenham, UK: Edward Elgar.

Long, C. P., Burton, R. M., and Cardinal, L. B. 2002. Three controls are better than one: a computational model of complex control systems. *Computational and Mathematical Organization Theory*, 8: 197–220.

Mayer, R. C., Davis, J. H., and Schoorman, D. 1995. An integrative model of organizational trust. *Academy of Management Review*, 20: 709–734.

Meindl, J. R. 1989. Managing to be fair: an exploration of values, motives, and leadership. *Administrative Science Quarterly*, 34: 252–276.

Merchant, K. A. 1985. *Control in business organizations*. Marshfield, MA: Pitman.

Mintzberg, H. 1979. *The structuring of organizations*. Englewood Cliffs, NJ: Prentice-Hall.

Noorderhaven, N. G. 1992. The problem of contract enforcement in economic organization theory. *Organization Studies*, 13: 292–343.

Ocasio, W. 1997. Toward an attention-based view of the firm. *Strategic Management Journal*, 18: 187–206.

Ouchi, W. G. 1979. A conceptual framework for the design of organizational control mechanisms. *Management Science*, 25: 833–848.

1980. Markets, bureaucracies, and clans. *Administrative Science Quarterly*, 25: 129–141.

Perrow, C. 1986. *Organizations: a critical essay*. New York, NY: McGraw-Hill.

Rousseau, D. M., Sitkin, S. B., Burt, R., and Camerer, C. 1998. Not so different after all: a cross-discipline view of trust. *Academy of Management Review*, 23: 393–404.

Scandura, T. A., Graen, G. B., and Novak, M. A. 1986. When managers decide not to decide autocratically: an investigation of leader-member exchange and decision influence. *Journal of Applied Psychology*, 71: 579–584.

Schriesheim, C. A., Neider, L. L., and Scandura, T. A. 1998. A within- and between-groups analysis of leader-member exchange as a correlate of delegation and as a moderator of delegation relationships with performance and satisfaction. *Academy of Management Journal*, 41: 298–318.

Sengun, A. E. and Wasti, S. N. 2007. Trust, control and risk: a test of Das and Teng's conceptual framework for pharmaceutical buyer–supplier relationships. *Group and Organization Management*, 32: 430–464.

Shapiro, D., Sheppard, B. H., and Cheraskin, L. 1992. Business in a handshake. *Negotiation Journal*, 8: 365–377.

Sitkin, S. B. 1995. On the positive effect of legalization on trust. In R. J. Bies, R. J. Lewicki, and B. H. Sheppard (eds.), *Research on negotiations in organizations*: 185–217. Greenwich, CT: JAI Press.

Sitkin, S. B. and Bies, R. J. 1994. The legalization of organizations: a multi-theoretical perspective. In S. B. Sitkin and R. J. Bies (eds.), *The legalistic organization*: 19–49. Thousand Oaks, CA: Sage.

Sitkin, S. B. and George, E. 2005. Managerial trust-building through the use of legitimating formal and informal control mechanisms. *International Sociology*, 20: 307–338.

Sitkin, S. B. and Roth, N. L. 1993. Explaining the limited effectiveness of legalistic remedies for trust/distrust. *Organization Science*, 4: 367–392.

Sitkin, S. B. and Stickel, D. 1996. The road to hell: the dynamics of distrust in an era of quality. In R. M. Kramer and T. R. Tyler (eds.), *Trust in organizations: frontiers in theory and research*: 196–215. Thousand Oaks, CA: Sage.

Snell, S. A. 1992. Control theory in strategic human resource management: the mediating effect of administrative information. *Academy of Management Journal*, 35: 292–327.

Spreitzer, G. M. and Mishra, A. K. 1999. Giving up control without losing control: trust and its substitutes' effects on managers involving employees in decision making. *Group and Organization Management*, 24: 155–187.

Suchman, M. A. 1995. Managing legitimacy: strategic and institutional approaches. *Academy of Management Review*, 20: 571–610.

Tyler, T. R. and Lind, E. A. 1992. A relational model of authority in groups. In M. P. Zanna (ed.), *Advances in experimental social psychology*: 151–191. New York, NY: Academic Press.

Van Maanen, J. and Schein, E. H. 1979. Toward a theory of organizational socialization. In B. M. Staw and L. L. Cummings (eds.), *Research in organizational behavior*: 209–264. Greenwich, CT: JAI Press.

Weber, M. 1968. *Economy and society*. Berkeley, CA: University of California Press (original work published in 1918).

Whitener, E. M., Brodt, S. E., Korsgaard, M. A., and Werner, J. M. 1998. Managers as initiators of trust: an exchange relationship framework for understanding managerial trustworthy behavior. *Academy of Management Review*, 23: 513–530.

Wicks, A. C., Berman, S. L., and Jones, T. M. 1999. The structure of optimal trust: moral and strategic implications. *Academy of Management Review*, 24: 99–116.

Wilkins, A. L. and Ouchi, W. G. 1983. Efficient cultures: exploring the relationship between culture and organizational performance. *Administrative Science Quarterly*, 28: 468–481.

Williamson, O. E. 1975. *Markets and hierarchies*. New York, NY: Free Press.

Zucker, L. 1986. Production of trust: institutional sources of economic structure, 1840–1920. In B. M. Staw and L. L. Cummings (eds.), *Research in organizational behavior*: 53–111. Greenwich, CT: JAI Press.

13 Consequences and antecedents of managerial and employee legitimacy interpretations of control: a natural open system approach

KATINKA M. BIJLSMA-FRANKEMA
VU University, Amsterdam

ANA CRISTINA COSTA
Brunel University, London

In this chapter we present a natural open system approach to organizational control, as opposed to dominant approaches, which can be typified as either rational system approaches, closed system approaches (Scott, 1987), or both. Our aim is to promote scholarly understanding of organizational control by drawing on a wider range of possible insights than dominant approaches do.

Two scholarly traditions, both with rather strong foci on certain aspects of control, have been prominent in the field. The first tradition, represented by agency theory and rational choice models of human behavior (Eisenhardt, 1989), focuses on rational choice of control mechanisms by managers, with the underlying assumption that control choices are driven by effectiveness and efficiency concerns. This focus typifies a rational system approach. The second tradition, represented by bureaucracy studies, draws on agency theory and the critical management tradition (for an overview of this tradition see Delbridge, Chapter 4) to focus on reactions to managerial control by those subjected to it. The studies in this tradition have mainly highlighted the constraining, harnessing, distrust-signaling perceptions of control. Both traditions can be typified as closed system approaches, since factors outside the organization, such as organizational environments, are not included in the analysis of employee reactions.

We propose to move from these rather narrow rational and closed system approaches to a more encompassing understanding of factors involved in shaping managerial choices and reactions of employees. Following Scott's (1987) distinction between natural versus rational

396

system perspectives and open versus closed system perspectives, resulting in four possible combinations, our approach can be typified as *natural open*, given the theories we draw on. These theories, institutional theory and organizational culture theory, represent an *open* system approach given the ample attention paid to the relation between organizations and the environment they are embedded in as a source of understanding internal structures and procedures, such as control mechanisms. Closed system approaches, on the contrary, concentrate on internal factors to understand structures and procedures. Open system approaches conceive managerial tasks and challenges differently. Institutional theory argues that, next to a technical environment that poses effectiveness and efficiency demands, organizations are also embedded in an institutional environment which poses legitimacy demands. Managers must deal with these two types of demands and with tensions that may occur between them.

Institutional theory and organizational culture theory also represent a *natural* system approach because, contrary to a rational system approach which sees organizations as shaped by rational choices managers make, these theories see organizations as social systems in which all organizational members contribute to shaping the organization in both interaction- and meaning-giving processes. This means that research on organizational control focuses on matters such as relations between controllers and controlled, both groups' interpretations of control, and their perceptions of legitimacy. The history of the organization, moreover, is studied as a source of understanding the present.

In the *natural open* system approach chosen, positive and negative interpretations of and reactions to control can surface in the analysis, while these interpretations are seen as partly dependent on current interpretations within the environment of the organization and the wider society. We expect our approach to make positive interpretations of control as understandable as the constraining, distrust signaling aspects mainly focused on so far. This proposed direction is in accord with a slight shift in the control field toward acknowledging beneficial effects of control, experienced by subordinates, as well as detrimental effects (Adler and Borys, 1996; Bijlsma-Frankema and Van de Bunt, 2003; Cardinal, 2001; Chalykoff and Kochan, 1989; Niehoff and Moorman, 1993; Sitkin and Pablo, 1992; Sitkin, 1995).

A second aim of this chapter is to develop a framework for research. Our framework is based on two core ideas. First, we contend that in order to understand organizational control, a core question to be answered is: *Why does control work in some situations and not in others?* Following Cardinal *et al.* (2004), who build on Cyert and March (1963) and Merchant (1985, in Cardinal *et al.*, 2004), we define control as "a system through which managers seek to align employee capabilities, activities, and performance with the organization's goals and aspirations." In order to answer this core question, one cannot focus only on managerial choices and neglect how those controlled interpret control and react to it. This means that *the relation between* managers and subordinates deserves more attention than has been paid lately. More specifically, the framework should allow analysis of the relation between *managerial control choices,* which involve *managerial considerations,* and *interpretations of and reactions to control by subordinates.* These matters are typically studied in an approach that is characterized as natural.

With these goals in mind we build on the seminal work of Alvin Gouldner (1954) who, in his study of a gypsum mine, distinguished three types of bureaucracy, representative-centered, punishment-centered, and mock bureaucracy, based on the question whether organizational rules and procedures served the interests of managers and/or of workers or neither party. By this way of framing his analysis, Gouldner put the matter of *appropriateness interpretations by managers and employees* central in the study of managerial control and consequences of control. Building on his work, the concept of *legitimacy interpretations* is central to our framework. The concept of legitimacy is, furthermore, a core concept in institutional theory.

A second idea underlying our framework is that studying organizational control should involve understanding how control choices and considerations of managers on the one hand and interpretations and reactions of employees on the other hand, are co-shaped, not only by the efficiency and effectiveness demands of the technical environment, as rational system approaches tend to stress, but also by the demands of the institutional field, of which legitimacy is a core demand. Building on institutional theory, we contend that key to the valence of interpretations and behavioral consequences of control is whether, given the explicit or implicit *legitimization* of a control mechanism by management, it is *legitimate* in the eyes of those controlled.[1] If a control mechanism is deemed appropriate by organizational members, they will accept it, rather than involuntarily comply, and positive consequences for the organization can be expected in the form of in-role and extra-role behaviors (Chalykoff and Kochan, 1989; Niehoff and Moorman, 1993). We will build on research in which these effects are shown to support the credibility of our approach.

This chapter will be structured into five parts. In the first part, we will explain managerial control as a multi-faceted phenomenon, involving managing tensions between different, sometimes contradictory, meanings. We will discuss four sources of legitimacy that, in the history of management and organization, have been accumulated in the institutional field, available for managers to draw on. In the second part, employee interpretations of control are discussed, and the relevance and effects of the four sources of legitimacy are validated with theory and research findings. In the third part, we introduce the concepts of salience structure and culture to understand how these four sources influence legitimacy experiences of managers and employees and how the experiences of both groups are related. In the fourth part, several of the insights developed are illustrated with a case of a dairy plant. In the last part, conclusions will be drawn and directions for future research will be outlined.

Managerial control

A *natural open approach*

The theories we draw on in this chapter, institutional theory and organizational culture theory, can both be typified as *natural open* system approaches. As mentioned before, they represent an *open* system approach given the ample attention paid to the relation between organizations and the environment they are embedded in as a source of understanding control mechanisms. Institutional theory argues that, next to a technical environment that poses effectiveness and efficiency demands, organizations are also embedded in an institutional environment that poses legitimacy demands.

Next to *open* system approaches, institutional theory and organizational culture theory can be typified as *natural* system approaches. First, both theories are interpretative in nature. This means that, contrary to rational system approaches, human beings are seen less as driven by calculation and benefit maximizing, and more as actively engaged in sense making and interpretation of the situations they are in. "Legitimacy is in the eyes of the beholder" is a characteristic argument in a natural approach. A second characteristic, applicable to both theories, is that organizations are seen as social systems. Legitimacy of a control mechanism is not seen as an individual, but as a socially constructed interpretation, a characteristic of a group or collective. This means that research on organizational control encompasses more than exploring considerations of individual managers and studying formal structures. Managers are not seen as isolated individuals, but as "actors in interaction, who constitute social structures, which, in turn, constitute actors" (Scott, 2001: 67). To understand why a specific control mechanism is applied in an organization, its embeddedness in the culture of the organization must be understood as well as how this control mechanism relates to the institutional field in which this organization is embedded.

This social system notion also implies that given different factors involved, tensions may arise in interpretation processes. For instance, tensions between groups, such as management and employees, may lead to different interpretations regarding the legitimacy of a control mechanism based on subcultures. Also within groups, actors may find themselves balancing different, sometimes contradictory, meanings at a time. In interpretative approaches, attention is paid to mechanisms people employ to deal with this problem. Implicit in our framework is the notion that selective interpretation, in which some features of the social world are made more salient than others, is such a mechanism. Weick (1995) denotes selectivity as one of the characteristics of sense making.

A third central notion in a natural system approach, which can be found in both institutional theory and organizational culture theory, is the relevance of history to understanding the present of an organization or an institutional field. This point is made very strongly in the theory of organizational culture, as proposed by Schein (1992). This theory argues that successful solutions to past problems shape present cultures, in which these solutions are preferred and taken-for-granted. In a similar vein, institutional theory argues that organizational procedures, such as control mechanisms, if proven successful or found legitimate by employees, will become laden with value and embraced based on tradition. In accord with this insight, we will research the history of the institutional field of organization and management to get insight in how ideas about legitimacy of managerial actions have developed, and to find the present sources of legitimacy on which managers can draw in choosing control mechanisms for their organization.

Institutional theory: balancing demands from two fields

In institutional theory, organizational control mechanisms are understood as codetermined by their effectiveness and perceived legitimacy within the institutional environment. Following Suchman (1995), legitimacy is defined as "a generalized perception or assumption that the actions of an entity are desirable, proper or appropriate within some socially constructed system of norms, values and definitions."[2] Legitimacy is in the eye of the beholders and a social constructed phenomenon. As Colyvas and Powell (2006: 309) note: "A central feature of legitimacy is that it resides in collectivities as widely shared presumptions."

Institutional theory argues that organizations face two different types of demands regarding the practices and processes they install within their firm, effectiveness and efficiency demands of the task environment, and legitimacy demands of the institutional environment. The institutional environment is seen as a warehouse full of legitimate examples of structures and processes managers can draw on in the design of their organization. "Do what successful others do" is the key to legitimacy. A core argument of institutional theory is that if the demands of the two environments turn out to be incongruent, the success of the organization will depend more strongly on meeting the demand for legitimacy than the demands of the task environment. As Meyer and Rowan (1977: 352) argued: "Organizational success depends on factors other than the efficient coordination and control of productive activities. Independent of their productive efficiency, organizations which exist in highly elaborated institutional environments and succeed in becoming isomorphic with these environments gain the legitimacy and resources needed to survive."

This argument implies that successful organizations will employ control mechanisms with a high level of legitimacy within the institutional environment they operate in. If the legitimacy claim implicit in the underlying managerial philosophy is accepted by organizational members, positive effects on organizational goal realization will follow. It can thus be expected that managers will take expected legitimacy in the eyes of employees into account in pondering on which control mechanisms to install in their organization. However, the legitimacy of a control mechanism in the institutional field, on which employees also draw in forming their interpretations of legitimacy, is not a static phenomenon. It can change under the influence of societal developments and the spirit of the age, developments in organizational forms, and changing experiences in the field of management, as the next paragraphs illustrate.

Developments within the institutional field: driven by paradox

From the start of the industrial revolution, a central challenge for organization theory and management has been the matter of how to control "the human factor," given the unique nature of this vital resource. Human resources cannot be purchased and owned by the employer like a raw material, because the service (labor energy) and the provider (the worker) are indivisible, which means that the workers have considerable control over how much physical and mental energy they will exert (Jaffee, 2001). This brings the matter of legitimacy of a control form to the fore, because if employees experience a control mechanism as appropriate, they will accept it and comply with it. Over time, the mode will become value-laden, that is, that they attach value to this practice and embrace it based on tradition or because it has become taken-for-granted, and is thought of as the only possible way to do things (Zucker, 1986). Eventually, a rationalized myth (Meyer and Rowan, 1977) may be built around it such that organizational members believe this embraced control mechanism is the most effective or efficient even if these claims are no longer clearly substantiated.

On the other hand, if legitimization fails, acceptance and compliance of employees can be expected to be negatively affected, and their control can be exerted against management. Jaffee (2001) provides a historic example, based on the study of R. Hoxie (as cited in Jaffee, 2001). Hoxie was a special investigator appointed by the US Commission on Industrial Relations, to examine the effectiveness of Taylor's system of factory management. He concluded that Taylor's "scientific management" had failed, because it curbed the autonomy of workers so strongly that it was deemed inappropriate by them. The legitimization proposed by Taylor and other advocates of scientific management, a combination of *scientific,* signifying a higher order value and neutrality of interests, and *democratic* (fairness), that is execution of control free of arbitrariness and fair rewards, failed to convince workers and their representatives as well. In their view, democratic would imply participation in decision-making by workers, which was not the case whatsoever in scientific management. Hoxie reported reactions such as turnover, absenteeism, sabotage, low levels of commitment, and collective resistance. These reactions prompted revisions in managerial strategies of control.

Given the vulnerability of managers to unproductive reactions of employees, it can be expected that in adopting control mechanisms, most managers will, next to considering criteria of effectiveness and efficiency, ponder on their appropriateness in the eyes of employees. Considering these two different matters simultaneously is often a matter of trying to balance factors that are hard to reconcile. History shows that since the industrial revolution, the matter of how employees will react to control has been an ongoing concern of managers, which is often in tension with the demands of rationality: "The imperative to plan and control production encourages the drive to rationalize, the human subjective response to rationalization, which often defeats the purpose of rationalization, prompts the implementation of alternative management strategies. The evolution of organization theory and strategy is driven by this basic contradiction or paradox" (Jaffee, 2001: 26).

The paradox proposed means that an organizational practice which may promote organizational goal attainment and success, may produce unintended consequences, as well, in the form of human reactions to the perceived inappropriateness of it, which may negatively influence the very goal attainment and success aimed at. The choice of a control mechanism appears especially prone to produce this paradox, given the host of negative behaviors in reaction to control bureaucracy studies have documented (Crozier, 1964; Gouldner, 1954; Reed, 1988; Vroom, 1980; Walton and Hackman, 1986). These studies support the vital role of legitimacy to employee acceptance of the control mechanisms used within an organization. Managerial philosophies provide the rationale on which the legitimacy claim of a control mechanism is based.

Managerial philosophies: shifting legitimization

A natural system approach pays attention to the history of institutions, in order to understand the present. What can history tell us in this case? The history of the institutional field of organization and management reveals that several management models are available in the institutional field for managers to adopt, each with a managerial philosophy as underlying legitimization. These management models have been developed in succession, in which a previous model lost part of its prominence to later models. Although through their different accents and legitimizations, the latter models diminished the general legitimacy of former models, the former models are still around in the institutional field to be applied, for instance, in subfields with a cultural fit to a specific model.

Creed and Miles (1996) described three models which, in succession, have dominated the field as the most legitimate way to think about and act in persuading organizational members to pursue organizational goals: the traditional model (1800-), the human relations model (1940-), and the human resources model (1960-). The fourth model they present, an emerging model called the human investment model, which is based on a network-of-organizations concept, will not be discussed here (for a discussion of control in networks of organizations, see Hagel et al., Chapter 9).

Creed and Miles show shifts in managerial thinking and proposed acting. The traditional model, of which Taylor's scientific management is an example, is characterized by behavioral control through close supervision and detailed prescriptions of simple tasks. The assumptions about human nature underlying this management model are drawn from theory X (McGregor, 1960), stating that humans are basically lazy and unwilling to work.

The traditional model was legitimized by the value employees attach to *justice* and the assumption that most people *do not value self-direction, self-control, and self-actualization* in a work context. It was expected that in the eyes of employees highly valued *fairness* of treatment and pay would outweigh the threat to the value of *autonomy*, which would result in the experience of appropriateness and compliant behavior.[3] The reactions to Taylor's model of scientific management, discussed above, suggests that – contrary to the expectations of managers who adopted the model – it so seriously threatened the value of autonomy that overall interpretations could not become positive. We contend, however, that contradictory meanings given to control mechanisms are a key to understand not only adverse reactions but positive reactions of organizational members as well. Both *autonomy* (Spreitzer, 1995) and *justice* (Cropanzano *et al.*, 2007; Mishra and Spreitzer, 1998) have been documented as highly valued within organizations. Contradictory meanings given to these characteristics of a control mechanism thus can be expected to prompt balancing on the part of employees to arrive at a collective interpretation of appropriateness or inappropriateness. In high risk organizations, for instance, close supervision and low autonomy for employees may be positively interpreted as curbing risks for employees, which, combined with a high value attached to fairness, interpreted as resulting from close supervision, may well lead to a positive interpretation of close supervision.

After publication of the Hawthorn studies (Mayo, 1933; Roethlisberger and Dickson, 1939), in which the value of human relations in the workplace surfaced as relevant to performance, the traditional model became criticized for not meeting the human need to belong, and gradually lost legitimacy to the human relations model. Now that providing belongingness had become salient as a source of legitimacy, next to autonomy and justice, all control mechanisms were judged on this legitimacy criterion.

Meeting the human value attached to *belongingness*, which is the backbone of the human relations model, is also widely documented in the literature as contributing to the well-being of organizational members, their self-esteem and their willingness to contribute to organizational goals (Ellemers *et al.*, 2004; Kramer, 1999; Lind and Tyler, 1998). The shift also brought changes in how relations between managers and subordinates were conceived of in relation to control. While in the traditional model managers tried to prevent group formation out of fear of "soldiering" (Taylor, 1911, p. 33, in Jaffee, 2001), the human relations model saw groups as sources of cooperation, if treated rightly. Moreover, where in the traditional model control was seen as to be exercised by managers only, the human relations model made some room for self-control by subordinates and a beginning of sharing responsibility for what happens on the work floor, signifying recognition of the importance of workers.

The implicit exchange offered to employees in this model seemed to be meeting the value attached to *belongingness,* be recognized as individuals, and a restricted degree of *autonomy,* in exchange for willing cooperation with managers. This model legitimizes control mechanisms which leave room for restricted delegation of responsibility to individuals and groups, as in combinations of individual and group output control with a more relaxed form of behavioral control. The human relations model thus added one source of legitimacy (i.e., *belongingness* or group *identification*) to *autonomy* and *justice,* already present in the institutional field as sources of legitimacy.

The shift from the human relations (HR) model to the human resources management (HRM) model took place around 1960, during the years of growing individualism (Hofstede, 1980), which was partly due to raised educational levels and increasing levels of prosperity in the western world. The higher educated employees appeared to be better motivated by intrinsic rewards and quality of work than by extrinsic rewards for "meaningless" work. Organization members' need for self-direction, in the form of competence exercise and development of competences, appeared to gain importance relative to their need to belong. These developments prompted the idea that stretching managerial controls to make room for competence input and development of employees would be a promising way to gain their commitment to organizational goals.

The HRM model signifies a clear break with the theory X (McGregor, 1960) assumptions about human nature underlying the traditional model. The HRM model is built on theory Y (McGregor, 1960), which assumes that employees are willing to contribute to organizational goals if they find their work meaningful and pleasant. This can be achieved by increasing their self-control, and offering them chances to exercise and develop their competences. Contrary to the traditional model, the value, attached to both *autonomy* and *competence exercise and development,* are seen as keys to make employees comply with in-role expectations and as a source of extra-role behaviors.

As in the HR model, the (expanded) subordinate influence and self-direction is present to meet the value attached to *belongingness,* but in the HRM model the centrality of this value is shifted to *competence exercise and development.* A second difference with the HR model is that compliance with organizational rules and goals is no longer the main aim. The HRM model aims at co-development and improvement of individual competences and organizational processes, by utilizing the hitherto untapped part of human resources more fully. The model thus added a fourth source of legitimacy, *competence exercise and development*, to the three sources of legitimacy already present in the institutional field, e.g., *autonomy, justice* and *identification*. In the next paragraph, the four sources of legitimacy will be further addressed from the perspective of the controlled.

Employee interpretations of control

Four sources of legitimacy

In this paragraph, we shift our focus from managerial understandings of legitimacy to the interpretations of legitimacy and reactions to control of employees. We contend that irrespective of the control mechanism, it is most important whether a control mechanism is experienced as appropriate by employees and why. For instance, a negative interpretation given to behavioral control is often grounded in a perceived lack of autonomy. Based on our approach, we argue that this is so only in cases where there is *too little* autonomy left in the eyes of employees, while in all other cases with sufficient autonomy levels in the eyes of employees, a positive interpretation of legitimacy, based on autonomy in the control mechanism can be expected.

We contend that the matter of legitimacy of a control mechanism will simultaneously involve four hypothetical questions: does the control mechanism leave enough *autonomy*? Does it serve *justice*? Does it serve *identification*? Does it promote *competence exercise and development*? In each of these sources of legitimacy it can be hypothesized that if the answer is yes, an interpretation of legitimacy is produced, if the answer is no, a legitimacy interpretation will not come about. So, in this line of argumentation, the difference between a positive or negative interpretation and meaning given to a control mechanism, and differential reactions in terms of commitment and effort is seen as strongly dependent on the answer to these four questions. Next to negative reactions to control, which dominated thinking about control, this approach can broaden our understanding of control to instances where positive meanings are attached to a control mechanism.

Legitimacy and control aim realization: research findings

We propose that the four sources of legitimacy serve as four possible sources of positive as well as negative evaluations. To support this claim we first examine how control could work to address these sources and the research literature support for the idea that realization of the aim of control will be promoted if the control mechanism is experienced as legitimate given a specific source of legitimacy.

Justice. Can control further justice? In general, the question can be answered affirmatively. Any form of control can promote the accuracy of the information managers have about their subordinates and accurate information, in turn, may further organizational justice shown in assessments by the manager and thus justice perceptions of employees, as Niehoff and Moorman (1993) and Reichman (2007) found. Justice has been found to promote institutional legitimacy experiences (Cropanzano *et al.*, 2007), and to positively impact commitment to team goals and efforts to realize them (Niehoff and Moorman, 1993), performance (Aryee *et al.*, 2002; Cohen-Charash and Spector, 2001; Colquit *et al.*, 2001; Kanfer *et al.*, 1987; Williams, 1999) and organizational citizenship behavior (Cropanzano *et al.*, 2007; Moorman, 1991).

Autonomy. Any form of control can be deemed appropriate if it leaves enough autonomy to the controlled in their eyes. This is mainly a matter of not controlling each and every thing subordinates do. The Hoxie study mentioned before showed that one reason why scientific management was not legitimate in the eyes of workers in around 1915 was that the autonomy of workers was reduced to almost zero in this management model. Autonomy is well documented as a basic human need within self-determination theory and hence a central concern of people. Self-determination theorists proposed (Gagné and Deci, 2005) and showed (Burton *et al.*, 2006; Lynch *et al.*, 2005; Williams and Deci, 1996) that if the need for autonomy is met by managerial actions, organizational members will willingly adopt managerial goals as their own and put in effort to realize these goals. The positive effect of autonomy on performance has also been proposed by empowerment theory and found in subsequent research (Spreitzer, 1995).

Identification. Belongingness, also referred to as identification with a group, is also documented as a fundamental human need (Ashforth and Maehl, 1989; Baumeister and Leary, 1995). Identification can be constrained, allowed, enabled, or promoted by control. On the negative side of the continuum, control mechanisms that leave little room to maneuver to subordinates may turn out to constrain the possibilities to feel positively connected to others within a group. On the positive side of the continuum, two paths from control to legitimacy surfaced from the literature. First, participation of organizational members in the design of control systems is believed to enable subordinates' experiences of appropriateness (Adler and Borys, 1996). Employee participation in work-related decision-making has been found to be positively related to performance (Locke and Schweiger, 1979). Second, managerial control can enable detection and restriction of deviant behaviors and free-riding by co-team members (Eisenhardt, 1989), which can curb negative feelings and promote positive feelings about the team, which in turn can enhance positive identification with the team and the manager (Bijlsma-Frankema et al., 2008; for a more extensive treatment of managerial actions which promote identification, see George and Quian, Chapter 6). Positive group identification is proposed and found to promote efforts to realize team goals and team performance (Ellemers et al., 2004; Haslam et al., 2003; Van Knippenberg and Van Schie, 2000).

Competence exercise and development. Of the last source of legitimacy, competence exercise, and development, competence exercise is documented as a fundamental human need in self-determination theory (Deci, 1985). Control can allow for or further competence in several ways. In general it can be argued that if control allows sufficient autonomy, competence can be exercised and to a certain degree developed. More specifically, social information processing theory proposes that managerial control provides cues to subordinates regarding which tasks are most relevant to managers. This can enhance the competence of subordinates to perform effectively. This effect was found by Larson and Callahan (1990). Another specific effect is that control can disclose suboptimal functioning of team members, in which case the manager can help these members to improve their competence. This effect was found by Bijlsma-Frankema and Van de Bunt (2003). Competence exercise and development are argued to have positive effects on commitment to organizational goals and efforts to realize them. Self-determination theory (Ryan and Deci, 2000) and empowerment theory (Spreitzer, 1995) both propose that if managers allow autonomy to employees, they will adopt managerial goals as their own and put in effort to realize these goals.

It can be concluded that all four sources of legitimacy are relevant in organizations nowadays. If managerial control is experienced to promote autonomy, justice, identification, or competence of organizational members, the interpretation of legitimacy will be enhanced. Legitimacy interpretations, in turn, promote members' commitment to organizational goals and their efforts to realize these goals. The four sources of legitimacy, however, do not always lead to similar legitimacy interpretations. In the next paragraph possible tensions will be discussed as well as how these tensions can be made manageable through a salience structure.

Balancing different interpretations: a matter of salience

For managers and employees alike, interpretations of a control mechanism, based on the four sources of legitimacy, may induce balancing, since the sources produce differential, sometimes contradictory, interpretations and meanings.[4] Organizational control configurations, which are a more complex phenomena comprising different control mechanisms, can be expected to further enhance the need to balance different interpretations in order to arrive at an overarching interpretation of the configuration's legitimacy. Yet, based on the notions of selectivity in "sensemaking" (Weick, 1995) and the notion of bounded rationality developed in decision-making theory by Simon, March, and Cyert (Cyert and March, 1963; March, 1994; Simon, 1955), it does not seem likely that all four sources are equally salient in every situation. From a decision-making perspective, March (1994) suggests that not all options are known, not all consequences are considered, and not all preferences are evoked at the same time. If these ideas are applied to how interpretations of legitimacy are formed, then it can be expected that in the balancing process, one or two sources, which are more salient than others, are considered most. We thus contend that a *salience structure*, in which the four sources of legitimacy are arranged by prominence, will simplify the balancing process (for a treatment of selectivity and salience, see Ocasio and Wohlgezogen, Chapter 7).

Yet, despite the presence of a salience structure, tensions between legitimacy interpretations, based on different sources, can be expected to surface. We discuss three of these *legitimacy tensions*: (a) autonomy-justice; (b) individual directed–group directed; and (c) compliance-development. An example of the first tension, autonomy-justice, was presented previously (the scientific management model). Very close supervision may be adequate to provide justice, but it may not be found appropriate by employees because of a perceived lack of autonomy. Conversely, managers who offer a great deal of autonomy and self-control to employees may have a hard time realizing justice, because they cannot observe employees closely enough to get adequate information about their performance. They may not be able to provide equity in the long run, which is needed to maintain employee commitment to organizational goals, as Wilkins and Ouchi (1983) notice about clan control.

The second tension that can be observed between the four sources of legitimacy is between a main focus on individuals or groups. A control mechanism which strongly serves the value of belongingness, for instance, by participation of employees in the design of the control mechanism, or by introducing peer control, may turn into a mode of governance which leaves little room for autonomy or self-development, as in cases of group-think (Janis, 1972) or strong concertive control (Barker, 1999). On the other hand, a control mechanism which allows high autonomy to employees, for instance, in individual output control of scientific researchers, may not be found appropriate by them because it is not effective in promoting belongingness, if that need is the most salient.

The third tension has to do with the aim of managerial actions, getting compliance of employees to what is expected of them, or furthering development of their competences. Groups for whom competence development is a highly salient source of appropriateness, may deem a control mechanism inappropriate because it is too compliance directed, prescribing too much and leaving too little autonomy for competence development. Conversely, groups with a high tendency to avoid uncertainty may find such a mode very appropriate, since for them competence development has low salience or even high negative salience, if they interpret development as a threatening aim because it evokes uncertainty.

A research agenda

Gouldner revisited: salience structures of managers and employees

What would our approach suggest in terms of a research agenda? In our research agenda the analysis in terms of a single control mechanism will be changed to fit the complexity of organizational life, in which more than one control mechanism is employed (Long, Chapter 12), mostly combined into control configurations (see Cardinal, Sitkin, and Long, Chapter 3). Furthermore, the theoretical approach we developed in this chapter is intended to promote a focus on several matters which, in our view, have been underattended in control research.

The first matter is to separately examine the interpretations of managers and employees of the control configuration present in an organization. To our knowledge, such an analysis has been seldom conducted since the seminal study of Gouldner (1954). The analysis would be aimed to answer questions, such as: which interpretations and meanings have managers and employees given to control? Which sources of legitimacy were more salient, which ones less salient (salience structure)? And can tensions be found between the interpretations?

The second matter is to study the consequences of congruence or incongruence of legitimacy interpretations of managers and employees. This matter is also inspired by the work of Gouldner (1954), who first analyzed which *consequences* interpretation congruence or incongruence could have for the functioning of organizations. Gouldner (1954) distinguished three different situations, which stand for three types of bureaucracy: (a) a representative bureaucracy, in which managers and employees experience the rules as appropriate, the rules are maintained and complied with by employees; (b) a punishment-centered bureaucracy, where one party sees the rules as appropriate, the other does not, but enforces the rules on the others; and (c) a mock bureaucracy, where neither party experiences the rules as appropriate and rules are neither maintained nor followed. The analysis we propose builds on Gouldner's (1954) work, but refines and extends the framework, by specifying theoretical ideas and theory-based questions underlying the analysis. We propose to examine how the interpretations of both groups are related, and whether there are differences regarding which sources of legitimacy are most salient, differences in tensions or differences in overall experiences of legitimacy. Second, the relation with performance-related employee behaviors and efforts should be closely examined, in order to understand the regularities in these relations. We contend that performance will benefit if employees interpret the control configuration as appropriate.

The third matter is to understand how legitimacy interpretations (in)congruence between managers and employees has come about and how these may be changed. We aim to analyze *why* management and employees are united in their experiences of legitimacy of managerial actions in some organizations and not in others. We thus extend Gouldner's framework to the study of *antecedents* of legitimacy interpretations (in)congruence of managers and employees. Based on the natural open system approach chosen, we argued before that to understand matters of legitimacy, the collectivity in which interpretations reside must be examined. We propose to include two collectivities in which legitimacy interpretations are embedded in our analysis. First, the institutional field which provides four sources of legitimacy for managers and employees to draw on a "warehouse of legitimate examples." The second collectivity is the organizational culture in which interpretations of legitimacy are embedded. The natural open system approach, furthermore, proposes that to understand the present, the past must be examined, that is, how legitimacy interpretations have come about, whether congruent, which integrates managers' and employees' interpretations, or incongruent, which can become a source of disintegration between them. An organizational culture analysis can provide insights in these three related aspects of legitimacy: collectivity, integration-differentiation, and cultural dynamics, as argued in the next paragraph.

Cultural dynamics

Why is it that in some organizations management and employees develop similar legitimacy interpretations of the control mechanisms used, promoting integration between them, resulting in willingness to comply on the part of employees (as in Gouldner's representative bureaucracy), while in other organizations incongruencies lead to employee interpretations of inappropriateness, disintegration, and low willingness to comply? This matter of integration and disintegration lies at the heart of a culture dynamic analysis (Martin, 2001).

Schein (1992) offers a theoretical framework to understand how similar (integrated) and dissimilar (disintegrated) interpretations of organizational actions, such as control mechanisms, are developed. He defines culture as "a pattern of basic assumptions – invented, discovered, or developed by a given group (organization) as it learns to cope with its problems of external adaptation and internal integration – that has worked well enough to be considered valid and, therefore, to be taught to new members as the correct way to perceive, think, and feel in relation to those problems" (Schein, 1992: 12). A basic assumption takes the form of an "if ... then ..." statement, in which the problem (if ...) is followed by the solution (then ...). If a group's solution to a problem has worked well over and over again, the assumption underlying it becomes taken for granted by the group and is added to the basic assumptions already taken for granted. Culture can thus unite employees and management *vis-à-vis* environmental demands and internal challenges, if these are coped with successfully. In such situations culture provides a shared lens, which determines which characteristics of the external and internal environment is focused on, which problems are seen as most salient, and which solutions are valued. The culture of an organization is partly unique and partly influenced by factors like the nature of the business, the type of product, risks involved in the production process, environmental culture, rules of the institutional field, and sources of legitimacy prominent in that field.

These notions about culture can be applied to the formation of legitimacy interpretations of an organizational control configuration. We contend that *justice, autonomy, identification,* and *competence exercise and development* signify simultaneously problems of *external adaptation* and of *internal integration.* On the one hand, the four sources of legitimacy are prominent within the institutional field, demanding to be addressed by managerial control in exchange for legitimacy. On the other hand, these four factors appear very relevant to employees, who also draw on the institutional field for their interpretations, and relevant to internal integration, because integration suffers if employees experience a control configuration as inappropriate.

Culture has a two-fold effect on manager–employee legitimacy interpretations. First, culture works as a lens, promoting selectivity in interpretations. By focusing on some problems, represented by one of the four sources of legitimacy, more strongly than on others, the culture provides an underlying salience structure, in which the four sources are differentially salient. If, for instance, the environmental culture is typified by "high power distance" (Hofstede, 1980), then it can be expected that the value of autonomy is less salient within the culture, while a low power distance environment will boost the salience of autonomy in legitimacy interpretation processes. Similarly, a low uncertainty avoidance environment will boost the salience of competence exercise and development. The second effect is that if the four sources of legitimacy, given their different salience, are successfully addressed by the control mechanisms used in an organization, the control mechanisms will be considered legitimate by all involved, and management and employees will come to share the basic assumptions that the problems of *justice, autonomy, identification,* and *competence exercise and development* can be best addressed by the control mechanisms installed.

Once shared interpretations of legitimacy are formed, they tend to become self-perpetuating and take the dynamics of a virtuous cycle (Gagliardi, 1986): in which "success further enhances sharing legitimacy interpretations and preferences for the control mechanisms concerned, and compliance with them." In a similar vein, Colyvas and Powell (2006) discuss the "conservative" character of legitimacy interpretations once agreed on by those concerned. They argue that a key feature of legitimacy is its self-reproduction. Once particular practices become legitimated, they are built into the social order, reproduced without substantial mobilization, and resistant to contestation (Jepperson, as cited in Suchman, 1995). In short, they become *taken-for-granted.* It must be noted, however, that strong cultures and strong experiences of legitimacy are not always beneficial for the organization. These conditions may foster rationalized myths (Meyer and Rowan, 1977), groupthink (Janis, 1972), and a weak ability to perceive or solve new problems that do not fit into the "lens" of the culture.

In organizations where success experiences are scarce, because a history of success is missing or where due to changes in the environment the culture has become obsolete, it can be expected that groups in the organization become divided. They will disagree on preferred solutions, and may develop distinct subcultures with dissimilar salience patterns in a self-reinforcing process of de-integration, a vicious cycle in the words of Gagliardi (1986). If incongruence grows, mutual distrust can be expected to develop between the groups. The chance that employees do not interpret the control mechanisms as appropriate grows, and with that the chance of non-compliant behavior. Our approach suggests that if a process of cultural change is initiated, realigning salience patterns seems an important aim to strive for.

Examining the viability of the proposed approach

In the next paragraph, a case of a dairy plant (Bijlsma-Frankema, 1997) is presented, to demonstrate several points that underscore the viability of the natural open approach chosen. A natural open approach is characterized by several distinguishing features. First, attention to positive next to negative interpretations of control and attention to processes in which tensions between interpretations may prompt balancing, enabled by a salience structure. Second, attention to embeddedness of individuals in social systems and collectivities, which may produce tensions between groups as well as harmony. Third, recognition of the relevance of history to understand the present. These three factors are not paid attention to by dominant rational approaches. A fourth characteristic is attention to both task and institutional environments, which pose demands that may be in tension, and consequences of success and failure in dealing with these external factors next to internal factors. This factor is not paid attention to by dominant closed system approaches.

In the analysis of the case we aim to demonstrate that these foci of attention further our understanding of control, control consequences, and control antecedents, beyond explanations that dominant approaches can offer.

Case of a dairy plant

Four years before the research took place, this plant, an autonomous family business with approximately ninety workers, was sold by the owners to a Dutch dairy cooperative. As a result, management of the plant lost its independent powers of decision about the relations with the external environment, planning, and investments, to the head office of the cooperative. For the workers, the takeover came as a complete surprise. They were informed the morning the new managers came in.

At the time of the research the productivity of the plant was low, the output quality was almost the lowest of all the dairy plants in the cooperative. Many mistakes were made on the shop floor, and machine failures often occurred. This was the reason the cooperative agreed to the research proposal.

The plant's future was very uncertain. Head office had plans to choose a site for a larger plant, to be formed by merging three plants, including this one, within three years. This decision was to be based on factors that could not be influenced by the workers or the management of the plant, such as the available infrastructure. In expectation of this decision, head office barely invested in the plant despite its outdated machines.

Key changes

After the takeover, the family left the company. They were replaced by a management team led by a plant manager. With the exception of two managers (including the plant manager), the members of the management team came from outside the old organization. A large part of the other executive jobs were taken over by employees from the cooperative.

The new management were given the task of "transforming" the old organization into an organization that would fit in with the cooperative. The rules and procedures existing in the cooperative had been introduced in the plant. This meant that some tasks were performed differently, especially quality management and the measurement of results. Besides, guidelines from the head office were applied to selection, promotion, and payment. In these guidelines schooling and diplomas were important. The company offered ample opportunities for employees to upgrade their education levels. Since the takeover, jobs had been reevaluated. Some functions had been degraded on the salary scale. Employees who did not meet the new schooling requirements of their jobs were offered other jobs, generally lower on the scale, but without loss of salary.

The new management intended to change the management style. On the one hand, greater distance was created between management and the other employees during daily business, since managers did not show themselves on the work floor as frequently as workers were used to. On the other hand, team meetings were introduced, in which employees were extensively consulted before decisions were taken. Employees were now encouraged to "think along."

Interviews: the workers

The old firm. The employees characterized the old company as a "genuine family business." Most employees knew each other well and were on a first-name basis. The atmosphere was personal, which included a feeling of togetherness. The market position of the relatively small company before the takeover made clients and suppliers extremely important. Flexibility and client-oriented behavior were considered both necessary and expected from employees. Employees proudly told about rush orders they worked on during evenings and weekends. During such times, the owners could also be found operating machines.

The money and equipment of the company had to be dealt with carefully. Things were always arranged as inexpensively as possible, careless handling of equipment (e.g., not cleaning it well) resulted in severe punishment. Despite the thrift, the employees received a salary above the minimum laid down in the collective labor agreement. Jubilees were celebrated extensively. Although good ideas, dedication, and hard work were rewarded with bonuses, some interviewees mentioned that these rewards were given rather arbitrarily. Management attached more importance to experience and commitment than to schooling and diplomas. Many employees had acquired their salaries and positions in the organization through hard work.

The management style of the old firm was typified as paternalistic. The management made decisions without much consultation, gave orders without giving explanations to employees, and expected these orders to be executed without criticism. There were not many written rules or procedures. The members of the board regularly walked around in the factory to inspect the production. Mistakes were heavily counted against employees. However, ill employees were cared for well and "if a baby was born somewhere, the managing director's wife would turn up on the doorstep with a bunch of flowers."

The plant after the takeover. The interviews showed that the employees felt much aversion toward the lack of clear guidance by management and the lack of strict supervision, which they had been used to. For the employees, the new management style was uncomfortable. Many of them could not even characterize it. In general, they wanted management to take firmer action and to manage more strictly. The management team was perceived to have little concern about the shop floor, the atmosphere in the company had become much more impersonal, and the new managers could be approached less easily. Workers felt that the new management did not make use of the experience and knowledge they embodied. Methods of working which "made the old company great" were discarded by new management. Money was wasted because things had to be arranged according to fixed guidelines (usually not the least expensive way), because overtime had to be paid now (also according to guidelines of the cooperative), and because mistakes were not given the same attention as they were in the past. Employees felt management did not provide the conditions for the plant to be successful. As a result, they had no trust in the management team's policies.

Employees indicated that they were less committed to the company and dedicated themselves less to it. Aversive feelings toward the bureaucratic reward system were strongly aired. In their view, commitment was not expected from them, in that "working hard is not rewarded any more."

Although they said that they did not work harder than strictly necessary, the employees also reacted negatively to the fact that the management allowed this unmotivated way of working. Compared to the severe punishments they were used to, hardly any sanctions were applied when rules were broken. Consequently, rules were regularly, even deliberately, broken. Customer complaints showed that cartons were filled with the wrong liquid, and even cigarette ends had been found in the finished products. An interesting observation was that the workers strongly resented the chances they had to break the rules.

Interviews: managers

The managers attributed the low productivity of the plant to two factors. First, as a consequence of the thrift of the former management, the machines had become outdated, and second, the shop-floor employees made too many mistakes and showed little motivation; there was too much grumbling and not enough good work.

The managers did not supervise in a strict style for several reasons. First, they were used to managing production workers who had been socialized in a workflow bureaucracy and, therefore, they did not need or want to exercise much supervision and control on top of the rules for the standardization of the work processes. They did not decode the grumbling of the production workers as a need for stronger leadership and instructions – and if they did, they rejected this need because they wanted workers to be more self-directive and less dependent on management. Second, they were sorry that the production workers had lost their preferred way of doing things overnight. The old plant was too small to survive independently, but the workers were never told this. They felt uneasy about the way their own company had handled the takeover. Third, they had not been able to convince headquarters that the future of the plant must be secured and investments had to be made. The uncertain future of the plant made them feel unable to offer the production workers the prospect of success in exchange for adaptation to the rules and regulations of the cooperative. They felt awkward about this and, as a consequence, did not react too strictly to mistakes and lack of commitment on the shop floor. Another consequence of the uncertain future of the plant was that the management team had not developed a shared strategy for solving the low-productivity problem. This was partly because they all reacted to the uncertainty of the plant's future with different strategies to keep their careers going.

Case analysis

We contended before that a natural open system approach would make positive interpretations of control mechanisms as understandable as the negative interpretations that have dominated studies of control reception by employees. The case showed findings which could not be made understandable from dominant approaches, especially the positive interpretations by the workers of the control configuration of the old plant. A most telling example is that the workers *resented that the close direct supervision they were used to in the old firm was not exercised any longer.* This observation clearly shows that close direct supervision *can be positively evaluated* and *can be experienced as highly appropriate by employees!*

Our approach concentrates on interpretations of workers to understand this reaction to close supervision. The combination of attention to history to understand the present, and the notions of tensions and salience, prominent in an interpretive approach, has produced an analytical framework for understanding interpretations of control. This framework encompasses four sources of legitimacy of which some are expected to be more salient than others. It is remarkable how well the framework fits the case description, made in the past (Bijlsma-Frankema, 1997), and how it promotes understanding of the findings beyond what other approaches could. Rational approaches of managerial choice, for instance, do not fit the indulgency pattern of the managers, who, feeling sorry for the workers because they lost their preferred way of doing things, did not supervise them as closely as they otherwise would have. The comparison of managerial and employee interpretations of the control configuration in use after the takeover, furthermore, prompts understanding of the low productivity of the plant. This low productivity was self-reported by workers (as having low dedication and regularly breaking rules), and was similarly interpreted by managers as a consequence of workers' mistakes, low motivation, and outdated machines. Table 13.1 gives an overview of managerial and employee interpretations of the control configuration and (in)congruence between them per source of legitimacy.

The table shows that while managers positively interpreted the control configuration as providing workers' *autonomy, justice,* and *competence development,* which all seemed to be salient in their view, the workers interpreted the configuration negatively on these sources of legitimacy. The interpretations of the workers showed that they did not value the autonomy, justice, and competence development provided by the control configuration as appropriate, because their preferences were focused on the control configuration they were used to. The increased autonomy granted to the workers, partly as a consequence of an indulgency pattern (Gouldner, 1954) employed by managers, did not add much to an interpretation of appropriateness of the present control configuration, because the autonomy given was interpreted negatively as a lack of valued close supervision. Justice considerations appeared salient, but not appropriately served, given the strongly negative feelings about the bureaucratic reward system: the workers felt that their competence, thrift, and hard work, which

Table 13.1 *Managerial and employee legitimacy interpretations of a control configuration*

Sources of legitimacy and consequences	Managerial interpretations	(In)congruence of interpretations	Employee interpretations: present firm	Employee interpretations: former firm
Autonomy	Indulgency (–/+), strict supervision not preferable (+).	*Incongruent:* autonomy not a salient preference of workers, they negatively value the absence of close supervision and guidance, while managers value workers who can handle autonomy.	Lack of supervision (–), more distance, less concern (–), lack of clear guidance (–).	Close direct supervision, punishment of carelessness.
Justice	Salary based on education (+), low arbitrariness (+), overtime paid (+), indulgency (–/+).	*Incongruent:* managers interpret the reward system as just, workers see injustice in not rewarding expertise and hard work, the base of the old reward system, and not punishing their deviant behavior.	Low appreciation of expertise (–), mistakes and rule breaking less often punished (–), aversion to bureaucratic reward system, working hard no longer rewarded (–).	Salary above minimum norms, based on experience and commitment, bonuses for good work (sometimes arbitrarily).

Identification	Cooperative good employer (+), consultation of workers and team meetings (+), uncertain future, no investments, hard to promise success (–).	*Partly congruent:* both groups regret that conditions for success cannot be provided. Managers positively value the identification opportunities offered by the cooperation, the workers do not interpret these opportunities as positive.	Management does not provide the conditions for success (–). They do not follow the old success formula of close supervision and reward of commitment and of experience-based competence (–).	Genuine family business, togetherness, working on rush orders, Jubilee celebrations, shared success experiences.
Competence exercise and development	Opportunities for training and education (+).	*Incongruent:* while management values the opportunities for competence exercise and development the cooperation offers, the workers miss the valuation of their competences, hard work, and commitment. Competence development in terms of education not salient.	Experience-based competence, commitment and working hard no longer valued (–).	Experience-based competence, working hard and commitment rewarded, not education *per se.*

Table 13.1 (*cont.*)

Sources of legitimacy and consequences	Managerial interpretations	(In)congruence of interpretations	Employee interpretations: present firm	Employee interpretations: former firm
Consequences for the organization	Low productivity due to worker mistakes, low motivation, sabotage, dated machines.	*Congruent:* both groups recognize low commitment of workers, breaking rules and making mistakes as antecedents of low productivity. Dated machines only mentioned by managers.	Low dedication, regularly breaking rules. Management should not allow these behaviors.	Shared success experiences shape salience structure and preferences: a success formula against which the present configuration is measured.

in the old plant underlied justice of reward allocation, were not valued any more. The workers also refuted the base for rewards because in their view it destroyed several factors their past success was based on, and with that their opportunities for positive identification in the present situation. The dairy cooperation offered another base for identification, by organizing team meetings and stimulating workers to think along. This base was neither seen nor recognized as appropriate by the workers. The dairy cooperation also offered ample opportunities for competence exercise, given the increased autonomy granted, and for development of competences by providing opportunities for education. The workers, who grounded the salience of competence exercise in their definition of experience-based competence, only perceived that their competence was not valued any more, resulting in an interpretation of inappropriateness.

For the workers, the most salient source of legitimacy appears providing identification, since their stories circle around the lack of shared success, a powerful opportunity for identification they experienced in the old firm. The managers did agree that they had not been able to provide positive future expectations, based on which the workers could have put in their best efforts to make these expectations come true. The managers were sorry for not having been able to persuade headquarters to invest in the plant, which for the workers would have been a tangible sign that the cooperation aimed the plant to survive and thrive. The managers expected, however, that the team meetings, worker consultation, and good secondary work conditions the cooperation offered would positively reconcile the workers with membership of the cooperation. This expectation did not materialize. Based on the four sources of legitimacy, the workers interpreted the control configuration as completely illegitimate. Our contention, that legitimacy interpretations of employees are key to the success of a control configuration, is thus illustrated by the case. Since dominant approaches do not pay attention to legitimacy interpretations, our approach adds insight that could not have been gained from these approaches.

Our argument that our understanding of managerial and employee legitimacy interpretations of control would benefit from attention to balancing of different interpretations, enabled by an underlying salience structure, cannot be properly demonstrated by the case data. The data do provide some preliminary signs that a salience structure underlies the legitimacy interpretations of the workers. *Identification* appears the most salient source of legitimacy, *justice* (based on reward of hard work, experience, and commitment) and experience-based *competence exercise and development* do seem salient but less so than identification, while *autonomy* does not seem salient at all.

A last aim of our approach is to add to the understanding of consequences of control configurations by studying antecedents of legitimacy interpretations. In this case the question can be asked how the salience structure and the legitimacy interpretations of the workers developed and why a high degree of incongruence was found with the interpretations of managers. The case data indicate that the legitimacy interpretations and the underlying salience structure of the workers are shaped by the culture developed in the old firm. In the old firm the problems were successfully solved by direct supervision, punishment of mistakes, rewards for hard work and thriftiness, experience-based competence, and flexibility. The shared success experience has confirmed the control configuration, infused it with value, and promoted its "taken-for-grantedness" (Schein, 1992; Zucker, 1986). This process makes the positive interpretations of close supervision by the workers understandable.

The old control configuration is retrospectively seen as the recipe for success and positive identification. Close supervision is a key, a factor that is seen as promoting hard work and commitment, which serves as an appropriate base of justice and a condition for the shared success experienced. The culture of the old plant underscored the low salience of the value of autonomy, the high salience of identification, and the salience of experience-based competence exercise. The salience of shared success as a powerful opportunity of identification and the lack of shared success with the present control configuration explains why such a high degree of incongruence was found between legitimacy interpretations of management and workers. Organizational culture theory argues that shared success with the present control configuration could have brought about congruence interpretations of managers and employees (Gagliardi, 1986; Schein, 1992), which would have resulted in willing compliance with managerial goals and increased trust in managers, further leading to success in a virtuous cycle (Gagliardi, 1986). Culture theory thus suggests that identification is an important source of legitimacy for employees, which if provided by a control configuration in an appropriate way, can produce clear performance benefits. This proposition could not have been gained by rational or closed system approaches.

Conclusions

This chapter presented a natural open system perspective on organizational control as a complement and an alternative to other perspectives, such as the rational system approach and the closed system approach. We have approached control as a multi-faceted phenomenon, involving the balancing of different and sometimes contradictory interpretations by managers and employees. The initial intention was on the one hand to challenge the idea that only rational choices and considerations are involved in managerial design of control mechanisms, and on the other hand that employees will mainly experience control as constraining and distrust signaling. Instead we proposed that, dependent on the perceived legitimacy of control mechanisms, these can be negatively and positively interpreted by different actors, with differential consequences. Based on an overview of managerial philosophies since the industrial revolution, we distinguished four sources of legitimacy available in the institutional field for managers to draw on in legitimizing the control mechanisms employed in their organization: justice, autonomy, identification, and competence exercise and development. The four sources may bring legitimacy tensions, as a consequence of which interpretations must be brought into balance. Based on principles of selective interpretation and bounded rationality we have contended that a salience structure, in which the four sources of legitimacy are differentially salient, will emerge in most situations.

In the second part of the chapter, we developed an agenda for research on the relation between legitimacy interpretations of managers and employees, building on the work of Gouldner (1954). First, we proposed to study the legitimacy interpretations of the control mechanisms of managers and employees and their characteristics separately. Next, we proposed to study congruence or incongruence between the legitimacy interpretations of the two groups and the consequences for the organization. Third, we proposed to examine the antecedents and development of management–employees legitimacy interpretations.

A cultural analysis was proposed to examine why in some situations managers and employees agree on the legitimacy of the control mechanisms used, and in other situations disagreement between the two groups can be found, where employees interpret the control mechanisms as inappropriate and react with diminished compliance. In the case of the dairy plant, next to other proposed insights, it was clearly demonstrated that the perceived success of the old firm had shaped the salience structure of the workers underlying their interpretations of the firm after the takeover, thus creating incongruence with the legitimacy interpretations of the managers.

In this chapter, an outline of how to understand the working of control mechanisms in terms of legitimacy, salience patterns, culture, and dynamics was sketched. Future work may further expand this preliminary attempt to outline this approach. Research is needed to test the framework and to further develop, refine, or redesign it. The matter, for instance of whether the framework developed can explain both positive and negative interpretations of control mechanisms based on the salience of sources of legitimacy, is a matter for future research. Different organizational structures and cultures can still be found in contemporary work environments and it would be relevant to explore under which conditions certain sources of legitimacy are more salient than others, and how the interpretation of control mechanisms between different organizational actors is affected by the underlying salience structure. A closer examination of how legitimacy matters are framed by managers and employees may present other characteristics of framing to be applicable to the data as well. The framework appears a promising step in developing a new, dynamic approach to control research.

Notes

1 The term control mechanism is used to refer to specific forms of control, such as behavioral control or output control. Although we acknowledge that organizations often simultaneously employ a variety of control mechanisms in a control configuration (see Cardinal *et al.*, Chapter 3; Long, Chapter 12), in the first part of this chapter we will use the term control mechanism mainly in a singular form to avoid over-complication of the argument we develop.
2 We will use the terms legitimacy and appropriateness as equivalents throughout the text.

3 Autonomy broadly refers to self-control and self-direction.

4 The relation between different sources of legitimacy is not exhaustively analyzed by focusing on possible contradictions, although we restrict ourselves to that here. Legitimacy interpretations based on one source may support and positively strengthen legitimacy interpretations based on another source. For instance, fairness interpretations may strengthen identification, as proposed by Lind and Tyler's (1988) group value justice model.

References

Adler, P. S. and Borys, B. 1996. Two types of bureaucracy: enabling and coercive. *Administrative Science Quarterly*, 41: 61–89.

Aryee, S., Budhwar, P. S., and Chen, Z. X. 2002. Trust as a mediator of the relationship between organizational justice and work outcomes: test of a social exchange model. *Journal of Organizational Behavior*, 23: 267–285.

Ashforth, B. E. and Maehl, F. A. 1989. Social identity theory and the organization. *Academy of Management Review*, 14 (1): 20–39.

Barker, J. R. 1999. *The discipline of teamwork: participation and concertive control*. Thousand Oaks, CA: Sage.

Baumeister, R. and Leary, M. R. 1995. The need to belong: desire for interpersonal attachments as a fundamental human motivation. *Psychological Bulletin*, 117: 497–529.

Bijlsma-Frankema, K. M. 1997. On costly frictions between organizational cultures and structure. In M. A. Rahim, R. T. Golembiewski, and L. E. Pate, *Current topics in management*, vol. II: 123–153. London: JAI Press.

Bijlsma-Frankema, K. M. and Van de Bunt, G. G. 2003. Antecedents of trust in managers: a "bottom up" approach. *Personnel Review*, 32: 638–664.

Bijlsma-Frankema, K. M., De Jong, B. A., and Van de Bunt, G. G. 2008. Heed, a missing link between trust, monitoring, and performance in knowledge intensive teams. *International Journal of Human Resources Management*, 19: 19–34.

Burton, K. D., Lydon, J. E., D'Alessandro, D. U., and Koestner, R. 2006. The differential effects of intrinsic and identified motivation and well-being on performance: prospective, experimental, and implicit approaches to self-determination theory. *Journal of Personality and Social Psychology*, 91: 750–762.

Cardinal, L. B. 2001. Technological innovation in the pharmaceutical industry: managing research and development using input, behavior, and output controls. *Organization Science*, 12: 19–36.

Cardinal, L. B., Sitkin, S. B., and Long, C. P. 2004. Balancing and rebalancing in the creation and evolution of organizational control. *Organization Science*, 15: 411–413.

Chalykoff, J. and Kochan, T. A. 1989. Computer-aided monitoring: its influences on employee satisfaction and turnover. *Personnel Psychology*, 42: 807–834.

Cohen-Charash, Y. and Spector, P. E. 2001. The role of justice in organizations: a meta-analysis. *Organizational Behavior and Human Decision Processes*, 86: 278–321.

Colquit, J. A., Conlon, D. E., Wesson, M. J., Porter, C. O. L. H., and Ng, K. Y. 2001. Justice at the millennium: a meta-analytic review of 25 years of organizational justice research. *Journal of Applied Psychology*, 86: 425–445.

Colyvas, J. A. and Powell, W. W. 2006. Roads to institutionalization: the remake of boundaries between public and private science. *Research in Organizational Behavior*, 27: 305–353.

Creed, W. E. D. and Miles, R. E. 1996. Trust in organizations: a conceptual framework. In R. M. Kramer and T. R. Tyler (eds.), *Trust in organizations: frontiers of theory and research*. London, UK: Sage.

Cropanzano, R., Bowen, D. E., and Gilliand, S. W. 2007. The management of organizational justice. *Academy of Management Perspectives*, 21: 34–48.

Crozier, M. 1964. *The bureaucratic phenomenon*. Chicago, IL: University of Chicago Press.

Cyert, R. M. and March, J. G. 1963. *A behavioral theory of the firm*. Englewood Cliffs, NJ: Prentice-Hall.

Deci, E. L. 1985. *Intrinsic motivation and self-determination in human behavior*. New York, NY: Plenum Press.

Deci, E. L., Eghari, H., Patrick, B. C., and Leone, D. R. 1994. Facilitating internalization: the self-determination theory perspective. *Journal of Personality*, 6: 119–142.

Eisenhardt, K. M. 1989. Agency theory: an assessment and review. *Academy of Management Review*, 14: 57–74.

Ellemers, N., de Gilder, D., and Haslam, S. A. 2004. Motivating individuals and groups at work: a social identity perspective on leadership and group performance. *Academy of Management Review*, 29: 64–74.

Gagliardi, P. 1986. The creation and change of organizational cultures: a conceptual framework. *Organization Studies*, 7: 117–134.

Gagné, M. and Deci, E. L. 2005. Self-determination theory and work motivation. *Journal of Organizational Behavior*, 26: 331–362.

Gouldner, A. 1954. *Patterns of industrial bureaucracy*. Glencoe, IL: Free Press.

Haslam, S. A., Eggins, R. A., and Reynolds, K. J. 2003. The ASPIRe model: actualizing social and personal identity resources to enhance organizational outcomes. *Journal of Occupational and Organizational Psychology*, 76: 83–113.

Hofstede, G. 1980. *Culture's consequences*. London, UK: Sage.

Jaffee, D. 2001. *Organization theory: tension and change*. New York, NY: McGraw-Hill.

Janis, I. L. 1972. *Victims of groupthink*. New York, NY: Houghton Mifflin.

Kanfer, R., Sawyer, J., Early, P. C., and Lind, E. A. 1987. Fairness and participation in evaluation procedures. Effects on task attitudes and performance. *Social Justice Research*, 1: 235–249.

Kramer, R. M. 1999. Trust and distrust in organizations: emerging perspectives, enduring questions. *Annual Review of Psychology*, 50: 569–598.

Larson, J. R. and Callahan, C. 1990. Performance monitoring: how it affects work productivity. *Journal of Applied Psychology*, 75: 530–538.

Lind, E. A. and Tyler, T. R. 1988. *The social psychology of procedural justice*. New York, NY: Plenum.

Locke, E. A. and Schweiger, D. M. 1979. Participation in decision-making: one more look. In B. M. Staw (ed.), *Research in organizational behavior*, I: Amsterdam: Elsevier. 265–339.

Lynch, M. F., Plant, R. W., and Ryan, R. M. 2005. Psychological needs and threats to safety: implications for staff and patients in a psychiatric hospital for youth. *Professional Psychology: Research and Practice*, 36: 415–525.

March, J. G. 1994. *A primer on decision making: how decisions happen*. New York, NY: Free Press.

Martin, J. 2001. *Organizational culture: mapping the terrain*. Thousand Oaks, CA: Sage.

Mayo, E. 1933. *The human problems of an industrial civilization*. New York, NY: Macmillan.

McGregor, D. 1960. *Human side of enterprise*. New York, NY: McGraw-Hill.

Merchant, K. A. 1985. *Control in business organizations*. Marshfield, MA: Pittman.

Meyer, J. W. and Rowan, B. 1977. Institutionalized organizations: formal structure as myth and ceremony. *American Journal of Sociology*, 83: 340–363.

Mishra, A. K. and Spreitzer, G. M. 1998. Explaining how survivors respond to downsizing: the roles of trust, empowerment, justice, and work redesign. *Academy of Management Review*, 23: 567–588.

Moorman, R. H. 1991. The relationship between organizational justice and organizational citizenship behaviors: do fairness perceptions influence employee citizenship? *Journal of Applied Psychology*, 76: 845–855.

Reed, M. 1988. The problem of human agency in organizational analysis. *Organization Studies*, 9: 33–46.

Reichman, I. 2007. Controle en vertrouwen, lang zo gek nog niet [Control and trust, a not so bad combination]. Unpublished Masters thesis, VU University, Amsterdam.

Roethlisberger, F. J. and Dickson, W. 1939. *Management and the worker*. Cambridge, MA: Harvard University Press.

Ryan, R. M. and Deci, E. L. 2000. Intrinsic and extrinsic motivations: classic definitions and new directions. *Contemporary Educational Psychology*, 25: 54–67.

Schein, E. H. 1992. *Organizational culture and leadership*. San Francisco, CA: Jossey-Bass.

Scott, W. R. 1987. *Organizations: rational, natural, and open systems* (2nd edn.). Englewood Cliffs, NJ: Prentice Hall.

2001. *Institutions and organizations*. Thousand Oaks, CA: Sage.

Simon, H. 1955. A behavioral model of rational choice. *Quarterly Journal of Economics*, 69: 99–118.

Sitkin, S. B. 1995. On the positive effect of legalization on trust. *Research on Negotiation in Organizations*, 5: 185–217.

Sitkin, S. B. and Pablo, A. L. 1992. Reconceptualizing the determinants of risk behavior. *Academy of Management Review*, 17: 9–38.

Spreitzer, G. M. 1995. Psychological empowerment in the workplace: dimensions, measurement, and validation. *Academy of Management Journal*, 38: 1,442–1,465.

Suchman, M. C. 1995. Managing legitimacy: strategic and institutional approaches. *Academy of Management Review*, 20: 571–610.

Taylor, F. W. 1911. *The principles of scientific management*. New York, NY: Norton.

Tyler, T. R. and Blader, S. 2005. Can business effectively regulate employee conduct? The antecedents of rule following in work settings. *Academy of Management Journal*, 48: 1,143–1,158.

Van Knippenberg, D. and Van Schie, E. C. M. 2000. Foci and correlates of organizational identification. *Journal of Occupational and Organizational Psychology*, 73: 137–147.

Vroom, C. W. 1980. *Bureaucratie, het veelzijdig instrument van de macht* [Bureaucracy, a many sided instrument of power]. Alphen aan de Rijn, The Netherlands: Samson.

Walton, R. and Hackman, J. R. 1986. Groups under contrasting management strategies. In P. S. Goodman *et al.* (eds.), *Designing effective workgroups*: 168–192. San Francisco, CA: Jossey-Bass.

Weick, K. E. 1995. *Sensemaking in organizations*. London, UK: Sage.

Wilkins, A. and Ouchi, W. 1983. Efficient cultures: exploring the relationship between culture and organizational performance. *Administrative Science Quarterly*, 28: 468–481.

Williams, G. C. and Deci, E. L. 1996. Internalization of bio-psychosocial values by medical students: a test of self-determination theory. *Journal of Personality and Social Psychology*, 70: 767–779.

Williams, S. 1999. The effects of distributive and procedural justice on performance. *The Journal of Psychology,* 133: 183–193.

Zucker, L. G. 1986. Production of trust: institutional sources of economic structure, 1840–1920. In B. M. Staw and L. L. Cummings (eds.), *Research in organizational behaviour,* VIII: 53–111. Greenwich, CT: JAI Press.

14 Managerial objectives of formal control: high motivation control mechanisms

ANTOINETTE WEIBEL
University of Liechtenstein

Formal managerial controls, though almost vanished as a subject in contemporary management science, are still a ubiquitous feature of modern organizations. Formal managerial control can be understood as the process by which managers officially define their subordinates' performance goals and standards, measure and monitor employees' conduct and output, and tie rewards and sanctions to goal attainment. Though interest in control scholarship has waned, it remains a popular and current topic for the practice of management. A possible reason for the high practical interest in this topic is that formal managerial controls are thought to solve the *cooperation problem*, a problem which has been referred to as the core of the managerial task (Miller, 1992). The cooperation problem stems from the organizational members having different and often conflicting goals, and these individual goals often conflict with the goals of the organization. This problem is most pronounced in the case of the corporate commons. The problem of the commons depicts a situation where benefits are jointly gained and shared but costs are borne individually. Because no employee can be excluded from the commons, some amount of free-riding is likely to occur (Hardin, 1968). Simon (1991) argues that the quality and success of an organization depends vitally on its ability to solve the problem of the commons.

Thus it can be argued that one of the main managerial objectives is to solve the problem of cooperation. In general *two solutions* are discussed. First, one way to handle the problem of cooperation is to achieve goal alignment by drawing on employees' *extrinsic motivation*. Extrinsic motivation is motivation to engage in an activity as an instrumental means to an end (Frey and Osterloh, 2002). In this case, employees' cooperative efforts are "bought" by tying their efforts or behavior to sanctions or rewards. Second, goal alignment also can be achieved by inciting employees' *intrinsic motivation.*

434

Cooperative behavior is intrinsically motivated when employees cooperate for their own sake, because they find it enjoyable or challenging, because they endorse the values underlying that behavior, or because they have an intrinsic desire to benefit another person (De Charms, 1968; Deci, 1975; Deutsch, 1960; Frey and Osterloh, 2002). In this case, employees' goals are aligned through goal compatibility or goal transformation.

In management science, the purpose of formal managerial control is to influence the probability that people will behave in ways that lead to the attainment of organizational goals by regulating activities through hierarchical authority (see for example Fayol and Urwick, 1963; Gulati, 1998; Snell, 1992) or through performance evaluation (see for example Eisenhardt, 1985; Jensen and Meckling, 1976). Thus, formal managerial control is thought to secure cooperative efforts by means of extrinsic motivation: common goals are defined, goal attainment is monitored by the management, and employees' compliance is rewarded or sanctioned depending on their compliance. According to this view, formal control is effective as long as individual behavior can be monitored or outcomes can be attributed accurately to individual behaviors (Eisenhardt, 1985). Yet monitoring and rewarding fall short in inducing employees' performance in the case of measurement and attribution difficulties. In this case, particular employees' intrinsic motivation to cooperate is the more effective way to solve the cooperation problem. With very few exceptions, however, formal control has not been discussed as a way to incite intrinsic motivation (for notable exceptions see Adler and Borys, 1996; Gittell, 2000b). Rather, formal control has often been modelled and demonstrated to destroy intrinsic motivation (Falk and Kosfeld, 2006; Gouldner, 1954; Kruglanski, 1970; McGregor, 1960). As a consequence formal managerial control might lose its function as a prime governance device: in modern knowledge-based firms measurement difficulties are inherent features of knowledge work and extrinsic motivation may not suffice to handle the corporate commons.

In contrast to this gloomy perspective, I argue that formal managerial control mechanisms can influence intrinsic motivation positively if enacted and combined in the right way. The influence of managerial control on intrinsic motivation is extrapolated from self-determination theory (SDT) (Deci and Flaste, 1995; Deci and Ryan, 2000; Frey, 1997b). This theory specifies under which conditions external interventions, such as formal control, facilitate and under which conditions they inhibit employees' intrinsic motivation. An external intervention which furthers intrinsic motivation must support employees' autonomy, competence experience, and feelings of relatedness. External interventions have a negative effect on intrinsic motivation if they restrict employees' self-determination and undermine feelings of relatedness. High motivation control mechanisms, therefore, which seek to promote intrinsic motivation, need to satisfy three objectives: autonomy support, competence support, and relatedness support. How such high motivation control mechanisms could look like by drawing on empirical evidence from organizational behavior and psychological economics will be discussed.

This chapter contributes to the literature in two ways. First, a more calibrated view of formal control than is common in the literature in managerial science is offered (for exceptions, see for example Kirsch and Choudhury, Chapter 10; Long, Chapter 12; Sitkin, 1995). Formal managerial control is still most often discussed to offer a punitive, carrot-and-stick approach to the cooperation problem with the potential danger to create self-fulfilling negative prophecies (Ghoshal and Moran, 1996), to create distrust spirals (Wells and Kipnis, 2001) and to destroy intrinsic motivation (Falk and Kosfeld, 2006). Formal managerial control – when designed to meet the aforementioned objectives – can also be an important facilitator of intrinsic motivation and thus might even create a positive self-fulfilling prophecy. Second, and in line with the overall purpose of this book, it is argued that researchers need to go beyond simple dichotomies, such as "behavior or output control," to understand the functions and effects of managerial control. Included in this discussion are the enactments of managerial control mechanisms and of the combination of managerial control mechanisms that in certain configurations will have a completely different effect than in other configurations and thereby offer a more fine-grained view on formal control.

The cooperation problem revisited – governing the corporate commons

Simon (1991) argues that the quality and success of an organization often depends to a high degree on how the problem of the organizational commons is handled. The problem of the commons depicts a situation where benefits are jointly gained and shared but costs are borne individually. Because no employee can be excluded from the commons, some amount of free-riding is likely to occur (Hardin, 1968). The governance of the commons is thus foremost a problem of cooperation in the sense that employees have to be convinced to join the collective action. This situation has been analyzed in more general terms in the literature on social dilemmas (for an overview see Dawes, 1980; Kollock, 1998). A social dilemma situation arises if the actions of self-interested individuals do not lead to socially desirable outcomes. Dawes (1980) defines social dilemmas as situations in which "a) each individual receives a higher pay-off for a socially defecting choice than for a socially cooperative choice, no matter what the other individuals in the society do, but b) all individuals are better off if all cooperate than if all defect" (Dawes, 1980: 169). Because self-interested actions have been proposed to be a fundamental aspect of motivation and behavior, social dilemmas present a serious problem to the organization of collective action in groups and organizations (Tyler and Degoey, 1995).

On a very general level there are two ways to handle a social dilemma: a "control" solution and a "motivation" solution. The first solution is to establish an overarching hierarchy, a Leviathan (Hobbes, 1909) or a central agent (Alchian and Demsetz, 1972) who is entitled to measure, monitor, and reward subordinates for their collective action. Cooperation in this first solution is essentially secured by means of formal managerial control. Social dilemma research has secondly been focused on developing an understanding of the conditions under which individuals will voluntarily cooperate because they are self-motivated to do so (e.g., De Cremer and Van Vugt, 1999). For example, Simon (1991) argues that many workers go voluntarily beyond commands, because doing the job well "is not mainly a matter of responding to commands, but is much more a matter of taking initiative to advance organizational objectives" (Simon, 1991: 32). Many employees seem to be motivated by something different than narrow material self-interest. These employees are intrinsically motivated to contribute to the corporate commons through their organizational identification or through their intrinsic involvement with their task.

What remains contested, however, is how both solutions act in combination. In the larger part of the literature, formal managerial control and employees' self-initiated intrinsic motivation are conceptualized as antagonistic concepts. Drawing on the human resources tradition (e.g., Argyris, 1964; McGregor, 1960) and the sociological tradition (e.g., Fox, 1974; Shapiro, 1987; Zucker, 1986), it is argued that formal managerial control signals distrust and that employees react to this distrust signal by reducing their intrinsic motivation and their voluntary engagement (Kruglanski, 1970). Indeed, field studies in a number of different disciplines (e.g., Barkema, 1995; Frey, 1997a; Ramaswami, 1996) as well as experimental data (Falk and Kosfeld, 2006) seem to support such a negative relation between formal control and intrinsic motivation. Yet there is also evidence that formal managerial control and intrinsic motivation relate positively. For example, Adler and Borys (1996) show that formal control may empower employees by providing guidance and helping them to be and feel more effective. In a similar vein, Sitkin and co-authors (Sitkin, 1995; Sitkin *et al.*, 1994) discuss how formal control might facilitate learning processes and thereby strengthen employees' self-initiated behaviors. Cardinal (2001) shows that formal, managerial control can be positively related to innovative behaviors, presumably because it facilitates rather than undermines intrinsic motivation for innovative activities.

A more thorough look at this debate shows that these contradictory results stem partially from the fact that research on managerial control "remains seriously underconceptualized" (Cardinal *et al.*, 2010: 3). First, control conceptualizations of different studies tend to vary greatly. Thus, the contradictory results may simply reflect a case of apples being compared to oranges (Cardinal *et al.*, Chapter 3). We will therefore suggest that in order to disentangle the effect of formal control on intrinsic motivation, a "molecular view" on control seems warranted: the units of analysis are different individual control mechanisms and their enactment. Second, existing molecular research on formal control often tests individual elements of control rather than configurations of control mechanisms, and thus important interactions between the different control mechanisms might have been missed. I suggest that the combination of individual control mechanisms matters in the sense that there exist complementarities between control mechanisms, for example, "high motivation control mechanisms" positively interact in their effect on employees' intrinsic motivation.

An important step toward a reconciliation of these diverging views on formal control and intrinsic motivation is thus to specify what is meant by "formal managerial control mechanisms." Managerial control is any process by which managers regulate or adjust the behavior of subordinates in the direction of the organization's objectives (Cardinal *et al.*, Chapter 3; Challagalla and Shervani, 1997). Formal control refers to that which is written and official and is defined as an officially sanctioned control mechanism (Cardinal *et al.*, 2010). Drawing on an early conceptualization of Edwards (1979; see also Eisenhardt, 1985; Kirsch, 2004), I distinguish three generic types of formal managerial control mechanisms: (1) standard specification; (2) measurement and evaluation; and (3) rewards. *Standard specification* essentially entails the definition and specification of either goals, means, or both. It involves mechanisms of defining outcomes, behavior patterns, and process enactment. *Measurement and evaluation* are designed to implement organizational standards and individual goal attainment. They mainly involve the exchange of information. Typical mechanisms are monitoring, evaluation of progress, and feedback. *Rewards* (and of course also sanctions) are applied to tie individual incentives to organizational goals. Typical mechanisms are contingent rewards and punishments by means of monetary incentives, praise, promotion, and acts of reprehension.

I posit that the way these control mechanisms are enacted and combined will affect their impact on employees' motivation decisively. First, managers will show different enactment patterns in relating to their subordinates (Tannenbaum and Schmid, 1958). For example, formal managerial control can be delivered either in a participative or an autocratic style. Second, control mechanisms can be combined in diverse ways. High motivation control mechanisms, I will show, are combinations of complementary control mechanisms, which are geared toward improving employees' intrinsic motivation (Pfeffer, 1994).

In the next section, I will draw on a framework based on self-determination theory to analyze how formal managerial control mechanisms can be enacted and combined to enhance rather than to destroy employees' intrinsic motivation.

Formal managerial control mechanisms and intrinsic motivation in the light of self-determination theory

Self-determination theory and intrinsic motivation

The main question self-determination theory seeks to answer is under which contextual conditions individuals motivate themselves (Deci *et al.*, 1999; Gagne and Deci, 2005; Ryan and Deci, 2000). This theory has been developed both inductively by building on empirical, mostly experimental studies (for an overview see Deci and Flaste, 1995; Deci and Ryan, 2002) as well as deductively by employing a framework "that highlights the importance of humans' evolved inner resources for personality development and behavioral self-regulation" (Ryan and Deci, 2000: 86). The line of argumentation, in a nutshell, goes as follows: organizational and social contexts that enable individual self-determination have a positive effect on intrinsic motivation. Self-determination is enabled if three innate psychological needs of individuals are satisfied: the need for autonomy, competence, and relatedness (Ryan, 1995).[1] In such a context human beings act agentic, that is, intrinsically motivated. They strive to learn and to extend themselves and thus to engage within and with the context in a positive self-reinforcing matter (Spreitzer *et al.*, 2005). A context that forestalls need satisfaction, however, undermines intrinsic motivation.

The need for *autonomy* plays a central role in self-determination theory (Ryan *et al.*, 1995). Individuals feel autonomous to the degree that they perceive their behavior to be truly self-chosen rather than imposed on them by others (Ryan *et al.*, 1996). The need for autonomy as a prerequisite for intrinsic motivation was first introduced by De Charms (1968). De Charms (1968) suggests that the fundamental requirement for internal motivation is perceiving oneself as the locus of causality for one's own behavior. Hackman and Oldham (1974) too argue that an experienced sense of self-responsibility, which is based on perceived autonomy, is important for voluntary engagement. Spreitzer *et al.* (2005) assume that autonomy enables employees to act agentic: they are more likely to stay focused on a task over a prolonged period of time and to explore new ways of handling tasks.

Intrinsically motivated task engagement is also dependent on how *competent* individuals feel in acting agentic. In self-determination theory the need for competence rests on two components: (a) the need to develop new skills and new mental frames; and (b) the need to feel a boost in self-esteem. The first aspect of competence – skill and frame development – can be traced back to earlier concepts such as White's concept of mastery (White, 1959) or Bandura's concept of self-efficacy (Bandura, 1977). This need is more likely to be satisfied if individuals see a relationship between their behavior and desired outcomes (Locke and Latham, 1990) and if they face optimal challenges (Deci, 1985). The second aspect of competence – self-esteem – has been suggested by writers of many theoretical traditions (e.g., Bijlsma-Frankema and Costa, Chapter 13). It has been proposed to be a strong pervasive motive to maintain a certain level of positive feelings about oneself to "increase, maintain, or confirm ... feeling of personal satisfaction, worth, and effectiveness" (Jones, 1973: 186). It is important to note, however, that in self-determination theory self-esteem is not focused on interpersonal comparisons but on intertemporal comparisons (Deci and Ryan, 2000). In other words, for individuals' intrinsic motivation it seems to be more important to feel good about the progress made at accomplishing a task rather than about the fact that "I am better than my colleague" at doing things. This type of self-esteem is boosted by positive task feedback (Deci, 1980).

Finally, according to self-determination theory, human beings also strive for *relatedness*. The need for relatedness is portrayed as the desire to feel connected to others – to love and care, and to be loved and cared for (Deci and Ryan, 2000). The basic quality of the need for relatedness is that it builds on mutuality, that is, it is characterized by mutual sharing of thoughts and feelings (see also Aldefer, 1969; Baumeister and Leary, 1995). Mutual understanding and respect is likely to strengthen intrinsically motivated agentic behavior as it pronounces the meaningfulness of certain tasks (Conger and Kanungo, 1988; Hackman and Lawler, 1971). In addition, Spreitzer *et al.* (2005) conjecture that individuals in a situation of mutual respect are more likely to feel autonomous and capable of mastering job demands and, thus, relatedness reinforces the fulfillment of the other two psychological needs.

In the next three sections this general framework from self-determination theory is linked to research on the impact of formal control mechanisms (respectively to their enactment and combination) on intrinsic motivation. Unfortunately, empirical researchers in the field of self-determination theory have mostly studied the interplay of context structure and motivation outside the work organization (see Gagne and Deci, 2005 for notable exception to this). Furthermore the lack of conceptual consensus and fragmentation in control research prevents us from conducting a comprehensive and complete review of the empirical findings of this field. I therefore picked existing research in a rather opportunistic way with the aim of demonstrating the usefulness of such an approach without claiming to offer a comprehensive set of "high motivation control mechanisms."

The undermining effect of formal control mechanisms on intrinsic motivation

A quick glance through control research shows that two arguments are often advanced to explain the possible negative effects of formal control on intrinsic motivation. First, formal control, almost by definition, is seen as a form of externally devised influence on the work context and the work process of employees, and thus to be naturally "at odds" with the need for autonomy (Argyris, 1957; Walton, 1985). Second, formal control is often portrayed to interrupt social relations (Bijlsma–Frankema and Costa, 2005; Fox, 1974). It potentially signals suspicion (Kramer, 1999; McGregor, 1960; Sitkin and Stickel, 1996) and exacerbates the hierarchical distance between the controller and the controllee.

Two control mechanisms in particular have been discussed to thwart autonomy and interrupt social relations: reward and monitoring mechanisms. First, although still fiercely debated, reward mechanisms – more specifically contingent rewarding – have been repeatedly shown to undermine intrinsic motivation. Second, close monitoring has also been shown to undermine intrinsic motivation. However, as I will discuss in the next sections, evidence suggests that it is not close monitoring *per se* that is causing this effect, but that it depends on the way close monitoring is enacted.

Reward mechanisms. Reward mechanisms are discussed as a main (negative) influence on intrinsic motivation. As a matter of fact, the influence of reward mechanisms on intrinsic motivation has sparked a heated debate – also known as the rewards controversy – on whether and in what form rewards undermine intrinsic motivation (see Deci *et al.*, 1999; Eisenberger and Cameron, 1996; Eisenberger *et al.*, 1999; Frey and Jegen, 2001). By now there seems to be some convergence in opinions about the negative effect of rewards on intrinsic motivation (a) in situations where individuals concerned have intrinsic motivation in the first place, which can then be undermined, and (b) in the case of expected tangible contingent rewards (contingent on the degree of standard fulfillment) with low informative content (Gagne and Deci, 2005; however for a different opinion see Rynes *et al.*, 2005). These types of incentives thwart individual's feelings of autonomy as they recurrently (in each performance review) highlight the fact that rewards are only given if employees follow a predefined path (Frey and

Osterloh, 2002; Kohn, 1993). In addition, contingent rewards may disrupt mutual social relations if, as Gneezy and Rustichini (2000b) suggest, the introduction of contingent rewards acts as a signal to the employee that a former incomplete work contract is now complete. Under a complete work contract, however, social interactions are based on a *quid pro quo* motive. Thus efforts are exerted only to the point as being specified and paid for and intrinsic motivation "to go an extra mile for the partner" is undermined.

These negative effects of contingent rewards on intrinsic motivation have been shown in many laboratory studies (Deci *et al.*, 1999) as well as in the field (Frey and Jegen, 2001; Gagne and Deci, 2005). For example, Gneezy and Rustichini (2000a) analyze the behavior of high school pupils collecting money voluntarily, that is, without monetary compensation (e.g., for cancer research or disabled children). When these children were promised a bonus of one percent of the money collected their efforts dropped by about 36 percent as – presumably – their intrinsic motivation to "do something for a good cause" was undermined by the reward offered. Burks *et al.* (2006) demonstrate the relationship-disrupting effect caused by contingent rewards: among bicycle messengers, they find that employees at firms that pay for performance are significantly less cooperative than those who are paid hourly or are members of cooperatives. Performance pay appears to make messengers between 12 and 15 percent more likely to behave egoistically towards their coworkers (Burks *et al.*, 2006: 9). These bicycle messengers when asked to play a sequential prisoner's dilemma were more likely to defect than those bicycle messengers paid by the hour or working in a cooperative. The authors suggest that in practice this could mean that performance-contingently rewarded messengers are more likely to "cherry pick" the best appointments, regardless of whether or not they are the best suited from the firm's perspective to make the delivery.

In research on managerial control, the effect of contingent reward mechanisms on employees' attitudes and motivation has been thoroughly studied in research on the effectiveness of sales control systems (for an overview see Baldauf *et al.*, 2005). Anderson and Oliver (1987), for example, study the effects of contingent rewards on sales personnel behavior and motivation. They argue that the formal control of sales personnel can be categorized as being either more outcome-based or behavior-based. In a formal control system that relies more on outcome control, objective results measures are often used as a basis for strong financial incentives (i.e., sales personnel are compensated to a high degree on a commission basis). In contrast, the object of evaluation in a behavior-based formal control system is the behavior of the employee, whereby the evaluation of behavior is typically more subjective and complex. The reason for this higher degree of subjectivity lies in the nature of the control object. Typically, behaviors are more difficult to measure. The transformation process, transforming inputs into outputs, is often not completely transparent. Oliver and Anderson (1994) show that commitment to the organization and to the team and a greater interest in serving the agency are higher in control systems that rely to a greater extent on behavior control and thus on more subjective and broader evaluations than in output control systems. Under the latter regime employees were more likely to be extrinsically motivated and less committed to the sales team as well as to the organization (Baldauf *et al.*, 2005; Oliver and Anderson, 1994).

I therefore propose:

Proposition 1a. Rewards and sanctions that are administered strictly contingent on the evaluation of standard fulfillment will undermine intrinsic motivation.

Proposition 1b. Rewards and sanctions that are administered on the basis of a broad and more subjective evaluation will not undermine intrinsic motivation.

Enactment of monitoring. Tight monitoring is often perceived to thwart individual needs for relatedness and autonomy. Monitoring is seen to signal distrust (Argyris, 1957; Ghoshal and Moran, 1996; Strickland, 1958), raise relational detachment (Thompson and Warhurst, 1998) and strengthen an "us versus them" perspective between management and employees (Bijlsma-Frankema *et al.*, 2008; Fox, 1974; Sitkin *et al.*, 1994). Furthermore, Argyris (1959) proposed that individuals in highly formalized and tightly monitored environments are frustrated as they are hindered in developing self-initiative and a sense of relative independence to "stand on one's own two feet" (Argyris, 1959: 147). At the same time, however, some authors argue that close monitoring, under certain conditions, augments perceptions of transparency and fairness (Niehoff and Moorman, 1993; Westin, 1992) and thereby feeds individuals' needs for competence and relatedness. The question is what makes the difference in these two rather opposite scenarios. I suggest that the effect of monitoring depends to a high degree on the enactment of monitoring.

Empirical research shows that monitoring seems to undermine intrinsic motivation only under the condition that the controller holds a "controlling," that is, suspicious intention. Current empirical work supports McGregor's (1960) conceptual model of the negative effect of monitoring on working relations and intrinsic work engagement under the condition that the controller initiates control with a "theory X" in mind, that is, a supicious and negative view about employees' work morale. For example, Falk and Kosfeld (2006) test the negative effect of managerial monitoring in a two-stage principal agent game. The principal can choose whether he/she wants to monitor the effort of the agent lightly, moderately, severely, or not at all. Those principals who choose to trust, that is not to monitor their agents at all, fare best. For example, agents who are trusted show twice the effort of agents who are lightly controlled. In an effort to understand the underlying reason for the performance reduction, the authors design two games with different types of control: in the first case monitoring is chosen by the principal, in the second case control is exogenously given. As a result, agents reduce their efforts only in the first case, that is, what agents really seem to react negatively to is the suspicious/controlling intention of the principal and not to monitoring *per se* (see also the studies of Strickland, 1958).

I therefore propose:

Proposition 2. Suspicious monitoring will undermine intrinsic motivation.

The strengthening effect of formal control mechanisms on intrinsic motivation

According to self-determination theory, formal control mechanisms and their enactment that support the needs of individuals for autonomy, competence, and relatedness will strengthen intrinsic motivation. In research on managerial control three areas have been observed to have such a positive effect: autonomy-enhancing control enactment, relatedness-enhancing control enactment, and constructive feedback as a competence-enhancing control mechanism.

Autonomy-enhancing control enactment. It has already been explained that formal control is bound to reduce employees' autonomy to some degree. Yet to what degree employees perceive formal control to be an outside pressure that limits their agentic behavior depends on the way formal control is enacted by managers. For example, Tannenbaum (1968) distinguished a number of control styles along a continuum of highly autocratic, managerial directed to highly participative, employee co-directed formal control. The expectation is that employees are more likely to feel empowered and self-motivated in a participative control system (Conger and Kanungo, 1988; Spreitzer and Mishra, 1999). Through participation, employees are given some control over the decision process (if not always over the resulting decision) and a possibility to express their concerns (for a related discussion see Lind and Tyler, 1988).

Empirical research on participation shows some fairly stable results in linking participation with perceived autonomy. Studies have shown that employees' participation in general is a strong predictor of internal motivation (Leana et al., 1992; Mayer and Schoorman, 1998; Rhodes and Steers, 1981). There is, however, only limited evidence linking employees' participation in the formal managerial control process to intrinsic motivation.

Conceptually, literature on participation in the development of a set of formal control mechanisms, that is, of the control system, must be distinguished from literature on participation in the execution of singular formal control mechanisms. Participation in the development of a formal control system and its effects are discussed by Adler and Borys (1996), who differentiate "coercive bureaucracies" from "enabling bureaucracies." Enabling bureaucracies are characterized by a high degree of participation by the employees in the constant redesign of organizational control systems. Workers in an enabling bureaucracy typically show higher internalized commitment to their work and their organization. Sitkin et al. (1994) differentiate total quality control systems from total quality learning systems. As opposed to total quality control systems, total quality learning systems offer opportunities for a continuous and participatory redesign of quality control principles and mechanisms. These opportunities for employees to have a say in the redesign of the control system are discussed to raise the incentives for innovative, self-driven behavior.

Participative execution of generic formal control mechanisms is also shown to strengthen intrinsic motivation. Pearson (1991), for example, finds positive links between internal motivation and participation in traditional performance monitoring processes. Frey (1997a) looks at participative standard setting. He compares the amount of civic virtue as displayed in the tax morale of different Swiss states and hypothesizes that the more extensive political participation possibilities are, the higher internalized tax morale will be. In states with a high degree of political control by citizens, tax morale was considerably higher than in states with a low degree of participation (for a recent overview see Feld and Frey, 2007). Thus:

Proposition 3a. Participative development of the formal control system will strengthen intrinsic motivation.

Proposition 3b. Participative execution of formal control mechanisms will strengthen intrinsic motivation.

Relatedness-enhancing control enactment. It has already been suggested that non-suspicious monitoring might be a necessary condition for a non-harmful effect of formal control on intrinsic motivation. This, however, does not yet explain why formal control, also in the form of tight monitoring, under certain conditions, even strengthens intrinsic motivation. It can be argued that formal control under certain conditions enhances feeling of relatedness and thus strengthens intrinsic motivation. I suggest that (a) benevolent acts of formal control (Deutsch, 1960), and/or (b) formal control focused on intrinsic job engagement (Frey and Osterloh, 2002) will strengthen intrinsic motivation.

The positive effect of formal control on intrinsic motivation seems to be connected first to what could be loosely described as "benevolent managerial intentions," that is, managerial intentions that are based on mutual interest and respect. For example, in gift-exchange experiments individuals are more inclined to intrinsically cooperate if they assume the other player to have benevolent intentions (for an overview see Fehr *et al.*, 2003). Also De Cremer and Van Knippenberg (2002) demonstrate that people are more willing to contribute to a public good if a leader makes personal sacrifices to achieve the collective vision rather than personally benefitting from his action. In the field of control science, Piercy *et al.* (2006) show that such benevolent monitoring leads to perceptions of organizational support and to higher voluntary engagement.

Second, research in self-determination theory suggests that employees feel socially connected if their intrinsic engagement for the job is valued (Frey and Osterloh, 2002). This implies that employees may value those control practices which put a spotlight on their overall (that is, their work-related, their contextual, and their voluntary) performance. Furthermore employees should react more positively if they are informed about their performance evaluation in a way that is fair and signals respect for their overall contribution (Bies and Moag, 1986). For example, Mayer and Davis (1999) demonstrate in a field experiment that a performance appraisal system which more adequately reflects the "true" overall performance of employees raises employees' positive perceptions of managers' care and benevolence. Pettijohn et al. (2001) identify fairness in the evaluation process as integral for employees' internal motivation.

I therefore propose:

Proposition 4a. Benevolent-minded acts of formal control strengthen intrinsic motivation.

Proposition 4b. Formal control focused on intrinsic work engagement will strengthen intrinsic motivation.

Competence-enhancing control mechanisms. Employees feel competent with respect to an activity if they understand reliable ways to achieve desired outcomes. Feedback as part of the control system can play an important role in initializing self-efficacy-enhancing feelings. In a meta-analysis, Kluger and DeNisi (1996) conclude that feedback has on average a moderately positive effect on job outcomes. However, more than 38 percent of the effects found in the literature were negative. From a self-determination perspective there are two reasons why feedback seems to not always affect self-motivation as hoped for: (a) it does not support individuals sufficiently in their self-development and learning, and/or (b) it does not boost self-esteem.

First, Sitkin et al. (1994) distinguish two different feedback systems: a controlling feedback system, which is geared toward increasing reliability and small-scale learning, and a learning feedback system, which is geared toward exploration and large-scale learning. Of these two types of feedback system the latter system appears to be better equipped to assist individuals in their self-development and learning. It thus should affect intrinsic motivation positively. This relationship between learning feedback systems and intrinsic motivation has also been extensively researched in didactics. For example, Higgins et al. (2002) show that formative feedback in teaching deepens students' learning and students' intrinsic motivation to learn. Hattie and Timperley (2007) conclude in a recent overview on this literature that this learning-oriented feedback is enhancing a deeper learning process, and it enables intrinsically motivated behavior to a much higher degree than controlling feedback.

Second, Kluger and DeNisi (1996) believe that only constructive feedback can have positive effects because constructive feedback boosts self-esteem. Baron (1993) characterizes constructive feedback as feedback that is specific in content, timely, delivered in an appropriate setting, and does not contain threats and attributions concerning causes of poor performance. Empirical findings on the effects of constructive feedback on internalization are, however, not entirely conclusive. Oldham and Cummings (1996) find that manufacturing employees produced the most creative outcomes when they worked on complex, challenging jobs and were given positive and mainly informational feedback. Such feedback, according to Oldham and Cummings (1996), encourages employees' feelings of self-determination. Also, in a theoretical article referring to earlier studies, London and Smither (1999) state that organizations can encourage self-development and internalization processes by providing non-threatening performance feedback. In their own empirical study, however, they were not able to show that constructive feedback had a positive effect on intrinsic motivation (London *et al.*, 1999).

Based on this evidence, I propose:

Proposition 5a. Learning-oriented feedback will strengthen intrinsic motivation.

Proposition 5b. Constructive feedback will strengthen intrinsic motivation.

Combinations of control mechanisms – high or low motivation control mechanisms?

Up until now we have focused on the effect of single control mechanisms or the enactment of these on intrinsic motivation. In practice, however, managers are combining several control mechanisms into a control system (Cardinal *et al.*, Chapter 3; Long, Chapter 12). Such an assemblage of control mechanisms may have a unique effect on intrinsic motivation, as such combinations can be *complementary*, that is, reinforcing each other in their effect on intrinsic motivation, or *substitutive*, that is, weakening each other in their effect on intrinsic motivation. We refer to such a complementary combination as "high motivation control mechanisms" in the remainder of this paper.

The combination of control mechanisms with the aim to augment their impact on motivation and individual performance is not trivial as the meta-analysis of Stajkovic and Luthans (1997) shows. These researchers, in the behavioral management tradition, assume that the combination of three control mechanisms – namely performance feedback, recognition of work and contextual performance, and contingent rewards – should have a complementary effect on employee performance. They find, however, that feedback and recognition have a smaller effect on task performance when combined with contingent rewards than if used on their own (Stajkovic and Luthans, 1997: 1,141). In a follow-up study, they show slightly different results but nonetheless discover that certain combinations of control mechanisms produce unanticipated effects (Stajkovic and Luthans, 2003).

An explanation for this "riddle" may be found by reinterpreting the findings in terms of self-determination theory. In their studies, Deci and Ryan (2000) emphasize that a context conducive to intrinsic motivation always needs to show some autonomy-supportive characteristics. Intrinsic motivation is not encouraged if employees learn to be more competent, yet for a lack of autonomy are not able to attribute this learning success to their own doing. Also, intrinsic motivation is not furthered to the same degree if employees feel socially supported but cannot attribute this feeling of relatedness to a genuine interest in their personality. Drawing on the background of self-determination theory, the findings of Stajkovic and Luthans (1997) might be explained by a mismatch of control mechanisms as autonomy-thwarting contingent rewards are combined with competence- and relatedness-furthering feedback and recognition. A complementary control system would thus consist of autonomy-supportive control mechanisms as well as of either competence- or relatedness-supportive control mechanisms or both.

We find some evidence of these complementary combinations in the control literature. Empirical evidence for such an interactive effect of autonomy support on the effect of competence support (as signaled by constructive feedback) on intrinsic motivation can be found in the studies of Gittell (2000a; 2000b). She compares several formal control systems in the airline industry. All airlines typically train their management in giving constructive feedback. However, airlines differ considerably in the ways they combine evaluation and sanctions/rewards (Gittell, 2000b). For example, American Airlines used to rely on a system of high individual accountability and contingent rewards. Their policy was to trace each outcome to the function responsible and to tie reinforcement closely to performance. As a consequence employees' intrinsic motivation seems to have suffered as they spent most of their non-task-related working time with finger-pointing and cover-up activities. Southwest Airlines, in contrast, refrained from such a high degree of individual accountability. Problems (such as flight delays) were purposely not attributed to specific employees. Rather, these problems were understood to be a difficulty of coordination between functional teams. As a consequence, intrinsic motivation seems to have been strengthened. To conclude, although feedback might contribute to a better understanding of causal linkages between behavior and outcomes in either case and thus heighten experience of competence, it might have affected intrinsic motivation negatively by this system of individual blaming and autonomy-thwarting reward mechanisms.

We also suggest that the combination of formal control mechanisms which signal relatedness with formal control mechanisms which support employees' autonomy should result in positive complementarities. We find, however, only very few studies to ground such a claim. Empirical researchers in the field of organizational support theory discuss how perceived organizational support raises employees' internalized commitment (for an overview see Rhoades and Eisenberger, 2002). As a possible explanation for this phenomenon, Rhoades and Eisenberger (2002) theorize that perceived organizational support fulfills socio-emotional needs and is thus met by heightened commitment. The two most important antecedents to perceived organizational support are supervisor support and procedural fairness. A benevolent and receptive supervisor is perceived to be supportive. Procedural fairness in this approach is conceptualized and measured as the degree of participation (in decision processes in general). In another study Rhoades *et al.* (2001) scrutinize the interplay of these variables: both supervisory care and participation were found to contribute strongly and in conjunction to perceived organizational support and commitment. Furthermore, Feld and Frey (2007) find (intrinsic) tax morale to be a function of citizens' participation rights in the tax process and of a relatedness-enhancing respectful treatment of citizens by the tax authorities. Yet this effect of the relatedness-supporting actions of the tax authorities became significantly less important once citizens were not given extensive participation rights in the political process.

I therefore propose:

Proposition 6. A combination of formal control mechanisms is complementary in their effect on intrinsic motivation if autonomy-supportive control mechanisms are combined with competence- and/ or relatedness-supportive ones.

Discussion and conclusion

Managers can handle corporate commons by either relying on formal control to draw on the extrinsic motivation of their employees to cooperate or by influencing employees' intrinsic motivation to cooperate voluntarily. The application of formal managerial control mechanisms, though, seems to be a double-edged sword. It may enhance employees' extrinsic motivation, but it also often destroys their intrinsic motivation. In this article, I argue that a better understanding of the underlying mechanisms can be gained by drawing on self-determination theory. Through the lens of self-determination theory, formal control is seen to influence three drivers of intrinsic motivation: autonomy, competence, and relatedness support. If all three drivers are addressed, intrinsic motivation is strengthened by formal control. Thereby a formal control system can be established that addresses both extrinsic and intrinsic motivation adequately.

Implications for research

There are several avenues for future research. First, in this chapter the effects that two types of formal control have on intrinsic motivation are analyzed: behavior and output control. We have not investigated the effect of a third type of formal control – namely input control – on intrinsic motivation. We expect two effects in this case. First, a selection criterion for input control could be individuals' autonomy orientation (Deci and Ryan, 1985). Research in self-determination theory suggests that people high in autonomy orientation tend to develop intrinsic motivation for a task more easily than people low in autonomy orientation (Lam and Gurland, 2008). Second, recurrent acts of formal input control can serve to expel adamant free-riders from the group. This might be an important condition to maintain intrinsic motivation of the other group members for their cooperative efforts (Robbins, 1995).

Second, in this chapter the motivational consequences of formal control mechanisms were focused on. A more complete picture, however, would also reflect on the competence- and learning-related consequences of formal control. Sitkin *et al.* (1994) have suggested how different formal control mechanisms can produce different forms of learning. Formal control thus is clearly influencing the abilities of employees in a systematic way. Some learning theories, for example the theory of assimilation and accommodation, a learning theory developed by Piaget (1971), assume that in a context providing autonomy, competence and relatedness is also conducive to ability development. Empirical studies have shown that autonomy-, competence-, and relatedness-supporting contexts are correlated with more efficient learning (e.g., Black and Deci, 2000). Studies in the tradition of the human resources movement even explicitly link characteristics of formal control to learning: ability development is furthered by participation, delegation, and feedback (for an overview see Creed and Miles, 1996). Thus, I suggest that this motivation-focused view on formal managerial control could be easily complemented by a focus on the effects of formal control on individual learning.

Third, that high motivation control mechanisms may not only strengthen employees' intrinsic motivation but may also prevent what has been referred to as the "dilemma of the supervisor" is proposed. The dilemma of the supervisor is shown to arise if managerial formal control is carried out in a more "traditional" way, that is, with virtually no possibilities for employees' participation in the control process (Strickland, 1958). A manager, who is foremost concerned with supervision, may become victimized by his own controlling behavior. Employees' behavior (especially that which is consistent with management's objectives) is seen by management as motivated by the formal managerial controls in place, as there are hardly any opportunities for the employee to prove himself to be trustworthy beyond pure compliance (Kruglanski, 1970). Managers may develop a "jaundiced" view of their subordinates (Ghoshal and Moran, 1996). Further research should clarify whether a solution to this dilemma of the supervisor would be to apply high motivation control mechanisms and in particular autonomy-enhancing control. Autonomy-enhancing control, which is dependent on participation, collective standard setting, and collective standard supervision, should enable the manager to observe the employees' behavior in "non-controlled" work efforts and thus may alter his/her perceptions. This may ultimately even fuel a virtuous cycle of formal control as described in positive psychology in which high motivation control mechanisms fuel employees' intrinsic motivation and happiness, which result in higher performance and ultimately signal to the manager that a need-supportive enactment of formal control is the right way to go (Gavin and Mason, 2004).

Practical implications

The framework put forward has several practical implications. First, concrete guidance is given for managers and organizations under what conditions formal control and intrinsic motivation guide employees' behavior in a complementary way.

Second, in the light of the framework introduced in this paper, several tradeoffs when introducing formal managerial control mechanisms can be identified. For example, investing in training managers to provide constructive feedback might yield only very modest returns if at the same time autonomy-thwarting control practices offset the positive effect of constructive feedback. Also, the widespread use of contingent rewards in the form of pay-for-performance systems can lead to adverse effects which are often not fully accounted for in the literature (Osterloh and Bruno, 2000). Pay-for-performance as discussed in this article may reduce employees' intrinsic motivation. It is hitherto unclear how lasting this effect is. Preliminary evidence suggests that intrinsic motivation might be reduced for a longer period of time (Gneezy and Rustichini, 2000b). If this effect is of long-lasting quality, consequences for the temporal development of a control system may arise in that it would be unwise to introduce contingent rewards prematurely as they may create strong path dependencies. This effect may offset the better known positive effects of pay-for-performance (Rynes et al., 2005).

Note

1 In contrast to most other need theories, self-determination theory defines needs as universal necessities that are essential for optimal human development and integrity. While in most organizational theories, needs have typically been treated as individual differences (that is, people are viewed

as differing in the strength of particular needs) in SDT each individual is thought to thrive on the fulfillment of these same three basic needs.

References

Adler, P. S. and Borys, B. 1996. Two types of bureaucracy: enabling and coercive. *Administrative Science Quarterly*, 41: 61–89.

Alchian, A. A. and Demsetz, H. 1972. Production, information costs and economic organization. *American Economic Review*, 62: 777–795.

Aldefer, C. P. 1969. Empirical test of a new theory of human needs. *Organizational Behavior and Human Performance*, 4 (2): 142–175.

Anderson, E. and Oliver, R. L. 1987. Perspectives on behavior-based versus outcome-based salesforce control systems. *Journal of Marketing*, 51: 76–88.

Argyris, C. 1957. The individual and organization – some problems of mutual adjustment. *Administrative Science Quarterly*, 2 (1): 1–24.

  1959. The individual and organization – an empirical test. *Administrative Science Quarterly*, 4 (2): 145–167.

  1964. *Integrating the individual and the organization.* New York, NY: Wiley.

Baldauf, A., Cravens, D. W., and Piercy, N. F. 2005. Sales management control research – synthesis and an agenda for future research. *Journal of Personal Selling and Sales Management*, 25 (1): 7–26.

Bandura, A. 1977. Self-efficacy: toward a unifying theory of behavioral change. *Psychological Review*, 84 (2): 191–215.

Barkema, H. G. 1995. Do executives work harder when they are monitored? *Kyklos*, 48: 19–42.

Baron, J. N. 1993. Criticism (informal negative feedback) as a source of perceived unfairness in organizations: effects, mechanisms, and countermeasures. In R. Cropanzano (ed.), *Justice in the workplace:* 150–170. Hillsdale, NJ: Erlbaum Associates.

Baumeister, R. F. and Leary, M. R. 1995. The need to belong: desire for interpersonal attachments as a fundamental human motivation. *Psychological Bulletin*, 117: 497–529.

Bies, R. J. and Moag, J. S. 1986. Interactional justice: communication criteria of fairness. In R. J. Lewicki, B. H. Sheppard, and B. H. Bazerman (eds.), *Research on negotiations in organizations*, I: 43–55. Greenwich CT: JAI.

Bijlsma-Frankema, K. and Costa, A. C. 2005. Understanding the trust-control nexus. *International Sociology*, 20 (3): 259–282.

Bijlsma-Frankema, K., Sitkin, S. B., and Weibel, A. 2008. Breaking out of inter-group distrust: judges and administrators in a court of law. *Hochschule Liechtenstein*, 1–54.

Black, A. E. and Deci, E. L. 2000. The effects of instructors' autonomy support and students' autonomous motivation on learning organic chemistry: a self-determination theory perspective. *Science Education*, 84 (6): 740–756.

Burks, S., Carpenter, J., and Goette, L. 2006. *Performance pay and the erosion of worker cooperation field experimental evidence.* Bonn: IZA.

Cardinal, L. B. 2001. Technological innovation in the pharmaceutical industry: the use of organizational control in managing research and development. *Organization Science*, 12 (1): 19–36.

Cardinal, L. B., Sitkin, S. B., Long, C. P., and Miller, C. C. 2010. The genesis of control configurations during organizational founding. Working paper.

Challagalla, G. N. and Shervani, T. A. 1997. A measurement model of the dimensions and types of output and behavior control: an empirical test in a salesforce context. *Journal of Business Research*, 39 (3): 159–172.

Conger, J. A. and Kanungo, R. N. 1988. The empowerment process: integrating theory and practice. *Academy of Management Review*, 13 (3): 471–482.

Creed, W. E. D. and Miles, E. R. 1996. Trust in organizations. A conceptual framework linking organizational forms, managerial philosophies, and the opportunity costs of control. In R. M. Kramer and T. Tyler (eds.), *Trust in organizations: frontiers of theory and research:* 16–38. Thousand Oaks, CA: Sage Publications.

Dawes, R. M. 1980. Social dilemmas. *Annual Review of Psychology*, 31: 169–193.

De Charms, R. 1968. *Personal causation: the internal affective determinants of behavior.* New York, NY: Academic Press.

De Cremer, D. and Van Knippenberg, D. 2002. How do leaders promote cooperation? The effects of charisma and procedural fairness. *Journal of Applied Psychology*, 87 (5): 858–866.

De Cremer, D. and Van Vugt, M. 1999. Social identification effects in social dilemmas: a transformation of motives. *European Journal of Social Psychology*, 29 (7): 871–893.

Deci, E. L. 1975. *Intrinsic motivation.* New York, NY: Plenum Press.
  1980. *The psychology of self-determination.* Lexington, MA: D. C. Heath Lexington Books.
  1985. *Intrinsic motivation and self-determination in human behavior.* New York, NY: Plenum Press.

Deci, E. L. and Flaste, R. 1995. *Why we do what we do: understanding self-motivation.* Rochester, NY: Penguin Books.

Deci, E. L. and Ryan, R. M. 1985. The general causality orientations scale – self-determination in personality. *Journal of Research in Personality*, 19 (2): 109–134.

2000. The "what" and "why" of goal pursuits: human needs and the self-determination of behavior. *Psychological Inquiry*, 11: 227–268.

(eds.). 2002. *Handbook of self-determination research.* Rochester, NY: University of Rochester Press.

Deci, E. L., Koestner, R., and Ryan, R. M. 1999. A meta-analytic review of experiments examining the effects of extrinsic rewards on intrinsic motivation. *Psychological Bulletin*, 125: 627–668.

Deutsch, M. 1960. The effect of motivational orientation upon trust and suspicion. *Human Relations*, 13: 123–139.

Edwards, R. 1979. *Contested terrain: the transformation of the workplace in the twentieth century.* London: Heinemann.

Eisenberger, R. and Cameron, J. 1996. Detrimental effects of rewards: reality or myth? *American Psychologist*, 51 (11): 1,153–1,166.

Eisenberger, R., Pierce, W. D., and Cameron, J. 1999. Effects of reward on intrinsic motivation – negative, neutral, and positive: comment on Deci, Koestner, and Ryan (1999). *Psychological Bulletin*, 125 (6): 677–691.

Eisenhardt, K. M. 1985. Control: organizational and economic approaches. *Management Science*, 31 (2): 134–149.

Falk, A. and Kosfeld, M. 2006. The hidden costs of control. *American Economic Review*, 96 (5): 1,611–1,630.

Fayol, H. and Urwick, L. F. 1963. *General and industrial management.* London, UK: Pitman.

Fehr, E., Falk, A., and Fischbacher, U. 2003. On the nature of fair behavior. *Economic Inquiry*, 41: 20–26.

Feld, L. P. and Frey, B. S. 2007. Tax compliance as the result of a psychological tax contract: the role of incentives and responsive regulation. *Law and Policy*, 29 (1): 102–120.

Fox, A. 1974. *Beyond contract: work, power and trust relations.* London: Faber & Faber.

Frey, B. S. 1997a. A constitution for knaves crowds out civic virtues. *Economic Journal*, 107 (443): 1,043–1,053.

1997b. *Not just for the money: an economic theory of personal motivation.* Cheltenham, UK: Edward Elgar.

Frey, B. S. and Jegen, R. 2001. Motivation crowding theory: a survey of empirical evidence. *Journal of Economic Surveys*, 15 (5): 589–611.

Frey, B. S. and Osterloh, M. F. 2002. *Successful management by motivation. Balancing intrinsic and extrinsic incentives.* Berlin/Heidelberg/New York: Springer.

Gagne, M. and Deci, E. L. 2005. Self-determination theory and work motivation. *Journal of Organizational Behavior*, 26 (4): 331–362.

Gavin, J. H. and Mason, R. O. 2004. The virtuous organization: the value of happiness in the workplace. *Organizational Dynamics*, 33 (4): 379–392.

Ghoshal, S. and Moran, P. 1996. Bad practice: a critique of the transaction cost theory. *Academy of Management Review*, 21: 13–47.

Gittell, J. H. 2000a. Organizing work to support relational coordination. *International Journal of Human Resource Management*, 11 (3): 517–539.

2000b. Paradox of coordination and control. *California Management Review*, 42 (3): 101–117.

Gneezy, U. and Rustichini, A. 2000a. A fine is a price. *Journal of Legal Studies*, 29 (1): 1–17.

2000b. Pay enough or don't pay at all. *Quarterly Journal of Economics*, 115 (3): 791–810.

Gouldner, A. W. 1954. *Patterns of industrial bureaucracy*. Glencoe, IL: Free Press.

Gulati, R. 1998. Alliances and networks. *Strategic Management Journal*, 19: 293–317.

Hackman, J. R. and Lawler, E. E. 1971. Employee reactions to job characteristics. *Journal of Applied Psychology*, 55 (3): 259–286.

Hackman, J. R. and Oldham, G. R. 1974. *The job diagnostic survey: an instrument for the diagnosis of jobs and the evaluation of job redesign projects*. New Haven, CT: Yale University.

Hardin, G. 1968. The tragedy of the commons. *Science*, 162: 1,243–1,248.

Hattie, J. and Timperley, H. 2007. The power of feedback. *Review of Educational Research*, 77 (1): 81–112.

Higgins, R., Hartley, P., and Skelton, A. 2002. The conscientious consumer: reconsidering the role of assessment feedback in student learning. *Studies in Higher Education*, 27 (1): 53–64.

Hobbes, T. 1909. Leviathan. In W. G. Pogson (ed.), *Leviathan*. Oxford: The Clarendon Press.

Jensen, M. C. and Meckling, W. H. 1976. Theory of the firm: managerial behavior, agency costs, and ownership structure. *Journal of Financial Economics*, 3: 305–360.

Jones, S. C. 1973. Self- and interpersonal evaluations: esteem theories versus consistency theories. *Psychological Bulletin*, 79 (3): 185–199.

Kirsch, L. J. 2004. Deploying common systems globally: the dynamics of control. *Information Systems Research*, 15 (4): 374–395.

Kluger, A. N. and DeNisi, A. 1996. The effects of feedback interventions on performance: a historical review, a meta-analysis, and a preliminary feedback intervention theory. *Psychological Bulletin*, 119 (2): 254–284.

Kohn, A. 1993. *Punished by rewards: the trouble with gold stars, incentive plans, As, praise, and other bribes*. Boston, MA: Houghton Mifflin.

Kollock, P. 1998. Social dilemmas: the anatomy of cooperation. *Annual Review of Sociology*, 22: 183–205.

Kramer, R. M. 1999. Trust and distrust in organizations: emerging perspectives, enduring questions. *Annual Review of Psychology*, 50: 569–598.

Kruglanski, A. W. 1970. Attributing trustworthiness in supervisor–worker relations. *Journal of Experimental Social Psychology*, 6: 214–232.

Lam, C. F. and Gurland, S. T. 2008. Self-determined work motivation predicts job outcomes, but what predicts self-determined work motivation? *Journal of Research in Personality*, 42 (4): 1,109–1,115.

Leana, C. R., Ahlbrandt, R. S., and Murrell, A. J. 1992. The effects of employee involvement programs on unionized workers' attitudes, perceptions, and preferences in decision making. *Academy of Management Journal*, 35: 861–873.

Lind, E. A. and Tyler, T. R. 1988. *The social psychology of procedural justice*. New York, NY: Plenum Press.

Locke, E. A. and Latham, G. P. 1990. *A theory of goal setting and task performance*. Englewood Cliffs, NJ: Prentice-Hall.

London, M. and Smither, J. W. 1999. Empowered self-development and continuous learning. *Human Resource Management*, 38 (1): 3–15.

London, M., Larsen, H. H., and Thisted, L. N. 1999. Relationships between feedback and self-development. *Group and Organization Management*, 24 (1): 5–27.

Mayer, R. C. and Davis, J. H. 1999. The effect of the performance appraisal system on trust for management: a field quasi experiment. *Journal of Applied Psychology*, 84 (1): 123–136.

Mayer, R. C. and Schoorman, F. D. 1998. Differentiating antecedents of organizational commitment: a test of March and Simon's model. *Journal of Organizational Behavior*, 19: 15–28.

McGregor, D. 1960. *The human side of enterprise*. New York, NY: McGraw Hill.

Miller, G. 1992. *Managerial dilemmas. The political economy of hierarchy*. Cambridge University Press.

Niehoff, B. P. and Moorman, R. H. 1993. Justice as a mediator of the relationship between methods of monitoring and organizational citizenship behavior. *Academy of Management Journal*, 36: 527–556.

Oldham, G. R. and Cummings, A. 1996. Employee creativity: personal and contextual factors at work. *Academy of Management Journal*, 39 (3): 607–634.

Oliver, R. L. and Anderson, E. 1994. An empirical test of the consequences of behavior and outcome-based sales control systems. *Journal of Marketing*, 58: 53–67.

Osterloh, M. F. and Bruno, S. 2000. Motivation, knowledge transfer and organizational form. *Organization Science*, 11: 538–550.

Pearson, C. A. L. 1991. An assessment of extrinsic feedback on participation, role perceptions, motivation, and job-satisfaction in a self-managed system for monitoring group achievement. *Human Relations*, 44 (5): 517–537.

Pettijohn, C., Pettijohn, L. S., Taylor, A. J., and Keillor, B. D. 2001. Are performance appraisals a bureaucratic exercise or can they be used to enhance sales-force satisfaction and commitment? *Psychology and Marketing*, 18 (4): 337–364.

Pfeffer, J. 1994. *Competitive advantage through people: unleashing the power of the work force.* Boston, MA: Harvard Business School Press.

Piaget, J. 1971. *Biology and knowledge.* Chicago: University of Chicago Press.

Piercy, N. F., Cravens, D. W., Lane, N., and Vorhies, D. W. 2006. Driving organizational citizenship behaviors and salesperson in-role behavior performance: the role of management control and perceived organizational support. *Journal of the Academy of Marketing Science*, 34 (2): 244–262.

Ramaswami, S. N. 1996. Marketing controls and dysfunctional employee behaviors: a test of traditional and contingency theory postulates. *Journal of Marketing*, 60 (2): 105–120.

Rhoades, L. and Eisenberger, R. 2002. Perceived organizational support: a review of the literature. *Journal of Applied Psychology*, 87 (4): 698–714.

Rhoades, L., Eisenberger, R., and Armeli, S. 2001. Affective commitment to the organization: the contribution of perceived organizational support. *Journal of Applied Psychology*, 86 (5): 825–836.

Rhodes, S. R. and Steers, R. M. 1981. Conventional vs. worker-owned organizations. *Human Relations*, 34 (12): 1,013–1,035.

Robbins, T. L. 1995. Social loafing on cognitive tasks – an examination of the sucker effect. *Journal of Business and Psychology*, 9 (3): 337–342.

Ryan, R. M. 1995. Psychological needs and the facilitation of integrative processes. *Journal of Personality*, 63 (3): 397–427.

Ryan, R. M. and Deci, E. L. 2000. Self-determination theory and the facilitating of intrinsic motivation. *American Psychologist*, 55: 68–78.

Ryan, R. M., Deci, E. L., and Grolnick, W. S. 1995. Autonomy, relatedness and the self: their relation to development and psychopathology. In D. Cicchetti and D. J. Cohen (eds.), *Manual of developmental psychopathology:* 618–655. New York, NY: Wiley.

Ryan, R. M., Sheldon, K. M., Kasser, T., and Deci, E. L. 1996. All goals are not created equal: an organismic perspective in the nature of goals and their regulation. In P. M. Gollwitzer and J. A. Bargh (eds.), *The psychology of action. Linking cognition and motivation to behavior:* 7–26. New York, NY: Guildford Press.

Rynes, S. L., Gerhart, B., and Parks, L. 2005. Personnel psychology: performance evaluation and pay for performance. *Annual Review of Psychology*, 56: 571–600.

Shapiro, S. P. 1987. The social control of impersonal trust. *American Journal of Sociology*, 93 (3): 623–658.

Simon, H. A. 1991. Organization and markets. *Journal of Economic Perspectives*, 5 (2): 25–44.

Sitkin, S. B. 1995. On the positive effect of legalization on trust. *Research on Negotiation in Organizations*, 5: 185–217.

Sitkin, S. B. and Stickel, D. 1996. The road to hell: the dynamics of distrust in an era of quality. In R. Kramer and T. Tyler (eds.), *Trust in organizations: frontiers of theory and research:* 196–215. London, UK: Sage.

Sitkin, S. B., Sutcliffe, K. M., and Schroeder, R. G. 1994. Distinguishing control from learning in total quality management: a contingency perspective. *Academy of Management Review*, 19 (3): 537–564.

Snell, S. A. 1992. Control-theory in strategic human-resource management – the mediating effect of administrative information. *Academy of Management Journal*, 35 (2): 292–327.

Spreitzer, G. M. and Mishra, A. K. 1999. Giving up control without losing control – trust and its substitutes' effects on managers' involving employees in decision making. *Group and Organization Management*, 24 (2): 155–187.

Spreitzer, G. M., Sutcliffe, K., Dutton, J., Sonenshein, S., and Grant, A. M. 2005. A socially embedded model of thriving at work. *Organization Science*, 16 (5): 537–549.

Stajkovic, A. O. and Luthans, F. 1997. A meta-analysis of the effects of organizational behavior modification on task performance. *Academy of Management Journal*, 40: 1,122–1,149.

2003. Behavioral management and task performance in organizations: conceptual background, meta-analysis, and test of alternative models. *Personnel Psychology*, 56 (1): 155–194.

Strickland, L. H. 1958. Surveillance and trust. *Journal of Personality*, 26 (2): 200–215.

Tannenbaum, A. S. 1968. *Control in organizations*. New York, NY: McGraw Hill.

Tannenbaum, R. and Schmid, W. H. 1958. How to choose a leadership pattern. *Harvard Business Review*, 36 (2): 94–101.

Thompson, P. J. and Warhurst, C. 1998. *Workplaces of the future*. Basingstoke: Macmillan Business.

Tyler, T. R. and Degoey, P. 1995. Collective restraint in social dilemmas: procedural justice and social identification effects on support for authorities. *Journal of Personal and Social Psychology*, 69: 482–497.

Walton, R. E. 1985. From control to commitment in the workplace. *Harvard Business Review*, 63 (Mar-Apr): 77–84.

Wells, C. V. and Kipnis, D. 2001. Trust, dependency, and control in the contemporary organization. *Journal of Business and Psychology*, 15 (4): 593–603.

Westin, A. F. 1992. Two key factors that belong in a macroergonomic analysis of electronic monitoring – employee perceptions of fairness and the climate of organizational trust or distrust. *Applied Ergonomics*, 23 (1): 35–42.

White, R. W. 1959. Motivation reconsidered: the concept of competence. *Psychological Review*, 66: 297–333.

Zucker, L. G. 1986. Production of trust: institutional sources of economic structure, 1840–1920. *Research in Organizational Behavior*, 8: 53–111.

15 | Control configurations and strategic initiatives

MARKUS KREUTZER AND
CHRISTOPH LECHNER
University of St. Gallen

Strategic initiatives are central building blocks for both scholarly research as well as managerial practice (Birkinshaw, 1997; Burgelman, 2002; Lovas and Ghoshal, 2000). They are defined as coordinated undertakings to develop or renew the capabilities associated with competitive advantage and above-average performance (Lechner and Floyd, 2007; Lechner *et al.*, 2010). In contrast to minor projects, they have characteristics such as substantial investment needs, partial non-reversibility, internal complexity, substantial risk taking, and a significant (positive or negative) impact on organizational performance.

Research on strategic initiatives has been mainly conducted in the realm of corporate entrepreneurship and strategic renewal (Zahra, 1996). Previous studies on initiatives have focused on learning activities (McGrath, 2001), resource allocation procedures (Noda and Bower, 1996), or the interplay of autonomous versus induced initiatives in the ecology of corporations (e.g., Burgelman, 1991, 2002). Although some of these studies emphasized the importance of the organizational context, our knowledge about the impact of managerial control mechanisms on strategic initiatives remains limited.

In order to advance our understanding, we draw on multiple control perspectives (Eisenhardt, 1985; Ouchi, 1977; Ouchi and Maguire, 1975) and focus on six specific control mechanisms (e.g., Cardinal *et al.*, Chapter 3; Long *et al.*, 2002). Based on the distinction between degree of formality and target of control, these control mechanisms are called formal and informal input control, behavior control, and output control (Cardinal *et al.*, 2004). As managerial control can be understood as all means by which firms align the behavior of organizational members with the goals of the firm (Flamholtz *et al.*, 1985; Tannenbaum, 1968), these control mechanisms enable us to study initiatives in a comprehensive and consistent way.

With this chapter, we intend to contribute in several ways. First, we add to research on organizational control by departing from traditional arguments of single target focus, which emphasized an either/or logic and proposed only one dominant and ideal control target for a specific situation (Eisenhardt, 1985; Ouchi, 1979; Thompson, 1967). Instead, we follow the recently emerging "broader" theory of organizational control, which assumes that organizational performance can be improved by focusing on multiple control targets (e.g., Cardinal et al., 2004; Long, Chapter 12; Long et al., 2002; Simons, 1994).

Second, instead of outlining one control mechanism after the other, we propose control configurations in the tradition of the "Gestaltansatz" of management research (Meyer et al., 1993). Building on work by Cardinal et al. (2004; Chapter 3), we extend existing research by developing control configurations and by examining their use for the execution of various types of strategic initiatives. By accounting for the multi-dimensional nature of control and the linkages between mechanisms, we try to set the stage for a theory of control that is amenable to more accurate, and predictive theoretical and empirical work (Doty et al., 1993).

Third, we also add to research on strategic initiatives by proposing a typology of strategic initiatives, based on the financial concept of return on invested capital (ROIC). This approach will enable us to derive several generic types of initiatives that resonate well with managerial practice. We complement previous distinctions, such as autonomous versus induced, by offering a typology based on concrete managerial issues, such as growth, cost cutting, and so forth. Such a typology is helpful, as initiatives cover a broad set of managerial topics requiring detailed specifications.

Fourth, based on anecdotal evidence, we explore typical traps and obstacles preventing firms from applying optimal matches between control mechanisms and strategic initiatives. As we examine causal linkages between managerial action, initiatives, and control types, we need to know why firms struggle in creating optimal constellations among these elements. This is also useful in deriving managerial guidelines for steering initiatives effectively through control mechanisms.

Strategic initiatives in corporate entrepreneurship research

As a firm-level phenomenon, research on corporate entrepreneurship is concerned with three major issues (Birkinshaw, 1997; Covin and Miles, 1999; Guth and Ginsberg, 1990; Lumpkin and Dess, 1996; Zahra and Covin, 1995). Corporate venturing (intrapreneurship) deals with the creation of new businesses within an organization. Strategic renewal is concerned with the transformation of existing businesses. Key ideas and capabilities on which a business is built are questioned, revised, and reshaped. Finally, changing industry rules is an entrepreneurial attempt to introduce frame-breaking new approaches for competition in an industry.

Often, those entrepreneurial activities are pursued in the form of strategic initiatives. These undertakings are created by the recognition of an entrepreneurial opportunity (Birkinshaw, 1997; Wielemaker, 2003; Wielemaker *et al.*, 2003). They are managerial vehicles for tapping into new sources of value creation and for focusing corporate entrepreneurship. As coordinated undertakings are conducted to develop or renew the capabilities, their locus can be on the business, corporate, or network level. The widespread application of initiatives in research and practice results from several reasons.

First, compared to constructs such as corporate entrepreneurship (or strategy) itself, strategic initiatives represent more easily identifiable and empirically observable elements. They often receive concrete names (e.g., Imagination Breakthroughs at General Electric, Shifting Gears at Munich Reinsurance Dynamo at Helvetia Insurance), are led by teams within the organization, and are equipped with their own profit and loss responsibility. This all makes them well traceable for empirical research. Second, compared to constructs such as routines, strategic initiatives are not only concerned with internal processes and practices, but also directly link these elements to external environments. Put differently, initiatives are not detached internal projects; however, their internal functioning is directly connected with their external achievements in the marketplace. They serve as linking pins between internal organizational events and external market developments. Third, strategic initiatives are at the forefront of altering existing resource configurations and changing established practices. They are not part of the activities related to running the ongoing, established business, but quite the opposite: they deal with fundamentally changing the *status quo* or significantly expanding the scope of the organization.

Some previous studies have partly used a conceptualization of initiatives including emergent processes based on self-organization (Burgelman, 1983b, 1983a; Floyd and Wooldridge, 2000; Mintzberg and Waters, 1985). Although we recognize this phenomenon, we focus on initiatives that have become visible in the organization, are pursued by an identifiable group of people (initiative team), and use corporate resources in a substantial way (e.g., time or funds). Skunk work, non-deliberate developments, or chance events are not part of this study, as they lack the above-mentioned characteristics of strategic initiatives.

Toward a typology of strategic initiatives

A look into the business world shows that initiatives exist in various forms, covering a broad set of managerial topics. Due to their apparent heterogeneity, we expect, as we will outline in the next paragraphs, that each type of strategic initiative is likely to benefit from a distinct control configuration able to accommodate its needs. Most classifications of initiatives are based on dichotomies, such as deliberate versus improvisational (Birkinshaw, 1997), induced versus autonomous (Burgelman, 1983b, 1983a), exploratory versus exploitive (McGrath, 2001), or entrepreneurial versus non-entrepreneurial (Zahra *et al.*, 1999). Even though every distinction has its particular strength, they build on a single continuum and, therefore, they are only to a certain degree able to capture the complexities of such undertakings in the empirical world. Further, these conceptual classifications are difficult in their application, as managers generally do not perceive their initiatives as autonomous or induced, but connect them with specific business objectives they are trying to achieve.

Therefore, we require a classification that is both theoretically as well as managerially relevant. For that purpose, we start with the financial ROIC classification and subsequently break it into its components, deriving a typology of strategic initiatives. ROIC is a measure of the return of invested capital in a business or corporate entity. It deals with the question of how much profit a company is able to

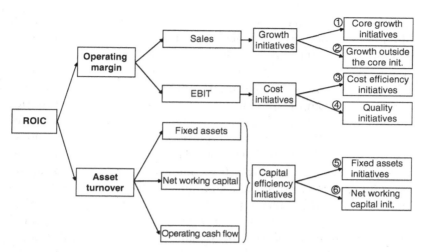

Figure 15.1 Typology of strategic initiatives based on a ROIC classification schema

generate with each dollar of capital. It is calculated by dividing the net operating profit after tax by the amount of invested capital that supports this business. The analysis of ROIC involves looking beyond the costs itemized in the financial statements. The cost of capital employed by the business and the efficiency with which capital is used are important factors to consider in corporate entrepreneurship (Dess *et al.*, 2003: 362; Lehn and Makhija, 1996).

There are several ways management may attempt to improve a firm's ROIC (see Figure 15.1). *Growth initiatives* are directed toward enlarging the revenue (top-line) of the organization to generate additional sales on the existing capital base (e.g., Kim and Mauborgne, 2004; Lechner and Kreutzer, 2010; Zook and Allen, 2003). They range from scaling up the core business, moving into adjacent areas, developing new products, entering new markets, and so on, with internal growth, alliances, or merger and acquisition (M&A) activities. Thus, growth initiatives can be further differentiated, among others, by the growth mechanism in use (organic, M&A, alliances) (Treacy, 2003), the product-market combination (Ansoff, 1965), or the distance to the core business (Zook and Allen, 2003). We use the final option to differentiate growth initiatives in the core business from those intended to increase sales outside the core business.

Cost initiatives include activities launched to improve the margins of an organization. They are generally directly reflected in the profit and loss account (Birkinshaw, 1997; Dess *et al.*, 1997). Cost initiatives consist of two types: efficiency and quality-enhancing initiatives. *Efficiency initiatives* are selected to enhance a firm's cost position relative to its competitors. They are frequently targeted on overhead functions (Nimocks *et al.*, 2005), including finance (e.g., move from detailed monthly to quarterly reporting), information technology (IT) (e.g., enforce IT-purchasing standard or outsourcing employee IT support), human resources (e.g., implement new travel expense standards), and marketing (e.g., consolidate advertising agency work, eliminate high-cost outliers). *Quality initiatives* also target the profit-and-loss (P&L) bottom line, but with a specific focus on quality improvements, especially of process management practices. Examples of initiatives elevating quality to a strategic competitive variable include six sigma (e.g., Bartlett and Wozny, 2002), total quality management (TQM) (e.g., Chenhall, 1997; Sitkin *et al.*, 1994), or business process reengineering (e.g., Benner and Tushman, 2003).

Capital initiatives serve to lower the capital employed in a business. There are two types. The first deals with the optimization of fixed assets, the latter with the optimizations of net working capital. To improve asset turns, it is important to identify "big ticket" items such as reducing accounts receivable (e.g., collecting overdue accounts, shortening payment terms), increasing accounts payable (e.g., delaying payment, getting longer payment terms), or reducing inventory (e.g., optimizing planning parameters, improving planning procedures). In the beginning of the 1990s, Dell, for example, started one major initiative to improve current assets by collecting early (resulting in low accounts receivable) and by paying late (resulting in high accounts payable). Today, Dell is using these increased accounts payable to finance inventories and accounts receivable by paying its suppliers late.

In sum, the ROIC typology facilitates a better understanding of the strategic initiative construct moving beyond simple continua. It is applicable in scientific research, providing us with a comprehensive set of initiative types, as well as managerial practice due to its direct connection with managerial objectives. In the next section, therefore, we will employ this typology consisting of six types of initiatives for deriving optimal control configurations.

Control and control configurations

A substantial body of theoretical and empirical research has accumulated on control, going back to the seminal work of Ouchi and Maguire (1975). In our study we define *managerial control* relatively broadly (e.g., Cardinal, 2001; Eisenhardt, 1985; Ouchi, 1977, 1979; Snell, 1992) as "any mechanism that managers use to direct attention, motivate, and encourage organizational members to act in desired ways to meet an organization's objectives" (Long *et al.*, 2002: 198). Control mechanisms are specific methods governing individual actions and acting as a fundamental unit of analysis in control research. Several dimensions are relevant.

First, by distinguishing control mechanisms by the organizational target that they influence, we receive a classification of input, behavior, and output control. *Behavior control* ensures that the process is appropriate. The firm attempts to influence the means to achieve desired ends by monitoring ongoing employee activities and behaviors and regulating how work gets done (Cardinal, 2001; Eisenhardt, 1985; Ouchi, 1977; Snell, 1992). The focus of *output control*, unlike that of behavior control, is on the end results as opposed to the means by which outcomes are achieved (Cardinal, 2001; Eisenhardt, 1985; Ouchi, 1977; Snell, 1992). It is applied by setting performance standards, defining the dimensions of desired results, measuring how well output aligns with the set standards, and providing respective rewards and punishment for success and failure in goal attainment (Cardinal, 2001; Merchant, 1985). The distinction between behavior and output control is well established and commonly used in control research (Turner and Makhija, 2006). *Input control* is the third control target and includes actions taken by firms prior to the implementation of an activity, such as searching for and selecting people who fit a firm's needs exactly as well as training and developing them before they assume responsibility in initiatives (Cardinal *et al.*, 2004; Long *et al.*, 2002).

In studying these control mechanisms, early control theorists concluded that one target of control should be preferred over others depending upon the given task (Eisenhardt, 1985; Ouchi, 1979; Snell, 1992). An emerging broader control theory recently questioned this either/or tendency in the literature. Theorists argue that a single focus contradicts both theoretical arguments and practical evidence; rather, controls have to be thought of as complements and as simultaneously active, at least in reasonably complex organizations, to influence the attainment of a specific goal (Alvesson and Karreman, 2004; Cardinal, 2001; Jaworski, 1988; Kirsch, 1996; Long, Chapter 12; Long *et al.*, 2002). We follow this broader theory of organizational control and assume that different control mechanisms coexist or even sustain each other, rather than being subsumed and marginalized by a dominant form; they can be thought of as a continuum ranging from low to high levels.

The three control targets can be further classified by the level of formality (Eisenhardt, 1985). *Formal controls* emphasize the establishment and utilization of formal rules, procedures, and policies to monitor and reward desirable performance. It has been the predominant focus of existing research. *Informal controls* rely on the establishment of organizational norms, values, culture, and the internalization of goals to encourage desirable behavior and outcome.

Following recent research by Long and colleagues and the results of their simulation study, we argue that input, behavior, and output controls can be applied not only formally but also informally (Cardinal *et al.*, 2004; Long *et al.*, 2002). In more uncertain and complex working environments (such as strategic initiatives), controls cannot only be static and formal. Rather, they have to be complemented by informal social control mechanisms (Davila, 2005). We thereby try to answer a call for research by combining formal and informal control mechanisms (Jaworski, 1988; Jaworski *et al.*, 1993; Pappas and Flaherty, 2005; Roth *et al.*, 1994; Sitkin and George, 2005).

Toward a configurational approach of control

Researchers (e.g., Cardinal, 2001; Cardinal *et al.*, 2004; Snell, 1992; Snell and Youndt, 1995) have significantly advanced control theory by focusing not only on one or two specific elements of control (e.g., only formal output control mechanisms) but on multiplicative relationships between control and other organizational phenomena. However, all of the studies only analyzed the direct influence of a single control mechanism on outcome variables without accounting for the linkages and interrelationships between control mechanisms. Whether control mechanisms tend to appear in predictable clusters or dispersed is still an unresolved issue. Cardinal and colleagues (Cardinal *et al.*, Chapter 3) advocate that control is best depicted as configurational, i.e., a "multidimensional constellation of conceptually distinct characteristics that commonly occur together" (Meyer *et al.*, 1993: 1,175). By basing the control configuration on the six control mechanisms, the two key principles to classifying configurations – coherence and holism (Meyer *et al.*, 1993) are met (Cardinal *et al.*, Chapter 3). A specific configuration can be built if the theoretical attributes (each possibly being low, middle, or high) reach coherence among them (Venkatraman, 1989).

Empirical research on the role of managerial control in the performance of strategic initiatives is relatively rare, despite the fact that the guiding and monitoring of strategic initiatives is considered one of top managers' main roles (Lovas and Ghoshal, 2000; Noda and Bower, 1996). As one of the few exceptions, McGrath (2001) analyzed the question of how managerial oversight processes influence exploratory learning in new business development projects. Differentiating between goal and supervision autonomy, she found both types of autonomy to be positively related to performance. Burgers *et al.* (2008) refined these results and showed that the optimal degree of autonomy of new business development projects depends on the newness of required technological and market knowledge. Floyd and Lane (2000) theoretically examined situations in which managers' inconsistent perceptions about the need for change create strategic role conflict. In those situations, organizational controls (socialization, market, bureaucratic, and clan) are the primary means used by managers to clarify and align role expectations. Related research shows how self- and professional controls can be used to get employees to go above and beyond traditional job roles and effect strategic renewal (Pappas and Flaherty, 2005). Focusing on TQM, Sitkin and colleagues took a contingency perspective to theorize how TQM has an impact on organizational effectiveness dependent on the uncertainty of the situation (Sitkin *et al.*, 1994). They propose that TQM comprises two fundamentally different goals, namely control (in routine situations) and learning (in non-routine situations), and suggest a balance between these two goals that should match the situational uncertainty faced by organizations.

The focus of this chapter is on understanding which control configurations are optimal for the six types of strategic initiatives. Therefore, we theoretically derive optimal configurations from numerous possible combinations that represent internally consistent combinations along the six distinct control mechanisms. By taking a configurational approach, we want to provide a theoretical basis for systematic empirical studies in the future which should be more predictive of firm success because they, by definition, take into account more potentially relevant variables (Dess *et al.*, 1997).

How,ever, by taking such a broader perspective and aiming for a more holistic model, we cannot draw on a single paradigm, as there is not a unified control theory up to now (and one is unlikely to emerge). Rather, we have to draw on multiple theoretical perspectives dealing with managerial control. Thus, we deliberately choose a kind of eclectic theory approach as we see the potential to generate richer insights for an understanding of our "dependent variable." Such an eclectic approach is well known in management research and especially in strategic management:

Strategic management research is characterized by [theoretical] eclecticism . . . Scholars draw theory . . . from economics, sociology, behavioral science, and to a lesser extent, other social sciences . . . For many strategic management problems . . . carefully combining multiple perspectives can generate richer insights (Maritan and Peteraf, 2008: 71).

Following this call, we use multiple theoretical perspectives, drawing on agency theory (Eisenhardt, 1985), transaction cost economics (Williamson, 1981), different psychologically based theories (Merchant and Simons, 1986), behavioral theory (Cyert and March, 1963), and the resource-based perspective (Barney, 1991) to better understand the implications of certain control configurations for initiative performance.

The majority of control researchers have assumed that managers apply control mechanisms to address the *agency problems* inherent in organizations. Based on the premise of goal incongruence between principals and agents, and the assumed opportunistic behavior of the latter, which are motivated to misrepresent both their abilities (i.e., adverse selection) and their efforts (i.e., moral hazard), (formal) control is necessary to align the interests of the agents with that of the principals (Barney and Ouchi, 1986; Eisenhardt, 1985). We use the agency theory paradigm to explore how to minimize total agency costs in the different initiative settings and how to maximize the objective function of the top management (principal) and the initiative team members (agents).

Transaction cost theory has focused on the limitations of markets and contracts for allocating resources and analyzes the conditions under which a hierarchy is a better way of controlling multiple actions than a market. The basic premise of transaction cost theory is that firms choose efficient organizational forms or governance structures based on transactional issues such as relation-specific investments or external and internal uncertainty. According to this theory, performance is enhanced when there is congruence between the governance structure and underlying dimensions of the exchange (Williamson, 1981).

Control is also one of the four conceptual pillars of the *behavioral theory of the firm* along with theories of organizational goals, expectations, and choice (Cyert and March, 1963: 22). The behavioral theory assumes bounded rationality and perceives organizations as coalitions involving a variety of stakeholders. It proposes that a firm's search behavior – in terms of generating and pursuing choices – is triggered by the difference between the goals aspired to and expected performance (Greve, 2003; Lant, 1992). Control is needed in order to specify differences between search alternatives (choices) and their actual outcomes (i.e., deficiencies of an actual value in comparison with its target).

Recently, a *resource-based perspective* has also been applied to control (Henri, 2006). We apply this perspective's basic logic in interpreting certain balanced control configurations as (contributing to the creation and maintenance of) a valuable resource or a capability-providing competitive advantage (Barney, 1991). Overall, we apply in this chapter such an eclectic approach, as it is our main objective to explain performance levels of strategic initiatives (phenomena), and less to apply and extend one theoretical control conception.

Control configuration and strategic initiatives

In this section, we outline for each type of strategic initiative, which aspects of the three formal and informal control mechanisms are most important and why (for a summary, see Table 15.1). We argue that a configuration that exhibits just the right combination of control attributes, that is, a situation of fit between strategic initiatives and control, is positively related to the performance of the specific initiative type.

Table 15.1 *Strategic initiatives control configurations*

	Input control formal	Input control informal	Behavior control formal	Behavior control informal	Output control formal	Output control informal
	Low	Low	Medium	Low	High	Low
Core growth initiatives	• No need for explicit selection criteria as there exists knowledge about the strengths and weaknesses of lower level managers. • Restricted need to learn and acquire new knowledge and to train team members as the business model is already in place.	• No need for informal selection processes as there exists knowledge about the strengths and weaknesses of lower level managers. • Restricted need to learn and acquire new knowledge and to train team members as the business model is already in place.	• Positive effects by involving top managers in discussion processes. • Can be used to set boundary conditions (e.g., to narrow the scope of exploration). • But, market units have some standard operating procedures in place for scaling their business up.	• Market units have some standard operating procedures in place for scaling their business up. • Relatively low requirement to learn and acquire new knowledge.	• Output is observable and measurable. • Strong signal to team that they have a stake in the product's financial and market success. • Motivation by tying both targets and rewards to initiative performance.	• As targets can be formally tracked, an informal output control focus might only be a source of additional costs.

Growth outside the core initiatives	High	High	Low	Medium	Low to medium	Low to medium
	• Clear selection criteria to staff teams with the needed knowledge and skills. • Provides a variety of perspectives (e.g., cross-functional teams).	• Internalization of organizational values and goals through socialization processes. • Higher commitment. • Higher trust level increasing the willingness to cooperate.	• Incomplete cause–effect knowledge. • No possibility to standardize actions *a priori.* • No basis upon which to evaluate the appropriateness of subordinates' behavior. • Impeding flexibility, experimentation, and creativity. • Signals lacking trust in team's ability to do their jobs.	• Informality induces team members to exercise greater individual discretion. • Higher motivation and commitment. • Top management as information broker and boundary spanner. • But, if too high, perceived as "foreign body," which might undermine team culture.	• Ambiguous standards of desirable performance. • Long time horizon. • Focus on results-oriented incentives could increase manipulation of information. • But, certain level necessary to define "stop-criteria."	• Ambiguous standards of desirable performance. • Long time horizon. • But still, certain level necessary to define "stop-criteria."

Table 15.1 (*cont.*)

	Input control formal	Input control informal	Behavior control formal	Behavior control informal	Output control formal	Output control informal
Quality initiatives	Medium • Training of team members in quality aspects. • No need for explicit selection criteria as quality initiatives are less conflict-laden and, therefore, personal aspects are less important.	Low • No need for informal selection processes as quality initiatives are less conflict-laden and, therefore, personal aspects are less important.	High • Existence of explicit cause–effect relationships in quality exercises. • Standard operating procedures. • Allows for early feedback. • Eliminates uncertainty and increases predictability. • Raises discipline.	Medium • Supports formal behavior control but is less relevant for formalized quality exercises.	Medium • Output is measurable (e.g., defect rates, quality of final product). • Preprogrammed corrective actions if outputs are not acceptable. • Supports quality improvements.	Medium • Used to keep a focus on the necessity to reach quality-related targets. • Allows for early output information and feedback.
Efficiency initiatives	High • Selection of initiative members with the right skills and	Low • Limited need for learning and building of new knowledge.	Low • Danger of legitimating the *status quo*. • Entails costs that might reduce the	Low • Danger of legitimating the *status quo*. • Entails costs that might	High • Output is easily observable and measurable (e.g., manufacturing	Low • Informal interactions between top managers and initiative

	gains of the exercise. • Informal interactions between top managers and initiative team members might be inefficient and a source of additional cost.			reduce the gains of the exercise. • Limited need for learning and building of new knowledge.	costs per unit). • Possibility to set minimal requirements for solutions to trim the duration of the search.		team members might be inefficient and a source of additional cost.
Working capital initiatives	characteristics (able to do the "dirty work"). • Necessity to define a clear initiative owner. • Integration of "neutral" perspectives (e.g., external consultants).	Medium • Limited need for explicit selection criteria as working capital initiatives are less conflict-laden and, therefore, the personal aspect is less important.	Medium to high • Top management can transfer its tacit knowledge. • Facilitates organizational learning. • Aligns shared values and beliefs. • Higher commitment.	High • Working capital related issues can be conducted with formal, standardized procedures. • Practicability of rules of thumb.	High • Top management can transfer its tacit knowledge. • Helps avoid unintended side effects or harsh counter-reactions. • Aligns shared values and beliefs. • Higher commitment.	High • Output is easily observable and measurable. • Stretch goals influence the aspiration levels of the individuals engaged and can lead to higher motivation.	Medium to high • Top management can transfer its tacit knowledge. • Fosters output focus and commitment to targets.

Table 15.1 (*cont.*)

	Input control formal	Input control informal	Behavior control formal	Behavior control informal	Output control formal	Output control informal
Fixed asset initiatives	High • Necessity to centrally bundle responsibility (key success factor of divestments). • Teams can be adequately composed. • Securing the required access to internal and external experts.	Low • By initiating timely and costly discussion processes, they undermine the positive influence of the formal triangulation.	High • Explicit criteria and stages facilitate a flawless execution. • Well structured situations to which analytical techniques such as capital budgeting can be readily applied.	Low • By initiating timely and costly discussion processes, they undermine the positive influence of the formal triangulation.	High • Output is easily observable and measurable. • Well structured situations to which analytical techniques such as capital budgeting can be readily applied. • Definition of outcome goals is possible.	Low • By initiating timely and costly discussion processes, they undermine the positive influence of the formal triangulation.

Control configuration for "core growth" initiatives

Growth initiatives in the core are about extending and replicating existing business. As we will argue in this section, a control configuration with a high level of formal output control complemented by a medium level of formal behavior control, and only low levels of input and all informal control mechanisms, might be best suited to this type of initiative.

The heavy emphasis on formal output controls constitutes a strong signal to initiative teams that they have a stake in the product's financial and market success (Bonner, 2005). By tying both targets and rewards to initiative performance, initiative teams are motivated to interact with customers because this interactivity is paramount to achieving success in the market. The high focus on output control depends on top managers having crystallized standards of desirable performance (Thompson, 1967: 84), i.e., outcome observability (Eisenhardt, 1985) and measurability (Ouchi, 1977). In growth initiatives in the core, this is normally possible. For example, specific sales targets can be set and monitored for each business unit, existing market, or customer segment.

Also, due to the lower uncertainty associated with such growth initiatives, top management only periodically keeps track of processes, for example, through meetings of steering committees. It is not necessary to prescribe each single step of the initiative team; instead, top management relies on being involved in discussing and monitoring actions. This medium level of process control can also be used to set boundary conditions. For example, as the case of Whirlpool reveals, new process mechanisms were put in place to narrow the scope of exploration and to restrain the organization to the core of its current business (Siggelkow and Rivkin, 2006).

Further, the requirement to learn and acquire novel knowledge is relatively weak for core growth initiatives (Sitkin and Bies, 1994). Most necessary knowledge is available, and only minor adaptations are likely to occur. Consequently, there is less need for additional informal controls through social interaction as well as an emphasis on input controls. Two main reasons support this: first, when growing the existing core business, the business model is well established, and the market units have some standard operating procedures in place for scaling the business up. These can build on the internal technical

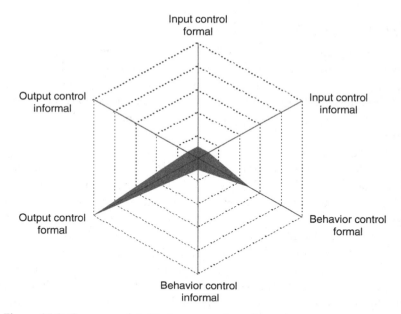

Figure 15.2 Core growth initiatives control configuration

knowledge, that is, the insights about the properties of specific activities that are vital for sustained regeneration (Dess *et al.*, 2003). Thus, it is less important for top managers to train the team members. Second, top management generally knows the strengths and weaknesses of lower level managers quite well and has a fairly good idea about optimal team compositions. Thus, there is less necessity to install explicit selection criteria.

In sum, we argue that the combination of the three formal and informal control mechanisms displayed in Figure 15.2 is best suited to core growth initiatives.

Control configuration for "growth outside the core" initiatives

Growing beyond the established core requires an organization to move into "uncharted waters." We argue that such initiatives are most successful if the top management understands its role as creating a positive context for these initiatives, allowing for their discretion, and enabling their developmental path. This is represented by a control configuration that puts strong emphasis on formal and informal input control, with medium to low levels of the other dimensions. The main reasons for the optimal match between this configuration and the performance of growth outside the core initiatives are:

First, these undertakings require initiative members that are able to cope fast and flexibly with unforeseen events that are likely to emerge. The degree of exploration is high and entrepreneurial learning is required, as the organization normally does not possess all relevant knowledge (Bonner *et al.*, 2002). Consequently, issues related to staffing, training, and preparing this journey are of major importance, as the evolution of such initiatives is likely to be volatile. High degrees of input control are crucial, because they set the context for subsequent actions of initiative teams, for example, initiative members might be obliged to run through obligatory training sessions prior to undertaking responsibilities. Top management can systematically use formal input control to establish teams with the variety of perspectives needed to generate innovative solutions to novel problems (Snell and Youndt, 1995).

Further, as senior managers only have a general idea of the qualifications required of team members (Snell, 1992), decisions about selection and training must be based on or at least enforced by, informal input control to be performance enhancing. This includes rituals, tradition, convention, and the like (Ouchi, 1977; Snell, 1992). Inherent socializing processes can facilitate the internalization of organizational values and goals by organizational members (Collins, 1982; Ouchi, 1979). Goal congruence between individual team members and the firm will increase the probability that individual and group behaviors will lead to the attainment of organizational objectives (Flamholtz *et al.*, 1985). The socialization process might also contribute to a more committed team; the level of trust between team members will rise, thereby increasing the willingness to cooperate (Ghoshal and Bartlett, 1994).

As cause–effect knowledge is incomplete and standards of desirable performance are ambiguous, neither high degrees of behavior nor output control are likely to be a viable option for such initiatives (Eisenhardt, 1985; Ouchi, 1977; Thompson, 1967). Top managers cannot standardize actions *a priori*, and they have no basis upon which to evaluate the appropriateness of subordinates' behavior *vis-à-vis* their intentions. Similarly, no clear output criteria or goals can be established *ex ante* because the range of outcomes and their probabilities are not known (McGrath, 2001); success or failure is only measurable in the long term (Ouchi, 1977; Snell, 1992). In an empirical study (Ramaswami, 1996), marketing employees were found to behave in dysfunctional ways when they were subject to both output and process controls in such situations. Close supervision was viewed as an expression of lacking trust in their ability to do their jobs, and the relevance of uncertain and not completely controllable outcomes for their evaluation and rewards was inducing them to manipulate information. Although we agree in principle with these arguments, we see the necessity for a limited focus on formal output control in order to define "stop criteria" for these initiatives. Otherwise, there are no mechanisms in place to end further investments and to avoid the well-known phenomenon of throwing good money after bad.

Further, prescribed processes (i.e., high behavior controls) are likely to be counterproductive for these growth initiatives, since they impede the creativity and flexibility commonly needed when driving growth to respond to changing situations, new internal or external circumstances, and the inherent uncertainty in the initiative type (Adler and Borys, 1996; Sitkin and Bies, 1994). The presence of detailed procedural guidelines and their strict monitoring by top management will reduce the likelihood that team members will deviate from established behavior patterns (Weick, 1979). The abdication of experimentation with new behaviors comprises the risk of losing an important source of variation and innovative ways to deliver more valuable solutions through the autonomous behavior of initiative managers (Burgelman, 1983a; Floyd and Lane, 2000; Inkpen and Choudhury, 1995; Sitkin *et al.*, 1994). Initiative teams with the goal to grow outside the core business require a certain agility, enabling creative thinking that overcomes key cognitive barriers and administrative rigidities (Leonard-Barton, 1992). They need to think differently about the industry, its structure, and competitive dynamics, and different scenarios have to be probed (Zahra, 2005: xiv).

Finally, although formal processes might be counterproductive, a certain degree of informal behavior control is likely to be helpful. Informality induces team members to exercise greater individual discretion (Thompson, 1967) and has been associated with greater motivation and commitment (McGrath, 2001). In addition, top managers take the role as information brokers by spanning boundaries (e.g., between different departments) and thereby they provide initiative teams with relevant information. However, there are limits to boundary-spanning activity, as a higher level of informal behavior control might be perceived as a "foreign body" undermining team cultures, which might be significantly different from established ones.

Empirical results support our arguments; for example, Bonner and colleagues (2002) showed that for highly innovative new product development (NPD) projects, decentralized and participative decision processes and a minimum reliance on formal rules and procedures had positive performance outcomes. Creativity, cross-functional integration, and serendipity on the part of the NPD team were critical determinants of project success. Also, Siggelkow and Rivkin (2006) stressed the superiority of a control situation in which lower levels were empowered and only a limited degree of control was retained at a higher level to prevent various departments of a firm from exerting negative externalities on each other. Thus, we conclude that the control configuration displayed in Figure 15.3 is the most valuable for steering growth outside the core initiatives.

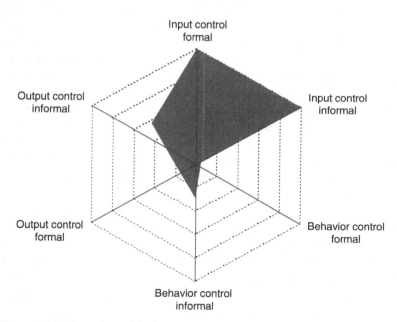

Figure 15.3 Growth outside the core initiatives control configuration

Control configuration for quality initiatives

We argue that a control configuration determined primarily by a high level of behavior control accompanied by a medium level of output control is most beneficial for quality initiatives. It is based on the conviction that behavioral improvements are key and that these influence the likelihood of reaching objectives.

This configuration's positive impact on quality initiative performance rests on the existence of explicit cause–effect relationships in quality exercises. These cause–effect maps are generally developed beforehand in detail and laid out crystal-clear in the form of process guidelines, tests, risk management procedures, and so on. The knowledge for the transformation and improvement of organizational tasks and processes is available. In such contexts, control research has supported the significance of high behavior control (Ouchi and Maguire, 1975; Sitkin et al., 1994; Snell, 1992). It allows for early feedback by recognizing when specific parts of the operating process are moving out of control. The need for process adjustments is signaled back, and this feedback can be used to further advance the process (Chenhall, 1997).

The routinization of transformation processes eliminates uncertainty and increases predictability (Ouchi, 1977, 1978; Ouchi and Maguire, 1975). *Routines*, defined as standard operating procedures that make employee responses to the task environment highly predictable (Cyert and March, 1963), are installed through close supervision, ensuring that repeated practices become semiautomatic and reliable. Behavioral performance appraisals and feedback help to correct procedural problems (Snell and Youndt, 1995). Research argues that the establishment of clear standards of behavior, a system of open and fast-cycle feedback, and consistency in the application of sanctions contribute to the establishment of discipline and the emergence of reliable practices (Ghoshal and Bartlett, 1994).

Further, the proposed optimal quality initiatives control configuration supports quality improvements (fewer errors or defects) through its reliance on formal output controls. For example, in total quality settings, measures of manufacturing performance typically focus on delivering quality products, such as customer satisfaction measured by quality of final products, on-time delivery, responsiveness to customer needs, and various aspects of the value chain associated with quality production, such as defect-free production (Chenhall, 1997: 188).

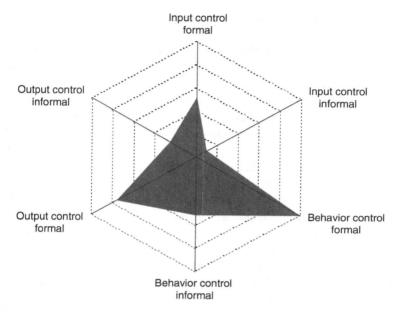

Figure 15.4 Quality initiatives control configuration

This mechanism is used to include all important aspects of manufacturing operations and thereby directs the attention of managers to its antecedents (Chenhall, 1997). Defect rates are measured against expectations, and if they are unacceptable, actions can be put in place to ensure that appropriate levels are achieved. This type of measurement has been referred to as a type of cybernetic feedback loop, which may involve some form of preprogrammed corrective action (Green and Welsh, 1988; Sitkin *et al.*, 1994).

Empirical evidence seems to support this line of reasoning. It has shown that the introduction and use of technologies characterized by standardized and automated processes benefited from highly developed behavioral control and medium levels of output controls (Merchant, 1985). Figure 15.4 displays the best suited control configuration for quality initiatives.

Control configuration for efficiency initiatives

Efficiency initiatives take their blunt and most classical form as cost-cutting exercises. Triggers are unsatisfactory profit margins, or preparation for increased competitive pressure. We argue that such initiatives require people in charge of control to take drastic action if targets are missed. High degrees of formal output and input control, and relatively low levels of other control mechanisms characterize this configuration.

First, researchers see output measurability as an important antecedent of formal output control. Generally, these initiatives can be well measured and have transparent objectives. Precise milestones are defined and tracked; for example, firms focus on factors such as "manufacturing costs per unit," or "percentage of raw materials to total costs." Initiative teams pursuing these initiatives receive defined objectives and deadlines. Top managers can deliberately set minimal requirements for solutions in order to trim the duration of search (Greve, 2003: 157).

In addition, formal input control enables top management to install the right types of initiative members. This matters, because such "unpleasant" acts are often not well regarded in the organization. Doing the "dirty work" of restoring profitability by reducing the economic structure of the organization and being able "to bear the brunt" requires skills that not every manager has. Not surprisingly, such initiatives are often heavily staffed with external consultants who are less involved in the micro-political fabric of an organization and are more likely to offer more "neutral" perspectives than insiders.

Finally, as cost-cutting exercises do not require learning and the build-up of new knowledge, a lower level of all informal controls and of behavior control is sufficient. Even more important, experienced cost-cutters deliberately restrain strong involvement in all details and particularities of business operations in order to avoid the legitimating of the current *status quo*. Further, intensive process monitoring creates costs that might reduce the gains of the exercise. It is often too costly and practically impossible for top management to dive deeply into all of the facts. In such situations, behavior control is an inefficient way to regulate performance (Snell, 1992).

It is interesting to note that a study of the implementation of cost-leadership strategies stressed the importance of tight budgetary controls, structured sets of organizational responsibilities (input control), and incentives based on meeting strict quantitative targets and frequent, detailed control reports (Govindarajan and Fisher, 1990). In sum, we argue that the combination of the three formal and informal control mechanisms displayed in Figure 15.5 is best suited to efficiency initiatives.

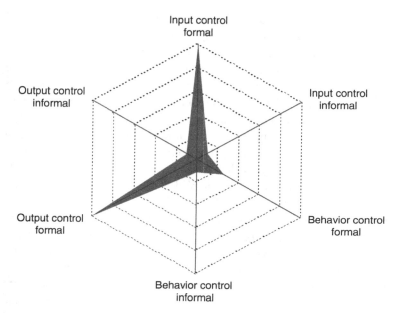

Figure 15.5 Efficiency initiatives control configuration

Control configuration for working capital initiatives

We argue that working capital initiatives benefit mostly from a control configuration entailing a high degree of informal and formal control mechanisms with a specific focus on behavior control. Informal input and output control are also relatively high while formal input control is medium to low. The top management team in charge of control should have diplomatic skills, which can be used in the plurality of formal and informal interactions, including the process of resolving disputes, crafting outcomes to satisfy various interests, and bargaining for organizational advantages. The main reasons why this configuration is beneficial for working capital initiatives follow.

First, it stresses the significance of behavior and output control, since these means are critical for issues such as extending/reducing payment schedules for creditors and debtors. It is possible to measure these objectives and conduct them with formal, standardized procedures. For example, rules such as, "focus on slow movers and on the first 80 percent of the inventory level," or "clarify internal rules for committing cash to those kind of inventories where the organization has no or limited sales visibility," are practical rules of thumb. Formal measures can be set up in the form of objectives such as "achieve on average a fifteen-day period to collect your bills."

In addition, the negotiator is able to set stretch goals. These have been found to have positive performance implications in activities such as innovative net capital improvements by being a motivational tool in individual or group-level, goal-setting tasks (Locke and Latham, 1990). Through stretch goals, managers are able to influence the aspiration levels of the individuals engaged. Often, team members voluntarily strive for more, rather than less, ambitious objectives if these goals are perceived as somehow realistic and if the members are equipped with the means to achieve them (Ghoshal and Bartlett, 1994).

Further, working capital initiatives benefit from all three informal mechanisms, but especially from informal behavior control, because top managers can transfer their knowledge grounded in memory, history, and organizational routines informally to initiative team members (Dess *et al.*, 2003). Informally based clan controls were argued to be superior in transferring tacit and sticky knowledge (e.g., on the complex relationships and best negotiation strategies) across organizational members (Turner and Makhija, 2006) and to facilitate organizational learning (Abernethy and Brownell, 1999).

This knowledge transfer is essential, because working capital initiatives deal primarily with suppliers and customers, and managing these relationships requires a substantial amount of flair and sensitivity to single actors. This knowledge might support initiative teams with fine-grained information and help to avoid unintended side effects or harsh counter-reactions. Working capital initiatives are mostly dependent on the support or negotiation power toward clients and suppliers.

Finally, a high degree of informal control is also beneficial in fostering commitment and aligning shared values and beliefs toward such initiatives (Cravens *et al.*, 2004). Empirical support for the superiority of this control configuration is provided by marketing research. Salespeople who had to fulfill similar tasks performed better under a more visible, high control system consisting of both formal output and behavior control and more informal professional and cultural control (Cravens *et al.*, 2004). They were also more satisfied and displayed lower burnout and role stress, compared to salespeople working under exclusively formal or exclusively informal control

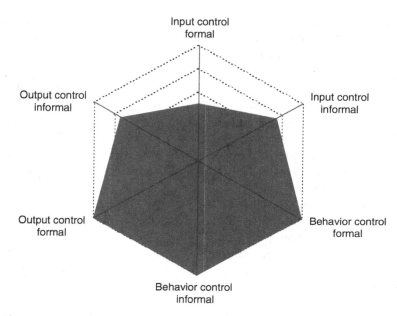

Figure 15.6 Working capital initiatives control configuration

combinations or low control combinations. Thus, we conclude that the control configuration displayed in Figure 15.6 is most valuable for steering working capital initiatives.

Control configuration for fixed asset initiatives

Examples of fixed asset initiatives include the acquisition or divestment of assets or sell-and-lease-back arrangements of plants or physical equipment. We argue that a kind of bureaucratic control configuration (i.e., a situation similar to bureaucracies with a formal division of power), rule following, and targets setting, is positively related to their performance. Thus, the optimal configuration is characterized by a strong focus on all three formal targets of control mainly for three reasons.

First, based on control research, the nature of fixed asset initiatives implies the adequacy of formal output and behavior controls (Eisenhardt, 1985; Ouchi, 1977; Thompson, 1967). Fixed asset initiatives tend to be well-structured situations to which the analytical techniques such as capital budgeting can be and are readily applied (Duhaime and Schwenk, 1985). For example, the selling of machinery is a multi-step process defined by clear, formal stages and outcome goals. Strict cost–benefit analyses form the basis of decision-making and there exists the possibility of controlling final performance by the level of the selling price or the improvement in the ROIC ratio. Just consider e-based spot markets for manufacturing equipment, and it becomes obvious that the disposal of such machinery is regulated through a set of legal and procedural elements. Initiative teams do not have to reflect about the "smartness" of the asset disposal. Their responsibility is restricted to a flawless execution of such decisions based on explicit criteria and stages.

Second, if responsibilities are clearly defined and bundled/concentrated (in one person, group, etc.) firms are more successful and the early participation of legal and tax experts are key success factors in the divestment process (Schiereck and Stienemann, 2004). With a bureaucratic configuration, top management can bundle responsibility centrally and with the implied focus on formal input control ensure that teams are adequately composed and have the required access to internal and external experts (Snell and Youndt, 1995).

Third, informal controls have the potential to be detrimental if applied in addition to steering this type of initiative. With their tendency to initiate timely and costly discussion processes and other micro-political activities (Cyert and March, 1963), they undermine the positive influences of the formal triangulation in the management of fixed asset initiatives. Therefore, the control configuration displayed in Figure 15.7 exhibits just this right combination of attributes and is proposed to be best suited to fixed asset initiatives.

Managerial traps in applying control configurations

In the previous section, we argued that particular control configurations might best benefit particular types of strategic initiatives, and we elaborated on optimal matches between these two elements. However, can we reasonably expect that corporations will be able to select or gradually find such optimal configurations? Or, are there reasons leading to deviations from those optimal matches? In the following section and based on anecdotal cases, we will outline several managerial traps that prevent firms from achieving such fits.

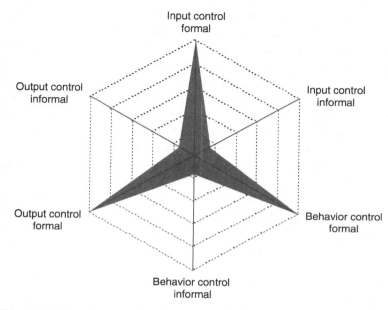

Figure 15.7 Fixed asset initiatives control configuration

One-size-fits-all trap

The first trap deals with the application of one control configuration for all strategic initiatives, regardless of their type. This trap is especially likely if firms pursue simultaneously a broad set of initiatives and impose a kind of overarching governance structure. Typically, such firms install a steering committee and an initiative officer who oversees and is ultimately responsible for all strategic initiatives. The implicit assumption is that strategic initiatives can be best controlled if managed with the same approach, which allows for comparison and a homogenous set of control devices (common templates, reporting guidelines, etc.). The desire for coherence and efficiency guides this approach. Sometimes, this approach also results from the unreflective use of best practices provided, for example, by external consultants, competitor analysis, or benchmarking studies, as these contain generalized, context-free guidelines (Nickerson and Zenger, 2002).

In the most extreme case, firms might also reduce their control configuration to a single control mechanism, while other dimensions are neglected. Cardinal and colleagues (2010) observed that firms with an almost myopic utilization of a single set of configurational attributes became less effective. They refer to Miller's (1987: 697–698) more general consideration that there exists a tendency to extend and zoom in on the original theme, for example, bureaucracies strive to become even more bureaucratic. Empirical evidence also suggests that many corporations focus on output controls, even in situations where control researchers have argued that they are imperfect and should not be relied upon (Cardinal *et al.*, Chapter 3; Chung *et al.*, 1999; Sitkin and Bies, 1994). One explanation for this behavior might be the comfort zone provided by frequent output reporting (Chung *et al.*, 1999).

Overall, firms falling into the "one-size-fits-all" trap underestimate the particular demands that each type of strategic initiative requires and end up with suboptimal matches between their dominant control configurations and initiatives.

Inertia trap

A further trap emerges when firms undergo strategic renewal, but continue to apply their established type of control configuration. For example, a corporation in the cement industry moved, after years of intensive cost cutting, into a period of international growth by launching a series of growth initiatives. For each of them, the same rigid control configuration that had served them well during the adverse business cycle, was applied. Not surprisingly, the performance of most growth initiatives was far below expectations due to the mismatch to the cost initiative control configuration. An explanation for this dysfunctional behavior might be related to the well-known "structural inertia" of organizations. Established processes and structure reinforce current behavior and impede changes in the *status quo*. Because the rigid control configuration was deeply embedded in that firm, its continued application had to be expected.

This trap becomes most pressing if firms have experienced positive results with their previous actions (e.g., Cardinal *et al.*, 2004). Miller speaks of the "Icarus paradox" (Miller and Chen, 1994), where firms facing a long period of (outstanding) success inherently develop the fatal tendency to (over)simplify their operational procedures and to blind the organization to discrepant feedback. A once successful pattern mutates into its opposite. The cause of failure, paradoxically, resides in what was once the source of success (Leonard-Barton, 1992; Miller and Chen, 1994; Schreyögg and Kliesch-Eberl, 2007). Behavioral theory supports this argument (Cyert and March, 1963; Greve, 2003) and argues that the *status quo* is generally perceived as a low-risk alternative, since it operates with established, widely known, and functioning standard operating procedures. In an empirical study, Audia and colleagues showed that firms with a successful past even avoided strategic changes in the face of major environmental shifts (Audia *et al.*, 2000).

Over-reaction trap

On the other hand, if the past performance of firms is below their aspiration level, the trap of "over-reaction" is likely to unfold (Levitt and March, 1988). It manifests itself as an extensive increase in all kinds of control mechanisms, and might be interpreted as a desperate attempt by senior managers to "turn the ship around." Although this is understandable, these managers are often not aware that their information capacity has limits, because too much information needs to be digested (Rivkin and Siggelkow, 2003). This might slow decisions and reduce the internal motivation of initiative teams (Child, 1984). Empirical evidence reveals that managers have neither the time nor the capacity to process all the information available to them. Two concepts well established in the literature support this notion (Simon, 1947). First, managers are rational only within their cognitive boundaries and are only equipped with limited information-processing capabilities. Second, managers engage in many concurrent activities, and consequently, strategic initiatives only represent a subset of their available time and attention.

Behavioral theory offers further support for this trap. It argues that performance decreases are associated with control increases – regardless of their cause (Cardinal *et al.*, 2004). For example, Snell and Youndt (1995) observed in an empirical study a negative, mutually enhancing spiral of lower performance and the subsequent increase of control. They showed that executives in poorly performing firms (at time 1) increased their amount of output control, which, in turn, led to even poorer performance (at time 2). They especially favored output control as a form of threat-rigid behavior (Staw *et al.*, 1981) and short-term orientation under conditions of decline to become more focused on the "bottom line" (Snell and Youndt, 1995).

Rustiness trap

Let us assume that a firm has been able to develop a strong capability in controlling its strategic initiatives. As we have outlined, such a capability would require first knowing which control configuration to apply, and second, conducting it effectively. As Winter (2003) points out, each capability requires some kind of training and nurturing if a reliable and repeatable pattern of activities (routines) is to be guaranteed. Clearly, firms not exercising a certain routine might slowly unlearn these necessary details and end up being confronted with the rustiness trap – the unlearning of routines. For example, after several pleasant years of a boom phase, a recession kicked in and forced a specialty chemical firm to radically pursue cost-cutting initiatives. Less surprising, the firm was ill-prepared for executing such initiatives, because such skills were in the meantime unlearned and had gotten "rusty." It took the firm some time to acquire necessary skills, methods, and processes for making this shift. The same apparently holds for the other case, where firms have lost their skills in growing their business after extended periods of stagnation and recession in which they were used to cost cutting and downsizing.

Slack trap

Organizational slack represents excess resources beyond those needed to maintain the organizational coalition. It provides firms with the ability to buffer setbacks and negative exogenous shocks (Cyert and March, 1963). In good times, firms tend to build up and store slack in financial instruments, excess staffing, excess pay, or tap into their slack resources to advance risky undertakings that they would not have done otherwise. The main problem associated with slack is the increased likelihood of more "lenient" control configurations than would be optimal. For example, output targets might be reduced or delayed, or less care might be taken in assessing the behavior of initiative teams. Overall, slack might lead to a general reduction of controls due to the reduced fear of failure (Nohria and Gulati, 1996; Singh, 1986).

Fine-tuning trap

A final trap deals with incremental changes in the chosen control configuration over time. Such a behavior might result if the monitored strategic initiatives are not fully progressing as expected and might lure senior managers into slightly modifying one or several control mechanisms. There are two risks associated with this. First, through a sequence of such changes, a control configuration can become insufficiently coherent, and eventually be transformed into another gestalt. Piecemeal changes could destroy the complementarities among the many elements of configurations (Miller, 1986: 235–236). Second, changes in control configurations might lead to unintended consequences: for example, initiative team members might misinterpret a change in one control dimension and alter their behavior.

Conclusion and implications for future research

In this chapter, we extended control research beyond the predominating focus on single elements' effects and their contingencies, by proposing several control configurations based on six control mechanisms. We related these ideal forms to distinct types of strategic initiatives. Based on the financial concept of ROIC, we distinguished six types of strategic initiatives that are relevant for both scientific research as well as managerial practice. We argued that the effectiveness of executing strategic initiatives is dependent on the tailor-made match between control configuration and initiative types. We concluded by elaborating on some common managerial traps responsible for deviations for these optimal matches. Overall, we think that this chapter offers detailed insights about control activities related to strategic initiatives and is helpful in reducing their failure rate. Our configurational approach is in line with recent work setting the stage for a theory of control that is amenable to more detailed and predictive theoretical and empirical work. Such an evolution of the field is necessary if we want to derive normative implications for executives charged with controlling strategic initiatives.

Several avenues for further research exist. First, research might empirically validate the control configurations and support or reject our theoretically developed propositions. Three appropriate statistical techniques are available (Roca-Puig *et al.*, 2007; Venkatraman, 1989). Numerical taxonomic methods, such as cluster analysis, are most appropriate to examine alignment from a configurational perspective and to analyze whether a misfit penalty exists for organizations in which the theoretically derived control configuration for a specific strategic initiative type deviates (Raymond and Croteau, 2006). Beside this "fit as gestalt" technique, research might follow the "fit as profile deviation" and assess the amount of variance from an ideal form. Further, "fit as covariation" would include a factorial analysis (Meyer *et al.*, 1993).

Second, future research could explore the impact of moderating variables on the configuration-initiative relationship. For example, control configurations characterized by lower amounts of formal control might be less effective in more hostile environments, and more effective in gentler environments (Lumpkin and Dess, 1996).

Third, we might deepen our understanding of antecedent variables (e.g., top management team characteristics) (Hambrick *et al.*, 1996), such as aspiration levels, tolerance for ambiguity, need for achievement, or political acumen, which might influence strategic choices and the exercise of discretion and control in organizations (Gray, 1990).

Fourth, future research might also move from the study of single initiatives toward the examination of whole portfolios of initiatives, or corporate programs. Firms frequently pursue partially homogenous, partially heterogeneous types of strategic initiatives under the heading of a corporate program. Based on our arguments, these firms will be confronted with apparent complexities and contradictions in steering diverse initiatives. However, our knowledge is limited about the consequences of such situations. Is it possible to spatially and temporally separate such initiatives within firms? Can members of steering committees simultaneously employ diverging control configurations?

This chapter has built on the extensive prior work on control and especially its recent development into a broader configurational approach and applied it to the initiative level. Based on the concept of fit, we proposed that each of the six types of strategic initiatives is likely to benefit from a distinct control configuration able to accommodate its needs.

References

Abernethy, M. A. and Brownell, P. 1999. The role of budgets in organizations facing strategic change: an exploratory study. *Accounting, Organizations and Society*, 24 (3): 189–204.

Adler, P. S. and Borys, B. 1996. Two types of bureaucracy: enabling and coercive. *Administrative Science Quarterly*, 41 (1): 61–89.

Alvesson, M. and Karreman, D. 2004. Interfaces of control. Technocratic and socio-ideological control in a global management consultancy firm. *Accounting, Organizations and Society*, 29 (3–4): 423–444.

Ansoff, H. I. 1965. *Corporate strategy: an analytical approach to business policy for growth and expansion.* New York, NY: McGraw-Hill.

Audia, P. G., Locke, E. A., and Smith, K. G. 2000. The paradox of success: an archival and a laboratory study of strategic persistence following radical environmental change. *Academy of Management Journal,* 43 (5): 837–853.

Barney, J. 1991. Firm resources and sustained competitive advantage. *Journal of Management,* 17 (1): 99–120.

Barney, J. and Ouchi, W. 1986. *Organizational economics.* San Francisco, CA: Jossey-Bass.

Bartlett, C. A. and Wozny, M. 2002. GE's two-decade transformation: Jack Welch's leadership. Harvard Business School Case Study.

Benner, M. J. and Tushman, M. L. 2003. Exploitation, exploration, and process management: the productivity dilemma revisited. *Academy of Management Review,* 28 (2): 238–256.

Birkinshaw, J. 1997. Entrepreneurship in multinational corporations: the characteristics of subsidiary initiatives. *Strategic Management Journal,* 18 (3): 207–229.

Bonner, J. M. 2005. The influence of formal controls on customer interactivity in new product development. *Industrial Marketing Management,* 34 (1): 63–69.

Bonner, J. M., Ruekert, R. W., and Walker, O. C. 2002. Upper management control of new product development projects and project performance. *Journal of Product Innovation Management,* 19 (3): 233–245.

Burgelman, R. A. 1983a. A process model of internal corporate venturing in the diversified major firm. *Administrative Science Quarterly,* 28 (2): 223–244.

1983b. A model of the interaction of strategic behavior, corporate context, and the concept of strategy. *Academy of Management Review,* 8 (1): 61–70.

1991. Intraorganizational ecology of strategy making and organizational adaptation: theory and field research. *Organization Science,* 2 (3): 239–262.

2002. Strategy as vector and the inertia of coevolutionary lock-in. *Administrative Science Quarterly,* 47 (2): 325–357.

Burgers, J. H., Van Den Bosch, F. A. J., and Volberda, H. W. 2008. Why new business development projects fail: coping with the differences of technological versus market knowledge. *Long Range Planning,* 41 (1): 55–73.

Cardinal, L. B. 2001. Technology innovation in the pharmaceutical industry: the use of organizational control in managing research and development. *Organization Science,* 12 (1): 1–18.

Cardinal, L. B., Sitkin, S. B., and Long, C. P. 2004. Balancing and rebalancing in the creation and evolution of organizational control. *Organization Science*, 15 (4): 411–431.

2010. The genesis of control configurations during organizational founding. Working paper.

Chenhall, R. H. 1997. Reliance on manufacturing performance measures, total quality management and organizational performance. *Management Accounting Research*, 8 (2): 187–206.

Child, J. 1984. *Organization: a guide to problems and practice*. New York, NY: Harper and Row.

Chung, L. H., Gibbons, P. T., and Schoch, H. P. 1999. The influence of subsidiary context and head office strategic management style on control of MNCs: the experience in Australia. *Accounting, Auditing and Accountability Journal*, 13 (5): 647–666.

Collins, F. 1982. Managerial accounting systems in organizational control: a role perspective. *Accounting, Organizations and Society*, 7 (2): 107–122.

Covin, J. G. and Miles, M. P. 1999. Corporate entrepreneurship and the pursuit of competitive advantage. *Entrepreneurship Theory and Practice*, 23 (3): 47–63.

Cravens, D. W., Lassk, F. G., Low, G. S., Marshall, G. W., and Moncrief, W. C. 2004. Formal and informal management control combinations in sales organizations – the impact on salesperson consequences. *Journal of Business Research*, 57 (3): 241–248.

Cyert, R. M. and March, J. G. 1963. *A behavioral theory of the firm*. Englewood Cliffs, NJ: Prentice Hall.

Davila, T. 2005. The promise of management control systems for innovation and strategic change. In C. S. Chapman (ed.), *Controlling strategy: management, accounting, and performance measurement*: 37–61. New York, NY: Oxford University Press.

Dess, G. G., Ireland, R. D., Zahra, S. A., Floyd, S. W., Janney, J. J., and Lane, P. J. 2003. Emerging issues in corporate entrepreneurship. *Journal of Management*, 29 (3): 351–378.

Dess, G. G., Lumpkin, G. T., and Covin, J. G. 1997. Entrepreneurial strategy making and firm performance: tests of contingency and configurational models. *Strategic Management Journal*, 18 (9): 677–695.

Doty, D. H., Glick, W. H., and Huber, G. P. 1993. Fit, equifinality, and organizational effectiveness – a test of two configurational theories. *Academy of Management Journal*, 36 (6): 1,196–1,250.

Duhaime, I. M. and Schwenk, C. R. 1985. Conjectures on cognitive simplification in acquisition and divestment decision-making. *Academy of Management Review*, 10 (2): 287–295.

Eisenhardt, K. M. 1985. Control – organizational and economic approaches. *Management Science*, 31 (2): 134–149.

Flamholtz, E. G., Das, T. K., and Tsui, A. S. 1985. Toward an integrative framework of organizational control. *Accounting, Organizations and Society*, 10 (1): 35–50.

Floyd, S. W. and Lane, P. J. 2000. Strategizing throughout the organization: managing role conflict in strategic renewal. *Academy of Management Review*, 25 (1): 154–177.

Floyd, S. W. and Wooldridge, B. 2000. *Building strategy from the middle: reconceptualizing strategy process*. Thousand Oaks, CA: Sage.

Ghoshal, S. and Bartlett, C. A. 1994. Linking organizational context and managerial action – the dimensions of quality of management. *Strategic Management Journal*, 15 (Special Issue): 91–112.

Govindarajan, V. and Fisher, J. 1990. Strategy, control systems, and resource sharing – effects on business-unit performance. *Academy of Management Journal*, 33 (2): 259–285.

Gray, B. 1990. The enactment of management control systems: a critique of Simons. *Accounting, Organizations and Society*, 15 (1–2): 145–148.

Green, S. G. and Welsh, M. A. 1988. Cybernetics and dependence: reframing the control concept. *Academy of Management Review*, 13 (2): 287–301.

Greve, H. R. 2003. *Organizational learning from performance feedback: a behavioral perspective on innovation and change*. Cambridge University Press.

Guth, W. D. and Ginsberg, A. 1990. Corporate entrepreneurship – introduction. *Strategic Management Journal*, 11 (Special Issue): 5–15.

Hambrick, D. C., Cho, T. S., and Chen, M. J. 1996. The influence of top management team heterogeneity on firms' competitive moves. *Administrative Science Quarterly*, 41 (4): 659–684.

Henri, J. F. 2006. Management control systems and strategy: a resource-based perspective. *Accounting, Organizations and Society*, 31 (6): 529–558.

Inkpen, A. and Choudhury, N. 1995. The seeking of strategy where it is not – towards a theory of strategy absence. *Strategic Management Journal*, 16 (4): 313–323.

Jaworski, B. J. 1988. Toward a theory of marketing control: environmental context, control types, and consequences. *Journal of Marketing*, 52 (3): 23–39.

Jaworski, B. J., Stathakopoulos, V., and Krishnan, H. S. 1993. Control combinations in marketing: conceptual framework and empirical evidence. *Journal of Marketing*, 57 (1): 57–69.

Kim, W. C. and Mauborgne, R. 2004. Blue ocean strategy. *Harvard Business Review*, 82 (10): 76–84.

Kirsch, L. J. 1996. The management of complex tasks in organizations: controlling the systems development process. *Organization Science*, 7 (1): 1–21.

Lant, T. K. 1992. Aspiration level adaptation – an empirical exploration. *Management Science*, 38 (5): 623–644.

Lechner, C. and Floyd, S. W. 2007. Searching, processing, codifying and practicing – key learning activities in exploratory initiatives. *Long Range Planning*, 40 (1): 9–29.

Lechner, C., Frankenberger, K., and Floyd, S. W. 2010. Task contingencies in the curvilinear relationships between inter-group networks and performance. *Academy of Management Journal*, 53 (4).

Lechner, C. and Kreutzer, M. 2010. Coordinating growth initiatives in multi-unit firms. *Long Range Planning*, 43 (1): 6–32.

Lehn, K. and Makhija, A. K. 1996. EVA and MVA as performance measures and signals for strategic change. *Strategy and Leadership* (May/June): 34–38.

Leonard-Barton, D. 1992. Core capabilities and core rigidities: a paradox in managing new product development. *Strategic Management Journal*, 13 (Special Issue): 111–125.

Levitt, B. and March, J. G. 1988. Organizational learning. In W. R. Scott and J. F. Short (eds.), *Annual review of sociology*, XIV: 319–340. Palo Alto, CA: Annual Reviews Inc.

Locke, E. A. and Latham, G. P. 1990. *A theory of goal setting and task performance*. Englewood Cliffs, NJ: Prentice-Hall.

Long, C. P., Burton, R. M., and Cardinal, L. B. 2002. Three controls are better than one: a computational model of complex control systems. *Computational and Mathematical Organization Theory*, 8 (3): 197–220.

Lovas, B. and Ghoshal, S. 2000. Strategy as guided evolution. *Strategic Management Journal*, 21 (9): 875–896.

Lumpkin, G. T. and Dess, G. G. 1996. Clarifying the entrepreneurial orientation construct and linking it to performance. *Academy of Management Review*, 21 (1): 135–172.

Maritan, C. A. and Peteraf, M. A. 2008. Frontiers of strategic management research: introduction to the special issue. *Managerial and Decision Economics*, 29: 71–77.

McGrath, R. G. 2001. Exploratory learning, innovative capacity, and managerial oversight. *Academy of Management Journal*, 44 (1): 118–131.

Merchant, K. A. 1985. Organizational controls and discretionary program decision making: a field study. *Accounting, Organizations and Society*, 10 (1): 67–85.

Merchant, K. A. and Simons, R. 1986. Research and control in complex organizations: an overview. *Journal of Accounting Literature*, 5: 183–203.

Meyer, A. D., Tsui, A. S., and Hinings, C. R. 1993. Configurational approaches to organizational analysis. *Academy of Management Journal*, 36 (6): 1,175–1,195.

Miller, D. 1986. Configurations of strategy and structure – towards a synthesis. *Strategic Management Journal*, 7 (3): 233–249.

1987. The genesis of configuration. *Academy of Management Review*, 12 (4): 686–701.

Miller, D. and Chen, M. J. 1994. Sources and consequences of competitive inertia – a study of the United States airline industry. *Administrative Science Quarterly*, 39 (1): 1–23.

Mintzberg, H. and Waters, J. A. 1985. Of strategies, deliberate and emergent. *Strategic Management Journal*, 6 (3): 257–272.

Nickerson, J. A. and Zenger, T. R. 2002. Being efficiently fickle: a dynamic theory of organizational choice. *Organization Science*, 13 (5): 547–566.

Nimocks, S. P., Rosiello, R. L., and Wright, O. 2005. Managing overhead costs. *McKinsey Quarterly*, 2: 106–117.

Noda, T. and Bower, J. L. 1996. Strategy making as iterated processes of resource allocation. *Strategic Management Journal*, 17 (Special Issue): 159–192.

Nohria, N. and Gulati, R. 1996. Is slack good or bad for innovation? *Academy of Management Journal*, 39 (5): 1,245–1,264.

Ouchi, W. G. 1977. Relationship between organizational structure and organizational control. *Administrative Science Quarterly*, 22 (1): 95–113.

1979. Conceptual framework for the design of organizational control mechanisms. *Management Science*, 25 (9): 833–848.

Ouchi, W. G. and Maguire, M. A. 1975. Organizational control – two functions. *Administrative Science Quarterly*, 20 (4): 559–569.

Pappas, J. M. and Flaherty, K. E. 2005. Informal controls at work: affecting behavior amidst uncertainty. In S. W. Floyd, J. Roos, C. D. Jacobs and F. W. Kellermanns (eds.), *Innovating strategy process*. Oxford, UK: Blackwell.

Ramaswami, S. N. 1996. Marketing controls and dysfunctional employee behaviors: a test of traditional and contingency theory postulates. *Journal of Marketing*, 60 (2): 105–120.

Raymond, L. and Croteau, A. M. 2006. Enabling the strategic development of SMEs through advanced manufacturing systems – a configurational perspective. *Industrial Management and Data Systems*, 106 (7): 1,012–1,032.

Rivkin, J. W. and Siggelkow, N. 2003. Balancing search and stability: interdependencies among elements of organizational design. *Management Science*, 49 (3): 290–311.

Roca-Puig, V., Beltran-Martin, I., Escrig-Tena, A. B., and Bou-Llusar, J. C. 2007. Organizational commitment to employees and organizational performance – a simultaneous test of configurative and universalistic propositions. _Personnel Review,_ 36 (5–6): 867–886.

Roth, N. L., Sitkin, S. B., and House, A. 1994. Stigma as a determinant of legalization. In S. B. Sitkin and R. J. Bies (eds.), _The legalistic organization:_ 137–168. Thousand Oaks, CA: Sage.

Schiereck, D. and Stienemann, M. 2004. Desinvestitionsmanagement grosser deutscher konzerne. _Zeitschrift Führung und Organisation_ (1): 13–18.

Schreyögg, G. and Kliesch-Eberl, M. 2007. How dynamic can organizational capabilities be? Towards a dual-process model of capability dynamization. _Strategic Management Journal,_ 28 (9): 913–933.

Siggelkow, N. and Rivkin, J. W. 2006. When exploration backfires: unintended consequences of multilevel organizational search. _Academy of Management Journal,_ 49 (4): 779–795.

Simon, H. A. 1947. _Administrative behavior._ New York, NY: Macmillan.

Simons, R. 1994. How new top managers use control systems as levers of strategic renewal. _Strategic Management Journal,_ 15 (3): 169–189.

Singh, J. V. 1986. Performance, slack, and risk-taking in organizational decision-making. _Academy of Management Journal,_ 29 (3): 562–585.

Sitkin, S. B. and Bies, R. J. (eds.). 1994. _The legalistic organization._ Thousand Oaks, CA: Sage.

Sitkin, S. B. and George, E. 2005. Managerial trust-building through the use of legitimating formal and informal control mechanisms. _International Sociology,_ 20 (3): 307–338.

Sitkin, S. B., Sutcliffe, K. M. and Schroeder, R. G. 1994. Distinguishing control from learning in total quality management – a contingency perspective. _Academy of Management Review,_ 19 (3): 537–564.

Smit, S., Thompson, C. M., and Viguerie, S. P. 2005. The do-or-die struggle for growth. _McKinsey Quarterly_ 3: 35–45.

Snell, S. A. 1992. Control theory in strategic human resource management – the mediating effect of administrative information. _Academy of Management Journal,_ 35 (2): 292–327.

Snell, S. A. and Youndt, M. A. 1995. Human resource management and firm performance: testing a contingency model of executive controls. _Journal of Management,_ 21 (4): 711–737.

Staw, B. M., Sandelands, L. E., and Dutton, J. E. 1981. Threat-rigidity effects in organizational behavior – a multilevel analysis. _Administrative Science Quarterly,_ 26 (4): 501–524.

Tannenbaum, A. 1968. _Control in organizations._ New York, NY: McGraw-Hill.

Thompson, J. D. 1967. _Organizations in action._ New York, NY: McGraw-Hill.

Treacy, M. 2003. *Double-digit growth: how great companies achieve it – no matter what.* New York, NY: Penguin.

Turner, K. L. and Makhija, M. V. 2006. The role of organizational controls in managing knowledge. *Academy of Management Review,* 31 (1): 197–217.

Venkatraman, N. 1989. The concept of fit in strategy research – toward verbal and statistical correspondence. *Academy of Management Review,* 14 (3): 423–444.

Weick, K. E. 1979. *The social psychology of organizing.* Reading, MA: Addison-Wesley.

Wielemaker, M. W. 2003. *Managing initiatives: a synthesis of the conditioning and knowledge-creating view.* Rotterdam, Netherlands: Erasmus University Rotterdam.

Wielemaker, M. W., Volberda, H. W., Elfring, T., and Baden-Fuller, C. 2003. The conditioning and knowledge-creating view: managing strategic initiatives in large firms. In A. M. Pettigrew, H. Thomas and R. Whittington (eds.), *Handbook of strategy and management,* I: 164–190. Thousand Oaks, CA: Sage Publications.

Williamson, O. E. 1981. The economics of organization: the transaction cost approach. *American Journal of Sociology,* 87 (3): 548–577.

Winter, S. G. 2003. Understanding dynamic capabilities. *Strategic Management Journal,* 24 (10): 991–995.

Zahra, S. A. 1996. Governance, ownership, and corporate entrepreneurship: the moderating impact of industry technological opportunities. *Academy of Management Journal,* 39 (6): 1,713–1,735.

2005. Introduction. In S. A. Zahra (ed.), *Corporate entrepreneurship and growth:* xiv–xxvi. Cheltenham, UK: Edward Elgar.

Zahra, S. A. and Covin, J. G. 1995. Contextual influences on the corporate entrepreneurship performance relationship – a longitudinal analysis. *Journal of Business Venturing,* 10 (1): 43–58.

Zahra, S. A., Nielsen, A. P., and Bogner, W. C. 1999. Corporate entrepreneurship, knowledge, and competence development. *Entrepreneurship Theory and Practice,* 23 (3): 169–189.

Zook, C. and Allen, J. 2003. Growth outside the core. *Harvard Business Review,* 81 (12): 66–73.

Index of terms

Author index